MW01260115

A Limited Edition
of

THE LIFE OF HERBERT HOOVER
Keeper of the Torch, 1933–1964

Presented by the Herbert Hoover
Presidential Library Association, Inc.

To:

*Copy Number*_____.

THE LIFE OF HERBERT HOOVER
Keeper of the Torch
1933–1964

THE LIFE OF
HERBERT HOOVER

★★★★★★

KEEPER OF THE TORCH

1933–1964

GARY DEAN BEST

palgrave
macmillan

First published in 2013 by PALGRAVE MACMILLAN® in the United States—a division of St. Martin's Press LLC, 175 Fifth Avenue, New York, NY 10010.

Where this book is distributed in the UK, Europe and the rest of the world, this is by Palgrave Macmillan, a division of Macmillan Publishers Limited, registered in England, company number 785998, of Houndmills, Basingstoke, Hampshire RG21 6XS.

Palgrave Macmillan is the global academic imprint of the above companies and has companies and representatives throughout the world.

Palgrave® and Macmillan® are registered trademarks in the United States, the United Kingdom, Europe and other countries.

ISBN: 978-0-230-10310-8

Library of Congress Cataloging-in-Publication Data is available from the Library of Congress.

A catalogue record of the book is available from the British Library.

Design by Scribe Inc.

First edition: January 2013

10 9 8 7 6 5 4 3 2 1

Contents

Photo section between pages 266 and 267

About the Author

by Glen Jeansonne

Gary Dean Best's fine volume, *The Life of Herbert Hoover: Keeper of the Torch, 1933–1964*, consummates the six-volume biographical series covering the life of Herbert Hoover sponsored by the Hoover Library Association. The series is characterized by meticulous primary research and quality writing, bringing more detail about Hoover's life to light than exists in any previous publications. The books also contribute original insights into Hoover and attempt to revise long-ingrained stereotypes. Each volume is the interpretation of its author alone, yet the series constitutes a corpus of information unavailable elsewhere.

Best, the nation's leading expert on Hoover's postpresidential decades, is a fitting author for this volume. An eminent historian who specialized in the era of the Great Depression, most of his 15 books and many of his numerous articles deal with the arch rivals of the era, Hoover and Franklin D. Roosevelt. Best's most memorable contribution to Hoover scholarship prior to the present volume is his two-volume study *Herbert Hoover: The Post-Presidential Years, 1933–1964* (1983). This new study, his final book and the capstone to a prolific career, is partly condensation and partly elaboration, complemented by additional research, reorganization, and stylistic editing. It will become the standard resource on Hoover's last years for the foreseeable future.

Best died on February 10, 2010, after completing the manuscript but before its publication. Subsequently, academic referees did not consider it appropriate to propose revisions without his permission. Thus the book stands as Best wrote it. Although it is doubtful anyone of the present generation will equal Best's accomplishment, his work commends other scholars to engage on research about Hoover rather than deters them. There have been only a handful of Hoover scholars of Best's stature. His presence is missed, but his legacy lives on in his books.

Like Hoover, Best was born in Iowa, and like his favorite president, he moved west, spending most of his teaching career at the University of Hawaii at Hilo. The transplanted Iowan, who received his PhD from the University of Hawaii in 1973, lectured at Sophia University in Tokyo (1973–1974) and was a Fulbright Scholar in Japan (1974–1975). Best held a National Endowment for the Humanities fellowship in 1982–1983 and was awarded research grants by the Hoover Presidential Library Association and the Hoover Institution of War, Peace and Revolution. Known as a spirited lecturer who entertained undergraduates with his wry sense of humor, Gary won the University of Hawaii Board of Regents Award for Excellence in Teaching in 1978 and the Award for Excellence in Scholarly/Creative Activities in 1994. Mentoring and writing never became routine; they were heartfelt.

In addition to his books on Hoover's postpresidency, Best published *The Politics of American Individualism: Herbert Hoover in Transition, 1918–1921* (1975), which launched his work as a Hoover scholar. Many of his books were devoted to Franklin D. Roosevelt and the New Deal, which he addressed critically from a conservative perspective, most notably in *Pride, Prejudice, and Politics, 1933–1938* (1990) and *The Critical Press and the New Deal: The Press Versus Presidential Power, 1933–1938* (1993). Best argued that the New Deal paralyzed the economy by overregulation and that Roosevelt crippled recovery by waging war on bankers and businessmen. The nation was beginning to recover when Hoover left office in March 1933, he believed. The conservative scholar was not daunted by the task of swimming against the historical tides of his times in his evaluations of both Hoover and his successor.

Despite his prodigious output, Best's studies were intricately undergirded by assiduous archival research. While working at distant repositories, he sometimes eschewed traditional methods of note-taking and dictated into a recorder. Later, he made transcripts. Unorthodox both in his methodology and in his interpretations, Gary broke precedents with his studies of the 1930s. With the solid foundation of books and articles he provides, written with intellectual honesty and innovative originality, his provocative and carefully crafted studies furnish momentum upon which scholars can build revisionist studies of the 1930s and of the final period of Herbert Hoover's life.

Glen Jeansonne
University of Wisconsin-Milwaukee
March 2012

The Herbert Hoover Presidential Library Association
and Palgrave Macmillan extend a special thank-you
to the following Hoover experts who were very
helpful in ensuring that Gary Dean Best's manuscript
was edited and prepared for publication: Spencer Howard,
Hoover Archivist; Dwight Miller, Retired Hoover Archivist;
Hal Wert, Hoover Scholar; Glen Jeansonne, Hoover
Scholar; George Nash, Hoover Scholar.

Introduction

Of all the presidents in American history, only John Adams lived longer than Herbert Hoover, and Adams's postpresidential life covered only about 25 years compared to Hoover's 31. Typically, American presidents come to the White House after a distinguished career and are little heard from thereafter. In the twentieth century, Theodore Roosevelt was active politically in the dozen years of his postpresidency, and William Howard Taft served as Chief Justice of the US Supreme Court. Wilson and Coolidge died soon after leaving office. No president in American history filled his postpresidential years with the activities and accomplishments of Herbert Hoover. Eisenhower and his successors were, and are, moderately active in public life, but their achievements are dwarfed by those of Herbert Hoover.

Hoover's postpresidential years were kaleidoscopic—filled with the activities of a man constantly on the move, both physically and mentally. He rarely turned from one activity to another, tending instead to work at a variety simultaneously. Much to the distress of liberals in his party (and of liberal historians ever since), Hoover exerted his considerable influence in the Republican Party to maintain the GOP as the bulwark of conservative principles in American politics between 1933 and 1952. The survival of conservatism in the Republican Party of the 1990s owes more to his stubborn adherence to the conservative creed (or traditional liberalism, as he would have put it) than to any other single factor or individual.

Simultaneously, Hoover was a leader of the opposition in two "Great Debates" over foreign policy during those years—the first over American involvement in World War II, and the second over committing US ground forces to the defense of Europe under the North Atlantic Treaty Organization in the 1950s. Although he was in both cases on the losing side, his voice captured the front pages of the nation's newspapers and the support of many prominent Americans. Years later, the policies that Hoover opposed have found less favor with historians and others.

Once the United States entered World War II, Hoover turned his attention to postwar planning and peacemaking. With Hugh Gibson he formulated a program that was largely embraced both by the Republican Party and by the Roosevelt administration. In advocating American participation in a postwar international organization, Hoover did more, perhaps, than any other individual to ensure that America's rejection of membership in the League of Nations was not repeated after World War II and to pave the way for a bipartisan foreign policy after the war.

In the midst of these activities, Hoover also pursued a theme that ran through much of his public life—a concern with children. In the postpresidential years this included his efforts to feed children in war-torn Europe before and after US involvement in the war and his work with the Boys' Clubs of America. As head of the Famine Emergency Committee after World War II, he waged a battle against hunger all over the world and exerted a powerful influence on US policy toward postwar Germany and Japan.

In addition, Hoover served under presidents of both parties as chairman of two commissions on reorganization of the executive branch of the federal government and was so influential in their work that both came to be known as the Hoover Commissions. Those efforts, undertaken when Hoover was in his seventies and eighties, brought about major reforms and restructuring in the federal government that have saved taxpayers billions of dollars. Perhaps no other individual in American history has exerted such an enduring influence on the reorganization of the federal government.

But even all these activities could not consume all the time of such a restless individual. Hoover was also a prolific author of articles and books. In addition to his three-volume memoirs, Hoover penned a multivolume history of the relief efforts he headed overseas in the twentieth century, a political manifesto titled *The Challenge to Liberty*, the influential proposal (with Hugh Gibson) for post–World War II peacemaking titled *The Problems of Lasting Peace*, and two books on post–World War I peacemaking at Versailles, including *The Ordeal of Woodrow Wilson*, besides other less important works. His productivity as a historian and writer alone eclipses that of all other former presidents, whose literary efforts after they left the White House tended, with some exceptions, to be limited to their memoirs.

It has often been said of Herbert Hoover that his accomplishments even before he became president were adequate to ensure him an important place in American history. It is equally true that his achievements during his postpresidential years are sufficient, in themselves, to make him an important historical figure without reference to all that happened before 1933. This is all the more remarkable when one considers that no president in the twentieth century, except Richard Nixon, left the White House as unpopular with so many of his fellow Americans as did the "depression president."

Hoover's postpresidential years are, in fact, so filled with activities and achievements that it is an impossible task to describe them all in one volume in sufficient detail. What follows is an attempt to chronicle as completely as possible the life and achievements of an incredibly productive life.

In researching and writing such a book as this an author is the object of many kindnesses and much assistance, without which the final work could not be written. In an earlier book, *Herbert Hoover: The Postpresidential Years* (2 volumes, Hoover Institution Press, 1983), I gratefully acknowledged the help of many who assisted with the earlier research. To those marvelous people at the Hoover Presidential Library and the Hoover Institution on War, Revolution and Peace, I should now like to add the name of the current director of the Hoover Presidential Library, Tim Walch, and the officers and staff of the Hoover Presidential Library Association who kindly asked me to do this book and supported me in doing so. As always, I am also indebted to the UHH Library, particularly its director Ken Herrick, for obtaining needed materials. And I am also grateful for the assistance of two student assistants, Tamra Rowcliffe and Sara Wessels, who helped with the research and other tasks involved with the book.

CHAPTER 1

The Silent Period

Home to California

Herbert Hoover was a spent man as he approached the end of his presidency. What Jordan Schwarz labeled "the interregnum of despair," with the stalemate caused by his continual conflicts with a Democratic organized Congress, had weighed heavily on him and despirited the nation.[1] His wife, Lou Henry, wrote son Allan that Hoover had "had a long, dull, deadly grind, and it will be a slow process getting back to normal under ordinary circumstances—like recovering from an illness."[2] Her husband, she wrote, could no longer participate in the "persiflage" that he was normally so adept at, and it made her realize "how utterly brain tired he was."[3]

To concerns about the country were added worries about the family's own economic situation. Over a dozen years of public service—first as food administrator under Wilson, then as secretary of commerce under Harding and Coolidge—and four years in the White House had drained, not added to, the family fortunes. The Depression had driven down the value and earnings of the Hoover investments, and taxes on them were now higher as a result of his own policies.[4]

Nor did the Hoovers contemplate that theirs would be a quiet and inexpensive retirement. Hoover was still a relatively young man at 58, the only living ex-president, and the titular head of the Republican Party for at least the next four years. The latter role, especially, would require the maintenance of an "establishment" and frequent travel. As Lou Henry observed, a man accustomed to being surrounded by experts and secretaries and stenographers could not easily adapt to the services of but one secretary/stenographer, nor would it be sufficient to support his activities. Yet where was the money to come from? This was well before the federal government began to provide an allowance to former presidents for such matters. It meant, Lou Henry wrote to her son, that the family would all "have to do our part to scrape together as much in the way of funds as we can manage."[5]

A month before they were to vacate the White House, Hoover contemplated a leisurely return to their home on the Stanford campus in California via a cruise through the Panama Canal with frequent stops for fishing in the Caribbean. His wife wrote their children that "he thinks he should get quite as far as possible from Washington as soon as his administration ends,—as fair play to the other man."[6] The trip would, she wrote, be like a "convalescence from an illness" for the former president.[7] But as the fishing aspect of the trip proved impracticable, it lost its attraction. And the onset of the banking crisis in the final two weeks of his presidency caused Hoover to abandon the plan entirely. The "interregnum of despair" still had its last and most painful act to perform.

After a bank "holiday" was declared in Michigan on February 14, 1933, runs on banks in other states led to similar closures elsewhere. Between February 15 and inauguration day, March 4, demands for currency amounted to over $1.6 billion, of which $300 million was for gold coins and certificates. According to the Federal Reserve Board, three-fourths of the demand occurred in the week before Franklin Delano Roosevelt's inauguration and more than half in the final three days before he entered the White House.[8]

While numerous factors certainly contributed to the banking crisis, the timing alone should dispose of any suggestion that it signified any "collapse of the old order." As the frenzy of withdrawals increased with the approach of FDR's inauguration, it is clear that concern over the new president's policies were uppermost in the minds of those lining up outside the banks. Aware of this, Hoover sought the cooperation of his successor in assuring anxious depositors that there would be no alterations in the value of the dollar after his inauguration, that the new administration would honor the pledges of a sound currency contained in the Democratic platform that accompanied his nomination in 1932.

Roosevelt, however, resisted all Hoover's efforts to enlist his cooperation in averting the bank panic by making such a pledge, telling one of his advisors that he "could see no reason why he should save these bankers" and ignoring the fact that it was the millions of depositors whose savings were at stake and only incidentally the fate of the bankers.[9]

It was in the midst of the banking crisis that the outgoing president accompanied his successor on the drive to the Capitol for the inauguration ceremony, with photographs showing the president-elect confident and smiling and Hoover looking solemn and distracted. One Roosevelt advisor remarked that Hoover appeared "close to death," with the "look of being done, but still of going on and on, driven by some damned fury." Another noted that the outgoing president looked "at the end, completely spent."[10]

Immediately following the inauguration, Lou Henry Hoover traveled to California with their son Herbert Jr., while Hoover left by train for New York City with his son Allan and was greeted at the station by an estimated 2,500 people.[11] He was clearly relieved at having the burdens of the presidency removed from his shoulders and slept for twelve hours his first night away from the White House. The next day he motored to the Connecticut home of his old friend and relief associate, Edgar Rickard, for a visit.[12] On March 6 he issued a short press statement calling on all Americans to cooperate in Roosevelt's closing of the banks.[13]

The next day the former president arose early and took a forty-minute walk through the nearly deserted streets of Manhattan with his secretary Lawrence Richey. The *New York Times* reported that Hoover looked "well rested and in fine spirits" and that he nodded and smiled at all those who recognized and greeted him. He then embarked on a series of meetings in his thirty-third floor suite at the Waldorf Astoria Towers with well-wishers, investment advisers, and representatives of the charitable trusts he was involved in.[14]

The following day Hoover ignored the fog that had settled over the city and embarked on another walk with his secretary over the damp sidewalks, stopping occasionally to window shop. Upon his return, Hoover again began a day of conferences concerning the affairs of the Belgian Scholarship Fund, the American Child Health Association, and the American Relief Association Children's Fund, as well as meetings with old friends.[15] The fog and rain of Wednesday was followed by snow swirls on Thursday, but the former president was out early again, clutching his soft hat, with the collar of his overcoat turned up, reiterating for reporters the need to support FDR's banking proposal. He then met with officials of the American Friends Service Committee concerning their relief work among coal miners in West Virginia, Kentucky, Virginia, and Illinois, a project in which the American Relief Association was involved to the extent of $20,000 per month.[16]

Although he publicly supported Roosevelt's actions in the banking crisis, Hoover was less than enthusiastic about them privately, writing Senator David Reed that he approved of the support Reed was giving the president but that he hoped Reed would "not get enthusiastic over it. The necessity for it could have been prevented; even when legislation became necessary due to their own conduct, a bill could have been devised which would do infinitely less harm."[17]

Hoover continued his daily routine of morning strolls while his plans to leave for California were continually delayed, first by the complications resulting from Roosevelt's closing of the banks and then by the death and funeral of French Strother, one of his White House secretaries and the man he had intended to be editor in chief of several publishing projects on the Hoover presidency.[18] During his stay in New York, Hoover was given a tour of Radio City Music Hall and took in a movie, thus beginning an infatuation with the Radio City Rockettes that stayed with him all his life (mentioned several times in the Rickard diaries). But at last, nearly two weeks after his departure from the White House, Hoover left for California on the train on March 16. The *New York Times* reported that several hundred persons saw him off but

that Hoover refused all requests that he say something to newsreel cameramen and reporters. His secretary, Lawrence Richey, told reporters that the
former president planned to "just take it easy for a month or so, maybe doing
a little fishing in the California mountains."[19]

After a two-day break in the trip west by a stop in Chicago to visit an old
friend, publisher Arch Shaw, the trip was resumed. At a stop in Utah, Hoover
was greeted by about five hundred Republicans but refused to give a political
speech, although he added that he might "some day . . . come to Utah and
make one that will be well worth listening to."[20]

When Hoover at last alit from the train in Oakland, California, reporters
said that the "years seemed to slip from his shoulders" as he was greeted by
a throng of well-wishers. Back at his home on San Juan Hill at the Stanford
University campus, after the drive from Oakland, Hoover said he believed he
would stay there "for at least twenty years." He wanted, he said, "to arise in
the morning without being informed that I have an engagement. I think I am
entitled to this." To questions from reporters, the former president replied,
"On economic and political questions I am silent. Even on fishing I am silent.
I am not going on a fishing expedition for a few days at least." He had, he said,
"no plans for the future" and warned reporters that they would not find his
home "much of a news centre."[21] Years later he recalled for a reporter that it
took him about "one week" to recover from the White House. "And then,"
he said, "there was a complete exultation and release at no longer having to
make ten vital decisions a day. I now could get into my automobile and drive
anywhere I liked."[22]

A New Life

Accompanying Hoover's departure from the White House were various
journalistic attempts to assess his presidency and his legacy. In general,
the assessments were charitable. The *Washington Post* pointed to Hoover's
positive accomplishments in turning the depression around, only to have
them undermined by the collapse of Europe in 1931. "Mr. Hoover," said
the *Post*, "has earned the gratitude of the country for his services. He has
battled with gigantic and unprecedented forces of destruction, without
sparing himself."[23] The *Chicago Tribune*, by contrast, found Hoover "one
of the most interesting paradoxes in our political history." He had contributed one of the "better expressions in our political literature of the
principles of American individualism," but "in practice and accomplishments he has been the greatest state socialist in our annals." Nor was it
all a result of the emergency caused by the depression, for Hoover had
shown "an enforced and persistent tendency, even before his presidency,
to increase the scope of federal activity and expenditure. He was, as one
political observer has said, government-minded." Moreover, on the issue of
prohibition Hoover had "sought compromise which was unsatisfactory to

anyone" and had allowed "a system of terrorism which violated the American spirit and the essential principles of American individual liberty which Mr. Hoover in speech repeatedly celebrated."[24] The *Baltimore Sun* found that Hoover's had been "an extremely unfortunate administration," which "at many possible turning points toward a safer national policy . . . took the wrong turn"—as in the case of the Smoot-Hawley tariff bill and the "ruinous ventures of the Federal Farm Board." It expected the Roosevelt administration to reject such "palliatives" and to "accept in full both the responsibility and the opportunity to correct our foundations."[25] The *New York Herald Tribune* agreed that Hoover had "failed to discipline his party in the writing of the Hawley-Smoot tariff" and in the process had lost the needed respect of Congress. But he had "fought for the right as he saw it with a singleness of devotion that has commanded the admiration even of those who disagreed with him" on such issues as prohibition. "The conscience of the country," it wrote, "never had a better spokesman." His "talent for organization and for direct appeal to individuals and groups" had enabled him to achieve "what no political skill could have accomplished." He had been opposed by "a foolish and surly Congress," and the whole country hoped "that a wiser Congress will uphold the new President's hands as it failed Mr. Hoover's." It concluded that in his "resolute, self-sacrificing devotion to the 'American system,' Mr. Hoover proved himself a great President."[26]

Although the stop in New York had appeared to be just a stage on his return to California, Hoover had already made plans before leaving to return to the Big Apple in order to complete various matters he had been unable to resolve during his brief stay. In fact, his trips to New York would soon become so frequent that Lou Henry Hoover would later describe her husband as a "commuter" between Palo Alto and Manhattan, and their lives as "nomadic."[27]

Once the adjustment had been made to life away from the White House, the lives of Herbert and Lou Henry Hoover settled into a routine that was anything but routine. The two were often on opposite coasts or somewhere in between. Lou Henry was constantly traveling because of her Girl Scout responsibilities, while Herbert was involved with his foundations that were centered in New York City and later with his board membership of New York Life and political activities. A letter from Lou Henry Hoover in 1937 illustrated their lives very well. She wrote Helen Boone, "Mr. Hoover is going east now, first to do a little fishing in Florida, and then to go up to New York for his various mid-month board meetings, including one that he is getting very much interested in now of the union or federation of Boys' Clubs. Before he returns I have to go east on a tour of Girl Scout Regional Conferences, from which I will not return in due course until early in June."[28]

As the years passed, the pace became more, rather than less, hectic when Hoover was increasingly called upon for testimony by Congress and was more in demand as a speaker. Lou Henry sometimes accompanied him on fishing trips, and they occasionally travelled together, but the two had very different approaches to travel. While Lou Henry enjoyed sightseeing, Herbert Hoover was interested primarily in getting from one point to another as quickly as possible. As Lou Henry wrote to their son Allan, "Daddy has always been a restless traveler,—traveling seems to be a process of going somewhere, with him, and looking at things along the way in a very casual and incidental matter. At that he does not miss having one glance at nearly everything! And one glance usually suffices. Even in Yosemite he does not want to look more than five minutes at any one thing."[29]

Of the two it was also Lou Henry Hoover who spent more time with their sons, Allan and Herbert Jr., and later with their grandchildren. Work was the focus of Hoover's life, and every other distraction from work—with the exception of fishing—was to receive as little time as possible. He spent a great deal of his time researching and writing speeches, even though he told Henry Allen that he didn't "value a lecture of mine as worth more than five cents and so I don't take any honorariums."[30]

Clarence Kelland later recalled that he had never known anybody so "capable of such patient labor and revision of his written word." He wrote,

> It has been my privilege to read, during the stages of preparation, many speeches to be delivered by Mr. Hoover. Always he has them printed in proof sheets. The first drafts seem to lack spontaneity and life and humor. You fear that here may be a failure. But then comes the first revision and the second and the third. Until at last you listen to the public presentation of the speech. It bears no relation to the first draft. It has everything, punch, humor, statesmanship, wisdom, terseness. It was not a spontaneous thing but a growth under his indomitable determination; his insistence upon perfection; his incredible patience and attention to detail. I have known him to rewrite an entire speech during the night hours that precede the day of delivery. If genius be an infinite capacity for taking pains, as someone said, then The Chief is indeed a genius.[31]

While Lou Henry Hoover was alive she helped her husband with his speeches, typing them on their Corona typewriter, then retyping them after Hoover had "cut it all up and added a lot more," then repeating the process until he was satisfied with it. She told their son Allan, "By the time it was finished I could have made the speech to an audience with my eyes shut!"[32]

But when there was a potential conflict between work and fishing, it was often the fish that won. In fishing, his secretary wrote, Hoover preferred "dry flies and always uses them. On land he likes any kind of fishing; at sea, he likes bonefish." On one fishing trip to British Columbia in 1938, the former president was made "Chief Bread Giver" by a local Indian tribe.[33]

Hoover was clearly a man torn between the relative peace and solitude of Palo Alto and the bustle of activity in New York City, and also between maintaining a dignified silence over the New Deal that was emerging in precisely the forms he had predicted during the campaign and lashing out at its destructiveness and silliness. Like his close friend columnist Mark Sullivan,

Hoover tended to believe that FDR deserved a chance and that premature criticism would only give the New Dealers a scapegoat when the inevitable failure came.[34]

Still, Hoover was acutely conscious of his position as titular leader of the opposition party, one of the few Republicans capable of reaching the front pages of the leading newspapers with his comments, and he deeply lamented the tendency of many Republicans in Washington to go along with the New Deal program. And he continued to harbor hopes of carrying the party's standard again in the 1936 campaign for the White House. But in those first months Jeremiah Milbank recalled that he was "a broken-hearted man when he left Washington. When I went to see him I would find him playing solitaire by himself. It made one feel like crying to see his low state of mind."[35]

Hoover's political dilemma was well expressed by Sullivan soon after Hoover's defeat in November, 1932, when he confided in a letter that most Republicans, from the party leaders to the rank and file, were eager to forget about Hoover and were absolutely opposed to nominating him again, despite a general appreciation of his ability. Hoover, Sullivan wrote, was regarded by most Republicans as an "intruder, an outsider who came in from a world other than politics, and not a member of "the politicians' union." They would seize upon his 1932 defeat as an excuse for passing him over in 1936 and insisting on a politician of the Coolidge type. Thus Hoover could only be nominated again if there was irresistible "pressure" from "the people" as in 1928. The likelihood of that happening would depend on Hoover's actions before 1936, during which time Hoover should not "act as in the faintest degree conscious of himself as a possibility for future office holding." Instead of campaigning for the nomination, Hoover should exert his political influence through "the weight of his ideas and of his voice."[36]

In short, Hoover's only prospect of gaining the nomination lay in acting as if he were not interested in it. This was a tall order, indeed, for a man whom friends and enemies alike agreed lacked the most rudimentary political skills. Milbank recalled that some of Hoover's "good friends" were telling him that "the Republican Party would never be the same while he was in it, and things like that . . . The early years were very difficult."[37]

Yet Hoover possessed a constituency of followers entirely apart from his political activities. Through years of service in the engineering profession, as head of Belgian Relief, the US Food Administration, and the American Relief Administration, Hoover had developed a large group of loyal supporters irrespective of party. Others might come to him, as Sullivan suggested, from "the weight of his ideas"—as an exponent of that traditional Americanism that seemed threatened by the statist polices of Roosevelt's New Deal. This threat was also a strong motivation for him to take up the role of leader of the opposition, and so was his desire for vindication.

The pursuit of vindication led Hoover to begin, even before he left the White House, to support a variety of publishing efforts by former members of his administration. French Strother, his former administrative secretary, completed an article for the *New York Times* before he died that summarized the achievements of the Hoover administration. Theodore Joslin was to write a series of articles for syndication by the North American Newspaper Alliance and edit a book of previously unpublished Hoover speeches.[38] Mark Sullivan was writing a piece aimed for the *Saturday Evening Post*, and several book projects were under way—one by former under secretary of state William R. Castle on the diplomatic accomplishments of the administration, another on its public works activities, and one on Hoover's humanitarian work from the days of Belgian relief down through his presidency. Strother's article was, in fact, published shortly before his death, but some of the others were aborted. The publication of the books was to be financed by asking donors to the Hoover War Library to temporarily divert their funds to HCH Publications, the instrument established to publish them.[39]

Strother's article appeared in the *New York Times* a week before Hoover left the White House. It was, of course, a highly biased essay, but the *Times* editorialized that it nevertheless contained "a certain direct element of authenticity of the kind which every biographer and historian is anxious to obtain and use." The *Times* hoped its readers would accept it in the spirit in which it was printed, "as an interesting and instructive contribution to our knowledge of what has been going on at Washington during the past four years."[40] Although the newspaper acknowledged itself as Democratic in its orientation, a majority of the letters to the editor in subsequent issues expressed appreciation to the *Times* for publishing the article and even showed a friendly attitude toward the former president. Democratic senator Hamilton Lewis, however, delivered a long and stinging rebuttal to Strother's points in an article a few days later.[41]

From his home on the Stanford campus, Hoover wrote to a confidant in Washington that once he had become "better organized" he hoped to begin providing analyses of the New Deal measures, since there "seems to be nobody to adequately analyze" them.[42] But Hoover felt acutely the handicaps of being so distant from the center of activity in Washington. Edgar Rickard, his longtime friend, relief collaborator, and investment adviser in New York City, wrote in his diary that Hoover was "feeling the isolation and craves news and cannot get information he is accustomed to in order to maintain touch with national and world affairs and cannot get it from local papers or local people." Nevertheless, the former president was "constantly in touch with Washington" and providing material for GOP senators and congressmen to use in fighting the New Deal legislation. His efforts seemed fruitless, however, since Congress was made of docile "newsmen infatuated" by FDR, so that no one seemed willing to support "Republican principles and Hoover policy."[43]

A few days later Rickard noted in his diary again that Hoover was "lonely beyond measure and feels terribly isolated" at Stanford; "he gets some satisfaction from browsing in [the Hoover] War Library, but after 22 years in constant touch with national and international affairs and association with men of importance and position it is [a] terrible letdown."[44] Yet when the *Associated Press* wanted to do a story on Hoover's activities since he left the presidency, including "little glimpses of his daily life, what he is doing, whether following politics closely, future plans, etc.," the former president's secretary responded that "Mr. Hoover does not consider that his present occupations have any public interest and hopes he may be undisturbed unless occasions of importance arise."[45]

While he shunned public attention and refrained from public comment on the New Deal, Hoover was actively encouraging others to make the points he refused to make himself. He was making suggestions for, and revisions of, editorial attacks on the New Deal by Harry Chandler of the *Los Angeles Times*, and he warmly encouraged George Horace Lorimer of the *Saturday Evening Post* for pointing out the dangers of Roosevelt's inflationary policies, telling him that he was "about the only person who can save this country from the tragedy of inflation."[46]

Business indices turned upward after the banking panic, but largely as a result of another and different panic—business concern over the higher prices that would result from the New Deal's inflationary policies and legislation, which caused manufacturers to buy raw materials and wholesalers and retailers to submit orders at present prices. For the unwary it was easy to conclude that the upturn was the result of confidence, when in fact it derived from fear. Hoover wrote of the situation in mid-May 1933 that "Some inflation, speculation, and seasonal improvement in business are evident. The great question is, has real demand come into real action—is there real confidence abroad in the land?" Hoover doubted it and concluded that the public was mostly "engaged in erecting storm shelters, including bunk statistics."[47]

Akin with others, Hoover agonized over the usurpation of congressional authority by the executive branch that he saw taking place during the "hundred days." Little escaped his criticism, but the Agricultural Adjustment Act (AAA) and the National Industrial Recovery Act (NIRA) were special targets. The AAA, he wrote privately, was "a strong forward march to Moscow," while the NIRA was "likely to be worse than socialism itself and in any event will only lead it." In seeking to raise farm prices the AAA would "diminish the purchasing power of the urban population by a billion five hundred million dollars a year," while the NIRA would be "ruinous to small business" and favored big business while it added little or nothing to employment.[48]

When National Recovery Administration (NRA) head General Hugh Johnson sought to speed up compliance with the NIRA by applying a "blanket code" to regulate the practices of all business in the nation through the threat of consumer boycotts against businesses failing to comply, Hoover wrote sarcastically that "I have thought that it would be desirable for me to join in the blanket code, more especially as I am the sole occupant of this industry of being an Ex-President. I have therefore responded by advancing my wages to $36.00 a week and decreasing my working time to minus nothing."[49]

Hoover's contacts with businessmen, especially small ones, soon caused him to be incensed over the effects of the NRA, however. Driving around California in early August he found

> the hideous immorality and tyranny of the boycott provisions, the stirring up of suspicion and hate between competitors in small business, conflicts between employers and employees in small businesses, and the burdens placed upon small business by which they are not able to compete with big business—all of them are creating a spirit in the community that is perfectly terrible. I have the most pathetic appeals for advice from people who wish to comply, and yet to whom it is ruin, or who have been subject to persecution in their communities. There has never been anything in our history that has so set neighbor against neighbor as this act.[50]

He wrote Lewis Strauss that bankruptcies were destined to rise among small businessmen if the code were carried out, since it was "almost impossible for employers of less than ten men to honestly go through with it without ruin."[51]

And yet Hoover held his public silence, because he was convinced the American people were still hopeful and were not yet willing to listen to the truth. Ninety percent of the people, he concluded, believed that "the millennium has come," and critics would only be reviled if they awakened the people from their New Deal–induced "hypnotism."

But if the people could not yet be roused from their hypnotism, did the Republican Party not need to be roused from its stupor? The titular leader despaired for the party he led. Too many had begun to act as if their leader was the man in the White House instead of the one in Palo Alto, or as if the party could only survive by trying to "compete in demagoguery and socialism" with the Democrats. The GOP, Hoover insisted, must continue to defend "constitutional methods" and oppose the centralization of power in the Roosevelt administration that smacked of dictatorship, to fight against the regimentation of society and in favor of "sound" economic and fiscal practices.[52] Few Republicans, however, were standing up in behalf of these principles in 1933; on the contrary, Hoover was told, there was "unanimity among Republicans in the House in opposition to any vigorous publicity campaign," arguing that "the country was still for Roosevelt."[53] The Republican National Committee, too, was taking the position that "the time had not been ripe to criticize too sharply," that "it would have been bad politics to go against insistent public opinion in favor of Mr. Roosevelt and his administration."[54]

Yet many rank-and-file Republicans were growing restive at the party's failure to act in opposition, and the reluctance of the party's elected officials to take a stand made their titular leader "itch to make a few remarks." Instead, he wrote GOP national chairman Everett Sanders that there were "two or three directions in which constructive criticism, as distinguished from the Democratic practice of smearing, should be made clear in the hope that it would save certain essentials . . . The first is the extraordinary misrepresentation—the misrepresentation as to administrative economies, the setting up of the 'extraordinary' budget, and the disguise of current expenditures by means of it; the destruction of the Civil Service; the character of men being appointed to public office; the misrepresentation that they had secured a tariff truce; etc., etc.—might induce the administration to return to that path of truth which is the first essential of government." Even the former president did not believe that the party should go beyond that at present but "must await a greater receptivity of public mind."[55]

Late in June, House Minority Leader Bertram Snell, of New York, issued a statement critical of the enormous expenditures of the first "hundred days" of the Roosevelt administration and received an appreciative letter from Hoover. Snell replied that his statement had received "some pretty severe criticism on the party of Democrats," and he went on to say, "the press and the radio all seem to be muzzled and absolutely afraid to say anything, or even present the facts in regard to the present administration. If any individual puts out a statement everyone says it is partisan criticism, but personally I think the time is pretty near ripe to give the facts to the country, and when I have any that I am sure of I propose to give them out." He asked the former president for any "suggestions anytime or any information you think I ought to have."[56]

Hoover's reluctance to make any public statements extended even to human rights matters. When Lewis Strauss asked the former president to speak out concerning the Nazi persecution of Jews in Germany, Hoover recalled that in the final weeks of his administration he had asked his ambassador to Germany "to exert every influence of our government." In the present circumstance, however, he could not know what "action the present Administration has taken" and did "not wish to embarrass them with public statements."[57]

The alternative to speaking out himself on issues was to continue to encourage others to do so and to furnish them with arguments they might use. In part this could be accomplished by rejuvenating the Republican National Committee, which through early 1933 seemed as reluctant as the party's titular leader to attack the New Deal. Hoover argued that the national committee and its chairman Everett Sanders "should begin stating facts, not destructive criticism, but in order that the country may have a full appreciation of what is going on."[58] The illness of Sanders, however, foreclosed the possibility of action from that direction until June, when the chairman began to schedule meetings with members of the national committee and chairmen of state committees in regional meetings across the nation.

After this brief burst of activity, however, which culminated in a regional GOP conference in Chicago on July 11, Sanders left on an extended vacation to Europe, arguing that politics were at a low ebb during the summer. The activities of the Republican National Committee ceased until he returned in mid-August, whereupon Hoover and some other GOP leaders groped for ways to forge the party into a more effective instrument of opposition. In mid-July the GOP was coming under increasing criticism from the *New York*

Times and others for not putting up a fight against inflation and the National Industrial Recovery Act.[59]

But Hoover's days were not all spent in monitoring the New Deal or encouraging opposition to it. The former president now had more time to indulge his greatest passion—fishing. In May he travelled with Lou Henry to a fishing stream in the California mountains and they returned with some "lovely rainbow trout" he caught.[60] In August Hoover was off again, this time to the Rogue River.[61]

Next the Hoovers were off to the Chicago World's Fair, and the titular leader of the GOP decided to combine it with a meeting of other Republican members in an effort to organize some activity that would rally the party around sound principles and strengthen its chances in the 1934 congressional elections. The Hoovers spent ten days in Chicago viewing the fair in between his political meetings. After several short trips to the fair, Lou Henry confessed to being "bored." The architecture of the fair she found "all singularly reminiscent of California Highway architecture as practiced by filling stations and hot dog stands," although at night some of it was "lighted very picturesquely."[62]

In his meetings with GOP leaders, Hoover suggested the creation of a finance committee to secure adequate funds for the party and also discussed with former treasury secretary Ogden Mills his idea of a declaration of party principles before the opening of Congress. Hoover's own suggestion was that such a declaration be limited to three subjects: "1. Restoration of constitutional practices; 2. Fiscal and monetary practices; 3. Opposition to socialistic programs." The method for issuing such a statement was not decided, nor was the question of whether Hoover's name should be associated with it.[63]

During his ten days in Chicago, Hoover also participated with his friend Arch Shaw in the creation of the Committee on Monetary Policies, a group of businessmen and economists mobilized to oppose the New Deal's inflationary policies. He wrote Lewis Strauss that a "fine opposition" had thus been created that he believed would halt inflationary policies in Washington.[64]

Hoover's close friend and Republican National Committee aide, John Callan O'Laughlin, urged Hoover to abandon his silence since "the time for leadership in opposition to the menacing theories and acts of the Roosevelt Administration has arrived." There was, he told the former president, no one but Hoover available to rally the opposition. O'Laughlin proposed recruiting one hundred prominent Republicans to address a request to Hoover that he express the policies he proposed for America. Hoover's reply to that request would, he said, "constitute the declaration of principles for the Republican Party to observe."[65] Such a close friend and New Deal critic as columnist Mark Sullivan, however, warned Hoover against such a course. O'Laughlin, he said was "overeagerly" advocating that something be done. Sullivan advised moderation, especially against any speech or statement from Hoover on current issues. "The President," he insisted, "is still entitled to the opportunity to push his own measures without partisan interference." The time was com-ing, but was not yet arrived, when "the people should have before them two alternative programs."66

However, it developed that other GOP leaders, including Mills and Elihu Root, had pursued Hoover's suggestion and were drafting their own proposed Republican principles. Mills and others had met with Sanders to suggest that the various drafts be reconciled and put "in composite form," and that they then be circulated to "loyal members of the Senate and House" after approval by the executive committee of the GOP National Committee.

Hoover quickly submitted his own rough draft and suggested that the final version should be released over the signatures of perhaps one hundred GOP leaders, with his own name, if it appeared at all, in alphabetical order with the rest.67 Hoover's draft was not, however, limited to a declaration of principles. It was also a vindication of his administration in its insistence that recovery from the depression had begun during his presidency, only to be aborted by the election of Roosevelt. Then, as in his earlier suggestion, Hoover confined the principles to three: "the restoration of the Constitution of the United States," "the re-establishment of a sound monetary, financial and fiscal system," and "the repeal or amendment of all emergency legis-lation [so] that the country shall no longer be plunged into socialism and collectivism with its destruction of human liberty which pursuance of these measures are bringing." His draft offered no alternatives to the New Deal other than an insistence that progressive action be taken "within the spirit and letter of the Constitution" and that the Constitution should be amended, if necessary.68

But aside from offering to participate as one of many signers of the dec-laration, Hoover was unwilling to go publicly on the attack against the New Deal. And when Roosevelt briefly flirted with attempting to induce inflation by playing with the price of gold in October, the former president took off for the Mexican coast for two weeks of fishing while the experiment was going on. Meanwhile, he was considerably happier with his situation at Stanford, with new sources of information available to him. As he wrote to investment banker Lewis Strauss, "I . . . have a statistical department consisting of the leading brokerage houses in San Francisco who, out of patriotism (they cer-tainly get no income), send me this data every morning often by telephone. They seem to have a desire to keep me in on economic trends and I read all of the personal dispatches that come over their private wires until I feel at times that I sit in with the New York Stock Exchange."69 And the former president was doubtless flattered when in September he was suggested for the post of high commissioner for German refugees, which the Dutch were trying to get the League of Nations to establish to deal with the large numbers of such refugees who were taxing the resources of neighboring countries like the Netherlands. Hoover's response to the proposal was, however, "not encourag-ing," according to the *New York Times*.70

14

Meanwhile, Hoover was closely monitoring the activities of the new Committee on Monetary Policies formed at the instance of his Chicago friend, industrialist Arch Shaw. The remote origins of the committee lay in the President's Conference on Unemployment, established by Harding in 1921, which became in 1927 the Committee on Recent Economic Changes under Secretary of Commerce Herbert Hoover, who had also chaired the earlier group. When Hoover entered the White House in 1929 he designated Shaw as his successor to chair the committee. At Shaw's suggestion, the committee formed a cooperative relationship with the Economic Club of Chicago, a group composed of Chicago-area bankers and business executives and economists.[71] The Committee on Monetary Policies was an outgrowth of this cooperative relationship and included many members of the Committee on Recent Economic Changes and the Economic Club of Chicago.[72] Late in 1933 it joined in the opposition to Roosevelt's inflationary policies and did so, the *Chicago Tribune* observed, "not a moment too soon."[73]

O'Laughlin and others, however, were growing increasingly strident in their insistence that Hoover himself go on the attack, while at the same time the former president was growing more concerned with the situation. He wrote Will Irwin in December, "If the real liberals of the United States would only awaken to the fact that none of this stuff is liberalism, that all of it is fascism, there would be more hope for the future."[74] He wrote another friend a long reflective later in the month,

> One thing always stands out in these economic experiences of the last five years—that is the part which fear plays in the whole system. The growth of instantaneous communication, the interdependence of every segment, have given it an importance in economic life never hitherto experienced or appreciated. Any policies which create fear will submerge every other effort. Today fear of unstable currency has paralyzed the capital goods industry. This same fear has turned the minds of the people from prudent investment to speculation in equities. Fear of the mounting public debt induces still other reactions. And in it all these things paralyze employment and bring more misery to new firesides . . . What troubles me more than all else is that liberty is drying up for the myth of utopia . . . [D]aily the world goes back toward the regimentations of the Middle Ages, whether it be Bolshevism, Hitlerism, Fascism, or the New Deal.[75]

Signs of discord in the Democratic Party late in the year encouraged Hoover but also caused him to reevaluate the desirability of any Republican initiative that might cause the other side to rally together again. The difficulty was that Republicans in and out of Congress were even more divided than the Democrats. An attempt to unify Republicans might simultaneously create more unity among Democrats and greater disunity among Republicans! As one Republican leader pointed out to Hoover, the principal obstacle to the formulation of a set of GOP principles was coming from Republicans in Congress, "where unity on fundamental principles may be impossible and at best only lukewarm."[76]

Despairing over the absence of opposition from the GOP to the New Deal, the *Saturday Evening Post*, in a Lorimer editorial and in articles by Sam Blythe, advocated the creation of a new political party. Lorimer and Blythe were convinced, O'Laughlin told Hoover, "that the brunt of the fight against the Roosevelt policies had been carried by the *Post* and that it had received no support from the Party that ought without question to have been active along the same line." Their call for a new party, he told Hoover, was designed primarily "to organize and encourage the opposition to the Administration." But O'Laughlin thought he saw hopeful signs of growing GOP unity and opposition in Congress.[77]

While some, including Hoover, continued to push for the declaration to be issued, other GOP leaders meeting with Sanders in late November in Washington thought they detected a shift in public sentiment away from the New Deal as a result of the downturn in the economy that occurred after the effects of the AAA and NIRA began to be felt, and the speculative boom caused by fear of inflation collapsed. They therefore questioned the wisdom of issuing the declaration of principles at such a time. Senatorial and congressional participants in the meeting also suggested that the declaration should be issued by the GOP National Committee, since they were certain not all Republican legislators would subscribe to it. The meeting agreed to postpone the issuance of the declaration until January.[78]

If the declaration of principles was to be delayed, however, it made it all the more imperative to Hoover that Republicans in the House and Senate should attack the New Deal, even while he maintained his own public silence. Republican legislators, however, showed themselves no more willing than the former president to go on the attack. Nor was Hoover successful in obtaining from other Republicans a defense of his administration against what he described as the "continual misrepresentation" of it by Democrats, until on February 1, 1934, GOP Minority Leader Bertram Snell of New York delivered a brief speech in the House in which he declared that Hoover's antidepression policies as president had been

the most constructive, complete recovery program that has ever been presented during my service by any President to the American Congress. I want further to say that the basis of the great proportion of your [the Democrat's] recovery acts came from Republican Herbert Hoover, whom you are trying to condemn in the eyes of the people at the present time. They were definite recommendations and he asked for cooperation of a Democratic Congress and did not get it. The depression was on then and I want someone to tell me where was your [the Democrat's] great interest in the people at that time? I know—you were absolutely unwilling for political reasons to give the chance to a Republican President you are now asking for a Democratic President. Except so far as the Reconstruction Finance Corporation is concerned, he never received a particle of cooperation. If you gentlemen had been as patriotic then as you are asking us to be patriotic now, the recovery would have begun a long time ago, and the delay in that is entirely up to you because you are absolutely responsible for the legislation in this House at that time.[79]

Hoover wired Snell his appreciation, but it was only one speech by one man.[80]

In the meantime, Hoover had begun to write a book. As Lou Henry described the inspiration, "we finally succeeded in getting my husband to get to work on his view of the present condition of our country and how it came to get there, and how it could get out,—all, of course, in rather general terms." Hoover had "got quite interested in it and has spent quite a little time arranging, rearranging, deleting and what not." She feared, however, that her husband had made it "perhaps a bit too condensed to be as effective as it might be to the average citizen," and that he "may have taken too much for granted in the average citizens' knowledge,—rather than in intelligence."[81] At one point, Lou Henry wrote their son Allan that "Daddy has barricaded the ink,—and is so engrossed in a book I don't want to disturb him."[82]

By Hoover's account he was stimulated to write the book because he was disturbed that so few books used for a "citizenship" class at Stanford University expounded what he regarded as the "American ideology."[83] He also felt a need to correct distortions in the media of his own public philosophy, first expressed a decade earlier in his small book *American Individualism*. Hoover decided that before he could be "of much help in advising the American people as to courses they should pursue, it seems to me that my position must be clarified." The new book project, eventually titled *The Challenge to Liberty*, was intended to serve both these purposes.[84]

Publicly, though, the former president rejected all efforts to break down his silence. He had, he told John Wheeler of the North American Newspaper Alliance, "resolved when I left the White House that no word of mine, nor any act, should weigh in even the slightest degree, directly or indirectly, against recovery," and he had adhered "faithfully to that resolution." His own efforts to produce recovery, he told Wheeler, had been "sabotaged for political ends at enormous losses to the American people," and he was "determined that no such thing should happen to the present Administration," ignoring his own efforts to get Republicans in Congress to oppose New Deal measures and to speak out against the Roosevelt administration's programs and policies.[85] Thus Hoover continued to reject all attempts to get him to speak or to write magazine articles.[86] He was, he told one friend, glad to see others criticize the New Deal policies, but he was convinced "that before criticism can sink in the American people must out of their own experience get an understanding of what is going on and have actual experience with the experiments being put forward. It is no use trying to fight against promises and ballyhoo."[87] As one Hoover friend described it, the former president was "keeping the cork in." But by early April Hoover had decided that "the time is coming some time in the next three months when I ought to take the cork out or alternatively make up my mind to retire altogether from any effort to remedy the situation."[88]

Hoover was, moreover, outraged over the apparent efforts of some of those around Roosevelt to "smear" his administration. Examples were the investigation of former postmaster general Walter Brown's handling of airmail contracts, attempts to prosecute former secretary of the treasury Andrew Mellon for income tax evasion, and other lesser attacks launched on other Hoover cabinet members. Hoover was correct in assuming that all these efforts would come to naught, writing a friend that his administration had represented "four years of the highest probity and freedom from improper influence that the Federal Government has ever seen."[89]

While the Republican National Committee continued to be moribund, a bill introduced in Congress by Senator Arthur Vandenberg put pressure on Sanders to resign as chairman. Vandenberg's bill would prohibit the chairmen of the two national committees from practicing law before departments of the federal government, and it forced Sanders to choose between the chairmanship and his livelihood. Sanders called a meeting of the GOP National Committee for June 5, 1934. At the meeting, Hoover supporters on the committee pressed for the release, finally, of a declaration of principles. A drafting committee headed by Charles Hilles put together a declaration that incorporated the points contained in previous drafts. While it contained the items that Hoover had insisted upon, it also went somewhat beyond his earlier draft in calling for "a broad, liberal, and progressive spirit, unhampered by dead formulas or too obstinately clinging to the past" in dealing with the economic problems that faced the nation. But such approaches must also be "within the framework of American institutions, in accordance with the spirit and principles of the founders of the Republic, without destruction of individual freedom."

The declaration warned, "A small group in Washington, vested with temporary authority, is seeking covertly to alter the framework of American institutions. They seek to expand to the utmost limit the powers of the central government. In place of individual initiative, they seek to substitute complete government control of all agricultural production, of all business activity." It put the Republican Party on record as favoring free enterprise, free speech, a free press, and a radio free from censorship, and it called "upon all who believe in the maintenance of these principles to unite in the election of senators and representatives who will support them." The declaration was approved and issued by the Republican National Committee.[90]

Predictably, press reaction followed party lines, with the Democratic *New York Times* dismissing it as "solemn emptiness" and the Republican *New York Herald Tribune* greeting it as "fresh in language and courageous in spirit."[91] The veteran Kansas Progressive newspaper publisher William Allen White applauded the declaration for incorporating the "old Bull Moose program of 1912" and added, "Who was back of all these liberal, highly democratic pronouncements? None other than the Hoover group."

The committee then turned to the task of electing a new chairman to replace the resigning Everett Sanders. Although former diplomat Henry P. Fletcher was not Hoover's first choice, he was widely regarded as a Hoover man and those on the committee who could be regarded as "Hooverites"—Mark Requa of California, Walter Brown of Ohio, R. B. Creager of Texas, and Harrison Spangler of Iowa—seconded Fletcher's nomination and then voted for him. Fletcher defeated his opponent, Kansas GOP chairman John D. M. Hamilton, 68 to 24.[92] Creager wired Hoover that Fletcher's selection meant the "retention by you of [a] powerful influence in [the] nation,"[93] while William Allen White regarded Fletcher as "Hoover's personal friend and political protégé," with his choice as chairman representing "a Hoover victory." The *New York Herald Tribune* agreed that Fletcher was known "as a Hoover man" but added that he was "a neutral so far as the schisms and quarrels of the party go" and likely to "unite all the elements of the party regardless of past disputes and present ambitions."[94] Clearly, the selection of Fletcher could not be construed as a rebuff for the titular leader of the party.

In April, Hoover ventured from Palo Alto for an extensive trip to the Midwest. William Allen White, a longtime Hoover friend, wrote that the former president

> started out about a week ago drifting east in his second-hand Cadillac, got as far as Arizona and ran into a bunch of politicians. Then went up to Albuquerque to see some friends and over to Santa Fe on business; heard some talk about the wheat money in Kansas and started east to see what was going on. He stopped off to see Polly Tincher [a Kansas statesman of credit and renown] at Hutchinson, came on up to Emporia, then went to Topeka to visit a cousin whom he had not seen for several years, who used to live in Lawrence when Hoover visited there as a boy. The Governor [Alfred Landon] naturally had him on for lunch. Tonight he will go to Kansas City to see The Star people and Arthur Hyde.

According to White, Hoover spent sixteen hours with him and they "talked about everything on earth except party politics."[95] From there he went on to Iowa, Nebraska, and Chicago, arousing great speculation as to the possible political motives behind the trip. The *New York Times*, however, thought "to suppose that he has already begun in his second-hand Cadillac to hunt a third nomination, is a little too fantastic, even for these days, so rich in cock-and-bull stories."[96] Hoover himself denied that there was any political significance in the trip and said that he had "nothing to say about public policies anymore." Exhausted from traveling nearly three thousand miles by automobile, he took the train back to Palo Alto.[97] After the trip he wrote a friend that he was "enormously amused to see how excited the Republicans in Washington can get when I leave the basement of this house."[98]

The Gospel of Palo Alto

Happy that the Republican National Committee had finally shown some signs of life and was under new leadership, Hoover resumed work on the book outlining his public philosophy, mailing off drafts to friends for their comments, then making revisions. His purpose in writing the book he explained to friends:

> It is my last shot at public service, and must be made now before I go on to other occupations finally, and they [sic] do not contemplate a literary career. I do not overestimate the book's usefulness; but it clears my own conscience and does what I can for people groping in the dark. Privately, I have no expectation that a nation which has once cut loose from its moorings to definite human rights and placed them at the disposal of the state will ever return to them. History does not move that way, and those who cling to such a philosophy are just part of the wreckage. We can nevertheless yell "help, help." With ten million unemployed and the destruction of business confidence after all this stuff, the most likely drive is toward more and more suppression of rights and more gospel from Walter Lippmann that it is the true interpretation of the forefathers; that is all for our good; that it is deserved punishment for our sins; that it is the discovery by Hebraic philosophers of genius who can compound collectivism and individual rights and make the waters of life.[99]

Hoover confided to William Allen White that he had "originally written the book with more quip and epigram, but on consideration I concluded that wherever it could be interpreted as containing the slightest degree of bitterness that it should be eliminated." The book, though probably duller, was "perhaps more useful for its purpose."[100]

Still, Hoover had not made the book as bland as some had suggested he should. Many of those to whom he had sent drafts for suggestions had recommended "that the Chapter devoted to National Regimentation, being an attack on the New Deal, should be suppressed," but Hoover felt that to do so would result in the book being reduced "merely to an essay on Liberty, of which there have been many before and many of them better." Thus he was willing to leave the chapter in, despite contrary recommendations, in hopes that it would be "a contribution to a re-adjustment of public thinking."[101]

The book first saw daylight as a series of articles in the *Saturday Evening Post*, which Hoover chose over American Magazine even though the latter offered $25,000 compared to the former's $10,000, perhaps because he regarded the *Post* as "our mainstay and hope in dealing with the problems of the day."[102] The articles summarized its major points, after which *The Challenge to Liberty* was released by Scribner's in mid-September of 1934. While the book did not attack the New Deal on specific points, it appealed to the American people to reject the trend away from individual liberty that was apparent everywhere in the world, including the United States. In short, the book championed "American Liberalism" and the "American System" against the new forces of fascism, nazism, and communism in Europe and the New Deal in America.

In his summation Hoover wrote,

> We cannot extend the mastery of government over the daily life of a people without somewhere making it master of people's souls and thoughts. That is going on today. It is part of all regimentation.
>
> Even if the government conduct of business could give us the maximum of efficiency instead of least efficiency, it would be purchased at the cost of freedom. It would increase rather than decrease abuse and corruption, stifle initiative and invention, undermine the development of leadership, cripple the mental and spiritual energies of our people, extinguish equality of opportunity, and dry up the spirit of liberty and the forces which make progress.
>
> It is a false liberalism that interprets itself into government dictation, or operation of commerce, industry and agriculture. Every move in that direction poisons the very springs of true Liberalism. It poisons political equality, free thought, free press, and equality of opportunity. It is the road not to liberty but to less liberty. True Liberalism is found not in striving to spread bureaucracy, but in striving to set bounds to it. Liberalism is a force proceeding from the deep realization that economic freedom cannot be sacrificed if political freedom is to be preserved. True Liberalism seeks all legitimate freedom first in the confident belief that without such freedom the pursuit of other blessings is in vain.
>
> The nation seeks for solutions of its many difficulties. These solutions can come alone through the constructive forces from the system built upon Liberty. They cannot be achieved by the destructive forces of Regimentation. The purification of Liberty from abuses, the restoration of confidence in the rights of men, the release of the dynamic forces of initiative and enterprise are alone the methods by which these solutions can be found and the purpose of American life assured.[103]

Largely as a result of the influence of William Allen White, a member of its selection committee, *The Challenge to Liberty* was adopted as a selection of the Book-of-the-Month Club, thus gaining wide circulation.[104] Hoover told White he was "mightily obliged for all the help you are giving to spread the gospel according to Palo Alto." He also urged the Kansas editor to say something in the press about the book to offset the inevitable criticism from the opposition that it was "'reactionary,' 'standpat,' etc."[105]

The appearance of the first of the *Saturday Evening Post* articles seemed to signal that Hoover's silence had at last been broken. In welcoming Hoover's reappearance, the Republican *New York Herald Tribune* noted that the former president had not mentioned the New Deal in his article but had pointed out the dangers that arose from the planning and centralization that so captivated those in the Roosevelt administration. It concluded,

> Mr. Hoover's views are those of an old-fashioned liberal, firmly devoted to the philosophy of government which evolved our Constitution and to the social philosophy under which the United States grew strong. Insofar as he is unwilling to see either materially modified he will arouse the scorn of the New Dealers and the experimentalists. But no thoughtful student of American affairs can afford to ignore the reflections of a man who had four years of practical experience in the supervision of our constitutional and social system and whose knowledge of world problems is unequaled.

They were the "impersonal and philosophical reflections on politics of a thoughtful man in retirement," the *Herald Tribune* wrote.[106]

Predictions like those of Hoover and the *Herald Tribune* that the book would not be universally welcomed were well founded. In retrospect there seems little about the book that could be criticized except by one avowedly intent on regimenting and collectivizing the nation, which few even in the New Deal would admit to being. From in and around the New Deal came attacks by Interior Secretary Harold Ickes and Agriculture Secretary Wallace, as well as Congressman Joseph Byrns, Democratic majority leader in the House. The criticism of Broadus Mitchell, Socialist candidate for governor of Maryland, was not surprising. Mitchell wrote in *The Nation* that *The Challenge to Liberty* was "a sorry performance. It is worse than dull. It is numb . . . Mr. Hoover's lips are automatically forming syllables which are familiar to him, but which have little enough application to what has recently taken place."[107]

The fact that Mitchell's essay was published by the editors of the respected liberal journal *The Nation* was indicative of the change that was taking place within liberalism in the 1930s—a change that alienated many of the liberals associated with the progressive period and tradition of less than a generation earlier. Traditional American liberalism had sought to curb business malpractices but had not been directed against the free enterprise system or against businessmen and bankers as a class. The new Rooseveltian brand of liberalism was, however, both antibusiness and antibanking, set class against class, and yet articulated no coherent alternative to the free enterprise economy it set out systematically to sabotage. It attracted to its banner, however, those who, like Mitchell, did advocate an alternative and who were quite willing in the meantime to join the saboteurs.[108]

Veteran liberals like Amos Pinchot and, later, Walter Lippmann, were uncomfortable with the new theories that had begun to masquerade as liberalism in the 1930s. Pinchot scolded the editors of *The Nation* for going "clean away from liberalism into communism." He broke with the new breed of "liberals" when asked to join organizations or to sign statements that he regarded as antibusiness. He rejected an overture from the National Unemployment League because they did "not really believe in private industry or in the profit system, and, therefore, they are in another pew from me." He also resigned as chairman of the People's League for Economic Security when it drifted "too far to the left." Genuine liberals like Pinchot thus found themselves in the uncomfortable position of siding with the very people they had formerly opposed in politics to defend free enterprise against the "bogus liberalism" of the Roosevelt administration.[109]

Moreover, there were some who could agree with Hoover's attack on regimentation but who were still convinced in late 1934 that the New Deal's assumption of power over business and agriculture was only for the duration of the "emergency" and that it would be surrendered once recovery was under way. This naive view was expressed in the review by historian Allan Nevins in the *Saturday Review*, when he wrote that Hoover had almost totally ignored the crisis in which the nation was embroiled and was mistaken in treating "an emergency assumption of authority as a calculated and sustained assault on liberty."[110]

No reviewer, however, was quite so colorful in his language as British socialist Harold Laski, who wrote in the *Manchester Guardian* that Hoover's book represented "the terrified anger of a high priest of the Ptolemaic astronomy watching the growth of the Copernican hypothesis. Mr. Hoover has no idea of what is happening in the States. He has notions of economics and sociology which might have been partially appropriate about the years after the Civil War, but have not since that time borne any relation to the situation they are intended to control."[111]

On balance, however, the positive reviews outbalanced the negative ones by over two to one, as measured by the *United States News*. Popular historian Will Durant wrote Hoover that his book was "amazingly eloquent and I cannot understand why the critics have not recognized its high literary quality."[112] Glenn Frank, president of the University of Wisconsin, called it "a great document!" It would so stand, he said, "as the judgment of posterity."[113] It is possible that if, as columnist Elliott Thurston observed in the *Washington Post*, the book had been written by anyone but Hoover it would have been more appreciated. Thurston opined that "an omniscient man from Mars might have written this book and been hailed as a prophet or a Moses. As a prophet in his own land, Mr. Hoover's fate at the moment seems to be the proverbial one. And the hour is not yet ripe for a popular uprising, even if Mr. Hoover were prepared to lead it."[114]

The Democratic *St. Louis Post-Dispatch* showed remarkable equanimity in writing,

> Mr. Hoover's conduct as a former President has been unexceptionable. During the seventeen months since the Roosevelt administration came in he has uttered no public word of criticism of its policies. He has opened himself to no faintest suspicion of trying to embarrass his successor for partisan gain. If Mr. Hoover now wishes to speak out he can do so without a trace of impropriety. Some might say it is his duty to speak out; he

is the titular head of his party, and many of his followers of 1932 look to him for guidance.

On any ground, Mr. Hoover is entitled to his book. The winner of the election has published two books. Certainly the loser, with plenty of time on his hands, should be allowed one.[115]

To the distress of its critics and Hoover's detractors, *The Challenge to Liberty* made the best-seller lists and 135,000 copies were printed.[116] When Hoover intimate Edgar Rickard talked with Scribner's in late February, 1935, he was told that "the books written by cabinet members and Roosevelt himself have not gone over well and [it is] safe to estimate that more Challenges have been sold than all the other books combined."[117] And though the book does not seem to have had the desired impact on the 1934 congressional elections, in which the Democrats added to their already top-heavy majorities in both houses, it may have exerted an influence later. In the 1950s, Chadwick Hall (formerly of *The Nation*) traced Eisenhower's victory in 1952 as a culmination of the successful "businessmen's crusade against the New Deal" that began in "1934 with the publication of Herbert Hoover's *The Challenge to Liberty*."[118]

During the summer Hoover paid his annual visit to the Bohemian Club summer encampment amid the redwoods of Northern California. In this cathedral-like setting of 2,800 acres were located approximately 250 camps of congenial friends, supplemented by guests. Its members and their guests made up the elite from journalism, government, commerce, industry, and finance. Hoover's affiliation was with Caveman's Camp, which included his two sons, Allan and Herbert Jr., as well as Dr. Ray Lyman Wilbur, writers Clarence Kelland and Charles Fields, and oilman Bert Mattei. It was a carefree time, devoted to conversation, speeches, golf, and theatrical productions, but it was also an opportunity for making important contacts.[119] Hoover would continue his visits there until his last appearance in 1962 when he was nearly 88. The former president also never relaxed in his pursuit of finned creatures, ranging from the trout of the mountain streams of the West to the billfish of the Gulf of Mexico. Lou Henry wrote a friend in late October 1933 that her husband was "trying his luck at sword fishing. The last time he did not even see the one the friendly press gave them credit for glimpsing."[120] In May of 1934 he was fishing on the Feather River.[121] And he had begun to contemplate writing another book, this one "on my own and some other person's activities during the Armistice." That book, however, was still over seven years away.[122]

Hoover's silence continued to make him enigmatic to many friends and foes alike. In May 1934, Duncan Aikman wrote in *The New York Times Magazine*,

No other ex-President within living memory has made the suppression of his views and public interests such an objective. In comparison with

Mr. Hoover's self-determined seclusion, Messrs. Taft and Coolidge with
their syndicated columns and "availability" for press statements were pri-
ma donnas of publicity; Colonel Roosevelt, with his intensive literary and
political activity, was a perpetual sunburst. Even Mr. Harrison and Mr.
Cleveland managed now and then to be accessible to reporters after the
pompous fashion of the mauve decade, and there were rare but significant
expressions from the Wilson house on S Street.

Mr. Hoover, however, has chosen to convert retirement from the
Presidency into a silence. It is a silence which envelops not only his views
on public questions but his daily interests and activities, his business
concerns—everything, in short, but his hobbies of fishing and motoring
and the bare route of his journeys when he goes visiting. As a result, the
silence has become crowded with legends.

In fact, Aikman observed, the silence resulted from the fact that Hoover's
mind was now more engrossed in political science than in practical politics.
Revealing of that were indications that the former president planned to take
no role in either the 1934 congressional elections or the 1936 presidential
race. There seemed so little partisanship about him that one visitor had complained, "He's so darned objective that he might as well be a historian."[123]

"Objective," Aikman agreed, seemed to be the term that best described the
"new Hoover mood," but the former president was too absorbed in the present to be described as a historian. Any bitterness seemed to have been sub-
merged "in the philosopher, the student, the scientific critic of government."
He had become "the New Deal's most attentive student." Aikman wrote,

It is known at the Hoover War Library, for instance, that practically the whole
school of literature on which the idea of economic planning is based, from
the most radically Communist works to the "corporative State" protagonists
of government by big business on the right, has passed under his eyes during
the past year. Translators are at work daily giving him the latest reports from
Moscow newspapers and periodicals on contemporary developments in the
Russian experiment, and to a lesser extent from Berlin and Rome newspapers
on German and Italian affairs. With peculiar zest the considerable subdepart-
ment which might be described as "anti-Hoover literature" has been examined. In addition, an irregular but vast quantity of reports from both official
and confidential sources pours in on the current activities of our government.

The result, Aikman reported, was that Hoover had been described by a confidant as "a man able to converse on the New Deal with an expertise possible
only to one who does not have to work in it," and he did so with considerable
objectivity.[124]

"But," Aikman wrote,

it would be incorrect to assume that a tanned gentleman not yet 60 and
bristling with energy does nothing but watch his world from the perch of

an aging philosopher. Beyond studies which would tax aPh.D. candidate's powers of absorption, Mr. Hoover finds time to be acutely busy.

He has swung into his old duties as a trustee of Stanford in a way that makes him almost a de facto subexecutive of the university.

At the Hoover war library he is the active head of a document and literature collecting organization which would absorb the full time of many an active business man. His correspondence is prodigious—so much so that he is reported to have complained recently that the mail bombardment of San Juan Hill must be coming from the same guns as that received by the White House. Even his motor and fishing trips are considerably more strenuous than the usual drowsy expeditions of sportsmen and scenery connoisseurs.

His constant contacts with a variety of people, including "hitch-hikers, CWA workers, county aid beneficiaries, country storekeepers and lonely ranchers," as well as visiting politicians, meant that "Mr. Hoover may be more alive to his times in 1934 than it was ever possible for him to be in the midst of his responsibilities in the White House." Thus if the former president did decide to make a fresh appearance in public life, "there may be a good many of all political persuasions who will be amazed at Student Hoover's extraordinary state of preparedness."[125]

Nationally syndicated columnist Raymond Clapper wrote similarly in July of Hoover's life in Palo Alto. The former president continued to receive an average of 200 letters per day, with up to 1,500 on days when a major issue was before the country. He also made frequent automobile trips into the surrounding area to keep in touch with grassroots sentiment. Clapper concluded,

> The outside world thinks of Mr. Hoover as a man brooding in silence. He is silent so far as the outside world is concerned and he has firmly rejected all offers to write or to discuss National affairs. But it is not a brooding silence. Nor the silence of a man who has lost his interest in life. It is the calm self-restraint of a man who is observing and thinking a great deal. It is a relaxed and attentive silence like that of a performer who has had his turn on the stage and is now watching the performance of others.[126]

To his wife, Clapper wrote that Hoover

> keeps in closest touch with everything and knows all about what's going on in this state—quite a contrast to Coolidge when I saw him after being out of the White House a couple of years. He had lost touch complete [sic] and was not interested except in the most casual way. Hoover reads the news closely and knows everything that is happening. I can't figure out whether he has the hope of another try or not—I am inclined to think that he would take the chance if it came but will not try for it—but I'm not very sure of that diagnosis. He does say that the people will rise up in rebellion against the administration.[127]

Hoover might well have been amused, too, by observations that much of the New Deal had originated in his own administration. Arthur Krock pointed in a July column to the fact that "the RFC [Reconstruction Finance Corporation], the first and most powerful of the alphabetical agencies, was a creation of the Hoover administration and hence a child of the Old Deal," making Hoover, "in this respect the father of the prodigal New Deal."[128] A month later an economist told a conference on recovery that it was "not generally recognized how much of the foundation work of the NRA was carried on under Mr. Hoover, first as Secretary of Commerce and afterward as President." Professor W. D. Ennis noted that Hoover's "trade practice conferences, between trade associations and the Federal Trade Commission, suggested a partnership of business with government; called attention to the unduly restrictive effect of our Anti-Trust Laws, stressed 'unfair competition' and did valuable work in standardization of product and aided in the introduction of adequate cost accounting." In fact, Ennis noted, the word "code came into use in its present connection while Hoover was Secretary of Commerce."[129]

In the late spring of 1934 business conditions began to flatten and in late summer and in early fall there was a sharp downturn that brought economic indices close to the worst levels in the summer of 1932. Lewis Strauss wrote Hoover from Wall Street that the "loss of momentum in the New Deal is now becoming pretty well apparent even to the casual observer. Most all lines of business are showing a very considerable deceleration as compared with March figures."[130] Hoover referred to it in May as "another sinking spell" and wrote, "The failure to secure movement in the capital goods industries has begun to have its effect."[131] It was causing "considerable loss" in the former president's stock holdings.[132] By the end of July the American Federation of Labor estimated that 10.3 million workers were still unemployed. The *New York Herald Tribune* business index had dropped below 50 only twice during the depression—to near 48 in July 1932, at the depth of the depression, and to 43 as a result of the bank holiday in March 1933. On September 28, 1934, it fell to 49. The *New York Times* reported that its own index had fallen "back approximately to the level of January, 1933, a few weeks before the bank closings." This, it reported, was in sharp contrast with Canada where business indexes were well over 50 percent above those for January 1933. The number requiring federal relief was, meanwhile, growing, and the *Wall Street Journal* wondered if Roosevelt realized that their growing numbers were "the measure of the New Deal's failure to launch lasting or continuing recovery."[133]

Criticism of the New Deal mounted in the face of its obvious failure to produce recovery. Much of that criticism seemed to echo the points made in *The Challenge to Liberty*. As Hoover put it, "The wells of criticism have begun to bubble and the terrorization does not work so effectively as it did a few months ago."[134] The American Bar Association, for example, charged, the "judicial branch of the federal government is being rapidly and seriously undermined" by the National Recovery Administration, Agricultural Adjustment Act, and other New Deal agencies. By delegating to such agencies vast judicial and legislative powers, Congress had removed large areas of legal controversy from the jurisdiction of the courts and had, instead, "substituted a labyrinth in which the rights of individuals, while preserved in form, can easily be nullified in practice."[135]

When a fireside chat by FDR tried to put a rosy appearance on the situation by ignoring that the nation was beset by crippling labor strife, rising unemployment, and business indices that were flirting with the lowest point of the depression, others filled in the details the president had omitted. Comparing the state of the economy in the midst of what it called the "Roosevelt depression" with that at the peak of the Roosevelt "recovery" in June 1933, the *New York Herald Tribune* pointed out, "We have just passed through a contraction in industrial activity that has amounted to more than 22 percent and that has been roughly comparable, statistically, with the major depression experienced in 1920–21. In other words, the hundreds of millions in government funds that have been spent have not primed the pump at all; they have maintained retail business at a fairly good level, but they have, so far as priming heavy industries is concerned, been like so much water spilled on the ground." The lesson to be learned was that "there is no legislative legerdemain, whether it be monetary manipulation, price fixing or regulation, that is a sound substitute for business confidence." The New Deal had failed.[136]

For Hoover it was only confirmation that his policies had been correct, and those of Roosevelt, wrong. The number of unemployed in September 1934, he noted, was "about the same as September, 1932," but in 1932 the number had been decreasing, while in 1934 it was increasing.

Hoover's own analysis of the situation in late August compared it with that in November 1932, when FDR was elected:

> Unemployment at that date according to the American Federation of Labor was about 11,500,000. Today it is still 10,500,000 according to the same authority. On the basis of gold values, the price of farmers' commodities are lower today than they were on the first of November, 1932. I haven't looked it up, but I venture to say that the rate of wages, if we take into consideration the cost of living, is less today than at that time. And above all, if we look at the progress made by the other nations, we find that our situation today is on a fictitious basis while they are far ahead with sound foundations under them.[137]

And this lack of progress was despite the vast expenditures poured out by the Roosevelt administration. Hoover also noted that the New Deal's destruction of food was "now becoming a larger issue in the West as it is silhouetted against the drought. The continuation of the AAA now that the surplus has been removed by Providence is going also to loom large. On one count or the other, both consumer and farmer is going to complain. However, with 80% of the mid-west and western population directly or indirectly upon subsidy, Al Smith's appraisal of shooting Santa Claus is going to weigh in the elections."

Thus the situation did not seem to bode well for Republican chances in the 1934 congressional races. An electorate grown increasingly dependent on the New Deal Santa Claus was not likely to shoot him. The new GOP National Chairman, Henry Fletcher, reported from Washington a lack of funds and an absence of interest or courage on the part of those with the means to help and who ought to be dedicated to preserving the free enterprise system. Some money that might have gone to the party was clearly being drained away by the new American Liberty League, which had been launched by leading businessmen and political opponents of the New Deal during the summer.[138] Prominent in the new organization were people anathema to Hoover because of their opposition to his reelection in 1932. Moreover, the former president objected to the Liberty League's overemphasis, as he saw it, on property rights. He was, he said, "neither for the Wall Street model nor the Pennsylvania Avenue model" of liberty.

Hoover decided to take no role in the congressional elections, other than whatever influence *The Challenge to Liberty* might exert. He concluded that the GOP campaign committees regarded him as a liability and decided that they were probably right so long as most of the party's candidates seemed so determined to run as partial New Dealers. He wrote to former governor Henry Allen of Kansas that the Republican Party might be tracing the path to extinction followed by the Whig Party in the mid-nineteenth century, as its candidates were "afraid of or are refusing to fight these questions on principle." If the GOP did not stand up for its principles and offer an alternative to the New Deal, it would "slide down the same precipices which engulfed the Whig Party in 1856." Nevertheless, even Hoover recognized the "difficulties of making a campaign of opposition where Santa Claus is visiting each household, and I realize that many people in this world would rather be elected than to be right."[139] Senator Lester Dickinson of Iowa confirmed that "for the first time we are experiencing Tammany methods in national politics. They are buying favoritism."[140]

Republican pessimism was validated when they lost even more seats in the 1934 election, contrary to the tradition of off-year electoral gains by the opposition. It marked the third successive defeat for the Republican Party, dating back to 1930. Hoover, even though titular leader of the party, had taken no part in the election, and with the exception of his book he had done nothing to present the issues to the voters. No doubt he felt some measure of responsibility for the defeat as a result of silence on political issues during the twenty months after he had left the White House. Perhaps it was time for the titular leader to become less titular and more leader.

From Arch Shaw came word that the publication of *The Challenge to Liberty* had led several people to ask about the possibility of getting the former president to give speeches. He told Hoover, "The president of the [Chicago] Commercial Club has spoken to me three or four times and is very anxious that you speak before that organization. The chairman of the program committee of the Economic Club [of Chicago] is also very excited about your speaking at one of the four meetings that they hold during the winter. At the last dinner something over 1200 men attended. One of the officers of the Illinois Manufacturers' Association was in and is very anxious to get you to speak."[141]

Hoover had begun to cast about for ways that he could reappear dramatically on the political stage. Reports that the appearance of his image on movie theater newsreels was causing enthusiastic applause encouraged him to believe that there might, perhaps, be an audience at last for what he had to say. He was also becoming concerned over the emergence of Kansas governor Alfred Landon's candidacy for the GOP nomination in 1936 in the vacuum created by his own inactivity, and by suggestions in the media that the Republican debacle in 1934 was proof that the party needed to swing to the "left" if it were to compete with the Democrats.[142] Hoover, however, was not sanguine that anything would be able to break the hold of the Democrats for years. He told the Stanford University debate team in mid-January of 1935 that by its use of direct federal relief funds the New Deal had built "an unbeatable political machine" that the Republicans would not be able to defeat "for two or three elections," because the Democrats had "the people bought off for that long."[143]

An invitation to join the New York Life Insurance Company board of directors now gave Hoover an excuse for frequent trips to the east coast that would not arouse suspicions of political motives. In January 1935 he traveled to New York City by train, reviewing en route the material to be included in a book by William Starr Myers and Water Newton on the record of his administration. In New York City the former president received an enthusiastic welcome from old friends. Ogden Mills hosted a large dinner for him that included former officials of his administration and journalistic friends. To a query from Mills whether the time had come for Hoover to reappear on the public scene, the majority responded that no one except the former president could get a hearing from the newspapers and the public for criticism of the New Deal.[144] Hoover also attended the Lincoln Day dinner of the National Republican Club, at which an overflow crowd greeted him enthusiastically. In a few brief remarks, he lauded Abraham Lincoln and called for personal liberty, warning that the people must be masters of the government rather than "pawns of the state."[145]

Hoover wrote William Allen White that he had been "promoted to the life insurance business, which necessitates my going east once in a while and I shall thereby come nearer Emporia—and if the White family is not strongly insulated, I may be in to sell you a policy."[146] To another friend he wrote, with considerable irony, "I am now the joint trustee with Alfred E. Smith and Nicholas Murray Butler of the fate of millions."[147]

While Hoover was returning to Palo Alto the Supreme Court ruled that the Roosevelt administration's repudiation of the clause requiring that government bonds be redeemable in gold upon maturity was unconstitutional, but it simultaneously denied recourse through the courts for those seeking bond redemption in gold. As he travelled through the towns of the West, the former president was continually asked by newsmen for his reaction to the decision. Finally, in Tucson, Arizona, Hoover dictated a statement for the wire services in which he called for restoration of the gold standard at the present value of 59 cents for a dollar. He pointed out that most of the unemployment was centered in the capital goods and construction industries, that these were dependent upon long-term capital for recovery, but that capital for them would not be forthcoming so long as "people are hesitant to invest their savings and take long-term risks because there is uncertainty in what value they will be repaid." Such an action would, he argued, "put more men to work out of the twelve million who still remain unemployed than any other single action." Hoover ended his statement with this observation: "We can get in appearance a false prosperity out of inflation. There is much inflation poison in the national blood through the combined effect of the devaluation, expanded bank deposits through government borrowing, and the Federal Reserve credit policies. The fever may grow at any time. There is no real recovery on inflation medicine. If the currency were made convertible it would tend to check inflation, replace relief with real employment, and contribute materially to a general recovery."[148] As predicted, the words of the former president did instantly capture the front pages of the leading newspapers, the *New York Times* observing that it was "one of the few public pronouncements made by Mr. Hoover since leaving the White House in March, 1933."[149] The *New York Herald Tribune* found "much to be said for Mr. Hoover's solution," but it would work best if Hoover himself with his "sound economics" were president. On the other hand, if Roosevelt continued his unbalanced budgets, "no amount of gold can save the dollar from depreciation or the country from currency inflation." It concluded, "As a means of testing the will to end extravagance and maintain the dollar, Mr. Hoover's demand is fairly put and rightly timed. Only by such challenges as those uttered by the former President and by the Senator [Carter Glass] from Virginia can the truth be smoked out of the financial murk center over the White House and the Treasury Department."[150]

The chairmen of the House and Senate GOP campaign committees quickly followed his lead in declaring for immediate restoration of the gold standard, to the considerable embarrassment of those Republicans in Congress who had supported the New Deal financial policies.[151] As for Hoover, he had resolved to stay on the attack now that he had tasted battle. He told Arthur Hyde, he would "not keep still any longer" but would instead "periodically shoot at the situation." He had begun to gather material for future attacks on the Roosevelt administration's handling of relief and on the NRA. While some complained that it was "not good politics," he had "not noticed any Republican in Washington or New York raise his voice in protest of the Moral issue."[152]

Thus was unleashed five years of intense political activity by the former president, which would include the pursuit of his party's nomination for the presidency in 1936 and 1940. The political scientist was about to have another go at practical politics.

CHAPTER 2

The Politician

On The Attack

In retrospect, it should have been as obvious to Hoover and his close associates then, as it is to historians now, that the former president faced an insurmountable hurdle in his efforts to be credible either as a critic of the New Deal or as a candidate again for the presidency. That obstacle lay in the very different memory that public opinion had of his presidency from that of Hoover himself. Hoover's memory was of an administration that had conquered the depression in the summer of 1932 only to have the recovery nipped in the bud by Roosevelt's election in November and uncertainties over his policies.

The memory of the American public, however, was of an administration that had grappled with the depression for over three years without notable success. The upturn in economic indices during the summer of 1932 had been but numbers on paper for most Americans, unaccompanied by any real improvement in their condition before it was aborted. Frustratingly for the former president, he was in the position of a physician whose prescriptions had almost killed the patient once but who was now asking for another chance from a highly skeptical family. And those around Roosevelt wasted no opportunities to portray the former president in this light. Thus as the *New York Times* editorialized after his statement on gold, Hoover's advocacy of a cause was more likely to hurt it than to help it.[1]

Nothing that Hoover and his friends could do was sufficient to convince many Americans that he had produced recovery in the summer of 1932, nor has that point of view made noticeable headway over a half century later. In that situation, the former president's cause was a hopeless one and he might have exerted greater influence on the situation had he continued in the role of political scientist and philosopher instead of entering the political arena.

But Hoover had made his choice. His second "shot" at the New Deal was in the form of a public letter to a meeting of the California Republican Assembly in Sacramento. He could not be at the meeting in person because he was involved with Charter Day exercises at the University of California. In his letter, Hoover sounded a "call to arms" for Republicans. By contrast with his first stab at the New Deal, this one was fashioned with greater deliberation and was more comprehensive. The Republican Party, he told his audience, must furnish the "rallying point" for all Americans who favored "fundamental American principles" of "orderly individual liberty under constitutionally conducted government" against "the newly created system of regimentation and bureaucratic domination in which men and women are not masters of government but are the pawns or dependents of a centralized and potential self-perpetuating government." Hoover listed for Republicans the objectives they must champion:

> to upbuild and protect the family and the home, whether farmer, worker, or business man . . . The fundamental protection of these homes is the spirit as well as the letter of the Bill of Rights, with the supports from the framework of the Constitution. They must be given peace with the world. There must be confidence in the security of the job, of the business, of the savings which sustain these homes. Increased standards of living, leisure, and security can come to the home through unshackling the productive genius of our people. The advancement of knowledge must be translated into increasing health and education for the children. There must be constantly improved safeguards to the family from the dislocations of economic life and of old age. With the growth of great industrial forces we must continue to add increasing protections from abuse and exploitation. We must be liberal in reward to those who add service, material or spiritual wealth to these homes . . . The windows of these homes must bright with hope. Their doors must be open outward to initiative, enterprise, opportunity, unbounded by regimentation and socialism. Today there must be restoration of faith, the removal of fear and uncertainty that these ideals and these hopes will be open to those who strive.

It was primarily the responsibility of young men and women to ensure that liberty was preserved and responsible constitutional government restored in the United States.[2]

One gets the impression that Hoover's entry into the political foray was as much a surprise to him as to others. The impulsive act of the statement to reporters at Tucson seems to have pulled him onto a course that he had been steadfastly resisting. Just a month before that statement he remarked that he hesitated "greatly to make extemporaneous remarks" and "was too lazy to prepare an address."[3] In February he refused an invitation from William Allen White to give a speech in Kansas, saying that he had recently turned down "about 9,000 opportunities to speak" and was afraid of what would happen if he ever broke his rule against public addresses.[4]

The reception of his first two attacks on the New Deal, however, seems to have encouraged him to continue on with a course of action he had formerly been so dubious of pursuing. His seemed, he mused, to be the "only voice in the party which carries nationally" and to capture the front pages of the newspapers, even if it also brought the expected attacks on his ideas and speculation about his ambitions for 1936. As William Allen White noted, Hoover's position on gold had been attacked by "the inflationists and certain jealous elements in the Republican Party."[5] And the *New York Times*, in a front page story, reported that his statement to the California Republicans "was construed by Republicans and Democrats alike as a determined move by the titular Republican leader to lay down a course of action for his party and bring himself to the fore as the champion of such issues." It had, however, "failed to arouse aggressive interest . . . among many members of his party in Congress."[6] And it editorialized that, though Hoover was the titular leader of the GOP, "the balance of political opinion remains against him."[7] Hoover, however, concluded that the Sacramento statement had produced a "very good response . . . except from certain Republican groups—old guard and 'liberals.'"[8]

Hoover was encouraged by supportive communications he received after his first two efforts and resolved to continue "to fire a blast occasionally."[9] His travels in the Midwest and West, he told Rickard, had put him in touch with the "grass roots," where he had found considerable disillusionment by Republicans with the national committee and with the GOP members of Congress, because they did "not fight for the Republican Party." He reported receiving "thousands of laudatory letters" for his first two statements. Rickard was impressed by the change that had taken place in Hoover in a few months— his "vigorous statements and confidence in himself." Obviously being on the attack agreed with the former president.[10]

When Gertrude Lane asked him to write a guest editorial for *American Magazine*, Hoover responded that he was already committed "to three speeches and two blasts during the next month" and so had no time for such a project as she had in mind. He was also busy, he told her, "traveling about trying to persuade publishers of newspapers that this country is in real jeopardy" and to get them involved in the fight.[11]

In late May and early June, in fact, Hoover did travel through the West and Midwest, meeting with publishers of Republican newspapers, including the *Portland Oregonian*, *Spokane Review*, *Idaho Statesman*, *Rocky Mountain News*, *Des Moines Register*, and others. He told them that, among other matters, they should concentrate attention on the expenditure of relief funds. He arrived in New York encouraged by the aggressiveness he found on the part of the newspapers.[12]

When Christopher Morley, brother of Hoover's friend Felix Morley, wrote to him in February to ask if the former president would write a book review for *Saturday Review* of the autobiography of John Hays Hammond, Hoover could not resist the chance to chide Morley for the negative review *Saturday Review* had published of *The Challenge to Liberty*. He wrote Morley that he had never written a review in his life, and then added, tongue in cheek, "Anyway your journal (from its reviews of my small efforts at authorship) seems to have little opinion of either my moral character or my ability to write or think. It will take me quite a while to reform the first and to learn the second and third before I would be eligible to your columns. And besides, your readers might be astonished at your inconsistency!" Hoover then invited him to that summer's Bohemian Club encampment.[13] By mid-May, Hoover could write to Ashmun Brown, "I see that some Washington columnists . . . think my little book was a failure. There is at least the sardonic humor that it has reached 125,000 copies, whereas 'On Our Way' by FDR reached 14,700 and the publisher went broke. Likewise, [Interior Secretary Harold] Ickes sold 2,400."[14]

Hoover had also in mid-January begun efforts to influence the course of the Republican Party in 1935–1936 by encouraging constructive activity by Midwest Republicans. These activities resulted in the calling of a midwestern Republican "grass-roots" conference in Springfield, Illinois, in June and other conferences in various regions of the country.[15] Predictably, Hoover sought from the Springfield conference a declaration that would vindicate his presidency. The declaration, he told William Allen White, should include the assertion that the depression was international in scope and a result of World War I, a statement that the United States had been on the road to recovery in 1932 before it had been aborted by the election of Roosevelt, and "a detailed blast of [sic] the New Deal actions." It must also point out that the New Deal was leading "nowhere but to Fascism or Socialism" and that recovery could only come from putting "people back to work on real jobs."[16]

White, however, refused to draft a declaration that was so largely an indictment rather than a constructive program.[17] The platform produced by the conference was not nearly as forthright as Hoover had hoped, being a mixture of attacks on some parts of the New Deal with tacit approval of other parts.[18] Still, Hoover was buoyed by his success in getting constructive action begun and publicity for the party that would "keep the Republican lamp alight," and on the strength of that success and the reception to his first two attacks on the New Deal he began to consider a bid for the party's nomination in 1936.[19]

By June it was apparent to Edgar Rickard that Hoover wanted the 1936 nomination, even though the former president was not willing to work openly for it or to give any open encouragement to those who wanted to work in his behalf. Only if there was manifestation of strong support for his nomination, he said, would be consent to carry the party's banner, because he was convinced that Roosevelt's successor would be "the most hated man in the country" because of the policies he would have to follow to pay for the New Deal's extravagance. Even some good things the New Deal had done would have to be abolished until the government was solvent enough to afford them. He told Rickard that he would not "undertake that burden unless he was thoroughly supported by his friends."[20]

The odds of that happening were, however, infinitesimal, as many of his most dedicated supporters recognized, for there seemed no point in nominating a candidate who could not possibly be elected. As William Allen White observed,

> This is a strange world in which we are living today, and one of the saddest and yet one of the most curious phenomenon is that the great mass of American people hold even after three years the rancor of 1932 which overcame Hoover. Nothing more terrible, more disheartening to our democratic ideals has ever happened in the history of the republic than this mob rage at an honest, earnest, courageous man. Yet it is here. It still hangs on. And everything he says, as well as everything his friends say, is discounted. It is unbelievable.[21]

White's perspective, however, was at least slightly clouded by the fact that he had become interested in the campaign of his fellow Kansan, Governor Alf Landon, for the Republican nomination. In June, Hoover wrote dramatist/ author Channing Pollock that it was a problem to be "constantly presenting higher economics and higher sociology to a great mass of people who are at least slow of understanding. It is folks like yourself who can present these things in such a fashion as to stir people's emotions. In the short view, the voter moves on emotions."[22]

Typical of the attitude revealed by some of the press was a Harry Brown article in the Salt Lake City Tribune in late June:

> How can Herbert Hoover be muzzled? That question is heard in Washington many times a day; it is heard wherever Republicans meet, be they Senators, Congressmen, Progressives, or Old Liners; it is heard in all walks where one Republican encounters another, and it is significant for it indicates clearly that the former president since he began to talk has made himself a serious handicap for his party to carry and by the same token has become a real invaluable asset of the Democracy. The Washington opinion is nigh onto universal that Hoover talking is a party menace . . . Now that Hoover has gotten the habit, he is talking on the slightest provocation. For one thing, Hoover has fully established the suspicion that he is a candidate for the Republican nomination next year . . . The fact is that every time Hoover speaks, cold shivers run up and down the spines of Republicans who have begun to take heart and who are beginning to believe that they may have a chance in the 1936 election.[23]

Hoover was not in the least put off by what he described as the "college yell 'muzzle Hoover'" on which Democrats and conservative and radical Republicans alike had attained "real unity." "For good or evil," he wrote a friend, "I have one of the few voices that can make the front pages. If ever there was an obligation of conscience on an individual citizen, it is right here," and he proposed, he said, "to use that voice in any fashion that will contribute to a halt."[24]

What did incense Hoover, however, was the fact that Harry Brown was hired by the Republican National Committee to handle its publicity. This was an affront the former president could not allow to pass. He quickly wrote to several members of the national committee to protest. To Harrison Spangler, of Iowa, he wrote, "How in the devil Republicans can expect to win this campaign by driving my friends out of the party I do not yet see."[25]

The letters and newspaper comments on his public statements did not paint quite the dismal picture that Brown presented. On the other hand, they revealed considerable confusion over the former president's objective. The combination of his public attacks on the New Deal and his unwillingness to publicly encourage a political movement in his own behalf led many to wonder whether he sought to be kingmaker or king.[26] In either case, time had already by late 1935 become critical for action on Hoover's part—either to forthrightly declare for the nomination and pursue it, or to decline consideration of it and throw his support behind the candidate he favored. But Hoover refused either course, and while his intimates compiled mailing lists, distributed copies of his speeches and publications, arranged meetings for him, and tried to enlist new supporters under his banner, Hoover himself continued his attacks on the New Deal with a speech before the California Republican Assembly on October 5, 1935.[27]

The issue, Hoover told the assembled Republicans, was "between straight and muddled thinking." Common sense was the only solution to America's problems, and the New Deal's combination of "gigantic spending" and "unbalanced budgets" was "the most subtle and one of the most powerful dangers which has been set in motion by the administration." One test should be applied to all legislation: "Will these measures restore the prosperity of America? Will they restore agriculture? Will they give you real jobs instead of the dole? Will they make America a happier, a better place in which to live?"[28]

The New Hoover

Time magazine looked at the potential GOP nominees in mid-October and wrote of the Hoover who had delivered the speech in California,

> The Herbert Hoover his listeners saw was not the grey-faced, discouraged oldster of 58 who drove down Washington's Pennsylvania Avenue and out of public life on March 4, 1933, but a vigorous figure of 61 with rosy cheeks filled out to their rotund par. The Hoover health had been restored solely by short morning walks near his Palo Alto home with his elkhounds "Weegie" and "Negri," by 45 min. drives up to San Francisco in his tan Buick touring car, Mr. Hoover at the wheel. The Hoover state of mind, while still definitely solemn, had been improved by the tranquility of his surroundings, his gardens, the view from his window of the quiet Coast Range and placid San Francisco Bay.
>
> But Herbert Hoover had not returned to Palo Alto to dodder his days away . . . [T]o keep in touch with the rest of the nation he had evolved a comprehensive, businesslike system which now keeps two stenographers and a pair of secretaries busy. Mrs. Dare Stark McMullin, an old friend

of Mrs. Hoover, is the secretary who culls the Hoover mail. Secretary Paul Sexson, a handsome young Stanford graduate, goes through a dozen newspapers airmailed daily from the East and a sheaf of pertinent editorials which Hoover friends also airmail in from all over the country. In addition, to keep the "Chief" posted on national and world affairs, the Stanford [sic] War Library, which Trustee Hoover helped to endow, is required to send in a daily report on the mutations of Fascism, Communism and the New Deal, all equally horrendous to Mr. Hoover. Furthermore, any member of the Stanford faculty who has returned from an Eastern trip may expect within a few hours an invitation to dine with the Hoover that night.

At 623 Mirada Road, Hoover's "unguarded, unmarked house on the side of Palo Alto's San Juan Hill," the upper floor was the entrance floor, where Hoover had "his study-office, a gracious paneled room with easy chairs, a Laszlo portrait of his wife and access to the secretarial offices below."[29]

Writing in Collier's in mid-October, also, George Creel examined the implications of Hoover's sudden reappearance on the scene for the Republican Party. The former president was, Creel wrote, the source of "mounting Republican panic," a "cloud that threatens to blot out their sun; the skeleton that bids fair to make a mess of their feast." He quoted one Republican as allegedly having said, "We know now just what the Democrats suffered with William J. Bryan. Lord, if Hoover would only get out and leave us alone." But Hoover had no such intention, Creel wrote, "Planted firm in a comfortable chair on the front porch of his pleasant home in Palo Alto, he looks out over the Republican Party in full confidence that it is still his demesne. Stouter than when he quit the presidency, his face has lost its querulousness, and that curiously lunar terrain is broken up at intervals by an actual smile. From all appearance he is both a happy man and hopeful."

Hoover was determined, Creel said, not to be "pushed aside or minimized" as titular leader of the party and considered that he was unpopular only with "crack-brained, radical element that has no proper place in Republican councils." He was also convinced that the American people now recognized that he had been "a great Chief Executive, who had the misfortune to run into a set of tragic circumstances over which he had no control, and that these circumstances were capitalized by unscrupulous demagogues to his discredit and defeat" and that they might well demand his renomination in 1936.[30]

The next month, Hoover ventured outside California to address the Ohio Society dinner in New York, after telling them that he had "no interest in these times in making just another speech, that I shall deal with some phase of public questions and with gloves off, otherwise they should get somebody else."[31] After attending a football game with Lou Henry and friends, the former president sat at the head table for the dinner and spoke for 43 minutes, with his speech interrupted 41 times with applause.

The speech dealt with New Deal economic planning. The National Industrial Recovery Act had been invalidated by the Supreme Court earlier in the year, thus removing one of the thorniest issues for which the Roosevelt administration had been criticized. Entirely apart from the regimentation that was so odious to Hoover and others, even such eminent economists as John Maynard Keynes had faulted the NRA for retarding recovery. But, unwilling to let the issue die, Hoover lambasted New Deal economic planning as a product of "starry-eyed young men in Washington" who thought they knew what was good for the country, and "a collegiate oligarchy" who used the term *planning* "to sanctify by a phrase a muddle of uncoordinated reckless adventures in government—flavored with unctuous claims to monopoly in devotion to their fellow men." The only thing the two types had in common, Hoover said, was their "habit of carefree scattering of public money" unchecked by "the old guest of a balanced budget." The New Deal had turned "the treasury into a national grab bag," had raised the cost of living for all, had eroded the purchasing power of wages, and had created strikes and class conflict.

Hoover had concluded, he told his audience, that

> a government should have in financial matters the same standards that an honorable man has. A government must realize that money must be earned before it is spent, that a nation's word in finance must be sacredly kept, that a nation is immoral if it repudiates its obligations or inflates its mediums of exchange or borrows without regard to prosperity; and, finally, that a nation which violates these simple principles will, like a man, end in dishonor and disaster. A government cannot expect financial honor in its people unless it maintains honor itself. A large part of the world's misery in all ages has come from the acts of government that ignored these principles and entered upon policies of reckless spending and debasement and repudiation.

The former president called for the abandonment of such financial and fiscal policies and of unnecessary expenditures on public works, a return of relief responsibility to local authorities, an end to "spending for visionary and unAmerican experiments," reduction of the size of the bureaucracy, balancing of the budget, readoption of the gold standard, and an end to inflation of the currency, as well as other reforms.[32]

The reaction to the Ohio Society speech was undoubtedly the most enthusiastic to date. The congratulatory telegrams were already pouring in when the former president returned to his Waldorf suite, many of them approving of his "change of style" and asking who was responsible.[33] Hoover himself considered the reaction "rather stupendous" and decided to deliver two more speeches attacking other aspects of the New Deal.[34] Demands for copies of the speech taxed the abilities of his Palo Alto staff to meet them, and Charles Hilles, hardly a Hoover intimate, recommended to the Republican National Committee that it begin to print and distribute Hoover's speeches since there was such a demand for them.[35] But the former president was pessimistic about the future, writing to Ballard Dunn that "the question is where the 'gimme' class is as potent as the pretorian guard," for "even the most 'political' Republican cannot outbid the Democrat. And if the 'gimme' group now dominates the future, the history of the Decline and Fall will be the same in either case."[36] To another correspondent he wrote, "Class conflicts on one hand and dependency on the other have been built up to a degree that makes one question as to whether a Democracy can survive."[37]

Newsweek magazine examined the reappearance of Herbert Hoover a few days after the Ohio Society speech and wrote,

> Seven weeks ago at Palo Alto, Calif., Herbert Clark Hoover blasted away at the New Deal in his first political speech since 1932. Last week in New York he again lambasted the New Deal.
>
> Throughout the country editorial writers interpreted the two broadsides as proof that the Hermit of Palo Alto was again going into action.
>
> The truth is that since 1933 the ex-President has been about as inactive as Notre Dame's rambling football team. He has crossed the continent twelve times, made innumerable trips about the West, and practically commuted between Palo Alto and Chicago.

"Of late," *Newsweek* reported, Hoover's Palo Alto home had "become a political beehive."[38] The *Literary Digest* made Hoover's movements even more graphic by reprinting a map from *Today* on which were outlined his many trips from 1933 through 1935. Writing in *Today*, Don Wharton pointed out that Hoover had "traveled more than 45,000 miles since he went into retirement," had "visited some twenty-eight States," and had been "in every section of the country . . . In New York, he is rated as one of the most regular guests of the Waldorf-Astoria."[39] But Hoover did not just stay in New York City during his trips east. In October, for example, he took the train to Philadelphia with friends, met with Stanford alumni, and attended the football game between Yale and Pennsylvania. He received a spontaneous reception at the game and autographed hundreds of programs and cards.[40]

Arthur Sears Henning of the *Chicago Tribune* visited Hoover in Palo Alto in November and wrote,

> I talked for two hours with former President Hoover today and came away with a clear impression that here is a man who is not seeking the Republican nomination for President next year. But as to the Republican nomination seeking him, that is another matter. If the convention should turn to him as its candidate, Mr. Hoover would accept, grateful for vindication at the hands of his own party, deeply sensitive of the responsibility of leadership, and wired with the determination to save his country as he views it from ruin at the hands of the New Deal. Not that he said so, for he would not discuss the question of his renomination . . . I am merely setting down my own impressions and conclusions formed in the

course of a conversation that ranged all the way from the idiosyncrasies of euca-
lyptus trees to the monetary manipulations of the Roosevelt administration . . .
I carried away the conviction that the paramount and all-consuming subject of
his thought is the ways and means to bring home to the people the national peril
of the New Deal nostrums, and that his last and least concern is his own political
fortune . . . He is convinced that unless the Roosevelt revolution be arrested no
later than next year, the continuing deficits, inevitably as they always have, will
produce an inflation in some form that will impoverish all but the speculators
who profit from such catastrophes. And as he talked he turned away from me
and gazed a long time out of the broad window overlooking the valley and I saw
that there were tears in his eyes.[41]

In September Hoover wrote a supporter that he was having trouble decid-
ing on subjects for his speeches and badly needed "Mr. Roosevelt to make
another speech as that helps powerfully."[42] Obligingly, Roosevelt presented
Hoover with a theme for his next speech, when the president responded to
critics of the New Deal with an address in Atlanta, Georgia that the *New York
Times* described as a defense of his administration and especially of its fiscal
affairs. Roosevelt argued that the "mechanics of civilization" had come to a
"dead stop" by the day of his inauguration, culminating a long spiral that had
begun with the stock market crash late in 1929. The New Deal had, however,
reversed the downward trend, Roosevelt asserted, increasing farm income by
$3 billion since 1932, with a resultant "rebirth of city business, the reopening
of closed factories, the doubling of automobile production, the improvement
of transportation and the giving of employment to millions of people." The
worst of the depression was over, and America was again in the "black."[43]
While the speech did not mention Hoover by name, it was clearly a response
to Hoover's attacks. O'Laughlin wrote him that "a situation has been created
by Roosevelt where you and he are crossing swords; that is an excellent development."[44] Hoover agreed and said he would "take the Atlanta speech for a
trimming on December 16th at St. Louis."[45]

Roosevelt's speech was made to order for Hoover, and the former president
clearly relished the opportunity it furnished not only to attack the New Deal
but also to defend his own administration against Roosevelt's assertions. Much
of the speech dealt with past themes he had covered, including the regimentation and fiscal irresponsibility of the New Deal. Then he turned to FDR's
charges that the economy had drifted unrelentingly downward under Hoover,
culminating in the bank panic of 1933. He again asserted that the depression
had been turned around in June and July of 1932 all over the world, including
the United States, and had continued its upward march everywhere but in
this country. After the 1932 presidential election, American recovery "beat a
retreat." Why had the panic of bank depositors come in March of 1933?

Hoover answered, "Because they [the depositors] were scared. We had no
bank panic from the crash of the boom in 1929. We had no panic at the financial collapse of Europe in 1931. We had no panic at the most dangerous point

in the depression when our banks were weakest in the spring of 1932. There was no panic before the election of November 1932. When did they become frightened? They became scared a few weeks before the inauguration of the New Deal on March 4, 1933." They had become frightened, Hoover argued, because the people awoke to the fact that the Roosevelt administration planned to violate its campaign pledges—that the gold standard would be abandoned, that the value of the American dollar would be tinkered with, and that "a wholesale orgy of spending of public money would be undertaken." The bank panic had been an attempt by depositors to protect themselves. Hoover also excoriated the waste and political uses of relief under the New Deal.[46]

For his next speech, Hoover decided to attack Roosevelt's agricultural policies, a course many had been urging upon him for some time. The speech was delivered in Lincoln, Nebraska, on January 16, 1936, by which time the AAA had already been found unconstitutional by the Supreme Court. The New Deal agricultural policies, Hoover charged, had "advanced from cajolery with a gentle rain of checks to open coercion. Men who planted on their own farms and sold in their own way . . . could have been sent to jail for doing just that. That is not liberty. That is collectivism." The processing tax levied to support the AAA had been a burden on the homes of 15 million workers and had "set boiling the witches' cauldron of class conflict of town against the farmers." Again making the case for a recovery during his presidency, Hoover argued that agriculture prices "arose in a state toward equality with industrial prices" in the summer of 1932, only to have that recovery retarded by the New Deal. The result of the New Deal's agricultural policies had been, said Hoover, "that the farmer has less to sell and pays more for what he buys. Labor pays for it in increased cost of living. By this device we have got the Economic Dog running around in circles chasing its tail." Exports of agricultural products had fallen, while imports of those products had risen. While American farmers were being forced to produce less, the American market was being increasingly opened by reciprocity treaties to the farmers of foreign countries.[47]

Getting Personal

Despite the enthusiastic reception the speech received in the press, Hoover found it attracting little support from Republicans in Washington.[48] And the former president also realized that Roosevelt was a good deal more popular than his New Deal programs.[49] It was not enough to attack the New Deal; the president must be linked to the programs in order to drive home to the voters Roosevelt's responsibility for the New Deal. But two of the most controversial of the New Deal programs had already been eliminated from the 1936 campaign by the actions of the Supreme Court. Roosevelt could no longer be hurt by them.

Meanwhile, Hoover's own prospects for winning the Republican nomination in 1936 seemed to be limping, despite his speeches. Even after the speech in Lincoln on agriculture, polls of Nebraska farm voters showed FDR the clear choice with them, with Hoover trailing both Landon and Senator William Borah of Idaho on the Republican side.[50] By early 1936, Landon had emerged as the clear favorite for the GOP nomination and was being supported by William Randolph Hearst's newspapers, a source of support that was anathema to Hoover and other leading Republicans like William Allen White.[51] Hoover's own "campaign" for the nomination seemed dead in the water. As one supporter wrote, the campaign was without a candidate and a rallying point, and without them there was no way to "bring out and evidence the support" for Hoover.[52]

In January, Hoover was aroused by a speech from Secretary of Interior Harold Ickes, in which Ickes had tried to deflect criticism away from FDR by telling his audience that Congress under Presidents Harding, Coolidge, and Hoover had "passed laws that were held unconstitutional, but it was not urged against these Presidents 'that they were deliberately trying to undermine the Constitution and erect a dictatorship' on the soil of free America because the courts disapproved some of their laws."[53] Hoover immediately challenged Ickes's statement where his presidency was concerned and demanded an apology to the public from the secretary of interior. He wired Ickes, "Not one of several hundred acts of that period has been held unconstitutional. I never signed a law without bearing in mind the special obligation which rested upon the President to protect the Constitution."[54] Ickes at first refused to respond to Hoover's wire, and when he did finally respond, on January 16, he admitted that he was wrong, but gracelessly added, "I am the more willing to accept your statement that no law passed during your administration has been declared unconstitutional in view of the fact that that administration was notable as do-nothing administration . . . It is entirely constitutional to do nothing."[55]

On February 12, 1936, Hoover responded to Roosevelt's State of the Union address with a speech of his own. The New Deal, he charged, had been a "veritable fountain of fear" from the interregnum onward, and it was only "the Supreme Court decisions crashing through New Deal tyrannies which brought a gleam of confidence from the fears that had retarded recovery." By implication, then, it was the Supreme Court and not the New Deal that was responsible for the upturn in the economy that had begun shortly the NRA decision and was continuing on into 1936. In other respects, this speech repeated the themes expressed in Hoover's previous four major speeches on the New Deal.[56]

Two weeks later the inner circle of the Hoover campaign met in the offices of the banking firm of Kuhn, Loeb and Company in New York City. In attendance were Lewis Strauss, banker and veteran of Hoover's relief activities, Edgar Rickard, Walter Brown, Larry Richey, and California oilman Bert Mattei. The latter reported failure in obtaining sufficient funds to continue to print and distribute Hoover's speeches. Brown presented discouraging news from his state of Ohio, where a poll of 1,600 Republicans had garnered only 4 percent support of Hoover as the nominee. It was clear that Landon had a lock on the nomination, and the conferees agreed that if the situation remained hopeless as of May 1, Hoover should renounce any interest in the nomination and pledge his support to whomever the nominee turned out to be.[57] Hoover, however, seems to have been more amenable to suggestions from others who were not included in the meeting that he continue to fight to the end. Such a course might lead him to be nominated in the event of a deadlock, and at the least, they argued, it should permit him to exercise a strong influence on the choice of the nominee.[58]

Meanwhile, Hoover continued to the most visible of any Republican in his attacks on the New Deal. In March he addressed Young Republicans in Colorado Springs and lambasted Roosevelt's betrayal of the 1932 Democratic platform on which he was elected. He deplored the tendency apparent in America toward personalized government at the expense of liberty, arguing that "almost every one of the world's mistakes had its origin in personal government. Violation of treaties, great wars, persecution of Jews, and other religionists, and so on down to the fantastic laws by a Must Congress, and the slaughter of pigs." There were, he told his young audience, three alternatives before Americans: unregulated business, government-regulated business, and government-dictated business. Government-regulated business was the "American System," whereas government-dictated business was the New Deal method, with its ideas "dipped from the cauldrons of European Fascism or Socialism."[59]

By the middle of March Hoover was convinced both that his chances of winning the Republican nomination were dismal and that FDR had so gained in strength that the nomination was of little value in any case.[60] Ironically, recognition that Hoover was the leading Republican critic of the New Deal had not caused him to become the logical Republican nominee in 1936 in the minds of any but a small minority of voters. At the same time, the campaign of Governor Landon was gaining momentum and Hoover was confronted by a challenge from the Kansan in his home state of California. An uncommitted slate of delegates had been put together there with Hoover's approval, and it contained delegate candidates who were committed to a variety of potential nominees or none at all. A rival slate of Landon delegates was now entered by Governor Frank Merriam and newspaper publisher William Randolph Hearst to try to win the state's convention votes for the Kansan, despite promises from Landon's California managers that they would not contest for the state's delegates.[61] When Landon refused to repudiate the Merriam-Hearst slate, Hoover returned to California to fight for the unpledged slate in the primary. All recognized that if Landon were able to win the delegates of Hoover's own state the former president's hopes for the nomination would be dead. Hoover's only hope of keeping even the faintest prospect of a renomination alive was to deal a symbolic defeat to Landon in California.[62]

In that same month, John Flynn scrutinized the former president for the liberal *New Republic* magazine. Who, Flynn wondered, was this person whose speeches were going out over the airwaves purportedly in the name of Herbert Hoover? Clearly it was "not the same person who gloomed his way through four tearful years as President." That Hoover's

> countenance was perhaps almost the worst possible one in America for use in connection with the theory that the way to end a depression was by raising public confidence. The poor man had in his vocal repertoire just two notes, one of which he used to intone nearly all the syllables of the sentence and the other, several tones lower than the first, he saved for the final syllable. The effect on listeners was to suggest thoughts of suicide or bankruptcy. How many men went out and hung up the shutters on the store after listening to a Hoover speech, no one will ever know.
>
> However, in the fullness of time he was squelched by the people and the air waves heard his two notes no more. Now three years have elapsed. He yearns for renovization. And now, apparently, a crew has gone to work to produce another "new Hoover." This time it is to be a gay Hoover, full of bright, cheery quirks and merry quips. The voice has been supplied with several more notes. The face has been rebuilt and a new system of lighting installed. In other words, Mr. Hoover has resorted to the art of make-up. The new package is labeled—H. Hoover, Happy Engineer.
>
> But after all, is this the real Hoover? There ought to be an investigation. We ought to determine how far we wish to introduce the make-up methods of Hollywood and the stage dressing room into the business of solving our national difficulties. We ought to discover if this voice we hear over the air and these oratorical caprices we read in the papers are coming from a real person or a synthetic robot who delivers the combined talents of a group of showmen.[63]

Meanwhile, Hoover had postponed a planned fishing trip to Florida in order to write and deliver another blistering attack on the New Deal in a speech at Fort Wayne, Indiana on April 4. Roosevelt's campaign in 1932, he charged, had been based "upon the implication that the depression was caused by me personally," and "continuously, day in and day out, before and even since the inauguration, and in the evening by the fireside, Mr. Roosevelt has condemned with great bitterness the policies and methods of the last Republican Administration." But the "saddest blow of all," Hoover told his audience, was that "certain New Dealers now arise and say that I was the father of the New Deal." And the former president admitted that "omitting their monetary and spending debauch, about all the agencies they will have left after the Supreme Court finishes cleaning up the unconstitutional actions will be the institutions and ideas they got from the Republican Administration." The Roosevelt administration had not only failed to keep its promises to the American people but it had made a worse record in solving the depression than Hoover's own administration. He would, Hoover said, "be glad if the thinking American people would soberly consider if the Republican Elephant, even though he has made mistakes, is not more surefooted toward recovery and progress than the bounding white rabbits of the New Deal. I recommend that magician's animal as the symbol of the New Deal party. It travels in uncertain directions at high speed. It multiplies rapidly."[64] At the end of the speech it was to be announced that a 96-page booklet containing Hoover's recent speeches was available by mail from NBC. Rickard reported that funds had been obtained to print ten thousand of them, though he hoped "the demand will be for a million of them, even though I don't know where the funds are coming from to print them."[65] In fact, however, the NBC announcer gave the impression that it was only that night's speech that was available, and only about three thousand copies were requested.[66]

Hoover then delayed his Florida fishing trip even further to hurry back to California in order to orchestrate the campaign for the uncommitted slate of GOP delegates.[67] The optimism of Hoover and his supporters took a giant leap when on May 5 the Landon slate of delegates went down to defeat before the uninstructed slate backed by Hoover. This symbolic victory over Landon was perceived by Hoover's supporters as keeping him in the thick of the race for the nomination.[68] Buoyed by the California result, Hoover delivered his final preconvention speech in Philadelphia nine days later, in which he again set forth his concept of the proper GOP alternative to the New Deal. Disaffected Democrats should join with Republicans in putting "the republic on the road to safety," which meant that the GOP platform should be a platform for "the American people" and not just for Republicans. The "five horsemen" of the New Deal Apocalypse—"Profligacy, Propaganda, Patronage, Politics, and Power"—or "Pork-barrel, Poppy-cock, Privileges, Panaceas, and Poverty"—must be reversed. The GOP should go on record in support of abolition of child labor and the provision of old-age pensions and better housing.[69]

From Ballard Dunn at the GOP National Committee came the observation that in a recent speech FDR had sneered at Hoover's campaign comment concerning "that grass which was to grow in the city streets." He told Hoover, "At Sioux City, Iowa on the 14th, April, there was held the first of a series of conferences protesting against the flood of imports of farm products— protesting against the Canadian trade treaty and like treaties . . . Enclosed is a copy of the resolutions adopted at Sioux City. George Peek talked there— Mr. Peek believes that tragedy will be the result of this flood of imports—as you put it, unless they are stopped, grass will grow in our city streets."[70]

By now it was apparent that the only hope of a Hoover renomination lay in a deadlock at the convention. To encourage such a deadlock, the former president apparently encouraged Frank Knox's candidacy, leading Knox to believe that Hoover would swing the California delegates behind him.[71] On May 18, nearly a month before the convention, Hoover took himself out of the active pursuit of the nomination by telling the press,

> It should be evident by this time that I am not a candidate. I have stated many times that I have no interest but to get these critical issues before the country. I have rigidly prevented my friends from setting up any organization and from presenting my name in any state convention and so not a single delegate from California or any other state is pledged to me. That should end such discussion and get one thing straight, I am not opposing any of the candidates. My concern is with principles. The convention will be composed of a most unusual and able personnel. The seriousness of the convention is evidenced by the fact that the large majority of the delegates are being sent by the people of the states without other instructions than to find the right thing to do for our country in the greatest crisis we have met in two generations.[72]

Hoover explained later that the statement had been made "just to keep in line with the realities of the situation. The politicians in this country still run it." But despite his disclaimer, efforts were still under way to convince the delegates that Hoover's nomination would be "the right thing to do for" their country.

Against the opposition of many Republicans, both Old Guard and New Guard, Hoover's friends were able to secure him an invitation to address the convention at Cleveland. Throughout the evening and late into the night before his arrival, a sound truck roamed the streets announcing the time of his train's arrival. When he descended from the train a crowd estimated by Edgar Rickard, perhaps optimistically, at eight thousand was there to greet him. According to Rickard's diary, Hoover was visited on June 10 by representatives of Borah, Knox, and Vandenberg who urged him to join in a stop-Landon movement, but the former president refused. At 8:30 that evening, Hoover appeared on the platform of the convention for his speech and was greeted by a wildly enthusiastic demonstration.[73]

On the shoulders of the delegates, Hoover declared, rested "the greatest responsibility that has come to a body of Americans in three generations," the responsibility "to determine the fate of those ideals for which this nation was founded." Their titular leader then took Republicans through a survey of the New Deal and observed, "The New Deal may be a revolutionary design to replace the American System with despotism. It may be the dream stuff of a false liberalism. It may be the valor of muddle. Their relationship to each other, however, is exactly the sistership of the witches who brewed the cauldron of powerful trouble for Macbeth. Their product is the poisoning of Americanism." And the New Deal had failed, so that it was now up to Republicans "to set the country on the road of genuine recovery from the paths of instability." If the GOP temporized over the principles of freedom it would deserve the same fate as the Whig Party a century earlier. And then came the attempt at a Patrick Henry-like ending:

Republicans and fellow Americans! This is your call. Stop the retreat. In the chaos of doubt, confusion, and fear, yours is the task to command. Stop the retreat, and turn the eyes of your fellow Americans to the sunlight of freedom, lead the attack to retake, recapture, and remain the citadels of liberty. Thus can America be preserved. Thus can the peace, plenty, and security be re-established and expanded. Thus can the opportunity, the inheritance, and the spiritual force of your children be guaranteed. And thus you will win the gratitude of posterity, and the blessing of Almighty God.[74]

Hoover's speech was followed by another enthusiastic demonstration and repeated cries of "We Want Hoover!" The demonstration could not be gaveled into silence and efforts to bring on the next speaker were fruitless even after it was announced that Hoover had left the hall and was returning to New York. Since nothing could still the boisterous demonstrators the convention had to be adjourned until the following day.[75]

This demonstration of Hoover's popularity apparently caused Knox and Vandenberg to seek his support in a common cause with Borah to stop Landon's nomination. According to Chester Rowell, Hoover replied that even if he joined them in such a statement, "probably Landon would be nominated anyway, as both of them had already shot their bolt. Then he, as the former President, who had just reminded the party of its great mission, would have been the one who disrupted that party and prevented it from carrying out that mission."[76] The nomination the next day was a cut-and-dried affair.[77] Landon was nominated, and Knox was chosen as his running mate. Although he was named as the vice presidential candidate, Knox apparently never forgave Hoover for what he regarded as a "double cross" of his own attempt at the nomination.[78]

Hoover had long since formed an unflattering opinion of the Kansas governor's fitness for the White House, regarding him as woefully inexperienced to handle the foreign and domestic responsibilities that fell to the president of the United States.[79] He also worried over the direction that Landon and his followers might lead the Republican Party, fearing that their course might be away from that charted by Hoover. To block such designs, the former president sought to exert influence on key planks in the party's platform, particularly insisting that it support the gold standard and a stable currency. When Borah managed to prevent any mention of gold in the platform, Hoover insisted that he would not support the ticket unless it was included. The term "sound money" had been used to "mislead the people by the New Deal," he charged. "It is a weasel word." The impasse was only settled when Landon wired his campaign chairman, John D. M. Hamilton, his interpretation of the platform to be read to the delegates in which he pledged to regard the platform reference to "sound money" as meaning "a currency expressed in terms of gold and convertible into gold."[80]

In early December, Hoover gave William Starr Myer his "inside news" of the campaign. Landon, he said, had been "a weak candidate," who had "evaded every issue to get the nomination" and had been "built up by a synthetic process like one would sell soap." After leaving the convention, Hoover learned of the capitulation in the platform to Borah over sound money and had threatened to "walk out" on the candidate. Landon at first refused to make a statement in favor of the gold standard, but John Hamilton refused to make his nominating speech unless he did. Hoover had advised the California delegation to "fight on the floor for sound money and walk out if defeated." He praised John Hamilton but told Myer that Hamilton had no control over the Landon campaign, that he was "dictated to from Topeka, getting up in the morning to find his work already laid out." Hoover thought Landon could have been elected if the election had been held in July, but his campaign was badly managed and "went to pieces."[81]

Ex-Titular Leader

Dethroned as titular leader of his party, Hoover could now only wait to see if he would be called upon to play a part in Landon's campaign. Despite his hard-hitting speeches before the convention and praise for his convention address, Hoover distinctly felt that he was out of harmony with those around Landon.[82] Despite indirect feelers that he and his supporters put out to the nominee, there came no requests for his participation in the campaign from either Landon headquarters or the Republican National Committee.[83] And so, for the first time since he had broken his silence over a year earlier, Hoover was out of public life until the latter stages of the campaign. He was restive, however, writing to Walter Brown, "My funeral eulogies have now been preached by all the press. As a last flower on the grave they have elected me elder statesman. How would it do to organize that office a bit and make it a live, militant job? It would surely chagrin the funeral directors and it might be made of some service to the American people."[84]

On Independence Day, Hoover trekked back to the gold country of California where he had worked as student mining engineer during his Stanford days and described it as "one of the happiest days of my life. I have been received not as a former President but as one coming back to his old friends." In what he billed as a nonpartisan speech, Hoover spoke to a crowd of six thousand on the subject of liberty. Liberty, he noted, was on the defensive throughout the world, including in the United States, and he told his audience, "It is not reactionary to hold fast to these fundamentals, to oppose tyranny and to support liberty. We realize that life is different in 1935 from 1776. The functions of government must always be expanded to restrain the strong and protect the weak. That is the preservation of liberty itself . . . But there are things that must be permanent if we would attain these purposes. The first of these is liberty." It was the "transcendent mission" of the United States "to hold bright the light of individual liberty" as a beacon for the rest of the world."[85]

In July, journalist Willard Kiplinger passed to Hoover, via Ben Allen, news that former New Dealer and now New Deal critic Raymond Moley would like to establish contact with Hoover. Kiplinger assumed that it was not a political initiative but a journalistic one.[86] Allen reported to Kiplinger that when Hoover saw the latter's letter "his only response was a broad grin, but I figure he understands exactly what you were driving at and I know he appreciates your analysis of the reason why Mr. Moley wants to see him." Allen promised to do everything he could to arrange it.[87] Thus was laid the groundwork for a close and longtime association between Hoover and Moley.

Republicans friendly to both Hoover and Landon worked to find a basis for the former president's participation in the campaign. According to Charles P. Taft, of the Landon camp, one part of the problem lay in the nominee's conviction that Hoover had tried to swing the Cleveland convention behind his own nomination and that Hoover supporters had tried to win over the anti-Landon forces to his candidacy. The result, Taft said, was that Landon did "not feel enthusiastic about begging Mr. Hoover to help and Mr. Hoover on the other hand, as the only ex-President, thinks the approach should come from this end." Taft threw the problem into the lap of his nephew, Robert A. Taft, for suggestions.[88]

Robert Taft had served with Hoover in the Food Administration during World War I and in the American Relief Administration in Europe after the war. He agreed that Hoover had probably sought the nomination at Cleveland but said he had seen no evidence of an organized campaign on Hoover's part to derail Landon at the convention. He told his uncle that he did not think it would hurt Landon to "invite him, without begging, to speak during the campaign."[89]

Thereafter friendly overtures began to emanate from Topeka, designed to smooth over any animosities between Landon and Hoover. On August 7 the nominee wrote Hoover a note of appreciation for a statement the former president had made about the improvement that could be expected in the unemployment situation with the election of a Republican president. Landon told Hoover that he "would appreciate your views as the campaign progresses."[90] When GOP chairman John Hamilton asked Hoover in mid-August to get into the campaign, Hoover insisted on a telegram from Landon inviting him to do so. Hoover told a friend, "The time has arrived to have a showdown over all this gossip as to whether I am a liability to Governor Landon or not. I informed Hamilton that if I did not receive the telegram, form of which I gave him, I would take it that they did not want me in this campaign; that I prefer to stay out of it, that I would make no difficulties for them whatever, but that I was getting completely fed-up with the constant gossip that comes out of Topeka." Hamilton had asked for several speeches from him, and Hoover was convinced that he was sincere, since he gave many reasons Hoover's participation would be valuable.[91] For his part, Hoover actually yearned to go on the stump against Roosevelt. He regarded FDR's acceptance speech as a reply to his own speech at the Cleveland convention and was eager to tear "that acceptance speech into small pieces."[92]

On September 2, the two Republican leaders found themselves on opposite ends of a telephone connection, although it is not clear who placed the call, and Landon asked Hoover's assistance in the campaign, especially "in October when the fighting gets hard on the home stretch." The two also agreed that the former president would stop off in Topeka to discuss the campaign on his return from a trip to New York.[93] After the telephone conversation, Hoover wrote to Landon, "I beg to confirm my answer to your telephone message of today that you urgently want my help and activity in this campaign. I shall be glad to help. Somewhere along the line I shall take occasion to indicate that you have made such a request as certain members of the Republican Publicity organization are giving a contrary color and are damaging the party and your interests. I will take up the question of visiting Topeka when I pass through Chicago on my way to New York."[94] Clearly the atmosphere between the two men was less than cordial. Hoover was disappointed at not receiving a greater role in the campaign.

On September 30, Hoover delivered a speech in Denver to the American Mining Congress that was unrelated to the campaign. In the speech the former president attacked Roosevelt's new undistributed profits tax for tending to "stifle honest enterprise, to lessen national assets, to help the powerful instead of the weak, to cost men jobs." He was, he told his listeners, not giving a partisan speech but merely relating objective sociology and economics. Hoover noted that there were "times when every business will lose money. It is at just such times that they cannot secure capital. If they have cash reserves they can hold staff and workmen together until things improve." Businesses had done that during the depression, but if they had been forced by an undistributed profits tax to pay all their profits out in dividends they would have lacked the cushion to do so, and there would have been many more bankruptcies and workers on relief. But now the Roosevelt administration proposed to penalize businesses for maintaining reserve funds by placing a heavy tax upon them, thus forcing them to pay those funds out in dividends that could then be taxed by the government.[95]

Through the remainder of September there was no word from Topeka on Hoover's participation in the campaign. Then late in the month Walter Newton reported to Palo Alto on a campaign swing through Iowa and Minnesota by the candidate and on a conversation with Landon and his lieutenants. Newton found concern being expressed in the Landon camp that Hoover was not involved in the campaign, and Newton had responded that if the former president was not active it was their own fault.[96] Two days later, Hoover was informed that Landon wished him to deliver his first speech in Philadelphia on October 16. The former president was elated.[97] On October 1, Hoover visited the candidate in Topeka to discuss the campaign. He came away convinced that Landon was but little versed in either American political history or foreign affairs and a man capable of little more than the management of a small business.[98]

Meanwhile, Hoover's supporters had arranged the finances for Hoover to participate in the campaign if called upon. His wealthy backers, primarily in California, had established Constitutional Publications, Inc., as the agency for printing Hoover's speeches and underwriting the costs of his travel and other expenses.[99]

Two weeks after his visit with Landon, Hoover delivered the first of his two campaign speeches, lashing out at the "intellectual dishonesty" of the New Deal. During the 1932 campaign Roosevelt had charged Hoover with "reckless and extravagant" spending, ignoring the fact "that Federal revenues had precipitously dropped off by two billion through a worldwide calamity":

> He denied us any quarter because we had placed humanity first in the American budget and spent and loaned public funds to a people in distress. Now he claims a patent on that idea. He gave us no credit marks for fighting a Pork Barrel Democratic Congress to get a balanced budget. He has patented many improvements on that barrel. With solemnity he promised to save 25 percent a year from expenditures of the government and to at once balance the budget. And he tearfully appealed to the woman in her home struggling to balance her budget. And he vigorously asserted he would never conceal anything.

But now Roosevelt "dismisses his own immensely greater deficits and all the evidences of his wastes and follies by the pious remark [that] for him and his supine Congress to have balanced his budget would 'have been a crime against the American people.' Thus he changes the rules between these two innings." After reviewing Roosevelt's failure to produce recovery and the shoddy bookkeeping of the New Deal, the former president told his listeners that the "hypocritical, misleading" figures used by the administration represented a "new deal in American public life . . . If an income taxpayer or any corporation kept books like this administration, that is if they showed similar morals in juggling their accounts, they would be put in jail." He called for the election of the Republican ticket in November, as well as the election of GOP Congressman and Senators to "drive these expenses down toward the Republican levels, balance the budget, put back the integrity of government accounting, and above all restore truth and morals to government."[100]

In Denver on October 30, Hoover delivered his second and final address of the campaign on a familiar theme, "The Challenge to Liberty."

Roosevelt, the former president observed, "on the eve of the election has started using the phrases of freedom. He talks sweetly of personal liberty, of individualism, of the American system, of the profit system. He says now that he thinks well of capitalism, and individual enterprise. His devotion to private property seems to be increasing. He has suddenly found good economic royalists. And he is a staunch supporter of the Constitution. Two days ago he rededicated the Statue of Liberty in New York. She has been the forgotten woman." But he pointed out that Roosevelt had made many statements in the 1932 campaign, too, that had turned out "not to mean what they were thought to have meant." Roosevelt should state "in plain words" whether he intended to revive the acts that the Supreme Court had invalidated, and whether he intended "to stuff the Court itself." The American people should be told whether Roosevelt had really abandoned "this 'new order,' this 'planned economy.'"

Then the former president closed out his speech, and his part in the campaign, on a familiar note: "Many of the problems discussed in this campaign concern our material welfare. That is right. But there are things far more important than material welfare. It is possible to have a prosperous country under a dictatorship. It is not possible to have a free country. No great question will ever be settled in dollars and cents. Great questions must be settled on moral grounds and the test of what makes free men. What is the nation profited if it shall gain the world and lose its own soul?" The election was not just between Landon and Roosevelt but "between two philosophies of government," between "a system of personal centralized government" and "the ideals of liberty."[101]

Landon, however, had not made the division between himself and Roosevelt in his speeches that Hoover had delineated in his own, having chosen to follow the path of what the former president called "me-too-but-cheaper." Hoover wrote in his memoirs years later that his Denver speech and the one before the convention "reaped so many thousands of telegrams and letters from radio listeners over the country and so many editorials as to give me complete conviction that the rank and file of the Party realized the issue. If Governor Landon had made a speech along that line to open his campaign and had stuck to it, he might not have been elected, but he would have left the Republican Party with a substance of principle—and he would not have gone into quick oblivion."[102]

It is certainly true that after a brief lead in both the Gallup Poll and the polls of the Democratic National Committee, Landon's popularity fell rapidly until by the time Hoover joined the campaign the Kansan was clearly destined to be the victim of a landslide. The massive outpouring of funds by the Roosevelt administration during the final months before Election Day certainly had much to do with the shift in the polls, but Hoover clearly cannot be blamed. Landon's lead in the polls came at the end of Hoover's blistering attacks on the New Deal before and at the convention, it fell when Hoover was not part of the campaign, and it did not rise again when Hoover rejoined the campaign in its last two weeks. It is possible that Landon's campaign lost a great deal from Hoover's absence during the critical months after the convention.

It is unlikely that Hoover could have won against Roosevelt if renominated in 1936, but it is probable that he might have done better than Landon. Roosevelt and Vice President John Garner certainly thought so. The president regarded Hoover as the only formidable challenger among the Republican possibilities and bet Raymond Moley that he would be nominated.[103] He regarded Landon as the weakest of his potential opponents and instructed members of his administration neither to say nor do anything that might prevent the Kansan from being nominated.[104] Garner believed that the "politically smart" thing for the Republicans to do in 1936 was to nominate Hoover, for even though he could not win he might help other Republican candidates gain office. When Landon was nominated, instead, Garner concluded rightly that the GOP had "set the stage for a party debacle."[105]

And a debacle it was. In his last poll, Gallup found only three states certain for Landon. On Election Day Landon carried only two of them. The campaign, Hoover concluded, had been a "mess" that left the Republican Party in shambles without "either principle or party spirit—at the moment." The party must now regroup around the "real principles and realities" that had been absent from Landon's campaign if it were to survive.[106] Trying to "out-New Deal the New Deal" had clearly not worked. Judging from the total Republican vote in lesser contests, Landon had not even captured the entire Republican vote, since Republican gubernatorial, senatorial, and congressional candidates had won between three and five million more votes than the Kansan.[107]

Hoover's friend and Landon supporter, William Allen White, did not know if Hoover could have attracted more votes than his fellow Kansan but felt that the former president "would have made more of an intellectual appeal." He wrote, "Possibly, and here I am not sure, the Republican Party would be better off if it had mapped a course in this campaign that would point to a definite plan and program in the future. We are a minority party. Our minds are not negative. They are affirmative . . . If we needed a program and platform and, as the old song says, 'a cause to justify,' Hoover could have lined the hem better than Landon."[108]

Lewis Strauss wrote Hoover a few days after the election that in New York the "general effect of the election" had been "similar to a concussion." Although Landon's defeat had been anticipated, people were "nevertheless stupefied at the realization of its completeness and more particularly by the fact that the debacle in congressional representation had not been anticipated at all."[109]

Columnist George Sokolsky suggested that Hoover make no statement on the future of the party "until Governor Lowden and a group could be arranged to call upon you for the assumption of leadership." Yet Landon, not Hoover, was now the titular leader of the GOP and he could be expected to continue to lead the party in a New Deal direction if there was no effort made to stop him. Hoover decided, with considerable encouragement from his friends, that only he was capable of steering the party back in the direction of traditional party principles. During a visit to Chicago in December he gained encouragement from his followers to "jump in and raise hell." The next month Hoover wrote reflectively to Arthur M. Hyde, his former secretary of agriculture, that he and his followers could pursue one of two courses: he could "sit back like

Cincinnatus, hoping to heaven that nobody will ever come near us," or he could adopt the role "of an evangelist in a world that does not wish to listen." He shrank from the latter role, he told Hyde, because of the "deprivation of the normal joys of life which lies in it, and the mud that comes from it," yet he felt "anxiety for the future of a misguided people." He would take on the occupation of evangelist only if there was a demand that he do so.[110]

To William Allen White, Hoover wrote that he was "relieved" at not having been called to assist any more in the campaign, since to do so "would have associated me with what was being said and done." He added,

> When the Republican Party starts out to mix populism, oil, Hearst, munitions and the Liberty League, it is bound to come to grief. I was interested in what you have to say as to sound finance of the party. You used the exact phrase that I did to some of the gentlemen in charge—that is, that if the money was taken from DuPont, Pew & Company, they would "sell the party down the river." And I am not sure that it has not been sold. It was a sad day when the party departed from my old rule of no more money than $10,000 from any one giver. I am not horning anybody out of the party. I see no possibility of fighting a battle to organize a political party for good government with the knife of that party constantly in one's back. From my "office" as an "elder states-man," I shall take occasion some one of these days to say what I think about the Republican Party and its conduct, and I shall do it with utter abandon of all restraints which have governed me up to this last election.[111]

Looking at 1936 in retrospect, Edgar Rickard noted that Hoover's visits to New York were now of longer duration. He added, "He had a signal victory in the primaries in California and the ovation at Cleveland was a most manifest vindication of his popularity and sound position."[112]

When the Brookings Institution think tank issued its book *The Recovery Problem in the United States*, columnist Arthur Krock found that it offered "far more pleasant reading to Palo Alto than to the White House." He noted that the Brookings Institution economists "pretty well" supported the Hoover contention that the United States had begun to recover from the depression in the summer of 1932 during his presidency, that it had suffered from the lack of cooperation from Roosevelt during the interregnum, and that Roosevelt's policy of taking the United States off the gold standard had not necessarily contributed to recovery since it had, in fact, "disorganized international economic relations."

While Hoover contemplated the role of evangelist in steering the Republican Party back to its vital principles, Landon, as titular leader, was proposing to Republicans and anti–New Deal ("Jeffersonian") Democrats a round-table conference to be held during the summer of 1937 to "help formulate definite policies" that would be agreeable to both groups.[113] Nothing could better illustrate the fundamental conflict between the two men than Hoover's desire to "purify" the GOP and Landon's efforts to "taint" the party further by compromising its principles in a coalition with non-Republicans.

Landon's proposal ran into early difficulties for a variety of reasons and from a number of groups within the GOP. Some, like former Illinois governor Frank Lowden, believed that Hoover should take the leadership of the party in these trying times. After meeting with Hoover and some of the former president's supporters in Arizona, Lowden proposed inviting both Landon and Hoover to spend a day or two at his farm in the expectation that this would convince the Kansan of Hoover's "inevitable leadership" and cause Landon to "fall in line."[114]

Hoover then traveled to New York and had been there but a short time when Roosevelt made his transparent grab for control over the Supreme Court by attempting to "pack" it with additional appointees of his own choosing. For those who were opposed to the New Deal, the Supreme Court was the last defense against Roosevelt's apparent grasp for autocratic power. The elections of the 1930s had given the Democrats lopsided majorities in both houses of Congress that had rubber-stamped most of Roosevelt's legislative initiatives. Only the Supreme Court had remained free of the president's control, and it had demonstrated its independence by voiding key elements in the New Deal program, including the NIRA and the AAA. During the winter of 1936–37 the president hatched his plan to bring the court to heel despite his failure to raise the issue during his reelection campaign a few months earlier. Hoover had, of course, questioned Roosevelt's intentions in the matter during his October 30 speech.

The president's grasp for control over the Supreme Court created consternation among many, including members of his own party, amid fears that Roosevelt was "driving steadily toward a dictatorship." Hoover quickly sought to mobilize opposition among political leaders and journalists of both parties from coast to coast. Using the skill and contacts honed during years in the Food Administration and in food relief activities, as well as from politics, Hoover was quickly able to organize groups in thirty states to arouse public opinion against the court-packing proposal. In describing Hoover's efforts, Edgar Rickard recalled that he had "made a nationwide address over the radio on the Supreme Court issue which was reproduced in full in 250 dailies and reprinted in hundreds of thousands of copies. He was largely instrumental in the creation of a great number of non-partisan leagues for support of the Supreme Court and continued to cooperate with those bodies."

Encouraged by the sizable opposition to Roosevelt's proposal among Democrats in Congress, it became the strategy of congressional Republicans to allow the members of the president's own party to carry the burden of the battle against him, lest GOP opposition drive Democratic opponents into supporting the White House. Republican Senators like McNary, Borah, and Vandenberg also sought to mute the opposition of Republicans outside Congress for the same reason, and special concern was expressed that Hoover might disrupt this strategy by attacks that would convert it into a partisan issue. Clearly, on a straight party-line vote the president's proposal could not be defeated.[115]

Although he issued a statement on February 5 deploring the implication in the president's proposal that he was attempting to subordinate the
court "to the personal power of the Executive," Hoover recognized in his
statement that the issue was one that "transcends any questions of partisanship," and he was as careful to counsel Landon against making it a partisan issue in his Lincoln Day speech as the Republican senators had been
about his own public statements. When he learned that Senator Borah felt
it was undesirable for Republicans to be "over-conspicuous" in the fight,
Hoover agreed, but he encouraged Borah to go on the attack because he
felt Borah's opposition was less likely than that of any other Republican to
alienate Democrats.[116]

Still, it would not do for the GOP to be totally silent on such a momentous issue, and Hoover finally despaired of the apparent timidity of his
fellow Republicans and went against even the advice of many friends by
delivering a speech on the issue. On February 20, 1937, he told the Union
League Club of Chicago that the court-packing proposal was "the greatest
Constitutional question in . . . seventy years." He reiterated that the issue
was a nonpartisan one and emphasized that he was speaking not as a Republican but "as an American who has witnessed the decay and destruction of
human liberty in many lands." The former president dismissed the arguments that had been advanced by the administration in support of the proposal. The motives behind it were clear. The Supreme Court had refused
to rubber-stamp the New Deal. Hoover observed, "If Mr. Roosevelt can
change the Constitution to suit his purposes by adding to the members
of the Court, any succeeding President can do it to suit his purposes. If a
troop of 'President's judges' can be sent into the halls of justice to capture
political power, then his successor with the same device can also send a
troop of new 'President's judges' to capture some other power. That is not
judicial process. That is force." The Constitution and the Supreme Court
would become "the tool of the Executive and not the sword of the people."
America had "already gone far on the road of personal government. The
American people must halt when it is proposed to lay hands on the independence of the Supreme Court. That is the ultimate security of every
cottage. It is the last safeguard of free men." Roosevelt needed to be told,
"Hands off the Supreme Court."[117]

Republicans and Democrats alike in the Senate raged over Hoover's
speech and some claimed, with doubtful authenticity, that it had weakened
the opposition in Congress.[118] Hoover was unrepentant, arguing that "if the
'hush-hush' people in Washington have their way, not only are we going to be
defeated, but the Republican Party is going to give the greatest display of cow-
ardice in all history." Only an aroused public opinion could force Congress
to defeat the president's proposal, and that is what he was trying to orchestrate nationwide. Perhaps with some exaggeration, Hoover claimed that the
response to his court-packing speech had exceeded that for any other speech

he had given and that the support for it came from Republicans and Democrats alike. And he insisted that when Republicans campaigned for election in 1938 they would "be grateful that at least one Republican had the courage to speak" out on the issue.[119] But he made no further speeches on the subject, although he vowed to "speak again when this goes nearer the end, which I don't believe will arrive for another month."

Although Hoover's supporters continued to urge him to take the lead in rebuilding the Republican Party, the former president insisted that he would take on the role of "evangelist" only if he knew that he had sufficient support. But Hoover did call upon the Republican National Committee to convene a national convention that would give new life to the party through the formulation of a statement of Republican principles. Ex-governor Frank Lowden supported the proposal, but Landon did not. Instead, Landon continued to toy with the idea of his round-table conference and to wonder if the court fight might bring more Democrats into the coalition that he envisioned.[120]

But Landon's handpicked GOP national chairman, John Hamilton, was also amenable to the idea of some kind of off-year conference if not a convention. Hamilton had studied the example of the Conservative Party in England and had concluded that the GOP might well emulate their practice of annual meetings and restatements of party policy. The disastrous performance of Republican candidates in the 1934 congressional races suggested that the party's office seekers should not again be forced to fend for themselves against the obvious appeal of New Deal candidates during off-year elections. Moreover, Hamilton found great confusion among Republicans about what the party stood for when he tried to raise money for the national committee. Landon's speeches had deviated substantially from the 1936 GOP platform. Was it the platform that defined the party's position in 1937, or Landon's "New Dealish" speeches, or some new credo based on the changing circumstances of 1937?[121] Landon clearly hoped it would be his speeches, while Hoover sought a more traditionally Republican platform for 1938.

Hoover and Hamilton agreed, then, on the desirability of some kind of national meeting, although Hoover took a somewhat broader view of its scope. Hoover also suggested that the convention be called by Lowden, Landon, and himself. Lowden had already given his consent. On April 19, Hoover dined with Hamilton and outlined his proposal.[122] Hamilton then took the matter up with his fellow Kansan only to find that the titular leader objected to the idea. Hoover was disappointed. The GOP, he told Hamilton, could not wait until 1940 to act constructively. He had discussed his proposal with thirty leaders of the party, he said, and only Landon was not enthusiastic about it. He suggested, therefore, that they "march ahead" without Landon, if necessary.[123] But without the approval of the titular leader, Hamilton lost his enthusiasm for the scheme. Instead of the convention that Hoover envisioned, Hamilton now advocated a statement from a smaller policy committee that could be named by the Republican national committee.

Hoover addressed a long letter to William Allen White in May to make the case for some action by the GOP. He told the Kansan,

> It seems to me that you and I mean "Historical Liberalism"—the kind that exudes from the word liberty. In that light the Roosevelt Administration is more reactionary than George IV. It is the negation of all that the word means except in its minor dictionary connotation of giving away other people's money. The New Deal having corrupted the label of liberalism for collectivism, coercion, concentration of political power, it seems "Historical Liberalism" must be conservatism in contrast. In addition, there are acts and policies of the New Deal that are neither reactionary, conservative, liberal, nor radical. They are just crazy. With that explanation of what liberalism is we can pass on.
>
> I certainly agree with your three premises—a. That we must have two political parties or we die. b. The old politicians' slogan that elections can be won by "the vote against" blew up in the last campaign. No political party can live without affirmative principles. c. That the party other than the New Deal should adopt the position of my Colorado Springs speech.
>
> It seems to me for a dozen reasons the Republican Party cannot be abandoned as a practical thing. It has to be revitalized and ought to be purged a lot. Today nobody knows what it does stand for . . . It is certain that some time this whole American economic works is going to smash in a chaos from the artificial and crazy forces that have been put in motion. That means either the Fascist on horseback or a turn toward "Historic Liberalism." That turn will not come unless there is a party in the country with a banner up, with affirmative principles and a belief in its leadership. There is neither today. So why not try to erect that banner?[124]

Thwarted at least temporarily on one front, Hoover moved on another. By May, the "express desire" he had insisted upon before taking on the role of evangelist began to be mobilized. Movements were begun by Arthur Hyde, John Spargo, and William Starr Myers, as well as Dean Sommer and Professor Allison Reppy of the New York University School of Law, who began to mass mail hundreds of Republicans who were believed to be Hoover supporters in order to test their loyalty to "The Chief" and to see if they would join in the effort to draft Hoover as the "intellectual leader" of the GOP.[125]

In mid-May 1937, Hoover was on the front page of the *New York Times* in connection with a new activity. Recently named national chairman of the Boys Clubs of America, Inc., the former president appealed for a $15 million fund to build one hundred new clubs in fifty cities within three years. The clubs, which then consisted of 255,000 boys in 153 cities, were decreasing juvenile delinquency and producing leaders of merit. He told his audience of more than one thousand delegates and leaders of business, industry, and finance at New York's Hotel Commodore, "You picture that pavement boy

entering the door of that house of constructive joy. The light of his face—
the gleam of honest devilment in his eye—the feeling of trust and security
in his heart. And here is the sense of safety and gratitude which warms his
mother's heart also."[126] The *New York Times* editorialized that its readers
should scan every word of Hoover's address, since his "depiction of the boys
is likely to have a place in American literature." Not even Mark Twain, it
opined, had "a better understanding of the generic boy than does Herbert
Hoover." It added,

> History will remember that this sometime President of the United States orga-
> nized the administration for feeding millions of children during and following
> the war. It should remember also what he did in the framing of the Children's
> Charter, beginning with the recognition of the right of the child to spiritual
> and moral training "to help him stand firm under the pressure of life." But
> in taking the chairmanship of the Boys Clubs of America he is adding a con-
> structive practical service on behalf of the youth of a new generation that may
> surpass in its beneficent results more than the feeding of bodies and carry into
> higher fruition the chartered rights of boyhood preserving in him his "endless
> enthusiasm, his high store of idealism, his affections and his hopes." No man of
> his time has done more for the world in "the business of boys."[127]

A few days later Hoover told the Boys Club of Detroit that decent housing
for slum dwellers could only be provided through public subsidies, either "as
a contribution to the cost of the land and buildings or to the rents." He called
upon the nation's municipal governments to have "the courage to enact and
the courage to enforce proper health, sanitary and living requirements in slum
areas," thus eliminating the "speculative value of slum lands." Such pressure
would also "force land owners to put up better buildings and would contribute
at least something to housing problems."[128]

Meanwhile, Landon's efforts to forge a new party of Republicans and anti–
New Deal Democrats continued to concern Hoover. Landon was in contact,
directly and indirectly, with a number of Democrats, including Lewis Douglas, Newton Baker, and Raymond Moley. Hoover's former treasury secretary,
Ogden Mills, whose loyalty to the former president was often professed but
seldom manifested, supported Landon's round-table idea over Hoover's convention proposal, although they differed over details.[129] The former president
viewed such efforts as a betrayal of the party's traditions and an attempt to
freeze him out of political affairs. Increasingly he began to view his entire
political future as dependent upon the efforts of Hyde and the others to kindle
sentiment for his resumption of leadership of the party, and when those efforts
appeared in mid-May to be producing but scant results, Hoover contemplated
a retirement from public life.[130]

Then simultaneously Landon's round-table proposal foundered over Moley's opposition to the creation of a new political party, and Hoover's eastern
supporters stepped up their work and began to attract support. Hoover began

again to proselytize in behalf of his convention idea. On his way back to Palo Alto from New York he stopped in Chicago and found Lowden still favoring the idea. Meanwhile, other Democrats turned deaf ears to Landon's round-table proposal. In mid-June, William Hard, who was privy to Landon's efforts, wired Hoover, "All immediate national coalition attempts abandoned and no talks on anything at all just now."[131] Hoover replied that the news would now allow "us to pass the summer without great anxiety."[132]

Faced with Landon's apparently unrelenting opposition to the convention idea, Hoover turned to a new arena to try to rally sentiment for his proposal—one that would simultaneously furnish new fuel for those who were seeking to arouse support for his return to leadership of the GOP. This would be in the form of an article for the *Atlantic Monthly* that would describe his proposal and seek to stimulate support for it.[133] As proofs of the article became available, Hoover circulated them to his campaigners and to Harrison Spangler, GOP national committeeman from Iowa, who promised he would do everything possible to secure newspaper publicity for the article. The article, published in the September issue, appeared on the newsstands in late August, with arrangements quickly made by Hoover and his supporters to have 32,000 copies of the piece distributed. *Atlantic*, too, reported considerable interest in the article and numerous requests for reprints.[134]

In an obvious swipe at Landon, Hoover wrote that the 1936 presidential campaign had obscured the real issues in America, since the party had tried to out–New Deal the Democrats in its promises. Hoover described the primary weakness of the Republican Party as deriving from its unwillingness to stand up for its substantial history of service, its failure to replace with youth the deadwood that it had accumulated through its victorious years, and its failure to "crystallize an affirmative and consistent body of principle in the face of the new situation." Lacking any principles, some leaders had talked of a party realignment, but Hoover expressed opposition to such a course. The GOP should concentrate on presenting a meaningful alternative to the New Deal in order to attract voters, rather than on discussing meaningless "coalitions" with Democratic leaders who had no following. America needed a political party that would "clearly and courageously and constructively set out the affirmative alternative to the coercive direction of the New Deal." Hoover then recited his familiar list of desiderata for such a declaration and closed with his plea for a convention or conference to formulate those principles for the party. Such a conference and declaration, he wrote, "would infuse a renewed fighting courage in the party's own ranks; it would inspire an organization with which free men could join in coalition; it would lift the hearts of free men and women." America needed "a new and flaming declaration of the rights and responsibilities of free men."[135]

Hoover now sought to capitalize as much as possible on the article, calling it to the attention of national and state GOP leaders, in some cases asking state party officials to see that resolutions were passed in favor of the conference and that copies of these be sent to the Republican national committee and to other party leaders.[136] Meanwhile, his followers were mailing out tens of thousands of copies of the article to former delegates to national conventions, to national committeemen and committeewomen, and to other Republicans.

As the debate over Roosevelt's court-packing bill continued in the Senate, Hoover was repeatedly asked by opponents to speak out again. To one such request, Hoover responded,

> I do not know whether any volume of persuasion from the country would have any great weight before it comes to a vote. In any event, it is desirable that as much individual hammering as possible should be done against Senators and Representatives in opposition to the compromise. From the way the date is framing, I rather doubt whether it would be advisable for me to intervene at this time. It might draw a red herring across the trail and allay the bitter fight now going on . . . It is not clear in my mind that I should make a noise again. I should think the better time for an all around rally is after this battle passes the Senate and reaches the House.[137]

To another correspondent he wrote that "this idea of taking leadership on behalf of Republicans and then being slandered by Republicans within twenty-four hours gets nowhere. I am therefore going to spend more time fishing."[138]

Hoover now made another attempt to induce Landon to board the conference bandwagon, but the combination of the Hyde-Spargo-Reppy effort to restore Hoover to intellectual leadership (given national publicity in the "Washington Merry-go-Round" column of Drew Pearson and Robert Allen) and Hoover's campaign in behalf of a convention or conference had convinced the Kansan that "Hoover and the old guard" were "carrying on a deliberate organized campaign to get control of the Republican organization," using former jobholders in the Hoover administration as the nucleus for the effort.[139] Sentiment was also negative among congressional Republicans where there was, as usual, little imagination being shown, except by House Minority Leader Bertram Snell, who favored a conference as doing no harm and potentially some good.[140]

Blocked by Landon again, Hoover now directed the efforts of his supporters to concentrate on the conference proposal, since it was associated with him. The "drive," he told them, "now needs to be centered on this and the creation of fundamental principles and not on leadership. If this idea carries, it will have demonstrated leadership."[141] Thus Hoover proceeded now to gamble his bid for leadership of the Republican Party solely on the issue of the general conference. The new tactic called for those who had been organizing sentiment in behalf of Hoover as leader of the GOP to now use their mailing lists to generate support for the convention/conference idea. Copies of the *Atlantic Monthly* article were to be mailed to them, together with a questionnaire asking if they supported a conference and soliciting their reaction to the program Hoover had outlined in the article. In this way, Hoover believed he and his campaigners would determine "what the intelligent grassroots think of the proposal and what they think of these ideas, and thereby be able to prove to the world, one way or the other," whether there was support. And incidentally, if people on the lists did support Hoover's idea, his campaigners would have new "points of contact" for their other Hoover work.[142]

Having committed all to the success of the convention/conference proposal, Hoover now set out personally to rally support for it on a variety of fronts. Spangler promised to present the proposal at the next meeting of the GOP executive committee and to ascertain in advance the views of its members.[143] With numerous supporters on both the executive and the national committee, Hoover had good reason to assume that his idea would find favor there, but leaving nothing to chance he worked personally to round up votes among national committeemen in the western states and from GOP organizations.[144] He also called upon others to do "missionary work among national committeemen."[145] Early in September he wrote Chester Rowell, "I am leaving tonight for the East. I may be back in a month. I may not be back for several. I am going out to make a battle on the question of a Republican conference. I have in the last month been in contact with Republican officials in many of our Western states and I have lined up South Dakota, Wyoming, Montana, Oregon, Washington, California, Nevada, Arizona, Utah and Texas and Iowa. I now propose to invade this type of folk in the East."[146] Clearly the former president was pulling out all the stops in his campaign for the conference and considered that his prestige was on the line.

On his way East, Hoover stopped off in Chicago for conferences with supporters there and with Lowden. He learned that replies to the questionnaires were running about 90 percent in favor of his conference proposal.[147] Landon continued to oppose a conference and he was joined now by his 1936 running mate, Frank Knox.[148] Sentiment was running so strong in favor of a conference, though, that Landon began to waffle and to suggest that a conference might be appropriate for the spring of 1938, but not now when matters were in a state of "flux."[149] A Gallup poll released on September 18 gave a resounding push to Hoover's proposal, however, when 88 percent of a cross section of Republicans expressed support for holding a national convention in the spring of 1938. Hoover must surely have been disappointed, however, in the fact that only 22 percent listed him as their choice "to guide the policies of the Republican party" until 1940. Landon, however, was the only Republican ahead of Hoover, with 31 percent.[150]

After he met with Spangler in New York on September 22, Spangler issued a press statement saying that he would urge the executive committee "to call a meeting of the full National Committee at an early date to determine the advisability of calling a General Republican Conference within the next two months, for the purpose of uniting upon a declaration of fundamental princi-ples." Hoover's proposal, he added, had "met with an extraordinary response," and he cited both the Gallup poll and the samplings by Hoover's own cam-paigners, as well as the resolutions that had been passed in support of a confer-ence by various Republican groups.[151] The gauntlet was down. Would Landon and other opponents of Hoover and his proposal defy approximately 90 per-cent of the Republican Party by seeking to block the holding of a conference? Would the former president be checked in his bid to recapture leadership of the Republican Party?

CHAPTER 3

The Evangelist

The Conference Fight

Although many others had suggested the desirability of an off-year convention or conference, including GOP chairman Hamilton, Hoover's article in *Atlantic Monthly* had identified the proposal mainly with him. The result was that many who might otherwise have favored the idea felt it necessary, instead, to go into opposition against what they regarded as a scheme to advance the former president's political ambitions.[1] This opposition denied Hoover the victory he had sought in the GOP executive committee, when they referred the matter to a meeting of the entire GOP National Committee that was to be held in November. This did not mean the defeat of the idea, but it would obviously cause further delays in an action that Hoover was anxious should take place as soon as possible. The *New York Times* reported that "thirteen of the sixteen members" of the executive committee had supported the conference idea and it expected that the full committee would "call such a convention some time in the Summer of 1938."[2] Rickard came away from a visit with Hoover in late September convinced that he was consumed by a desire to "dominate the policy and to regain leadership of [the] party," but he worried that the former president "underestimates the bitterness of the members of the party against him and overestimates the power of his friends."[3]

Delayed in the matter of the conference, Hoover was also delayed in his desired ascendancy to leadership of the GOP. The former president now confronted his opposition within the party by recruiting journalists like David Lawrence and Arthur Krock in support of his cause.[4] One product of his efforts was a column by Boake Carter at the end of September that denounced the "old guard" in the GOP for their opposition to new ideas in the party and especially their opposition to Hoover's proposal for a conference. Carter wrote, "So far their chief effort . . . is to chant inanely that Hoover is leading the party revolt because he wants to take another crack at the Presidency. Instead of using what little brains they have left and examining the proposals made on their merits; instead of weighing the significance of the poll results among Republican citizens of the country; instead of taking stock of themselves, they descend to personal attacks."[5] While other newspaper comments tended to focus on the conflict between Hoover and Landon for leadership of the party, columnist Frank Kent echoed Carter in identifying the opposition as the "old guard," who were obstructing the conference proposal because they "seemed to fear that in some way the convention may redound to the credit of Mr. Hoover and apparently some of them are small enough to prefer scuttling the whole idea, shutting the door of hope on the party and on the country, as well, rather than have that happen."[6]

Arthur Krock found the dispute between Hoover and Landon over the proposed conference "discouraging to all who want to rebuild an effective opposition to the party in power." He continued,

> That has seemed to be the immediate purpose of Mr. Hoover and those who have associated themselves with the former President in calling for the conference. If this is so, then the national as well as the party interest should impel the Republican National Committee, at its November meeting, to call the meeting . . . And it would seem that Mr. Landon's objections . . . should be withdrawn . . . It is the only idea the party has had for ever so long, and the National Committee owes it to the millions who realize the necessity of two strong national parties to give it a trial.[7]

Landon, meanwhile, was being exhorted by one of his own key supporters to take back the leadership of the party that Hoover had assumed. Landon, he said, should have written the *Atlantic* article, instead of Hoover. As the former president had said, the party must "stand up and be counted on fundamental principles." "In that battle," Richard Lloyd Jones told the Kansan, "Hoover has started. You have stopped. The hour waits the marshal who will take command . . . There are leaders who are not long going to stand idle waiting. [Hamilton] Fish has spoken, [Arthur] Vandenberg has spoken, even Hoover, who has not the people's confidence, has spoken and spoken well. I believe in you. There are seventeen million who believe in you. You must justify this faith in your leadership. But as a leader you must now LEAD, SPEAK, CHALLENGE—CHARGE. Take COMMAND or remain in silent retirement."[8] Landon, however, was upset over the fact that Hamilton had ignored him in the whole convention proposal and was also irritated that Hoover had, in his *Atlantic* article, taken "a very adroit smack at the last campaign by saying we were trying to outdo Roosevelt."[9]

Another supporter, Frank Altschul, was warning Landon that many potential contributors to the party were reluctant to contribute until they knew what the GOP stood for and until its leaders stopped fighting among themselves. "To the man on the street," he wrote, "the whole thing looks like a sickening performance. It would seem as if, in the clash of personalities over perfectly trivial issues, the major objective of building up a united party of opposition in the face of a great national emergency was being completely overlooked." As for Landon's contention that congressional campaigns would be fought over local rather than national issues, Altschul told the Kansan that the campaign must be fought over national issues, since Republican candidates were "licked" before they started on local issues by Democrats who could promise more. Altschul encouraged Landon to "fall in" with the conference idea since it would "best serve the interests of the party."[10]

Landon was fond of referring to Hoover as a member of the old guard, but definitions of "old guard" clearly differed according to whom was queried, and it tended to be an epithet applied to all who disagreed with the respondent. Realistically, the term could only be applied to one of two groups: those perceived as ideological reactionaries in the party, or those who were identified with past GOP administrations as officeholders. The two were not necessarily synonymous, and while the former may have deserved some opprobrium, to reject the latter required that the party erase years of positive accomplishments in pursuit of a "new" image. Hoover himself was part amused and part insulted that the Landon camp put him in the "old guard" category. He wrote Theodore Roosevelt Jr.,

> I think you will have to be a little more precise as to who the old men of the sea are in the party, because I have no doubt that the Governor [Landon] believes it includes some of us who decline to accept such designations. I have been around Nevada, Wyoming, Montana, Washington, and Oregon, and I find the opposition to the New Deal growing although discontent with the lack of definite ideas in our party prevents them from joining with us. They are holding for a new party under new leadership and will not come with us unless we are able to define where we stand.[11]

Early in October, Hoover traveled to Illinois for a meeting with Lowden and Landon over the conference proposal. According to Lowden's memorandum of the meeting, Landon and Hoover each compromised over the issues that divided them, and both Lowden and Hoover came away from the meeting under the impression that the Kansan had entered into an agreement with them. Three days after their meeting, Hoover wrote to Hamilton that Landon had agreed that Hoover was to notify the chairman that they jointly favored the creation by the national committee of a group to draft a declaration of partly principles that would then be submitted to a conference of party leaders in the spring of 1938.[12]

Curiously enough, Landon did not recall having given the conference proposal his unqualified support, despite all the discussions and compromises. As Landon remembered his position, he had insisted that three conditions be met before he would agree to the proposal: (1) the committee that selected the membership of the general conference must be representative of all interests in the GOP; (2) congressional leaders must support it; (3) he must know in advance what the general conference was to do—he wanted "full accord on the plans and programs."[13]

It seems unlikely that both Lowden and Hoover could have missed three such specific conditions as Landon claimed to have insisted upon. More likely, the Kansan had second thoughts about the commitment he had entered into, or was persuaded to renege on it by others. In any case, Landon now exerted every effort to block approval of the general conference by the national committee. He also tried to delay the meeting of the national committee for a month, but failed.[14]

Besides Landon, the principal source of opposition to the conference idea came from Republicans in Washington. In a meeting with Senator Vandenberg, Hoover found the Michigan senator opposed to a conference on the grounds that it might embarrass the local stances of congressional candidates. Hoover countered that "every Republican candidate for Congress is beaten to a frazzle on local issues before he starts," because New Deal candidates could promise the sky and give evidence that they delivered. Thus the only hope of GOP candidates lay in running on national issues "beyond the narrow vision of local benefits."[15] However, Landon's new conditions, coupled with opposition in Congress, rendered unlikely the prospect of any constructive action by the Republican Party that did not have the support of a united party.

While Landon and Hoover marshaled their opposing forces for the November national committee meeting, the press increasingly viewed the conference proposal as a test of strength between them. The North American Newspaper Alliance (NANA) opined that if the two men could not reach a compromise before the national committee met, there was "likely to be an explosion among the party leaders." Neither of the two men, it noted, had ruled out a run for the nomination in 1940, and it appeared that "each is seeking recognition as the titular leader of the party."[16] The *New York Times* wrote that "the hostility between Mr. Hoover and Mr. Landon, both of whom appear to be determined to be the mouthpiece of the party, is reported to be deep seated." There was some apprehension within the party, it reported, "that this attempt [by Landon] to head off a convention to draft a declaration of principles for the 1938 Congressional campaign may create a situation not conducive to harmony in the minority party and further widen the breach in its ranks." When Landon went on the air in mid-October with a nationwide speech, Hoover and his supporters expected the Kansan to attack the midterm conference proposal. Instead, Landon lambasted the New Deal as befitted the titular leader of the opposition party. The *New York Times* reported that some Republicans regarded the speech as Landon's attempt "to assert his leadership of the Republican party and put himself in the role of titular leader." It added, "Now that he has urged the Republican members of Congress to curb the President's power, it is assumed that Mr. Landon will join the former President and others in a call for a party conference before the 1938 elections."[17] Columnist Delbert Clark described it as "the crisis in the half-hidden struggle between ex-Governor Landon and ex-President Hoover for supremacy in the councils of the party."[18]

Hoover conceded that Landon's was a "good speech" and set out to make sure that Republican leaders tuned into his own address in Boston on October 26.[19] At Boston Hoover spoke of the necessity for Republicans to have "a fighting cause," "an affirmative program," "effective methods," "a forward purpose," "idealism," and to be responsive "to the needs and crises of the people." Hoover assured his listeners that he was not seeking public office but intended to "keep on fighting for those things vital to the American people" even if to do so laid him open to charges that he was seeking the nomination. The Republican Party, he thundered, "must move forward or die. Therefore no party can be static. It must move forward with the times." And that was the purpose of his proposed Republican conference.[20]

Hoover's speech was featured on the front page of the *New York Times*, which took special note of his disclaimer concerning any interest in public office.[21] The former president was encouraged by the general press reaction to the speech and by the letters he received. *Time* magazine called the speech "a far better oratorical job than Landon had done the week before" and one filled with "the sarcasm that began to appear in his public utterances after he left the White House."[22] Ben Allen told Hoover that he had been deluged with favorable comments of everybody from stenographers to elevator operators.[23] But the real test of the speech's effectiveness would be the decision by the national committee on the conference proposal. A few days before the speech, Hoover had met with Connecticut GOP leaders and told them that the immediate objective of the conference was to increase Republican seats in Congress. He also suggested that a committee of one hundred should meet before the general conference to work out its policies.[24]

Ground between the conflicting ambitions of Landon and Hoover, GOP chairman John Hamilton groped for a compromise that would be acceptable to both camps. On November 2 he offered the two leaders two resolutions. The first would establish a policy committee that would "consider and report to the Chairman of the Republican National Committee its conclusions upon the pertinent questions now before the American people, said Committee to be composed of not less than one hundred members." The second would establish a committee of arrangements, made up of 25 members, "to determine the place, time and method of determining the membership" of a general conference to which the report of the policy committee would be submitted by the national chairman.[25]

At its meeting, the Republican national committee adopted a resolution that was a compromise, although it substantially met Hoover's desires. The proposed committee on arrangements was dropped, and the recommendations of the program committee would go to the national chairman who, under the compromise, would then call a meeting of the GOP National Committee "to determine the most effective and practical manner (a national general forum, conference, or otherwise) for preparing a report of the recommendations for the consideration of the nation." The motion for the compromise was carried without a dissenting vote, although Hooverite R. B. Creager of Texas expressed his disappointment with the compromise and his intention to fight for the calling of a general conference after the program committee had submitted its recommendations.[26]

Charles Michael wrote in the *New York Times* of the decision,

> Since the Republican party sank to its lowest ebb in the 1936 election, carrying but two States, Vermont and Maine, its leadership has grown cautious. Many of the men in Congress have become professional officeholders, unwilling to do anything that might disturb their incumbency, or frighten away groups of voters. The Republican members of Congress and the national committeemen seem to be hoping that the party can return to power through the mistakes of the Roosevelt administration . . . Even the Hoover followers were afraid to test their strength, although they entered the meeting with sixty of the 100 committeemen present favorable to a conference next year. John D. M. Hamilton, Republican chairman, directing the Hoover forces behind the scene, was averse to use his votes and his steam roller. He could have won the day for the Hoover proposal. He hesitated to do so because he foresaw a prolonged fight in the committee and unhealing scars . . . Impelled by newspaper demands and those of the younger men and women in the party, the committee may act quickly and promptly early next year. It was this feeling that partly influenced the Hoover group not to carry their fight to the floor.[27]

In short, the opponents of the conference proposal had won only a temporary victory.

Landon's biographer, Donald R. McCoy, has argued that the compromise passed by the national committee amounted to a "rebuff" for Hoover.[28] If so, it was much more a rebuff to the Kansan, who had consistently fought against any constructive activity by the Republican Party that did not include "Jeffersonian" Democrats. Moreover, Hoover had achieved much of what he sought, having already expressed the opinion before the meeting that the policy committee was the most important element in the proposal, and he reiterated this belief after the committee's decision. Republican rank and file, he told reporters, had pushed the party "the larger half of a strong movement forward from a policy of negation." He added,

> The program committee of 100 is to be appointed as proposed by myself and associates to formulate a declaration of convictions and an affirmative program for the party. General conference or no general conference, the declaration is the thing. The rank and file will probably take care of the conference question in time. The program committee can perform a great national service if it is appointed from unafraid men and women who will stand up and be counted . . .

The program committee will have a great opportunity to give life and vigor; to unify the Republican party; to realign it to the needs of the people; to lay the foundations of fusion to all forces who not only oppose many New Deal methods but who want a way out of the crisis.[29]

By whatever name—program committee, general conference, or mid-term convention—Hoover had succeeded in getting a representative group of Republicans at work on formulating principles for the Republican Party. This had been his objective from the beginning—some constructive activity on the part of the GOP that would attract public attention to the party. It remained to be determined whether a general conference or midterm convention would be convened, but it was now largely irrelevant since the program committee would draw up the declaration of principles that Hoover wanted.

The problem was that, even though Hoover knew he had scored a victory, the press focused on the failure of the general conference to be approved by the national committee and cast it as a defeat for the former president. When Landon's 1936 running mate, Frank Knox, gleefully did so in his *Chicago Daily News*, Hoover responded bitterly that the declaration of principles had always been his priority, not the general conference. He wrote Knox, "The National Committee did adopt that more important thing. After having been for months practically the sole voice of insurgency in the party against rotting inaction, you do not even mention the major thing that I have stood for but depict the minor thing. The result was to plaster me all over the country as having been defeated and turned down and generally humiliated. I presume that it is satisfactory enough to some of you, but I question whether it is for the good of the country."[30] Hoover was correct, but so was Knox in replying that since it was the midterm convention or conference idea that was associated with Hoover in the popular mind, he had in that sense the image of having been defeated.[31] And so it was regarded, too, by those like Spargo and Reppy who had labored to bring about Hoover's restoration to leadership of the GOP. They regretted that Hoover had pinned all his hopes, and their efforts, on the conference proposal, for the compromise of the national committee put their efforts right back where they had started.[32]

Predictably, the program committee now became an arena of contention between Hoover and Landon as each sought a committee staffed with members representative of his views, since the two GOP leaders would naturally try to influence the recommendations of the committee as much as possible.[33] The key issues between the two were as follows: (1) Would the program committee complete its deliberations early enough in 1938 for a general conference to be called, as Hoover wished, or would it be delayed into 1940, as Landon preferred? (2) If the deliberations were completed in 1938, would a general conference be called? Hoover of course pushed for rapid action by the program committee, while Landon sought delay in an effort to stalemate any general conference.[34] Despite Hoover's prodding, the program committee, under Chairman Dr. Glenn Frank, did not move quickly to formulate the program he sought.

Frank, though, in an interview with the press in mid-October, sounded very much like Herbert Hoover. According to the *New York Times*, Frank called upon the party to offer the country a restatement of the principles of "traditional liberalism," since the GOP was the only hope to champion "real liberalism." He explained, "Professional liberalism at the moment is moving toward the totalitarian state idea. One of the most critical needs is a complete, careful and honest restatement of—I dislike to call it the conservative position, because I mean the traditional liberal position adjusted to the circumstances of the times."[35]

Frustrated at the lack of movement, Hoover now returned to the speaking circuit to try to assert his leadership of the party. On November 8 he told an audience at Colby College that an "increasing darkness has descended upon free expression and free criticism in the world" since World War I, as governments perfected the use of propaganda and applied it to politics. It was the responsibility of newspaper editors, he said, to discriminate between "propaganda and real news, between untruth and truth." The responsibility was greater and more difficult with radio than it was for the newspapers, he told his listeners.[36] Four days later Hoover told an audience at Syracuse University that people trained in public service must be involved in "the hurly burly of political conflict," since it, too, was an aspect of public service.[37] Totally absorbed in writing and delivering his speeches and with monitoring the progress of the program committee, Hoover instructed his campaigners to limit their efforts. He knew they had been uncomfortable with his concentration on the conference idea, and he wrote John Spargo a lengthy letter of explanation for his actions:

> I know that you have not felt comfortable under the tactics which I have been following. After all, what we are fighting for is to hold certain precious fundamentals of personal liberty to the American people in the midst of a crumbling world. The time we have in which to do this is limited. It is not as if we could take years and years to build up. I came to a realization that despite all of the efforts of such devoted friends as yourself, there was little hope of building up, in the time we have, a personal leadership of these ideas which would dominate the American mind and control the direction which they would take. I felt in this limited time, we must get some great instrumentality pledged, or we would not succeed. The only possibility is the Republican Party. I realize that if the leadership and these ideas are handed over to a party, one gives over the role of John the Baptist, to become the supporter of a political mechanism. But I have thought it was in the interest of the country that it should be done this way. I have had to fight every inch of the way against pinhead politicians whose sole object is to get to the public trough by the easiest route. They, of course, attack me as a means to destroy the idea of the hard road. Whether the

policy committee . . . will serve effectually for this purpose or not, no one of us can tell. I am, of course, a great deal discouraged with what is going on. But anything that does come of it, is to the good in the great cause we have to fight. I have no intention of retiring for one minute from the battle and, of course, one accomplishes nothing unless one has a group of strong men such as you, who are willing to wade in at every moment to support such leadership as I can give. But peoples' ideas of leadership are still crystallized in the terms of ambition for political office, and they are not disposed to rally around people other than those they think are making a fight to secure office. Whether we can succeed in this sheer fighting for ideas as distinguished from personal ambitions I do not know. At the present, I have very great doubts about it.[38]

The Roosevelt Depression

By the time he delivered his next speech, in Chicago on December 16, there was no ignoring the economic collapse that had occurred in the previous months. From late spring the nation's economy had reeled under the effects of a massive wave of labor unrest and the spiraling wage-price inflation that was set off by a combination of the wage hikes (and accompanying price increases to pay for them) granted by industry to buy labor "peace" and the inflationary results of the gigantic federal spending (including the veterans' bonus) of 1936 to ensure Roosevelt's reelection. In the White House, the Treasury, and the Federal Reserve Board there was concern that the wave of inflation might threaten the government's credit and the solvency of the banking system, as banks tried to dispose of the low-interest government bonds that were virtually their only portfolio during the New Deal years in order to lend at the higher interest rates. As Hoover had predicted in March, "The forces making for higher rates are more powerful than those which maintain present levels. How far this rise in interest may go cannot be forecast, but a rise of 1% will create a serious fall in high grade bonds. Theoretically, such a rise would impair the the whole banking structure through their holdings of government issues and other bonds." After reviewing other economic conditions in the United States, Hoover wrote, "The practical question is, when is the smash coming?" He thought the Roosevelt administration would, through inflation, continue to make America "artificially happy during 1937."[39]

However, facing the consequences of over four years of business baiting and neglect of recovery, the Roosevelt administration felt forced to cut government spending to cool off the inflation even though the nation remained in the midst of a depression. An administration that had built the illusion of a recovery based on the increased purchasing power it had provided through deficit spending and legislative mandate now saw consumer purchasing power seriously eroding because of inflation and could find no course of action available but to cut that purchasing power even further by slashing government spending.[40] The consequences were predictable. In September, the stock market began to decline. Former Roosevelt brain truster Adolf Berle found Wall Street "scared to death" that a real downturn in business was in store. On October 11 the stock market staggered under a wave of what Secretary of Treasury Henry Morgenthau called "a type of relentless selling, all day long, which you couldn't see the end of." A week later the stock market collapse of 1929 was repeated, and the economy began the plunge that economists, businessmen, and journalists had predicted. Early in December a Gallup poll found that 58 percent of Americans believed the Roosevelt administration was entirely (19 percent) or partially (39 percent) to blame for the new collapse. An air of unreality settled over the White House, as if the president and his key advisers were unable or unwilling to admit the enormity of their failure.[41]

Hoover himself was suffering from the economic downturn as his own stock portfolio declined in value. Moreover, the accompanying drop in farm prices was affecting his son Allan's farm operation in California to the point where he was in danger of losing the farm.[42] In mid-October Rickard was convinced the market would go lower, although Hoover disagreed with him. Rickard, it turned out, was correct.[43] The next month he found even Hoover concerned about business conditions, with his gloomy outlook reinforced by his contacts with pessimistic businessmen.[44]

Early in November, Hoover responded to a query from John Bricker on what might be done to reverse the "increasing unemployment, the increasing suffering that is inevitable during this winter." He told Bricker,

> When experiments in government, no matter how well intentioned, begin to deprive hundreds of thousands of jobs, it would seem time for their reconsideration. Without going into long-view questions which would give stability and individual security, certain simple actions would greatly contribute to restore confidence and thus reverse the tide of increasing unemployment. They should be done immediately.
>
> 1. Prosecute individual dishonesty and abuse, but stop these incessant condemnations of honest business.
> 2. Assure the country that there will be no further attacks on the Supreme Court, and thus restore confidence in our institutions.
> 3. Repeal the tax on undistributed profits in order that businesses can invest their earnings in expansion of equipment and employment of men instead of dividends to stockholders.
> 4. Repeal the capital gains and loss tax. In the long view people take as much or more tax losses as they pay tax on profits. The government gains little if any direct revenue. It exaggerates booms and slumps and retards enterprise and employment. It is depriving people of jobs.
> 5. Suspend consideration of the wages and hours bill until legislation can be devised that will not destroy jobs.
> 6. Re-establish the administration of relief by voluntary local committees of distinguished citizens even if the Federal Government has to pay all

but a small percentage. The local communities will thus be enlisted to find jobs and to adapt relief to individual needs. It will save billions, and give real confidence that the budget will be balanced.[45]

Hoover found the consensus of opinion, though, was that "we will keep in the doldrums for a good many months." Everything depended on the actions of the federal government now, since the New Deal's actions and policies had replaced natural forces.[46] A few weeks later he wrote Ashmun Brown, of the *Providence Journal*, that the economic situation was bad: "the total failure of the Roosevelt Administration to grasp the fundamentals of what is needed is worse; and the disintegration of the Republican Party due to the efforts of a dozen pin-heads does not offer much hope for real leadership."[47] He told Mark Sullivan that if the New Dealers didn't "look out, they will turn this 'recession' into a tailspin." William Allen White wrote him, "I have always believed you had [the depression] licked and if you could have had even a year in the White House after '33 you would have put America along with England on the upgrade. The Lord only knows where we are going now."[48]

Hoover again addressed the economic situation in a speech in Chicago on December 16, 1937. He found Americans "torn with dissension and feelings of insecurity and even fear." The concern stemmed from something "far deeper in our national life than this immediate business recession." He preferred the new word "recession," he said, and he could "be wholly objective on this depression because certainly I did not create it." The problem was that under the New Deal the entire economic system had been "condemned without discrimination as to its strengths or its faults," and a planned economy had been instituted. This "brought a conflict between two fundamentally opposite philosophies of government and economics in operation at the same time." The planners in the New Deal sought "the gigantic shift of government from the function of umpire to the function of directing, dictating and competing in our economic life," through such devices as "politically managed currency, managed credit, managed interest rates, huge expenditures in pump priming and inflation of bank deposits," as well as the use of "relief funds to build the government into competitive business," the use of taxing powers to control business conduct, and the use of regulatory powers to dictate to business. The result had been "obvious violations of common sense."

Hoover warned his listeners that when "the government expands into business then in order to protect itself it is driven irresistibly toward control of men's thoughts and the press." Free enterprise, on the other hand, was the only economic system that did not limit intellectual and spiritual liberty. Government's role in a free enterprise economy must be limited to regulation; economic groups must voluntarily cooperate with one another and with non-economic groups, including the government. Taxing powers should be utilized by the government to ensure that no group received either too much or too little of the abundance produced. "It is difficult for timid minds to believe that free men can work out their own salvation," Hoover told his audience. "Arrogant minds seeking for power live upon this timidity."[49]

Reporters found the former president in a "jovial mood" when he arrived in California from Chicago. He told them the program committee was a "move in the right direction" and then quickly busied himself in the California political situation, looking ahead to the 1938 congressional elections.[50] While on the East Coast he had written Gertrude Lane of *Collier's* to suggest an editorial supporting the Republican program committee. "There is nothing the country needs more than to have a definite banner erected by the Republican Party," he wrote her, "to get it out of pure negation and pinhead politics into the field of constructive statesmanship." He hoped that Collier's would help in his drive to expedite the work of the committee.[51] Meanwhile, he warned the Hooverites on the committee, "There is a definite drive on the part of the Congressional and Topeka groups to defer any statement until after the Congressional election. The rank and file of the Republican Party would be disgusted with any such measures and the committee on policy would be hopelessly lost. Everywhere I go I find that the hope of the party lies in this committee and the disgust is chiefly centralized in the opposition group."[52]

At this crucial point, however, the former president made preparations for a trip to Europe. Arrangements for Hoover's return to the scene of his relief activities before and after World War I had originally been made in 1935 but had been canceled due to the death of the queen of Belgium.[53] Late in 1936 the planned trip was taken up again, with Hoover seeking an invitation from the Belgian government to revisit the nation he had fed during the early years of World War I.[54] However, that trip, too, fell through, since the Belgian government seemed reluctant to extend such an invitation to someone so obviously out of favor with the Roosevelt administration.[55] The Belgian reluctance to make an event of his return, coupled with the crisis over the Supreme Court and Hoover's involvement in the fight over a Republican conference, all caused a delay of the trip until 1938. But in January, Hoover finally received the desired invitation.

En route east to catch the ship for Europe, Hoover stopped over in Chicago for a visit with Glenn Frank, chairman of the GOP program committee, as he had grown anxious over the direction the committee seemed to be taking. At Landon's insistence, the committee was interpreting its mandate as only one of inquiry, whereas Hoover regarded this as contrary to the national committee's expressed intent in establishing it.[56] From John Callan O'Laughlin came the impression that "Landon is more interested in his effort to pull you down than he is to build up the Republican Party."[57] Hoover wrote H. Alexander Smith that the committee had "no use on earth unless it is prepared to make a bold declaration of principles at this time."[58] Curiously enough, House Minority Leader Bertram Snell agreed that the committee should "do something that attracts the attention of the country."[59] After meeting with Frank and impressing upon him the need to get out a statement as soon as possible, Hoover traveled on to New York and prepared to sail for Europe.

Meanwhile, the selection of the members of the program committee was proceeding. The *New York Times* reported,

> During the more than twenty-five hours in which the party's leaders have studiously and not without partisanship culled out prospects, the rivalry between the Hoover and the anti-Hoover forces has been apparent . . . While the Landon forces and the Congressional opponents to a national off-year convention are operating quietly, they are nevertheless most aggressive and vigilant in seeing to it that the Hoover faction does not gain control of the committee. If they should get control, the opposition feels that a draft of principles prepared by Mr. Hoover and aimed to advance him as a candidate, would emerge. Mr. Fletcher, the former national chairman, is directing the group that is fighting Hoover control. Indications now are that the Hoover faction will be defeated.[60]

As the members were named, Hoover wrote to some to congratulate them and heard from others who sought his advice. Hoover also made sure that members received copies of the Wilbur and Hyde book on the Hoover presidency, since it would "make a better background for new policies if they know what really has taken place under Republicans, not what the New Deal says has taken place."[61]

Meanwhile, Japanese aggression in China, the bombing of civilians, and particularly air attacks on the USS *Panay* and Standard Oil tankers on the Yangtze River, had aroused war sentiment in some circles in the Roosevelt administration. Hoover wrote O'Laughlin that he was "as yet undecided whether this war drive is on merely as Machiavelli's number one rule for diversion of a troubled public mind, or whether it leads through to a determination to get us involved. Either one is dangerous. If they do not get us involved before I come back [from Belgium] I will have a better background with which to make a head-on attack."[62]

Off to Europe

The former president had originally planned to visit only Belgium, but the trip grew longer and longer due to other invitations, some of them instigated by Hoover's associates, since the European trip was intended to further enhance his image in relation to Landon. Lou Henry did not accompany her husband since, she explained to a friend, she "realized that it could be much more easily and effectively taken without adjunct of ladies' parties on all occasions and all the way around." Those would have slowed "up the pace considerably," and Hoover was one who chomped at the bit when the pace got slowed.[63] Perrin Galpin recalled that Hoover had taken "a dozen books or so, mostly on political European questions" to read during the sea voyage to Europe. Galpin wrote, "He would skim these books through until he came to a passage on which he had special knowledge. If the author failed to come through with accuracy on a matter on which Mr. Hoover had special knowledge the Chief generally let the book go . . . With detective stories, Mr. Hoover would start at the beginning and if the first chapter did not interest him he would try the last chapter. Then, if there seemed to be no problem in the middle, the book was out."[64]

Hoover arrived first in Havre, France, where he was met by some of the veterans of his relief activities, and then drove to the Belgian frontier. *Newsweek* reported, "Every Belgian paper from Communist to Rexist [royalist], dropped its bickering to honor Herbert Clark Hoover, Belgium's Wartime Relief Administrator, with fulsome editorials. Every member of the Chamber of Representatives rose in his seat at word that Herbert Hoover had crossed the frontier . . . The Belgian Government issued a new stamp, bearing the portrait of the late great King Albert but dedicated to Herbert Hoover." *Newsweek* also noted that with a surplus of $25 million after it ceased operations, the Commission for Relief in Belgium (CRB) had contributed $9 million to rebuild Belgian universities, $6 million for a foundation for scientific research, and $10 million for exchange scholarships between Belgium and the United States.[65]

After a rousing reception in Belgium the Hoover party traveled to France, Switzerland, Austria, Czechoslovakia, Germany, Poland, Latvia and Estonia, Finland, Sweden, and England. Hoover was distressed to find that France had slipped considerably in power and prestige and wondered if it might not soon cease to be an important factor in European politics. In Switzerland he was surprised to find so little interest by League of Nations officials in their positions, with many searching for other jobs. Clearly the League of Nations was ceasing to fulfill the hopes of its founders. Hoover was in Austria only days before the Anschluss that brought it under German control, and he found a spirit of fatalism among its government officials as they awaited the inevitable fate. He found Czechoslovakia willing to give up the predominantly German-inhabited Sudeten area that had been forced upon her in the peace settlement ending World War I in an effort to weaken Germany, but she was prepared with a well-equipped army to defend the rest of her territory and counted on the help of the Soviet air force in doing so.[66]

In Germany, the former president was able to talk with Adolf Hitler for nearly an hour through an interpreter. Their conversation was cordial. According to Rickard's description of what Hoover told him, the former president found the German leader intelligent and determined, ideological and emotional.[67] After the chat with Hitler came one of the most extravagant events of the tour, when Hoover and his entourage were invited to lunch with Hermann Goering at his "hunting lodge," Carin Hall, located some forty miles from Berlin, set in a forest with a lake. As Perrin Galpin described it, the lodge was "built around a central court with low buildings on three side of the large court. On one side, opposite the Great Hall, are offices and rooms for the rather numerous staff of assistants that General Goring maintains." The Great Hall, where they met the other guests, was about two hundred feet long by fifty feet wide, with a huge fireplace at one end and a large plate glass window at the other through which the lake could be seen. Priceless paintings, tapestries, and statues lined the walls and the room. After sipping sherry and port in the Great Hall, they were ushered through a long hall, so filled with artwork that it reminded Galpin of a museum, to a thoroughly modernistic dining room where they had a lunch catered from a distinguished Berlin restaurant. After lunch they entered another large room for coffee, and this one was filled with trophies of the hunt.

Galpin wrote,

When it was time to go the General had arranged for from 12 to 16 huntsmen in green uniforms, each with his hunting horn, to assemble in line in the courtyard and play the Hunting song from Siegfried. It was a magnificent sight and we did not know whether to salute, stand at attention, or, as we did, get in the automobile and drive away . . . On comparing notes after the lunch we all decided that Carin Hall would put to shame the wildest dreams of any Hollywood magnate. The whole place was built in a year and one could estimate the cost of the whole thing, including the art, at anywhere from three to six million dollars.

Goering also spirited Hoover away for a conversation on the elimination of waste, a field in which the former president had established expertise while serving as secretary of commerce. Goering was quite proud of Germany's accomplishments in promoting self-sufficiency, showing Hoover examples of cloths and carpets made from cellulose yarns.[68]

Hoover told Edgar Rickard that he gained the impression that Hitler did not want to go to war with England and France, but that he would move east and south, instead, if they sought expansion. He also observed that he had "an uncomfortable feeling of repression from the moment he entered the country until he passed over the border." Germans, he found, were unwilling to talk freely as long as they were in the presence of even one other German.[69]

As there was so much interest in his conversation with Hitler, Hoover gave out a statement to the press:

I have had a great many conversations with leaders in Germany and other countries in Europe, and I shall have more such discussions. I never discuss the character of such private conversations. One cannot but sympathize deeply with all those peoples and different groups within them in their hundreds of acute problems and their inheritance from the World War. Despite their difficulties, most of these nations have done more in public health and housing for the lower income groups than we have in America. I can say further that I am even more reinforced in my belief that the progress of America rests in the principles of intellectual liberty and spiritual freedom, a system of free economy regulated to prevent abuse, and popular government. I shall discuss Americans relations to the European scene upon my return.[70]

As the Hoover party crossed the frontier into Poland, the former president recalled an American Relief Administration worker who had been abandoned in a village there after year. For six months the forlorn worker had counted railroad cars until he at last cabled Hoover at Stanford to ask for further orders!

Back in Belgium, Hoover and his entourage were guests at a gala dinner thrown by the king—the first such gala dinner given since the death of the queen a few years earlier. One hundred ten people were seated at the same table. "In Summary," Galpin wrote, "the places where the Chief received the finest receptions were, in my opinion, in Belgium, which we expected, but even a greater welcome in Czechoslovakia and in Finland. I was sold on the Finns."[71]

Hoover ended his trip in England where he was interviewed by the press. He told reporters that he had discussed the European situation "with the leading men of fifteen nations" and had "a deep consciousness of the many menaces to peace" but did not "believe that a widespread war is probable in the immediate future."[72] Hoover and his party returned to New York City on March 29. In almost all the countries visited he had met with the top government officials, US diplomatic representatives, and the press.

Before he left for the United States, Hoover received a wire from Lewis Strauss notifying him that he had been asked by Norman Davis, the president of the Council on Foreign Relations, to address that prestigious group upon his arrival in New York.[73] Hoover was also invited to address the Economic Club but chose the Council on Foreign Relations against advice of many of his supporters.[74] His speech, delivered on March 31 and nationally broadcast, was on the topic "Foreign Policies for America." The former president opened the speech by noting that he had received numerous invitations since World War I from various European countries, cities, and universities to visit but had until now no opportunity to accept. On this trip he had "welcomed the opportunity to observe at first hand the political, social, and economic forces now in motion nineteen years after my last day in Europe." He recounted for his listeners his earlier experiences there and described his return to those nations "to discuss the forces in motion with more than a hundred leaders whose friendship I had enjoyed in the past and probably another hundred whom I met for the first time." Europe had experienced a rise of dictatorships and was caught up in an arms race that was creating "increased government debts and deficits." Each nation there was striving for the maximum of self-sufficiency in industrial and food production. The failure of the League of Nations had led to a renewed dependency on old concepts of balance of power, which had produced fear and a steady increase in some nations "of brutality, of terrorism, and disregard for both life and justice." Although it was "an alarming and disheartening picture," Hoover did not believe a general war was in "immediate prospect." Military preparations were incomplete, and thinking seemed to be primarily defensive rather than offensive.

Beneath these visible aspects of the situation were "still deeper currents," which included the "injustices and unrealities of the Peace Treaties" that ended World War I, the economic chaos that had led to the economic collapse of the early 1930s, and the age-old hatreds and aspirations that festered among the racially mixed populations of Europe. In these conditions, the United States should make clear that it would not take part in another general European war, not even in alliance with the democracies against totalitarianism, for such a conflict would "have all the hideous elements of the old religious wars." "If the world is to keep the peace," Hoover declared, "then we must keep peace with dictatorships as well as with popular governments. The forms of government which other peoples pass through in working out their destinies is not our business." The United States should organize and join "in the collective moral forces to prevent war" and should encourage economic cooperation between nations, since "prosperity of nations is the best antidote for the poisons of fear and hate." Above all, the United States should "keep alight the flame of true liberalism": "the protection of democracy is that we live it, that we revitalize it within our own borders, that we keep it clean of infection, that we wipe out its corruptions, that we incessantly fight its abuses, that we insist upon intellectual honesty, that we build its morals, that we keep out of war." This was "the greatest service that this nation can give to the future of humanity."[75]

Arch Shaw wrote Hoover that the reaction to the speech was "the most favorable . . . and from a broader group of people than from any of your previous speeches, except perhaps the one at Cleveland [the convention] which, however, was given under the most dramatic of circumstances." He suggested that Hoover's next speech be given according to this same "approach."[76]

Columnist Raymond Clapper wrote William Allen White after the speech that "one of the most interesting things that is happening now, it seems to me, is the comeback which Hoover is making." Clapper thought his foreign affairs speech "an excellent job and when he was shown on the newsreels here delivering it he received a very enthusiastic hand from the audience. Maybe there's life in Hoover yet." A few days later Clapper wrote again that he had "several letters from widely scattered parts of the country reporting movie house applause for Hoover. Obviously something is going on in this country, but I still am not quite certain what it is." He found it a curious phenomenon after Hoover had "been considered as a dead one for some five or six years," and especially peculiar that it was "developing just as Roosevelt falls smack on his nose."[77] William Allen White told the former president his speech had been "a most effective one, probably the most effective you had delivered for a long time."[78]

Perhaps as an outcome of the "renaissance" of Herbert Hoover after his European trip, the former president was receiving more than the usual requests to write magazine articles. In response to one such request, he wrote, "At my point of life I do not need to get into print and I do not want to unless it is going to accomplish something. I can get my name in the papers anytime I want to by overspeeding an automobile."[79] To another he wrote, "My interest in writing anything is only for the purpose of getting something clearer in the American mind, and I think as far as my European experience is concerned I will have contributed everything in that direction within another two weeks of speaking."[80]

Roosevelt's attempt to pack the Supreme Court had been defeated in mid-June 1937 when the Senate Judiciary Committee reported out Roosevelt's court-packing bill with a report so negative that, columnist Raymond Clapper observed, it read "like a bill of impeachment except that [it] refers to [the] bill instead of Roosevelt by name." The *New York Herald Tribune* agreed that the committee's report "was far more than the disapproval of a bad bill. It was an indictment of the President of the United States by leaders of his own party, for long his supporters and advocates." Indeed, the report of the committee said of Roosevelt's bill, "It is a measure which should be so emphatically rejected that its parallel will never again be presented to the free representatives of the free people of America."[81]

Hoover was concerned, however, that Roosevelt would try again. If so, part of his strategy was likely to unfold in the 1938 election when he would try to defeat those Democrats who had opposed him in the Senate and obtain more quiescent votes in that body. Thus when the League for Supreme Court Independence queried the former president on whether it was time to disband after the defeat of Roosevelt's proposal, Hoover responded,

> These leagues and committees which we have formed throughout the country should not be dissolved yet. They have been of profound importance in mobilizing public opinion. They are non-partisan.
>
> In the elections of 1938 they should be prepared to support those Senators and Congressmen who have actively attacked this proposal, whether they be Democrats or Republicans. Likewise, they should demand the views of all the candidates for the Senate and House upon this question, whether they be Republicans or Democrats.
>
> The issue will not be settled if candidates are to be subjected to political reprisals on this issue, or until it is certain that it cannot be claimed from this election that the electorate supports packing of the Court. You should continue to stand on guard.[82]

Hoover had gotten the impression from his travels across the country that "if we put on a strong national campaign against the New Deal in this congressional election, we will certainly carry quite a number of seats."[83]

A new issue presented itself during the winter of 1937–1938, however, in the form of a White House bill seeking reorganization of the executive branch of the federal government. While the bill ostensibly sought to streamline the executive branch in the interest of greater efficiency, something that a former president like Hoover might have applauded, for opponents of the New Deal it represented yet another grab for power by the man in the White House, an effort to bring the various executive agencies even more tightly under his control and direction. Even critics admitted that it "would be a pretty good bill" if it placed the power in any other hands but Roosevelt's. Columnist Raymond Clapper acknowledged that opposition was based on "a growing lack of confidence in Roosevelt" and was "not so much a protest against reorganization as against Roosevelt personally."[84]

As the bill neared a vote in the House, Hoover went on the offensive. He wired Congressman J. William Ditter that it was "an attempt by indirection to increase the Presidential authority over legislative and judicial functions and to bring about an extension of the spoils system, which should render this bill wholly objectionable to the American people."[85] En route back to his Palo Alto home, Hoover told the press in Chicago that it represented "the reintroduction of the spoils system after 75 years of battle to set up the civil service commission" and was "a grab for more power by the President."[86] By the time he reached San Francisco the bill had become a step toward fascism. He told reporters there that any "encroachment upon the judicial and legislative areas of our government is an attempt to break down the democracy under which we live." The United States, he said, seemed to be "moving in the direction taken by every European state that has lost its liberty as the result of economic misery."[87]

A few days later the bill was defeated in the House of Representatives by a vote of 204 to 196, with 108 Democrats joining the Republicans in opposition. Hoover hailed GOP minority leader Bertram Snell for his "grand fight" and wrote, "You cannot appreciate in Washington, what a tremendous effect it has been [sic] throughout the country. It has lifted the spirits of everybody who has any devotion to the American form of government."[88] To William Castle he observed that the defeat of the bill was of importance primarily "because it indicates the turning of the public mind of this country from centralized authority."[89]

Meanwhile, Hoover had returned to the subject of foreign policy with an April 8 speech in San Francisco. To give his audience an appreciation of conditions in Europe, he compared it with California: "If we had 500,000 troops and 2,000 aeroplanes looking at us hatefully from over the Oregon line, another 400,000 men and 2,000 planes ready to march over the Nevada line, and another few hundred thousand being drilled in Arizona ready to pounce upon us, this would be a less comfortable place. And if we had to pay taxes for about 400,000 men in our own State to make faces at these sister States, then it would be still more uncomfortable." After describing the living conditions that resulted in Europe from this and from the readiness of the authoritarian countries there to throw anyone in a concentration camp who did not agree with the state, Hoover concluded that he was happy California was 7,200 miles from Europe. Hoover then described his European trip before turning to the American scene. He indicted the Roosevelt administration for the slow recovery of the United States from the depression as compared with the recoveries of democratic and totalitarian nations alike in Europe. Only by discarding the planned economy of the New Deal could "genuine self-respecting jobs in productive enterprises" be restored. The most prosperous democracies in Europe, he told his audience, were those who had "refused to adopt these courses of Planned Economy."[90]

Professor Allison Reppy wrote Hoover in early April that the former president's trip abroad and his subsequent speeches had struck a responsive chord in many people, particularly the foreign born, who had previously been in "the toils of the New Deal."[91] A number of others remarked on the continuing "renaissance" of Hoover's popularity with moviegoers. William Allen White applauded Hoover's March 31 speech and wrote that when the former president appeared in a newsreel in a Kansas City theater, "the audience burst into a cheer."[92] Arch Shaw called Hoover's attention to the fact that in the latest Gallup Poll he ranked second among Republicans, behind Vandenberg and ahead of Landon. "The Hoover curve has been moving up since your European trip," he wrote.[93]

The former president remained on the attack, berating the morals of the New Deal in a speech in Fresno, California. A dishonest government, he said, affected the morals of the people. Morality in government rested on the selection of officials under the merit system, but the Roosevelt administration had discarded "seventy years' effort to build up a national system of merit service." A moral government did not use government funds to try to influence elections, but the New Deal had used federal funds to pressure members of Congress to vote as it wished, to influence voters in "politically doubtful districts," and to aid corrupt urban political machines. A moral government practiced honest accounting of public funds, but the Roosevelt administration juggled accounts to deceive the American people. A moral government was "scrupulous in its financial transactions with the citizen," but the Roosevelt administration had welshed on its promises, using "public funds to manipulate its own bond market, rigged the currency." A moral government used its expenditures to build up the character of the people, not to "undermine the responsibility, the self-respect, the dignity that marks free men." Instead, the New Deal policies had enticed every community into "a conspiracy to get its share from the Federal grab bag," undermining the responsibility of states, communities, and individuals. A moral government did not connive "at lawlessness and sit-down strikes," nor foment class animosity, setting one group against another and dividing the people by hate. Under the Roosevelt administration intellectual dishonesty had "become an art under the heading of propaganda." He told his audience, "These are grave hours. We are in a moral recession in government. Beyond this we have for five years listened to a continuous defamation of everything that has gone before. Honest achievement of men has been belittled and attributed to improper motives. Ideals embedded in our patriotism are smeared with contempt. We are told that the frontiers of initiative and enterprise are closed. We are told that we are in ruins and we must begin anew. We are told the government must do it for us." But Hoover told his listeners that, on the contrary, with a restoration of morals the nation could do even more in another generation.[94]

The former president continued the attack a few days later with a speech to twenty thousand in Oklahoma City, pointing out that none of the fourteen European nations then under authoritarian governments had set out to surrender their liberties. Each had, however, undertaken "New Deals under some title, usually Planned Economy," and gradually, by the same course the United States seemed to be following, their governments had "sapped the vitality of free enterprise by government experiments in dictation and socialistic competition." They had sacrificed free enterprise in order to pursue the utopias of both fascism and socialism, with each step "accompanied by greater corruption of the electorate, increasing intellectual and moral dishonesty in government." Permanent economic recovery was impossible in such a situation, and only further collapse resulted, with new calls for the people to surrender more liberties to "some man or group of men who promised security, moral regeneration, discipline, and hope." It was only a short, easy step "from experimental dictation by government to farmers, workers and business into a full Fascist system," when free enterprise, "demoralized by fear," had to be compelled to produce "by more fear and coercion." By contrast, the most prosperous nations in the world were those democracies who had practiced belt tightening, balanced budgets, and had "refused new deals and planned economies." The American people would, Hoover told his audience, be shocked if they had "a detailed list of the powers over their daily life they had surrendered to the President and his bureaucracy." It was this "creeping collectivism" of the New Deal that had aborted the economic recovery begun in 1932 by sickening initiative and enterprise, substituting fear, and destroying millions of jobs. Now faced with a depression of his own making, Roosevelt could only propose "more bureaucratic dictation to businessmen, more inflation, more pump-priming, more Planned Economy." These failed devices must be discarded completely so that confidence could be restored and the initiative and enterprise of men could be released once again.[95] From a businessman friend in San Francisco came praise for "one of the most inspiring [speeches] that you have ever delivered over the radio."[96]

As Hoover's speeches indicate, the economy had continued downward in 1938 after the crash in late 1937. By early May 1938 the Barron's business index had slid to 53.7, lower than in October 1932 and very near the 46.7 of the banking crisis in 1933. The economy had by now "erased all the recovery gains it had made since the late spring of 1933, just following the bank holiday," said *Barron's*. The *New York Times* index dipped to 75.4 in late April, the lowest figure since the week ended May 6, 1933, lower than in the depths of the 1934 recession. Between September of 1937 and June 1938, industrial production fell by 33 percent, national income by 13 percent, profits by 78 percent, payrolls by 35 percent, industrial stock averages by over 50 percent, and manufacturing employment by 23 percent. Yet, as Walter Lippmann wrote in early April, "incredible as it sounds, the New Deal does not have any program, good, bad, or indifferent, which even pretends to have any relation to the economic crisis. One would scarcely know from the President's utterances that there is a crisis." For *Barron's*, the "Democratic jokes about the Hoover depression and 'prosperity just around the corner' don't seem so funny as they did $18,000,000,000 ago."[97]

In early May another columnist found that "almost every distinguished Democratic chieftain has now broken with Mr. Roosevelt on major policies. Never before in American history has a Chief executive been so utterly repudiated by the men who should be serving as his front-line figures, or at least concealing their differences from the gaze of the public." Not only were the Democratic leaders insisting now on a "live-and-let-live attitude toward big and little business—toward productive sources of employment" but their position had "caught the imagination of the public." The protests of Democratic leaders, he wrote, reflected "a conviction that the President heads a wrecking rather than a rescuing squad."[98] If so, it seems certain that Hoover's attacks on the New Deal must have helped them reach that conclusion.

By mid-June the *Barron's* index had dropped to 50, only 1.5 above "the historic low-point of six years ago" and below the figure for October 1932. All the recovery gains since May 1933 had been erased. The *New York Times* pointed out early in the month that cotton was selling at "the lowest level in history in terms of the old gold dollar." The new lows to which the economy was falling, combined with Roosevelt's obstinance in the face of criticism of his policies, led to questions about whether the president of the United States genuinely sought economic recovery. A Gallup poll found 79 percent of the people in favor of assistance to business through reduction of taxes. From this and other such polls it became apparent by mid-1938 that Roosevelt's anti-business policies were losing their popularity with the public.[99]

With the New Deal in disarray, Hoover pressed for action within the Republican Party, again encouraging Glenn Frank to move on an early preliminary declaration of principles. Despite obvious reluctance, the chairman began to work on a preliminary statement in consultation with the former president. In late June, Frank wired Hoover that he had rewritten the document four times but was "reluctant to send it until I felt it was somewhere near worthy of the fight you have waged."[100] Hoover found Frank's draft lacked force, however, and he asked Chester Rowell to revise it.[101] He hoped that the preliminary declaration could be ready for a meeting of the full committee that was scheduled for August 1.[102] However, the declaration encountered a rocky road through the executive committee and the program committee itself, and it emerged in a form quite disappointing to the former president and his supporters.[103]

Issued in a press release on August 5, 1938, the statement declared, "The Committee has the conviction that, under present trends in legislation and administration, the United States may suffer the two-fold disaster which has overtaken peoples quite as sure of their destiny as we have been—the breakdown of an elaborate economic system and the disintegration of responsible and effective government." Despite five years of New Deal spending and "a freedom to act without parallel in our political history," there were still 12 million unemployed Americans—a number that threatened "the continued employment and income of every American who now has a job." They were unemployed, the declaration averred, because of "the confusion and uncertainty in which the present Administration has plunged us" through untested policies "hastily conceived, wastefully financed, ineffectively administered," and in conflict with one another. No solution was possible until there was "complete assurance that the nation's life and enterprise are to be operated under a program founded on the principles of a balanced representative government, an adequately regulated and just system of private enterprise, a workable economics of plenty, and an inviolate code of civil liberties." Having stated these basic principles, the press release concluded, the Republican program committee would now get to work at the task of formulating specific policies that would implement these principles. The statement disclaimed any intent to commit the GOP National Committee or any candidates for office to the principles expressed.[104]

Hoover's supporters on the committee had labored so hard to get even this innocuous press release that they congratulated themselves over it.[105] Chester Rowell, however, considered that it had "so little vitality that it is barely able to speak." It was, he said, "an apology for saying anything, with the defense that it really does not say anything important nor bind anybody," and it betrayed not the slightest recognition "that we are at a crisis in American life, which may determine toward which way of liberty, of political and economic structure, and of place in the world, the American people are to be committed, perhaps irrevocably." Nor did it reveal any assertion of leadership by the Republican Party "of those who wish to go forward on the basis of what has been, until now, universally recognized as the American way." Americans, Rowell said, needed to be told "that we are at the parting of the ways between one system, political and economic, and another, and that the choice must be made by 1940 "or it may be forever too late to choose at all." Since the committee had defaulted in that responsibility, Rowell concluded that Hoover would have to continue to put the issue before the American people.[106]

The declaration read very much like a Hoover speech, but as noted earlier, Hoover sought a declaration of principles, not an indictment of the New Deal, and so he shared Rowell's disappointment. However, the former president was also charitable toward his supporters who had labored with such difficulty even to produce any statement at all. He wrote one of them,

Considering the opposition which you encountered, I think you did well to get a statement of any kind through. Of course, it is far from what you would have and what many of our friends would have, but I am never disposed to quarrel with fine men because they do not win everything. We have to bear in mind that those destroying the Republican Party, either through determination or ineptitude, had started out deliberately to lick this Program Committee, and that they had done considerable work in advance to prevent the August meeting from having importance or value.[107]

A few days later Hoover wrote Arch Shaw, another member of the committee, that "having read and reread the text of the committee's statement, I think better and better of it. You and Alex [Smith] certainly went down into the pit to rescue this much from that crowd." He told Shaw he was considering using the principles enunciated in the statement for a speech.[108] The former president's long battle for a declaration of GOP principles before the 1938 elections had been capped with at least this minor accomplishment.

Hoover had decided that he would not again repeat his silence during the 1934 congressional elections and had scheduled three major speeches for the 1938 campaign. One of the problems, he wrote columnist Mark Sullivan in mid-July, was

the fact that Roosevelt is more popular than the New Deal. This is due in considerable extent to the fact that the responsibility for the New Deal has not been laid to him, and that he has succeeded in completely divorcing himself from its failure and its more malevolent acts. I am beginning to have the belief that if we are going to get rid of him we are going to have to associate him with the responsibility that is really his. I agree with you as to the weight of this flood of money and its influence on the voters. While millions of people will agree collectively that it is wrong, the personal benefit they receive still holds them within the Roosevelt ranks. It may be that there will be no relief except bankruptcy. The difficulty with bankruptcy in a democracy is that it is the end of democracy. If it were only the money involved I could view it with more complacency.[109]

Hoover asked John Spargo how far "he should go in bringing personal responsibility on Mr. Roosevelt" and was encouraged by Spargo that "bold and uncompromising attack upon Mr. Roosevelt himself is the best political strategy."[110]

Liberty Magazine on July 16, 1938, published an article on Hoover by his old friend from Stanford days, Will Irwin, who wrote,

When I entered Herbert Hoover's room in the hotel which he makes his headquarters in New York, I found him at a small desk in the corner, grinding out his speech for the Benjamin Franklin celebration in Philadelphia. He looked up, grinned his greeting, waved the hand that held the lead pencil and went on writing. Literary composition comes hard with him, as with us all. As usual, he twirled a lock of his front hair, clenched his feet round the legs of his chair, and when he broke the lead of his pencil, cast away the offending tools as though it had done him wrong.

Interviewed, Hoover noted that the principal need of the nation was to find jobs for the millions still out of work. "But," he told Irwin, "private enterprise will function to give jobs only in an atmosphere of reasonable optimism and confidence." He continued,

> You remember that Kipling title, *Rewards and Fairies*? Business lives— we all live—on rewards and fairies. We become demoralized as soon as some one locks up the rewards and poisons the fairies. You remember that one about "We have nothing to fear but fear." You might paraphrase it a little—"We have nothing to feed upon but fear" . . . If we could see into the hearts of millions of American people you'd find that they're afraid of something the government has done or may do. Different people and groups, of course, have different reasons for fear.
>
> There are the attacks on the independence of the Supreme Court. There are the government policies as to money and credit, which make a venture in business or even an investment a bad bet on what Washington will do next. There are artificial prices, and jobs that people know can't last. There is the idea you have more if you produce less. The average citizen knows that such a proposition doesn't make sense. There are taxes which run beyond the point where enterprise is worth while. There is the bulldozing of New Deal speeches, which don't scare the wicked and which take the heart out of the upright. There are the dictation, threats, and unfair practices of government boards. There are the thousands of prowlers and their questionnaires which violate the old principle that a man's house is his castle. There is the corruption of elections by subtle coercion of the voter on relief and of farmers, which creates fear for democracy itself. There is the systematic stirring of strife between trade-unions and between workers and employers, which demoralizes all production . . . Look at the losses of workers, employers, and consumers in strikes and lockouts . . . Add in the sit-down strike, and haven't we cause for fear?
>
> There is the intimidation of the farmers. There is the government interference in prices of commodities. This throws calculations of many industries completely out of joint. There are the increasing hidden taxes, which take the buying power of workers and farmers.

At this point, Hoover scraped out his pipe and filled it with tobacco, lit it, "and slumped down in his chair. He has," Irwin wrote, "a curious habit of jingling small coins while he is thinking hard, and he was doing this now." Then Hoover continued that another source of fear was government competition with business: "Who wants to invest in an industry with the government as a competitor?" He continued, "Let's lump off some of the rest—the decadence of morals in public affairs, local corruption and futility in the administration of relief, cumbersome centralization, tendencies in the administration toward the European insanities of Fascism and Socialism. Don't forget the debts and deficits caused by reckless spending and futile pump-priming. Every citizens knows in the bottom of his heart that if this continues to mount up, the government must in the end either impose more taxes, go bankrupt, or inflate the currency." "It is little wonder," Hoover concluded, "that the country is jittery." And there would be no "restoration of real confidence and faith until our people know that the government has changed its direction." Irwin was impressed to find five people waiting outside to see Hoover when he left and was told by his secretary that it was one of his slow days.[111] Edgar Rickard, too, found Hoover "insatiable as to work and [he] does not relax."[112]

In July, another old Hoover friend, humorist Irvin S. Cobb, introduced the former president before his talk to the Bohemian Grove Encampment. Calling Hoover "the first citizen of California and in the minds of millions of his admirers the first gentleman of the United States," Cobb told him, "Mr. Hoover, I voted against you twice in the last two campaigns. The first time was a party gesture as an old line Democrat; the second time it was a grievous error as an American citizen which I have repented in sack-cloth and ashes." He did not, Cobb said, wish to bring politics into "this friendly scene," but he thanked Hoover "because you never got the idea of burning down the temple of our forefathers in order to get rid of a few cockroaches in the basement."

In a speech before Montana Republicans early in August, Hoover slightly toughened his approach to the president, offering seven reasons why there should be "a radical change in the membership of the next Congress":

1. To restore the independence of the legislative arm of government, which had been abandoned by the "rubber-stamp majority" in Congress for the previous six years.
2. To restore "sober consideration and effective debate of legislation," which could only be achieved by the existence in Congress of "a substantial opposition" that could delay legislation it had been duly considered.
3. To restore legislative control of the national purse.
4. To provide Congress with "responsible law makers" and not "rubber stamps."
5. The rubber-stamp Congress had "frightened and scared" the business community, thus acting as "a potent agency for producing unemployment."
6. To defend independent-minded members of Congress against the Roosevelt doctrine, which said, "If Congress is not subjective to the Executive then the Executive Branch may use its vast powers and its control of expenditures to defeat candidates who have dared respect their responsibilities and conscience."
7. "If the people do not want centralization, personal power and dictation in this government, now is the time to act."[113]

Hoover was convinced that the congressional elections of 1938 were of crucial importance for both the nation and the Republican Party. If the small

GOP minorities in the House and the Senate were allowed to slip any further there would be virtually no check any longer of Roosevelt's apparent thirst for power. And if the Republican Party suffered another defeat, after the successive ones of 1930, 1932, 1934, and 1936, it might well spell the end of the party. In August he traveled through the western states, meeting with GOP leaders in an effort to invigorate the congressional campaigns of candidates in Idaho, Montana, and Utah, where he concluded that the party might pick up four seats in Congress.

In late September Hoover delivered the first of the three major speeches he had planned for the campaign. He would, he told his audience, explore Roosevelt's New Deal in his speeches, using as a yardstick "the test of the greatest Leader humanity has ever known [Jesus Christ], who said: 'By their fruits ye shall know them.'" The first of the speeches would deal with "morals in government," the second with the "destruction of government of free men," and the third with the "economic consequences." Hoover indicted the New Deal for what he described as its "alphabetical morals," which he described as "The G.E.A.A.—Get Elected Anyhow Anyway." The Roosevelt administration had used the spoils system to appoint three hundred thousand officeholders for whom political affiliation had been the only test of "merit." Federal agencies like the Works Progress Administration (WPA) had been shamelessly used for political purposes, while the administration was also coercing corporations into making political contributions. The New Deal had shown no morals in its financial practices, was deceptive in its dealings with the public, and was actively propagandizing itself at the expense of taxpayers. And it preached class hatred. Hoover concluded, "Mr. Roosevelt denounces and accuses all of us who do not believe in these methods and these actions as conservatives. If being conservative on dragging America into the morass of political immorality or into the Dead Sea of reaction is Conservative then I cheerfully join that party."[114] Hoover wrote to a friend that "the response to the speech shows it to be the issue. American people may be amateurs in politics but they are professionals when it comes to morals."[115]

On October 17 in Hartford, Connecticut, Hoover found the familiar faults with the New Deal: the degeneration of political morals, "the malignant growth of personal power," the fomenting of class divisions, "a creeping collectivism," and failure, despite all that it had inflicted upon the country, in ending the depression. The former president concluded,

> The New Deal and its yes-yes men in Congress have been experimenting with the American way of life for six years at dreadful cost in human misery and despair. It would seem that the experiment has not been a success.
>
> The voter might well experiment for himself for once. He might vote for men who would halt this whole movement. For a nation to take the next two years to stop, look, and listen is an experiment that could not

make the situation worse. It is not a very great risk for the voter to take . . .

It might prove the experiment that saved the freedom of the men and women of a great nation.[116]

The speech made the front page of the *New York Times*, which printed the full text.[117]

Before the next campaign speech, Hoover gave a talk to the eighth annual Forum on Current Problems sponsored by the *New York Herald Tribune* in the Waldorf Astoria on October 26. In his speech, Hoover had insisted that war was not in prospect and that the United States must remain aloof from any European conflict. Arthur Krock regarded the speech as building a bridge to Senate Republicans like Hiram Johnson and William Borah.[118]

In his third speech, given in Philadelphia in November, Hoover delivered his most biting remarks. Roosevelt had delivered a speech the previous night in which he had claimed success in "creating economic stability, prosperity, and security for the average man." Hoover retorted to the president's claims by pointing out that he had somehow neglected to mention "the 11,000,000 unemployed, or farmers' prices, or some other instabilities and insecurities." Hoover would demonstrate, he declared, "that the consequences of New Deal morals, their undermining of representative government and their economic policies not only cancel out the humanitarian objectives which it professes and to which all Americans aspire, but that they undermine all hopes for progress in standards of living to all our people." Of the two methods of providing the necessities of a people—through an economy of liberty or through an economy of government compulsion— Hoover favored, he said, the former, "because I know it is inseparable from intellectual and spiritual liberty" and was the "only road to higher standards of living" and to the survival of "morals and self-respect of men." Despite the weaknesses of the free enterprise system, it was the only one that stimulated technology and efficiency and resulted in productivity and a higher standard of living. "Free enterprise," he observed, "can well be called the economy of plenty."

Roosevelt, however, had produced a conflict between the two types of systems through the imposition of a planned economy atop the free enterprise system in America, and after six years of the New Deal, America alone of all the surviving democracies was still mired in the depression. Roosevelt's policies had undermined the long-term confidence of men, and the humanitarian objectives of the New Deal had been distorted by the growth in personal power and the lack of morality in government. "The people grow poor in personal liberty when its officials grow rich in personal power," Hoover charged. He called upon his listeners to elect an independent Congress: "That will be a sign to America that we have changed our national road from compelled men to free men. It will bring new confidence in the future and will quickly make jobs." He pleaded for the "election of a new Congress of independent men" so that America could "come back."[119]

As the elections approached, Hoover was deeply distressed by an issue on the California political scene. A proposition had been placed on the California ballot that was described as a "Labor Peace Initiative" but that was clearly designed to curb the power and activities of labor unions in that state by severely restricting strikes and boycotting activities.[120] The former president had friends who were deeply committed to both sides of the issue. His own disposition was to oppose the proposition. "In the broad sense, I have always felt that laws which step over the line of mere correction of obvious abuse and enter the field of dictating conduct are in themselves a contradiction of true American ideals," he wrote, and he placed some aspects of the proposition in this category.[121] He briefly considered issuing a statement in opposition to the proposition if the presidents of Stanford University and the University of California would join in a request for his views on it, but he was dissuaded by President Ray Lyman Wilbur of Stanford, who argued that no good could come to Hoover by taking a position on the issue.[122] In the end, the former president decided to "keep still and hope to be of service later."[123]

In mid-October, *Newsweek* magazine polled 45 newsmen and 8 politicians (4 from each party) and found the consensus predicting a 50-seat gain in the House for the GOP and a 4-seat gain in the Senate. Mark Sullivan decided that if the Republicans did not pick up at least 50 seats in the House it would be difficult to argue that there had been any slippage in Roosevelt's popularity. *New York Times* columnist Arthur Krock predicted that "if the House increase [of Republicans] goes above fifty, the Senate as much as four, and the present eleven Republican governors are joined by fellow-partisans in certain States, the political consequences to the Administration will be serious." In fact, the Republican gains in the 1938 elections exceeded the expectations of the most optimistic Republicans and other New Deal critics. Republicans gained 81 seats in the House of Representatives and 8 in the Senate and added 13 governorships.[124]

The sense of crisis that had followed four successive electoral defeats was somewhat lessened. Both Hoover and Landon found in the election results vindication for the courses they had followed in 1937 and 1938. For Landon, it was confirmation that he and his followers had been correct in their opposition to a midterm Republican convention or conference.[125] For Hoover and his supporters, the gains were directly attributable to the former president's speeches and articles attacking the New Deal and putting forth Republican principles, as well as to his successful and well-publicized efforts to bring about some constructive activity on the part of the party organization.[126] The Republican Party, in which Hoover had performed the role of evangelist after Landon's disastrous defeat in 1936, had demonstrated during the two years between elections durability and vigor, defying the views of those like Landon who believed its only future lay in coalition. Whatever factors contributed to the Republican resurgence in 1938—the court fight, the recession of 1937–1938, or the international crisis of late 1938, to name a few—Hoover had justification for believing that his vision of the party's future had been vindicated and that he had aided more than any other Republican in the resurgence of the GOP in 1938.

CHAPTER 4

Crises Abroad,
Politics at Home

New Hope

Typically the election results of 1938 were viewed as a defeat for Roosevelt rather than a victory for the Republicans. Arthur Krock wrote in the *New York Times*, "One-party government, under the domination of the President as leader of that party—a domination often exercised through young doctrinaires who never faced a poll—was emphatically abolished after trial by the voters of the United States last Tuesday. The average taxpayers who form what is loosely called the 'middle class,' shifted their allegiance from the President and the post-1936 New Deal to accomplish this." The Democratic *Omaha World-Herald* agreed that "it was not the Republican Party that won the victories, rather it was the Administration that suffered defeats. Millions who had supported Roosevelt and his party turned to Republican candidates because there was no other available way of making evident their distrust and alarm." But as columnist Joseph Alsop, a Roosevelt relative, confided, "New Dealers rather defiantly refuse to recognize its full significance, but I don't see how you can get around the fact that . . . the election is a repudiation of precisely the intellectual liberalism for which the New Dealers stand."[1]

Republicans, including Hoover, were naturally encouraged by the outcome, although the former president was disappointed that Thomas Dewey had failed narrowly in his bid for the governorship of New York. A GOP victory there, he felt, "would have been practically a final blow to the New Deal."[2] His press statement after the election agreed with the general view that the result was more anti–New Deal than pro-Republican. He said,

The returns indicate that a majority of the American people voted for Governors, Senators or Congressmen, either Republicans or Democrats, who are opposed to the New Deal. This protest should enable the beginning of the end of this waste of public money, these policies of coercion, political corruption and undermining of representative government. The reinvigorated Republican party is now in a position to join effectively with the anti–New Deal Democrats to check these policies in the Congress and thereby contribute to restore employment and agriculture, to reestablish confidence in business and above all to restore faith in America. Over the next two years, it is the duty of the Republican party not alone to join in this check, but to develop a constructive program which will commend itself to the country for 1940.[3]

Besides the victories, an analysis of the gubernatorial returns prepared for him showed that in the 28 states where there were contests, the GOP had outpolled the Democrats by 12 million votes to 10.6 million.[4] Hoover's own analysis concluded that where candidates for office campaigned against the New Deal they invariably won out, except for one race in California.[5]

The former president opined that "if we keep up the battle for the next two years, I believe we shall end this episode in American life in its destructive aspects."[6] Others, however, were not as confident that the election spelled the end for FDR. The acerbic H. L. Mencken, a bitter Roosevelt opponent, wrote William Allen White that "Roosevelt got a beating on election day, but he still has two years to go, and in that time he may convert the boobs all over again. In particular I suspect him of a scheme to get the country into war. The trick will be easy if he really wants to perform it."[7]

If Hoover's efforts to wrest control of the GOP from Landon in 1937 and 1938 had failed, they had nevertheless given the former president tremendous visibility, and he clearly entered 1939 as a leading figure in the party. Many party members commended him for his contribution to the turnaround in the GOP's fortunes in 1938. Will Irwin wrote Hoover that he wondered "if anyone appreciates how much your speeches have had to do with the unexpectedly brilliant victory. Certainly a lot of people in private life have sensed it. I am hearing about them on all hands."[8] A Republican national committeeman wrote him that "beyond question" his speeches "did more to influence public sentiment than did the efforts of any half dozen others."[9] But Hoover wrote Will Irwin, "I am getting an enormous amount of mail insisting that I carried the election, but I haven't seen any account of that in the newspapers."[10] Julius Klein, however, called his attention to such an observation in the *Washington Post* and added, "There's no doubt whatever but that a goodly portion of the avalanche which swept down on our 'red' friends last Tuesday was started by your forceful blows during the campaign."[11]

A Hoover supporter wrote Edgar Rickard that the result showed how "utterly foolish and completely unrelated to political realism" had been the comments of political commentators and politicians during the past two years in their eulogies for the GOP and their insistence on a new party that would include Republicans and anti–New Deal Democrats. John Spargo wrote,

> Not only has the party revived with an amazing demonstration of strength and vitality, but it is now clearly evident that only its own folly the next eighteen months is likely to prevent its return to power in 1940 . . . And I should be less than honest if I did not acknowledge to myself that most of those who held to that view and who kept plodding along drew our inspiration, our faith, and our courage from the Chief . . . I have been unable to evade one significant conclusion. It is that without a single exception, whenever I have received a letter from anybody, whether friend or stranger, who expressed confidence in Herbert Hoover and any measure of admiration for him, I have found that person to be firm in the conviction that loyal and unwavering insistence upon fundamental democratic ideals and principles must inevitably win and that the Republican Party could save our democratic institutions to the nation if, and only if, it took the high ground of uncompromising devotion to fundamental principles . . . On the other hand, the cynics, the pessimists, and the proposers of desperate experiments, have with scarcely an exception belittled Mr. Hoover and included him with the useless and outmoded elements to be relegated to the scrap heap. Because of these things, while fully aware that it cannot be statistically demonstrated, in my inmost soul there is profound conviction that the sturdy and uncompromising intellectual and moral leadership of the Chief contributed more to the recent victory than all the efforts of the national committee and more than all the funds that were spent for the party campaign. And that conviction necessarily carried with it the belief that those of us who have stood with the Chief, refusing to be turned aside, carrying on despite setbacks and discouragements, have a right to feel that our faith and our constancy have not been in vain, but have borne fruits of victory even greater than most of us dared believe.[12]

Having labored so hard to achieve the electoral result, it would have been easy for Hoover to overestimate his contribution to the GOP success, if indeed he did overestimate it. He was much sought after as a speaker, he maintained a loyal following and close ties with Republican leaders both in and out of Congress, and as the international situation in 1939 brought the introduction of various defense and foreign affairs proposals in Congress, the former president was increasingly consulted for his views by Republicans in both houses of Congress. His relations with Landon, however, remained strained, despite Hoover's attempts to extend a "long arm" to him during the 1938 campaign.[13]

In January Hoover also continued his commitment to children by joining his former 1928 rival, Alfred Smith, and Senator Arthur Capper in an appeal for funds for the Save the Children Fund. That organization, formed in the early 1930s to provide food, clothing, and school supplies for the needy children of the Southern highlands, expressed an immediate need for $1 million.[14] Hoover and Smith spoke over the radio from New York City, Capper from Washington, DC.

Foreign Concerns

More than anything else, Hoover's prominent role in the debates over foreign policy kept him before the American public and contributed to his rise in popularity in 1939 and 1940. Even before he left for Europe in February, 1938, Hoover had addressed the darkening international situation in both Europe and Asia with a radio speech to the Republican women's clubs of New York, Chicago, and San Francisco on January 15, 1938. The world, he noted, was "filled with increasing distrust and rising disorder," with armies growing in size and international economic relations demoralized. In confronting the situation, the United States should learn from its experience with the Great War fought less than a generation earlier. It should realize that in such a war the winners suffer almost equally with the losers, that wars inevitably produced inflation, that democratic government in the Unites States "probably could not stand the shock of another great war and survive as a democracy." The United States should fight only to defend its own independence and against violations of the Monroe Doctrine in the Western Hemisphere. It was a position from which the former president would deviate only slightly during the remainder of his life.

Somewhat surprisingly, in view of his distrust of Roosevelt, Hoover opposed the Ludlow Amendment, a proposal by Congressman Louis Ludlow of Indiana that would have required a nationwide referendum on the issue of American participation in a war, except in the event of an invasion of the United States, before a congressional declaration of war could be made. The former president argued, somewhat irrelevantly, that the device was workable only if all nations of the world were democracies and agreed to similar referendums. The greatest assurance that the United States would not be attacked lay in preparedness for defense and the determination of the nation to use its arms "solely to repel aggression against the Western Hemisphere." In all other situations the United States must preserve its neutrality. The United States should "cooperate in every sane international effort to advance the economic and social welfare of the world," since the "prosperity of nations is the best sedative to hate." Such international cooperation had been his goal in arranging the 1933 World Economic Conference, only to have the conference sabotaged by Roosevelt. Such conferences, Hoover insisted, remained the best answer to international economic friction.[15]

Hoover's short and relatively minor speech to the GOP women launched him into an area that would loom increasingly important in 1939 and the years that followed. It aroused a good deal of favorable comment, and Congressman Hamilton Fish Jr. inserted it into the *Congressional Record*, noting in a telegram to Hoover that he was pleased to see the former president did not agree with the internationalism of his former secretary of state, Henry Stimson, who continued to support the use of embargoes, armed force, and the "quarantining" of other nations.[16]

In the fall of 1938, as Europe seemed to be teetering on the verge of war over German demands for the Sudeten region of Czechoslovakia, Hoover addressed the crisis in a speech to the Forum on Current Problems on October 26 in New York City. His message was by now familiar. The question Americans must ask themselves, he said, was "Do these totalitarian governments threaten our safety?" Hoover answered the question in the negative and opposed any American involvement in a European war. Instead, the United States should provide "moral force" behind the principle that international relations should be based on law and free agreement, rather than on force, and should assist in providing international economic cooperation to bring economic prosperity to the world. Economic improvement would not only contribute to peace but also "relax these philosophies of despotism" and "remove their brutalities" more than "all of the armies and navies in the world."[17] While the Roosevelt administration apparently believed that the Munich settlement of the Sudeten question had averted war, Hoover was less optimistic. He wrote a friend, "I do not think the world has anything to congratulate itself about at any point over the whole European episode, and of course my impression is that it is only a porten[t] of worse to come. I would like to persuade myself otherwise."[18]

In November he went on the air over a San Francisco radio station to express his outrage over Nazi assaults on Jews in Germany. He told his listeners, "This rise of intolerance today, the suffering being inflicted on an innocent and helpless people, grieves every decent American. It raises our every sense of indignation and resentment. It makes us fearful for the whole progress of civilization. It is our hope that those springs of tolerance and morals, of human compassion which lie deep in the German people may rise to control. But in the meantime our condemnation of these leaders should be without reserve. They are bringing to Germany a moral isolation from the entire world."[19] Lewis Strauss tried to convince Hoover that he should head up an organization to look after Jewish refugees from Germany, but Hoover argued that such a privately funded effort would be insufficient because if it were mounted the Germans would use it as an excuse to dump their six hundred thousand Jews on it overnight, and Poland would follow with four million. Hoover was convinced that it was a problem solvable only by governments, and that Great Britain should take the lead.[20]

But Hoover did add his voice to that of other distinguished Americans in January 1939 in supporting legislation that would permit America to receive refugee children from Europe, saying that it should be "supported by every American. There can be no criticism that this action adds distress to our unemployed. It benefits the American wish to aid suffering, it answers the appeal to every American heart for the protection of children."[21] And in April he wired his support of the Wagner-Rogers resolution in Congress, which would favor accepting twenty thousand German refugee children outside of the immigration quota. Hoover's wire said, "As you know, I strongly favor this bill providing for the admission into the United States of 20,000 refugee children. No harm, and only good, can come to a nation by such humane action. I have no doubt of their adoption into American homes. I am glad to see support of the measure by such great influences as both the Protestant and Catholic churches and the American Federation of Labor."[22]

In February 1939, Hoover appeared before the Council on Foreign Relations again and outlined for them what he defined as the traditional foreign policy of the United States: (1) remaining free of foreign entanglements and other peoples' wars; (2) concentrating on self-defense, not on intervention in others' wars; (3) defining the Western Hemisphere as part of American defense under the Monroe Doctrine; (4) protecting the lives of Americans abroad by force, if necessary, but relying upon peaceful negotiations to protect American rights and property; (5) cooperating in "peaceful movements to promote peace and in economic movements to promote world prosperity" but without threats of force to attain these objects; and (6) prohibiting, under the neutrality laws, the purchase of armaments in the United States by belligerents. To Hoover it seemed that Roosevelt was deviating from these traditional policies and the inevitable result, if continued, would be the involvement of the United States in war. Hoover saw no threat to the United States or the Western Hemisphere that justified the administration's policies, and he worried that personal liberty and economic freedom would disappear in this country under the conditions of modern warfare. Thus one inevitable outcome of an American war against fascism would be the transformation of the United States "into practically a Fascist state." Instead, the United States should stand as a beacon of liberty for the rest of the world.[23]

The speech to the Council on Foreign Relations attracted considerable praise. The editor of the *Los Angeles Times* called it "the most illuminating and penetrating analysis of our miscalled foreign policy yet made by anyone," and he suggested that the former president write a syndicated weekly column on world affairs.[24] Frederick J. Libby, executive secretary of the American Council for Prevention of War, believed that the speech had "checked temporarily [the] war trend [of the] Roosevelt administration" and told Hoover he was distributing 25,000 copies of it.[25] Congressman Hamilton Fish inserted the speech in the *Congressional Record* and told Hoover that if he "wanted it printed to be sent out in franked envelopes" he was welcome "to use my franking privilege if you do not have one. You can get your speech at actual printing cost."[26] Hoover told columnist Boake Carter he was afraid his speech marked "the beginning of a long and difficult fight to keep America out of grave danger."[27]

By the end of 1938 Hoover had already begun to counsel congressional Republicans on foreign policy, traveling to Washington early in December for a breakfast meeting with them that had been arranged by his former undersecretary of state, William Castle.[28] In January, Republicans in Congress formed a GOP Policy Committee for National Defense and again sought Hoover's advice.[29] Senator Styles Bridges of New Hampshire was one who echoed Hoover's position in the Senate, addressing that body in February along lines he had discussed with the former president. Bridges, too, argued that the United States must stay out of war and follow a realistic foreign policy "based upon fundamental proven principles and maintained for a longer time than necessary to deliver a 'fireside chat.'" The United States should not, he insisted, "act in the cause of peace as though we intended to fight."[30]

Support even came from the other side of the aisle, with Democratic Senator Thomas Walsh approving what he called Hoover's "militant pro-American views and his broad liberal and patriotic attitude."[31] The former president welcomed allies in the struggle to keep America out of war regardless of where they came from and regardless of their motives. He commended to O'Laughlin's attention an article by "that left-winger, Professor [Charles] Beard in the 'America Mercury,'" because Beard, too, was "opposed to our going into war."[32]

Hoover pinned his hopes for peace in early 1939 on the British desire to avoid war. He was no critic of appeasement of Hitler by such European leaders as British Prime Minister Neville Chamberlain, writing, "Probably the one thing that will keep us out of war is the British. They have sanity. They do not want to go to war. And they are today the only outstanding skillful group of world diplomats. If Roosevelt had maintained at least the tone of voice of Chamberlain in this situation, he might have been in a position, at the proper moment, to have been of great service to the world in bringing these people around a council table."[33] Foreign affairs having begun to loom so importantly on the political scene, the former president was all the more anxious that the record in foreign policy of his administration should get wider dissemination. William Starr Myers now replaced William Castle as the person designated to bring out a book on the foreign policies of the Hoover presidency.[34]

Politics Again

Hoover left foreign relations to return to an attack on the New Deal in his Lincoln Day speech in New York, when he lashed out at Roosevelt's State of the Union message. Describing "The Real State of the Union," the former president charged that the nation was "more sadly divided and confused than at any since Lincoln's time." The 1938 elections had brought improvements, however, by demonstrating that Americans were still willing to use the ballot box to safeguard their liberties. The independence of Congress had been partially restored and guardians of the independence of the courts had been reelected to office. "The people," Hoover concluded, "have proved that elections cannot be controlled by government subsidies." Since the "first chore of a political party out of power" was to provide "corrective opposition" and the "exposure of the witchery of half-truth and the curb of arrogant and extreme action," Hoover pointed out that the New Deal had failed to produce recovery from the depression. Their only solution to their failure, he charged, was to call for even greater spending on a scale that meant "the most startling budget proposals ever laid before the American people in peace-time." The Republican Party, Hoover concluded, faced three great missions before it: the preservation of the principles of freedom, which were still being undermined by the New Deal; the economic recovery of the United States; and the avoidance by the United States of any entanglement in a foreign war.[35]

Afterward, Hoover wrote to the Ohio Republican national committeeman from Ohio,

> I think the Lincoln Day dinners did some good in indicating a solid front in the face of our divided enemies. The New Deal, of course, has been most industrious trying to provoke great schisms in the Republican Party as a sort of antidote of their troubles, but I see no more of it since the Lincoln Day dinners over the country. I think it would be advantageous if we could later on stage some more events of this kind where we can bring a large amount of our artillery to bear at the same moment.[36]

Dining with Hoover on February 22, Rickard found him "not at all interested in anything that does not bear upon his own prospects or just recognition as head of the Republican Party."[37]

Alf Landon was certain that Hoover was seeking the nomination and that if he didn't receive it himself, he wanted to be in a position to select the nominee.[38] The two men continued to be rivals, with part of that rivalry manifested in their mutual attempts to build close relations with the rising star of the party, Thomas Dewey of New York. The Hoovers, who by now were spending much of their time in New York City, had managed to develop something of a social relationship with the Deweys there, while Landon sought from distant Topeka, Kansas, to steer Dewey away from identification as a "Hoover" man.[39] Landon had supported the efforts of New York GOP national committeeman Kenneth Simpson in creating "fusion" tickets in New York in which Republicans and the left-wing American Labor Party cooperated to defeat Democrats.[40] Predictably, Hoover had opposed those efforts. When Dewey broke with Simpson early in 1939, it could be regarded as a victory of Hoover over Landon, although among those advising Dewey to make the break was Landon's fellow Kansan William Allen White.[41]

The division between Landon and Hoover was encouraged by some of the Kansan's supporters. One wrote him late in February that there were "two Republican Parties . . . one headed by Hoover and maybe Vandenburg, making speeches, snatching up banners and waving them with never a thought since 1932." The other GOP was headed by Landon and included people like House Minority Leader Joe Martin, which was making a "record which will be our bulwark in 1940." "The Hoover outfit will blow itself out," he wrote Landon. "Your boys have the offices and the organization."[42]

Hoover's 1936 aspirations for the nomination had not included any attempt to organize the grass roots, but 1939 saw such an attempt launched in the form of a group known as the Republican Circles. While ostensibly designed simply to impart new vigor into the Republican Party in the western states, it is clear that Hoover's supporters intended the organization to support his ambitions, whatever those turned out to be.[43] By late February, Circles had been organized in California from San Luis Obispo to the Mexican border, with each county having ten initial members, who, in turn, were creating new Circles. One inducement to join was the promise of an opportunity to meet with Hoover in "informal, confidential" conferences.[44] In mid-March, Hoover returned to California for the first series of such meetings.[45] That the Circles were intended to function as Hoover "shock troops" is clear from Ben Allen's remark: "Every man selected in this Circle had to be a Hoover devotee and pledge himself simply to a belief in the political philosophy and principles of the Chief and support of his leadership."[46]

While Landon's followers were not involved in such organizational activities, some were doing their best to sow suspicion among Republicans of Hoover's own activities. Landon and his supporters were convinced from the extent of the former president's activities that he was either seeking the 1940 nomination for himself or was determined to name the nominee.[47] Other Republicans, however, recognized the value of Hoover for the party, irrespective of any candidacy. As one wrote in late March,

> Prior to the last election a group of men got together in this county and determined to perfect an organization which would, if possible, take this state and other states, out of the grip of the Democrats. We consulted Mr. Hoover and he laid out a working plan which was followed by the group with the result that we elected a Republican member in Congress from this district by a 15,000 majority. This gave us courage and we decided to begin organizing for the 1940 election. We wondered whether or not Mr. Hoover would be able to put over the message to the people, and so the Crossley people conducted a poll during one of his speeches. This is done by having thousands of telephone messages sent into homes during the course of a program to find out just how many are listening . . . Charles McCarthy and Edgar Bergen have a 26,000,000 audience, President Roosevelt a 30,000,000 audience and very much to our surprise, after thirty minutes Mr. Hoover had an audience of 34,000,000. We decided that by these figures it would be a good plan to have some constructive talks made by him, as they would reach a large number of the people. We knew of no other Republican who could reach such a group, and so it was determined to have him make some speeches, which he has been doing. It was also determined that we would organize groups in every community of the State—groups which were willing to take his leadership. He was very frank in saying that he was not a candidate himself, but would cooperate in any constructive movement.[48]

In late March Hoover wrote Arch Shaw that he had just finished "a string of 13 meetings—one every night since I saw you."[49]

By now another potential candidate for the 1940 nomination had begun to make his presence felt. This was Robert A. Taft, son of former president

William Howard Taft, and a close Hoover friend since his association with the former president's food and relief work during and after World War I. Taft was one of those Republicans elected to the Senate in the GOP resurgence of November, 1938. Concerned that he might face a challenge from his own wing of the party, Hoover sought to discourage Taft's ambitions for 1940 as premature in view of his lack of a record in the Senate, but there was increasing talk of a Taft nomination in the absence of any other strong candidates.[50] There was also, however, considerable speculation concerning Hoover's own plans and prospects for 1940. Meanwhile, some tried to link him with Dewey's candidacy. In late April he wrote a friend that because he had dined with Dewey, "and for some reason it leaked out into the press, I am supposed to be backing him." Hoover was not, he insisted, "backing anybody," and he decried the tendency of politicians "to grasp for pretty small straws."[51]

The former president definitely considered the 1940 nomination worth attaining. Like many others, he sensed that the political trend in the nation in 1939 was in a conservative direction, and if the GOP did not drop the ball, the 1940 election could be won.[52] But his own ambitions aside, Hoover continued to seek a return by the Republican Party to its traditional principles by 1940—principles he believed had been abandoned by Landon in 1936. Thus while he was worried by Dewey's rising prominence in the party and the threat it posed to his own candidacy, he was also concerned that the Landon group (what Harrison Spangler called "the Sunflower Group of malcontents"[53]) might "control" Dewey and continue to steer the party away from traditional Republicanism. While the break between Dewey and Simpson somewhat lessened this possibility, Hoover continued to work to ensure that the GOP would reflect his own policy in 1940. Throughout 1939 he sought to shape the declaration of the Republican policy committee, which was now to be made in 1940, but his efforts had scant effect.

When blocked in one direction, Hoover always found others where he could move forward with his objective. In early 1939 this took the form of holding more of the small meetings with local groups of 50 to 150 participants at the site of each of his speeches, both to disseminate his philosophy and to advance his standing in the party. Included in the meetings were local civic leaders and molders of public opinion including, usually, the publisher of the local newspaper.[54] After one such meeting with small town publishers in Illinois, a participant wrote, "Meeting Mr. Hoover and hearing his intimate talk was just about the biggest thing that ever happened to some of the country publishers . . . He talked for an hour and a half and not a man left— they hardly stirred. More than one assured me after the meeting was over it would do more for sound Republicanism than anything that had happened in Illinois in years."[55]

When not writing or speaking, Hoover was monitoring the progress of the Republican Circles in the western states.[56] By mid-1939 Circles had been formed in Montana, Idaho, Washington, Oregon, and Colorado, in addition to California, and the group was cooperating with similar organizations in Arizona and Nevada.[57] Hoover busied himself raising funds to put representatives into the field in the western states to further promote the group. Former governor Thomas Campbell of Arizona was given the task of organizing groups in that state and in New Mexico.[58] Hoover also wrote to political leaders in the western states encouraging them to cooperate in the organization effort. In one such letter he told former governor C. C. Moore of Idaho that the Circles were "the only satisfactory form of Republican organization to fight the New Deal in 1940 that I have seen. It mobilizes the responsible men in each county and town for active campaigning and at the same time supports the regular organization and all other Republican organizations."[59] Dining with Hoover in June, Rickard found everything was "subordinated to his political ambitions and he is spending much time in writing, revising, and changing several speeches he has in hand."[60]

Back on the stump, the former president told graduating seniors at Lincoln University (Tennessee) on June 4 that they were "about to enter a world more confused as to its ideas and principles of life than has been the case for a long time." One of those confusions was over how to protect "personal liberty in the changing economic and social pressures." The American system of free enterprise, based on liberty, had produced greater productivity, more progress, and was, he argued, the only system with humor. The free enterprise system could not, however, survive when mixed with government compulsion. Hoover added, "Voluntary cooperation moves from a delicate mainspring. That mainspring is the initiative, enterprise and confidence of men. The moment any part of compulsion or coercion is directed at free men their fears rise, their energies slack, their productivity slows down, and the people suffer. Coercion feeds upon more coercion. Either out of desperation or design, governments apply more and more coercion once they have started. And they demand more and more power over men." Taking note of the war fears in the United States, the former president asserted that the real danger to America was not from "violent invasion of these systems from abroad" but rather from their "subtle growth" in the United States as a "means to remedy war dislocation and depression."[61]

Graduating seniors at Earlham College in Indiana heard from Hoover eight days later, when he tried to clarify for them the confused thinking of political labels like "reactionary, conservative, liberal, and radical." America, he noted, had no political parties organized under such labels, and he told his audience, "We use these terms politically mostly for slogans and oratory. They are used for eulogy and defamation. If you do not like somebody you consign him to the complexion most hated by your listener. These terms are used as refuges from ignorance or intellectual dishonesty. They are set up as pigeon-holes for men and groups to imply they are righteous, stingy, public-spirited, opposed to public interest, or generally sinful. They are dumdum words to assassinate men and then to plant bitter onions on their graves."

The former president then defined for his audience his concept of American liberalism, in familiar terms, and explored for them the "impure" forms of liberalism then current in America. Hoover suggested to his listeners that they eschew all such labels as *liberal, radical, reactionary*, or *conservative* and dedicate themselves instead to the American system of liberty. Where defense of that system required them to be liberal or conservative or reactionary or radical, they should not hesitate to be whatever was required.[62]

On his trips into Tennessee and Indiana for the commencement addresses, Hoover continued his practice of meeting with small local groups where he sounded public opinion and developed useful political contacts.[63] On his way back to California he concluded that "the general shift is toward the Republican party, but I think it is going to be more of a battle than most of our people believe at the moment."[64]

An American Foreign Policy

While he attacked the New Deal in his speeches, Hoover was criticizing Roosevelt's foreign policies in articles. In one published in Liberty magazine in April, the former president suggested that the United States could respond to a world crisis in either of two ways, neither of which he judged as isolationist. The first was to maintain neutrality and to seek to bring about a settlement of world tensions through peaceful methods, including economic cooperation. The other was "to depart from neutrality" and "to exert the physical force of the United States on one side of a conflict." The latter course must inevitably result in American involvement in war. The path of neutrality he defined as "the long view and the realistic view," while the use of force was "the short view and the emotional view." Hoover argued that the fascist states had no intention of attacking the Western democracies, but that if an attack came those democracies were entirely capable of their own defense.

Hoover expressed opposition to allying the United States with France, since that meant aligning itself also with the Soviet Union, a nation that had tried for twenty years to subvert the American government. Fascist though it might be, Italy had never done that. The former president also insisted that the destructive philosophies of Germany and the Soviet Union could not much longer survive. Then he added, "Moreover, the whole theory of stopping aggression is in fact an attempt to maintain the status quo in national boundaries all over the world. We need only to look back even one hundred years of history to see how many fights we could get into. In fact, we have been aggressive in our time. Otherwise parts of the Rocky Mountains and California would belong to Mexico today." Hoover concluded, "We cannot become the world's policeman unless we are prepared to sacrifice millions of American lives—and probably some day see all the world against us. In time they would envisage us as the world's greatest bully, not as the world's greatest idealist." The experience of World War I, moreover, should have demonstrated to Americans the folly of trying to "make the world safe for democracy."[65]

In that same month Hoover wrote his former undersecretary of state, William Castle,

> The whole situation seems to be getting worse. It appears now that the failure
> of the appeasement program [in Europe] is going to lead to a debacle. At least,
> [British prime minister] Mr. Chamberlain is trying to prove that there was no
> such antagonism toward Germany over Central and Eastern Europe, so as to
> enable him to build up such a program. I naturally hope he succeeds in his new
> undertaking but it looks pretty gloomy this morning. If the United States had
> stayed out of this controversy, the President of the United States would then
> have been in a position to propose mediation of the whole situation and prob-
> ably to make the greatest contribution to peace in this generation. As it stands,
> there is no one to make this contribution.[66]

Moreover, he wrote another friend, the Roosevelt administration had "given the country the jitters over the possibility of our going to war and these jitters are throwing hundreds of thousands of men out of work."[67] By June, Hoover was becoming concerned that Roosevelt's sword rattling was being "trans- ferred to Japan from Europe, which gives us another front on which we will have to fight."[68]

In July *American Magazine* published an article by the former president pointedly titled "Shall We Send Our Youth to War?" The Europeans, he wrote, were once again engaged in one of their historic power conflicts, and the United States must ensure that it did not again become a pawn of Euro- pean power politics as had been the case in 1917–18, whether as a result of foreign propaganda or of American diplomatic mistakes. Propaganda was already seeking to "fertilize our soil for our entry into war," and hostile words were being fired at "the nations we don't like" by American government offi- cials. Roosevelt's policies indicated that the president had "taken a seat at the table where power politics is being played. He has joined in the chessboard of Europe." Hoover reiterated his belief that the country could "never go through another great war without becoming a totalitarian state in order to fight effectively such a war. When we have finished we shall not have estab- lished peace in the world. We shall have sacrificed liberty for generations in the United States." America could stay out of a European war only if its peo- ple had "the resolute will to do so." He told his readers,

> Staying out is a matter of tactics and strategy almost as difficult as the strategy and
> tactics of war. And, if there is not the adamant will to stay out, no amount of law
> can keep us out. The first thing required is a vigorous, definite statement from
> all who have responsibility, both publicly and privately, that we are not going to
> war with anybody in Europe unless they attack the Western Hemisphere. The
> second thing is not to sit in this game of power Politics. These are the American
> policies that will make sure that we do not send our youth to Europe for war.[69]

On July 5, Hoover gave a summary of his *American Magazine* article over the radio on the "American Magazine Hour," and the following day he expanded on it in a speech before the International Convention of Christian Endeavor Societies in Cleveland. The former president touched on the inhumane and destructive aspects of modern warfare and proposed that all nations should agree to the following: (1) that food ships should be as immune to attack as hospitals, and that they should not be subject to blockade; (2) that there should be no bombing of civilian populations; and (3) that bombing should be restricted to "the field of actual fighting men on land or sea, and at works devoted strictly to munitions." Neutral nations should be responsible for ensuring that these conditions were not violated through their management of the shipment of food supplies and by monitoring conditions in belligerent countries "to determine the facts of any killing of civilians from the air." Moral force, the power of world public opinion, would be the "teeth" of enforcement, since Hoover maintained that under conditions of modern warfare "one of the utmost anxieties of both sides is to hold the good will of neutrals" in order to avoid influencing them to "aid or join the enemy." At the very least, the arousal of ill will in the neutral countries by violations could lead to "informal boycotts of credit and supplies even though they go no further."[70] Congressman Ralph Brewster wired Hoover that it was "one of the most compelling and timely documents ever penned. The issue is clearly drawn."[71]

In August, Hoover published an article, "Let's Keep Women and Children out of the Trenches," in the *Christian Herald*. "The violence of war is year by year falling more and more horribly upon the civilian populations," he pointed out. "Put bluntly that means killing of women and children," accomplished both by aerial bombing and by starving the civilian populations of enemy countries. After reviewing the arguments given for pursuing such tactics, Hoover asked, "Even supposing all these arguments are true, are we to accept defeat of international decency? Are we not to try every method, explore every channel, that might allay these causes of war and armament and that might protect the lives and minds of innocent women and children? Must we accept the despair of return to barbarism? Must we accept such a collapse of Western civilization?" Hoover called on all nations to agree to four tenets:

>   1. That vessels laden solely with food supplies should be placed upon the same basis of immunity [from attack] as hospital ships. They should go freely. Blockade should not apply to them. There should be no attack upon their passage by either warships or submarines.
>   2. That there shall be no bombing of civil populations and no bombing anywhere except in the field of actual fighting men on land or sea, and at works devoted strictly to munitions.
>   Neutral nations should participate in the enforcement of these provisions by the nations agreeing:

3. That the organization and shipment of food supplies in war should be full cargoes under the management and jurisdiction of a commission of the neutral nations.

4. That neutral observers should be continuously in session within every belligerent country to determine the facts of any killing of civilians from the air.

Belligerents, Hoover opined, would not dare risk losing the goodwill of the neutrals by violating these provisions, lest they drive the neutrals into alliance with their enemies. The United States should take the lead in insisting on these provisions, Hoover wrote, "We possess a great power and we should use it to save mankind from the barbarities of war. In this we will be right at all times."[72]

Encouragement for his foreign policy speeches and statements came from popular historian Will Durant, who expressed the hope that Hoover would "continue to arouse the country to the fact that it is once more being made the pawn and joke of British policy."[73] From John Callan O'Laughlin came word that his speeches and magazine articles had "created great interest in Washington" and that some Republican members of Congress had admitted to him that in their statements and votes "they were inspired by you."[74] The former president made sure that copies of his speeches and articles were mailed to selected members of Congress.[75]

Hoover was convinced, however, that Roosevelt's policies had brought Europe to the brink of war by giving the democracies confidence that the United States would support them. The result was that the democracies had abandoned their policy of appeasement and had begun to take a more aggressive stance toward Germany and Italy, despite the fact that neither had shown any intention of attacking the democracies. Thus in Hoover's view, Roosevelt's policies had "measurably advanced the possibilities of war in the world, and the end of that war to save democracy will be that there will be no democracy left."[76]

Some of Hoover's supporters now began to voice the suspicion that the international situation was being made into an issue by the Roosevelt administration in order to divert public attention from its failures domestically, and they expressed concern that Republicans, obviously including the former president, were "falling into the trap." For Hoover, however, the dominant issue in 1939 was keeping the United States out of war.[77] If European conditions were distracting the attention of Americans away from the New Deal's failures, they were also contributing to Hoover's emergence as the leading Republican critic of the Roosevelt foreign policies and enhancing his preeminence over Landon, who was obviously inexperienced and unprepared to contend with the former president in this arena. In late August, as the situation in Europe grew more critical, Hoover voiced concern that if war did break out there, it would instantly change "the color of American attitudes and interests" and make the fight to keep America neutral even more difficult.[78]

In late August, as the war scare intensified, Hoover told reporters after a fishing trip to Montana that "all this war talk is beginning to affect even the fish. They are getting nervous and excited, too."[79] Two days before war broke out in Europe, Hoover wrote a friend, "Assuming that Europe does not go to war, I would believe that my duty would be to combat the New Deal. If Europe does go to war, I would feel that I would have to be engaged in trying to keep the United States from going in." He concluded that things were "in an unholy mess."[80]

The invasion of Poland by Hitler's army on September 1, 1939, triggered the general European conflagration that Hoover had feared. In a press statement the former president described the time as "one of the saddest weeks that has come to humanity in a hundred years." It was, he avowed, a "senseless war" that not only would result in the deaths of millions but also would be followed by "another quarter of a century of impoverishment to the whole world." He foresaw a long war of slow attrition and feared that "there may come a time of desperation when all restraints go to the winds," when the war was likely to become "the most barbarous war that we have ever known." Nazism was repugnant to the American people, he observed, and American sympathies would naturally be with the democracies, but "whatever our sympathies are, we cannot solve the problems of Europe": "America must keep out of this war. The President and Congress should be supported in their every effort to keep us out. We can keep out if we have the resolute national will to do so. We can be of more service to Europe and to humanity if we preserve the vitality and strength of the United States for use in the period of peace which must sometime come, and we must keep out if we are to preserve for civilization the foundations of democracy and free men."[81]

A few days later Hoover wrote John Callan O'Laughlin his appraisal of the situation and his recommendations for Republicans in Congress. Americans, he pointed out, were "97% against Hitler" and "97% against joining in a war." This made for "a critical emotional situation which can be turned at any moment." He continued,

> If the Republican members of Congress have sense, they will do three things: First, they will abolish the limitation on the sale of arms as soon as possible; second, they will enact the cash and carry provision; and third, they will introduce a drastic policy of keeping out of war, expressed in such a manner as to be morally binding on the President when he signs the bill.
>
> If the allies could obtain arms in this country, it would give an emotional outlet to the American people. To refuse to sell arms will only dam up the tide which will break loose in a demand for participation.[82]

A few days later Hoover sketched for William Castle his thoughts on the neutrality issue then being debated in Congress. He told Castle,

The high issue before us is to keep out of these wars. We must judge every action in foreign relations from that standpoint alone, not only in the immediate setting but over a few years to come.

The heart of this controversy is whether we retain the present embargo against the shipment of weapons, or whether it be repealed. . . .

There are obviously grave dangers in either course proposed. The real question is whether it is possible to find a course that lessens the major dangers either way . . .

My own belief is that we need to take a different point of view from either of the present alternatives of embargo or no embargo. Such an entirely different point of view finds a part expression in certain principles which I proposed in June, 1932, on behalf of the United States to the Disarmament Conference in Europe. One of these proposals was that we should make a distinction between aggressive weapons and defensive weapons. At that time I proposed that aggressive weapons should be wholly abolished. I defined aggressive weapons as bombing planes, large mobile cannon, sub-marines, tanks, and poison gas . . . Forty-one nations agreed to the broad principles proposed. Two declined because it was not sufficiently drastic. Seven reserved their decision. Two or three opposed it. It at least had most serious acceptance. Had it been adopted this present war would have been impossible.

Subsequently, in May, 1933, President Roosevelt repeated this same proposal directly to all other governments in the world, strongly urging its adoption.

Part of the principles controlling these proposals can be applied to our present situation:

The first of such principles is that we in America should not sell aggressive weapons to anybody at any time, whether they be at war or peace . . . [T]hese aggressive weapons . . . are the instruments by which attacks are made upon civilians. America should not be, even by sale, an indirect or possible party to the killing of women, children, or civilians in general.

The plans I suggest would apply these principles to the Neutrality Act now before the Senate by amending it (a) to prevent the sale and shipment of bombing airplanes, aerial bombs, large mobile guns, submarines, tanks and poison gas; (b) it should not apply only upon a finding of the President that war exists, but should prohibit their sale to all nations at all times and irrespective of whether a state of war exists or not.

Hoover also insisted that the "preamble to this bill be revised into an emphatic declaration of policy by the United States of keeping out of war, in order that there may be no misapprehension on the part of any of the belligerents of our determination."[83]

Back to Politics

When Senator Robert A. Taft announced in August 1939 that he would be a candidate for the 1940 GOP presidential nomination, the Taft forces quickly put out feelers to the former president concerning the possibility of attracting convention delegates in California. Hoover expressed appreciation for Taft's consistent opposition to the New Deal and voiced doubts about the viability of Dewey and Vandenberg, but he insisted that the California delegation to the convention must be uninstructed, as in 1936, and the Taft camp concluded that it would be "suicide" to oppose the former president over this.[84] Hoover had managed to convince himself from his travels in the West that there was no real enthusiasm for Taft or any of the other apparent Republican candidates. Visitors to the former president came away with the impression that he intended to have a prominent voice in the selection of the party's candidate and that he might well be interested in being named the nominee himself.[85]

With the Republican convention less than a year away, the Hoover campaign for the nomination seemed much farther along in August 1939 than it had been at the same time in 1935. The grassroots organizations that his followers had created in the western states seemed to offer the prospect that he would go to the 1940 convention with a solid core of support within uninstructed delegations from those states. His writings and speeches continued to keep him at the forefront of Republican criticism of the New Deal, with copies of his speeches and publications distributed, as before, through his mailing lists. Moreover, he had carefully cultivated friendly relations with each of the emerging potential candidates, which offered the prospect that if their own bids for the nomination failed they would not be averse to Hoover's candidacy.

In addition, the German-Soviet invasion of Poland in September had provided new opportunities for Hoover in the public arena. His impact as a leading opponent of the New Deal had been blunted by the popularity of Roosevelt and many of the New Deal programs he attacked. But as a leading voice in opposition to American involvement in the European war, Hoover was solidly on the side of an overwhelming majority of American public opinion. As the only living ex-president, with the international expertise he had gained both in and out of that office, Hoover could expect to be looked to for leadership by Republicans and non-Republicans alike who were concerned about the war issue. Hoover recognized that foreign issues had now replaced domestic ones as the primary concern of most Americans, and he was determined to bend all his efforts to establishing himself as the leader in the fight to prevent American entry into the war.[86]

But could anything more be done to strengthen Hoover's position at the convention in 1940? The former president posed that question to several of his supporters. Distressingly, much of the advice repeated that of 1935—that Hoover should not allow his friends to openly seek the nomination for him. To do so, Nebraska Supreme Court Chief Justice Robert

Simmons counseled, would detract from his attacks on the New Deal, since those attacks would then appear to be solely designed to advance his personal political aspirations. Moreover, to do so would likely disrupt the former president's cordial relations with the other candidates and make it less likely that they would throw their support to Hoover if their own bids failed. An openly avowed candidacy would also make it apparent that his efforts in behalf of uninstructed delegations from the western states were motivated by his own ambitions and this would lead the other candidates to seek committed delegations. Simmons also warned that Hoover would lose the immense esteem in which he was held by many Americans. Thus the Nebraskan recommended, with arguments that were difficult to refute, that Hoover operate in 1939–1940 much as he had in 1935–1936, clarifying the issues, staying out of the way of other potential candidates, and remaining "in a position to inherit their strength and support," while continuing to seek a largely uninstructed convention.[87] The tactic had not worked in 1936; were the odds better in 1940?

Others, though, were looking for ways to increase the former president's influence at the convention. Public relations man James Selvage wrote Hoover in August suggesting the formation of a group that would "do a propaganda job favorable to you, designed to increase your influence at the convention." He felt that the task could be accomplished with the expenditure of from $20,000 to $25,000. Hoover wrote back that he would be in New York the following month and "we can discuss the various things about which you have written to me."[88]

Hoover now embarked on a combined fishing and political trip through Wyoming and Montana, where he had scheduled 3 meetings with political leaders but had been forced to increase the number to 11 because of the demand. In fact, the requests for his appearance had been so great that his difficulty, he reported, "was to get out of that region." Each of the meetings had been with groups of two hundred to four hundred men and women. "There can be no doubt," he wrote Simmons, "that Republicans are deeply moved and they are going to make a more determined campaign than ever before."[89]

Back in New York in mid-September, Hoover held meetings on his political future and launched the proposal that Selvage had suggested.[90] A few days after his return, Kenneth Simpson called on the former president and thereafter relations between the two men were more amicable.[91] Perhaps it was reflective of Hoover's rising stature in the country, in part the result of the international situation, that previously unfriendly GOP leaders like Simpson suddenly found reasons to build bridges to him. A good deal of evidence was accumulating that pro-Hoover sentiment was on the increase at the grassroots level.[92] Landon and his supporters were aware of the trend and were concerned. One supporter wrote the Kansan that he had found "men in the street" were saying "we need Hoover—too many of them," and because of this, he wrote, "we've got to walk carefully for some time, Alf."[93]

In September the former president faced a political problem in his own backyard when Republicans in Los Angeles began a movement to reduce to virtually nil his influence over the selection of the state's delegates to the 1940 convention. Hoover and his supporters moved quickly to respond to the challenge and by the end of the month the effort had been thwarted.[94] Meanwhile, the Republican Circles had invaded Utah, but after the Los Angeles challenge Hoover decided more effort was needed in that state to deal with any future challenges there. But money was running short, with the prospect that the whole movement might collapse by the middle of November for lack of funds. Thus Hoover's once-promising grassroots organization did not present a hopeful prospect as the end of September approached.[95]

As noted earlier, Hoover's own financial resources were not adequate to support his political activities. Yet it was true, as Landon and other critics so frequently observed, that the former president seemed well financed in those activities. Such financial support came from Hoover supporters located in many parts of the country, but a considerable part of it flowed from wealthy Californians such as mining engineers Harvey Mudd and William Honnold, oilman A. C. (Bert) Mattei, and financier and industrialist Henry M. Robinson. On the East Coast, investment banker Lewis Strauss, of Kuhn, Loeb and Company, was a conduit through which funds flowed to Constitutional Publications, Inc., the agency organized by his friends to print and distribute Hoover's speeches and publications and to furnish funds for his other political activities.[96] Cereals magnate W. K. Kellogg also aided the former president's efforts by paying for the publication of his speeches in the Addresses upon the American Road series.[97] The direct link between Hoover and the Republican Circles was made clear in September 1939, when, at his request, the Constitutional Publications group paid some of the bills of the Republican Circles.[98]

Late in September, Edgar Rickard wrote Lou Henry Hoover, in California, that her husband was "working extremely hard." He explained,

> He has just completed a "rush" order for an article for the *Saturday Evening Post*, which will appear in one of the late October issues, and now he has been asked by the *Scripps-Howard Syndicate* for a current article to run in their newspapers. I don't know whether he will give them any article, but at any rate he is working on it and that means that we try not to disturb him at the Waldorf any more than we can help. I am having a great time in taking care of some of his correspondence. It is a mighty difficult thing for the Chief to write any serious article, with the constant stream of visitors who dash into the Waldorf and many of them have no consideration for his time and merely want to gossip, while others of course he wants to see.[99]

Neutrality and Relief

Shortly after the German-Soviet invasion of Poland, Roosevelt met with legislators from both parties and with Landon and Knox, the 1936 GOP nominees, to seek bipartisan support for the repeal of the embargo clause in the neutrality law. After the meeting, the president met privately with Knox and informed him of his intention to form a coalition cabinet such as Knox's newspaper and others in the press had been advocating.[100] When rumors of Roosevelt's intention reached Hoover he wrote to Senator Charles W. Tobey late in the month on "the partisanship and coalition question" and suggested that Tobey keep the letter in his files "as against the day when this subject may become a live one and we may need an attack." In the letter, the former president expressed his views "on the position the Republican Party should take on the adjournment of partisanship and coalition government." If it was meant by adjournment of partisanship that "party action" should cease, Hoover wrote, "then a most serious question is raised. Virile organization of political parties has a vital function in sustaining the process of free government" and should "only be suspended if self-government has been abandoned." There would be monumental issues to be debated in the 1940 election, including foreign policy. "If there is to be no debate upon foreign policies when there is a difference of opinion, then we have again lost free government." If the purpose of coalition government was to suspend partisan action, then it would mean one-party government and "the start of totalitarian government." Coalition was of doubtful utility even in wartime, Hoover argued, and the United States was not at war. If Republicans did enter the administration, then both they and the president should know that they would not represent the Republican Party or Republicans in Congress. Hoover wrote, "If, to obtain greater skill in the Cabinet or greater confidence for his Administration, the President desires to select Republicans for those posts, there is no the slightest objection. If he desires to obtain advice from Republicans, likewise, there can be no objection. If he desires to explore what unity could be obtained upon special questions, that also is good. But these individuals would give this advice and sit in those positions solely for their skill and merit. They would not be acting for their party." While the United States remained at peace, Republicans should support the administration in its efforts to keep the nation out of war and to prepare for the defense of the nation, but political activity could not be adjourned since it would "adjourn free government in the United States."[101]

Roosevelt also made overtures in Hoover's direction after six and a half years of treating the former president like a pariah. Edgar Rickard recorded in his diary for September 14 that he had dined at Hoover's suite with the former president, Arch Shaw, and Norman Davis. It was, he observed, a "most interesting evening." Davis, head of the American Red Cross, "came direct from FDR with [a] request that HH take over [the] entire [European] relief problem," which was then being dealt with by the Red Cross. Accustomed to years of smearing and mistreatment by the White House, Hoover responded with suspicion and skepticism concerning the genuineness of the overture or its motives. He consented, instead, to take a place on the Red Cross committee, but with "no contact with FDR."[102] Hoover was concerned that while Davis was genuine in his request, Roosevelt might be trying to divert him into relief work to silence his opposition to the domestic and foreign policies of the White House. Meanwhile, Eleanor Roosevelt was also working through a mutual friend to encourage Hoover to take over the European relief problem.[103]

There was, moreover, no direct overture from president to former president, which Hoover would certainly have preferred. And there was no publicity given to the administration's offer from either side, prompting William Allen White to write after FDR's publicized meeting with Knox and other GOP leaders that he was "unhappy because the President did not include Hoover. I realize that Hoover is poison, that he is a sort of political typhoid carrier, but he is honest, intelligent and courageous. And intellectually the Democratic party cannot afford to slight him and the nation cannot afford to ignore that type of man."[104]

The outbreak of the war in Europe nevertheless brought Hoover new responsibilities in private relief work. This role, too, led to publicity for him, as the experienced director of relief activities relied on tested public relations technique to generate financial support for his efforts. These relief activities were not, however, as successful as those before America's entry into World War I, in part because of the antipathy toward him on the part of the Roosevelt administration and the effect this antipathy had in lessening his influence with foreign governments like that of Great Britain, whose cooperation was needed for effective relief. The British and others were unwilling to irritate Roosevelt by cooperating with Hoover, and the Roosevelt administration was unwilling to apply pressure in behalf of Hoover's efforts when it was needed to lower the British blockade of Europe so that food supplies go through. Thus Hoover's public role as an opponent of the Roosevelt administration worked to the detriment of his relief efforts.[105]

Hoover also busied himself with ensuring that his own position on the war and on American policies related to it was being publicized by columnists and inserted into congressional debates.[106] He also wrote more magazine articles. When Christian Herter suggested that he write a book based on the *American Magazine* article, Hoover replied that articles were preferable since they could reach four or five million readers, whereas the best that a serious book could obtain was a readership of ten or twelve thousand.[107]

In October the *Saturday Evening Post* published his article, "We Must Keep Out," in which Hoover again described the contradictory attitudes of Americans—their desire to stay out of the war on the one hand and their sympathy for the democracies in their war against the despised dictatorships on the other. The former was the attitude of reason, the latter that of emotion, and the danger to America was that "our indignation will displace our reason." European nations, he pointed out, had always put their own interests first during times of peace, refusing to repay their loans from America while at the same time accumulating "balances and assets in this country [worth] several times the amount of payments." And when World War I ended, the Europeans had tried to avoid purchasing the great agricultural surplus that had been created for them in the United States and had rushed to buy cheaper food from other nations. It was time that Americans recognized other nations put their own interests first and that Americans started doing the same. American sympathies for the European democracies would "be drawn upon heavily in the days to come," but America's duty to its sons was "to hold reason in power over emotion. It is to hold the long vision of America's future. It is to keep out of these wars."[108]

Hoover was confident that Britain and France could not be defeated and that the war in Europe would, at worst, resolve into a stalemate.[109] This complacency led him to exert his energies against total repeal of the embargo provisions in the neutrality laws. He was, he wrote in early October, "in day and night conferences with a great many national leaders over the very dangerous situation into which we are drifting over this neutrality legislation."[110] Roosevelt was not only seeking freedom from restrictions on the cash-and-carry sale of munitions but was also seeking a flexible law that would permit him to differentiate between aggressor and victim. Failing that, he sought repeal of the embargo provisions altogether, so that arms and munitions could be sold to belligerents, at least on a cash-and-carry basis like other exports, in a move that could only benefit the democracies whose navies controlled the seas.

Hoover continued to insist that such sales be limited only to defensive items, and he found support for his proposal from popular aviation heroes Charles Lindbergh and Eddie Rickenbacker. He also believed at least six senators would support his plan, but he was disappointed to find opposition to it from many upon whom he had counted for support.[111] For many of these latter there seemed to be no safe ground between repeal of the neutrality law and no law at all, so that the law must be preserved in its entirety as the only guarantee that America would not be drawn into the war.[112] Hoover himself regarded the particular legislation in force as less critical than the will of the administration and of the people. He advocated the sale of "defensive" weapons only because he hoped that this would provide an outlet for the emotions of a people who overwhelmingly supported the democracies and that, thus appeased, the public would continue to oppose actual American intervention in the war.

When Senator Styles Bridges solicited from the former president suggestions for the preamble of a proposed neutrality amendment he was submitting to the Senate, Hoover suggested it begin, "It is hereby declared to be the policy of the United States to remain absolutely neutral in wars between other nations. Whereas, in accordance with this policy the risks of becoming involved can be diminished by restricting the exercise of certain neutral rights of our citizens; Therefore be it . . ."[113]

Bridges also solicited Hoover's views on the proposed changes in the neutrality law, and the former president again offered his compromise on "defensive" weapons. Weapons used against civilian populations should be embargoed by the United States, but the weapons used for defense against such attacks should be sold—pursuit aircraft, antiaircraft guns, "and any other instruments of defense against attacks on civilians." Such a policy would not mean that the United States was taking sides in wars nor that it was moving toward participation in them, nor would it "inflate American industry" and contribute to "the creation of industrial and financial pressure groups interested in going deeper into war." It would not be an unneutral action and it would be consistent with the ideals of the United States, since it would mean the nation was "raising a standard against barbaric action." His proposal, he said, would keep "both our conscience and our neutrality right." In other respects he found the proposed neutrality bill generally "constructive."[114] Hoover also stated his proposal succinctly for newsreel cameras, arguing that his compromise would shift "this whole issue from power politics to foundations in morals and humanity. It is the only safe ground upon which to maintain American neutrality and to keep out of this war."[115]

Hoover's friend William Allen White organized and chaired the Non-Partisan Committee for Peace through the Revision of the Neutrality Law, but privately he supported the former president's proposal to embargo offensive weapons.[116] Even Senator Arthur Vandenberg, generally a Hoover opponent in the GOP power struggles, thought there was "much to be said" for the Hoover compromise, and he asked the former president to draft his ideas into legislative form. Hoover complied and told Vandenberg he had received "a very large response, particularly a seeming surprise that our Administration would dare propose to sell bombing planes, poison gas, and submarines." The senator placed Hoover's statement in the *Congressional Record* and solicited any further thoughts he might have as to the precise form that an amendment along this line might take. He would, Vandenberg told Hoover, "see what can be done at this end of the line."[117]

Hoover was discouraged, however, that his proposal had seemingly not altered the balance in the Senate over the repeal question, with a substantial majority still favoring repeal of the embargo, some of them under prodding from the White House. The compromise Hoover sought appealed only to some of those in the minority opposition who sought, thereby, a ground for blocking total repeal. Seeking to arouse public support for his proposal, the former president spoke over the radio on October 20. He told Vandenberg he did not expect to "change the course of events," but "it does seem to me that somebody has to voice moral standards in this country if we are not to slide down the same barbaric road that Europe has tread."[118] He told William Castle that he had "no doubt that I will receive volleys from all the Dorothy

Thompsons and the Walter Lippmanns and Mr. Roosevelt and everybody else of the pro-war party."[119]

In that speech, Hoover called for national unity in the face of the crisis abroad and explained his compromise proposal. As for the demarcation of defensive and offensive weapons, Hoover argued that every child in Europe could make the distinction between bombing planes and poison gas on the one hand and the "pursuit planes, observation planes, search-lights, anti-aircraft guns and gas masks" that were used in defense against such destruction. Aerial bombing of civilians meant that "the world has gone back to savagery, where armed men killed women and children and burned cities." Brave men, he insisted, did not "sneak around and kill unarmed men, women and children, and destroy their homes . . . Chivalry is certainly dying in our world." Hoover therefore not only sought to bar the sale of weapons used to commit such deeds but also intended to make their use as ineffective as possible by freely selling the devices that could be used in defense against them. His proposal, he insisted, would avoid many dangers and would above all contribute "something constructive to the world by way of humanity and moral standards."[120]

Even before he delivered the speech, however, the former president was disappointed by the reaction of some of his friends to advance drafts he sent them.[121] Many of them were disappointed by Hoover's willingness to countenance the sale of any weapons at all. According to this view there was no real distinction between one soldier killing another with a rifle and the murder of children by bombing planes—both were equally abhorrent and could only be dealt with by a total embargo on all weapons of war. As a Quaker, Hoover no doubt agreed with the idealism expressed in this position, but realistically he argued that the situation in Congress was such that in a straight vote on the repeal of the embargo it would pass the Senate by at least 60 votes and the House by a vote of about 235 to 180. What he was seeking was a compromise that might draw some votes away from total repeal. In the interest of practicality, then, as well as idealism, blind support of the embargo would accomplish nothing. Hoover's proposal probably did not do so, either, but it was at least an attempt to rescue something from the situation.[122] But Hoover knew it would arouse opposition from the interventionists.

Although he received considerable praise for his radio address, the rigid positions in Congress on both sides of the embargo question did not augur well for a compromise. When his substitute plan was introduced as an amendment in the Senate it was defeated on October 26 by a vote of 56 to 36.[123] Hoover now looked to the House, where he hoped that the vote would be closer. Late in the month he wrote, "While it may be too late, Republican leaders in the House have concluded that their best hope of handling this embargo is to ask the members to vote against the Senate report so as to give an opportunity to amend it to prohibit the export of poison gas and bombing planes. There is a bare possibility that they might get a majority on this basis. Otherwise they are licked by about twenty votes."[124] The congressional coalition of Republicans and anti–New Deal Democrats did not extend to foreign policy issues.

What is surprising is the division within the Republican Party over the issue. For once, Hoover was marching with congressional Republicans and it was Landon and Knox who were out of step. Knox argued that the injection of partisanship into what should be a nonpartisan issue was unwise and not in accord with public opinion. Republican opposition to repeal of the embargo had caused Knox to "wonder whether our party has not lost through inept and stupid leadership even the right to come back into dominance."[125] Because the fight was so obviously lost, some GOP leaders, including Landon, tried to ensure that "Republicans would not line up solidly against the bill" and encouraged GOP members in Congress to vote for repeal.[126] But Landon refused to publicly favor repeal because he was reluctant to take a position at odds with the sentiment of most Republicans in Congress. As for Hoover, he agreed with Castle that his proposal had not been "correctly timed" and told Castle that "we muffed the method of handling our proposal."[127]

Although the House joined the Senate in voting overwhelmingly for a new neutrality law along the lines the White House had requested, opponents succeeded in gaining some concessions. American citizens were barred from sailing on belligerent vessels and American ships were banned from sailing into belligerent ports. For Hoover, the failure to get his compromise proposal adopted was a defeat, but he still regarded the question of American involvement in the war as hinging more on the will of the American people and their leaders than on the enactment or repeal of laws. From Vandenberg came the encouraging belief that the expressions of opposition to American involvement in the war, voiced by both proponents and opponents of the embargo repeal, had registered with the White House and had set back any plans Roosevelt had to involve the United States in the war. "It remains to be seen how long the administration will be content to wear its latest disguise," he wrote Hoover. "Let us hope and pray that it may be permanent."[128]

Hoover responded that he agreed the vote in Congress had crystallized the anti-interventionists in the nation, but it had done the same for the pro-intervention group. At the moment the anti-intervention group was in the majority, "but it is in danger from an emotional invasion at any time."[129] And he was less optimistic about the intentions of the Roosevelt administration. "We must now await the next step toward taking us into war," he wrote O'Laughlin, and he predicted it would involve "either extending government credit to the Allies or presenting them with ammunitions." He predicted the war in Europe would "likely go to bed in the military sense until spring and that we will be deluged on the diplomatic front until that time. If there is no success in that direction, then we can expect to see a serious war that may last for many years."[130]

Politics

While he battled for his compromise on the neutrality legislation, Hoover was also meeting with intimates in New York City in October to get their views on whether or not the time had come to launch a campaign for the Republican nomination.[131] Later in the month, Alan Fox, who had sampled public opinion for the former president during the 1936 campaign, prepared to launch yet another effort. The plan called for sampling approximately forty different groups in New York state through some four thousand questionnaires.[132] As the questionnaires began to flow in, Fox found that more were "favorable to Hoover than any other one candidate and a good many of those who favor Hoover say they voted for Roosevelt last time."[133] Hoover pronounced himself "much interested in the poll," but he continued to maintain to all but his most intimate associates a complete lack of interest in the nomination. Thus when Daniel Willard, president of the Baltimore and Ohio Railway, wrote Hoover that of all the possible candidates for 1940, Hoover stood "so high above any of them as to be distinctly in a class by yourself," the former president responded that he was "not seeking for any such job—and one of the cardinals of politics is if you do not seek, nothing comes to you. Therefore, I am able to sleep nights."[134]

Some considered that Hoover was the ideal figure to try to mediate an end to the war in Europe. In November, 1939, the editor of *Zion's Herald*, a Methodist weekly, wrote that he was prepared to publish a plea for the former president to take the leadership in such a mediation and that a number of New England churches had already passed resolutions to that end. When he asked for Hoover's approval of the publication of such an appeal, the former president responded that he preferred not to "make any public statements on the matter." While he agreed that an early end to the war would be the "the greatest blessing that can come to civilization and no effort should be spared that has hope of constructive success," he did not feel that the time was ripe for such an effort. Later, he said, "a new situation might arise that would be more favorable," but for the present "the first obligation in this matter rests upon the administration in Washington." Moreover, he pointed out, "the law forbids any negotiations with foreign governments by private citizens."[135]

Still, Hoover was clearly not averse to the movement in behalf of such a mediation effort. On November 10 he had met with Howard P. Davis and apparently had not discouraged Davis's attempt to generate a mass appeal for Hoover to take steps to mediate an end to the war. The Davis effort took the form of petitions to be circulated in churches throughout the United States and through newspaper and magazine publicity. Davis wrote Hoover late in the month, "Presently you will hear this faint cry for your services in the greatest of world crises swell into a mighty roar."[136] True to his word, Davis was soon deluging Hoover with petitions and resolutions from churches all across the United States. Since nothing could obviously come of such appeals, one can only speculate concerning Hoover's motives in failing to squelch it. Perhaps he felt that such an outpouring of evidence of the desire for peace in Europe would be useful in opposing the administration's policies leaning toward intervention, or maybe he felt the movement could be useful for him politically.

The invasion of Finland by the Soviet Union late in November 1939 immediately aroused great sympathy in the United States for the Finns, the only Europeans who had repaid their World War I obligations to the United Sates. Hoover suggested the withdrawal of the American ambassador from Moscow to register American disapproval for the Soviet act of aggression. He wondered "why we are so tender towards communist Russia, especially in view of the rough treatment this present administration gave to Nazi Germany. We ought to express our national indignation both ways."[137] The former president quickly took the lead in organizing relief for the Finns by reassembling many of his old relief hands and launching a public appeal for relief funds.[138] The drive quickly won widespread support from many prominent in public life and from the press. Rather than establish local committees as in past efforts, Hoover sought speed and publicity by enlisting local newspapers to drive the appeal and receive contributions, with acknowledgment of the contributors on their pages. By late December he had over 1,200 newspapers actively engaged in raising funds for his Finnish Relief Fund, Inc.[139]

Such activities were double-edged, however. They gave further publicity to Hoover and enhanced his image as a humanitarian and director of such works, but they also detracted from the time and energy he could otherwise have devoted to politics. The diary of Edgar Rickard, filled with the topics discussed around the dinner table in Hoover's apartment at the Waldorf Towers, became increasingly devoted, late in 1939, to details of the relief effort, with political discussions becoming rare. More and more of Hoover's concerns were with raising private funds for the Finnish relief work and with disputes he was having with Norman Davis of the Red Cross over demarcating the responsibilities between that organization and Hoover's group. Thus during critical months in late 1939 and early 1940, politics became a minor concern of the former president, and his campaign for the 1940 nomination suffered neglect.

In a November press conference, Eleanor Roosevelt publicly called for Hoover to head a central agency to coordinate refugee relief work.[140] The following month a Washington newspaper reported that Hoover had turned down Roosevelt's invitation to head "all relief activities in the United States," because it would distract him from the 1940 presidential campaign and because he did not want to be identified with the New Deal. The New York Times reported,

> A little later it was said at the White House that the President, acting through Norman H. Davis, chairman of the American Red Cross, had

requested Mr. Hoover to take charge of all European war relief activities in this country, but apparently he did not want to accept.

Stephen T. Early, White House secretary, who explained Mr. Roosevelt's part in the effort to draft the former President for the relief job to be conducted in cooperation with the Red Cross, said that because Mr. Davis had not reported on the outcome of the conversations it was assumed Mr. Hoover was not interested in the proposal.

Hoover's secretary, Lawrence Richey, had responded that Early's statement seemed to deal with different questions. According to Richey, Hoover had suggested that the Red Cross expand its effort to cover all types of relief. Norman Davis had then issued a statement saying that Hoover had declined to head a proposed Red Cross committee on European war relief but had offered "to cooperate and assist the Red Cross." Having now established a Finnish Relief Fund, Hoover was cooperating with the Red Cross to avoid duplication and competition. Hoover, too, denied that there was any friction between the two organizations.[141] Taking note of the issue, columnist Arthur Krock correctly pointed out that whenever FDR and Hoover were "interested in the same subject a debate, a dispute or an actual controversy will always be the result because, so long as both are alive, they will probably be intense political adversaries."[142] *Newsweek* added, "If Hoover spurned Roosevelt overtures, as Davis insists, his motives were probably less Republican in texture than purely personal. Few Administrations in American history ever went to greater lengths to smear a predecessor than the present one, and the former President had every right to question the sincerity of a sudden peace gesture—especially at a time when President Roosevelt was making considerable capital of the so-called national non-partisan front. Certainly members of the Administration and self-styled friends of the Red Cross have contributed their share to the bad blood."[143]

On December 15, 1939, *Time* magazine devoted considerable attention to the revival of Herbert Hoover, noting that when he left office in March 1933 no predecessor except John Quincy Adams had been "so thoroughly unpopular." But now, less than seven years later, *Time* reported,

> Last week, when Republican leaders assembled in Washington correspondents were surprised to find that the biggest question was: What will Herbert Hoover do? General agreement was that at next year's convention he will control at least 200 of the 1,000 delegates. Of course the Republicans agreed that 1940 would see the New Deal's end. But general agreement, not only in Washington, D.C, but in Oregon, Illinois, Minnesota, Kansas, etc., was that, with stage set, audience waiting, super-spectacle prepared—with a fine cast of characters, a wonderful story, a happy ending—the star performer was poison at the box office.
>
> Nevertheless, it was as plain as a New Deal deficit to a Republican wheelhorse that in his exile Herbert Hoover had made himself a symbol

of the Republican Party. To the dismay of many an ardent Republican, to the positive frenzy of some, in spite of the efforts of a few, he had gone up & down through his seven years with the fortunes of the party itself. Dignified, unbending, difficult in his personal relations, vulnerable to attack, sensitive to slights, losing votes by his stiffness as fast as he won them by his integrity and intelligence, he remained the symbol of Republicanism— just as he had been the symbol of its defeat when the pent-up storm burst on his head in 1932. Left-wing Republicans looked on him as The Man Who Came to Dinner—when slights did not work, they tried to make him an Elder Statesman; when he still refused to go away, they agreed hastily that he was the ablest U.S. Republican, while they canvassed busily for somebody else. In spite of all, last week in Washington the biggest question among Republicans remained: What will Herbert Hoover do?

"Everywhere," *Time* found, Hoover's prestige was rising, "and with it the prestige of the party."

Time concluded,

At 65, he looks younger than when he left the White House. He is red-faced, cherubic, and still wears the high collars, high shoes, the slightly pained and embarrassed smile that have always made him an easy target for cartoonists. His only political characteristic is that he smokes cigars. But he hates to be photographed doing it. He sometimes drinks a cocktail. Reporters who interview him now find that he has few doubts—of himself, of his ideas, of the U.S., of the prospect that the G.O.P. can defeat the New Deal in 1940. The apostle of confidence has never lost his own.[144]

In mid-December Hoover decided to move permanently to the East Coast after the 1940 Republican convention and, if he were not the nominee, to retire from all political activities. He did not want to live in California and did not like the campus life, nor did he like the house in Palo Alto. He told business manager and confidant Rickard that he was "by instinct a city man."[145] According to Rickard, the former president was growing increasingly restless in late 1939 over what he regarded as the sabotage of his political ambitions by the professional politicians, and the Finnish relief activities had furnished a welcome diversion and convenient outlet for his prodigious energies.[146] So engrossed had he become in the relief effort that when columnist George Sokolsky asked the former president early in January how his name might be kept before the American people in preparation for the 1940 convention, Rickard found him totally uninterested in such political matters.[147] During these critical winter months, Hoover's campaign for the nomination was limping along without his active direction or involvement.

After the Soviet invasion of Finland, the Finnish Relief Committee was organized in December with Hoover as national chairman. New York City mayor, Fiorello LaGuardia, volunteered to serve as New York chairman, and arrangements were made for a massive rally to be held at Madison Square

Garden with leading Scandinavian singers from the Metropolitan Opera to entertain, along with an orchestra and nationwide speakers.[148] Hoover thought it a good idea to have some prominent Finns on the committee to deflect opposition and was glad for LaGuardia's participation, since it would stop "all criticism from labor and other elements and we will need all of that kind of help we can get for a sharp quick campaign."[149] *Time* wrote that Hoover "issued an appeal, got newspapers to accept contributions for Finnish relief, telephoned an address to a mass meeting in Manhattan."[150]

Editor and Publisher, the organ of the newspaper business, interviewed Hoover on December 23 concerning his use of newspapers in the new relief campaign. It wrote, "Mobilized overnight by former President Herbert Clark Hoover through an appeal sent out to all editors and publishers by the AP, UP and INS, the newspapers of the nation this week were almost solidly behind the task of organizing relief for the noncombatant civilians of war-torn Finland. More than 1,200 newspapers have launched appeals for contributions to the Finnish Relief Fund, Inc., of which Mr. Hoover is chairman." The participation of the newspapers had been launched by Hoover's appeal on December 7, in which he had noted that there was not sufficient time to follow the usual method of organizing committees in each town and city, which also involved considerable overhead expense. Therefore, Hoover had asked the nation's newspapers to lead the appeal and to accept cash contributions for forwarding to the central office. The press, Hoover told *Editor and Publisher*, had "responded in extraordinary fashion" and had "done the job wonderfully." He added that he had received support in conceiving and launching the campaign from Harry Chandler, publisher of the *Los Angeles Times*, Roy Howard of the Scripps-Howard chain, Paul Smith, editor and general manager of the *San Francisco Chronicle*, William Randolph Hearst, and others. Arthur Hays Sulzberger, president and publisher of the *New York Times*, was one of 75 national leaders who were serving on the national committee of the Finnish Relief organization, along with Dean Carl W. Ackerman of the Columbia University Graduate School of Journalism. Some newspapers had even organized benefits to raise relief funds.[151]

In mid-December, Rickard wrote that Davis and the Red Cross seemed out to sabotage their effort and that, while contributions were "rolling in in vast numbers," they were small gifts and the total of about $45,000 collected was "very discouraging."[152] But on December 18, 1939, Hoover's committee sent the Finnish Government $100,000 for "general civilian relief purposes."[153] And five days later he sent another $100,000 and told the Finnish Prime Minister, "In the dreadful crisis which the Finnish people are so bravely confronting, may I assure you of the unprecedented expressions of sympathy and prayer for their welfare which are flowing to them at their sad Christmas season from American homes in every part of our country."[154]

Late in November, Rabbi Stephen Wise, president of the American Jewish Congress, invited Hoover to address a rally at Madison Square Garden on

December 13 in protest of the "savagery directed by Nazidom against Jews within its domain and conquered territories as expressed in mass deportation."[155] Hoover responded that it was impossible for him to be in New York City that day, but he reminded Wise that he had expressed his feelings many times in radio addresses and public statements, and he would be "glad to have it repeated to the meeting that in common with an overwhelming majority of our fellow citizens I have been outraged by the bestialities visited upon the people of Jewish faith."[156] When a persistent Wise noted that Hoover had returned to New York City on December 13, he wired Hoover again asking him to participate in the rally, and Hoover did join Landon, LaGuardia, and others in addressing the crowd of twenty thousand, repeating essentially the same sentiments he had expressed in his letter to Wise.[157]

Hoover's supporters, however, continued their efforts and early in the year reported a "revolutionary change of attitude" in the country toward the former president.[158] For those accustomed to sitting on the fence, Hoover's rising popularity posed a problem. If those upon whom he was counting for support allied themselves with another candidate, they knew their disloyalty to "the Chief" would incur his wrath if he won the nomination. On the other hand, such fence sitters obviously hoped to have a hand in the nomination and election of a Republican president, and despite his apparent rise in popularity, Hoover seemed little interested in the nomination and to offer only an outside chance at best.[159] While critical decisions were being made over which candidate to support, Hoover declined all invitations to speak during the month of January, confining all his activities that month exclusively to Finnish relief.[160] Thus he continued to look less and less like a serious possibility for the nomination.

However, late in 1939 Hoover did find new sources of financial support for the Republican Circles and by this time he could count 85,000 members in the western states.[161] When western Republicans gathered to hold a regional conference in Salt Lake City in December, Circle members and other Hoover supporters were well represented and, according to one report Hoover received, had "strongly dominated" the conference, with the results "completely satisfactory" from his standpoint.[162] All but Oregon, Arizona, and New Mexico were represented at the conference, and Hoover backers experienced little difficulty in persuading the meeting to come out in support of uninstructed delegations to the 1940 GOP convention.[163]

CHAPTER 5

Campaigns

From Relief to Politics

The issue of financial assistance to beleagured Finland was dropped in the lap of Congress by President Roosevelt. The president seems to have favored such financial aid but to have recognized the opposition it would arouse if it were known that Roosevelt supported it. Very likely any discussion of aid to Finland would be regarded by opponents of the administration's foreign policies as a "backdoor" for extending similar aid to Great Britain and France. Ironically, despite their opposition to financial aid to these latter countries (due to the precedent of World War I), GOP leaders like Hoover and Robert A. Taft favored a loan to the Finns because, as Taft put it, "there is no conceivable excuse for the Russian attack, and America has always favored, and often aided, those who are fighting for their freedom."[1] The same argument could, of course, have been made in support of assistance to the British and French, but the proponents of aid for the Finns ignored the double standard they were applying to victims of Soviet as opposed to German aggression at the same time that they condemned the Roosevelt administration for its double standard toward the two. The loan, when passed by the House and Senate, was limited to $30 million, did not mention Finland by name, and excluded the purchase of "arms, ammunitions, or implements of war" with the money, under the provisions of the Neutrality Act. It was also passed too late to be of any assistance to the Finns as their valiant effort was being crushed under the superior numbers of the Red Army.[2]

The fall of Finland effectively ended Hoover's relief efforts in their behalf and the former president now divided his time between political activities and Polish relief. His efforts to get food relief to Poland were, however, stymied by a lack of money. The effort was one beyond the capabilities of private charity, since it would require about $50 million, he estimated. Hoover sought

$5 million to $10 million from the Polish Government in Exile to get the supply of food moving, but through May it had still not been received, and only small quantities could be shipped from private contributions.[3] Hoover's intimates were concerned with what the former president could do when he no longer had Finnish relief to keep his name before the people "between now and convention time." Rickard recorded in his diary, however, that it was "a problem which does not seem to bother HH as he is absorbed in the Finnish relief and will be satisfied only if he does a good clean job."[4] Earlier difficulties with the Red Cross seemed to have ended, with Norman Davis acknowledging to Hoover that the type of relief assistance furnished by Finnish Relief, Inc. "does not come within the scope of relief furnished by the Red Cross, and since it is meeting a very great need, I do hope you will be able to continue as long as the urgent need for civilian relief exists."[5]

With Finland's defeat and the conclusion of a peace treaty with the Soviet Union ending the war, Hoover issued a press statement:

> The terms imposed on Finland mark another sad day for civilization. The Finns have made a heroic defense that will live for all time, but the odds were insuperable. The Finnish Relief Fund must continue for the present to meet the civilian emergencies for which it was created. There will be thousands more of Finnish refugees from the Russian acquired territory for whom new homes must be found. Homes destroyed by air attack in every town and city must be rebuilt. There are many destitute who need to be carried over until employment can be resumed. I hope the Fund will continue to receive the united support of the American people as in the past.[6]

However, the end of the war seemed, in Hoover's words, to have had "some curious psychological effects on the country" and had "practically stopped all interest in the Finnish Relief Fund." Moreover, the American people seemed "sore about" Finland having made peace with the Russians, so that it would take "a lot of defending and explaining to restore the previous emotional devotion to the Finns." That being the case, Hoover recommended winding down the solicitation of funds.[7] However, he advocated going ahead with various fundraising events already scheduled that stretched into early June and he was against any announcement that the fund was ending its efforts since it would reduce interest in those events and lessen donations while also discouraging the Finns that America had lost interest in them. The fund, he told committee members and state chairmen, still had enough money on hand or likely to come in from the fundraising benefits to supply Finland with a minimum of $100,000 per week until early June.[8]

In March the two Hoovers convalesced in their Waldorf apartment. Lou Henry wrote friends, "We are very busy here—triply or quadruply because we both had these very bad colds that are prevalent in New York and so were out of commission for a good many days. At least the doctor told us to be and I was,—but of course Mr. Hoover went right along doing everything he should do even though he was barking and wheezing and looking really quite ill and a big blizzard was raging outside."[9]

Meanwhile the Republican Program Committee was at last nearing the end of its labors and its chairman, Glenn Frank, had circulated a draft of the final program to the various members for their comments. For the most part, the Hooverites seem to have approved the draft, although Lewis Strauss faulted it for its implied endorsement of the Securities and Exchange Commission, which he regarded as "busy harassing all legitimate business enterprises rather than just going after the wrongdoer," and its recommendation of purchase of submarginal lands, which he regarded as a New Deal project.[10] Later in the month, Arch Shaw wrote Hoover that the executive committee had met for three days, with "some meetings lasting from morning until late at night!" He found there was "now practically complete approval," with "every letter of consequence from the membership" having been "given careful consideration."[11] A month later, Frank wrote Hoover of "the gratitude of my heart for the privilege the chairmanship of this committee gave me of working with you and the other members who so unselfishly have given of your time and money to the production of our report which has had an unprecedented reception by press and public." He told Hoover, "The major metropolitan papers have given from one to five full pages to the report in addition to front-page news stories, editorials and cartoons. The reaction to the report even from the opposition press, has reflected a recognition of the fact that we tried to do an honest job quite above the battle of mere partisan bushwacking." He was, he said, closing the committee offices on March 1.[12]

The former president was convinced that no other candidate was emerging from the pack and that his own prospects for the nomination remained good. Fox's polls continued to support this impression, although they also indicated a widespread belief that Hoover could not win if nominated.[13] The former president was meanwhile defending himself against what he regarded as "smears." When a Life magazine article on the movie, "The Grapes of Wrath," captioned a picture of a fight to describe it as taking place in a "Hooverville," Hoover was tempted to sue Henry Luce, the publisher of the magazine. The former president wrote that "outside of every American city there has been for the last 75 years a tin-can-dump inhabited by hobos and tramps." He wrote,

> They did have more inhabitants during the depression. There were only four or five of them in the whole nation that had signs put on them called Hooverville. These signs were put up by the politicians during the 1932 campaign. They were most quickly taken down by the local people as being infamous. Every one of these localities had a relief committee looking after the destitute, but the normal hobo does not want to have relief. Furthermore, these dumps still exist after seven years of the New Deal relief and they have the same inhabitants and in some states they are even larger than ever before. Particularly, right at this moment in California there are one hundred towns which never had

them before, as a result of the New Deal policies in squeezing out sharecrop-
pers in the South. And incidentally, many of them over the country are now
labeled Rooseveltville, an equally infamous form of smearing.[14]

Two polls in New York City in mid-February registered very different
results. In one, Thomas Dewey outpolled Hoover by nearly two to one, and
a very definite shift was revealed away from Roosevelt and toward the Republican Party. In the other, which was confined to the Queens area of the city,
Hoover barely edged out Dewey 159 to 157, with no other candidates even
close.[15] Neither of these polls bore out the results Fox was reporting from his
own efforts. Another poll, taken in Indiana, asked two questions: who was
most qualified to be president of the United States and who should be nominated by the Republican Party in 1940? To the first question, the response
was overwhelming for Hoover, who polled 86 percent, with his nearest rival,
Senator Arthur Vandenberg, at only 10 percent. To the second question, however, the response was 36 percent for Vandenberg, 26 percent for Dewey, 23
percent for Taft, and only 9 percent for Hoover.[16] Clearly, qualifications were
not counting heavily with the voters of Indiana. Hoover, however, derived
some encouragement from both the New York and Indiana polls.

The former president finally returned to the stump on Lincoln's Day
with a speech in Omaha, Nebraska, after months of distraction from political
activities over relief and foreign affairs. The principal problem in America,
he told his audience, was unemployment, and getting the American people
back to work was "the greatest humanitarian action of our day and age." The
government could not support the unemployed forever, for the taxes required
to pay for the relief effort would eventually "asphyxiate the whole productive
system." The cause of unemployment was none of the reasons usually given,
like laborsaving devices. It arose from the absence of "certain dynamic forces"
that must be combined to create jobs, but three "notions" in recent years had
paralyzed those forces: (1) the notion that "the whole system is wrong and
must be made over"; (2) the notion that government officials should "plan,
direct or operate the economic life of the people"; and (3) the notion that
"governments can spend and spend and borrow and borrow without thought
of tomorrow." To solve the unemployment problem these notions must first
of all be discarded, and the drift toward statism must be reversed. Morals
and intellectual integrity must be reestablished in government. Unity must be
sought in place of class conflict and disunity. And finally, the American people
must stay out of the war.[17]

In California, Hoover's supporters had meanwhile fought back a challenge
to the uninstructed delegation he sought from the state to the GOP convention, and early in February he was told that 32 of the 44 delegates could
be counted on to support him.[18] Hoover congratulated them for "a fine job
considering the manipulations and disloyalties" with which they "had to contend." He thought that he could influence one or two more of the delegates,

and, revealing a vindictive strain, he added "that we may be able to do something to the people who have not played the game."[19] It was apparent that the former president was approaching the 1940 convention in a far different spirit from that in 1936.

Hoover busied himself now with discouraging any challenges to the unstructured slate from the Taft, Dewey, and Vandenberg camps, sometimes taking the opportunity to remind others of the fate that had befallen the Landon challenge in that state four years earlier. Taft supporters were especially incensed by Hoover's action, since they felt they could win the California delegation "within 48 hours" if Hoover would disclaim any interest in the nomination himself and pass the word that he was not opposed to Taft.[20] The suspicion was growing in the Taft camp, however, that Hoover either was seeking the nomination himself or wanted the nominee to be John Bricker, governor of Ohio.[21]

Late in February, Hoover traveled to Washington to confer with the State Department concerning Polish relief and to testify before the House Foreign Affairs Committee in support of financial aid for Poland to buy relief supplies. During his stay in the capital, Hoover talked with Secretary of State Cordell Hull and also held meetings with the Polish ambassador and others concerning the problems that might be encountered in administering relief to that country if financial assistance were arranged.[22] Throughout the month of March, Hoover was again almost totally absorbed with relief matters.[23] Despite attempts to keep the Finnish relief effort in operation to aid refugees from that country, the Soviet occupation of the country had caused American interest in the Finns to ebb, and funds were reduced to a trickle.[24]

A poll of midwestern and eastern newspapers in March encouraged the former president when it showed that 50 percent of the Republican journals considered him the candidate best qualified to handle the problems of the presidency.[25] The efforts of Hoover's followers to get uninstructed delegations to the convention from other states were also bearing fruit.[26] In early April, Rickard found the former president optimistic about his political prospects.[27] As the fast-moving events in Europe were making foreign relations loom even more importantly for the 1940 nomination and election, Hoover urged William Starr Myers to complete the book he was writing on the Hoover administration's foreign policies by spring so that it could be in the hands of delegates by convention time.[28]

By mid-April Hoover was mapping his strategy for the pursuit of delegates at the convention. The former president was convinced that many of the delegates would turn to him after the third ballot.[29] Pleased with initial results from the Fox polls, Hoover now decided to pursue them on a larger scale, while also sending "educational" material to each of the delegates.[30] He also explored the possibility of having some newspaper initiate a "call" for a Hoover draft during the month of May.[31] Public relations man James Selvage outlined the thinking in the Hoover camp:

It seems to some of us here that the time has come, or will have come early in May, to begin to activate the demand for the Chief which we know is there, and almost on every side you hear today that he is the ablest man and should be in the White House, coupled with that silly followup, "but he can't be elected." That is the thing that must be broken down and we have the feeling that if we concentrate our fire over a period of six or seven weeks before the convention, that a grass-roots demand can be built that will catch fire. In this connection . . . a survey has been made in New York in the vicinity of more than 10,000 voters—names taken from the official voting list . . . In all but one election district, Mr. Hoover is running ahead of Dewey by a sizable margin and on the first choice for head of the ticket he is far in front . . . A poll of the bar association went heavily for the Chief and against Dewey. If we know the demand is there under the surface, we must bring it upward and, by letting it be known that there are many who feel that the Chief is the man, give courage to those who are hesitant about speaking out. With this in view, several of us are writing to everyone we know and can trust, suggesting that starting soon after May 1st they do everything in their power to stir talk about the Chief.[32]

As part of the campaign, John Spargo was again enlisted into service, with letters and articles distributed to the mailing lists; but the effort in this respect was much reduced from the level in the 1936 campaign.[33] Efforts to actually influence delegates, however, were obviously greater than four years earlier. Hoover backers were in the field in the South and the West contacting delegates in his behalf.[34] Late in April, Hoover estimated that he would attract approximately ten votes on the first ballot in the convention but pick up sixty more on the second ballot due to shifts from California, New York, New Jersey, and Illinois. This did not include votes from Ohio, where he had been told by Governor Bricker that if Taft's momentum failed, the governor would try to carry the Ohio delegation into the Hoover camp. From every direction, Hoover was hearing that the grass roots were for him if only they could be convinced he was electable. Thus it seemed at the end of April that it required only the publicizing of the results of the opinion polls being conducted to bring Hoover's potential strength to the fore and assure his nomination.

As the Nazi juggernaut moved across Western Europe in the spring of 1940, Hoover spent every available moment in front of the radio monitoring the war news. By the middle of May, the former president also had a television set, although there was very limited programming yet in 1940. The events in Europe were of great potential significance for Hoover. On the one hand they would increase the number of countries and people needing food relief, even while making the British more reluctant to allow the food through their blockade. On the other hand, it was likely to strengthen Hoover's bid for the GOP nomination since "Dewey's lack of international experience" would be thrust into "greater prominence" and would probably "diminish his possibilities." Hoover was not willing to take the movement in behalf of Willkie seriously as of May, regarding it merely as "a reaction from disappointment" as to the other candidates available.[35]

As part of his strategy, the former president was also attempting again, as in 1936, to keep all the other candidates in the race to prevent anyone from gaining a clear majority. In a telephone call to O'Laughlin in late April, Hoover asked him to encourage Vandenberg to make two major speeches in May and to tell the Michigan senator that Dewey's delegate strength was not as much as the New Yorker claimed. It was desirable, Hoover said, for each candidate, including Vandenberg, to stay in the race and to "battle hard." O'Laughlin, however, found Vandenberg pessimistic and told Hoover he would need continuous prodding from the former president to stay in the race.[36]

Foreign Affairs and Defense

The foreign situation could not be ignored, and Hoover's longtime hatred and suspicion of the communist regime in the Soviet Union had been further fueled by its invasions of Poland and Finland. In an April article for *Collier's*, the former president lashed out at the Roosevelt administration for having extended diplomatic recognition to the Soviet government in 1933, breaking with the policies of FDR's four predecessors. In a moralistic approach to diplomatic recognition that echoed Woodrow Wilson, Hoover wrote,

> When our neighbors choose to live a life of disrepute, we do not shoot them up. But we can hold up the moral and social standards in the country a little better if we do not associate with them. Or take part in their parties. Or invite them in our homes. Or present them to our children.
>
> Recognition of new governments is thus more than reestablishment of legalistic or trade relations. It is a sign that we believe they are respectable members of the family of nations. It gives them the right of entry in our homes. It gives them a recommendation to our neighbors.

The communist regime had been immoral since its inception. The Bolshevik revolution had been a "liquidation" of liberalism in Russia, and ever since then the communists had ruled by terror, bloodshed, and murder, while attempting to undermine democratic governments abroad. Four successive American presidents and their secretaries of state had concurred in the nonrecognition policy by the United States, but Roosevelt had granted diplomatic recognition in exchange for a Soviet promise not to undermine the government of the United States. The Soviets had not kept that promise and had also revealed their utter lack of morality in foreign affairs by their rape of Poland, the destruction of the independence of Latvia and Estonia, and the invasion of Finland. Hoover again called for the recall of the American ambassador from Moscow, but he did not advocate breaking off diplomatic relations since it might be interpreted "at this time of a world aflame . . . as warlike."[37]

Vandenberg and Hoover harbored similar viewpoints, with the Michigan senator writing to the former president that he had written an article for *Liberty* similar to Hoover's in *Collier's*. "We are presenting substantially the same indictment and we reach substantially the same conclusion," he told Hoover. "I have been urging this viewpoint on the floor of the Senate for a long time."[38] Hoover responded that they were agreed on the need "to ventilate the follies of the foreign policies of this administration. It is not often in foreign policies that one is able to point to the direct consequences of wrong such as we are in this case."[39] The two continued their consultations on foreign policy both by letter and in personal meetings.

After struggling with the problems of Polish relief for the first five months of 1940, Hoover found those efforts both more complicated and more sought after once the Germans made their successful thrust westward in the spring of 1940. As the German juggernaut rolled over country after country the number of nations requesting relief grew accordingly. First Belgium joined Poland in calling for help, then the Netherlands, and later Norway.[40] The Commission for Polish Relief, Inc., organized on September 25, 1939, was soon joined by the revived Commission for Relief in Belgium on May 16, 1940, and the Queen Wilhelmina Fund for the Netherlands on May 13, 1940. And through these early months money was still flowing to Finland from Hoover's Finnish Relief Fund, Inc. Such requests for relief brought Hoover into increasing contact with his own and the British governments through 1940 and presented difficulties for the work of other agencies like the Red Cross. By the summer of 1940 the relief effort had been so blocked by the war, however, that when W. K. Kellogg, of cereal fame, offered to contribute $20,000 for children's relief, Hoover was forced to turn it down since it was, he said, "impossible to land supplies anywhere on the European continent of importance, and there is no more than normal destitution in England."[41]

The former president had also begun to concern himself with the issue of military preparedness. On May 17, 1940, he issued a press statement calling for there to be "no partisanship upon the principle of national defense." The United States should embark on a "thoughtful and scientific" armament based on the experience gained from the current war in Europe. While "undue haste" should be avoided, the nation must move forward rapidly with the "creation of facilities for production" under the leadership of industry, not the army and navy. "The job should be directed by a staff of tried leaders chosen from actual industrial production," Hoover argued, "not the financial leaders of the industry but the men who have come to the top through actual production experience on a large scale."[42]

Hoover told Congressman Joe Martin that if American industry could be "mobilized under some nonpartisan government agency in which [industry] had confidence, it could almost instantly double the production of aircraft."

He suggested the government encourage industrial expansion by permitting tax write-offs when wartime use of the equipment ended and by coordination of subcontracting. He suggested also that automobile manufacturers be encouraged to suspend new models for a year, thus turning "over their machine tool capacity and their machine tool machinists to making machine tools for expansion in the aviation field." It was vital, he told Martin, "to set up some sort of an agency that would have control of the entire production of all munitions of every kind," as the United States had discovered by the end of World War I and as every European nation was now doing. The former president favored overall control by one man, because "no board ever functions properly in executive matters unless all the powers are vested in the chairman and even then it is inefficient."[43]

Hoover pressed the issue in a speech on May 27, calling for the creation of a single-headed Munition Administration that would give the United States the appearance of having a "keep off the grass" sign and "a fierce dog plainly in sight." He noted the confession of the chief of staff that the US Army was not prepared to wage modern war. Of FDR's call for the manufacture of 50,000 warplanes, Hoover said the nation did not need 50,000 airplanes but did need American industry to be geared up to the point where it could produce that many a year if needed. Preparation for defense, he told his listeners, required

> first and foremost: This is a business requiring expert knowledge of manufacturing, industry, labor and transportation and agriculture. The lesson of the whole of the last World War and every step in the present war is that the procurement of munitions in any large volume must be separated from the army and navy establishment. It must be done by an organization separate and independent of either department. It is an industrial job—a manufacturing job, a mass production job—for management and labor. It requires that thousands of factories be coordinated to do their part . . .
>
> The second lesson learned over and over again out of all these recent years is that such operations cannot be controlled by boards or councils or conferences. They must be controlled by a single-handed trusted and experienced man . . .
>
> The third lesson taught by experience is that we must get these vast expenditures of money out of politics—get them out of sectional pressures and out of group pressure. We must get them focused into one place where the whole nation can look at it and watch the spending. That is the only way we can prevent profiteering. It is the only way we can eliminate waste and assure efficiency . . . We know only too well the use that can be made politically of favors to localities and to individuals in the expenditure of large sums of money.[44]

Congressional Republicans did press for such an organization of the defense effort, but Roosevelt chose, instead, an advisory defense council of seven coordinators, including Edward R. Stettinius and William S. Knudson. Moreover, Assistant Secretary of War Louis Johnson attacked Hoover's suggestion of a one-man defense administrator in a radio address on May 28, which was released in advance by the Democratic National Committee rather than by the War Department. Johnson blamed the nation's lack of preparedness on the Republican years of 1921–32 when battleships were scrapped and the army was starved to a mere skeleton. Johnson quoted Hoover's prediction in October 1939 that the Allies would be able to defend their empires and that the war would end, at the worst, in stalemate and said, "Tonight this analysis of the situation seems curiously unreal in the light of news from abroad that the King of Belgium has capitulated." There was, however, no need yet for a single administrator of the preparedness effort for the United Sates was not at war and the nation already had "agencies competent to do the job."[45] Hoover then responded with a press statement criticizing both the president's action and the Johnson speech. His press statement said,

> In view of the crisis we face and all the exposures of the past month, the country will be disappointed that President Roosevelt has chosen to set up another advisory committee instead of reorganizing the war and navy departments and appointing somebody from industry for the production of munitions. There are three or four good men on this committee, and the country will gain confidence in it if it boldly insists that these things be done at once. Certainly Assistant Secretary of War Johnson last night demonstrated that his capacities at political smearing exceed the capacities he has shown in past years in production of airplanes and guns. We need action now and not advisory reports for the file.[46]

Visiting him on May 29, William Starr Myers found that Hoover "looked more worn and weary than at any time since I saw him at Palo Alto in June, 1933. He seems very pessimistic."[47] Hoover wrote a friend, "The war overshadows everything. It is almost impossible to get people to take any interest in domestic questions except preparedness."[48]

On May 21 the *New York Times* reported that Roosevelt was on the verge of naming a coalition cabinet in which two places would be given to Republicans. Rumor had it that former 1936 vice presidential candidate Frank Knox would be offered the post as secretary of the navy and that Alf Landon had been asked to be secretary of war. Landon, however, had said he was "specifically opposed to any suggestion that the Republican party postpone its national convention or lend itself to any coalition which would tend to decrease party responsibility," and Hoover was also quoted as being opposed to any coalition movement. Senator Charles McNary and Congressman Joseph Martin, leaders of the GOP minorities in Congress, had expressed their agreement with the "titular leaders."[49] Knox among others had tried to get the GOP to postpone its convention until at least the first of August, since "we would know at least more about the war situation, and what ought to be done about it, and we would also have the advantage of knowing what the Democrats have done on July 15, which would be of no inconsiderable advantage to us."[50]

Hoover continued to be the leading GOP opponent of American entry into the war and was much sought after for advice from congressional and other Republicans, despite the inaccuracy of his prediction that the European democracies would be able to defend themselves. On June 7 the former president wrote to Governor Bricker to congratulate him on his "vigorous attacks on the President's notion that opposition" to his foreign policies "should cease" and added that Bricker's speeches had done "a lot of good."[51] In an article for *Liberty* magazine early in June, Hoover reiterated his warnings against American participation in the war and insisted that it was America's responsibility, instead, to "use our unimpaired resources, our courage, our moral strength to do mankind infinite service" in allaying "the destruction of war, and the ravages of Famine and Pestilence" afterward.[52] Congressman Karl Mundt of South Dakota congratulated him on the article and wrote, "Our minority group in Congress has gradually—too gradually, in my opinion—gotten back its fighting spirit and from now on until adjournment I hope we shall have power enough and policy enough to wage a head-on attack on FDR's steady usurpation of Congressional powers and his sure march toward American involvement in the war . . . I am convinced if we can keep out of war until next November, we can rid this country of Roosevelt and rescue it from the permanent loss of its own democratic processes and privileges."[53]

Other GOP leaders, including Landon and Knox, the 1936 nominees, supported bipartisanship in foreign policy, but Hoover was outspoken in calling for determined Republican opposition to the Roosevelt administration's march toward involvement in the war. As an articulate spokesman for a foreign policy based on reason rather than emotion, he won the support of many Republicans in and out of Congress, as well as that of many others who were opposed to American intervention. As on editorial described the Hoover position,

> Mr. Hoover sees our foreign policy marching with our preparations for defense. He is not isolationist. He firmly believes that isolation is impossible. He wants intensely to keep America out of war, but armed effectively to keep any threat away from this hemisphere. To keep out of war he wants America to act realistically and without emotion. He wants only cool, deliberate action. It is clear that he is not a man who would ever try to sweep American off its feet and into war. He sees only folly in talking offensively to other nations. The President's first responsibility, he says, is to evade war, not to stimulate it.[54]

A New Challenger

By May the Hoover campaign for the nomination consisted of the polls, letters mailed to delegates and GOP officeholders, and fieldwork on Hoover's behalf in the eastern, southern, and western states.[55] Reports from the West suggested that the former president would have a "trifle over a majority" of the delegates from the states there.[56] Hoover's confidence, however, gradually ebbed during that month. His expectations of winning the nomination had been based largely on the seeming inability of the other candidates to arouse enthusiasm. As a result, Hoover had good reason to anticipate that the delegates would turn to him as each of the others failed to gain the required majority. But in May a new and unforeseen challenge to those expectations began to surface. The name of Wendell Willkie began to increasingly appear in the former president's correspondence and in Rickard's diary accounts of his conversations with Hoover.

At first Hoover attached little importance to the boom for this former anti–New Deal Democrat, who was now a candidate for the GOP nomination. He wanted to believe that the enthusiasm for Willkie stemmed mainly from disappointment over the other candidates, and he could not "conceive that it will get anywhere in the convention, although it is very popular in business circles. Many of the people who have been backing Dewey financially have now switched over."[57] But by the end of May, Rickard found Hoover disturbed over Willkie's growing popularity and considering the organization of some draft-Hoover groups to counter it.[58] A few days later the former president was even forced to acknowledge numerous defections from his own supporters to Willkie.[59]

At dinner with the former president on May 29, Edgar Rickard found him for the first time willing to acknowledge that there had been a big surge for Willkie even among those he had been counting upon. On May 31, Rickard wrote that Hoover had grown "alarmed at Willkie's support." Rickard was glad, he wrote, that Hoover was "going on [a] fishing trip tomorrow as he is getting a bit jittery." By early June the former president's mind was consumed with the speech he was planning for the convention.[60]

While Hoover sought to keep the other candidates in the race, they, in turn, jockeyed for the former president's support. Early in May Robert A. Taft sent word to Hoover that if elected he wanted the former president for secretary of state, but Hoover regarded it as "wholly infeasible" and recognized that it was "nothing more than preconvention stuff."[61] Hoover continued graciously to entertain each of the aspirants who sought to call on him either in New York City or Palo Alto, and rumors abounded in the press after each such meeting, but he gave no indication of a favorite.

If Hoover had no preference, it was clear that many of his supporters favored Taft over the other candidates. In conflict with the former president's strategy of capturing Taft's delegates after the first ballot, some of

Hoover's lieutenants were now planning to throw any Hoover strength to Taft if Hoover showed no promise on the first ballot. Taft himself was confident that his former relief boss would "rather have me in than any other of the active candidates."[62]

Meanwhile, the credibility of the polls taken by the Hoover camp that had fed the former president's hopes of grassroots support was shattered late in May when the results of a Gallup poll taken that month were released. Instead of polling for opinions concerning the qualifications of the GOP candidates, as Hoover's supporters had urged, Gallup simply tested their popularity. The polls showed a slight drift away from the Democrats and toward the GOP, but it still found the Democrats supported by 54 percent of the people. Trial results showed either Roosevelt or Hull capable of eating any of the potential GOP candidates. Most damaging for the Hoover campaign, however, was the finding by Gallup that Dewey was the leading GOP choice, with 62 percent and gaining, while the former president was not a factor, lagging well behind the rest of the field as the choice of only 2 percent.[63] All the potential that had seemed to exist in the Alan Fox polls for influencing convention delegates had been destroyed by a single Gallup poll.

Crestfallen, the former president now counted heavily on the influence of the speech he was to deliver to the convention, and in early June Rickard found him absorbed in writing it. On June 4, Hoover lunched with Dewey and learned that the New Yorker claimed over four hundred delegates, which was nothing like Hoover's assessment of the situation. Renewed efforts were now made at the last moment to mobilize the support of the old Belgian Relief and American Relief Administration group, as well as all who had been involved in the newer Finnish relief effort. The Hoover camp began to take on a note of desperation as the Willkie challenge began to appear more and more threatening. Early in June, Helen Reid, wife of the editor of the Republican *New York Herald Tribune*, sought Hoover's support for the Willkie candidacy.[64] It was by now clear to Hoover that Willkie was his chief rival for the nomination, and he was receiving disturbing reports about the new challenger. One of his correspondents wrote in mid-June, "A local minor official of the local utility company brought me downtown yesterday morning. He swung right into Willkie talk. It ran something like this: 'We have had our orders. At the right time our employees, stockholders and bondholders will go to work. We have a nationwide campaign committee ready to go, and the heads are now laying the groundwork.'" The writer concluded that the Willkie boom was part of an "effort of the utilities to control things Republican."[65]

Hoover agreed that "the big business people have gone over to Willkie," thus dealing "a mortal blow to the Dewey boom." He still doubted, however, that Willkie would have many delegates.[66] Landon, too, thought that if Willkie "had ever held a public office and was not a utility man, he would be a real contender because of his robust personality and ability to express himself," but he still saw Dewey as "pretty strong at the grassroots."[67] Hoover was particularly upset to hear that in a speech in Nebraska, Willkie had attacked the GOP administrations from 1920–1932, putting them in the same category as the New Deal administration. The only difference was that Willkie attacked FDR by name, but not Coolidge and Hoover.[68]

Through the month of June, Hoover concentrated most of his attention on the campaign for the nomination. In the preconvention debates over the platform, one issue aroused his intervention, however. As headlines described the German conquest of Western Europe, the GOP delegates on the platform committee divided over the question of whether the party's platform should take a stand for supporting the beleaguered democracies. As the *New York Times* described it,

> A strong current toward a declaration of sympathy for the forces still battling Nazi domination of Europe, as well as for all possible material aid "short of war" developed quickly among the forty-odd members of the Republican Resolutions Committee as it convened informally today to begin drafting a platform to be presented to the national convention next week. Led openly by Alfred M. Landon of Kansas, Presidential nominee in 1936, and Walter E. Edge, former Senator from New Jersey and later Ambassador to France, the so-called "Aid-to-the-Allies" movement pushed into the background, for the time being at least, any serious agitation for a restatement of the traditional isolation policy for which the Republican party has been noted in recent years.[69]

Landon was subsequently named chairman of the subcommittee to draft the plank on foreign policy and national defense.[70]

The efforts of Landon and others to develop their pro-Allies plank were complicated, however, when the White House on June 20 announced that Republicans Frank Knox and Henry Stimson were joining the Roosevelt cabinet to head the Navy and War Departments, respectively, thus giving the appearance of a coalition cabinet in which Republicans would have the greatest responsibility for preparedness. The move was not unexpected, and in late May it had seemed so imminent that Hoover had given Senator Charles Tobey consent to release the letter on the topic he had written to him nearly a year earlier. When that letter was given to the press on May 23, Hoover felt that its release "did some good."[71] What was shocking for Republicans was the timing, which was practically on the eve of the GOP convention and just as the Resolutions Committee was debating the foreign policy plank of the platform. The result was that Knox and Stimson were "virtually read out of the Republican Party" by many party leaders for, as the *New York Times* reported, "party leaders, convention delegates and committee members regarded their course as an act of party treachery." Roosevelt's action, it was felt, had virtually forced the GOP into a position of opposition, as the party of peace as against FDR's apparent warlike intentions.[72]

Hoover's response was one of the more temperate and followed the line of his letter to Tobey. "Messrs. Stimson and Knox are, of course, entering the

Cabinet to give personal service, and not representing the Republican Party," he told the press. "There is no question of coalition involved. It has no effect on the 1940 campaign. The national issues remain exactly what they were."[73]

At the same time, Hoover's supporters were trying to overcome the negative effects on his campaign by the Gallup poll results by releasing on June 21 the results of the Alan Fox samplings. The press release reported that in matching Hoover against FDR, voters in 14 states had demonstrated that the former president would gain 16.7 percent over his 1932 vote and Roosevelt would lose 14.2 percent. The results of the poll were released by Richard Lawrence, publisher of *Printer's Ink*, Ruth Pratt, a former congresswoman, Everett Colby, a former GOP national committeeman from New Jersey, and John J. Hopkins, former assistant to the secretary of treasury in Hoover's cabinet.[74] The press release did not confide that the polls had been limited to middle-class suburban areas where Hoover's support could be expected to be strongest.

As the convention grew nearer, Hoover saw evidence that the Willkie boom was puncturing the bubble of other candidacies, especially Dewey's, but he still refused to concede the latecomer a chance. He estimated that the ex-Democrat would have forty delegates on the first ballot and that he would reach only one hundred at the most.[75] From many directions Hoover was hearing of delegate and grassroots and financial support for Willkie, but he continued to feel that the most serious challenge to his own chances would come from a Taft-Dewey combination.[76] He was also concerned that Landon had not been invited to address the convention and worried that the Kansan might feel he was responsible for the omission. He asked GOP National Committeeman R. B. Creager to correct any such impression in Landon's mind, telling Creager that Landon "is one of the great assets of the Republican party and we need teamwork now more than ever before."[77]

The Willkie camp predicted the nomination of their candidate on the sixth or seventh ballot, and there was growing evidence of defections in his direction from other candidates.[78] Hoover's chances, though, seemed to receive a major boost from the testimony of Congress of Industrial Organizations (CIO) leader John L. Lewis before the GOP platform committee. Lewis defended the Hoover administration against the charge that it had brought on the depression and done nothing to alleviate its effects. He also supported Hoover's claim that recovery from the depression had begun in 1932 but that the New Deal had prolonged it and transformed it into a chronic condition by its policies and weaknesses. According to the *New York Times*, Lewis had also suggested to numerous people that Hoover was the best qualified candidate to attack the New Deal in the campaign and to deal with the critical international problems that would face the next president.[79]

James A. Hagerty, a *New York Times* writer, now listed Hoover with Willkie in the "dark horse" category since Lewis's testimony had "brought the former President decidedly into the convention."[80] It was clear that much would depend on the effect of Hoover's speech to the convention. Would it kindle the kind of demonstration that his 1936 effort had? "On the effect of his speech, more than anything else," the *New York Times* opined, "will depend the possibility that Mr. Hoover may be put forward for the Presidential nomination."[81] A few days later it wrote,

> A decided threat to the candidates already in the field is seen in the scheduled appearance of former President Herbert Hoover before the convention tomorrow night. Friends who have read Mr. Hoover's speech declared that it will be the best and most forceful he ever has made. It is regarded as significant that Mr. Hoover will not leave Philadelphia immediately after his speech, as he did after addressing the national convention at Cleveland four years ago. Friends of Mr. Hoover—and they are in many State delegations—expect the speech to make a great impression, and possibly to make Mr. Hoover a candidate before the convention. With no candidate having a majority of the delegates and no one of those under present consideration entirely satisfactory to a majority, the situation is ripe for something in the nature of a stampede. It may not and probably will not be for Mr. Hoover, but if he chooses, his influence would be a powerful aid to any candidate.[82]

Alas, the potential influence of the former president's speech was as obvious to his foes and to the other camps as it was to the *New York Times*.

And down to the very end Hoover refused to allow an organized effort in his behalf at Philadelphia, trying to preserve the impression that he was not seeking the nomination when he was, in fact, actively pursuing it. Typically, he wrote to Ray Lyman Wilbur on the eve of the convention: "I have declined to take any part in these draft [Hoover] movements. That is the sort of thing that people have a right to do if they feel that they want to. The only way I would take a public position would be by a draft. We have no political organization and are not establishing one . . . The convention is entirely open and the delegates have come to no conclusions as yet."

Rickard lamented that there were lots of Hoover Indians at the convention but no chiefs in charge. It was, he wrote, "all terribly at loose ends."[83]

There was considerable speculation over what effect Hoover's speech might have on the foreign policy plank in the platform. The aid-the-Allies declaration had faded in the furor over FDR's appointment of Knox and Stimson to his cabinet, but it had now resurfaced again. GOP National Chairman John D. M. Hamilton called it the "chief plank in the platform." The *New York Times* reported, "Some leaders think the nomination of the candidate for President depends upon this plank."[84] A great deal, then, seemed to be hinging on Hoover's speech when he entered the convention hall at 9:37 p.m. on June 25 to address the convention.

The 1940 GOP convention in Philadelphia was the first political event ever televised in American history. From the cameras in Philadelphia the images were transmitted to New York City by NBC over a 10-mile wire circuit supplied by the Bell Telephone Laboratories, of which 93 miles were of coaxial cable. In New York the images were broadcast by station W2XBS from its transmitter high atop the Empire State Building. Television sets, which cost about $400 in 1940, or about the same as an automobile, were still comparatively rare, and telecasts could not often be tuned in outside the New York City metropolitan area. Expectations were high concerning Hoover's speech. One journalist reported that the "hall was jammed to the rafters for Mr. Hoover's speech. Even the press section was jammed with people exercising squatter's rights." "It seemed," he wrote, "that everybody in Philadelphia who could get near Convention Hall was present, hoping for an ultra-dramatic call by the former occupant of the White House. They were disappointed."[85]

Samuel F. Pryor, GOP national committeeman from Connecticut, chaired the committee on arrangements for the 1940 convention. Pryor was a dedicated supporter of Willkie for the nomination but also a longtime acquaintance and admirer of the former president. According to Pryor's recollection in 1980, Hoover began the evening badly by making his way to the podium too early. Pryor recalled, "When he came up to speak on the platform, he didn't wait for the signal to the television people, the signal from me to the people, he just walked up. All I heard was a lot of clapping, and I said, oh my God, is that Mr. Hoover coming? And he was walking up the aisle!"[86]

After the initial ovation and the introduction by convention chairman Joseph Martin, there was a demonstration for Hoover that lasted for several minutes—the first real show of life by the convention. Hoover stood before them in his familiar blue suit, self-consciously putting his hands in his pockets and then withdrawing them while he watched the demonstration before him. Then, as Martin gaveled the demonstration into silence, the smile vanished from the former president's face and he launched into his oration. He told his audience,

> We are faced with the task of saving America for free men. Two-thirds of the world is at war. Twenty nations have become the stamping ground of militant despotisms. Almost everywhere in the Old World the light of liberty . . . has gone into a long night. Men and nations have lost their moral and spiritual moorings. Even in America our system of liberty has been weakened. We are divided in mind and fearful. And confusion in liberal nations is made worse by the spread of incompetence in governments everywhere.

Hoover then made his familiar points against the New Deal's dictation to business. Governments could not dictate economic policies without also destroying "free speech, orderly justice and free government." The failures of these "totalitarian liberals," as Hoover referred to them, led inevitably to unemployment and class divisions and, finally, to the curtain dropping on liberty altogether when, "frustrating and despairing these hundreds of millions of people voluntarily voted the powers of government to the man on horseback as the only way out." America must learn from the experience of this happening in Europe.

The former president then launched into his familiar indictment of the morals of the New Dealers, the misuse of relief, the support of Democratic urban political machines through federal funds, and the use of taxpayer money for partisan political propaganda. He lambasted the New Deal spending policies, which included deficit, debts, and inflation, and pointed to the handicap that such a heavy debt posed on American's ability to defend itself. America must avoid becoming involved in any European or Asian wars but should supply materials and munitions to "those nations who are fighting for their freedom," but only if "it involves no action which takes us to war . . . and we must act within the law."

Four more years of the New Deal would be a disaster for America, Hoover told his audience:

> The New Deal has contributed to sapping of our stamina and making us soft. In quest of security they [the New Dealers] have retreated from liberty. In quest of reform they have abandoned justice and stirred class hate. In quest of relief they have injured self-reliance. In quest of an easy way out they have lessened the vision of America. The road to regeneration is burdensome and hard. It is straight and simple. It is a road paved with work and with sacrifice and consecration to the indefinable spirit that is America.

This was the road along which Republicans must lead the nation.[87]

Following the speech, Hoover was rewarded with applause and another demonstration. One reporter wrote that the convention had "found its lungs" in response to the speech, which had "provided a much-needed blood transfusion for what had been until then an anemic gathering of the Grand Old Party."[88] But the hoped-for stampede did not occur. James Hagerty wrote that the Hoover speech had "virtually challenged the delegates . . . to nominate him for President if they had the courage to make a real fight at the election in November . . . Indications that Mr. Hoover might be the leader for whom the convention is searching came from the warmth of his reception." However, even Hagerty found the enthusiasm in 1940 slightly milder than in 1936.[89] Another observer wrote, "Through all of the political atmosphere . . . ran a new factor based on the sudden realization that the speech delivered tonight by Mr. Hoover automatically put him among the contenders for the nomination." No demonstration comparable to that for Hoover had yet been seen for any of the other candidates.[90]

Perhaps one reason the response did not live up to expectations was because of poor sound amplification that caused many of the delegates to barely hear the former president. There were frequent calls for him to speak louder. This was, of course, particularly disastrous since Hoover counted so heavily upon the speech to create a bandwagon for his nomination. One reporter wrote that the "printed releases of Mr. Hoover's speech read much more interestingly than its spoken delivery. For some reason, Mr. Hoover stood too far back from the microphones, reading the typed sheets, it seemed, at a distance of more than two feet." He added, "For the first half-hour of his speech most of his words were inaudible to most of the press-stand occupants. Men sat with the typewriters before them, a copy of the speech on the pine desks, trying to follow the speaker paragraph by paragraph. Even with hands cupped to their ears, only an occasional phrase came through clearly. Then, as Mr. Hoover reached his peroration, Lawrence Richie, his former White House aide, stepped forward and adjusted the microphone setting. The improvement was immediate, but the damage had already been done."[91] James Selvage wrote years later, "Instead of his speech going over big, as it would have, there began to be cries from all over the auditorium—'We can't hear you—louder' . . . Well, his speech was a flop. Instead of being a good speech, it was a flop, and I am convinced—all of us were—that this had been deliberately rigged and the loudspeaker cut off."[92] Hoover and his secretary, Larry Richey, were also convinced that the sound system had been tampered with.[93] Pryor, who was the logical suspect, had a strange explanation for the poor sound quality when interviewed forty years later. According to Pryor, Hoover had not spoken into the microphone: "I had to go out and get the microphone and put it in his hand. He wouldn't pay any attention to the microphone . . . The microphone was perfectly all right. But he wouldn't talk into it. He would talk over this way and the microphone would be here, and I'd go out and bring the microphone over and put it in front of him."[94] Such an explanation might have rung true if applied to a high school freshman orator, but it hardly is credible when applied to an experienced speaker like the former president of the United States!

According to Pryor, another difficulty was that Hoover ignored the television cameras, much to the consternation of the cameramen and of Pryor. But this would have had no effect on the audience before him, and so many of Hoover's speeches had been filmed for newsreels that it is difficult to believe he would have ignored cameras of any kind. In view of other Willkie "dirty tricks" that occurred at the convention, one is left with the suspicion that the Willkie forces had done their best to sabotage a speech that the press and delegates alike agreed could be pivotal in gaining Hoover the nomination. Whether from sabotage or Hoover's own blunders, the opportunity for the 1940 nomination had slipped away.

Hoover's speech touched only briefly on foreign affairs, but the *New York Times* concluded that it had given little comfort to the "isolationists" in his party, editorializing,

> What [Hoover] had to say on the subject of foreign relations was clearly awaited with special interest by the audience which honored him with its reception. But what he had to say will not resolve the doubts now present in the minds of his fellow countrymen. For his discussion on foreign policy was not free from inherent contradictions, and it contained at least a little of something that will be pleasing to all sections of his party. But in one important respect—the matter of giving aid to European democracies, provided this is done within our law

> and provided it involves no risk of war—Mr. Hoover went much farther than the plank which is apparently to be recommended to the convention.[95]

On the contrary, the foreign policy plank adopted by the convention was virtually a statement of Hoover's views. It declared for nonintervention in foreign wars, attacked the Roosevelt administration for its foreign policies and lack of preparedness for national defense, and supported the extension of "such aid as shall not be in violation of international law or inconsistent with the requirements of our national defense" to all peoples fighting for freedom or whose liberty was threatened. It also called for orderly and realistic preparations for the defense of the United States, its possessions, and outposts, and for upholding the Monroe Doctrine.[96]

The day after his convention speech Hoover met with approximately 150 newsmen. When questioned about his availability for the nomination, the former president recalled for them that he had announced two years earlier he would not again seek public office, and he did not think, he said, that they would find any evidence at Philadelphia that he had changed his mind. He had, however, advocated an open convention because "of the seriousness of the times and the shifting problems that the country has to meet." The delegates had a number of able candidates to choose from, and Hoover promised to support their choice. When pressed to say whether he would accept the nomination if it were offered to him, Hoover replied that he had "no further comment to make upon it."[97] To the end, Hoover refused to leave himself publicly available for a nomination he was trying so desperately to win in secret. It is unlikely that the press conference did anything to advance his prospects for the nomination.

Rickard confided to his diary that the Hoover forces believed they had 150 to 200 delegates but would hold them back with only a few votes shown on the first two ballots. The hope was that the convention would then be adjourned, the Hoover forces mustered, and the former president's nomination put over in subsequent roll calls.[98] The desired adjournment, however, never took place. On the first ballot Hoover received 17 votes; his total rose to 21 on the second ballot and to 32 on the third and then began to decline. Dewey led all candidates on the first ballot and then steadily lost strength. Taft gained steadily, but Willkie, who began with 105 votes on the first ballot, gained more rapidly than Taft and reached 659 votes on the sixth ballot, thus winning the nomination. Most obvious from Hoover's tally was the costly failure of the whole Republican Circles effort in the western states, where Hoover at his high point received 13 votes in California and negligible votes in Colorado (3) and Utah (11). Hoover's "western strategy" had failed miserably.[99] Disappointed, Hoover now proposed to remain outside the campaign completely unless he was begged to participate and unless Willkie agreed to defend his administration and to give him a voice in political appointments in California.[100]

Much of Hoover's antagonism toward Willkie stemmed from the methods used by the nominee or his overzealous supporters to gain the nomination. This included not only the suspected tampering with the sound system for Hoover's speech but also the apparent printing of duplicate tickets so that the convention galleries could be packed with spectators hired off the street to chant "We Want Willkie" throughout the convention proceedings and the inundation of delegates with telegrams supporting Willkie's candidacy. John Hamilton recalled Hoover being upset in his hotel room over the piles of telegrams he had received. It was obviously done as a preconcerted plan, because Hoover had never received so many telegrams about anything in his life.[101]

The staggering volume of pro-Willkie telegrams that Hoover and other GOP leaders and delegates were inundated with before and during the convention was reminiscent of the tactics used by the utilities in lobbying Congress against the utilities act a few years earlier—an effort that was investigated and exposed by a congressional committee. Landon, who threw the support of Kansas to Willkie on the crucial and decisive sixth ballot, returned home to Topeka to find that many of the telegrams he had received were fabricated, as some 18 mail sacks containing his acknowledgments for these telegrams awaited him with their contents stamped "Addressee Unknown."[102] But it was too late now. Landon and the other delegates had fallen at Philadelphia for this bogus evidence of "grass roots" support.

Another source of Hoover's alienation stemmed from his conviction that Willkie's nomination signaled a further turn away from the ideals the former president felt should be championed by the GOP. Walter Brown described the disquietude in the Hoover camp: "I fear the Republican party as we have known it, is gone forever. Under the leadership of anti–New Deal Democrats there will be little to interest real Republicans."[103] Another wrote, "I feel that if the American people want a renegade Democrat and a representative of Wall Street as their leader, they are welcome to him."[104]

Hoover was noncommittal about supporting the GOP nominee. When he stopped in San Francisco on his way home to Palo Alto, the former president told reporters he would not "like to make any statement about Mr. Willkie without giving more careful thought to the matter."[105] From his home in Palo Alto, Hoover addressed a reflective and warm letter to the defeated Tom Dewey, encouraging him to stay in politics in order to maintain fundamental party principles in the GOP during a period in which the principles of the two parties seemed to be so fluid.[106]

Despite his chilliness toward the Republican candidate and the methods by which he had obtained the nomination, Hoover could not long maintain his neutrality in the race because of his concern that FDR should be evicted from the White House. But no overtures came from Willkie's campaign seeking Hoover's assistance. Hoover wrote Walter Brown late in July that he had received "a number of indirect and verbal messages but no direct communications from Mr. Willkie." It was reminiscent of 1936 and, as had been the case four years earlier, Hoover decided "to await [Willkie's] directly expressed wishes." He added, "There are many people among his friends who have the same feeling that Landon had in 1936. Having had one experience I shall not be put to the same humiliation."[107] Dewey, too, had not been asked to participate in the Willkie campaign, adding to his suspicion that it was to be a repeat of 1936, but Hoover was convinced that the election would "be lost if only Willkie [is] allowed on the radio."[108]

Hoover's attitude changed in mid-August when Willkie invited him on a fishing trip. When the trip had to be canceled, the nominee invited him to visit him in Colorado Springs. While the meeting between the two men was marred by Willkie's incredible faux pas of inviting Elliott Roosevelt, son of the president, to dine with them, Hoover predictably decided that Willkie was preferable to FDR in the White House.[109] He thought Willkie was "making a good candidate" and if nothing intervened in world affairs he thought it might be possible to elect him.[110] The former president agreed to make some speeches in Willkie's behalf and tentatively planned one for the middle of September.[111]

The Willkie campaign seemed disorganized and chaotic to him, however. The nominee antagonized the party regulars with impulsive and ill-advised remarks and seemed not to have any definite ideas on any subject. Moreover, there seemed in the Willkie campaign the same disposition to ignore Hoover and his followers as had been the case with Landon in 1936, though to a lesser extent.[112] But none of his reservations diverted Hoover from the primary objective, which was the defeat of FDR. He wrote one correspondent who had criticized Willkie, "I have one central thought at this moment. We must make the maximum effort to get this Blum regime out of Washington. A rebuke of these present policies and a change are of vast importance to the whole future of the country. I shall do any proper thing they want me to do. I don't think it will be very much."[113]

Foreign Concerns

When Roosevelt began to apply economic pressure on Japan in mid-1940 in an effort to discourage their expansion, Hoover worried that it might lead the United States into war in Asia. He wrote O'Laughlin early in August, "Shutting down scrap iron and octane gas exports to Japan is again only sticking a pin in a rattlesnake. As a great majority of her trade will go on anyway, she can obtain these supplies elsewhere. Either we should leave this thing alone, or we will be drawn into real trouble. However, there does not seem to be anything to be done about it at the moment."[114] As in 1931–1932, when he had opposed his secretary of state, Henry L. Stimson, over the issue of economic sanctions against the Japanese in response to the Manchurian incident, Hoover viewed such sanctions as leading inevitably to war.

There quickly followed the destroyers-for-bases swap with England proposed by FDR. While no one doubted that the British faced a critical situation with much of Europe under the control of Nazi Germany and the seas patrolled by her submarines, opponents of American intervention in the war argued that to give such vitally needed military assistance to one side was clearly an unneutral act and might even be regarded as hostile by Germany. If so, it could easily lead to American involvement in the war. However, Hoover did not publicly oppose the deal, even though he counseled Republicans not to support it, and when the exchange was made, Hoover issued a statement that omitted all reference to the destroyer part of the arrangement: He told the press, "The new naval and air bases are important contributions to our defense. The only criticism of the transaction is that it was not submitted to the Congress for approval. There can be no sound reasons why that should not have been done. The American government has sought such bases in the Caribbean but hitherto the British refused. I am very glad to see that all of these bases have been acquired."[115]

Neglected by the Willkie campaign, Hoover delivered a preparedness speech at the University of Pennsylvania on September 18. He argued again that the United States should not become involved in the wars in Europe and Asia. The United States could exist in freedom even though the rest of the world was awash with totalitarianism, but its freedom was likely to disappear for a generation if it entered the war. A free economy could continue to exist in the United States if this country competed with the totalitarian ones in goods produced cheaply through industrial efficiency. Such efficiency could be achieved through technological advances, the upgrading of plant equipment, the elimination of waste, the application of laborsaving devices, and the removal of government restrictions on capital and labor that impeded or penalized efficiency. Hoover also advocated reciprocal quotas to protect American jobs and to secure markets abroad for American good. America's "service to humanity," he concluded, "is to make this industrial revolution serve free men. We must prove that the purpose of science is to save mankind and not to destroy it. And we must prove that we can defend ourselves."[116]

The *New York Times* called the former president's speech "not only one of the most thoughtful statements to come from any American statesman in recent months but one of the most impressive speeches of his own career." The newspaper found his call for support of pure and applied scientific research in pursuit of greater industrial efficiency "a proposal that deserves immediate study."[117]

While Hoover was speaking in Pennsylvania, the GOP nominee was traversing California in search of votes, continually lauding Senator Hiram Johnson but making no mention of the other distinguished Californian, former president Hoover, thereby imperiling his campaign there. While Willkie sought to woo the support of Johnson and his followers, his studied refusal to mention Hoover's name was alienating the former president and his supporters.[118] And even with Willkie's effusive praise for him, Johnson had refused to commit his support to the nominee. The combination of Willkie's slight in California and the continued neglect of his potential role in the campaign led Hoover to briefly consider issuing a statement taking himself out of the campaign entirely. He was dissuaded from doing so by Edgar Rickard, who convinced him that to do so would be to eliminate any possibility of a Willkie victory.[119]

Hiram Johnson, never a close friend of Hoover, sent word to him through O'Laughlin that he had not been in contact with Willkie, had not known beforehand of Willkie's intentions in California, and considered Willkie's failure to mention Hoover an "outrage." But like Hoover, Johnson decided that he must support Willkie in order to defeat FDR.[120] Coincidentally, Willkie was visiting in New York City and spent the entire day there without so much as paying even a courtesy call on the Republican former president, although Hoover had anticipated that he would extend at least that slight courtesy.[121] By now Hoover had begun to grow pessimistic about Willkie's chances in November, perhaps because of his own absence from the campaign.[122]

Although it seemed that the Willkie campaign wanted two campaign speeches from the former president, it developed that the Willkie people were unwilling to pay for the broadcasting of his speeches as they had allotted all radio money for the nominee's speeches. Hoover explained to a friend,

> Inasmuch as the money was not provided for broadcasting at Columbus, I postponed that speech until later on. It appears they will have money enough to pay for a broadcast around the 25th of October. No allotment was made for national broadcasting of any major speeches except Mr. Willkie's, although some $700,000 was allotted to publicity. I think Mr. Dewey will probably go on twice on a national hookup and I am going on twice. I doubt whether there will be any other national hookups. Mr. Willkie is working himself to death and has fifteen more national broadcasts before the end of the campaign. If he could just get some men around him who would prevent his being run ragged, it would be better for everybody.[123]

It began to appear, however, that if Hoover was to participate in the campaign he might have to raise the money to pay for his own radio broadcasts, and the former president set out to do so. He also sought, unsuccessfully, to arrange for a joint appearance with Senator Hiram Johnson in Willkie's behalf, since he thought this "would represent the final healing of all Republican wounds in California and would create enthusiasm among the people." He was also sure it was the only way Willkie could carry the state.[124]

In the first of his speeches, in Columbus, Ohio, in late October, Hoover took up the third term issue, reviewing the tradition in American history of a two-term limitation on presidents and the implications of a third term for Roosevelt in 1940. The past eight years, he pointed out, had seen a great growth in executive power such as had undermined democratic government in the rest of the world. He did not mean, Hoover added, to "suggest that Mr. Roosevelt aspires to be dictator," but it was apparent that his power had been built "to a dangerous point in this Republic" and that there were men around him who were "implacably pushing further and further in that direction." The two-term tradition was a check on the growth of such personal power. "Is this any time for America to surrender forever this vital check upon power?" he asked. Hoover went on to charge that the New Deal had sought to intimidate and smear all those who had opposed this grab for power and had sought to purge from office those who did not agree with it. He added, "In building up these powers the independence of the Supreme Court, the Congress, and the local governments has been degraded. Methods of intellectual dishonesty have been used in creating this personal power. A political machine has been built which places all free elections in jeopardy. An economic system is being created with drifts steadily away from free men and free enterprise down the suicide road of National Socialism." And this personal power, Hoover warned, was now being used to steer the United States toward war. It was time, he declared, for the American people to stop this growth of personal power through the election of Wendell Willkie.[125]

From Mark Sullivan came praise, "for the content of the speech, its orderliness and force of thought, and its happy phrasing; for its humor and for its delivery . . . It was for many an unanticipated and highly agreeable experience to hear an audience laugh at practically every second or third sentence of a speech by Herbert Hoover." Hoover now had the freedom, Sullivan remarked, to "be the voice of most elevated thought of the American people with [his] words carrying the authority of complete disinterestedness, complete freedom from personal or party considerations. That any country at any time should have a voice of this kind is an immense asset. And to be that voice is a great satisfaction."[126]

Back in San Francisco, Hoover told the press that FDR was "taking his country steadily towards war," even though he had "been incompetent in providing defense for us in case of war." Hoover added, "This is the only democratic government in the world that defeated recovery from the world-wide depression except the French, and the French adopted a New Deal. This administration is steadily developing the same growth of personal power that has swept the world into nazism and fascism. The unwritten constitutional provision against third terms for presidents has been held resolutely ever since the foundation of the Republic for just precisely this sort of a situation. It must not be abandoned now."[127]

Now that he was active in the campaign, Hoover was more optimistic about Willkie's chances. On October 31, he traveled to Lincoln, Nebraska, to attack Roosevelt's foreign policies, but first he issued a statement in response to Roosevelt's speech on armament and defense in Boston the previous night, in which FDR had talked of the weaknesses in the nation's defenses he had inherited when assuming the presidency in March 1933. Roosevelt's memory was "at fault" Hoover said, because the United States had an army of 148,000 in 1933, and the number was not substantially increased until 1937, "and even then, after Congress had appropriated the necessary funds, Mr. Roosevelt did not budget the expenditures. Only six months ago the chief of staff reported to the Senate that we had full equipment for only about 75,000 men." As for the navy, Republican presidents had negotiated reductions agreements with Britain and Japan and provided for a US Navy as large as Great Britain's, and with Japan's "only 60 per cent of ours." Hoover added, "If Mr. Roosevelt's memory weren't faulty, he would recall that in 1932 he attacked the Republicans for spending too much on the army and the navy; that in 1934 he reduced expenditures for the armed forces by $100,000,000, of which $20,000,000 was cut from the air force."[128]

In his Lincoln speech Hoover accused the president of aiming "billingsgate" at foreign heads of government and thereby destroying the moral influence of the United States abroad and stimulating enmity toward the nation everywhere in the world. The president's involvement of the United States in the "power politics" of Europe had created an international alliance against the United States for the first time in history. Hoover lashed out at Roosevelt for sabotaging the London Economic Conference of 1933, the collapse of the Geneva disarmament conference, recognition of the Soviet Union, and the whole conduct of American foreign policy since the Munich Agreement in 1938. The threat to the United States in 1940 was minimal, he insisted, for if Germany could not cross the 25 miles of the English Channel to invade Britain, how could it contemplate an invasion of the Western Hemisphere thousands of miles away. The argument that Roosevelt should be reelected because of his experience in foreign relations was patently ridiculous, Hoover insisted, for all the president had demonstrated was his utter incompetence in that area. Hoover concluded for his listeners, "You are far more likely to get into war with Franklin Roosevelt as president than with Wendell Willkie."[129]

The following night Hoover summarized the major issues in the campaign with a speech in Salt Lake City. In familiar terms, Hoover told his listeners that upon the election hinged the preservation of democracy in America. The new Deal had started with three economic ideas: (1) "the whole American system was a wreck and wrong and must be made over," (2) "new frontiers of enterprise were gone and the job was to divide the existing pot," and (3) the federal government should control all economic life through a planned economy. These ideas had produced "attempts to control our courts, to control our Congress, to control our elections, to control our public opinion with mass propaganda and slogans, and finally to demand a third term." All this, he warned, had "a pronounced odor of totalitarian government." The New Deal had succeeded in making economic depression "a chronic way of American life." Willkie, he said, would "get this economic machine functioning, produce prosperity, give jobs, make a market for farm products in full stomachs . . . ,build up national income, create the production out of which taxes can be paid and deficits overcome."[130] After the speech, Hoover wrote Mark Sullivan with obvious relish that "Roosevelt invited an attack from me on personal grounds and I did it extemporaneously from Salt Lake City. The audience at least seemed to like it."[131]

Though Hoover felt the GOP candidate did not come forth emphatically enough in opposition to American intervention in the European war, he nevertheless counted heavily on Willkie's election to reverse Roosevelt's interventionist foreign policies and also to support his stalemated efforts to get food relief to the people of Europe. Of this latter, Hoover wrote Hugh Gibson,

> the future of our [relief] work depends much upon the American election. It looks at the moment to me as if Mr. Willkie will be elected. He would naturally be favorable to relief of these people. Mr. Roosevelt will follow American public opinion. I cannot let the fate of these 30 millions of people rest where it is. I have, therefore, been devoting my time to arranging with the spiritual and moral leadership in the United States for a widespread American demand that agreement be brought about by which they can be saved. I find universal support amongst these leaders and a resolution to put on an active campaign to stir up American opinion. I am making no statements in the press and I am exerting myself everywhere to keep this campaign from taking anti-British form. But I shall break loose as soon as the election is over.[132]

Hoover had long since come to the conclusion that Roosevelt was sabotaging his every effort to furnish food relief to Europe.[133]

Another source of opposition to his relief efforts, however, came from his old friend William Allen White, whose Committee to Defend America by Aiding the Allies regarded Hoover's relief plans as a source of assistance to the German war effort against the Allies and therefore opposed any relaxation of the British blockade of the European continent. Although the United States had furnished such relief to Belgium and northern France during the early years of World War I, White argued that the situation was different now because the Germans were systematically forcing the conquered peoples of Europe "to produce for Germany munitions, ships, planes, and other supplies to be used to destroy England and eventually menace America." Therefore, White felt it was not "wise to feed those enslaved populations actually engaged in producing implements and munitions that threaten our safety." His committee was, however, interested in finding "some formula under which . . . humanitarian relief medical and food supplies may enter the conquered countries." White insisted, "There is no black here and no white. We have all got to move in a gray area."[134]

On November 18, 1940, the National Committee on Food for the Small Democracies was organized at a meeting in New York. *Commonweal* magazine editorialized that Hoover "had given the country a formula to work on, one that seems sound in the main, and invites the respect accorded to experts. Moreover, he does not stand alone; the relief commissions for Belgium, Holland, Norway and Poland back his plea. It ought not to be shrugged off without at least testing the policy of the Germans and of the English and of the American people."[135] But less than a month later the British signaled their unwillingness, on December 10, to relax their blockade for food shipments.

Hoover was fairly confident of a Willkie victory as Election Day approached and was totally unprepared for the size of Roosevelt's convincing victory.[136] Analyzing the returns, however, he concluded the GOP had "capacity in it yet."[137] Republican candidates for governor, senator, and congressman had run ahead of Willkie in their total vote, and they had been closer to traditional Republicanism than the presidential candidate.[138] And if Willkie had obtained even one-half percent more of the votes in Ohio and the eastern states, Hoover calculated, he would have won the presidency.

Hoover decided that this "phenomena of running behind the regular Republican candidates stands out in this campaign even more vividly than it did in the Landon campaign. The aggregate vote was from 1 to 2 million greater than the vote for Willkie." From this he concluded again, as in 1936, that in courting the votes of anti–New Deal Democrats, independents, and New Dealers, Willkie had lost the votes of a significant number of Republicans.[139] The lesson of 1936 was reemphasized for the former president— GOP presidential candidates must stand for traditional Republican principles or they could not be elected.

In his press statement on the electoral results, however, Hoover tried to put the best face possible on the outcome, saying, "The election closed with both candidates and both parties pledged to the utmost national preparedness and to keep out of foreign wars. The transcendent duty now is the full cooperation of everybody in this vital purpose."[140]

A few days later the former president again addressed the issue of the need for partisanship even during the world crisis. He told the press that Republicans had a duty to oppose the drift toward centralization of power in the federal government. While Republicans agreed with Democrats on issues like peace, national preparedness, and aid to England short of war, there was still a necessity for debate on domestic issues. "The organization of all democracies has to revolve around two major parties," he said, "thus giving two different points of view for the people to thresh out at the ballot box." But he called for an end to "smearing and all that kind of opposition for all time." Coalition cabinets, such as Roosevelt had created by the appointment of Knox and Stimson, were "desirable," he said, "in case of war, but not in peace times—as they imply no pounding on the anvil of debate." "Individuals of exceptional ability" should be appointed to the cabinet at any time, regardless of party affiliation, but they should not be taken in as representatives of either party in the expectation that they would end partisan debate.[141]

One impact of the 1940 campaign and election on Hoover was a reinforcement of his earlier expressed determination to move to New York from Palo Alto. In mid-November, Rickard found both Hoover and his wife determined not to return to their Stanford home because they felt "their position has been largely damaged in that state by undermining in [the] last campaign where he was ignored." Rickard wrote, "He really does not know what to do, and I am distressed over his more or less defeatist attitude as to public opinion of him."[142] Willkie's forces had forged their own organization in California, ignoring Hoover and his supporters while cultivating relations, instead, with Senator Hiram Johnson. This was an affront that was intolerable to Hoover, and it left him with virtually no influence any longer in the politics of his home state. Beginning with 1941 the trips to California would become fewer and fewer.

CHAPTER 6

Leading the Loyal Opposition

Lend Lease

Two weeks after the election, Hoover invited Willkie to lunch and the two had an amicable visit. He also saw William Allen White and Thomas Lamont and "cautioned them to stick to their aid to Britain and not attack his relief plans."[1] As Thanksgiving approached Rickard wrote that Hoover "seems to disregard public holidays and outwardly at least does not seem to have much sentiment in family reunions." He found Hoover "restless" and uncertain what he wanted to do.[2] Hoover wrote a friend later in the month that he had "determined not to again engage in politics, but to devote myself as well as I can to the larger problems of the country," the greatest of which was "to keep out of war." He did "not see clearly where the Republican party is going, but certainly it ought to be a Republican party."[3] In early December he and Lou Henry moved into a new apartment in the Waldorf Towers that was more suitable as a permanent residence.[4]

Roosevelt's reelection presented new challenges for Hoover, and the continuation of old ones. He had hoped that Willkie's election would bring to the White House a supporter of his food relief efforts in occupied Europe. Instead, it continued the same obstacles. Hoover now sought to enlist so many prominent Americans in support of his efforts that their demand for the relaxation of the British blockade would be difficult for the Roosevelt administration and the British to resist. Contrary to William Allen White's assertion that there was no black or white in the issue, Hoover viewed it in stark terms. It was, in fact, in the interests of the British to feed the starving peoples of the occupied countries of Europe if they could only see beyond short-term wartime considerations. The war would end someday, and the British would then have to live with the peoples of Europe whom they had deprived of food. That did not bode well for long-term British interests on the Continent.[5]

Hoover had, however, little success in attracting prominent Americans to his cause. He received numerous responses that were negative to the idea of furnishing food to the malnourished people of Europe who might be of use to Hitler. Included among the opponents were the presidents of many major universities.[6] With emotions running high because of the war, humaneness suffered from many "isolationists." Hoover was successful in recruiting General John Pershing as a member of the committee, but he could not overcome British resistance to his relief proposals.[7] In late December he set off for a fishing trip in Florida in pursuit of "peace of mind" but determined to push on with his efforts after the first of the year.[8]

Meanwhile, the former president had continued his campaign to keep the United States out of war. Late in November he discussed with Joseph Kennedy, US ambassador to Great Britain, the British resistance to his relief plans. Kennedy agreed with him that the United States must stay out of the war, since the only result of American intervention would be the triumph of fascism in the United States. Kennedy confided to the former president that he intended to resign as ambassador within a few weeks to return to the United States and devote himself to opposing American intervention into the war. The two promised to say in close contact as they had a joint mission to keep America at peace.[9] But Hoover declined to join the America First movement, writing,

> In view of my obligation to organize a movement in the United States to break down the barriers against food to the five small democracies, I think it is desirable that for the present I should keep free of other connections. I am completely possessed with the necessity of making clear the facts and the truth of the relations of the United States to the European situation. It is indeed a difficult job in view of the furious emotions and the enormous amount of propaganda that is flooding the country. This is injected to destroy even so humane a question of trying to save the lives of millions of innocent people from famine.[10]

President Roosevelt floated the concept of lend-lease assistance to the Allies at a press conference on December 17, 1940, and then proposed the program to Congress in his annual address on January 6, 1941. Hoover was not opposed to granting aid to the Allies, but he was concerned with the precise details of whatever legislation was enacted. He wrote Senator Robert Taft that before the Senate approved lend-lease it ought first to learn about payment for materials already contracted for, payment for future supplies, and other payments. Britain's war objectives also needed to be defined—particularly their proposals for a peace settlement, their intentions regarding postwar disarmament, and what measures they proposed to bring about permanent peace in the world once the fighting had stopped.[11]

On December 21, Hoover spoke to the Pennsylvania Society of New York and told his audience that "in normal times such occasions as this should be devoted to the lighter side of life," but there was, he pointed out, "little to be gay about when madmen destroy in a day what it has taken the sweat and blood and tears of mankind a thousand years to erect. The stupendous sound track of this terrible moving picture drives its horrors into every home in every hour of our land." He could discuss the situation, he said, without fear of being accused of "partisan impulse," because he had "divorced myself from politics for the balance of my life—or have been divorced." The "ferocity" of the discussion of 1916–17 was being repeated in the United States in 1940, and as in the last war America was being "deluged with propaganda from both sides." America was "afflicted with slogans: 'war mongers,' 'appeasers,' 'pacifists,' and what not." Such smearing should not stifle debate over America's legitimate interests, since it was the "transcendent right of Americans, and their duty . . . to express their position on war and peace. It is the greatest issue that can come to any nation." It was America's "immediate and imperative task . . . to concentrate upon preparedness. Our defenses must be so strong that dictators singly or in combination must be convinced that it is impossible for them to cross these oceans. And we wish our industries to function for Britain, China and Greece." He continued,

> The enormous preparedness program we have undertaken amounts in some ways to as great an effort as war itself. Many of its problems of economic organization are war problems.
>
> It is so large an effort that it demands complete national unity. And a pertinent place for unity is in labor relations . . .
>
> We learned some bitter lessons on the method of organization of munitions and supplies in the last war. The principal one was that production could best be had by the mobilized cooperation of industry, not by force . . .
>
> But we learned that there must be responsible, single-handed leadership, not the indecision of boards.

The problem for America was to "carry the burden of arms without decreasing the standard of living." This could only be achieved by increasing production to meet the needs of war and of the impoverished world that would need help once the war was over. It must include "greatly expanded scientific research and invention" for "new methods in the saving of materials and labor." Free competition must be maintained to reduce costs to the consumer, and "every sort of restriction by both capital and labor which impedes or penalizes the use of better methods and better machines" must be eliminated, as well as all "unnecessary governmental restrictions which encumber protection and lessen the initiative of men." As for food, Hoover wrote,

Governments may deprecate, some cartoonists may sneer, some columnists may argue. But the hard, inexorable, stark fact is that before the next harvest millions of innocent children, women and men in Belgium and the other occupied democracies will be faced with complete starvation and disease. That fact cannot be dismissed. Nor can remedy be found overnight after these hideous calamities are upon us. They require months of organization. It is not my purpose to discuss that question here. But a great body of Americans will continue to search for a method of their saving. And there need be no feeding of Germans in that action.

Americans must also begin planning for the postwar world, to ensure that there would be an end to such wars. He told his audience, "Destiny has so ordered the course of events that much of the world's hope lies ultimately in our hands. We are the ultimate hope and sanctuary of human liberty."[12]

For Hoover, who monitored press reaction to his every speech, it was noteworthy that this one had "extraordinary unity of praise from such divergent corners as the *New York Times, News, Daily Mirror, Sun and World Telegram*, the *Chicago Tribune*, the *Chicago Sun*, the *Minneapolis Star Journal, Time*, and so forth."

After William Allen White resigned as chairman of the Committee to Defend America by Aiding the Allies, he wrote Ray Lyman Wilbur and confessed that he had "spent considerable time keeping more radical members of our committee from opposing [Hoover's relief plan], but not always with the success I should like to have had." It was those radical members, the "war mongers" as White called them, who had led him to resign from the committee.[13]

In a press statement of January 10, 1941, the former president expressed his major concern with the lend-lease proposal. Hoover questioned the necessity for the "enormous surrender" of congressional responsibilities that was involved in the White House plan, although this had by now become typical of Roosevelt's policies.[14] When the press reported that Congressman Sol Bloom would seek his testimony before the House Foreign Affairs Committee, Hoover sent a public letter to Bloom that expressed his views on the proposal. While he was "in favor of extending every practicable aid, short of war, to Britain to enable her to maintain her independence," he was also opposed to American intervention in the war. There were, he told Bloom, many questions about the proposed legislation and great confusion over what it would include. Hoover suggested that Congress should "at once draft into the bill positive definitions of what these powers are and specifically exclude what they are not, and thereby provide for concrete debate and eliminate much controversy and bitterness."[15]

Hoover hoped that the Republican minority in Congress would be able to amend the bill in such ways as to reduce Roosevelt's ability to use it to take the United States into the war.[16] To that end, the former president took an active role in rallying and counseling the GOP effort. As he described his efforts to one correspondent, "I have been in constant communication with Republicans in the House and Senate. We are developing a definite program. We have secured a continuous stream of able radio speakers and have more coming up. I think we are going to defeat the big issue in this bill, that is giving the President the power to make war."[17] When the America First Committee encouraged him to go on national radio to oppose lend-lease and offered to help with broadcast time, Hoover responded that he was "exerting" himself "in this matter day and night" and preferred to "let this situation develop a little" before going on the radio.[18]

The issue of lend-lease even produced a rare example of agreement between Hoover and Landon, when it caused the 1936 GOP nominee to defect from his lukewarm support of Roosevelt's foreign policies. Lend-lease seemed to Landon to be a step toward involvement in the war, similar to those that had preceded American entry into World War I. In a nationwide radio broadcast on January 11, Landon asserted that Willkie, who supported the lend-lease proposal, would not have been nominated by the GOP in 1940, nor would FDR have been elected, if the American people had known then what Willkie and Roosevelt would be saying now.[19] From friends like columnist Raymond Clapper came the predictable concern that Landon was identifying himself "as one of the Hoover-Lindbergh crowd," but Landon responded that he had "no illusions as to the popularity of my course." He had, Landon said, been willing to help England "in all material ways and in ways that will not involve us in actual combat," but the Lend-Lease Act he regarded as a step toward the latter.[20]

For Hoover and Landon, bitter political adversaries since 1935, the road was now open for cooperation in opposing Roosevelt's foreign policies during the remaining months until Pearl Harbor. At the same time, however, Hoover was seeing defections from his own camp, some by those among his most dedicated political supporters. John Spargo, for example, joined Willkie in wholeheartedly supporting lend-lease, although he assured Hoover that "[my] profound admiration for you and my loyalty to you are not and will not be in the least measure lessened."[21]

On January 24, Hoover sent Senator Arthur Vandenberg four proposed amendments for the lend-lease bill. It seemed, he said, "obvious that the minority opposition can only move effectually by amendments and by amendments we would aggregate great support from the public and possibly in Congress that cannot be had by attempts at substitute legislation." Hoover's proposed amendments would make it explicit that nothing in the Lend-Lease Act authored the president to convoy ships with the American navy, repair ships of belligerent nations in American harbors, transfer American naval vessels to other nations, or expend funds outside the United States.[22] Vandenberg wanted any more suggestions Hoover might have to offer and was meeting with him in a few days because he was "always most happy to have [Hoover's] effective cooperation."[23] While Senator Robert

Taft inclined toward offering a substitute bill, Hoover believed the amendments he had proposed would make the issues clear to the American public
and that sufficient support could be obtained for amending the bill in its most
vital provisions, thus eliminating the grant of such powers to the president
that could involve the United States in war.[24]

By contrast with Hoover and Landon, the GOP's 1940 nominee, Wendell Willkie, supported Roosevelt's foreign policies in late 1940 and early
1941, thereby increasing the suspicion and opposition toward him by other
Republicans. Immediately after Willkie's defeat by Roosevelt in November
1940, efforts were begun to strip the ex-Democrat of the mantle of titular GOP leader during the next four years. One group of party members
asked Hoover to state publicly that "as a matter of practical reality, principal Republican leadership [in] this country now resides or should reside in
Republican members of Congress where extremely slight loss compares most
favorably with [the] presidential verdict." Republicans in Congress, therefore, represented the "only Republican voice truly national in character and
possessing [a] mandate denied to both Landon and Willkie."[25] The former
president did issue a press statement on November 11, 1940, earlier cited,
commending the two-party system.[26] Although it did not take the form suggested, it was nevertheless applauded by anti-Willkie Republicans for having
made no mention of him.[27]

Privately, Hoover agreed that congressional Republicans must now bear
the responsibility for formulating GOP policies since "they have to vote on
these questions and they have to answer to their constituents for their vote."
They could still consult with GOP leaders outside of Congress, however, as
they were doing with Hoover. This was, of course, a far cry from the former president's attitude in prior years, and it no doubt derived from the fact
that GOP congressmen were now active in opposition and consulting him,
whereas earlier they had appeared complaisant or willing to let Democrats
lead any opposition. For some, inside and outside Congress, Willkie's defeat
and general discredit within the party meant that Hoover must again "point
the way" for Republicans.[28] This the former president clearly intended to do.
As part of the effort to reduce or eliminate Willkie's influence in the party,
Hoover and his followers set out to eliminate his supporters from any influence in California's Republican politics.[29]

Naturally, congressional Republicans were incensed over the fact that
they were leading the fight against Roosevelt's interventionist foreign policies, while their titular leader seemed to have gone over to the side of the
opposition.[30] In early 1941 this defection added further fuel to the movement to purge Willkieites of any influence in the party. Landon was at least
consistent in agreeing that congressional Republicans should plot the party's
future for the next four years, but to his earlier arguments was now added
the fact that it was especially necessary "with a titular leader who is not much
inclined to work with the party leadership in Congress."[31] Landon viewed the

situation as so critical that despite his reluctance to travel to Washington, he acceded to Senator Taft's request that he testify against the Lend-Lease Act before the Senate Foreign Relations Committee because, Taft told him, he was "the only Republican leader whose testimony will combat the idea that Willkie speaks for the party."[32]

The fight over the Lend-Lease Act continued through February and into March of 1941. Although he frequently considered delivering a public attack on the bill, Hoover was restrained by O'Laughlin's advice not to do so lest he further imperil his food relief objectives.[33] However, he continued to counsel GOP congressmen on ways to blunt the administration's proposal. Despite his attempts to rally them in presenting a unified front, Hoover despaired in late January that each of them seemed to be going his own way and that they did not have the cooperation of conservative Democrats over foreign policy issues that had been forged on domestic issues. Moreover, by the end of January he had begun to distract himself by working on his memoirs and, in Rickard's words, "trying to check on his varied and rapid movements."[34] By mid-February the former president confided to O'Laughlin his conclusion "that the country is losing interest in any amendments to the Lend-Lease Bill. It is unquestionably going to pass, and therefore a very large number of people have become discouraged and have given up the fight against it."[35]

Senator Taft was completely discouraged, writing to Hoover in response to the former president's suggested amendments concerning convoys that he expected to use it in the debate on the amendments: "I think it is important that some answer be made to the question that the President has unlimited authority to convoy as he pleases." He told Hoover that he thought the opponents "had made some headway in the last three or four days." Mail was "overwhelmingly opposed to the bill," so that it appeared likely the opponents would be able to attach some amendments to the bill even if they could not get a substitute bill instead.[36]

By March the former president, however, had abandoned hope that the bill could be amended. His concern, he wrote William Castle, was that "it is a war bill, yet 95 per cent of the people think it is only aid to Britain." He explained, "The bill [a] surrenders to the President the power to make war, any subsequent action by Congress will be rubber stamp work; [b] empowers the President to drive the country still further toward a national socialistic state; [c] empowers the President to become real dictator of opposition policies to the Axis. He can determine who, in what way and how much aid any nation may receive from the United States." Hoover preferred a policy that would give the British "all of our accumulated defense material which we could spare" and "an appropriation of anywhere from two to three billions [of dollars] with which to buy other things," allowing them "to spend the money directly themselves and to conduct their own war in the way that seems to them to be the wisest."

He concluded, "All that we can do is to use our energies and influence to keep down emotions and to hold the President to his promises not to spill American blood."[37]

Castle wrote Hoover that "a good many people" had told him the time had come for the former president "to make one or two nationwide radio speeches." He added, "There is a tremendous groping for the truth . . . among Congressmen and Senators just at this time." He suggested that if Hoover would "make a calmly reasoned speech which would show this country just where we are going, it might give a kind of leadership which is utterly lacking at the present time."[38]

When the bill was passed on March 11, however, it contained important amendments, including one that Hoover had sought. That amendment stated, "Nothing in this Act shall be construed to authorize or to permit the authorization of convoying vessels by naval vessels of the United States." Another amendment added, "Nothing in this Act shall be construed to authorize or to permit the authorization of any American vessel into a combat area in violation of section 3 of the Neutrality Act of 1939."[39] These amendments were small consolation for Hoover and other opponents of American involvement in the war who recognized that passage of the Lend-Lease Act had, even more clearly than the destroyer-for-bases deal, committed the United States to one side in the war. Under Roosevelt's prodding, the pattern of 1914–1917 had advanced another giant step.

Food Relief

Hoover's reticence about publicly attacking the Lend-Lease Act stemmed largely from his continuing effort to get food relief to the occupied areas of Europe. The debate over the Lend-Lease Act confronted him with the dilemmas of (1) opposing aspects of a bill that provided aid for Britain at the same time that he was seeking British cooperation in his food relief plans and (2) opposing the Roosevelt administration's bill at the same time that he was seeking assistance from the State Department in breaking down British resistance to relief. When Hoover's representatives H. Alexander Smith and William H. Tuck met with State Department officials in late January they found the department, including Secretary of State Cordell Hull, "interested and sympathetic in the maintenance of the effort, but at the same time" of the opinion "that everything should be done to have the Germans do their share of any relief work that might be decided upon." The problem, they were told, was to find "a formula which . . . would be acceptable to the British government." Smith and Tuck came away convinced that Hoover's relief efforts were "not being actively opposed by the State Department, but that on the contrary they are watching the situation with interest."[40]

In mid-February Hoover formulated a plan he felt sure could not be reasonably opposed by the British, since it seemed to meet their every objection to previous proposals. It called for the establishment of soup kitchens that would care only for the destitute and children and would "exclude all those working for Germany and all that sort of claptrap," which the British and other critics of food relief had raised as objections.[41] Meanwhile, Hoover's efforts to rally public support behind relief seemed to be showing results, as he found editorial opinion "running 7 or 8 to 1 in our favor," with only a few newspapers of any importance in opposition. Late in the month, however, he complained of "a deluge of British propaganda against us, and . . . the Administration has joined in the chorus." He now proposed to turn his fire on the Roosevelt administration once the lend-lease bill had been passed, because the "responsibility now belongs to them, as they are in a position [because of the Lend-Lease Act] to carry it through with the British."[42] By his control of the lend-lease effort, Roosevelt could, if he wished, Hoover felt, force the British to lower their blockade.

O'Laughlin, who was in close touch with Hull from his vantage point in Washington, counseled Hoover to withhold his attack on the administration, however, to avoid giving a political complexion to the relief effort. His impression was that Hull was sympathetic but that both Roosevelt and Undersecretary of State Sumner Welles were "most virulent in opposition to your [Hoover's] work and encouraging the British in their refusal to relax the blockade." O'Laughlin's advice to Hoover was for him to continue his course of "presenting the facts to the people and letting them place the responsibility where it belongs. As time goes on, and starvation increases abroad, the feeling thus aroused will force Administration action."[43] Others likewise counseled the former president "to pipe down for a while," lest he ruin "his chances to be used when the nation will need him most."[44]

Hoover laid before the American people his proposal to the British in a speech in Chicago on February 16. The plan called for (1) an initial experiment in Belgium to test whether food relief could be conducted without military benefit to either side; (2) soup kitchens "where the people come to get their food and thus there can be no question of feeding Germans"; (3) an initial feeding of one million adults and two million children with bread and soup; (4) an agreement from the German government not to requisition native food; (5) promises from both the British and Germans that relief ships would be safe from attacks; (6) supervision of the entire relief effort by some neutral body. Hoover argued that there was no possibility of military advantage to either side and no question of charity. The small democracies possessed financial reserves in the free world adequate to pay for the food, and no appropriations from the American government were needed. Nor would food relief deprive any Americans of food. The humanitarian reasons for feeding destitute Europeans were obvious enough, but Hoover restated them for his listeners. American self-interest was also involved, he argued, for Americans would have to live with the European nations after the war and needed their goodwill. He concluded by describing his own experience with famine in Europe and told his listeners, "I know starvation in the last war had a large part in the causes of the world's agony today. I had hoped it would never again come to the world. But it has come, and I would be untrue to myself and to my country if I did not fight it to the end."[45]

On February 28 Hoover traveled to Washington to meet with Hull in order to lobby in behalf of his relief plan. Much of their conversation, however, dealt with national and international affairs. Hull told Hoover he was convinced the Germans were out to conquer the world and that if England fell the Germans would first take South America into their "economic or political axis" and then attack the United States. Hoover responded with an entirely different theory, based on his discussions with Hitler and other German leaders in 1938. He viewed Germany as determined to dominate Russia if it succeeded in finishing off Britain, because Russia and the Balkan states together "possessed far greater undeveloped resources than the whole Western Hemisphere, that the Germans were a land people, a soldier people not a sea people, that Russia could be had with two Army Corps, while the Western Hemisphere would require gigantic sea equipment."[46]

Hoover regarded the meeting with Hull as "satisfactory," but if he harbored any expectations that their talk would end British resistance to food relief it was not long in being dashed.[47] A press release of March 7 from the British embassy rejected all appeals to lift the blockade of the Continent. Rickard viewed it as the worst blow yet to the relief efforts.[48] On March 10, Hoover responded with a press release of his own, reiterating that his relief plan would not impair any British war effort but would instead "uphold the ideals of democracy to the world and these little nations" and would "save the lives of multitudes of children and others." The food situation, he insisted, was worse on the Continent than the British realized.[49]

On March 25, Hoover and his relief lieutenants met to consider a letter he proposed to send to Secretary of State Hull.[50] The following day, Sir Gerald Campbell, British minister to the United States under Ambassador Lord Halifax, called on the former president to explain Britain's opposition once again. One thousand British children and women were being killed every day by German air attacks, he told Hoover, and he felt that Hoover was overlooking their interests. Hoover responded that the deaths of British children at the hands of the Germany enemy could not avenged by British complicity in the starvation of the children of Britain's allies. When Campbell criticized the propaganda of Hoover's committee as "distinctly anti-British and . . . injurious to the cause," Hoover responded that the British government had attacked him without giving him the opportunity to explain to the British people exactly what his plan entailed. When Campbell reiterated that the committee was anti-British in its propaganda, Hoover responded, "To disagree with British policies was a right even of Englishmen and certainly I had not surrendered that right by being an American."[51]

Hoover repeated these points in his letter to Hull the next day. He told the secretary of state,

> The passage of the lend lease act obviously involves us deeply in the consequences of the war. But it also gives our government a measure of responsibility to see that the policies pursued by the British are in the interest of both winning the war and winning a peace, and in the interests of the United States. The British have opened the blockade on food to southern France [via the Red Cross] and with that event 95% of all the so-called principles they have advanced for the absolute wall of food blockade to the democracies is negatived [sic]. I have considered the humanitarian question of saving millions of lives as the transcendent purpose and so long as our government had no responsibilities I felt it should be solved by private actions. But it now has other important and different aspects. In view of this changed situation I would like to present the bearings of this use of food control to aid in winning the war and the peace and in the special interest of the United States.

Hoover argued that if Germany would give the requisite guarantees, which the United States and Britain demanded, then the British should be pressed by the US government to allow the food relief in. As an extra inducement, Hoover added, "I know that it would bring to the British cause support [in America] that is now lukewarm or doubtful."[52]

When two Hoover aides visited the British embassy on March 28, however, they received the same response the former president had heard from Campbell. Under no circumstances would the British lift the blockade on food to the European continent. Rickard and the others now decided to propose to Hoover that the efforts of the relief committee be curtailed. Reluctantly, the former president decided to concentrate on educating Congress concerning the proposal while withdrawing the relief committee representatives from Europe. By the end of April, Hoover had decided to "gracefully" close down the relief efforts, while still refusing to acknowledge defeat, because he realized that relief was now a matter for governments to resolve and that private efforts were helpless in the face of British opposition and unrelenting British propaganda against relief.[53]

When a Hoover critic wrote in *The Nation* that the former president was a "stubborn helper of Hitler" and "merely an egotist who dislikes the Administration, dislikes the British, and loves to be world-important," William Henry Chamberlain was moved to respond with a letter to the editor. Chamberlain wrote that Hoover's generous impulses, as shown through years of food relief in Europe before, during, and after World War I, might be "incomprehensible to armchair strategists who have worked themselves up to the point of believing that the issue of the war depends on withholding from hungry French children shipments of oatmeal and bananas. Fortunately, the majority of the American people are not yet living in an atmosphere so divorced both from reality and from humanity."[54]

Back on the Attack

If Hoover was to abandon efforts to influence the American and British governments, however, it meant that he was now freed from the need for restraint in dealing with foreign relations questions and could resume his attack on the march of the United States toward intervention in the war. He was concerned that lend-lease, "aside from its direct purpose, will further channel the public mind into the rapids which lead inevitably to military war. The British propaganda, our natural sympathies, our indignations and fears over the Nazi regime have already conditioned thought to a readiness for that definite action." He still clung, however, to the hope that war might be avoided.[55] For Alf Landon, who had moved ever closer to Hoover's position on the international situation, statements that the lend-lease bill signified the end of an "era of isolation" was inaccurate. The Kansan recognized that the "only real period of isolation we have had" was "the period under Roosevelt, from the time we abandoned the London economic conference down to and including the signing of the neutrality act." The GOP had been labeled as isolationist in the 1920s because of its opposition to American participation in the League of Nations, but as Landon well knew, the foreign policies of Harding, Coolidge, and Hoover had, in other respects, been anything but isolationist.[56]

On March 19 Hoover's former undersecretary of state William Castle wrote to him that many had concluded it was time for him to go on the attack again with some speeches. Hoover replied that he had planned a speech for March 28 in which he was "trying to find a new approach to this problem that will ultimately cause the American people to stop, look and listen."[57]

In that speech, Hoover returned at last to the attack. The Lend-Lease Act, he pointed out, had "enormously changed the shape of things," and the United States was fast "driving into the psychosis of war." The nation now faced the same choice as in 1914–1917. Americans should confront a number of issues before making up their minds on the question of war. Was the United States determined to remake the world? Was it going to impose its will on the world by becoming a world policeman? If it did enter the war, how would it be able to restore economic prosperity to the world and to its own people with reduced resources after the war? How would it be able to "save a world ravaged by famine and pestilence?" How would it be able to restore liberty in its own land after the inevitable adoption of wartime socialism and fascism? How could a peace be made that would be any more permanent than the last one? In Hoover's view the United States ought not to spend its young men and resources in war but ought to preserve the "sanity and compassion" of a noncombatant for the peace table after the war and to maintain its resources intact so when the war ended "we may be able to contribute something to restore another and better world."[58] Privately, however, Hoover had no "expectations of stopping the American people from going to war or to stop them from making a mess out of peace. I do not know that any prophetic warning has ever had any importance in history. I am, however, going to die with my conscience alive."[59]

The former president recognized that his position was becoming increasingly unpopular as public sentiment grew for American participation in the war. He was convinced in early April that the United States would be in the war within ninety days.[60] He told Arthur Hyde that the nation was "backing into this war through a series of intellectual dishonesties. But so long as the people like to be fooled and are willing to be fooled by persons, I do not see what an isolated voice in the wilderness can do."[61]

A few days later Hoover predicted what the next six months would bring. He expected that during that period of time every American would come to want a British victory and a German defeat. The Germans would not be successful at invading England, but neither would the British air attacks on Germany break that country's morale. In the meantime, millions of men and women in the occupied European democracies would "die of starvation or become stunted in mind and body . . . —unless help is brought to them." The Germans would overrun Yugoslavia and Greece, while the British would defeat the Italians in Ethiopia and control East Africa and the Mediterranean. He predicted, correctly, that the United States would begin to convoy ships to Britain and that there would be incidents involving the sinking of American ships and the deaths of American sailors. The United States would likely send an expeditionary force to assist the British in their control of East Africa and the Mediterranean Sea. Hoover did not believe that Japan would join the war within the next six months, because he expected them to be sure that Hitler had won before they entered. "Western civilization," Hoover concluded, "has consecrated itself to making the world safe for Stalin." He despaired that "nothing can stop this landslide towards war now except a great reaction from the middle west, which has no way of expressing itself as there is no meeting at the ballot box in time."[62]

In Hoover's mind the crucial issue was convoying. If the American people voiced their opposition to convoying strenuously enough, then the incidents that might precipitate American involvement in the war could be avoided. But the American people were much more divided, confused, and uncertain in 1941 than they had been in 1917, so that the kind of unanimity of sentiment on the issue of convoying that was required probably could not be obtained. Meanwhile, defense preparations were lagging, and Hoover did not believe that the United States could hope to have adequate armed forces for one-and-a-half to four years. Still, Hoover was convinced that Hitler would not go to war with the United States unless this nation committed "an overt act or shooting [sic] his men." Thus if the United States avoided such a "shooting" situation as might occur during convoying, there remained a possibility of staying out of the war. As for the war in Europe, he concluded that it was, at best, a stalemate, and that the odds of it being broken in England's favor were not the best. England's defenses could not be improved by American entry into the war, and the cost of American intervention would be a reduced standard of living and the adoption of "totalitarian" methods to fight a war against totalitarianism. War's end would bring economic dislocations that would bring revolution to all the countries involved in the war and make them fertile grounds for the triumph of communism.[63]

On May 9 Hoover called Senator Charles Tobey's attention to a speech he was delivering on May 11 and asked Tobey to try once again to unite Senate Republicans in a "team fight" against Roosevelt's foreign policies.[64] In his speech, the former president made one of his strongest appeals yet against intervention. Recalling Roosevelt's campaign promise on October 23 not to participate in foreign wars or to send American boys to fight in foreign lands, Hoover insisted that the president's pledge could no longer be believed. Since the beginning of May the American people had been deluged with speeches and propaganda, "the meaning of which is to drive the American people into this war." Britain should be given "the maximum tools of war," but this could be done only if the United States stayed out of it. America was not prepared even for its own defense, and yet the use of American naval ships for convoy duty must inevitably lead to war. The situation, he pointed out, was very different in 1941 from what it had been in 1917. In 1917 Japan had been on the Allied side, and there had been no need for the United States to consider defense in the Pacific. Now, however, Japan was "openly allied to the Axis" powers, and if the United States entered the war it must provide for the defense of the Pacific as well. Hoover reviewed for his listeners the price he believed Americans would have to pay if it participated in the war—the sacrifice of lives and liberty and the inevitable postwar bankruptcy.[65]

Hoover's speech was hailed by opponents of American intervention. Charles Dawes issued a statement to the *Chicago Tribune* strongly endorsing Hoover's "voice of reason, of experience, of patriotism, and of statesmanship." It was, he said, "also the voice of wisdom and will be a guide to his fellow countrymen."[66] Senator Alexander Wiley praised the speech as "a polestar for an unemotional appraisal of the situation" and inserted it in the *Congressional Record*.[67] Former New Deal brain truster Raymond Moley called it "a magnificent summation of the reasons why the American people ought to put a restraining hand on their government." He told Hoover, "Whatever happens, you have made the record and it is a record with which you, your children, and your childrens' children can live in the sober years to come."[68] Robert Wood, head of the America First Committee, considered the speech "one of the very best utterances that has ever been given on the subject of our entry into the war" and added, "From all sides I hear that it had a very powerful effect." He asked Hoover to make another speech in June, as the America First Committee planned "to throw everything we have into the fight in June."[69]

In June of 1941 the German armies poured into the Soviet Union, just as Hoover had predicted to Hull that they would. The invasion furnished

Hoover and other opponents of American intervention with a powerful new rationale for the United States to remain out of the war. The Russian revolution in 1917 had transformed World War I into a war of democracies against autocracies. Now the German invasion of the Soviet Union transformed the war in Europe into one being fought primarily between two equally reprehensible totalitarian dictatorships—Nazi Germany and Communist Russia—with neither of whom the United States should make alliance. One of the first to raise this new issue was a Democrat, Senator Harry S. Truman of Missouri, who urged that the United States should back whichever side seemed to be losing: "If we see Germany is winning we ought to help Russia, and if we see Russia is winning, we ought to help Germany, and in that way, let them kill as many as possible, although I wouldn't want to see Hitler win under any circumstances. Neither of them think anything of their pledged word."[70]

Senator Robert A. Taft addressed the changed situation in a speech on June 25 in which he, too, pointed out that the war was now primarily between two totalitarian states, despite Roosevelt's attempts to paint the Soviet Union as a democracy. How, Taft asked, could the United States ally itself with the Soviet Union when "no country was more responsible for the present war and Germany's aggression than Russia itself?" It was the Russian nonaggression pact with Germany that had freed Hitler to unleash his aggression against Poland and the war with Britain and France. What's more, "Russia proved to be as much of an aggressor as Germany itself," with its invasions of Poland, Latvia, Estonia, and Finland. How could the United States, in the name of democracy, make an alliance "with the most ruthless dictator in the world?" If Germany won, it would be a victory for fascism. It Stalin won, it would be a victory for communism. If the United States would but stay out of the conflict, the German invasion of the Soviet Union could well turn out to be the solution to many of the problems of the world. Let the two totalitarian ideologies waste their energies fighting one another. Taft concluded, "The Russian war has weakened every argument for intervention."[71]

Hoover followed with a speech four days later, noting it was curious that the German invasion of Russia had intensified the "propaganda of fear or hate" designed to force the United States into the war, even as it had created less real justification for American intervention. While it was sensible for Great Britain and the Soviet Union to cooperate against their common enemy, it made "the whole argument of our joining the war to bring the four freedoms to mankind a gargantuan jest." The Soviets had demonstrated over and over that they were "one of the bloodiest tyrannies and terrors ever erected in history." They had "carried on a world conspiracy against all democracies including the United States," despite pledges to the United States at the time Roosevelt had extended them diplomatic recognition in 1933. "Is the word of Stalin any better than the word of Hitler?" Hoover asked his listeners. Stalin had joined Hitler in destroying the freedom of Poland, and then had invaded Latvia, Lithuania, Estonia, and Finland. If the

United States now joined the war on the side of the Soviet Union it would win "for Stalin the grip of communism on Russia, the enslavement of nations, and more opportunity for it to extend in the world." On the contrary, the United States should adopt a policy of "watchful waiting, armed to the teeth, while these men exhaust themselves."[72]

Hoover's prediction that Germany and the Soviet Union would "exhaust themselves" may have been buttressed by a conversation he had with Colonel Truman Smith, of Army Intelligence, just before the German invasion of Russia. According to Hoover's aide memoir of their conversation, Smith told him that "every indication is that Roosevelt intends to get into the war" and that "no member of the General Staff wants to go war but . . . they bring no great influence to bear on this situation." Smith had also dismissed any German threat to the United States and predicted that Hitler would invade the Soviet Union, whereupon the Germans and Russians "would destroy each other if left alone."[73]

Others, however, had a different view of the changed situation. The *New York Times* expressed that view in an editorial on July 1, 1941. A German victory in Russia, it pointed out, would lead Hitler to "come into possession of enormous resources, notably of oil, which would enable him to defy the British blockade." It would also raise Hitler's prestige in South America, end Russian assistance to China against Japan, and lead to Nazi-Japanese domination of Siberia, thereby exposing the United States to great dangers in the Pacific. For the *New York Times* this was the "time for action. With Hitler engaged at least temporarily in war upon two fronts we have an opportunity—never before, and perhaps never again available—to strike a blow to destroy the German war machine that constitutes the only immediate threat to our security."[74] For Landon, however, it all meant that the "only invasion this country has suffered since the war with England in 1812 is the organized propaganda invasion by Soviet Russia." And he told a CBS radio audience, "The most vicious part of this whole business is the attempted terrorization of all who dare to say that our participation in the war is still an issue."[75]

Hoover's efforts to keep the United States out of war were now consuming all his energies and attention. He wrote a friend after the June speech that he would welcome the opportunity not to have to deal with the international problem, but "as long as my voice will be heard I shall do the best with it that I can." He was convinced that Germany would make short work of Russia "and dispose of that infecting center of Communism," and once that was accomplished he expected Hitler to seek peace with the British. Meanwhile, he hoped that his speech would "help stay our hands from the trigger until these events arrive."[76]

The former president was obviously weary from his fight against intervention and his failures with the relief effort. But he recognized that his was one of the few influential voices still protesting the course the president was following, and he could not bring himself to turn from that responsibility.

Early in June he replied to an invitation to go on a welcome fishing trip to Canada that he doubted he would be able to make: "I am trying to fry a great number of fish—among them to keep this country from going into the war. I do not want to get away very far from the center of things so that I may use what little influence I have in that direction. If this country does get into war I would go out and fish for the balance of the war. But as long as there is the remotest possibility that we will stay out of it, I feel I must do what I can."[77] The former president's opposition to war had made him persona non grata in some social circles. He wrote a friend in late August, "I am sorry that I cannot approach Mr. John D. Rockefeller. He has cut me off his social list completely and violently because I do not want to go to war."[78]

Although Hoover's efforts to get food relief to the occupied democracies had attracted further support, it was not enough to break down the Roosevelt administration's opposition to relief. Gradually the work of the National Committee on Food for the Small Democracies was liquidated as a result of inaction and lack of funds. Early in June Hoover told Ben Allen that "we have to make a slaughter in this organization because we haven't the money to go on."[79] About the same time Hoover directed an angry letter to Secretary of State Hull:

> Not only am I deeply shocked at the present attitude of our government, but I know tens of millions of Americans would also be shocked. History will never justify the government of the United States siding with the starvation of these millions. What you have said, in effect, is that the American government accepts the view of Britain in this matter; that you will not even attempt to moderate these policies so as to save the lives of literally millions of women and children in these small democracies. Yet these countries have sacrificed their all for Britain and the cause against aggression which you properly state is also an American cause . . . We now apparently abandon these peoples to their fate and that without consideration of the sacrifice they have made against aggression or the importance of preserving among them confidence in the ideals of democracy itself. The fundamental question to be answered by our government is not whether the Germans are primarily responsible or the British blockade is responsible, but whether our government refuses to secure from these governments the remedy which it has the duty to urge and thus avert disaster from these peoples and their millions of children.[80]

Hull, however, viewed the situation through fundamentally different lenses from those of the former president. The responsibility for supplying food rested with the German occupiers, and in the case of Europe the Germans had removed vast quantities of foodstuffs for the use of those working in behalf of the German war effort. This was the cause of any shortage of food in the occupied countries, Hull argued, and Hoover's proposals would only "replace the stocks removed by the occupying authorities," an action that would naturally be welcomed by the Germans since it would also "release labor now required for food production to be used in furtherance of the German military effort."

The fundamental problem, Hull insisted, was the "overthrow of Hitlerism unless all Europe is soon to starve. It is this broader and more basic viewpoint that many of us visualize."[81] In this way, Hoover's emphasis on eliminating hunger was cleverly twisted into an argument for American intervention in the war—to hasten the defeat of Germany and thereby end hunger in the occupied countries.

Late in May a journalist suggested to Alf Landon that in order to counter the united front that had been formed in support of Roosevelt's interventionist policies, a counterpart united front should be formed in opposition to them. He suggested that Hoover, Landon, and former vice president Charles Dawes go on the radio from different parts of the country and during the same half hour of radio time attack FDR's foreign policies.[82] At the same time, Landon was being asked by Frank Knox, his running mate in 1936 and now one of FDR's in-house Republicans, to come out in support of Roosevelt's foreign policies. Knox argued that Landon could contribute greatly to much-needed national unity.[83] Landon agreed on the need for unity but blamed the lack thereof on the president.[84] Instead of pursuing the proposed joint radio address, Landon suggested to Moley that he and Hoover issue a joint statement to accomplish the same purpose. Moley passed the suggestion on to Hoover, and the former president agreed. Hoover suggested that Moley organize the statement, and he offered to try to recruit Dawes, University of Chicago president Robert Hutchins, and Ambassador Joseph Kennedy to participate in the statement, as well as others of "that caliber."[85]

At Hoover's request, Robert Hutchins quickly prepared a draft statement that contained most of the points Hoover had raised in his speeches, including the changed nature of the European conflict since Germany's invasion of the Soviet Union, which had left "little to choose between the domination of Europe by a Nazi dictatorship and its domination by a communistic dictatorship." Hutchins's draft statement placed the signers on the side of continued aid to China and Great Britain but argued that "American lives should be sacrificed only for American independence." American energies should be "devoted to preparing the defense of this hemisphere," and the president should "abstain from further war-like and provocative deeds, and . . . recognize that the country wants to aid Britain and China, defend itself—and stay out of war."[86]

Suggestions were incorporated as the statement circulated among potential signers, and various possibilities were considered for the role of organizer of the movement and issuer of the statement. Felix Morley, former editor of the *Washington Post*, and then president of Haverford College, was finally chosen.[87] The month of July was consumed with revising the draft, getting the views and consent of other influential figures, and settling on the mechanics for bringing the statement out. Late in the month, Morley pleaded the press of his other responsibilities and bowed out as organizer, so that the search began anew for his replacement.[88] Meanwhile the signers were also seeking unsuccessfully to attract leading Democrats to participate. Joseph Kennedy, an obvious choice, demurred, pleading that he preferred "to go my way alone," and no other prominent Democrat would participate if Kennedy did not, although CIO leader John L. Lewis did join in signing the statement.[89] The decision was made late in July to have the statement issued by Frank O. Lowden, one of the signers.[90]

The final draft of the statement was printed in the *New York Times* on August 6, 1941. It called for the American people to demand of Congress that it "put a stop to step-by-step projection of the United States into undeclared war." It called attention to the military initiatives taken by the Roosevelt administration without the sanction of Congress, which undermined the constitutional powers of the legislative branch. The European war was a matter of power politics, and "the American people want no part of it." The statement included all Hoover's recurring themes, including the argument that since the German invasion of Russia the war had ceased to be one between freedom and tyranny. The "appeal of the fifteen" was issued over the signatures of Hoover, Landon, Lowden, Dawes, and Lewis, as well as those of academicians Ray Lyman Wilbur (of Stanford), Felix Morley, and Robert Hutchins; opera singer Geraldine Farrar; writers Irvin S. Cobb and Clarence B. Kelland; former diplomats Reuben Clark and Henry Fletcher; and others.[91]

The response to Hoover's June 29 speech on the invasion of the Soviet Union by Germany was encouraging. Arch Shaw reported an "avalanche of enthusiastic comments" and a "flood of requests for copies." W. K. Kellogg contributed $5,000 to underwrite distribution costs and there were suggestions that five million copies of the speech be distributed.[92] The former president concluded that the speech had attracted a greater response than any other he had delivered since leaving the White House.[93] Senator Taft praised it as "a magnificent speech" and told Hoover he had "heard nothing but praise for it."[94] Rickard reported that Hoover's mail indicated his speech had changed many minds against intervention in the war.[95] Hoover now proposed, he told columnist Boake Carter, to "go on making nasty remarks until Congress finally declares war—even though it may only be a confirmation of a declaration of war."[96] But the former president also thought his speeches "had better not be too frequent and must be properly timed." He wrote one congressman, "You will remember that when we used to boil maple syrup as youngsters and the syrup reached the point at which it was about to crystallize, it would begin to sputter. The old New England custom was to pour a few drops of cold water and it would calm down. If I can be of that kind of service, I will have reached the only point of usefulness that I care about."[97]

Meanwhile, the former president continued to maintain close contact with Republicans in Congress. When FDR announced the stationing of US troops in Iceland in July, Hoover wrote Senator Taft that he was "wondering if it is not time for the Republicans to take up the question of limiting all appropriations for military operations to use entirely within the Western Hemisphere," and he told Congressman J. William Ditter that if House would do the same thing "it might be helpful." By this and other devices, he thought Congress might be able to "stop any further steps towards getting into this war."[98] Taft responded that he would "talk with some of the other Republicans to see whether we can hope to put a rider on the military appropriations bills to confine their use to the Western hemisphere."[99] Congressman Roy Woodruff, chairman of the House Republicans wrote Hoover, "Always the next few days following one of your address, we discuss them with interest, approval and enthusiasm, and I am sure I speak the mind of all our group when I express the wish that we may see something of you in the months and years to come." He was, he wrote, "greatly impressed . . . by the fact that your speeches are always timely; they seem to come to us at a time when they are most effective."[100]

While Republicans in Congress maintained a fair degree of unity in opposition to Roosevelt's foreign policies, the Republican Party in general was being torn apart by the division between interventionists and noninterventionists. Unfortunately for the latter, many large financial backers of the party were from the eastern interventionist wing of Republicanism. While they supported the position of Willkie and his followers, they were not eager to contribute to the fortunes of a party that would not follow its titular leader. The sad condition in which this left the party's finances was revealed by Franklyn Waltman, director of publicity for the GOP national committee, when he wrote Alf Landon in late July,

> There is a great deal of bitterness within the party against Wendell Willkie, and, on the other hand, he has some very militant supporters within the party. The national headquarters has not been at so low an ebb as it is now since the dark days after the Hoover defeat of 1932. The greatest difficulty apparently is being experienced in obtaining funds and, were it not for the fact that we came out of the last campaign with a surplus on which we have chiefly been living this year, I do not know where we would be. As it is, the staff has been reduced to skeleton proportions.

Republicans continued to be divided over Willkie's proper role in the GOP. Some continued to feel that Willkie and his supporters should be "read out of the party" he had so recently joined and that the Republican Party should unify as the party opposed to intervention in the war.[101] Others, however, argued that the salvation of the party lay in strengthening the Willkie wing and in following his leadership.[102] When Willkie paid a call on Hoover in late July at the Bohemian Grove encampment, Hoover gave him what Rickard described as "a very cold reception" and refused to discuss national affairs with him.[103]

connection have all been highly effective, and we can always feel the impact of them here in Washington by a revival of anti-war expressions from the people back home."[116] Hoover had just published three articles in the *Saturday Evening Post*, however, and he wanted to delay any further speechmaking until the articles "had settled into the American consciousness." He wanted "to do everything that can be done," he told Mundt. "Even if we can only delay the final collapse, we still have a chance for something to happen that might save us."[117] He was equally pessimistic in writing to Vandenberg: "All of our protests may be futile but the day will come when there will be retribution in the United States. It is vital for the future that men like yourself have stood steadfast."[118] Vandenberg wrote that he was experiencing "a great depression as I sit in my front seat at the greatest tragedy in history."[119]

Hoover's articles for the *Saturday Evening Post* did not address the world situation in 1941, except by implication. Titled "The First American Crusade," they dealt with the United States and World War I as viewed from Hoover's perspective as a member of President Woodrow Wilson's "war cabinet" and as an observer of the deliberations at the peace conference. His intention was clearly to dissuade the American people from embarking on a second "crusade" in 1941 by recalling the disparity between American ideals and European realities. As he wrote the editor of the *Post*, "the value of the articles is to set out the experiences of America with just such proposals as the present Four Freedoms and the Churchill-Roosevelt declaration."[120] Americans had rapidly become disillusioned and cynical after the idealism of the war years, and the former president obviously hoped to rekindle those emotions by reminding them of their recent past.

In the articles, Hoover pointed out that the United States was "the only nation since the crusades that had fought the battles of other peoples at her own gigantic loss." In the final installment, which appeared in the November 15 issue, he sought to demonstrate the futility of yet another such "crusade." America's ideals, he argued, had grown away from those of Europe during the 300 years of separation, and Americans were unaware of the "gigantic explosive forces" that existed in Europe as a result of 400 million people, of 26 different races, living in an area two-thirds the size of the United States and burdened with "age-old hatreds" and "economic and religious conflicts." In addition, there were growing populations, rebellious minorities, and other fears, all of which Hoover described as "the perpetual stimuli of war." America had proved during World War I that she had "the courage and genius to make war, and make it magnificently," and one system of militarism and despotism had been destroyed. But America had failed in trying to secure from European leaders after the war "the adoption of concepts of justice or that far-seeing statesmanship which replaces conflict with co-operation among nations." President Wilson had tried to do so but had failed. The United States had often been accused of "running out on Europe" for its failure to ratify the peace treaty and join the League of Nations, but the fact was that the

Europeans had earlier "run out" on America by refusing to make a just peace based on Wilson's Fourteen Points.[121]

By late October the battle in Congress was over outright repeal of the Neutrality Act, which would represent another giant step toward participation in the war. Mundt told Hoover that Republicans in Congress would "need all of the support we can get" in opposing repeal. He added, "Willkie's indefensible attempt to inject partisanship into the issue has put just one more hurdle in our way. But I am glad to report that his influence among the members of Congress is very, very insignificant. However, his repeated statements do stimulate some of the wealthy Republicans throughout the country to write in expressing support for his position. I am glad to say, though, that the great speeches which you and Mr. Landon have been giving more than offset the Willkie effort." He asked the former president to speak over the radio again "some time the first week in November, so that the full effect of it would be registered in the House before the fatal vote is cast on our side of the Capitol."[122]

When Julius Klein visited Hoover in early November, he found him pessimistic about the prospect of avoiding American intervention in the war. Hoover "took a most ominous view of the world situation, pointing out that even as we talked war in the Pacific was a possibility within three days." He thought that the American naval attacks on German submarines in the Atlantic might be used by Hitler to pressure Japan, under the terms of their alliance, "into open warfare against the United States and Russia." Hoover told Klein, "Whether the break comes now, next week, or next month, we must face the inexorable fact that war is inevitable." He still believed that Hitler could be beaten without the assistance of the United States, but it was obvious that Roosevelt would take America into the war. Asked what his role would be once war was declared, Hoover affirmed that he would support President Roosevelt and would do everything he could do to help. However, he was confident that Roosevelt would not ask anything of him, since the people around the president hated Hoover personally. Klein wrote after their meeting,

> In his mature wisdom he has come to the regretted conclusion that war cannot be averted. He is thinking how that war can be won; how can the American standard of living be preserved; how can a peace be established that will really outlaw war in the future. He feels that immediate attention must be given now to that peace; that even now some special groups should be considering the problems that must be faced in the final settlement that the next generation shall not face a world such as we do today.[123]

On October 9, 1941, Roosevelt requested of Congress that it revise the 1939 Neutrality Act to permit the arming of US merchant ships, although this was only the opening wedge for requesting a good deal more. Further incidents involving the sinking of American ships by German submarines during the month led to pressures for additional changes in the act, and later in the month the abolition of combat zones was added to the proposed changes. By convoying ships in direct violation of congressional restrictions imposed in the Lend-Lease Act, Roosevelt himself had created the situation in which Americans and Germans were killing one another in the North Atlantic, and now he sought to exploit the situation created by his illegal acts in order to draw the United States further into the war.

In letters to members of the Senate in November, Hoover rallied opposition to the revisions. To Senator Wallace Whyte Jr. he wrote that he had not favored the Neutrality Act when it was before Congress, because he had "felt certain it would lead to difficulties." But now,

> be that as it may, the whole thing has taken an entirely new aspect today. The only practical purpose of repeal would now be to carry supplies to the British in American flag ships. The validity of this vanishes entirely under the lend lease law which authorizes the handing over of ships to the British to be operated under their flag. The British have plenty of crews or they can obtain plenty of foreign crews to supply any number of ships. The intentions of the Congress in the neutrality act, as you know, have been deliberately evaded and flouted by Panama register. Whether this was done to make sure that incidents would occur, I don't know. Obviously these Panama register ships were put to carrying contraband and they met the fate which comes to contraband ships in war . . . Repeal now amounts to ratification of this attempt to defeat congressional will and this use of these incidents. The repeal of the act, however, moves us into even higher dimensions. That act by the Congress will be claimed as a species of constitutional authority to take further steps toward war. The inevitable consequence of sending the American flag ships to Britain will be innumerable incidents of sinking of these ships with American crews. They will furnish further fuel for the fire. The clamor for an expeditionary force is the next step we have to face . . . The actual importance of each step taken has small importance compared with the direction in which we are being taken. The ultimate of that road is an expeditionary force unless Congress puts the brakes on now. And it means all out war by a mere Congressional rubber stamp of executive action. It seems to me that it is the last chance of Congress to hold its real position.[124]

But the Democrat-controlled Congress abdicated its control over war making to Roosevelt once more. The revision was passed on November 13 and became law four days later.

A few days after the vote, Hoover spoke over the radio. As he did so, it appeared that his earlier prediction of a German victory over the Soviet Union was in store, but he argued that even such an eventuality did not pose dangers for the United States. It also proved the folly of believing that the United States could defeat Germany in a land war thousands of miles away, when the Soviet Union, with its "10 million men, 20 thousand tanks, 20 thousand planes, fighting on her own soil behind her own fortifications" could not do so. Moreover, his conquest of the Soviet Union would mean Hitler must now contend with 100 million potentially rebellious subjects to add to the 230 million he already ruled in Europe. Their potential for trouble, he suggested, would be the strongest deterrent against his dreams of further conquest. Meanwhile, there was nowhere in Hoover's speech a hint of sympathy for the plight of the Russians and no identification of the United States with the Soviet Union as a common enemy of fascism. On the contrary, in Hoover's view communism continued to be identified with its enemies as an enemy of the United States. As Hoover put it, "we want the end of these evil and brutal ideas of Nazism, Fascism and Communism." He asked for assurances from Roosevelt that there would be no American forces sent overseas without the approval of Congress, and he also called for planning to begin immediately for the peace conference that would follow the war. It was Hoover's last speech before Pearl Harbor.[125]

Although the former president's speeches on the issue of war or peace had been devoted to the problems posed by Roosevelt's policies in the Atlantic, at least as early as February 1938 he had begun to be concerned that the White House was seeking to involve the United States in a conflict with Japan.[126] When the Roosevelt administration gave the required notice of abrogation of the US-Japan Treaty of Commerce in mid-1939, it left Hoover with "a foreboding that we have taken on a situation from which sooner or later we will see outrages upon American citizens and other incidents which will inflame the country and draw us into war in the east." If it was the president's desire to cause a war with Japan, Hoover was certain that the abrogation of the treaty was "one step on the road."[127] He expressed similar concern once economic sanctions began to be applied to Japan.[128] By July 1941 William Castle, the undersecretary of state in his administration, had concluded, "Certainly Roosevelt is doing everything he can to make Japan attack us—and the Japanese don't want to."[129] Hoover did not sympathize with Japan's occupation of French Indo-China, and he supported Roosevelt's response, but he also felt that the president's "continuous sticking of vocal pins in this tiger" had contributed to Japan's action and made a solution to the problem more difficult. Still, he hoped that a modus vivendi might be reached with the Japanese.[130]

Meanwhile, Hoover's counsel was also being sought by Congress concerning possible domestic economic policies during wartime. On August 3, Hoover responded to a query from Senator Taft by writing that the Roosevelt administration's proposal to apply price controls would be "perfectly futile," as proved by the experiences of other countries during World War I. On the contrary, he wrote Taft,

> in the passage of our own law in 1917 we rested on four theories. The first was voluntary agreements which were applied to the great major commodities where there were comparatively few manufacturers . . . The second one, which we applied so largely in the Food Administration, was the control of margins on manufacturers, wholesalers and retailers. By this device we prevented any considerable profiteering and held prices astonishingly stable . . . The third

method was to prevent hoarding and withholding and thereby maintain an even flow of commodities. The fourth device used was in those cases where we bought and sold for the Government, such as wheat, sugar and meat products, where we were purchasers of such large quantities for export we could dominate the market.

The Roosevelt administration's bill, by contrast, put the emphasis on "the fixing of prices at the final outlet," an approach that would "fill the country with bootleggers and . . . commodities at the fixed prices will rapidly disappear." However, he told Taft that he didn't "know whether it is worth bothering much about. Nothing will teach these people anything. Perhaps the best thing is to let the worst happen and then the people will do something about getting rid of the lot" of them.[131]

Three months before the Japanese attack on Pearl Harbor, Hoover was convinced that Roosevelt was doing everything he could to "get us into war through the Japanese back door."[132] He was certain, however, that the Japanese would prefer to await the unfolding of developments in Europe before they entered[133] the war, unless they felt forced by Roosevelt to do so earlier.[133] This was the danger. Three weeks before Pearl Harbor, Hoover wrote O'Laughlin, "There is no sense in having a war with Japan. But I am afraid that our people [the Roosevelt administration] are so anxious to get into the war somewhere that they will project it. They know there will be less public resistance to this [war with Japan] than to expeditionary forces to Europe."[134]

In late November Chester Bowles suggested to Hoover that he draw up a peace proposal as a basis for negotiations between the Allies and Axis. "The Interventionists," he wrote, "have actually done everything in their power to confuse the issues. As a result many Americans in a hazy sort of way believe that our only choice lies between a Nazi dominated world if Germany wins, and a return to the old European boundaries if Germany is beaten." Hoover, Bowles said, had "laid the groundwork for such a proposal in your speech a week or two ago in which you suggested that the war had reached a stalemate and that we must, at any cost, resist all pressure to send an Expeditionary Force in an attempt to break the stalemate." Bowles suggested that Hoover deliver a speech "sometime between now and Christmas briefly reviewing the present world situation and offering a tentative outline of terms on which peace might be discussed."[135] Hoover, however, felt "that the time has not yet come when such a presentation would be of use. It may come before the winter is over."[136] In fact, it would not come at all.

Hoover later compiled a diary of the final days before Pearl Harbor in which he described his involvement in one final attempt to avert the break between the United States and Japan. According to the diary, Raoul Desvernine, a prominent New York attorney and businessman who had served on the executive committee of the Liberty League, phoned Hoover on November

23 to acquaint him with the dangerous state of the talks between the United States and Japan. Desvernine had been present at interviews that the Japanese negotiators, Ambassador Nomura and Admiral Kurusu, had with Roosevelt and Hull. According to Hoover's diary,

> [Desvernine] insisted that the Ambassador and Kurusu, the newly arrived special Ambassador, were personally absolutely genuine in seeking a solution; that they represented the naval and civilian elements; that these elements strenuously wished to avoid war; that they realized the future of Japan lay in cooperation with the great naval powers; that they had a most difficult corner to turn and save national face and dignity; that their thesis was that urgent action should be taken at once to ease the situation; that Hull was driving absolutely to war; that Roosevelt was apparently hanging back.

When Desvernine asked if Hoover had any suggestions, the former president suggested to him, according to his diary,

> that he find out if the Japanese would agree to a six-months' standstill agreement on all military action, they to have civilian supplies through the sanctions, a Five-Power Conference to be called at Honolulu or somewhere for the purpose of finding a formula for peace in the Pacific. The Powers to be represented being the United States, the Netherlands, Britain, Japan and Chiang-Kai-Shek's [sic] Government to represent China. I stated this was the test of their good faith. If they would agree to this, then the thing to do was for him or friends to see Roosevelt and suggest to Roosevelt that he propose it and take the glory. Also that his negotiation had to be gotten into Roosevelt's hands and out of the State Department.[137]

Three days later, on November 26, Hull handed the Japanese emissaries what they regarded as an ultimatum. Desvernine was convinced that the ultimatum "undoubtedly meant war, as it left no way out for the Japanese to save their face." Again he asked Hoover for advice, and again Hoover told him to get in touch with Roosevelt at once, to ask him "to take the reins." Roosevelt was then vacationing at Warm Springs, Georgia.[138] At Hoover's suggestion, Desvernine sought an opening to the president through Bernard Baruch and met with him on December 1, a Monday. Baruch consented to meet with Desvernine and Kurusu that afternoon, but told Desvernine he "could not go to the President without the detailed proposals reduced to a memorandum and that he could not purport to state the Japanese proposals on his own authority." Desvernine and the two Japanese envoys thereupon worked until 1 a.m. the next day preparing the memorandum, which, according to Desvernine's recollection of it, proposed (1) a gradual withdrawal of Japanese troops from China under the supervision of a joint US-Japanese commission, with the Japanese to retain three or four garrisons in China in locations and sizes to be agreed upon with the United States; (2) agreement to a memorandum with the United States on an interpretation of the Tripartite Pact among Japan, Germany, and Italy

---

that "would make it impossible for any war between the United States and Japan to arise from that Treaty"; (3) settlement by negotiation of the trade situation and the embargoes against Japan; (4) an international conference to be held at some neutral place, mutually agreed upon, pending which there would be "an economic and military standstill agreement"; (5) "that pending the solutions of this Conference, there should be a relaxation of the embargo in respect to non-military commodities to be imported in normal quantities."[139]

Desvernine gave Baruch the memorandum, one copy of which had been initialed by Kurusu, and that evening Baruch's secretary phoned Desvernine that an appointment would be arranged for the Japanese to see the president. On Wednesday, December 3, Baruch phoned Desvernine that the president had seen the memorandum and wanted to talk to Desvernine alone. Desvernine met with Roosevelt the next day and was told by the president that the memorandum indicated the basis for a solution. That afternoon Kurusu and Nomura met with the president, and the next day—December 5—Roosevelt met with the two Japanese again. According to Hoover's diary,

> Desvernine talked with Nomura and Kurusu after their meeting with Roosevelt and Desvernine believed that the memorandum had solved the entire situation. Some collateral questions arose in those discussions, one of them was whether the Japanese would negotiate with Chiang-Kai-Shek [sic], Roosevelt using the expression: "Perhaps he might 'introduce them to Chiang-Kai-Shek [sic]'" to which Kurusu replied that "No one could refuse to meet and discuss matters after an introduction by the President of the United States." All seemed settled, and the next day Desvernine came to New York.[140]

Desvernine returned to New York on December 6. The next day, Japanese carrier-based aircraft attacked American naval and military installations in Hawaii and elsewhere in the Pacific. If Hoover's diary is correct, he had suggested the basis on which conversations might, at least, have gone on, had the Japanese not already felt forced to make their fateful attack against the United States because of Hull's ultimatum. Emphasis must be placed on the *might*, however, since it cannot be known whether at this late point Kurusu and Nomura accurately reflected the temper of their government in Tokyo. In any case, the effort was too late, and the United States was at war. Herbert Hoover had labored mightily to prevent American entry into the war, but the dropping of the first Japanese bomb at Pearl Harbor on December 7, 1941, exploded his efforts.

Nearly forty years later, Robert Sherrill, Washington editor of the liberal journal *The Nation*, wrote,

> All admirers of Roosevelt, and even many of his critics, will contend that how or why he manipulated us into World War II really doesn't matter because it was inevitable that we would eventually get in, and the sooner the better, for the cause was just and the results noble. It is time we begin seriously to question

that old argument. Far from being noble, the results of World War II, like the effluence of Love Canal, have poisoned our earth seemingly forever. Most of the negative forces that make our national life so unhappy and irrational—the military-industrial waste, the impenetrable federal budget, the "national security" hysteria that is supposed to excuse FBI excesses, the covert insanity of the CIA, the incredibly unwieldy federal bureaucracy, the flatulent patriotism of our educators—became permanent fixtures with World War II.[141]

CHAPTER 7

███████████████████████████████

The War Years

On the Defensive

It was difficult for anti-interventionists like Hoover to maintain a public presence after Japan's attack on Pearl Harbor. It did not matter that their predictions concerning the consequences of Roosevelt's foreign policies had proven correct; the mood in the nation was intolerant, and those who had argued all along that the Axis powers were the enemies of the United States now felt they had a monopoly on patriotism. Some anti-interventionists sought to escape the smears by retreating from public life. Hoover had by now become so accustomed to smears that they had little effect on him, and the former president busied himself with planning for the peace that would follow the war, determined that the errors of the Versailles peace conference that followed World War I should not be repeated. Hoover's efforts would influence the mechanics of peacemaking after World War II and also contribute to the willingness of the GOP to accept an American role in postwar international cooperation such as he had sought, and the party had rejected, after World War I. As an experienced participant in the mobilization for World War I, the former president also found himself consulted frequently by officials in the Roosevelt administration and also by congressional Republicans seeking advice on legislation.

The attack on Pearl Harbor caught the Hoovers at lunch with the John Hamiltons in Pennsylvania. Unaware of the attack, Hoover was met by reporters with the news when he returned to the Waldorf Astoria.[1] He was quick to express his support for President Roosevelt in confronting the war. Privately, however, he continued to feel that Roosevelt's policies had provoked the attack and that if the United States had not indulged in "this constant sticking of pins in rattlesnakes, the Japanese would have totally collapsed without loss of a single American life."[2] He told his former undersecretary of state William

Castle that it was "of vast importance" that an account of the process by which this tragedy had been brought upon America should be written and he asked him to "preserve every record and every recollection that bears on the whole question and get as much documentary support for it as you can."[3] Hoover hoped initially that the war might be confined to Japan, but this soon proved chimerical as the Germans and Italians honored their alliance with their Asian ally by declaring war on the United States.[4]

While he told the press that America had been "treacherously attacked by Japan" and that the United States "must fight with everything we have" in the war thus forced upon her, Hoover still could not resist pointing out that he had opposed Roosevelt's foreign policies in the belief that other approaches might have avoided the situation in which the nation now found itself. Still, it was time, he said, to put such differences aside and to unite in full support of the president to ensure victory.[5] Privately, however, Hoover was certain that history would eventually vindicate the position of the anti-interventionists.[6]

Wartime meant the imposition of economic controls, and as former US Food Administrator during World War I, Hoover quickly found his advice sought by congressional Republicans and others as they dealt with administration initiatives in that area.[7] Senator Robert Taft's position on the Senate Finance Committee meant that he was intimately involved in such questions when they reached that body. Hoover counseled Taft that any legislation concerning food control should be based on two principles: (1) that a single person should be appointed to supervise all "food production, distribution, rationing, price control, government purchases and foreign relief" and (2) that the agency administering food "should be based primarily upon cooperation with the people and the trades" involved.[8] Landon wrote Hoover that his testimony "was very timely, and in the best spirit of patriotism."[9]

As criticism of the mobilization effort mounted, Roosevelt appointed the War Production Board as the major agency for that purpose. Hoover was not impressed, writing, "These members were the heads of government agencies, each reporting and taking independent direction from the President. They will exactly continue to do so. It will probably work worse than even before. Especially as [Donald] Nelson is not a strong man. He has become a thorough New Dealer and is a victory for the New Order which is to further make the country over with war as its instrument."[10] In February the chief of the sugar section, food supply branch, of the War Production Board, wrote Hoover for advice "as to the activities of the various phases of your Food Administration program" during World War I.[11] Hoover responded that household conservation could be organized "through cooperation with householders and grocers," thus avoiding the necessity for "ration tickets with their enormous staff requirements."[12]

When Congressman Joe Martin, sounding very much Hoover, wanted to make the Lincoln Day celebration in Washington "a great patriotic meeting," with "politics out of the picture as much as possible," Alf Landon expressed one of his rare disagreements with the congressman. On the contrary, he wrote, the meeting should "proclaim the necessity of politics; that we can't abandon our form of Republican processes; that politics is as essential in war as it is in peace," but of course only "highminded patriotic politics." He approved of Martin's tactics, however, in "letting the Democrats and administration supporters like the New Republic take the lead in pounding the delinquencies and inefficiencies and confusion of the administration's handling of our war efforts. There is a great question in the minds of everyone whether we are getting the job done or not." And all the while that the Democrats were "whooping it up" that "people should forget politics," the Roosevelt administration was "carrying on vigorous political activities through the AAA, the NYA, the WPA, FSA, etc."[13] Landon was to be the featured speaker at the dinner in Washington.

Hoover was certain that any contribution he might make to the war effort would be limited to responding to requests for advice from GOP congressmen. The Roosevelt administration clearly had its "enemies" list, with Hoover at the top, and it was unlikely that the president would call upon those "whom they deem as outside the New Deal aura, except for a few minor lights from the business world who can be picked up and shoved around." Though he accepted this as fact, Hoover was nevertheless disturbed by it, since he felt it would inevitably "lead to stupendous mistakes and ultimate demoralization."[14] Nevertheless, the animosity of the White House was apparently not shared by congressional Democrats, for after Hoover testified before the Senate Finance Committee on the price control bill, Taft wrote him that even Democrats like Senators Barkley and Glass were quoting his testimony. They had not necessarily understood what Hoover was saying, Taft observed, but "they all accepted you as an authority on the subject." Hoover's visit to the Senate had "left a very fine personal feeling among all the Senators, Republican and Democratic, with whom you came in contact."[15]

The timing of the Pearl Harbor attack utterly disrupted the meaning and impact of Hoover's latest book-publishing effort. His articles for the *Saturday Evening Post* on the tragic results of peacemaking after World War I were scheduled for publication in book form as *The Halls of Peacemaking*, which was subsequently changed to *America's First Crusade*.[16] Unfortunately, the book was not ready for release until after Pearl Harbor, by which time what appeared to be a sound warning against American entry into the war no longer seemed appropriate to some at a time when the United States was fighting for its survival. Because he was aware of the hostility that his book could expect from reviewers for the New York newspapers, Hoover tried to keep it from being sent to them for review.[17] He wrote the publisher, "I have no doubt as to the scolding that will come to this book in view of the event of December 7."[18] When the expected "scolding" did occur, the former president described it as "a fine exhibit of how far free speech can get intimidated or destroyed by an intolerance of war psychosis." The book still had value, he pointed out, in showing the mistakes of one peacemaking attempt that ought to be avoided after the present war. He wrote, "These reviewers' attitudes are the attitudes of men afraid to face that problem and fearful that the American people would be corrupted by discussion of it until victory—when, God knows, it will be too late to prepare."[19] To get even for their opposition, he decided to get the book "as wide a distribution as possible."[20]

It soon became apparent, however, that the publisher harbored the same doubts about the timing of the book, largely as a result of "certain financial and social interests in New York who were pushing our going into war to the aid of England before Pearl Harbor." A book that was supposed to be published in October had, it turned out, been deliberately delayed "on one pretext or another,—which were later found to be all fictitious." When it was discovered that "practically none of the bookstores had it, it was discovered that Scribner's had not put it on their own advertising lists, nor in the principal publishers' general list," an "omission" that could "only be made deliberately from the publisher's office."[21]

Raymond Moley agreed with Hoover's comments about what Moley described as "book reviewers who seem to be arrogating to themselves the function of statesmen in that they attempt to decide when a book should be published and what the motives are in writing it," as especially manifested by reviewers for the *New York Times* and *Herald Tribune*. He expected to "pay my respects" to such reviewers in a piece he was writing on the book for the *Wall Street Journal* and the *Chicago Journal of Commerce*, because he thought what Hoover had "said needed to be said and now."[22]

William Barrett's review of the book for the *Boston Post* was, however, a sympathetic one that ended with some pertinent comments on the former president. He wrote,

> History will deal kindly, too, with Herbert Hoover. The most misunderstood man of his generation, he has become more warm and human in the public consciousness since he left the White House. A people walking the hard road of another crusade will learn slowly and write it for History to read that in offering them only a weary climb from the depths of the depression, Herbert Hoover shared with them the only reality. All else was delusion and when the mirage lifted, the same hard climb was still there and yet to be walked.[23]

Reading the book brought back to Robert Taft memories of "those days in Paris and the complete shamelessness with which the Allies went after our money." He hoped "the significance of the title and the working out of our idealism may sink in on the American people before we finally have to send ten million men to Europe."[24] Hoover found it interesting that, although the "left-wingers" were "making dive bombs" on his book, they were simultaneously praising a New York play, *In Time to Come*, which he described as "a dramatizing of this book or Ray Standard [sic] Baker's more violent *Life of Wilson*—I don't know which."[25]

Late in January Hoover wrote a friend that the "left-wingers all over the country have put on a drive against that little book because it is somewhat of an answer to Union Now and other nonsensical schemes. They have so frightened Scribner's, that these publishers have apparently done little to distribute the book." And the *New York Times* was "making another assault on it next Sunday!" It was all, he observed, "simply a demonstration of war psychosis."[26] To another friend he wrote that the bad reviews of the book were "book burning of the Hitler type."[27]

Collections of Hoover's major speeches and articles had been published under the title *Addresses upon the American Road* and were being financed by cereal magnate W. K. Kellogg. One of these volumes, too, was released soon after Pearl Harbor, causing some consternation for Hoover over what to do about its distribution since it contained his speeches opposing FDR's interventionist policies and actions. He wrote Kellogg that to "distribute it generally at present might create the impression of continuing division at a time when we need to submerge our views to the immediate necessity." He had, therefore, sent it to some three thousand reference libraries but had not released it to the press or to the public.[28]

Planning for Peace

Having examined the errors of peacemaking in 1919, Hoover now turned his attention to ensuring that the next peace would be made on a planned and rational basis. Even before Pearl Harbor, some of his 1941 speeches had called for consideration of the peace to be made at the end of the war. As noted earlier, Chester Bowles had encouraged Hoover as early as September 1941 to devote a speech "to the kind of world organization toward which we should all work after the war and perhaps, more definitely, how the war could best be brought to a close."[29] Shortly before Pearl Harbor Bowles wrote again, "Like yourself I am ardently opposed to our participation in the war. I am a member of the National Committee of America First. I am not, however, an Isolationist. I believe that after the war we must make every effort to contribute towards the gradual creation of a sounder and more cooperative world."[30] Bowles's description of himself applied equally to Hoover. The simultaneous commitment of such individuals to both nonintervention in the war and to international peacemaking machinery after it ended demonstrates the bankruptcy of such simplistic terms as "isolationist" and "internationalist" to describe the noninterventionists and their opponents. The issue prior to Pearl Harbor was not "isolationism" or "internationalism"—it was war or peace.

Since it was a logical development from his articles and speeches and his book on the "first crusade," it is not surprising that Hoover had already begun before Pearl Harbor to work with former diplomat and longtime friend Hugh Gibson on a book that would set forth the principles that should be followed in fashioning a durable peace. Hoover hoped their efforts would "be a contribution to sanity," but he wanted others to consider the problems of the postwar world as well.[31] One suspects that the former president was so accustomed to smearing that he wanted some public expression of the necessity for such planning from an authoritative source beforehand. In January 1942 he began to press the Council on Foreign Relations to take up the issue of planning for postwar peacemaking. He refused to renew his membership in the council, he told its secretary, Allen Dulles, because there was no reason for its continued existence unless the council was "prepared to come out emphatically with a public statement that the problems and project for the forthcoming peace must have full and frank discussion by the public now." Efforts by the press to stifle consideration of such questions until after the war was over would only lead to a repeat of the situation after World War I when "we went to the peace conference badly prepared for what we had to meet, and as a result so bad a peace was made that we are now in a second world war."[32] Dulles agreed and pointed out that the council was also pursuing such studies, but he refused to make such a public statement as the former president had demanded.[33] However, Hoover was sufficiently encouraged by news of the studies in progress that he renewed his membership.

An administration that had bungled eight years of dealing with the depression was hardly one to inspire confidence in its ability to wage a foreign war. In February 1942, Hoover wrote Richard Lloyd Jones of the *Tulsa Tribune*, "This war belongs to the God-seekers and the New Dealers. It will be ours when they lose it. And lose it they will (in its foreign aspects) if they keep charge of it." The war could have been avoided by wiser policies, Hoover argued, but that could not be helped now. He concluded, "We can pray that new men come to leadership quickly both here and in England or we shall fail."[34] He was sure that 1942 would see "an unending series of disaster," and from these disasters he believed would come "a yearning in the American mind for more effective conduct of this war." But he did not feel that the yearning was yet "great enough to yield anything but curses upon those who would encourage it." He looked to the possibility of that attitude changing by the 1942 congressional elections.[35]

Wartime conditions might be expected to have impelled even such a spite-filled group as that around the Roosevelt White House to leave no stones unturned in a search for national unity. But despite the passage of nine years since he left the presidency, Hoover was still persona non grata with the Roosevelt clique, a continuous slight that led him to write O'Laughlin in Washington, "Quite aside from everything else, this would seem to indicate that they are unaware of the old standard of courtesy from the White House. That is, former Presidents, irrespective of party should be periodically invited and welcomed to indicate the continuity of government and sportsmanship in the

White House. In my time it was taken for granted that the President should take the initiative in courtesies of this sort." The former president found it curious that Roosevelt had extended such invitations to other opposition leaders but not to him. However, Hoover would, he said, continue to give "any possible support to the war efforts" and would even defend Roosevelt against unwarranted attacks by Republicans. "If I find it necessary to engage in comment on the conduct of the war," he wrote, "it will be entirely constructive, upon no petty issues and never below the belt."[36] John Callan O'Laughlin sympathized with the former president's bitterness over his treatment by the White House but added, "Now that we are at war, don't you think it is desirable to forget past precedent and procedure, and in spite of the nasty and inexcusable smearing you have suffered, put yourself in a position which will clearly show that in this tragic time you are prepared to go all the way in support of the war effort? It would be like you, who are so big, to do this. I gather this to be your attitude, but it does seem to me that its expression would be worthwhile."[37]

Landon and Hoover continued the close contacts they had forged before Pearl Harbor through their common opposition to Roosevelt's foreign policies. In 1942 their primary concern was with the GOP and with preparing for the congressional elections in November. Hoover was concerned that Republicans in Congress who had opposed Roosevelt's interventionist policies before Pearl Harbor, and who had been smeared as isolationists, should not be purged in the wartime hysteria and intolerance.[38] Typical was the effort in Illinois to "purge" Senator C. Wayland Brooks for his prewar "isolationism," the *Chicago Sun* arguing that there was "no excuse for a United States Senator who does not know what is going on in the world" and that Brooks should not even seek renomination.[39] Hoover was made somewhat optimistic from the fact that the inadequacies of the Roosevelt administration were being brought into sharp relief by setbacks in the war and hoped that these would offset the domestic political situation. Late in February, Congressman Joseph Martin thought he saw an excellent opportunity for the GOP to capture the House of Representatives in November, a conclusion he reached as a result of a swing through the western states.[40]

Landon, too, saw the prospect of sweeping gains for the GOP in November, but despite urging from Hoover and Taft, he refused to become GOP national chairman in the belief that he could contribute more as an individual than as chairman toward healing the schism between prewar interventionists and anti-interventionists.[41] Landon and Hoover were both concerned that Willkie seemed intent on maintaining the division within the GOP between the two groups to the detriment of the party.[42] That, Landon remarked, was Willkie's "only stock in trade." Obviously referring to Willkie, Hoover wrote to Mrs. Ogden Reid that "there is a small element of Republicans who believe that every Republican who was against any part of Roosevelt's foreign policies before Pearl Harbor is a leper" and that in taking that attitude such

Republicans were "doing great disservice, not only to the party, but to the country, for it is an implication of lack of patriotism." What the party needed was "a healing process, not the keeping of old wounds open," so that the GOP might be "welded into a real force in national service, not split by internal fights."[43]

Landon was taking the same position in his correspondence, but columnist Raymond Clapper responded that if there was "any point in having elections it is to pass on the candidates," and a congressman "naturally must run on his record. If he seemed to have misjudged the situation, it is only fair for voters to hold that against him and choose a man in whose judgment they have more confidence." Clapper agreed that "the pre-Pearl Harbor attitude should not be the sole test, but I think it is totally beside the purpose of elections to ignore it."[44] Landon agreed but added that "by the same token that opens up the lavish peace promises of Mr. Roosevelt, and that is the thing I had hoped to avoid now."[45] Meanwhile, Hoover found it ironic that the result of the delays in the Roosevelt administration's mobilization of the nation meant that it "may become not an isolationist nation, but an isolated nation."[46]

Early in April, Hoover and Hugh Gibson traveled to the former president's home on the Stanford University campus and then northward to Oregon where they combined fishing with work on the book dealing with the problems of a lasting peace.[47] Gibson wrote Perrin Galpin in mid-April, "We're off for Oregon tomorrow and hope to meet up with some fish. It has rained pretty steadily since we got to California and we should not be surprised to find the fish have all been washed out to sea. Nonetheless, we are all going strong and are getting on with the book which ought to be in shape by the time we get back. I think you will find it improved and reading more smoothly."[48] They had already finished a first draft, had printed it out on linotype, and had mailed copies to various people for comments and suggestions.[49]

At the same time the GOP National Committee was meeting in Chicago and seeking a compromise between the Willkie group and the more traditional Republicans. Resolutions were proposed by both Willkie and Taft; the former put emphasis on the prosecution of the war and America's postwar role; the latter focused on the need to preserve the two-party system during wartime. Taft's resolution also called for opposition to "any effort by the Administration to use the war as an excuse for the extension to domestic affairs of unsound economic panaceas disapproved by the great majority of the people." Taft's draft tended to be more combative, while the Willkie one was more supportive of Roosevelt. The final resolution adopted by the committee straddled the two drafts, incorporating language from both.[50] Hoover claimed credit for "the critical paragraph on post-war relations," which he described as "a long way from Willkie's draft."[51] That paragraph read, "We realize that after this war the responsibility of the nation will not be circumscribed within the territorial limits of the United States, that our nation has an obligation to assist in the bringing about of understanding, comity and cooperation among the nations of the world in order that our own liberty may be preserved and that the blighting and destructive forces of war may not again be forced upon us and upon the free and peaceloving peoples of the earth."[52] This was a paragraph as ambiguous as anything that Harding had uttered in the 1920 campaign for the presidency, one that could mean a variety of things according to the perception of the reader. In truth, the paragraph was also not far from Willkie's own proposal and contained much of the language of Willkie's own resolution. The animosity between the two men, however, made it impossible for them to recognize the closeness of their views concerning the postwar role of the United States.

Hoover did not make his first wartime speech until May 20, 1942, when he warned a New York City audience that it would be necessary for Americans to suspend some of their liberties at home even while they fought for liberty overseas. It was imperative that the president should have dictatorial economic powers in order to win a total war, and there must be "no hesitation in giving them to him and upholding him in them." Freedom of press and speech, too, must be limited in order to withhold vital information from the enemy, but "criticism of the conduct of the war is necessary if we are to win the war." Blunders could not be covered up nor incompetent leaders be kept in control, lest such contribute to defeat. Not even the president should be immune from criticism. The former president opposed any attempts "to reform freedom and to make America over anew socially and economically during the war." Instead, all efforts should be concentrated on winning the war, and there would be "plenty of time to exercise the spirit of reform after the war is over." Taking "on the load of a new social and economic order in the middle of this dangerous stream," he warned, would "not help us to get across."

Hoover also opposed any return to the "rabid intolerance" that had affected the country during World War I, particularly that being shown toward those, like himself, who had opposed American participation in the war. Such intolerance did not contribute to the national unity that was vital during wartime. He ended the speech with four suggestions: (1) that the war effort be more effectively organized than it was at present; (2) that the nation begin already to plan for the reconstruction that must follow the war; (3) that preparations be made now for ensuring that the peace would be an enduring one; and (4) that all "surplus food producing" countries prepare for the demands of the war and the peace, because "unless there be food there will be no foundation for peace."[53] In making the latter suggestion Hoover could not know in 1942 how deeply involved he would be in the search for food supplies in the postwar years. The speech received compliments from many quarters and was printed in the *Congressional Record* at Senator Taft's initiative.[54]

It was about this time, also, that the former president began to receive periodic briefings from the War Department on the progress of the war effort.

These briefings apparently came at the insistence of Harry Hopkins, who suggested it to General George Marshall on a flight from London in April, 1942. General Albert Wedemeyer was designated to give the briefings to Hoover and visited him at his Waldorf Astoria suite. Hoover, said Wedemeyer years later, "was very grateful" and "asked many intelligent questions."[55]

Politics

If Willkie's group was willing to sacrifice GOP unity by continuing its criticism of past "isolationists," it was natural that Democrats should seize upon the same issue in campaigning against Republicans in the 1942 elections. Taft wrote Hoover that the Democratic strategy had to be "met head on," but he could generate no interest among GOP senators and congressmen in going on the attack.[56] Hoover's May 20 speech, delivered five days after Taft's letter, seems to have been an effort in the direction of what the senator felt was necessary. That speech, Hoover wrote Landon, had been intended to test a number of propositions:

> My very proper designation of these economic measures as Fascist (a hateful word) has raised the ire of the Left Wing who foresee trouble in holding these measures after the war if this label is made to stick. Likewise the statement that the President "must have many dictatorial powers" went sour with the reactionary interventionists who had assured the country than no such measures would be necessary and who don't like them anyway. It also raised the hope of the Freedom House group, who have organized to defeat all Republican Congressmen and Senators who were opposed to war before Pearl Harbor. This group is an unnatural combination of reactionaries and the left-wingers who, for entirely different points of view, worked to get the country into war—and want a monopoly on patriotism now.[57]

O'Laughlin wrote that he had "heard many admiring comments upon your address" at the Capitol and would see Steve Early [FDR's secretary] within the next day or two to learn the White House reaction.[58] Senator Capper agreed that the address was "one of your best" and noted that Taft had printed it in the *Congressional Record*.[59]

A few days after the May 20 speech Hoover suggested to Landon that in his Flag Day speech the Kansan take up points similar to those he had raised. The former president suggested the basis of a national program to guide Republicans during the war years, which would include support for winning the war, the end of name-calling, submission to economic fascism during the war years but not once the war was over, no radical experiments by the government during wartime, the slashing of all unnecessary government expenditures during the war, the provision of a lasting peace when the war was ended, and the laying of foundations "for economic recovery after the war based on economic liberty." Without this latter, Hoover told Landon, "there will be no liberty of any kind." Landon sent the former president a draft of his proposed speech asking for comments, and Hoover responded with numerous suggested revisions.[60]

Meanwhile, Hoover and Gibson had brought *The Problems of Lasting Peace* to completion. The Hoover War Library had agreed to pay the cost of publishing the book in order to keep its price low, and *Reader's Digest* had expressed interest in carrying a condensed version.[61] The latter offered the prospect that the fundamentals of the book would be brought into the homes of over five million Americans.[62] The authors had circulated early drafts of the book in order to obtain comments, and the reception had been enthusiastic. However, the publisher also sent advance copies of the book to some sixty leading figures interested in foreign affairs, including Under Secretary of State Sumner Welles. Welles received the book on May 20 and ten days later delivered a speech on foreign affairs that received wide comment and acclaim. Distressing to Hoover and Gibson was the fact that the Welles speech advanced many of the same proposals contained in the as-yet-undistributed *Problems of Lasting Peace*. Hoover remarked, "It may be just a coincidence. But if it is, it is an extraordinary one in view of Mr. Welles' previous views on this subject."[63] To prove his point, the former president drew up a memorandum that compared portions of Welles's speeches of May 30 and June 17 with the corresponding comments in the Hoover-Gibson book. Hoover concluded by writing, "It is understood that these two speeches were the beginning of a series to be delivered to enlighten public opinion and clarify public thought as to our peace objectives. It is to be hoped that in future addresses he will give us his views on the remainder of the program for peacemaking formulated in the book. Since he has following along so willingly thus far it is perhaps not unreasonable to anticipate that he will propose the rest of the program."[64]

Hoover was determined to make *The Problems of Lasting Peace* into a best seller. Perhaps there was a certain amount of personal vanity involved, but certainly the former president recognized that the book was likely to have a greater impact if it reached the best-seller list. In June, Hoover sent advance copies of the book to people he thought might be willing to underwrite its promotion. As he wrote to Robert Wood of the old America First Committee,

> It has appeared to us that it is worth some effort to secure its widespread distribution. That can only be done by non-publishing methods. You will realize that a successful serious book (which we have reduced to $2.00 in order to get it before the public as cheaply as possible) can not be adequately promoted out of any publisher's profits. There ought to be from $5,000 to $10,000 spent in promotion . . . We need to publish full page advertisements over the country of these views. And 20,000 to 25,000 copies should be sent out to cover all the colleges, high schools and public libraries in every town and village and every association and group engaged in this . . . To do the whole job some $25,000 should be provided. Hugh and I have stretched our resources in costly research work and preparation of the book. After you have read the book and satisfied

yourself that it is a contribution, if you know of any quarter that might help us, I believe it would be a public service.[65]

Wood did attempt to find financial support for the promotion.[66] At a dinner with Hoover and Gibson at the Waldorf, Rickard found the conversation entirely taken up with finding ways to promote the book. The former president was still trying to raise $10,000 for promotion.[67] Rickard soon had a representative contacting bookstores in western cities in behalf of the book. Sales were promising, but Rickard found that Hoover would be satisfied with nothing less than the top of the best-seller list.[68] Lou Henry Hoover was happy to see that Doubleday was pushing the book "to the best of their ability," in contrast with the Scribner handling of *America's First Crusade*.[69]

The former president was also busy trying to obtain supportive "blurbs" from such figures as Admiral Pratt and General Pershing, since they would "go a long ways to keep down the senseless type of destructive criticism."[70] He also suggested to John Callan O'Laughlin, "In view of Welles' action, would it be a good thing for you to see [Secretary of State] Hull when the book is out; take him a copy, inscribed or not by me, and see if he would, after reading, possibly make a favorable remark in a press conference? He could take some wind out of Welles if he did it right."[71]

To Landon, Hoover wrote, "There are some 200 associations listed in the country which are discussing peace terms—and a dozen Government Departments working on them. The purpose of the book is to try to induce some sanity in these discussions and the peace-making." He asked Landon to mention that it was forthcoming when the Kansan gave a speech on June 14 and then added

> We are going to have a battle over it with Willkie's "Freedom House" and the Left Wingers generally. If people can only be induced to read it, I think it answers much of their mushy thinking.
>
> I stirred up the wasps in my [May 20] speech when I lit upon the "intolerance" of those who want to excommunicate (except for taxes, military services and labor) all those who opposed war before Pearl Harbor. I did not then know how far they had organized to fight our Congressmen and Senators in the next election. I would have made it even stiffer if I had known what they are doing. The Christian Science Monitor has gotten out the voting record, pre-Pearl Harbor, of every member of Congress. Some one is spreading it nationally. The Luce publications are joining in the campaign. Freedom House has put men on the radio to smear my speech and denounce the election of all "isolationists."
>
> If two-party government is to exist it must exist upon free debate and the right of opposition. If we are to win this war there must be criticism of misconduct in the war. If the American people are going to penalize men for conscientious beliefs on such issues as peace and war and for criticism of the war and foreign relations, then the foundations

of opposition and, in this case party government have gone by the board because most of the men to be penalized are Republicans. The professions of this group "Freedom House" of non-partisanship are a fraud. Certainly it does not make for national unity and should be denounced as such.

He suggested to Landon that they begin to "formulate a national program which can guide the Republicans" and suggested,

1. Now we are in war, we must win.
2. We must have the end of name-calling, smearing and challenging the patriotism of decent men.
3. We must submit to economic Fascism in order to win the war.
4. We intend to wipe this Fascism off the slate when war is over and to restore decent economic liberty in America.
5. We don't want [Francis] Biddle-ism and radicalism diverting the energies of the Government or people from war.
6. We want to cut out the wholly unnecessary government expenditures during the war.
7. We want a lasting peace this time, built upon sanity and cooperation which protects American ideals and American life.
8. We want foundations laid for economic recovery after the war based upon economic liberty or there will be no liberty of any kind.

He asked for ideas from Landon and suggested that the Kansan's forthcoming speech might be a good opportunity to outline them.[72]

The Book-of-the-Month Club took up the Hoover-Gibson book and it quickly went into a sixth printing.[73] Hoover's promotion efforts were bearing results and he wrote Taft on July 9 that the book was receiving "an astonishingly good reception. No serious book has ever sold the way this one is. One would hardly expect it to become one of the best sellers—but that is the fact."[74] That a good part of the book's popularity stemmed from Hoover's own well-managed and well-financed promotion campaign, as well as the purchase of books for donation to libraries and organizations, went unmentioned in Hoover's letter. More important, though, is the fact that from a combination of the condensation in *Reader's Digest* and the circulation of the book by the Book-of-the-Month Club, *The Problems of a Lasting Peace* did reach an audience quite remarkable for a book of its type, and one should not underestimate its influence on public opinion. Hoover wrote a friend in mid-July that the book had a received "a most extraordinary reception—having been recommended by over four hundred newspapers and journals of one kind or another."[75] *Time* magazine wrote, "The Elder Statesman Herbert Hoover now stood committed to sweeping US participation in world affairs. Columnists and reviewers, in long columns of praise, found no discrepancy between the Hoover-Gibson principles and those of Under Secretary Sumner Welles and Henry Wallace. Remarked Columnist Walter Lippmann: 'This is a notable event: Governor

Landon has already endorsed the Hoover-Gibson book; Mr. Willkie's position has never been in doubt. Thus we may take great comfort in the fact that there is a high degree of unity of opinion among our political leaders.'"[76]

The book began by reviewing the previous 140 years of history and then turned to a description of the dynamics of peacemaking at the Versailles Conference after World War I. In the third and final section of the book, the authors addressed the foundations of lasting peace, the methods of peace negotiations and peace preservation. "Any structure of lasting peace," they wrote, "must consist of two parts. The first is its foundation of political, territorial, military, economic and ideological settlements which restore order and recovery to the world. The second is the erection thereon of some instrumentality to preserve peace." The Allies should be clear on their aims and principles in peacemaking and should reduce them to specific and practical terms before the peacemaking began. They should also agree on the methods by which it was to be conducted. Any peace treaties should "initiate" and "nurture" representative government in the enemy countries and establish free enterprise economies. Control of international trade should be restored to free enterprise. There should be international cooperation to ensure monetary stability, and tariffs should be "equal to all nations" and "no higher than will preserve fair competition of imports with domestic production." This ruled out reciprocal trade agreements, which were discriminatory. All nations should have access to raw materials without the interference of monopolistic controls. Germany should not be dismembered.[77]

The book went on to suggest that those areas of the Pacific and Africa that offered little prospect of immediate self-government should be put under "international government with equal access to all nations for immigration, trade, and development of natural resources." As an ideal they realized was probably impossible to attain, Hoover and Gibson proposed the complete disarmament of the enemy countries and the establishment "of a constabulary of the police type" for the maintenance of domestic order. They also supported consultation before the end of the war on concrete steps that could be taken toward disarmament within weeks after the war ended. Experience showed that if it were not done at that time, effective disarmament was unlikely to occur. The leaders of the Axis powers and their lieutenants must be dealt with no differently from "common criminals conspiring to murder."

As for reparations, Hoover and Gibson argued that placing nations in economic bondage was not the way to lasting peace. They wrote, "Certainly experience shows that no nation can be punished as a whole and at the same time leave any hope of lasting peace. This endless treadmill of punishment must be stopped in the world if there is to be real peace." The authors favored arbitration of future disputes, and there must be a provision for revising the peace treaties, they wrote, since "experience shows that peace can best be preserved, not by preventing change and putting the future in a straitjacket, but by seeking to control change and direct it. Obviously, any attempt to maintain the status quo indefinitely is a direct invitation to war—for peaceful means being denied, the change can come only through force." They would, therefore, build into international law a provision for the mechanics of treaty revision, along with arbitration, mediation, and other peacekeeping methods.

Hoover and Gibson pointed out that the forces destructive to the goal of establishing a long-term basis for peace were at their apex immediately after hostilities ceased. Thus they argued "the desirability of working under more favorable conditions, of giving time for destructive forces to abate and gaining time for reflection and negotiation in solving long-range problems." They would divide peacemaking into three steps: "first, immediate settlements of certain problems which will not brook delay; second, an intermediate period for rebuilding of political life and economic recovery; and third, a subsequent period, of more or less indefinite duration, for settlement of the long-view problems which require a cooling off of emotions, deliberation and careful development."

Among the problems that would require immediate settlement they listed demobilization and disarmament, the establishment of de facto states within "empirically determined" temporary boundaries, the establishment of representative governments, elimination of famine and pestilence, and the "restarting of industrial production." The long-range problems, they suggested, should be assigned to "separate international commissions, their conclusions to be brought in after political and economic life has begun to recuperate and destructive emotions given time to cool off." They viewed these long-range problems as including provision for the governing of areas not yet ready for self-government, long-range economic problems, boundary disputes, "readjustment of intergovernmental debts, settlement of private property questions, and damages from the war," as well as the "building of international machinery to preserve peace." Until political order had been restored, economic recovery attained, and the long-range problems solved, they saw no alternative but for the victorious Allies to "maintain order in the world by military force."

Entirely apart from the efforts exerted to promote it, leading Republicans viewed The Problems of Lasting Peace as a valuable contribution. William Allen White immediately set out to promote the book among leading Republicans both in and out of Congress, since he found the views outlined synonymous with his own.[78] He found many in agreement with him as to its merits, including some unlikely converts to the proposal for "international machinery to preserve peace."[79] Senator Capper, who had opposed American participation in the League of Nations after World War I, praised it as "a marvelous book" that would "have a far-reaching effect in this country," and Senator Taft hailed it as "a foundation on which all Republicans can stand."[80] Hoover told Taft that he personally regarded the provision for a "cooling off" period before the actual peacemaking proceeded as one of the book's most valuable contributions.[81]

Leon Stolz, chief editorial writer for Robert McCormick's *Chicago Tribune*, generally regarded as a bastion of isolationism, thought that the most valuable aspect of the book was "its emphasis on the importance of the terms of peace as distinguished from any all-embracing scheme of world organization. Unless the terms are livable, no scheme of world security will work. We mustn't be allowed to forget that."[82] One of the problems with the League of Nations Covenant after World War I was, of course, that it sat atop a treaty that was grotesque in its provisions. Senator Harold Burton, who in 1943 would cosponsor the important Burton-Ball-Hatch-Hill resolution in the US Senate in favor of American participation in a postwar world organization, wrote Hoover and Gibson in mid-August 1942 that he had read the book during a trip to Alaska "with great interest and profit." He continued, "I thank you for it. I believe it will be of great value to all concerned. It is priceless to me."[83] Later in the month Burton wrote again that he had lately had "several opportunities to consider some of the material in your book" and that he was "sure that I will find it valuable to me in many ways." He had also heard Senator Alexander Wiley speak highly of the book.[84]

In June an Arthur Krock column in the *New York Times* reviewed the positions of Sumner Welles and of the Hoover-Gibson book and found that "no responsible American voice has been raised in dissent" to the proposal that "a long armistice precede the making of peace after victory." And though two members of the "battalion of death" who had fought against American entry into the League of Nations were still in the Senate, there had likewise been no objection raised to the proposal that the United States enter "a collective security organization of nations" after the conclusion of peace. Krock called it the "Welles-Hoover-Gibson proposal" and predicted that "the existing chorus of general approval will grow for the three stages of armistice that are recommended." Anne O'Hare McCormick also noted the similarities between the Welles and Hoover-Gibson positions in her review of the book for the same newspaper. She called it "an honest, courageous and comprehensive contribution to a debate that will determine the future course of our own country and the world. What matters is that it be widely read and discussed."[85]

Hoover wrote Hugh Gibson in mid-July that the *Baltimore Sun* had been "the only paper which realized we have punctured the old lie that American was responsible for WWII for lack of cooperation after WWI." He had, he told his coauthor, "raised some more money to promote the book," but he felt that "further advertising better be delayed until fall."[86] He also thought it would be "a good thing if the Army would distribute" the book, since it "at least gives them something definite to fight for."[87]

William Allen White hoped to forge an agreement between Hoover and Willkie over postwar policy. He wrote Hoover that there was "enough difference between your plan for an international peace and the plans of [Vice President Henry A.] Wallace to make a real issue. The trouble is that we may be confronted on the one hand with a proposal for purely utopian world revolution, and on the other hand merely a continental hemispheric isolation-ism. Either would bring disaster. Sometimes when I think of it, I am more scared of the peace than of the war."[88]

The War

Hoover watched the succession of Allied defeats during the first half of 1942 with alarm, blaming them in large part on the mishandling of the war by the Roosevelt administration. When Singapore and the Dutch East Indies fell to the Japanese, Hoover blamed it on the strategic error of "too little and too late." He now feared that Australia, China, and India would also fall.[89] Roosevelt's slowness in equipping an army and constructing ships raised the possibility that by the time the United States could exert an influence on the war it would be an isolated nation.[90] He did not feel comfortable in alliance with the Soviet Union, considering that nation untrustworthy as an ally and likely to make a separate peace with Hitler at any moment as it had done during World War I.[91] The former president found the American people confused over the purpose of the war, partly because they could not "reconcile a crusade for liberty with a Russian partner," and partly because they could not appreciate the idea "of giving millions of American lives to restore [British] mastery over the Malay races instead of [giving them] their freedom."[92] Yet he found it "very difficult for those of us who have been in opposition to criticize as we will only be discredited as being in opposition to everything. However, sooner or later the subject will have to be raised or we may have terrible consequences."[93]

Hoover found it difficult to conceive of a "land invasion of Europe" in 1942, since it could not be done "on a sufficient scale to really reduce the pressure on Stalin." Instead, it would "probably result in the Japanese reluctantly making an attack on Stalin under German urging" and a defeat of inadequate forces was likely to "leave England open to invasion," because Russia could not "in any event be a very effective force in 1943," and because there was "not yet enough shipping to do a real job." The war, he insisted, could "be won by attrition and the decomposition of enemy nations under [the] long strain of total war. We have," he wrote O'Laughlin, "no right to adventure, nor right to slaughter uselessly American youth." But Hoover doubted that any "amount of sanity can protect America from the chanting forms of left-wing political pressure to which the present Administration is susceptible from both domestic and foreign quarters."[94]

In September the former president grew increasingly distraught over the mobilization situation. He told Arch Shaw that he paced "the floor wondering if" he did not "owe it to the country to blow off," only to realize that "it would not carry much weight."[95] But he wrote Arthur Sulzberger, publisher of the *New York Times*, to remind him that in December 1941 he had called Sulzberger's attention to the fact that the management of commodities by the Roosevelt administration "was wrong and would bring utter confusion."

Now his prediction was coming true, as revealed by the "rubber folly," and he pointed out that the Baruch committee had recommended reorganization along precisely the lines that Hoover had recommended to the Senate Finance Committee in December. Now he urged that the *New York Times* push for a similar reorganization of "all other critical commodities, services, or groups of them." He told Sulzberger, "Unless these things are done and done promptly we will have a catastrophe."[96]

Hoover had also suggested to Taft changes in the tax codes that would allow "all debtors a deduction from income or corporation taxes equal to 8 1/4 percent of their indebtedness, provided they invested this amount in government securities and provided they placed these securities in the hands of a trustee to be used as payments on principal of their debts." He would, he said, like to see more than 8 1/4 percent, but the economic effect of even this limited proposal would be "to bring the same immediate cash to government," reduce "private debt and increase government to an equal amount." After the war the government could "better handle its financial affairs than can private debtors handle them through foreclosures and the bankruptcy courts."[97]

Later in the month he added the recommendation that corporations "of less than $500,000 (or even $1,000,000) capital, with less than say 10 individual stock holders" should be classed as partnerships in the new tax bill as it would relieve them "of double taxation and the excess profits tax," with the stockholders only "subject to income taxes on any profits," so "individual losses on venture business could thus be set off against gains." The result might be some loss of revenue for the government, but the amount of new minerals produced would "be greater than that induced by the present program of government loans and subsidies," and farmers would "produce more food and keep prices down," and inventions would be stimulated. It would aid with the preservation of small business instead of driving prospects and inventions into the hands of big business."[98] Taft agreed with Hoover but felt that "within the New Deal there is a deliberate attempt to reduce corporations to a point where after the war they will be dependent on the government for their very existence."[99]

Hoover had been doing considerable fishing during the first eight months of 1942, including over his sixty-eighth birthday, and when Arch Shaw wrote to ask if he had left any fish in the Madison River, the former president responded that the trouble was "all the neighbors want to line the banks and to talk about the war."[100] He told Gibson, "Fishing is not much good anywhere, anytime, anyhow. We caught lots of fish, but the population insisted on gathering along the bank to discuss the war."[101] As for the war itself, Hoover had begun to sense that the Roosevelt administration was beginning to realize the "utter confusion in the economic organization for the war." "The Army, Navy and Industry are doing their job," he wrote O'Laughlin, "and could win this war if it were not for the economic and political interference by the Administration." He considered the American invasion of the Solomon Islands "an accomplishment" and assumed that the British failure at Dieppe had provided a useful "warning on the difficulties of the Second Front."[102]

A month before the election, Landon came to the conclusion that if the GOP did not win control of the House of Representatives it was "going to be right close."[103] Hoover, meanwhile, was predicting gubernatorial victories in California, Colorado, Pennsylvania, Delaware, Ohio, New York, Massachusetts, and other states, as well as an increase of 6 to 8 Republican seats in the Senate and 25 to 50 in the House. He was pleased by the prospect that any such GOP victories, except in California, would be by "anti-Willkie men."[104]

The election actually resulted in the GOP increasing its seats in the Senate by 10, and in the House by 47. Hoover was pleased, but he quickly issued a statement to the press in which he pointed out that the Republican victories should give no comfort to the Axis, since every candidate in the election, from whichever party, had run on a platform of "vigorous, efficient prosecution of the war." He admitted that there was "a strong element of protest in the vote, but it was the protest of insistence upon more effective organization of the war and that can be of no comfort for the enemy."[105] He told Congressman Joseph Martin that the victory gave Republicans two great opportunities: (1) "to insist upon a reorganization of the war agencies so as to stop this blundering delay and the loss of lives in this war," and (2) "to stop the use of war measures to permanently collectivize this country."[106] The former president was especially delighted that Senator George Norris of Nebraska had been defeated, Norris having been a thorn in his side as president.[107]

Rumors abounded that Roosevelt had pared his "hate list" due to the exigencies of war and that Hoover might now be tapped by the president to assist with relief efforts in Europe, perhaps as head of the United Nations Relief and Rehabilitation Agency (UNRRA). Instead, that post was given to another Herbert, former governor of New York Herbert Lehman. Hoover considered it "a rotten appointment from any point of view" and disappointedly considered addressing a public letter to Lehman outlining his own views on relief.[108] Dissuaded by Gibson and Rickard, the former president instead wrote a private letter to Lehman and received in response an invitation to lunch to discuss relief problems.[109] Prior to their luncheon, Hoover wrote Lehman again to press the project dear to his heart: the relief of women, unemployed men, and children in the occupied democracies, as well as an increase of supplies to Greece. He also brought up his prewar proposal, which had been clocked by the British but had been supported by many leading Americans.[110]

At the luncheon in Hoover's Waldorf suite on December 3, the former president reiterated his concern for the fate of those in the occupied areas. The question, he told Lehman, was whether the Allies were "fighting to liberate oppressed peoples or to liberate vast cemeteries."[111] When Lehman left the Waldorf he refused to comment to reporters on Hoover's proposal.[112] Meanwhile, a similar initiative had been launched to provide food relief for the occupied areas by Socialist Party leader Norman Thomas, who was chairman of the Post-War World Council.[113]

Hoover wrote Ray Lyman Wilbur that the "powers of the new Food Administrator leave out vital segments of the OPM, the OPA, the Lend Lease, and the Army and Navy food controls. It will continue to be a mess. They read my first recommendation and ignored the second. [Secretary of Agriculture] Wickard is a weak sister and will fail. So will Lehman. Already Hopkins has taken North Africa from him and appointed his war administrator."[114]

The division between the Willkie wing of Republicans and traditional Republicans continued to plague the party at the end of 1942. After the election, Hoover set out to ensure that the Willkieites should not gain control of the Republican National Committee.[115] The problem was to find a new chairman who would be acceptable to both camps. Landon was an obvious choice, supported by Hoover, but the Kansan refused to take on the responsibility.[116] Werner Schroeder, national committeeman from Illinois, was widely supported by anti-Willkie Republicans for the chairmanship and was believed to be capable of winning in a straight pro versus anti-Willkie vote, but he was anathema to the Willkieites for his alleged ties to the isolationist Robert McCormick of the *Chicago Tribune* and his election would not provide the desired unity.[117] As Hoover remarked, "the Willkie forces are on the job, preparing to smear and accuse Schroeder. The first blast is against anybody that does not embrace Willkie's all-out but undefined 'after war policies.'"[118]

Hoover preferred that there not be a bitter confrontation over the chairmanship that could prove detrimental to the party. He sought, therefore, a compromise candidate whose allegiance was just as strongly to the anti-Willkie camp but whose election could be viewed as a compromise once the Willkieites had the satisfaction of feeling they had "blocked" Schroeder. Thus the rumor was floated that although Schroeder had enough votes to win, he would be asked to withdraw in favor of a compromise candidate of unity.[119] At the meeting of the committee in December, two ballots were divided between Schroeder and Fred Baker of Washington, the choice of the Willkieites, with Harrison Spangler of Iowa a distant third. After a recess, Spangler was elected by a unanimous vote. Hoover claimed credit for breaking the deadlock in the committee and for the resulting election of the Iowan.[120] From the beginning, the strategy had been to block Willkie's candidate with Schroeder and then offer Spangler as a compromise. The former president celebrated Spangler's election as a victory over Willkie, and certainly Hoover had every reason to smile for Spangler had been a "Hoover man" ever since the days of the battle over Hoover's GOP conference proposal in 1934.[121] A week after the meeting he wrote Ray Lyman Wilbur, "Spangler's election tickles my funnybone in many places. Willkie fell into a complete trap and is just now beginning to awake to it."[122] Taft agreed that "Spangler believes in a direct attack on the New Deal and his views are almost exactly the same as those of Schroeder."[123]

A new chairman elected, the committee next reaffirmed the commitment to postwar international cooperation it had passed on April 20. The motion for this reaffirmation was made by Senator Robert Taft, who had opposed the resolution in April.[124] The combination of this resolution and the defeat to Schroeder made Willkie feel that he had been victorious in the committee meeting, but the election of Spangler was certainly no victory and, in reality, neither was the adoption of the resolution. Between the April and December meetings *The Problems of Lasting Peace* had been published and it clearly accepted some role for the United States in international cooperation. There were, by any reasonable definition, few isolationists in the party, although there were certainly grounds for serious differences of opinion over what America's precise role should be in the postwar world. Certainly, neither Hoover nor Taft were recent converts to the cause of international cooperation, both having championed it at the end of World War I. If Willkie was under the impression, shared by his biographers and too many historians of this period, that Republican leaders like Hoover and Taft were being dragged by his leadership into reluctant acceptance of postwar international cooperation, he was badly mistaken. The sizable gulf that had existed between interventionists and noninterventionists before Pearl Harbor was clearly not very wide at all over postwar policy, nor did their pre–Pearl Harbor labels have any relevance to their positions on peacetime international cooperation.

Meanwhile, on December 16 Hoover delivered another nationally broadcast speech in Chicago that expanded on the Hoover-Gibson program. He told his audience that there were "two separate problems" involved in avoiding the tragic experience at Versailles. The one was the "method of the machinery by which we make peace and the other is the settlement of the problems of peace themselves." The essence of the Hoover-Gibson approach, he said, was that it dispensed with any armistice, and there would be no general peace conference such as at Versailles. There would first be a "conditional peace" during which the world would be turned "toward political and economic and spiritual recovery," after which there would be a cooling off period to "work out one by one and separately the solutions of lasting peace." This would involve such matters as disarmament of the enemy, provisions for repatriation of prisoners and displaced persons, relief of famine, aid in reconstruction, and the restoration of trade. He found widespread agreement on certain propositions necessary to "gain a real peace this time." Those included a determination to make a peace that would last and "which assures freedom among men and the establishment of machinery for cooperation between nations."[125] Willkie wrote Hoover the next day that he had "read with great interest your very provocative address of yesterday," and he asked to have a talk with him when he returned to the city.[126] Hoover responded that he had "a bunch of grandchildren to shepherd over the holidays, but soon thereafter I would be glad if you would have lunch with me." Of the speech he told Willkie, "It is at least a novel incident when a proposal simultaneously wins high approval from the *New York Times, News, Daily Mirror, Sun, World Telegram,* the *Chicago Tribune, Sun,* and the *Emporia Gazette!* Aside from the Communist press, the only critic is the *New York Tribune.*"[127] That was a group, he told Landon, that "cannot usually be said to be a sweet chorus."[128]

William Allen White was convinced that it was important to get Republicans lined up in support of the Hoover-Gibson program outlined in *The Problems of Lasting Peace* to ensure that the fate of international cooperation after World War II was not the same as after World War I. To that end, White wrote Landon late in December 1942 to encourage him to join with a dozen GOP leaders, including Hoover and Willkie, in signing a manifesto that "would justify Republicans in feeling that the Hoover statement was our party policy so that in 1944 we need not have a convention row [as in 1920] and a probable split on the question of foreign policy, and can devote ourselves entirely in that platform largely to domestic issues."[129] This, of course, was entirely acceptable to Hoover. Meanwhile, the former president was correcting the incredible impression of columnist Walter Lippmann that he and Gibson had borrowed the ideas of Sumner Welles, rather than vice versa! He wrote Lippmann, "Despite the *New York Herald Tribune,* our proposals were in print before his [Welles's] or Mr. [Henry A.] Wallaces's speeches so we did not steal Welles's expression of a 'cooling off period.' I even used the expression 'a period to cool off' a year before."[130] From O'Laughlin came word that neither Roosevelt nor Welles would concede that the inspiration for Welles's speech mentioned earlier had come from Hoover and Gibson, but he wrote that "both welcome your attitude because they feel it will contribute to a policy that the country generally will accept."[131]

To further White's initiative, Hoover send him a condensation of *The Problems of Lasting Peace,* in hopes that it might constitute, as White intended, "a program upon which all substantial Republicans might agree." The former president suggested that Landon send a letter to leading Republicans to ask their views of the program set forth in the condensation.[132] White, meanwhile, was seeking a rapprochement between Hoover and Willkie by offering to host a luncheon for the two men; he also passed along to Hoover some friendly comments Willkie had made concerning him.[133]

While Landon was not enthusiastic about White's proposal, he supported it. He wrote Hoover that he wasn't certain the timing was right but also affirmed that he was willing to join the movement. The Kansan proposed to sound out Minnesota governor Harold Stassen, a rising star in the party, before writing Hoover more fully.[134] GOP national chairman Harrison Spangler also expressed hope "that leading Republicans everywhere will be able to be in substantial agreement on our duties and obligations after the war is over." He found many of the alleged disagreements among Republicans concerning the issue to be "quite mythical" and likely to be "easily forgotten as time goes on." He did not, however, express a commitment specifically to the Hoover-Gibson plan as the basis for such a Republican agreement.[135]

Hoover entered 1943 in a far better frame of mind from a year earlier. In January 1942 the former president was on the defensive for his "isolationist" views before Pearl Harbor, but a year later he had gained a prominent role in discussions concerning postwar foreign policy as a result of his writings and speeches. Moreover, during the previous year he had been frequently called upon for advice not only in connection with postwar policy but also over relief and domestic mobilization questions. He now resolved to press once again for food relief to the occupied democracies. Early in January 1943 the executive committees of the Commission for Relief in Belgium and the American Children's Fund (an outgrowth of the old American Relief Administration) met and agreed to revive the National Committee on Food for the Small Democracies and also to promote the Hoover-Gibson plan for peacemaking.[136]

Meanwhile, in January Hoover published a series of six articles in the press under the title "The Home Fronts and Global Strategy" that appeared between January 11 and 16, 1943. Hoover pointed out that the home fronts of both the Allies and the enemy were important to the strategy of the war, since under conditions of total war nations pitted not only their military forces against each other but also "the total emotions, the skill, and sacrifice, the work of every adult citizen." It was a contest of "strength, spirit and endurance of civilians against civilians, as well as between armies and navies." The war with the Axis had now become one of "attrition" that was "just as vital on the home front as on the military front." And the powers of attrition were increasing more rapidly for the Allies than for the Axis. After reviewing the home fronts of the Axis and other Allies, Hoover turned to the American home front, which he found "in a more favored position than our Allies in one great particular"—the United States need fear neither aerial attack nor "being starved out by submarine blockade." But the United States must "not only raise large military forces, equip them and transport them overseas" but must also "furnish finance, food and munitions to the other United Nations" and must simultaneously "support our civil population in such a fashion that their physical strength and spirit are not exhausted." These responsibilities offered "no margins for the waste of blunders or mismanagement on our home front." "Our job," Hoover pointed out, "is production, production and more production" if the Allies were to win the war of attrition. But the "conduct and organization" of the home front was less than satisfactory. While the armed forces had learned the lessons of World War I, those lessons had "been largely ignored and even repudiated on our home front." Hoover then restated the principles of effective home front organization that he had advocated in speeches, press statements, and congressional testimony. Above all he warned against "endangering the food supply to ourselves and our Allies by excessive drafts of manpower from agriculture."[137]

Taft wrote that he was reading the articles "with interest," and he added, "Stimson and Patterson are more military than the generals and have no appreciation of the part which a civilian population plays in the war."[138] Hoover wrote to William Castle that he didn't like the "looks of things" either abroad or at home. He added, "Washington is trying to do too much too fast. The 'raison d'etre' of those articles was to build up reasons why they ought to go slower."[139] The articles, he told Ben Allen, had been "written at the joint request of the A.P., U.P., I.N.S., and N.E.A.," with the "actual engineering of the matter . . . done by Roy Howard."

A few days later he joined in an appeal for funds for the Salvation Army, arguing that he had found its canteens "nearest the front line" and that its "moral support is welcomed by every branch of our armies."[140] Hoover also spoke to the National Industrial Conference Board in New York and over NBC to the nation. He had difficulty getting air time and was finally able to do so only by displacing the Abbott and Costello program.[141] He was speaking, he told O'Laughlin, because "unless something is done very promptly to assure the farmer that he will have labor, we are going to be too late to help the next crop."[142] In his speech Hoover had, he said, been asked by the board "to say something on our war food problem." Food, he remarked, had "now become secondary only to military operations in determining the outcome of the war. And it will take first place in saving the world from anarchy after the war." He pointed out that when the conflict ended, the United States would "be faced with three or four hundred million starving people." In addition to preparing for that responsibility the United States must meanwhile feed the Allies and its own population. There was already an "acute shortage especially in meats and fats in the world," since "all over Europe the flocks and herds are being consumed." And there was also a shortage in the United States. The American home front was "confronted with the fact that our shortage of labor, of machinery and methods of price control are limiting the vitally essential expansion of this production and the flocks and herds upon which productions depends." Unless "these limiting forces" were reversed there were "dangers to the conduct of the war and winning the peace." But not enough progress was being made in this direction. The problem, Hoover told his listeners, stemmed from four primary causes:

> First. Some 2,000,000 men have been drained from the farm labor supply into arms and munitions.
> Second. The methods of food price control by which prices to the farmer in many instances are lower than cost of production.
> Third. The manufacture of farm machinery has been reduced by 75%.
> Fourth. We still go on subsidizing the farmer to restrict production in some commodities.

Besides changing the policies under numbers 2, 3, and 4, Hoover advocated increasing the manpower supply by ending the draft of farm labor into the military, improving the utilization of labor by industry, and furloughing farmers in the military during planting and harvesting times. Hoover concluded, "We urgently need to determine what we can do within our strength of manpower, materials, shops, and agriculture, and the bottlenecks with which we must contend. We need to determine which of our tasks comes first. And if we determine rightly we will place agriculture in the first rank of the war effort alongside of planes and ships. Our imperative necessity is the maximum food production. The American farmer will do it if he is given a chance. And the fate of the world may depend upon it."[143] Rickard thought it was "the best presented speech in his career."[144]

In that same month, Hoover attempted to put to rest any speculation that his activities were part of an effort to capture the 1944 GOP nomination. For the first time, he ruled out well in advance of a convention any political aspirations, when he wrote Kent Cooper of the *Associated Press* of such rumors, "There is not an atom of truth in these rumors. I wish to reiterate again my statement that I will not again accept political office. I hope such misstatements will cease. I believe I can be of more service to my country at my time of life with an occasional discussion or advice upon public affairs. I should like to be able to do so free from political imputation."[145] For the first time since he left the White House, Hoover was no longer a candidate for the GOP nomination.

On January 8 Hoover lunched with the British ambassador, Lord Halifax, at the latter's request. It appeared that GOP gains in the 1942 congressional elections had prompted the British to take a renewed interest in the Republicans, especially in the one who was apparently exerting such an influence on GOP attitudes toward postwar policy. The conversation ranged over a number of topics, with Halifax expressing concern that the United States might take an "isolationist" course after the war ended. Hoover told him he "thought even in the Middle West there would be a readiness to accept a Council of Nations . . . something like the League of Nations without force, sanctions[,] and that there would be readiness to look after the police aspect of our problems through the maintenance of a British-American air force." The former president told Halifax further that he did not believe the American people were ready for an international military force that would be directed by such a mixed international body "but that this difficulty could be avoided by having us friendly to determine our own action in cooperation with Britain." According to Hoover's aide-memoir of the conversation, Halifax was so astonished "at this statement of readiness to cooperate with Britain that he went over the ground again."[146]

When Halifax queried him concerning the reasons behind such anti-British sentiment as did exist in the United States, the former president explained that Americans wanted nothing to do with either socialism or collectivism and were appalled at evidence that Britain was moving to the left. Hoover cast doubt upon the sincerity of the "left-wingers" around Roosevelt, suggesting that they were more committed to close relations with the Soviet Union after the war than with Britain. Hoover also took advantage of the opportunity to once again press the issue of food relief. However, contrary to intimations Hoover had earlier received that the British had relaxed their position, the ambassador refused to commit himself or his government to any relaxation of the blockade of the Continent. Still, Hoover believed that the British had been shaken by the GOP gains in 1942 and might be more receptive now to pressure for the relaxation of the blockade.[147]

Hoover's conversation with Lord Halifax reveals some rather remarkable views for the first time. In suggesting Anglo-American cooperation to enforce peace in the postwar years, Hoover anticipated Thomas Dewey's call for a postwar Anglo-American alliance eight months later. In putting his emphasis on air power as the vehicle for maintaining peace, Hoover was anticipating the position he would take during the Great Debate over strategy and foreign policy in the early 1950s. The former statement, however, is somewhat suspect, given the coolness the former president exhibited toward the British before, during, and after the war, and may have been a ploy to break through the British blockade of the European continent so that food relief might reach the occupied democracies. If so, it did not have the desired effect.

In January the State Department published a "white paper," "Peace and War," which was a compilation of the documents related to the coming of American involvement in the war. While Hugh Gibson was mentioned in it, Herbert Hoover was not. For Hoover, the failure to mention him was "merely the usual evidence of vindictiveness." He told O'Laughlin, "More important is the disclosure of the fact that Roosevelt now claims to know war was inevitable at the time he was promising the country he would never send American boys overseas. Some day someone will publish another White Paper and make some corrections in these so-called historical records." He also wrote that the "economic program in the country is going even worse." Hoover had heard that Donald Nelson was telling people "his position was hopeless due to constant interference of Mr. Roosevelt and was gloomy indeed over the whole outlook."[148] Taft wrote Hoover that the "legislative investigating work is discouraging because, after all, the war problems are principally administrative in nature, and it makes very little difference what Congress does if the administrators make a mess of them. About all we can do is show up the worst abuses"[149]

In January Landon held the promised meeting with Stassen and brought up the joint statement on postwar policy that White had suggested. He sent Hoover a memorandum of their discussion, which seemed to indicate Stassen's approval of the Hoover-Gibson program. Landon sent Stassen the memorandum for his approval, and Hoover told Landon he would "be greatly interested to know Governor Stassen's reaction."[150] No reply came from the Minnesotan.

Meanwhile, Hoover had declined an invitation by House Minority Leader Joseph Martin to meet with Republican members of the House, arguing that matters needed to be clarified "a little before we go into a huddle." He told Martin, "This is an era of investigation rather than policies."[151] A small group of GOP senators traveled to New York for dinner with him late in the month, however, including George Aiken, Rufus Holman, John Thomas, Hugh Butler, and Chris J. Abbot.[152] And contrary to his reply to Martin, Hoover was eager to meet with new GOP members of the House but sought some way to do so "outside Joe Martin." William Castle set to work to arrange such a meeting since he felt that they were "pretty hard to manage, and if they could have some kind of clear directive it might help."[153]

In mid-January Martin wrote Hoover for his advice on the idea of a "war cabinet" such as Hoover had served in under President Wilson, several people having written to suggest the idea. The former president promised to send him something "in a few days" but added that it seemed to him the "hottest iron the Republicans can strike is this whole food situation. It is a mess much greater than any press discussions would indicate. There are meat and milk famines all over the country due to mismanagement." He was taking the issue up in a speech that week, he told Martin, "which ventilates some parts of it— with the indignation I feel left out."[154]

Hoover had been for some time receiving complaints about the handling of consumer needs at home by the Roosevelt administration. One newspaper reporter wrote, "In this war, the government is committed to rationing commodities and regimenting the people. During the First World War, there never was a ration card although there were shortages. How did you [Hoover] do it, and why can't they [Roosevelt's administration] do it now? I believe that voluntary cooperation worked for you and would work today."[155] The former president was pessimistic by mid-January, writing that he didn't "like the looks of things abroad," nor did he "like the looks of them at home." The administration, he repeated, was "trying to do too much too fast."[156]

A few days later Hoover sent Martin his views on war organization and suggested that his memorandum might furnish material for a speech by one of the GOP congressmen. "The American people might be appalled if the men who are really conducting the war were visualized by being collected into a war council and daily exhibited," he told Martin. "That might in itself promote change."[157] In his memorandum, Hoover again called for the division of civilian activities under functional groupings, each headed by a single administrator who would be responsible for all functions of government related to his group of activities. He also called for the creation of a war council, or war cabinet, and basing all mobilization activities on the maximum cooperation of the people in order to avoid the creation of a huge bureaucracy. This latter aim could also be promoted through decentralization down to the state level.[158]

Hoover told Martin he found it curious that the organization of the army and navy had been built upon the experience and men of World War I, while in the area of civilian mobilization "the whole experience of the last war has been rejected or avoided," and the men involved in the earlier war had been excluded from Washington during this one. "We have today," he told Martin, "a confusion of boards, commissions, divided functions in organization, masses of futile coordinators and bureaucrats. There has been no War Cabinet or War Council and in consequence, lack of policies, overlap," and bickering had become rampant. Compulsion had been used instead of cooperation, with the result that people did not cooperate and the country was "rampant with snoopers and enforcers." The productive powers of industry were not being utilized and futile bureaucracy had been substituted with a consequent growth in the number of federal employees." Martin expressed pleasure at receiving Hoover's indictment of the war effort and agreed with the former president that it would "be very helpful to one of the boys in preparing a speech."[159]

Meanwhile, the effort continued to gather Republicans behind the Hoover-Gibson formula as the basis for the postwar policy of the GOP. Hoover was now taking a more active role in the effort. Following his meeting with the Republican senators at the Waldorf, the former present sent each of them a synopsis of the Hoover-Gibson plan and asked each if he thought it "might constitute a Republican policy in this connection."[160] Senator Hugh Butler now invited Hoover to travel to Washington for a meeting with nine GOP senators whom Hoover had labeled the "young Turks." The meeting was scheduled for early February, at which time he was also to appear before a Senate committee to discuss mobilization.[161] In Kansas, William Allen White continued to do his part in behalf of the program, writing Hoover in early February that he thought "the time is right to put the foreign relations position of the Republican party on ice for the duration under your plan." He had gotten the impression from both Willkie and Landon that they supported the plan, and he believed that most other leading Republicans would follow. He told Hoover, "It would be a great service to your party if you would get the danger averted of a major row in the Republican convention about foreign policy."[162]

Hoover was busy during his few days in Washington in early February. First, there was his testimony before a subcommittee of the Senate Appropriations Committee, which Democratic senator Elmer Thomas of Oklahoma said would "carry great weight throughout the country," because, Hoover had "studied the problem of supplies thoroughly in the last war and he is not involved with the government now. Most of the testimony we have received so far has been from men who are taking orders from the government."[163] Warning that the United States probably faced three to five more years of war, Hoover urged a revision of military manpower policies to free one million more workers for agriculture, mining, and oil drilling during the next year. Roosevelt's goal of 11 million men in uniform by the end of the year was too high, he asserted, since shipping bottlenecks would prevent their being carried overseas or supplied. Roosevelt needed to provide incentives for the production of urgently needed meats and fats. The home front was just as important as the war front, he argued. Time was on the side of the Allies, and there was no need to attempt to do everything at once, thus overstraining the home front.[164] Hoover's views won endorsement from two Southern Democratic members of the farm bloc, Senator John Bankhead remarking that he agreed "wholeheartedly" with the former president.

Hoover's testimony was, however, quickly criticized by Secretary of War Stimson and other administration spokesmen, who challenged his conclusions. Columnist Arthur Krock supported Hoover in the *New York Times*, writing, "Yet in that very period this correspondent, who for two months had been making diligent inquiry among informed persons, reported that many of those 'charged with the heavy responsibility of winning the war'" agreed with Mr. Hoover. "This correspondent based his report on the testimony of civilian war administrators, who also bear a heavy share of the burden of winning the war, and of men experienced in the national resources and the solutions reached during the World War." Krock wrote these words in September, at a time when even the Roosevelt administration had implicitly acknowledged, at last, the accuracy of Hoover's comments by reducing their military manpower levels.[165]

Besides meeting with the GOP "young Turks," Hoover also met with Secretary of Agriculture Claude R. Wickard about the food situation at Wickard's request.[166] He also arranged for the introduction of a resolution in the Senate by Senators Gillette (Democrat) and Taft (Republican) supporting his attempts to arrange food relief for the small European democracies.[167] To the support of the resolution came the National Council for Prevention of War and Socialist Party leader Norman Thomas.[168] So congenial did Hoover find Washington during this trip that he decided to move there if a Republican won the presidency in 1944.[169]

Others, however, contemplated an earlier move by the former president. In mid-February Senator Arthur Capper publicly called upon Roosevelt to designate Hoover as a "super efficiency expert" to eliminate waste and duplication in government and to "weed out useless bureaus and useless activities." Capper insisted it was "a crying shame that Mr. Hoover's services have not been pressed into use to accelerate a victory over the Axis. Everyone familiar with his record knows he is an extremely able administrator. Even his political foes concede that." A similar plea had been made a week earlier by Senator Davis of Pennsylvania, who had been Hoover's secretary of labor.[170]

Another possible avenue of service seemed in prospect in February 1943, as rumors circulated of the imminent resignation of Senator Hiram Johnson. Citing such rumors in California, Hoover wrote John Callan O'Laughlin,

"I have been approached by two or three responsible groups to know whether I would accept an appointment to fill out [Johnson's] term until January 1943 [sic]. Before even thinking about it, I was wondering if you could discreetly

inquire what Senator Johnson's plans are. Certainly, he is no longer contributing much in the Senate. I am not sure what I could do with the job if I got a
chance. However, I would like very much to know what his plans are, what he
thinks and what the facts really are."[171]

O'Laughlin found, however, that Johnson could not resign for financial reasons, even though he was unable to contribute as much in the Senate as he
wanted. O'Laughlin, therefore, did not explore with Johnson or his wife the
suggestion Hoover had made, although, he said, "there is no doubt Hiram is
a sick man."[172]

GOP national chairman Harrison Spangler had meanwhile injected himself into the effort to bring Republican leaders into a unified position on postwar policy. He wrote Landon,"I had hoped that I could have you, Mr. Hoover,
and Mr. Willkie as my guests at dinner in New York, at which we could have
a frank discussion and at least ascertain how far apart we might be. This idea
was give me by Mr. William Allen White, and Mr. Hoover thinks it might be
worthwhile. I had hoped you would be here soon . . . As soon as you can give
me a somewhat definite time you will be here, I will arrange with Mr. Hoover
and Mr. Willkie."[173] However, the former president was leaving for California,
and this meeting had to be postponed.[174]

The irrepressible White fired off a new round of letters to GOP leaders
in mid-March, asking that they read and make marginal comments upon
the Hoover-Gibson condensation. He wrote Senator Charles McNary,
"If I could know where our open-minded Republican friends balk at the
Hoover program, I believe some of us could get out a statement that all of
us would sign."[175] Meanwhile, GOP senators Joseph Ball and Harold Burton had joined with two Democratic colleagues to introduce a resolution
in the Senate favoring the development of machinery for the settlement of
peacetime disputes between nations and for the creation and maintenance of
an international military force to be used against aggression by any nation.
Burton wrote Hoover on March 19, enclosing a copy of an article he had
written for *The Republican* entitled "The Roads to Lasting Peace." He had,
he told Hoover, taken "my text from your book on 'The Problems of Lasting Peace,' and had submitted a draft of the article to Hugh Gibson for
approval before publishing." He also sent the former president a copy of the
Burton-Ball-Hatch-Hill (B2H2) resolution, saying that he believed it was
consistent with the article he had written. If Burton believed his article was
based on the Hoover-Gibson book, it follows that he considered the resolution consistent with it also. He told Hoover that he was "hopeful you believe
that this Resolution or some reasonable modification of it is a helpful step
in the right direction."[176]

Burton's article did, in fact, follow the Hoover-Gibson program very
closely, but the B2H2 resolution was not as acceptable to the former president. The resolution (S Res. 114) read,

Resolved, that the Senate advises that the United States take the initiative in calling meetings of representatives of the United Nations [Allies] for the purpose of forming an organization of the United Nations with specific and limited authority—

1. To assist in coordinating and fully utilizing the military and economic resources of all member nations in the prosecution of the war against the Axis.
2. To establish temporary administration for Axis-controlled areas of the world as these are occupied by United Nations forces, until such time as permanent governments can be established.
3. To administer relief and assistance in economic rehabilitation in territories of member nations needing such aid and in Axis territories occupied by United Nations forces.
4. To establish procedures and machinery for peaceful settlement of disputes and disagreements between nations.
5. To provide for the assembly and maintenance of a United Nations military force and to suppress by immediate use of such force any future attempts at military aggression by any nation.

That the Senate further advises that any establishment of such United Nations organization provide machinery for its modification, for the delegation of additional specific and limited functions to such organization, and for admission of other nations to membership, and that member nations should commit themselves to seek no territorial aggrandizement.[177]

Hoover apparently had no quarrel with the resolution through item 4, but his marginalia indicate that he believed revisions were required in the remaining items. Those marginalia show that he sought submission of any agreements between the United States and the other United Nations to the US Senate for approval; that he believed item 5 should be modified to read, "To establish the terms and machinery for making a conditional peace to be enforced by the United Governments and for the subsequent development of machinery for settlement of disputes and controversies among nations, and for the development of economic aid and other relations which will bring a permanent peace"; and that he sought an additional item, which would call for the disarmament of the enemy and provide for temporary governments in liberated enemy territory. In his reply to Burton, Hoover wrote that the purpose of the resolution was "fine," but as to the contents, he thought "it should be strengthened somewhat and the independence of the Congress and the Senate [should be] better safeguarded." He feared that the resolution, as written, would be taken by the Roosevelt administration "as a blank check to make commitments and then the Senate would be called upon to make them good even though such commitments depart from the concepts which you have in mind."[178]

Hoover's actual suggestions to Burton departed somewhat from his marginalia, with insertion of "representative" to make item 2 read, "permanent representative governments," a reference to "cooling-off periods," and other changes. The former president's principal objection, it seems, was that not all the proposals of *The Problems of Lasting Peace* were included in the short resolution. However, the former president was not alone in his reservations about the B2H2 resolution. Senator Vandenberg also questioned it, and it was apparent from polls of the Senate that the resolution would not pass.[179] The introduction of the resolution had the effect, however, of sidelining Hoover's plan to rally Republicans behind the Hoover-Gibson plan, since it "might be misinterpreted by the evilminded as trying to offset or discount Senators Burton and Ball's resolution." No one would consider William Allen White's actions as driven from such base motives, however, and Hoover suggested it might be better if the Kansan took the planned initiative.[180]

Meanwhile the former president continued to deliver speeches and to write articles for publication. In mid-March he addressed the Iowa legislature and a meeting of the Midwest Governors' Conference. In those speeches Hoover warned that the United States faced a food deficit and must increase its food production for a long war and for the momentous task of feeding the world after the war ended. He also told his listeners that America must be prepared to help police the world in the immediate postwar period and should begin now to plan for a peace that would end economic barriers and disarm the aggressors. As in his testimony before Congress the previous month, Hoover warned that the government was diverting too much farm labor to the armed forces and to factories, as well as too much steel from farm machinery to munitions production and too much fertilizer for use in producing explosives. The administration needed to realize that the same priority must be given to food production as to munitions manufacture for manpower and materials. He also called again for consolidation of all authority over food under the secretary of agriculture, and he, of course, pressed for adoption of the Hoover-Gibson formula for peacemaking.[181]

When British Prime Minister Winston Churchill suggested a few days later the creation of postwar regional councils to deal with the problems of Europe and Asia, Hoover and Gibson quickly expressed approval and added Churchill's proposal to their own peace program, adding such a council for the Western Hemisphere, as well, with the Pan American Union the logical agency on which to build such a council.[182] In an article for the *New York Times Magazine* in April, they suggested that such regional councils should bear the primary responsibility for the resolution of disputes within their regions, with recourse to a world institution only in the event of failure by the regional councils.[183]

In March Hoover traveled to Washington for meetings with GOP congressmen and senators, including Senators McNary and Butler, and Congressmen Martin, Vorys, and Ditter.[184] He was encouraged to feel that there was a "Southern Revolt from the New Deal" within the Democratic Party and, sounding somewhat like Landon in 1936, he thought there was now an "opportunity to build a real coalition or a national ticket."[185] After the meetings, William Castle reported that the congressmen had been enthusiastic about their visit with him.[186] Having learned from his conversations in Washington that the B2H2 resolution was dead, Hoover resolved to press on again with getting agreement on the Hoover-Gibson plan, writing William Allen White that he could not now be accused of interfering with the Ball and Burton proposal.[187]

White had already written a number of GOP leaders and by early April he was encouraged that "the whole thing seems to be working out about as we want it to go." He was also continuing his efforts to bring Willkie, Hoover, and Landon together, but Landon, "who has so much fox blood in him that he is skittish of his own tail," was "more or less coy." Nevertheless, White was confident that the three could be joined together "on some statement of foreign policy," and he was certain "the Republican expression of our foreign policy will in the end rally under Hoover's leadership, and that the Hoover proposals, with most unimportant reservations, will finally be accepted as the party's position."[188] Hoover seems to have grown somewhat pessimistic, however, writing a friend that the country was "about to go crazy on both the peace settlements and on the postwar planning questions, to say nothing of the mismanagement of the home front in the meantime. I do not know that any of us can contribute much sanity to the situation, but it seems to me important that I devote myself to that job."[189]

The possibility of a meeting with Landon arose when the Kansan decided to travel east to deliver a speech on foreign policy he had been preparing with Hoover's assistance. He thought that a meeting with Willkie might be held in Hoover's Waldorf suite, with no attempt at secrecy but that the contents of their discussion should be "entirely confidential and off the record."[190] Hoover responded that both he and Spangler hoped Landon would come east, whether the meeting with Willkie was held or not, but that such a meeting could be arranged "if it seems wise."[191] Landon left for the east in early April, although he had decided to postpone his speech until after British foreign secretary Anthony Eden's visit to Washington. During his visit, Landon conferred with Hoover, but without Willkie. A joint statement was not forthcoming, then, from the three GOP leaders, perhaps because of the imminent publication of Willkie's book, *One World*.

Willkie's book was released in April 1943 and contained much that Hoover could applaud but also a great deal that must have been disturbing. Willkie's naive acceptance of Stalin's expressions of support for the territorial integrity of all nations, their right to arrange their affairs as they wished, the restoration of democratic liberties, and all the rest must necessarily have grated on the sensibilities of those who, like Hoover, could recall the Soviet Union's naked aggression against such principles in the cases of Poland, Latvia, Estonia, Lithuania, and Finland.[192] Moreover, the two leaders disagreed on the timing for creating the international machinery for peacekeeping, which both advocated. Hoover called for the creation of such machinery late in the peace-making process, while Willkie advocated creating it now, while the war was still in progress. Willkie wrote that it was "idle to talk about creating after the war is over a machinery for preventing economic warfare and promoting peace between nations, unless . . . part of that machinery had been assembled under the unifying effort and common purpose of seeking to defeat the enemy."[193] The distance between the two over this proposition meant that any basis for a common statement on postwar policy was lacking, although both could continue to work toward the same ultimate objective—the creation of an international organization.

Willkie's book began immediately to sell at a staggering rate, apparently absent any of the promotion that had supported the Hoover-Gibson volume. By early May it was also apparent that the 1940 nominee was angling for the 1944 nomination. Landon and Spangler were rumored to be part of a "stop Willkie" movement, and it seemed apparent that those rumors had originated with Willkie or his supporters in an effort to advance his own candidacy.[194]

Among the proposals for peacemaking after the war, Hoover found one introduced by Senator Wilson in the Senate better than most, for it provided "the Senate and House shall have a voice in these discussions." Hoover, though, was convinced that "we would get further—and—faster if these discussions were limited to the methods and machinery for making the peace. Everybody seems to want to make the peace itself." He thought that the Roosevelt administration would oppose any resolution that would take peacemaking out of their own hands, but there would be less objection if "the resolution was directed towards setting up the machinery for making peace" rather than the content of the peace itself.[195]

In March, Herbert Lehman also queried Hoover for advice in dealing with accounting and statistics in his foreign relief and rehabilitation operations, based on Hoover's American Recovery Administration experiences.[196] Hoover responded by suggesting that Lehman contact Dr. Frank Surface, who had been "one of our leading statisticians and who still is."[197]

In May Landon finally delivered his delayed speech on foreign policy and was praised by William Allen White who lauded him for having "unqualifiedly landed with Hoover and Willkie, or at least between them, a little to the right of Willkie and a little to the left of Hoover."[198] Hoover agreed, wiring Landon that the "speech came over fine" and asking for copies so that it could be given more publicity.[199] For White, Landon's speech symbolized that "Hoover, Willkie and Landon, who certainly are officially leaders of the Republican party, are unanimous in their feeling against isolation." He thought it now would be possible to get their agreement on the long-desired statement and that 25 to 30 other leaders of the GOP might be induced to join them. White even thought Hoover might be a potential Republican nominee for 1944 and that he could win against Roosevelt.[200] Even Landon conceded late in March that Hoover "is stronger in the country today than he has been at any time since 1932. I hear it on all sides."[201]

GOP National Chairman Harrison Spangler had been for some time considering the creation of a Republican Post-War Advisory Council. The cumulative effects of the efforts in behalf of the Hoover-Gibson plan, the groping of Senate Republicans for a postwar policy through such devices as the B2H2 resolution, Willkie's book, and Landon's speech, apparently convinced him that the time was ripe for such an initiative. He wrote Landon that the council would now begin its work and that Senator McNary and Congressman Martin had designated committees from the Senate and House to work with GOP governors in developing a postwar program for the Republican Party in both domestic and foreign areas.[202]

Some historians have wrongly concluded that Spangler's initiative resulted from the pressure of public opinion generated by Willkie's book, but it should be clear that the movement in behalf of a postwar GOP policy long predated the appearance of Willkie's book and that in seeking to base the foreign policy on the Hoover-Gibson book the movement was anything but isolationist. William Allen White, hardly an isolationist, was at the center of that movement, determined that the fate of international cooperation should not be the same as it had been nearly a quarter of a century earlier. In those efforts, White was in close cooperation with Spangler. On April 6, two days before the Willkie book was released, White wrote Spangler,

> I feel reasonably certain that if Hoover, Landon, and Willkie would agree on a statement we could bring in with them on the statement 8 or 10 Senators and the most important leaders in the House. The publication of such a statement signed by such men would do much to take the bitterness out of the platform fight on foreign policy. I can't conceive of much serious difference on domestic policy—which perhaps might be better said: I can't conceive that even a bitter fight on matters of domestic policy would leave the party badly shaken. The big issue is foreign policy. The split, if any, will come there and it seems to me most important that we who feel these matters seriously should do what we can to iron out the honest differences.[203]

Making such unity difficult, however, were the efforts of Willkie and his followers to continue their war against the other Republican leaders and the GOP organization, apparently as determined as Willkie's biographers have been to develop the image of Willkie as the lone "internationalist" in the Republican Party battling against the "isolationism" of the "Old Guard." Willkie's smears were increasingly alienating his fellow Republicans. One against Landon in June disturbed the Kansan so much that he almost considered an open break with the man whose nomination he had assisted so greatly three years before. But Landon still felt it was necessary to "preserve a reasonable unity in the Republican Party," even though Willkie had by now "broken with all those who had most to do with his nomination" and had shown during the 1940 campaign and ever since that he lacked an understanding of those principles of political leadership that were requisite in a president of the United States.[204]

The Willkie wing of the party involved itself in the creation of a Republican Postwar Policies Association, which, though it adopted the *One World* line, claimed that it had no candidate for 1944 and received no Willkie money. The divisive tactics and smears of the Willkie faction led both Hoover and Landon to cast about for a candidate for 1944 who could derail Willkie's drive for renomination. Late in May Hoover began to connive with other Republicans in an effort to undermine Willkie's popularity, first by trying to drive a wedge between Willkie and California governor Earl Warren, and then by giving Governor John Bricker of Ohio his covert support.[205] He was also working once again for an uninstructed delegation from California to the Republican convention.

The B2H2 resolution having failed to make any headway, Senator Arthur Vandenberg joined with Senator Wallace White to draft an alternative that they presented to the Senate on July 2, 1943. The new resolution differed from B2H2 in a number of particulars, but of special note is the fact that it met one of Hoover's primary objections to the earlier resolution by averring that all American peace actions should be by "due Constitutional processes," which, as Vandenberg put it, eliminated "the Roosevelt habit and desire to bypass Congress in these respects." It also pledged "faithful recognition of American interests" and called for cooperation among sovereign states, thus precluding the possibility of a world state such as some of the more idealistic and utopian were demanding.[206]

Hoover had remained constructively critical of the New Deal's mishandling of the home front in newspaper and magazine articles, in testimony before congressional committees, and in speeches. In early June, one of his associates on Wilson's "war cabinet" was at last called to duty by the Roosevelt administration, when the president finally appointed Bernard Baruch to be an advisor to the Office of War Mobilization. In reporting the event, the *New York Times* did not see in it any "special basis for hope that many more members of the country's 'first team' will be taken into the war administration," but it added, "As has been demonstrated positively, in the last few months, some of these [first team members] can be very effective on the sidelines. The most recent contributions of former President Hoover to a solution of the problems of food and—in collaboration with Hugh Gibson—of post-war planning have been valuable. The comment could fairly be made that clearer and more constructive ideas are to be found in these utterances than in any that have come on the same topics from members of the administration." The newspaper went on to say that the difference between Hoover's and Roosevelt's speeches on the food problem represented the "difference between facts and good intentions," while the Hoover-Gibson peace plan was "more soundly imaginative and promising than any that has come from an official source." It concluded, "Thus from the sidelines men like Mr. Hoover, whose talents are not wanted officially, can serve the nation and the world in abundant measure." But how much more effective might the war effort have been if this member of the nation's "first team" had been called to serve?[207]

The recognition of Hoover's value was increasing, however, even with the Roosevelt administration. The day following the observations of the *New York Times*, Chester C. Davis, administrator of the War Food Administration, wrote Hoover, "If and when conditions here become stabilized so that I can discuss policy with some assurance, I hope very much to have the opportunity to counsel with you." In the meantime, he had directed his assistant to call on Hoover in California for advice.[208] The former president responded that he "would be glad to be of any service at any time, in any way that I can." He could not believe, Hoover told Davis, "that the seriousness of the situation is being realized by the people with whom you have to work."[209] Viewing the situation on the home front, Hoover wrote one correspondent that the slogan of World War I had been "Win the war by cooperation," while in the present one it seemed to be "Win the war by suffering."[210]

Spangler's Republican Advisory Council now appeared to be the best vehicle for adoption of the Hoover-Gibson program for peacemaking, and in late July Hoover pressed it upon him. The party must take new and constructive action, he warned, in order to dispel once and for all the charge that it was isolationist. He wrote writer Clarence Kelland, "The way to kill off phrase-makers is to produce something new and worthwhile out of the Advisory Committee. This program is not only sound but new and prevents a thousand frictions."[211] Former GOP chairman John Hamilton agreed, saying, "We should do all we can, and the Republican [Advisory] committee seems the proper place to do it to dispel any thought that the Republican Party is isolationist in any respect."[212] Hoover also lobbied others on behalf of his plan, including New Jersey Senator Albert Hawkes, who promised that he "would follow through on the plan suggested by you . . . because it is very sound and practical."[213]

On August 5 Senator H. Alexander Smith wrote Senator Warren Austin, of the Willkie camp, that he had been asked by Spangler to draft some formal resolutions for the Republican Advisory Council. He sent to Austin his draft on postwar policy, pointing out that its recommendations were general as the forthcoming meeting of the council on Mackinac Island in Michigan would go into specifics, but he felt his draft should "indicate the general framework in which we propose to present our report."[214] Smith's draft called for "the participation of the United States in postwar cooperation between sovereign nations to prevent by any necessary means the recurrence of military aggression and to establish permanent peace with justice in a free world." There was no mention of participation in an international organization, and Austin made certain that he penciled in this addition to the Smith draft.[215] By now,

however, even Austin realized that the GOP was far removed from isolationism and that the question before the Republican Advisory Council would be
how the United States would cooperate with the rest of the world rather than
whether it would do so.[216] Austin noted that the resolutions Smith proposed
indicated a "broader vision," which he concluded "the country at large is rapidly embracing, however reluctantly, in all but a notably and admittedly very
important group of fine midwestern states."[217]

As the date for the Mackinac Conference approached, Hoover exerted
all his efforts in seeking to ensure that the postwar program adopted would
embrace the Hoover-Gibson proposals.[218] Writing to Governor Bricker,
who would be at Mackinac but was not on the foreign policy committee, he
expressed concern over the foreign relations plank that would be adopted,
writing that it was likely to be similar to the resolutions that had been introduced in Congress. Hoover had no objection to those but regarded them as
insufficient. What was needed, he told Bricker, was "some bold, constructive,
specific proposals that will get outside of words and their traps and will give
the Party some distinction of determination." He suggested the essence of the
Hoover-Gibson program should be included in any resolution of the council,
including the specification of a provisional peace, or "cooling-off period," and
"the development of a world institution to preserve peace."

If these were included in the council's resolution, Hoover argued, they would

> accomplish six things: (a) Prevent commitment of the Party to New Deal peace
> plans until we have had a chance to consider them. (b) Give a distinctive and
> new approach to the whole problem of peace. (c) It will be in effect an assertion
> that we must get away from the futile methods of the past. (d) It avoids throw-
> ing the Republican Party into a debate as to how much national sovereignty
> will be parted with by "policing the world" because that question cannot arise
> until the world has had a chance to cool off and do its job constructively. (e) It is
> a program upon which we could get much unity. It would not conflict with any
> known proposals of the New Deal and, therefore, could not be charged with
> dividing the country's unity. (f) It would demonstrate that the Conference had
> not been dominated by certain destructive persons.

He was making a speech over the radio on September 3, Hoover told Bricker,
which would go further into the reasons for his proposal, and he was also
writing to other members of the council to urge that his plan be taken up at
Mackinac.[219] Clearly Hoover hoped that his speech, too, would influence the
deliberations of the Mackinac Conference.

CHAPTER 8

Planning for Peace

Mackinac

In June, John Callan O'Laughlin wrote Hoover that the Roosevelt adminis-tration had "mixed feelings" about the GOP forming a committee to develop a postwar program. O'Laughlin wrote that while they felt its program might be coordinated with that of the administration, there were likely also to be "irreconcilable differences." The administration welcomed Hoover's absence from the committee but was disappointed that Willkie was not on it, since it felt that he could be relied on to influence the committee toward the admin-istration's program. Hull and others in the administratrion, O'Laughlin said, were "apprehensive . . . that the Republican attitude will show the world that there is division amongst our people about the kind of peace we will accept, and this will cause embarrassment to the President in the negotiations he is conducting and has in mind."[1]

The speech that Hoover delivered in Minneapolis on September 3 was, by timing and content, clearly designed to influence the discussion about to begin on Mackinac Island, and he had mailed off advance copies of the address to members of the council, including Senators Austin and Vandenberg.[2] The American people, Hoover said, were "alive to the need and determined that we must have a lasting peace this time." The discussion over postwar policies was being dominated by two kinds of people—those who had looked to the past and were attempting to propose "something definite and positive" and those who "live in the indefinite or the infinite," whose ideas were mostly "nebulous words" about the need to preserve peace and restore prosper-ity. Nations that were successful at war making were all too often failures at peacemaking. It was time for a new approach to peacemaking—one that "must leave the century-old bright lights of eloquence and nebular words and explore the hard road of experience." Hoover then went on to describe the Hoover-Gibson program for his listeners, including the program's fourth step—the creation of a world institution to preserve peace.[3]

A few days later he wired Arch Shaw that the speech had received a great deal of favorable editorial comment in the nation's newspapers. Hoover added, "At yesterday's press conference the President practically adopted the line himself. The newspapers here comment on the fact that it is my proposal." Hoover wondered if Kellogg, the cereal manufacturer, might be interested in underwriting the printing and distribution of one-half-million copies since it seemed possible that the program in the speech was something on "which we might get common agreement throughout the country."[4] The former president apparently did not feel that the nation had yet been sufficiently saturated with the Hoover-Gibson proposal, despite its distribution in book and article form, as well as in speeches and in the numerous condensations he had circulated throughout the country. He wrote a friend early in April, "There is still a lot to do in this world and perhaps the day will come when we older men may have more of a voice than we do today—even though we remain on the sidelines."[5]

Since the speech had no air outlet in Chicago, the *Chicago Tribune* reproduced it in full in its pages at the insistence of Arch Shaw and Chauncey McCormick, brother of the *Tribune's* publisher, Colonel Robert McCormick. Chauncey McCormick wrote Hoover that he "knew nothing better than your speech to stymie the Willkie boys." The *Tribune* had also editorialized in support of Hoover's position, and McCormick had "found keen enthusiasm" for the speech.[6]

The Mackinac Conference was held on the island by that name and attended by 49 delegates and 100 newspapermen—2 reporters for every Republican delegate. Since no cars were permitted, all traveled around in 50 horse-drawn carriages after traveling to the island by lake steamers.[7] Much to Hoover's disappointment, the conference ignored the Hoover-Gibson four-step peacemaking process, although it did embrace their concept of a postwar international organization of sovereign nations. The conference produced a document that was largely lacking in content and certainly devoid of anything new. The product of a committee that consisted of Senators Vandenberg and Austin, Governors Dwight Green and Edward Marvin, Congressman Charles Eaton, and Congresswoman Frances Bolton, the resolution disclaimed any attempt "at this time" to put forth "a detailed program for the accomplishment" of the great aims it envisioned. Instead, the council went on record in support of the prosecution of the war "to conclusive victory over all our enemies" and looked to "responsible participation by the United States in post-war cooperative organization among sovereign nations to prevent military aggression and to attain permanent peace with organized justice in a free world." Participation in the "post-war cooperative organization among sovereign nations" was, moreover, hedged with numerous Hooverian qualifiers relating to the national interest and the Constitution.[8] Historian Robert

Divine has described the statement as "the most important step yet taken toward American involvement in a future international organization."[9] Clearly Hoover had been a major influence in moving the GOP to an acceptance of that role for the United States.

The attempts of Willkie and his supporters in politics and journalism to make internationalism a divisive issue in the GOP that Willkie might exploit for his own political benefit have obscured for many historians the consensus among Republicans regarding the postwar role the United States should play in an international organization, as well as the fact that Hoover and his supporters, like William Allen White, played a far more important role than Willkie in bringing about that consensus and the declaration at Mackinac. While Willkie's influence with GOP leaders was by now minimal, those same leaders had been deluged with the Hoover-Gibson postwar program and with appeals from those like William Allen White that the program should be made the basis for Republican postwar policy. As for the Mackinac Conference itself, Hoover later claimed to have been the one "probably responsible for the committee which resulted in the Mackinac conference," and his claim cannot be easily dismissed when it is recalled that it was longtime Hoover ally Harrison Spangler who spearheaded the call for the Republican advisory committee that led to the conference.[10]

The Mackinac declaration fell short, in fact, of the position Hoover had taken. While "internationalist" Senator Warren Austin was encouraged that the declaration had abandoned "cooperation" for "cooperative organization," Hoover's draft statement and his speech of September 3 had called for "a world institution."[11] William Allen White agreed that Hoover's draft and speech were preferable to the declaration issued by the conference, which he described as an "innocuous straddle," necessary to reconcile the extreme internationalists with the extreme nationalists. "But," White concluded, "because I felt the straddle was going in the right direction, I didn't complain much."[12] Indeed, he had little about which to complain, for with the help of another Hoover ally, Harrison Spangler, his efforts on behalf of the Hoover-Gibson program had been rewarded in what he regarded as their most important aspect, the commitment of the GOP to international cooperation. The United Nations organization would not meet the fate that had crippled the League of Nations at its birth.

All but a small minority of Republicans were pleased with the Mackinac Conference statement, with approval registered in GOP newspapers ranging from the *Chicago Tribune*, widely regarded as isolationist, to the "internationalist" *New York Herald Tribune*.[13] Hoover's friends on the council were apologetic over their failure to go further in adopting Hoover's suggestions. Taft explained that the committee on foreign affairs had been "faced by a very difficult problem which superseded every other consideration"—the desire of Vandenberg to obtain unity on a statement that would assert "the continued sovereignty of the United States." According to Taft, Vandenberg's efforts to bring Austin and his group to agreement on this had used up all his energy, or else he would have tried to incorporate more of the Hoover-Gibson plan. Still, Taft was pleased that the declaration excluded "extreme isolation on one side and the Stassen international state on the other."[14]

The Mackinac statement was only intended as a preliminary declaration, and the committees were now to work out a more detailed platform for the Republican convention in 1944. Hoover was encouraged to believe that his other proposals might be adopted when Senator Warren Austin wrote him a few days after Mackinac to ask for a copy of the Hoover-Gibson program "for my use in future meetings of the permanent committee on Foreign Policy."[15] The former president responded with a copy of *The Problems of Lasting Peace*, a condensation that had appeared in *Collier's*, a copy of his September 3 speech, and a paragraph he had suggested for the Mackinac declaration.[16]

Hoover also derived some satisfaction that his clipping service reported more newspaper editorial support for his Minneapolis speech than for the Mackinac declaration.[17] Another source of satisfaction, but also of some chagrin, was the increasing evidence that the Roosevelt administration seemed to be committing itself to the Hoover-Gibson program. The day after the Mackinac Conference had failed to incorporate his peacemaking proposals in its declaration, Roosevelt had, in Hoover's view, "snapped it up" at his press conference. It seemed that Hoover's ideas on postwar peacemaking were finding more support in the Roosevelt administration than in the GOP. Willkie's own book, *One World*, was published in 1943 and attracted little positive attention from Republicans. Observing that Willkie had "sunk to such a low ebb . . . despite the 'claque' which has unceasingly boosted him privately and publicly," Landon did not "think his book is going to help him."[18] Henry Allen wrote Hoover likewise that he did not think the book was "doing him any good now. There is a growing conviction that his book indicates that he desires America to be the social security headquarters for the world. Men compare it with Wallace's demand that every child in the world should have a bottle of milk."[19]

Neither Roosevelt nor undersecretary of state Sumner Welles would, of course, credit Hoover and Gibson with paternity of their own expressions of support for a transitional period before peacemaking, although they apparently appreciated the contribution Hoover was making to acceptance of the idea by public opinion.[20] Shortly before the Mackinac Conference, Hoover received via John Callan O'Laughlin evidence that his stance on postwar policy was receiving a sympathetic ear within the State Department. O'Laughlin passed on a message from Secretary of State Hull, which he said was "substantially as follows":

> Please say to President Hoover that I deeply appreciate his approval of what I am trying to do, and that I am grateful for his kind offer to help me. I think his proposal for a transitional period in connection with the peace is one of

very great importance, and he may be sure that I will give it my most earnest consideration . . . I think the contributions Mr. Hoover and Mr. Gibson made in their book were admirable. Unfortunately, in these times the crackpots rise to the surface, and it is gratifying that sane men are giving their thought to the important subject of the peace terms.[21]

When the *Kansas City Star* published an editorial supporting Hoover's postwar plan, the former president wrote the editor, "That was a helpful editorial. Now we have to go to work on what kind of a world institution—and caution our people not to be in hurry. They need to see the shifting scene for a year or two or three before taking this, the most important act of all human action in our time except the defeat of the enemy."[22] Radio commentator H. V. Kaltenborn also thought Hoover's *Collier's* articles represented "an important contribution to the peace problem" and said he would "be happy to refer to them in my broadcasts." The problem, he told Hoover, was to harness idealism "to the step by step procedures which are our only promise of permanent results."[23]

Foreign Affairs

Thomas Dewey had called, on the eve of the Mackinac Conference, for a postwar alliance between the United States and Great Britain. Despite Hoover's suggestion of something very similar during his discussion with the British ambassador the previous year, the former president was now opposed to the idea. He considered that Dewey had "got off wrong on this line" and did not consider it "helpful either to him or the country."[24] Columnist Walter Lippmann had taken a similar line in his book, *U.S. Foreign Policy: Shield of the Republic*, and Hoover wondered if J. Reuben Clark could not write a critical response to it. Hoover told Clark, "The whole book is built upon the premise that the British have been our friends and guardians over 120 years and consequently we ought to do various things with Great Britain. Lippmann belongs to a great clan developing in the United States who would like to see our reentry into the British Empire." He told William Allen White that he and Hugh Gibson agreed with many of Lippmann's conclusions, but Lippmann "leaves the world a continuous armed camp basing peace on power politics. To me it is a counsel of despair, a destruction of all hope."[25]

A few months later John Foster Dulles, then chairman of the Commission to Study Bases of a Just and Durable Peace, established by the Federal Council of the Churches of Christ in American, thanked Hoover and Gibson for the opportunity to meet with them and exchange views. He was, he told Hoover, doing his best to combat Walter Lippmann's thesis through his speeches. He was confident that Lippmann's thesis would "not prevail and that the work which our commission is doing will be one of the major reasons why it will not prevail."[26] Dulles would soon emerge as a major foreign policy advisor to Thomas Dewey.

During 1943, Hoover and other Republicans became concerned that the Roosevelt administration was deserting the noble ideals of the Atlantic Charter for a reliance on alliances and balance of power politics in postwar international relations. They were especially alarmed at what this might mean for Soviet domination of Eastern Europe. This concern began with Hoover at least as early as June of 1942, when it became clear to him that the Soviets aspired after the war to extend their boundaries to "include half of Poland, half of Finland, Estonia, Latvia, Lithuania and Bessarabia." He regarded the negotiations that month between Britain and the USSR as indicating a "return to the old ways of military alliances and balances of power. Those American wishful thinkers who believe this is an abolished practice in the world should have a rude jolt."[27]

One peace organization, the National Council for the Prevention of War, which had supported Hoover's efforts to get food relief to the occupied democracies, began to campaign in February 1943 for a negotiated peace, since it argued that "a war in Europe fought to the bitter end can result only in the triumph of communism" and that the conquest of Japan "would merely extend communism throughout China and neighboring countries." The organization argued that five more years of war would also "leave our country denuded of much of its youth, impoverished and thoroughly regimented under either a Nazi or a communist type of dictatorship."[28] Hoover was certain that Stalin had no intention of giving up any of the territories he had acquired by force in 1939 and that Poland was doomed, while "all the New Deal and British columnists and radio commentators are now busy conditioning the American and British mind to the notion that this rape is no violation of the Atlantic Charter or the purpose for which Britain declared war."[29]

Landon, too, had become convinced by mid-1943 that Roosevelt was "shifting to a balance of power policy and is himself abandoning the Four Freedoms and the Atlantic Charter to that effect."[30] Even Walter Lippmann was predicting a postwar world that would be a continuous armed camp with the only peace based on power politics.[31] The realities of the emerging world situation in 1943 were already clearly at variance with the Atlantic Charter, which Americans had been led to believe embodied the ideals for which they were fighting. In late October, Landon attacked the new direction he perceived international relations were taking in a speech and he received warm approval from Hoover, who told him, "I thought it was a good thing that you challenged Roosevelt on the question of military alliances. It brought that subject out where it ought to be."[32]

Hoover was somewhat encouraged by the results of the foreign ministers' meeting in Moscow in November 1943. The declaration at the end of that meeting indicated that Hull had adopted the Hoover-Gibson formula for peacemaking and had succeeded in getting the approval of the Soviet Union as well. O'Laughlin recalled the message that Hull had earlier sent via him to Hoover and wrote, "Obviously the proposal which you and Hugh made guided Mr. Hull in the highly successful negotiations he concluded at Moscow."[33] Taft agreed that there was "no doubt that Secretary Hull had followed your pioneering thought in the Moscow provisions dealing with the method of peace."[34] Landon, too, said he was glad to see Hoover "getting the credit you deserve out of the Moscow Declaration."[35]

The former president agreed that the only significant difference between the Hoover-Gibson plan and that enunciated at Moscow was that "Mr. Hull himself elected the four powers to guide the world over the Transition Period instead of waiting to go through the form we suggested of having the United Nations elect them!" He wrote publisher Roy Howard that the Moscow Declaration had followed the approach to peacemaking

> in exactly the methods that Hugh and I have been agitating during the last 18 months. You will find it in the following approach:
>
> In its peace phases the Declaration is notable by the absence of any reference to a general peace conference or any armistice or any long-term military alliances. Instead it envisages:
>
> a. The leadership in restoring order in the world by the four leading powers—their action to proceed by consultation and collaboration;
> b. A transition period after surrender and pending the establishment of some sort of world institution to preserve peace during which the leading nations will establish law and order;
> c. The creation of such a world institution "based on the principle of the sovereign equality . . . and open to membership by all nations."[36]

Hoover also wrote to other newspaper editors and publishers to point out the similarities. H. J. Haskell of the *Kansas City Star* wrote the former president to thank him for the material he had received "calling attention to the striking similarities of your peace plan and the plan adopted at Moscow." He sent Hoover a copy of an editorial the *Star* had published on the subject and told the former president, "It must be a real satisfaction to have made such a contribution on this vital subject."[37] The editor of *Woman's Home Companion* wrote Hoover, "Congratulations on the deserved recognition that you and Hugh Gibson got in Arthur Krock's column . . . in connection with the Declaration of Moscow." He told Hoover that he planned "to weave a few paragraphs from the *New York Times* piece into the editor's note that we will publish as a foreword to the important article you and Mr. Gibson have written for us."[38] Hoover responded by sending Anthony even more editorials, to which the editor responded that they were "a thrilling testimonial to what a lot of us have considered one of your greatest public services,—one that will have far-reaching consequences in the years to come."[39]

The *New York Times* agreed that while the State Department committee that drafted the Moscow Declaration "did not include Herbert Hoover or

Wendell Willkie," the text did reveal "how directly both contributed to the great achievement, giving the Republican party the right to claim a large and important share." The *Times* erroneously credited Willkie with being chiefly responsible for the GOP's support for postwar international cooperation, but it added, "The part played by Mr. Hoover, however, in association with Hugh Gibson is not so well realized, but the blueprint of Moscow bears, among others, the Hoover-Gibson signature, and in very large letters . . . A comparison of their proposals with the Declaration of Moscow reveals a striking parallel. Except for the fact that the Four Powers assigned the transition world leadership to themselves instead of having themselves elected by the United Nations, no important disparity is visible."[40]

From Secretary of State Hull, via O'Laughlin, came "keen satisfaction" that Hoover approved of the Moscow Declaration. He did not think there was any substantial difference between the declaration and the Hoover-Gibson plan even in the selection of nations assigned to "guide the world over the transition period," since the United Nations might still be called upon to select the four trustee powers. While he had drawn on all quarters for advice, Hull told O'Laughlin he had found the Hoover-Gibson "proposal especially acceptable, and it guided him in the formulation of the paragraph of the agreement cited above." O'Laughlin concluded that Hull was obviously "grateful for the transition period idea."[41]

When Landon issued a statement critical of the Moscow agreements, Hoover was concerned that the Kansan had given "Willkie another chance to start a cry of isolation in the Republican Party," which leading newspapers like the *New York Herald Tribune* and *New York Times* had taken up in order "to further Willkie." The former president quickly got "Alf on the carpet" and then issued an explanatory statement in which he said Landon was not opposed to the Moscow Declaration but had "rightly objected to advance pledges of Republicans to commitments on peace settlements until these proposals are made known."[42] His own statement, Hoover claimed, had "served to stop division that would only have added confusion in the public mind on the whole foreign situation. The Governor went a considerable distance. He feels deeply that the New York press is trying to stop free discussion. The important thing is to keep the forty or fifty prominent Republican leaders on the constructive side. It is not so easy when criticism is so easy and most men so suspicious of the Administration." He had found it necessary, he told O'Laughlin, "to stop outbreaks from eight different Republican Governors during the last four days. I have felt that some semblance of solidarity on foreign relations must be maintained."[43] The former president was clearly seeking to still GOP criticism of a foreign policy that he considered to be essentially of his own design.

Late in July, Hoover broadcast a speech before the Emergency Conference to Save the Jews of Europe. Of the Jews, Hoover said that there was "no language which will either portray their agonies or describe their oppressors . . . To find relief for them is one of the great human problems of today." He continued,

> There should be more systematic temporary measures. There are groups of Jews who have escaped into the neutral countries of Europe. Others might be gotten out, and an effort should be made. They and any other refugees from the persecution of Fascism should be assured of support by the United Nations. This should go farther. Definite refugee-stations should be arranged in these neutral countries for those who may escape. But these measures should be accompanied by arrangements to steadily transfer them from these refugee-stations in neutral countries to other quarters. Possibly the release of greater numbers of refugees could be secured from the Nazi countries by European neutrals.

Then Hoover joined the plight of the Jews with his efforts to get food relief to Europe:

> There is another direction of temporary aid to these distressed people. For two years I have urged the systematic food-relief of starving women, children and unemployed men in the occupied countries. That would have included several million Jews. Relief was refused on the ground that such action would aid the Germans. We proposed conditions that would have prevented this. Relief was however finally permitted to one of these countries—that is, Greece—under the exact conditions which we stipulated . . . And our State Department says officially that it is not benefiting the Germans. Does not this experience warrant its extension to other occupied countries? It would save the lives of thousands of Jews.
>
> Long-view relief resolves itself into two phases: where to migrate these people so as to find permanent security; how to establish them in living.
>
> We must accept the fact that the older and more fully settled countries have no longer any land and opportunity to absorb the migration of the oppressed. Most Jews recognize that it is not in their interest to force such an issue. Palestine could take more of them. But after all Palestine would absorb only a part of the three or four millions whom this Conference has been discussing as needing relief. That could be accomplished only by moving the Arab population to some other quarter. These are problems impossible to settle during the war . . . There should be some place where they may build a new civilization as they did on this continent during the last century. The newest continent, from point of view of development, is Africa . . . Large areas of this upland are suitable for a white civilization. They are rich in material resources. But if we are to make use of them, there must be vast preparation. Men, women and children today cannot be dumped into new lands. There must be definitely organized advance preparation of housing, transportation, industrial establishments and agriculture on a huge scale. Many of these great African areas are mandates established from the last war, in trust for all the world. Such an area in Africa could be considered sentimentally an annex to Palestine.

The Allies, he said, should "undertake to finance and manage a real solution as part of the war." After the war, the Axis powers should "be required to restore the property of these persecuted peoples and help financially their new settlement."[44]

After the Teheran Conference later that year between FDR, Stalin, and Churchill, O'Laughlin wrote Hoover that the agreement there seemed to have "advanced farther toward your plan . . . Certainly the communique proves Teheran to be an anti-climax to the Moscow Conference, unless there were secret agreements of which we will know nothing."[45] Hoover, however, thought the "whole thing looks like secret verbal agreements."[46]

Food Questions

Much of Hoover's attention during 1943 was also occupied with food questions, both foreign and domestic. On the domestic front, he urged House Minority Leader Joseph Martin to establish a Republican food committee of House members in order to monitor management by the Roosevelt administration of the nation's food supply. He suggested the committee be given "a consumers' complexion" by the appointment of half its members from consumer states, the other half from agricultural areas.[47] Martin did appoint such a committee and named Congressman Thomas A. Jenkins as chairman, since his New York district was both urban and rural. The former president wrote a friend in early April that "the whole meat question has been so badly administered that it is a mess." New York City, he said, "has not had 30 percent of its normal supply for a month."[48] Hoover wrote Taft in April that the "food situation is getting worse and worse for having started down the line of [the Roosevelt administration's] particular idea of ceiling prices at retail outlets," and now the government was "plunging deeper and deeper into the mire." All such approaches by other countries during World War I had failed, Hoover recalled, and under his leadership the US Food Administration had concentrated instead on "stimulating production, in smooth distribution, in preventing black markets and local famines, and in protecting both the farmer and consumer." He sent Taft a memorandum on the methods used during World War I in handling meats and wondered if it were not time for Taft to "make an effective speech on this subject and at an early date."[49] Bernard Baruch wrote Hoover that the Hoover-Gibson postwar program "really ought to be sent far and wide." He added, "At the moment, I am trying to get order in Washington. One of the things I am trying to do is to get Chester Davis appointed as Secretary of Agriculture and Food Administration and get the whole thing under one head just as you advised."[50]

In mid-June Hoover wrote columnist Arthur Krock that he had been in the mining states checking on the Roosevelt administration's handling of the metals industry. He found "zinc, lead and copper ore production" were declining and would "decline more under the same chaos that affects food." Numerous critics, including Hoover, had offered "alternative plans, but his opposition, as you indicated, is congenial." Hoover predicted, though, that events would "crowd him. Food supplies will continue to diminish, black markets will increase, prices will rise (and hell itself may break loose in our seaboard cities) before another year is over. I am indeed greatly disturbed that we may weaken the whole war effort on the home front."[51]

In a speech to the Federated Farm Bureaus in June, Hoover demanded reorganization of the administration's food program to clear up "this muddle of uncontrolled food prices, local famines, profiteering, black markets and stifled farm production." His suggestions included (1) consolidation of all authority over food production and distribution under one responsible administrator, in the person of food administrator Chester Davis, who should be Secretary of Agriculture and a member of the Office of Manpower Mobilization; (2) decentralization of the work under state, municipal, and county administrators; (3) increase in farm manpower over the prewar level and the planting of forty to fifty million more acres in 1944 than in 1943; (4) shift of industrial production to provide large additions of farm machinery; (5) abolition of the system of retail and wholesale price ceilings; (6) encouragement of farmers to appoint war committees to engage in collective bargaining on prices, with parities abandoned for the duration of the war; (7) fixed rationing to balance consumption with production; (8) establishment of war committees in the processing and distributing trades to keep the flow of food moving to the right places and enforcement of the dealer licensing system to stop black markets; (9) abandonment of subsidies to either farmers, traders, or consumers.[52]

Hoover's speech was interrupted many times by applause, and American Farm Bureau president Edward A. O'Neal told him, "Most of the farmers of the nation are for you and the program you have announced."[53] The speech received favorable comments from Republicans, but a few days later Roosevelt labeled Hoover's criticism of his administration's food management as absurd. Hoover wrote to his former secretary of agriculture, Arthur Hyde,

> The speech apparently got under the President's hide and he made an extraordinary statement about it just the other day. I can quite well believe that it all sounds "absurd" to him and especially when we in the last war had no black markets, no local famines, we were shipping more supplies to our allies than we are now, when prices rose less, and when even after the armistice we were able to ship 30 billion pounds to Europe, and now just the reverse of these things is happening under the machinery in motion in Washington.[54]

But FDR had insisted on ignoring the tested methods and the experienced men of World War I. The food situation would remain in chaos through the war years, with serious consequences when a world famine loomed in the postwar years.

In September 1943 Hoover wrote Krock that the "manpower situation in the country is much worse than Washington would like to admit or even than Mr. Baruch's notable report discloses." Almost every essential industry was short of labor that was showing up in inadequate maintenance of the railroads and would later show up in food shortages.[55] In that same month the Roosevelt administration did, however, retreat on the manpower front. Arthur Krock reported in the *New York Times* that the US army was planning to cut its projected strength down from 8.2 million troops to 7.7 million in order to prevent disruption on the home front. Krock pointed out that those who had "pointed out obvious flaws in the domestic program met with stubborn opposition and were called hard names. Former President Hoover was one of these." The columnist recalled Hoover's testimony before a Senate subcommittee in February 1943, when he had criticized the mobilization plan for taking needed workers away from the farms, mines, and petroleum fields. That testimony had been quickly challenged by Undersecretary of War Patterson, but Krock had found even then that "many of those 'charged with the heavy responsibility of winning the war' agreed with Hoover."[56]

The Roosevelt administration and its allies in Congress had, however, been "totally uncompromising" and had made clumsy attempts to smear the former president by citing a memorandum Hoover had sent to Colonel Edward House during World War I advocating that priority be given to food and munitions shipments to Europe over the transport of troops. Roosevelt himself had encouraged Secretary of War Robert Patterson to use the memorandum, and Patterson had charged that if Hoover's advice had been followed in 1917 "the Germans would have won the war in the summer of 1918." Hoover's advice in 1943, however, was not the same as in 1917, and there was disagreement between Hoover and the administration over when the 1917 memorandum had been written—in March or in October. That the administration was willing to dig through the House Papers at Yale University for the memorandum, however, evidencing the extent to which it felt itself to be on the defensive.[57] The cut in the projected army size was proof even the Roosevelt administration belatedly recognized that Hoover and the other critics had been correct.

In late September Congressman Jenkins solicited Hoover's views on the food situation and suggested that a member of the committee consult with the former president in New York.[58] Hoover welcomed such a visit and wrote Jenkins that the situation had only changed for the worse: "The folly of divided administrative responsibilities is more evident every day. The folly of subsidies of the farmers from the public's point of view is the same. Their political purpose is just as evident. The driving of cattle away from feed lots, the use of a vastly unnecessary amount of skim milk for hogs, the famines in beef and dairy products are all samples of mismanagement."[59] Following Hoover's recommendations, Jenkins told him the committee would introduce legislation in Congress that would centralize food activities under one head and would seek immediate steps to increase food production in 1944. It also planned to give ample publicity to the follies of the Roosevelt administration's food policies and their consequences. Even if their efforts produced no changes in the policies of the administration, Jenkins was hopeful that they would have an effect on the 1944 election.[60]

There was also little abatement of Hoover's desire to get food relief to the women, children, and unemployed men in the occupied areas of Europe. The Gillette-Taft resolution, favoring food relief to the occupied democracies, was still pending in the Senate Foreign Relations Committee. When the Women's International League for Peace and Freedom expressed support for the resolution, Gillette asked Taft if it were not time to push for its passage by scheduling hearings before a subcommittee and scheduling testimony. While Taft and Gillette worked within the Senate, other expressions of support for the resolution began to arrive from a number of directions, including organizations, congressmen, and state legislatures.[61]

Hoover's efforts to provide wartime food relief to the democracies were, however, now faced with new opposition from an organization called Food for Freedom, Inc., which advocated building up food reserves for the postwar years rather than providing food relief during the war. And it seemed to be another irritation for the former president from the Willkie camp. Hoover wrote Ray Lyman Wilbur in late April, "Food for Freedom, Inc. is the old Freedom House—Willkie group in another disguise and is mainly to oppose food for the small democracies."[62] Wilbur thereupon declined an invitation to serve as a member of their board.[63]

Hoover also continued to monitor the United Nations Relief and Rehabilitation Agency and postwar plans for relief. He wrote to Lehman late in June that it would "be desirable in the United Nations agreement for relief that provisions should be made which will prevent the consumer nations (which are a majority) from determining the prices of good to the American farmers in supplying nations. The experience after the last war indicates the urgent need for such protection," he wrote. Hoover also argued for selling food on credit, as opposed to making it an outright gift, since the use of loans stimulated efforts at productivity and conservation in the recipient countries and encouraged an early return "to a commercial basis of living" there. Lehman had been taking the position that anything but outright gifts would burden the recipient countries with impairment of their credit and make them less able to borrow for reconstruction, thus making economic recovery difficult. But Hoover insisted it was "rather the excessive credits used for non-productive purposes . . . in the post-war period which brought about the ills you suggest and not credits for food relief."[64]

Hearings did begin at last on the Gillette-Taft resolution in November.[65] Rumors continued to reach Hoover that Roosevelt was, himself, interested in getting food relief to the occupied democracies and that he hoped sufficient sentiment might be developed in the United States to "force" his hand in taking it up with Churchill, who remained adamantly opposed.[66] But the hearings themselves were a disappointment and brought protests from many who supported the food relief proposal. From Nevin Sayre, secretary of the Fellowship of Reconciliation, came a demand that the hearings last for more than the mere two days that had been scheduled, for Sayre argued, "They must give opportunity for public expression to others besides Mr. Hoover and the Quakers. Everyone knows of their valiant fight since 1940 to get permission to send milk, vitamins, etc., through the American-Anglo blockade. What Congress and the country need to hear is the expression in favor of feeding by leading Democrats, labor and farm groups, non-Quaker churches, peace organizations, etc."[67] Socialist Norman Thomas, chairman of the executive committee of the Post-War World Council, also wrote the chairman of the subcommittee that he considered it "unfortunate that your subcommittee is so greatly curtailing hearings on the Gillette-Taft resolution." By doing so, the committee was making the resolution look "too much like an exclusive Hoover" proposal and greatly reduced "the give and take of opinion between the country and your subcommittee."[68] Obviously Hoover was not alone in the struggle and a profound spirit of humanity still existed in many Americans even in the midst of the barbarism of war. The resolution was finally adopted by the Senate on February 15, 1944, but had no apparent effect on either the Roosevelt administration or the Churchill government. Still, as Hoover remarked in his history of the relief effort, "devoted men were demonstrating that compassion was not dead in America."[69] But that compassion counted for little since it was not shared by Roosevelt.

As for United Nations Relief and Rehabilitation Agency (UNRRA), Hoover outlined his reservations in letters to members of Congress. To Congressman John Taber he wrote in May 1944 that UNRRA's constitution made it impossible for Congress, "after an appropriation is made, to have any check whatever." Moreover, the Director General was "practically irremovable and therefore cannot be made responsible to the Congress for his actions." This seemed to make it desirable for Congress to avoid appropriating large sums to UNRRA and to, instead, make such appropriations "from time to time." Also, in order to make sure that other countries were contributing their share to UNRRA's operations, Congress should make America's "contributions in installments so that the situation can be periodically sized up." More important, though, Hoover told Taber that "under this mismanagement of agriculture there will be no consequential surplus of American supplies when the European emergency comes."[70]

Politics

As 1944 neared, Hoover began to monitor the political situation. From the GOP national committeeman from Minnesota, who had talked with Willkie for two and a half hours, Hoover heard the opinion that the 1940 nominee was finally becoming more orthodox in his Republicanism and more willing to listen to experienced GOP leaders.[71] But Hoover responded that "the gentleman you mention could never be elected despite his sudden getting of religion."[72] Hoover was certain the Mackinac Conference had strengthened the party by showing the country it possessed "leadership and cohesion." He told John Bricker that the GOP in 1944 should strive for the support of the Jeffersonian wing of the Democrats but should "not try for the New Dealers whom we can never get."[73] In May of 1943, William Allen White thought "that either one of four men could beat Roosevelt—Willkie, Dewey, Hoover, or Stassen." He found "a lot of strength all over the country for Hoover."[74] Landon also reported to Hoover rumors that "there is a bitter feeling developing between Stassen and Willkie" that had "been growing for some time, [as] evidently Mr. Willkie considerably sensed it in Governor Stassen's review of his book which appeared in the *New York Times Magazine*."[75] Landon was irate over an attempt by Willkie to smear him by linking his name with a former "lieutenant" of Huey Long, but despite this affront by the man he had helped put over for the nomination in 1940, Landon did not feel it was "time for an open break with Mr. Willkie" and was concerned that the Republicans "preserve a reasonable unity."[76]

Hoover was also working closely with Dewey, writing him in mid-October 1943 to suggest that he telephone California Governor Earl Warren to suggest that he choose and lead the GOP delegation from that state to the 1944 convention.[77] Dewey agreed to do so.[78] Hoover clearly intended by his action to try to separate Warren from Willkie. It was important, Hoover told Dewey, to counter Willkie's claim of having the support of the California delegation, since such claims were "making an impression in other areas."[79]

After the November 1943 elections Hoover wrote Henry Allen, "There's not only a trend, there is a revolution in motion . . . The American mass revolution proved a mild infection due to inherent qualities. We have not had the bloody passages and we have passed into the reaction stages without military dictatorship. But the underlying movement is here and it is much deeper than politics."[80] But Landon wondered at the intolerance of the so-called liberals and feared that after World War II the nation would see a return to the witch hunts of 1918 and 1919.[81]

The year 1944 began on a tragic note for Herbert Hoover. On the evening of January 7, as he prepared to depart for a dinner with Edgar Rickard and Hugh Gibson, the former president found his beloved wife Lou Henry collapsed on the floor of her dressing roof. The Waldorf Astoria hotel doctor pronounced her dead.[82] Friends and family rushed to the side of the former president to help him through the difficult days that followed, and the tragedy even elicited a telegram of condolence from President Roosevelt.[83] Fifteen hundred mourners attended her funeral service at St. Bartholomew's Episcopal Church in New York City, including two hundred Girl Scouts. Hoover sat with their sons, Allan and Herbert Jr. and later in the day left for California to escort her body to the burial place at Stanford.[84]

A close family friend wrote years later,

> Mrs. Hoover's death left a great void in her husband's life. It so happened that my husband [Jeremiah Milbank], our daughter Nancy, and I were with him at a mine in Pioche, Nevada shortly after Mrs. Hoover's passing. Nancy had just learned the game of Canasta and one evening offered to teach it to us while we were playing gin rummy with Mr. Hoover. He had enjoyed gin rummy as a means of diversion and relaxation and told Nancy he thought gin rummy was a pretty good game but he would be glad to try one game of Canasta.

The result was that Hoover quickly became "addicted" to the game and had enjoyed "evening foursomes at the game ever since." She added, "When the telephone rings now, after his three secretaries have gone off duty for the evening, the telephone operators at the Waldorf Towers—on Mr. Hoover's instructions—will not put any call through which would interrupt his evening's recreation [of Canasta] unless the caller gives a secret password."[85] According to Clarence Kelland, Hoover made up his own rules for the game, which his friends called "the Park Avenue rules," and the stakes were a tenth of a cent per point, with Hoover deeply depressed if he lost as much as thirty cents.[86]

For a man so deeply involved in so many issues of importance, there was little time to be spared away from public life, no matter how deep the sorrow, and work soon proved to be the best cure for Hoover's grief. By January 24, he was back in New York at the Waldorf. On the surface, at least, life seemed to be restoring to normal by the end of the month.[87]

One issue that began to divide the Republican Party in early 1944 was the question of when the contemplated international organization should be formed. Many Republicans had begun to feel that its formation should not be delayed until after the end of the war, as had been advocated in the Hoover-Gibson program. Hoover continued to take the position that the timing for its creation should depend on world conditions that could not be predicted in advance. As he wrote to David Lawrence in November 1943, Hoover believed "we must this time establish fundamental order before we load such an institution with an impossible task . . . for I believe that is what destroyed the ultimate effectiveness of the League—not because it was incorporated in the Treaty of Versailles, but because the world did not first establish order before giving it that job."[88] But growing suspicion of Soviet intentions led others to advocate an early formation of the postwar peacekeeping organization. Hoover's former undersecretary of state William R. Castle favored a six-month limit on the transition period because he had concluded that Hull was being duped by the Soviets, while Stalin had "done nothing to show that he intended to live up to whatever promises he may have made in Moscow." Under such circumstances, the prospect of the Soviet Union acting as one of the peacekeepers during the transition period was not appealing.[89] There was, though, no apparent opposition to maintaining a "cooling-off" period before concluding the actual treaties of peace, such as Hoover and Gibson had suggested.

Postwar Policy

In the committee on international postwar problems that had been established by the Mackinac Conference, the Hoover-Gibson approach of delaying the creation of the international organization was submitted, but immediately "there were a number of challenges to the idea of waiting for any considerable length of time before setting up an international organization to preserve the peace." The majority appeared to favor the establishment of such an organization "within six months or so." Castle was one of those who supported the shorter period. After some debate, the matter was postponed until a later meeting.

Although Hoover's own suspicions of the Soviet Union were of long standing, he did not allow them to distract him from pursing the Hoover-Gibson formula for peacemaking. If his fellow Americans were now growing aware of Russia's expansionist designs and untrustworthiness, it was only after Hoover had warned them since 1933 when Roosevelt had extended diplomatic recognition to the Soviet Union. When the Supreme Soviet, Russia's rubber-stamp "parliament," announced that it was granting greater autonomy to the Soviet Union's member republics, Hoover noted the addition to the list of Latvia, Estonia, and Lithuania. The American people, he told O'Laughlin, had not yet "grasped the import of Stalin's sixteen republic declaration," but it mean "Communist enslavement of five—and possibly nine—formerly independent nations." The United States dared not challenge the Soviet Union over the issue because of wartime exigencies, but the declaration had "changed the whole course of international relations; it has destroyed the Atlantic Charter completely; it has abolished the whole idealistic concept of the American purpose in this war." The world, he noted, was now left with "three great centers of power committed to sheer Imperialism under new names and methods."[90]

James Reston, in Moscow, agreed. He wrote in the *New York Times*,

> Soviet Russia . . . has not accepted the principles that spheres of influence should be abandoned and that a general European settlement is to be arranged with each power having an equal say in the settlement of every area on the Continent. There is, in fact, a growing feeling that Russia, while willing to cooperate with the United States and Britain in other parts of the world, is demanding the right to establish a Russian sphere of influence to the east of the line running from Trieste to Prague and Stettin and that east of that line she is going to insist upon the creation of "friendly" governments that would form a sort of cordon sanitaire in reverse, a chain of states, not to protect western Europe from Russia but to protect Russia from the possibility of any coalition that might be formed in western Europe.

The consensus among Western diplomats in Moscow, Reston wrote, was that the Soviet Union was "laying the groundwork for an even greater empire than she now has and is pointing the way, not to a system of the present collective security but toward a world divided" into four great spheres of influence.[91] Stalin had apparently not read Willkie's *One World*. But Hoover refused to be discouraged, writing Gibson in mid-February 1944, that since the US and USSR had been "cooperating and collaborating in the conduct of war, there is no reason why we should not cooperate and collaborate from war to peace— the ultimate aim of which must be to establish some world institution for the maintenance of peace."[92]

Prospects for 1944

Republicans looked ahead with some optimism to the 1944 presidential election. Willkie was clearly a candidate for the nomination, but both Landon and Hoover were determined that Willkie should not again carry the party's banner. Landon strongly supported Thomas Dewey for the nomination, while Hoover seems to have preferred Governor John Bricker of Ohio, although he maintained close relations with Dewey. Both Landon and Hoover seemed less committed to particular candidates, however, than to denying the nomination to Willkie. When Willkie was able to win only 6 of New Hampshire's 11 delegates, despite having "twice stumped that state, had a large organization and had no opposition," Hoover concluded that Dewey was in the best position for gaining the nomination, although he believed "Bricker ought to be in a substantial position."[93]

Late in March Dewey dined with Hoover in New York and the two discussed the political situation. The former president gathered that Dewey preferred to be drafted by the convention but that "he was going to see that the draft machinery was in high gear." Dewey sought advice from Hoover on what his tactics should be before the convention and afterward, apparently taking it for granted that he would be the nominee, probably on the first ballot, confiding that he wanted Earl Warren for his running mate. Hoover was appalled to find that John Foster Dulles had drafted a foreign relations speech for Dewey to be given the following month. He recorded in his aide-memoir of their conversation, "I told him that John Foster Dulles was filled with a lot of fuzzy ideas; that he was living in a dream-land which had been completely knocked into a cocked hat by Joe Stalin; that the outlook for the world had been changed; that there would nothing in the nature of a 'world government' and that there would be no surrendering of sovereignty; that irrespective of what might be the attitude of the United States, neither Russia nor Britain would accept any such fuzzy ideas."[94]

Hoover told Dewey that if he were elected president "he would have to create a special bureau of 600 lawyers and 2000 detectives to expose at least one case per day of the corruption of the present regime; that this would be the only method of preventing the New Dealers from undermining him during the next four years and thus defeat him for a second term." Dewey responded that Hoover was wrong; it would take "6,000 lawyers and 20,000 detectives and some new jails." Hoover suggested General Douglas MacArthur as possible vice presidential nominee, but Dewey did not take to the idea. Hoover wrote in his aide-memoir, "I came out of the long discussion with confirmation of my high esteem for Dewey's intellectual capacities, his energy, and his political ability, but in some way I have a reservation as to his character. Nevertheless, at the moment, he seems to be the inevitable candidate, and the spiritual winds that blow through the White House may strengthen any of the deficiencies on the character side. He has fewer of the human qualities than Bricker has. Whatever humanitarism [sic] he has is coldly calculated in terms of votes." But Hoover was convinced that some of Dewey's negative qualities seemed to have softened since 1940, and he believed the New Yorker to be a better candidate now than he would have been four years earlier. "The great contrast between Bricker and Dewey as candidates," Hoover wrote, "can be seen in the political management Dewey has already set up around himself whereas Bricker has none of importance."

Hoover believed that the dominant mood at the Republican convention would be opposition to a candidate (Willkie) rather than support for anyone.[95] Most observers agreed with the Hoover-Landon assessment that Dewey was the likely nominee, but Hoover continued to supply Bricker with ideas for his speeches.[96] Then, when Willkie withdrew from the race in early April after a disappointing showing in the primaries, Dewey's prospects seemed even better.[97] Hoover, at least, was considerably relieved at Willkie's withdrawal, writing to Richard Lloyd Jones that he could now devote more time to nonpolitical matters since "Mr. Willkie has been retired as a national danger."[98] With Dewey now clearly the front-runner, Hoover felt it was important to check some of Dulles's idealistic influence on the New Yorker's foreign policy. He cautioned him against making a speech on foreign policy, noting that Dewey was already a signatory to the Mackinac declaration, that the international situation was confused, and that the Roosevelt administration still had not produced a definite postwar program of its own to criticize.[99]

However, Governor Bricker before the Ohio Society of New York City on April 25 had called for American participation "in a cooperative organization of sovereign nations." Hoover's influence on the Ohioan was obvious.[100] If Bricker was to speak on foreign policy, there was certainly nothing to bar Dewey from doing the same, and despite Hoover's advice to the contrary he delivered his speech two days after Bricker's. Hoover concluded from the speech that his concerns had been unfounded. He wrote Dewey that the New Yorker's "judgment was better as to the timing of that speech than mine." He lauded Dewey for steering "between the rocks about which I have been particularly fearful at this time. I do not pretend that you are adopting my ideas, but the central theme of it has been my steady agitation for the last two years and therefore I could not help but approve."[101]

Whether or not the former president was being completely honest in his praise is not entirely clear. Others certainly had no enthusiasm for the speech. Robert E. Wood wrote Vandenberg,

> If Dewey in his New York speech had had the sense to adhere strictly to the Mackinac declaration, which any sensible nationalist or, for that matter, any sensible internationalist can subscribe to, he would be on safe ground, but when he made the speech he did on foreign policy, which was primarily intended for New York City listeners, it looks to me as if he is in the hands of the very same group that supported Willkie, and it indicates that he will lose out in the middle west. Without the middle west he cannot be elected.[102]

Unless Dewey stood on the Mackinac declaration, Wood added, "I will not trust his foreign policy any more than I do F.D.R.'s."[103] Others, too, regarded Dewey's speeches as showing far too much of a Dulles influence on him, with the result, one Hoover friend wrote, that people were saying, "Hell, it looks like 1940 all over again," while others remarked that "Dewey has thrown away all the fruits of the Wisconsin victory over Willkie because Willkie-ism is still in the saddle."[104] In other words, having defeated Willkie, Dewey now seemed to be donning his clothes. Some Republicans called upon Hoover to try to influence Dewey away from the Willkieite variety of "internationalism" that Dewey had begun to expound, but Hoover refused to do so.[105]

On May 25, 1944, Hoover removed himself from the candidate selection process with a statement to the press: "Until now I have ignored the continuous efforts by ill-informed people to link my name with various possible nominees for President, including Governor Bricker, Governor Dewey, and General MacArthur. I am taking and expect to take no part in the selection of the Republican nominee. The people and their duly elected delegates will take care of that themselves."[106] The statement was apparently issued at the request of Dewey, who hoped thereby to avoid being linked by the Democrats to the former president. It was apparent that the 1944 campaign would follow the pattern of 1936 and 1940, when the GOP candidates sought to distance themselves as much as possible from Hoover.[107] But Dewey continued to seek the former president's advice, and especially his assistance in getting Earl Warren to agree to join the ticket as vice presidential nominee.[108] Wearied by the general attitude, Hoover decided to write into his convention speech a farewell to public life, only to change his mind a few weeks later.[109]

When Hoover addressed the Republican convention on June 27 there was no mention of withdrawing from public life. Instead, he recalled for his audience,

> At each of the great rallies of our party in 1936, in 1940 and today in 1944 I have been called to speak upon the encroachments and dangers to freedom in our country. Each time I knew before I spoke that our people would not believe that the impairment of freedom could happen here. Yet each subsequent four years has shown those warnings to have been too reserved, too cautious. The

reason why these warnings have been accurate is simple. From the beginning the New Deal in a milder form has followed the tactics of European revolutions which have gone before. The direction being set, the destination is not difficult to foresee.

After reviewing the encroachments upon American liberties under the New Deal, Hoover asked, "With the blessings of the Attorney General, the Communists and the fellow travelers are spending vast sums to re-elect this regime. Would they spend their money to support the freedom of men?" True, many of the liberties had been lost under the guise of wartime emergency, but "can a regime which forged 'shackles on the liberties of the people' in peacetime be trusted to return freedom to the people from the shackles of war?" On the contrary, Hoover asserted,

> already the New Dealers have planned a large number of Trojan horses labeled "liberalism" and "freedom" stuffed with a mixture of totalitarian economics and doubtful statistics. The easiest task of government is to suppress individuals, subject them to bureaucracy and subsidize them to lean on governments— or a political party. If a government has enough power, it can always do that. The hard task of government and the really liberal task, is to build self-reliance, stimulate initiative, and thereby create men and women of energy, of dignity and of independence. That is the motive power of America.

The decision between these two philosophies of government had to be made now, Hoover argued, because now was the time to begin planning for postwar America so that the returning service men should "find no delays in productive jobs."

As for foreign policy, Hoover pointed out that the resurgence of nationalism meant that peace "must be based upon cooperation between independent sovereign nations." He advocated a world organization, but one split into three divisions—Europe, Asia, and the Western Hemisphere —with each division primarily responsible for preserving peace in its area. This was especially important for Europe, "where the dangers of world wars come from." He advocated again a long transition period in which to lay the foundations for a stable peace. Then he lashed out at Roosevelt's foreign policies, especially the agreements at Teheran. Roosevelt, he charged, was following the method of "power politics and balance-of-power diplomacy," and worse yet, the United States was apparently "to furnish the balance between Britain and Russia." That was sure to earn for the United States the enmity of both. He ended his speech by pointing out that the convention was "handing the leadership of the Republican party to a new generation" that would soon be swelled in numbers by millions of returned servicemen. This was as close as he came to a farewell.[110]

The foreign policy platform adopted at the convention rejected participation in the kind of "world state" advocated by Stassen and Willkie, and in most details it followed the Hoover-Gibson program. While the Republican delegates were meeting, Roosevelt, too, at last enunciated his own general proposals concerning postwar policy, and these were similar to the plank adopted by the GOP convention. Journalist Anne O'Hare McCormick examined both the Republican and Roosevelt programs and concluded, "In a way it may be said to be his [Hoover's] program, for he was the first to outline the procedure and set the limits of American participation that are now embodied in both proposals."[111]

As in 1936 and 1940, the former president's speech was well received by the convention, and he was pleased by the response. Bascom Timmons recalled that Hoover got a "big" and "long demonstration with such cheering that when he started to make his speech they just kept on." Timmons was sitting directly in front of Hoover and said he "felt almost like crying." He told Hoover, "You are getting such a demonstration up there you have about got the tears coming to me," and Hoover responded, "Well imagine how I feel. This certainly can make any man feel very happy."[112] Dewey received the expected nomination, but Earl Warren declined the second spot. Hoover claimed credit for obtaining Bricker's consent to take the vice presidential nomination, although his actual contribution may have been less than he thought.[113] In sum, Hoover was more pleased with the results of the 1944 convention than with its predecessors in 1936 and 1940, but he told the press that he did not expect to take an active part in the campaign. He was, he told reporters, busy writing a book, but he would do whatever the nominees asked of him.[114] He was also approaching his seventieth birthday. To one correspondent he wrote, "It has been a long road to get the party back on the track again;—the futility of Landon; the extraordinary machinations of Willkie; the sudden dropping out of Warren and the quick action necessary to complete the ticket; but finally we have at last a fighting team and I think we can win."[115]

In letters to both Bricker and Dewey, Hoover repeated a recommendation he had earlier discussed with both of them. In pursuit of a coalition with conservative Democrats in the 1944 election, the former president suggested that ten to twenty "Democratic leaders of first rank" and a similar number of leading Republicans should announce that "the thirty principal offices of Cabinet and War Agencies would be appointed equally from the two sides but no specific position or appointments" would be announced. Sounding like Landon, seven years earlier, Hoover believed such a proposal for a coalition government would attract numerous anti–New Deal Democrats.[116] Hoover had for some time been in close touch with the American Democratic National Committee, a movement within the Democratic Party to capture the party from the New Dealers and to oppose a fourth term for Roosevelt. The group had indicated they planned to support the Republican nominee in 1944 if Roosevelt were renominated but seemed to prefer Taft over Dewey due to the latter's comparative youth and inexperience.[117] Dewey responded that the proposal contained "fascinating possibilities," but he noted that FDR was creating some drama over his choice of a vice presidential nominee. He thought it best to await the outcome of the Democratic convention.[118] When Roosevelt dropped Henry A. Wallace for Harry S. Truman of Missouri, the move placated many of those, especially southerners, who might have deserted the Democratic ticket for such a coalition proposal.

The Campaign

Hoover anticipated that he would have no role in the 1944 campaign, and he wrote John Hamilton that he believed he had paved the way for his absence by his speech to the convention.[119] When the new GOP national chairman, Herbert Brownell, sent him the plans for the campaign, there was, indeed, no mention of a role for Hoover.[120] Brownell later recalled that while Dewey admired Hoover's mind, he felt that "the Republican Party and the country generally were more liberal in their approach to the political issues of the day than Mr. Hoover was." Brownell also felt that Dewey was fearful of being "dominated by any personality, and it was pretty easy to be dominated by Mr. Hoover because he knew so much about every issue."[121] As for Hoover, according to Bonner Fellers, he felt that Dewey "had no inner reservoir of knowledge on which to draw for his thinking." And Hoover told Fellers, "a man couldn't wear a mustache like that without having it affect his mind."[122] The former president told John Hamilton that during the 1944 campaign Dewey actually visited Hoover at the Waldorf and asked him not speak during the campaign.[123]

When the press asked Dewey about Hoover's support of the ticket during an interview in Spokane, Dewey responded that he had not seen the former president since the convention and had no plans to see him again.[124] From such evidence, Hoover wrote to Ruth Hanna McCormick Simms, "It having been plainly indicated that I was a liability, I naturally (like you) took to the mountains. I have no such serious duties as looking after cows, but have given great attention to the fish. Of course, every new candidate has to make his own campaign and the problems, of course, are new and the experience of other campaigns never seems very real. I have great confidence in the political abilities of both Dewey and Brownell."[125] Privately, however, Hoover was annoyed by Dewey's neglect of him, and he grew increasingly disenchanted over the nominee's willingness to commend some aspects of the New Deal as Willkie had done.[126]

Still, the former president's view of the nominee waxed and waned with the speeches Dewey made.[127] And no less than with Landon and Willkie, he viewed Dewey's election as vital if the United States were "to stop this stampede to the left and turn in some degree toward the right."[128] The world badly needed an example that would lead it in a conservative direction, and only a Republican administration offered any hope of checking the spread of communism through the world.[129] Hoover wrote one correspondent, "The Stalin form of Communism seems certain for Poland, Estonia, Latvia, Lithuania, Jugo-Slavia, Bulgaria and Roumania. DeGaulle looks like the introducer of it to France, and if the 'Free Germany Committee' in Moscow is installed in Berlin, it probably will pervade there also. The Communist sections of China seem to be a base for its extension there. Altogether these left-wing ideas are sweeping the world. The only stop I see is to win this election in the United States."[130]

Meanwhile, Hoover and Gibson had begun to write a series of two articles for *Collier's* magazine on postwar planning for peacemaking. The difficulty, as Hoover wrote Gibson, was trying to anticipate Roosevelt's policies, for he seemed to have no foreign policy. This meant that Hoover and Gibson were "rather up a stump about these articles for Collier's," until it became more apparent whether FDR's "plan" was for the peace, or a "plan of organization for making the peace."[131] Gibson responded that Sumner Welles seemed "to be plodding along in our footsteps" with the notion of a "transition" period and had even used their expression "trustees of peace." Gibson wrote that Welles ought to "at least put his own label on the bottle" and that he and Hoover should get into their *Collier's* article "the statement that these ideas were put out by us—none genuine without our trademark."[132] Hoover agreed the point should be made "that if they have any foreign policy they took it from us—transition period in the Moscow Declaration, and even some items in the league plan."

Early in October 1944 Wendell Willkie died. Hoover's statement to the press concealed the antagonism he had long felt toward the man: "The death of Mr. Willkie deprives the nation of a great and deeply patriotic citizen. His colorful personality, his indomitable energy, and his active mind have stirred national consideration and understanding of the difficult problems of our time. His passing will be a great loss in finding their solution."[133] Willkie's funeral brought together the leading figures of both political parties in a rare gathering. Dewey, who shared the same pew with the former president, avoided speaking to Hoover, while Eleanor Roosevelt, by contrast, was very friendly toward him.[134]

To the end Hoover was not invited to participate in the campaign, for the first time since he had left office. Despite the persistent snub of him by Dewey, the New Yorker was defeated in the presidential election the following month, although Roosevelt's vote was below that in 1940. For Hoover, Dewey's defeat was only further evidence that it was folly for a Republican candidate to straddle the New Deal and to refuse to tackle the Democrats head-on in defense of pre–New Deal Republicanism. Hoover saw the only consolation for Republicans in FDR's reduced vote, which he hoped might restrain him in his policies.[135] To William Castle, Hoover wrote that it was time "to start pushing the stone uphill again."[136] He was now convinced more than ever that the salvation of the nation required "a coalition of the conservative forces."[137] Toward this end he encouraged the launching of a journal of conservative ideas, since "our universities and other intellectual centers are impregnated weekly by the New Republic, the Nation, the New Masses, and other journals, and in this last battle we had to meet not only the professors but a generation of students."[138]

Yalta

John Callan O'Laughlin remained Hoover's principal source of information on the administration's foreign policy and military strategy, from information that the publisher gained from his many contacts in Washington. But as noted earlier, Hoover was also receiving unofficial briefings from the War Department.[139] At least as early as December 1944 he knew of the race between the United States and Germany to develop the atomic bomb. He continued to decry Roosevelt's willingness to meddle in "European power politics," especially when it seemed to benefit the Soviet Union, since it could only mean "disaster for Europe."[140] When FDR left for the historic Yalta Conference, Hoover predicted that the president would "come back with a lot of Uncle Joe's [Stalin's] promises which will fade out as fast as the so-called Moscow Declaration faded. At the moment it is useless to say anything without being justifiably accused of creating difficulties, so I am keeping still."[141]

Nevertheless, when the first public details of the Yalta agreement were released, Hoover expressed publicly the belief that "it comprises a strong foundation on which to rebuild the world. If the agreements, promises, and ideals which are expressed shall be carried out, it will open a great hope to the world."[142] Privately he had little expectation that they would, in fact, be carried out, but his public statement had been worded in such a way, he explained, as to be in a "more strategic position when I have to challenge their failure."[143] His public statement, however, provoked negative comment from many friends. William Castle wrote, "I have had any number of people ask me how you happened to make the statement about the Crimea Conference which the papers here quoted, something along the line of preparing the way for a better world." Among those who had expressed surprise was the Polish ambassador. "People come and ask me every day about it," Castle wrote, "and I don't want to try to interpret what you intended to say, especially as I have nothing to go on except the one or two sentences published here." He asked Hoover for guidance on what line he should take when questioned. Castle's reaction to Yalta was that if "there ever was a time when Roosevelt simply ate out of the hands of Stalin it was this last conference." The distribution of territory at the conference he found "just about as contrary to the principles of the so-called Atlantic Charter as anything could be."[144]

Landon also wrote to Hoover to ask his opinion of the Yalta declaration, and when Hoover replied he sent a copy of his reply to Castle. Hoover explained that the American people yearned for peace and the Roosevelt administration was trying to construct machinery for peace in the postwar world. Admittedly that machinery contained "many faults and weaknesses that are dangerous both as to peace and to our country," but to correct them required that they be amended, and "blind and futile opposition" was not the answer. Hoover wrote,

> The Atlantic Charter, the Moscow pact, Dumbarton Oaks, the Yalta declaration, etc. all reiterate certain ideals and principles which, if carried out in good faith, comprise a foundation for such an organization. The odds are that they will not be carried out in good faith. And in that case these promises come to nothing. But at least we can hold up the ideals and promises as a basis of real peace and hold them to carrying them out . . . To take the attitude of withdrawing from the whole mess at this time would not get support from the American people and it would be only a futile gesture to urge it . . . Put another way, I am for helping design an experiment. If it has the elements of success, to support it; if it is hopeless, then to damn it. And I want to see it succeed.[145]

In his letter to Castle, Hoover added that it was important for the three centers of power to cooperate until Germany was defeated. As for Poland, "is there any hope that voices of protest now will alter the result?" Hoover concluded that Poland's only hope was that her situation might be corrected through the international organization that would be created after the war.[146] Castle confessed that he could not quarrel with anything Hoover had said in his letter to Landon, because it is "all true," but he wished Hoover's press statement had contained more of the reasoning outlined in that letter.[147] From Hoover's explanation to Landon and Castle, it is clear that the former president had abandoned one of the principles he had advocated so strongly in his speeches and writings since before Pearl Harbor—his insistence that no international organization could correct, or should be based on, a bad peace. Increasingly, as the wartime agreements continued to violate the principles of the Atlantic Charter and what Hoover regarded as right, he was forced to fall back upon the international organization for their correction, even as Wilson had been forced to do at Versailles. America's "second crusade" was in this sense, at least, following the course of the first.

A Change in the White House

On April 12, 1945, President Franklin Delano Roosevelt died. Hoover's statement to the press read, "The nation sorrows at the passing of its President. Whatever differences there may have been, they end in the regrets of death. It is fortunate that in this great crisis of war our Armies and Navies are under such magnificent leadership that we shall not hesitate. The new President will have the backing of the country. While we mourn Mr. Roosevelt's death, we shall march forward."[148] The man who had sought constantly to discredit Hoover, who had denied to him even the minimum of courtesies expected of a president to a former occupant of the White House, and who had ignored his abilities in peace and in war, was gone from the scene, replaced by Harry S. Truman. Although eight years older then Roosevelt, Hoover had outlived his nemesis.

According to Joseph Greene, Mrs. Cordell Hull told him that Eleanor Roosevelt had attempted in the final days of Roosevelt's presidency to bring about an official reconciliation between her husband and Hoover, but she was unsuccessful. Until the very end Franklin Delano Roosevelt would not agree to any kind of official reconciliation.[149]

CHAPTER 9

████████████████████████

A New Attitude in Washington

A New President

In the midst of the eulogies for the departed president, Hoover received evidence of a new attitude in Washington when he was extended an invitation from Secretary of State Edward Stettinius Jr. to accept a box in the San Francisco opera house for the opening session of the conference on international organization set for April 25.[1] It is inconceivable that Roosevelt would have approved such an invitation, despite Hoover's contribution to American foreign policy during the war years. Conditioned by years of deceit and neglect and abuse from Washington, Hoover at first suspected that the invitation was either "evidence of offensive ineptitude—or a foundation for smearing" and declined the invitation, noting in his reply that he was not in Palo Alto (where the telegram was sent) but in New York City.[2]

Only hours before Roosevelt died, Hoover had told Felix Morley he hoped the president "would live long enough to reap where he had sown."[3] Now he was certain Truman would be an improvement, and he approved of the new president's initial speech to Congress. Intrigued by Roosevelt's successor, Hoover wrote Truman's fellow Missourian, Arthur Hyde, to ask about him.[4] Hyde replied that he had no firsthand knowledge concerning Truman, but he entertained "a considerable hope for his administration" and believed that his background would lead him to be somewhat more conservative than Roosevelt had been.[5] Optimistically, Hoover wrote to his sister, "Now that there has been a change in Washington, I may be on the move often." He added, "Time moves on and I can feel 71 in my bones, especially when I go fishing."[6] The former president could have had no idea how prophetic his prediction of being "on the move" would be.

The former president approved of Truman's first speech to Congress and thought the new president's advisers were trying to give him the image of "a man of humility purposely to contrast him with F.D.R." Hoover may have harbored hopes that Truman would appoint him secretary of war, since the command of shipping that job would entail could help him speed food relief to Europe.[7] Others likewise hoped that Truman would take advantage of the opportunity "to make for an era of good feeling and show his breadth of thought by appointing [Hoover] to a key position in the post-war activity, or better still, as an additional member to the United States Delegation to San Francisco."[8]

While no such invitation came, Hoover nevertheless had good reason to feel that his life had turned a corner in April 1945. The war was clearly in its final months. He had outlived his longtime antagonist in the White House, and there was every reason to hope that Roosevelt's successor would lead the nation away from the leftward drift it had taken under Roosevelt and would also rally the free world against Soviet expansionism. And Hoover could sense, in other ways, a conservative revival in the United States. For a year he had been supporting Frank G. Hanighen's new conservative journal *Human Events* and was also involved in an attempt to bring out another to compete with such liberal and left-of-liberal journals as the *New Republic*, *Nation*, and *New Masses* in the universities and other intellectual centers.[9]

Foreign Relations

A week before the beginning of the San Francisco Conference Hoover delivered a speech in Philadelphia to reiterate his views concerning the proposed international organization. It was, as Rickard noted, "to give his views on Dumbarton Oaks prior to the San Francisco Conference."[10] Three weeks earlier, between March 25 and 28, he had published four articles outlining his suggested amendments to the Dumbarton Oaks plan for a United Nations organization. In those articles he made seven suggestions he believed would "greatly strengthen this charter of peace":

> First: Positive standards of the political rights of men and women and the establishment of a World Committee to promote these political rights. The Committee to rank with the Economic and Social Committees already proposed in the Dumbarton Oaks plan.
> Second: Provision for revision of onerous treaties between nations at, say, ten year intervals, in order to assure that the peace settlements are dynamic and not static.
> Third: Regional organizations of the organization to preserve peace into three areas, Asia, Europe and the Western Hemisphere; the regional organizations to be subject of course to the Security Council.
> Fourth: Absolute disarmament of the enemy powers.

Fifth: Immediate relative disarmament of the United Nations and the establishment of maximum limit of armies, navies and air power among them.

Sixth: While it is probably not a part of the charter itself, when it is adopted by the Congress the authority to use force should not be given the American delegate on the Security Council, but that power should be delegated to the President of the United States with the provision that he be bound by the majority of the joint Foreign Relations Committees of the Senate and the House as to whether a vote to employ American force shall be submitted to the Congress as a whole.

Seventh: Take enough time in formulating the Charter of Peace to do it right.[11]

Hoover told Arthur Krock he was glad to see that Vandenberg, one of the delegates to the San Francisco Conference, had embraced "two of my proposals: a. Political rights of nations and of men. b. Provisions for review of war settlements and treaties." He was, however, fearful that the thinking about the new international organization seemed to be "steadily drifting closely to the pattern of the League of Nations." He could not understand why there was no member of the US delegation who "from experience knows the weaknesses and the strength of the League," even though there were several available who were "not connected with political parties."[12]

In his Philadelphia speech, Hoover pointed out that his suggestions had also been "put forward by the representatives of the peace committees of the three great religious groups, the Protestants, the Catholics, and the Jews." Now he wished to add two more suggestions to the original seven: "There should be a control of military alliances. There should be a definition of aggression." He also agreed with Senator Vandenberg's suggestion that the General Assembly be given "freedom of initiative." Hoover added, "The purpose of these additions is: First, to surround the mechanistic bones of the Charter with moral and spiritual forces. Second, to create those standards of conduct which should be the basis of decision by the Security Council. Third, to reach into the causes of war much more deeply than just the settling of quarrels and the curbing of gangsters. And fourth, to simplify the work of the organization." The "primary weakness of the Holy Alliance, the League of Nations and Dumbarton Oaks proposals," Hoover said, was "the failure to face the facts as to the real causes of war." He reiterated the points made in *The Problems of Lasting Peace* and in subsequent changes and additions to it. A weakness of the League of Nations Covenant had been "its failure to incorporate a bill of rights and standards of conduct of nations and men." Such a bill of rights ought to be incorporated in the new charter. The league had also made no "adequate provision to ease strains by orderly change in agreements between nations when they become onerous or inapplicable," and such a provision should be made in the new charter.

The council of the League of Nations had been "overburdened with all the minor troubles and confused voice of the world at every session," but this could be avoided in the new charter by putting the first responsibility for peacekeeping on regional suborganizations, thus freeing the United Nations organization "to deal only with questions that contain dangers of world war," giving smaller nations a greater voice, and relieving "America and other nations from the strains of many a minor dispute." He noted that Churchill had endorsed such a principle.[13]

The League of Nations had also failed to include adequate provision for disarmament or the control of alliances, and it was the "multitude of these alliances after the last war [that] inspired fear, counter-alliances, increase of armaments. They made for balances of power, and they created voting blocs in the League. They not only weakened the League but they contributed to World War II." The new charter should include such provisions. Meanwhile, the changed nature of aggression required that it be defined in the charter in all its forms, including "direct or indirect subsidized governmental propaganda in other nations." Finally, Hoover cautioned the framers of the charter not to hurry, saying, "If we take six years to make war it might be a good idea to take a few more months to build a sound organization to keep the peace." Ex–New Dealer Raymond Moley considered the speech "exactly what is needed at this time of confusion and drift." He told Hoover that "the country never needed you more than it needs you right now and I hope you will not be silent as in the months past."[14]

The National Council for Prevention of War, which included a number of church groups as participating organizations, presented its own list of proposed revisions to the Dumbarton Oaks agreement—revisions that were heavily influenced by Hoover's views. Frederick Libby, the executive secretary of the organization, wrote that he had tried to incorporate Hoover's main points, because "whatever Mr. Hoover says in this field deserves very close consideration."[15] Hoover, however, was disappointed by the lack of diplomatic experience reflected in the American delegation to San Francisco. He was hopeful, he told Senator Homer Capehart, that "things may be some better under President Truman" but added that it was "only a hope as I am not encouraged over the outlook for good legislation over the next couple of years."[16]

New Responsibilities

Further evidence of the changed attitude in Washington came when Secretary of War Henry Stimson phoned Hoover in late April to invite the former president to spend the day at his Long Island home. Still suspicious, Hoover declined the invitation. A few days later Stimson invited Hoover to travel to Washington to "discuss with him the postwar situation of Europe, which he said had degenerated into a dreadful state." The situation in Europe was, of course, exactly what Hoover had predicted. Stimson told Hoover he had discussed his invitation with President Truman and that the president believed the former president's advice would be valuable. Hoover refused to go to Washington, however, unless the invitation came directly from the president and was specifically to see Truman himself. Hoover wanted the nation to know that he was "not a seeker of interviews," and if, after the two had met, the president directed him "to talk to the Secretary of War that I would be delighted to do so."[17]

By way of explanation for his reluctance and his imposition of such conditions, Hoover recounted for Stimson an incident O'Laughlin had related to him. O'Laughlin had urged Steve Early, Truman's holdover press secretary from Roosevelt's presidency, that the administration should seek Hoover's advice. According to O'Laughlin, Early had responded "that if Hoover wanted anything he would have to come down on his knees to get it." That this was the attitude of a Roosevelt New Dealer did not surprise Hoover, but that advisers like Early remained around the new president convinced him that "whatever good intentions the President may have about this, he has been coaxed by the men around him into the old vindictiveness." His "only protection from the left-wingers and people like Early," he told Stimson, "would be to have an invitation from the President and . . . if Truman did not think it worth while to pay this small courtesy to me for the benefit of my advice, they had better not continue to attempt to get it."

Others were also suggesting to Truman that Hoover's counsel be sought as a method of creating "an era of good feeling." Senator Ralph Brewster took the subject up with the president and found him interested but insistent that it was Hoover who must take the initiative in calling on him, in which event, Truman assured Brewster, the former president would have an "A-priority" on his time. However, the Republican elder statesman continued to hold out for an invitation from the White House.[18] Meanwhile, in a V. E. Day speech at Carnegie Hall on May 8, Hoover appealed for immediate action, now that the war in Europe was ended, to rush food relief to the destitute people there and particularly to the millions of impoverished children. Speaking under the auspices of the Save the Children Federation, Inc., Hoover told his audience that if UNRRA could not start the flow of food at once, then the War Department should take on the responsibility. It was fine, Hoover said, to debate about postwar trade and the structure of peace, but the more important thing to do and now was to rush food to Europe, for it was "now 11:59 on the clock of starvation." He intended no reflection on Herbert Lehman, director of UNRRA, Hoover insisted, but he had "been hampered by power politics" with the result that "precious time has been lost."[19]

A week later Hoover followed with a radio address that called for the shipment of food immediately from the United States and Canada by the US Army if the people of Europe were to be carried through the next ninety days. The principal need, he told his audience, was for bread. None of the countries of Western Europe, he said, had "produced enough food in the harvest of last August to last them until the harvest of the coming August. In the meantime, only a trickle of food has been sent to them." Since farmers would make sure that their own needs were cared for first, the cities would be the areas most distressed, and in the cities it would be the working people who would suffer the greatest privation. While the Europeans also needed meat and fats, they could get through the next ninety days with mainly bread and whatever vegetables they could obtain. Meat and fats, though, were necessary for the children, and Americans should "tighten our belt a little and supply this comparatively small amount," but Americans could not "supply meats and fats to everybody in Europe." Hoover concluded, "I repeat, this is a problem of the next ninety days; it is urgent. It is urgent as a matter of humanity. It is urgent as a matter of preserving order. It is urgent in protection of our boys in Europe. It is a job so long delayed that only the American Army can solve it."[20]

Earlier he had sent Taft figures from the Department of Agriculture showing greater per capita consumption of meat, chicken, fats, and sugar under the compulsory rationing of World War II than under the voluntary program he had followed during World War I. And the World War I program had been accomplished without "ration boards, ration cards, harassment" and with "only trivial expense."[21] In a memorandum he sent to Congressman Jenkins, head of the Food Committee, Hoover reiterated these points and recalled his speeches and testimony in behalf of the World War I plan that had been ignored by the administration despite deteriorating food conditions. The consequence, he pointed out, was that food consumption was up over World War I, the country was "rife in black markets," there was less meat, and there was now "a paid bureaucracy of at least 200,000 in food controls as against under 10,000 paid employees in the last war."[22]

Between his two addresses on the food problem, Hoover finally met with Stimson at the latter's request. On May 13 the former president motored to Stimson's home where he found the secretary of war still insistent that Hoover should call on Truman. Stimson assured the former president that Truman was eager to see him and to discuss the food situation. Hoover, however, was equally insistent on an invitation from Truman. Stimson told Hoover that Truman agreed with the suggestion the former president had made in his speech that the army should take over the European relief effort.[23] Stimson was apparently very complimentary in describing the new president, for though Hoover refused to yield in the matter of an invitation, he came away from the meeting feeling that Truman might actually be a better president than Dewey would have been.[24]

In that same month Hoover began to consider the terms under which peace might advantageously be made with Japan. In a memorandum of a discussion with Joseph Kennedy, former ambassador to Great Britain, in mid-May, Hoover wrote that he and Kennedy had agreed on the urgency of making peace with Japan under terms that would require her evacuation from China and disarmament for "at least 30 to 40 years," but that would allow her to keep Taiwan and Korea "to save her face and recover her economic life."[25] That same day, Hoover furnished Secretary of War Stimson with a memorandum that outlined his views. Hoover argued that as a result of the war the "British, French, Belgian and Dutch Empires are safe for a while," while the Soviets had, by annexations and the creation of puppet governments, extended their political domination over Latvia, Estonia, Lithuania, eastern Poland and Bessarabia, Rumania, Bulgaria, Yugoslavia, Finland, Czechoslovakia, and Austria. This meant that there would "no longer be an opportunity for American or British enterprise therein." This left only "three great areas in the world where the Americans and British might have freedom and opportunity in economic life": the European colonial empires, the Western Hemisphere, and "Asia outside of Russia." However, the likely outcome of a total defeat of Japan would be Russia's seizure of Manchuria, North China, and Korea, from which she would probably expand to take the balance of China and even "Japan by ideological penetration." The likelihood of this happening increased "every day the war with Japan [continued]." Prolonging the war would require millions of Americans for the invasion of Japan, and the result was likely to be that we "have won the war for Russia's benefit just as we have done in Europe."[26]

Hoover suggested that Chiang Kai-shek and his Anglo-American allies should make peace with Japan on the terms he had discussed with Kennedy. The result for the United States would be the saving of lives and resources that would otherwise be spent in continued war with Japan; the United States would be spared the prostration that might make it impossible for her aid in the recovery of other nations. On the other hand, everything would be gained that could be obtained by fighting the war to the finish, and Russian expansion would be checked, Japan would recover economically, and the Japanese would be in a position to govern themselves without the intervention of a joint Allied military government—and "under such terms there would be the hope that Japan would return to cooperation with Western Civilization and not agitate for revenge for another century as is likely to be the case otherwise."

Meanwhile, Hoover found himself increasingly drawn into the food situation, as alarm grew in Washington over conditions in Europe. The former president had frequently expressed his disgust with the UNRRA for its handling of relief, most recently in a letter and memorandum to Congressman John Taber on May 15. Taft, too, was "tremendously concerned" over the administration's policy. As he wrote Hoover on May 23,

> As you know, it is dominated by the idea that retail prices must be practically frozen, and every consideration has been sacrificed to that fetish. They have cared nothing about decreasing badly needed production, and they have cared nothing about putting men out of business if they thought it necessary for the freeze policy . . . The policy originated as an appeasement to labor. In beliefs today it is dominated by New Deal economists who want a continued regulation

of profits. I have protested against a continuation, but I have not felt like putting on a major battle during the war which would appear to the public to be a battle for profits against the interests of war workers . . . Now, however, we are moving into the post-war period, and sometime before long the reconversion problems will outweigh war production in importance. If the present policy is not changed, it is perfectly hopeless to expect businessmen to expand their plants or any man to go into business to provide the jobs which will be essential. Industry after industry has been here proving that they are beginning to lose money . . . I don't really see any solution except to change the whole management of the inflation program, I do not have much hope that Truman will do it.[27]

Hoover agreed that the policy was "a plain ruin. Even as a war measure it is a totally wrong method—and it is not effective either."[28] On May 18th he wrote the vice chairman of the Foreign Policy Association, "I think you will see the adoption of my recommendations as to relief."[29]

On May 23 a delegation from the War Department sent by Stimson called on him. It included Assistant Secretary of War John J. McCloy. Despite Stimson's comment to Hoover earlier in the month that Truman had accepted the former president's advice that the army take over all responsibility for European relief, Hoover now concluded that this meeting was for the purpose of convincing him "that the Army would not take over the relief of the liberated countries during the next 90 day emergency." The army blamed UNRRA for the problem and discussed the problems faced in the next ninety days. Hoover adhered to his original insistence that the army must "furnish the Staff" for the relief effort and also insisted that one man should be assigned "dictatorial" powers over the economic life of "the liberated countries from Italy to Norway, with Shipping, Transportation, Food, Coal and other divisions under strong men," with a man in Washington "to coordinate and direct the American agencies." He also recommended that an American railway president be put in charge of shipments of food and other necessities to American ports. Unless his recommendations were followed, Hoover warned, "the liberated countries are likely to go communist."[30]

On May 25 Truman penned the sought-after invitation to the former president, writing, "If you should be in Washington, I would be most happy to talk over the European food situation with you. Also, it would be a pleasure to me to become acquainted with you."[31] After a dozen years, Hoover found himself no longer considered a pariah by the White House, and the stage was set for his reemergence into public service. Hoover quickly accepted the invitation and was pleased by the attention given to the forthcoming meeting by the media.[32] He busied himself with gathering material for the meetings in Washington and lunched with Bernard Baruch to get his backing, if necessary, for the recommendations he planned to make. Rickard found the former president elated at the opportunity to give advice to Truman and at the recognition being given his experience.[33] The *New York Times* noted, "Mr. Hoover has not been in the White House since the inauguration of Franklin D. Roosevelt in

1933. He has been in Washington many times in the past twelve years, sometimes appearing as a witness before Congressional committees. So far as ever
was disclosed he was never invited to the White House by his immediate predecessor." The *Times* noted that the invitation was being hailed in Congress as
a "fine nonpartisan gesture" on the part of the new president.[34]

On May 28, 1945, Herbert Hoover stepped into the White House for the
first time since he had vacated it for Franklin Delano Roosevelt over a dozen
years earlier. According to Hoover's aide-memoir of the conversation with
Truman, the president wanted his views on "the whole situation." Hoover told
him that the "situation was degenerating all over the world, partly, of course,
due to the war and partly due to mismanagement, but that [Truman] had to
take it as it is and that there was no time to be bothered with recriminations as
to what might have been." Truman agreed with him that the parts of Europe
that were under the Soviets should be left to them to feed. In the rest of
Europe, including US-occupied Germany, the emergency would last for the
next ninety days until the harvest was in, and a long-term approach would be
required after that. The present emergency could not be dealt with as he had
done during the post–World War I armistice, Hoover noted, because there
was no peace conference in session now to grant the kind of authority he had
possessed then. Therefore, Hoover argued again that the army must deal with
the emergency, since it was already handling part of the problem and was
the only agency capable of cutting through red tape. The former president
then repeated his earlier recommendations to Stimson and McCloy.[35] Truman
agreed that, although Stimson was opposed to army involvement in relief,
Hoover's arguments had persuaded him that there was no choice. He asked
Hoover to talk to Stimson.

As for the domestic food situation, Hoover told the president that it was
"terrible." Fats should have been the top priority of wartime food production,
he said, but the number of hogs in the United States had, instead, declined
from 82 million to 60 million in the past 12 months. Hoover again suggested,
as he had so many times during the war, the creation of an economic war
council to determine broad economic and other related policies. The conversation then turned to the foreign situation, whereupon Hoover expressed
his distrust of the Russians, who were "Asiatics," without the "reverence for
agreements" that Western nations entertained. The Russians, however, must
be taken as they were and the United States ought not to go to war with them,
nor should this country try to bluff them or follow policies just "short of war."
A war with the Soviet Union, he told Truman, was unthinkable and would
"mean the extinction of Western civilization or what there is left of it." The
former president also argued in behalf of the negotiated peace with Japan that
he had suggested to Stimson earlier in the month. He repeated his view that
the Soviet Union would not "come into the war with Japan except perhaps in
the last few minutes."

Although his meeting with Truman lasted for nearly an hour, Hoover had no illusions that his advice would be followed, writing that the president had been "simply endeavoring to establish a feeling of good will in the country, that nothing more would come of it so far as I or my views were concerned." No position in the administration had been offered to him, and he concluded that the meeting had been held by Truman for purely political advantages. Still, he felt that both he and Truman had reaped advantages from the meeting. The president had given the impression of being broad-minded and above partisan politics, by comparison with his predecessor, while in Hoover's case those people who had continually smeared him would no longer feel they had the active support (or even encouragement) from the occupant of the White House.[36] The *New York Times* editorialized that Truman's "wise and generous gesture in calling the former President into council is a recognition that partisanship must wait on the threshold of humanity. Mr. Hoover's advice has been available but unsought for a long time. Mr. Truman promptly welcomes it."[37]

As Truman had requested, Hoover also met with Stimson and McCloy again concerning the worsening food problem in Europe. Hoover told Stimson that the only way the army could extricate itself eventually from relief and transportation and other related functions "was to go deeper in; that they should take over very much larger responsibilities . . . I could see no one else who could bring this food to the seaboards and no one else who could have at its command the necessary authorities." He repeated the suggestions he had earlier made to both men and now found them in agreement with him, perhaps because of the president's support for his position.[38]

Hoover also sent Truman a memorandum (at Truman's request) dealing with the subjects they had discussed. The memorandum summarized their discussion and Hoover's recommendations. This memorandum, dated May 30, differed slightly from one Hoover had earlier submitted to Stimson in its discussion of the Japan question. The Truman memorandum did not argue for a negotiated peace from the standpoint of preserving an "open door" for British and American enterprise in East Asia but instead advocated it solely on the basis of saving American lives and resources. It did not mention the Soviet Union, or the threat of communism spreading to China, Korea, and Japan in the event of a prolonged war. There was now provision for trials of war criminals and for the ceding of "certain islands held by Japan," and Japan's retention of Korea and Taiwan would now be under a trusteeship, probably under the new international organization. The Japanese government should be warned that if it did not accept the terms proposed, "they are unfit to remain in control . . . and we must need proceed to their ultimate destruction."[39] Truman responded that the memorandum would "be very useful to me" and scribbled across the bottom of his letter to Hoover, "I appreciate it very much your coming to see me. It gave me a lift."[40]

On June 6, Hoover told a press conference that Truman was doing an "admirable" job in responding to the food problem. Hoover told the press that there would "soon be enough food to get along comfortably, unless climactic reasons cause a drop in production." Truman had taken "two very wise steps" in appointing Clinton P. Anderson as Secretary of Agriculture and in consolidating the War Food Administration under that department. Hoover denied that he was taking on an active role in the food crisis, telling reporters, "My position in the world today as a 71-year-old man is in an advisory capacity only."[41] The former president did not know that he was speaking too soon.

Politics

While in Washington for his meeting with Truman, the former president also met with nine GOP senators at William Castle's home, including Taft, H. Alexander Smith, Bourke Hickenlooper, and Alexander Wiley. At that meeting he also advocated a negotiated settlement with Japan, and Castle wrote him a few days later,

> I am . . . sure that what you have to say about Japan will sink into the minds of the Senators who were here and will do good. Yesterday afternoon I was discussing the matter at some length with Hugh Wilson who, as you know, is the advisor on foreign matters for the Republican National Committee. He is very enthusiastic over your plan and says that it would seem to him to give an opportunity for the minority in Congress really to take the lead, that probably Vandenberg would be the man to introduce the matter. The speech would have to be written with the greatest care so that the general public would not feel that we were backing down in our demands on Japan; that we were asking what we must have as a result of the war; but not in a way which will prolong the war.

Castle also reported a great deal of favorable comment in Washington concerning the Hoover-Truman meeting and that it had also stirred a great deal of attention in the media.[42] When Senator Wallace White publicly supported a negotiated peace with Japan, Hoover wrote him that it was "a most helpful statement," and he added that if Truman would make a similar statement and "include no desire on our part to destroy the emperor or his position, I believe we would get immediate results." His travels across the country had led him to believe that the war with Japan was "not very popular." He had also found, however, that "every conversation finally drifts onto some outrage by the OPA in its management of food."[43]

Hoover had contributed ideas to the postwar policies of the Roosevelt administration and had publicly supported FDR's postwar policies as long as they seemed to echo his own position, as at the Moscow Conference, even as he sought to mute opposition on the part of other Republicans to those policies. Though neglected by most historians, the former president's contribution to the forging of a bipartisan approach to postwar policy was already

obvious even before Roosevelt's death. His influence as a potential leader of
opposition to the wartime agreements forged under Roosevelt had not only
been stilled but such influence as he exerted was supportive. With Truman
in the White House, it was even easier to support bipartisanship in foreign
policy and the administration openly sought his assistance. Early in June 1945
Dean Acheson and William Clayton of the State Department lunched with
Hoover and asked him to use his influence with Republicans in Congress to
help the administration get approval of renewal of the Reciprocal Trade Act (a
New Deal measure) and the Bretton Woods agreement that provided for the
creation of the International Monetary Fund and the International Bank for
Reconstruction and Development.

Hoover sent O'Laughlin an account of the meeting and reported,

> I told them that I was on the other side of the fence as far as the reciprocal tariff
> was concerned, but had taken no active part in the discussion, and that I could
> not, therefore, be of much help in that particular. I said that I would intervene
> with my friends on the Hill in the matter of Bretton Woods. I subsequently
> telephoned several of our friends on both sides and urged them to put up no
> organized opposition but to let it go as a nonpartisan measure. I noticed that
> [Congressman Joe] Martin announced this policy the next day.

Hoover suggested that O'Laughlin might want to report what he had done
"to the proper quarters," by which he clearly meant the State Department.[44]

Hoover was cheered by the more conservative and cooperative attitude in
the White House and said kind words about Truman in an interview with the
press. Privately, however, Hoover told intimates that he had to talk to Truman
"in words of one syllable."[45] O'Laughlin wrote that the former president's
statement, combined with similar ones from Dewey and Landon in support of
Truman's foreign policies, had led "Capitol Republicans to wonder what has
happened to the GOP."[46] Hoover told California Republican publisher William F. Knowland, "Never has this country ever felt so relieved as during the
last 90 days. The new President is rapidly altering the 'party line' and there is
a much more hopeful feeling that we will pull through the postwar troubles.
It is not going to be easy."[47]

Food Conditions

There had, however, been no improvement in the domestic food situation,
and without improvement in America the foreign food situation must remain
critical. In late June Congressman Jenkins, chairman of the GOP Congressional Food Study Committee, again solicited Hoover's suggestions, writing
that some of his former recommendations had "been accepted in principle
by the Administration and with very good results. But the Administration
still stubbornly clings to most of its politicies and practices in spite of the
fact that the situation is getting worse and worse." Jenkins asked that Hoover

Left to Right: Herbert, Jr; Herbert III; Margaret; Joan; Lou Henry; Allan; Peggy Ann; and Herbert Hoover at the family home in Palo Alto, CA on Christmas Eve (1933). Courtesy of the Herbert Hoover Presidential Library-Museum. 1933–62

Lou Henry Hoover in Girl Scout uniform with dog Weegie (1937). Courtesy of the Herbert Hoover Presidential Library-Museum. 1937–31

Herbert Hoover with Field Marshal Hermann Göring (in white) in Karin Hall on Goring's forest estate (March 9, 1938). Courtesy of the Herbert Hoover Presidential Library-Museum. 1938–35

Herbert Hoover, head of the Finnish Relief Fund, is introduced to Popeye (Harry F. Welch) by Ward Greene of King Features Syndicate, enlisting children's support in Finnish relief (January 9, 1940). Courtesy of the Herbert Hoover Presidential Library-Museum. 1940–10

Herbert Hoover is surrounded by Polish war orphans during his tour of the devastated city of Warsaw (April 2, 1946). Courtesy of the Herbert Hoover Presidential Library-Museum. 1946–51

Herbert Hoover and his team tour the remains of the "Old City" of Warsaw—the two women are gathering firewood (April 2, 1946). Courtesy of the Herbert Hoover Presidential Library-Museum. 1946–77

Herbert Hoover and Gandhi leave the Viceroys' House following a conference on India's food problems (April 23, 1946). Courtesy of the Herbert Hoover Presidential Library-Museum. 1946–A72A

Herbert Hoover and the crew of the "Faithful Cow" pose in front of the plane which brought Herbert Hoover from Japan (May 7, 1946). Courtesy of the Herbert Hoover Presidential Library-Museum. 1946–B17B

The First Hoover Commission including (seated L to R): Herbert Hoover, President Truman, Joseph Kennedy, and Dean Acheson (standing third from right) (ca. 1948). Courtesy of the Herbert Hoover Presidential Library-Museum. 1948–60

The Hoover family poses in front of the birthplace cottage - L to R: Herbert Hoover III, Herbert Hoover Jr., Allan Hoover, Stephen Hoover, Herbert Hoover, Andrew Hoover, Allan, Jr., Margaret C. Hoover, Margaret Hoover, Mrs. Herbert Hoover III (August 10, 1954). Courtesy of the Herbert Hoover Presidential Library-Museum. 1954–60

Herbert Hoover with his secretary, Bernice (Bunny) Miller, on his 86th birthday (August 10, 1960). Courtesy of the Herbert Hoover Presidential Library-Museum. 1960–62

Herbert Hoover walking through the crowd during the Hoover Presidential Library dedication. Courtesy of the Herbert Hoover Presidential Library-Museum. 1962–B47B

again "outline for us how best to organize the Animal Products Industry of the Nation so as to relieve the terrible meat situation." The shortage of fats and oils from animal production was "fast becoming distressing since it involves the production of baked products, such as bread, and sanitary products, such as soap."[48]

Hoover responded on June 20, 1945, by pointing out that the food problem was not a partisan matter but one involving both the well-being of the American people and their ability to handle the problems of relief in the liberated areas of Europe. Many of the problems were the result of mismanagement by the Roosevelt administration, and the results were declines in hog, sheep, chicken, and beef production; difficulties with distribution that were creating shortages across the nation; the existence of black markets in meats and fats "in every city of the country" as a result of the "breakdown in control of both distribution and prices"; and continuance of the policy of subsidies to producers, which came from taxpayers' pockets and helped nothing. The Roosevelt administration had tried to fix prices at the retail level and then work backward to the farmers, while using "subsidies and constantly changing prices to open the multitude of bottlenecks." Hoover's method in World War I had been "to fix prices as near the farmer as possible and to work forward to the consumer by additions of normal trade differentials and without subsidies." World War I had produced no black markets, he claimed, nor famines, ration cards, or rapid inflation, while it had led to less consumption per capita than was the case in 1944 and to constantly increasing production of all animal products so that it had been possible not only to feed Americans also to save the children of Europe.[49]

Hoover suggested reconstructing the World War I method and administration even at this late date, with the secretary of agriculture granted all the powers and staff of the Office of Price Administrator, as well as control of all "allocation and buying of major animal products for the Armed forces, Lend-Lease and relief," in addition to his authority as food administrator. There should be an administrator of animal products, with an advisory committee representing the military, lend-lease, and relief allocations, as well as committees of the major agricultural units from growers to retailers. Prices to farmers by packers should be set, packers should be allowed an agreed markup to cover their costs, and a proper profit, and the same should apply to retailers. Reminding Jenkins that he had been advocating this approach on the administration since the outbreak of the war, he told him that the results would be lower prices, a normal flow of trade, no local famines, no need for subsidies, increased production, and a minimum of policing by the government. That Hoover's plan worked was shown by World War I. That Roosevelt's plan did not work was shown by World War II. If Roosevelt's plan were not abandoned, the difficulties would only continue to multiply "and the hope of aid in meats and fats to women and children abroad becomes hopeless."

Foreign Relations

When Truman prepared to leave for the Potsdam conference, Hoover joined with other prominent Americans in signing a memorial to the president that asked the three heads of state to agree on terms that would permit free elections in the areas "liberated" by the Soviet Union; ensure the right of all democratic parties to participate; provide for freedom of speech and press, international supervision of the first election, the withdrawal of Soviet troops before the election (or joint occupation with US and British troops during the electoral period); and establish the right of news correspondents and representatives of the Red Cross and other charitable organizations to operate in Poland and other Soviet-occupied territories, as well as other provisions.[50] Here was a clear expression of America's mistrust of the objectives of the Soviet Union, but given Hoover's realism concerning that regime, it is doubtful he held much faith that such provisions would be honored by the Russians even if they accepted them at Potsdam.

On July 18 Hoover spoke on behalf of the United Nations Charter in San Francisco. The former president had, of course, advocated that the new international organization not be created until after a "cooling-off period," and so he described the new charter as "probably as good as could be obtained under the existing emotions, the present governments, the conflicting ideas and ambitions in the world." He called for the Senate to vote to ratify it "promptly" but also warned the American people they "should be under no illusions that the Charter assures lasting peace." It was at best only "an expression of desire and machinery to advance peace." Peace would also require "economic and political settlements among nations by which this war is liquidated," and those would have much more effect on questions of peace or war than the charter, since, as he had pointed out before, "the Charter could not preserve a bad peace." The charter did not contain the "bill of rights" for nations and peoples that he had advocated, and the veto power in the Security Council was likely to hamper its efforts to respond to military aggression. The charter had also failed to even define aggression or contain any commitment to disarmament. In voting for it, the Senate must also ensure that the US delegate to the Security Council did not have the power to commit US military forces without recourse to the congressional responsibility for declarations of war under the Constitution.[51]

Hoover told Americans that "the plain fact" was that the success of the United Nations and of peacemaking and peacekeeping would still depend on the "successful collaboration of the three centers of power—that is, Russia, Britain and the United States"—and that would continue to be the case for "many years to come." Hoover added,

> But lasting peace cannot be based upon the dominance of three or four or even five powers forever. The Charter will offer a forum for world opinion and advice to these responsible powers. The retreat from the Atlantic Charter, the

ambitions and emotions of war, the omissions from the San Francisco Charter emphasize that these three great powers are really the trustees of world peace rather than the Charter itself. There must be a transition period where this collaboration will require much patience, it will require great firmness. It will take time and much good will to find lasting settlements after the high emotions of war, of national ambitions, of differing national purposes.

Contrary to Hoover's advice, the international organization had been formed even before the end of the war. But the former president pointed out, correctly, that with or without the international organization the transition would be a reality, with the three "trustees" responsible for peace rather than the United Nations Organization.

Late in July Henry Allen wrote Hoover that it was time for him "to get up a speech about America's opportunity to reemphasize leadership and democracy," since it appeared "as though socialism has captured the imagination of the European world and of course, under the New Deal leadership, it has made tremendous progress in this country." Allen worried that the "advocates of democracy are getting mealy-mouthed."[52] Hoover was, he told Henry Allen, speaking to fifty thousand people on that familiar theme but was having "difficulty rephrasing the subject in new terms sufficiently vigorous and appealing to meet the danger." He asked for suggestions from Allen so that he could go on "another track instead of beating my old phrases over again," but Allen's suggestions arrived too late to help.[53] On August 11 Hoover spoke to the Iowa Association of Southern California in Long Beach, California. In his speech on "The Challenge to Free Men," the former president pointed out that the "specters of war and revolution stand behind every shoulder. They haunt every thought and our every word." "Communism or Creeping Socialism are sweeping over Europe," he told his audience, and they were "beginning in Asia." "A score of Fascist nations have shifted to Communism; and half a dozen nations once liberty-loving are shifting to Socialism." And the same kind of thinking had infested the United States under the New Deal, to which had been added the government controls of wartime. Hoover them championed the liberties of the "American System." Americans had sacrificed and fought and died for that system, he pointed out, adding, "Is it not a faith? Is it not a belief for which men die? Is freedom to be defeated by slogans, or foreign propaganda, or Fifth Columns? You and I must not be marked as the generation who surrendered the heritage of America."[54]

In that same month there briefly appeared to be a prospect that the former president might have an opportunity to deal with postwar problems from the vantage point of a seat in the United States Senate. Hiram Johnson's poor health led him to express interest at least as early as January1945 in being appointed to the Senate from California if Johnson died.[55] When Johnson did die, in August, O'Laughlin was pressed into service to ascertain if the senator's widow and son might intervene with Governor Earl Warren in supporting Hoover's appointment to fill out the unexpired years of Johnson's term.[56]

Many letters were sent to Warren in Hoover's behalf, and the *New York Times* supported his appointment in an editorial.[57] Warren, however, appointed publisher William Knowland, instead. Hoover expressed an insincere sense of relief to disguise his disappointment at not being chosen.[58] However, political considerations aside, Hoover's age (he was 71) and his long absence from California during his residency in New York made him in an unlikely prospect to represent the people of that state.

Shortly before V. J. Day, Hoover penned his views on the agreements reached at Potsdam and on the use of the atomic bomb against Japan. The Potsdam agreements he found to be simply further confirmation of his earlier suspicions that the Soviets intended to annex east Finland, east Poland, Latvia, Estonia, Lithuania, and Bessarabia, as well as proof that Rumania, Bulgaria, Finland, Yugoslavia, and Hungary would be under communist-controlled governments, while the election to be held in Poland would be so manipulated as to take that country, too, into the Russian orbit. Germany was left with little hope of economic recovery, with the result that the rest of Europe would probably be impoverished and unstable, too. Of the possibility of dropping of the atomic bomb on Japan, he wrote, "The use of the Atomic bomb, with its indiscriminate killing of women and children, revolts my soul." The only difference between the use of the bomb and poison gas was, in the fact, that the United States alone possessed the bomb and therefore need not fear retaliation. He suspected that the bomb was "being exploited beyond its real possibilities to frighten the Japs."[59]

In mid-September, Hoover told the Executives Club of Chicago that the United States must aid the war-ravaged nations of the world to the best of their ability, but there were limits, he pointed out, to what the thirty million families of the United States could do for the three hundred million families who needed help. The United States had also been impoverished by the war, and Europeans should not ignore that or the fact that "American recovery and financial stability is the first need of the world. Unless we recover no one will recover." American assistance would be in the form of loans, he told his audience, and repayment would have to be in the form of goods except for a relatively small amount of gold. But the period of destitution was not the time to demand repayment of any kind. Instead, Hoover advocated a five-year moratorium on Allied debts, including those under lend-lease, and "five years hence when the shape of the world is more clear, we should joint our Allies in the disposition of such debts. And as a price for American assistance, foreign governments should be required not to erect any trade barriers against American goods, and should not undertake "dumping" or cartel operations at the expense of the United States." He concluded,

> We must help. We should use common sense. We should limit our help to
> what our taxpayers can afford. We should consider our own employment

situation. We should limit our aid to the minimum necessary. We should limit it to the direct purpose of restoring their domestic needs through commodities.

We should organize the help so as to minimize the ill-will over repayment. We should do it with the knowledge that we are doing it at a loss to ourselves but to aid mankind to recover from the greatest disaster of all history.[60]

Politics

Late in September 1945 Hoover responded to a request from Norman Chandler of the *Los Angeles Times* for an editorial by issuing a new manifesto for Republicans. In it, Hoover argued that "one of the first necessities of successful democratic process is two major political parties," but they must also present real alternative programs and issues. He wrote,

> Today the radicals on the "left" are organized and vigorous. The conservatives on the "right" are unorganized and impotent. The American people need and have a right to organized expression of conservative thought. Being a conservative is not a sin. It is not "fascism" or "reaction." It means today the conservation of representative government, of intellectual freedom and of economic freedom within the limits of what does not harm fellow men. It means the conservation of natural resources, of national health, education and employment. A conservative is not allergic to new ideas. He wants to try them slowly without destroying what is already good.

The American people deserved "an opportunity to express the conservative point of view" when voting, and a conservative party might eventually "come into power against the radical excesses and the accumulation of errors and blunders which are the inevitable result of long continuance of one party in power." The GOP should therefore represent conservatism "and do it with pride in its principles and in the service it can perform for the country." It should not shrink from the smears it would attract from the "left" at use of the term *conservative*, because Americans would "see through the smears sooner or later." Republicans should disdain use of the word *liberal* since it had been corrupted beyond utility and distorted to mean the reverse of its original ideals. The socialists and communists, Hoover suggested, "have nested in this word until it stinks. Let them have the word. It no longer makes sense."[61]

Hoover was doing his best to steer the Republican Party in a conservative direction. When he learned that House Republicans were formulating a platform or declaration of principles for the party, he sent Congressman Jenkins a six-point program that included (1) support for an international organization to prevent future wars; (2) opposition to the collectivism and regimentation "imposed upon the American people by Franklin Roosevelt and its unnecessary enlargement during the war"; (3) elimination of waste and corruption

from the federal government, reduction of the federal work force, reestablish-
ment of solid national finances, and independence of the judiciary; (4) encouragement of private enterprise and opposition to government competition with
business, but regulation of business and the right of labor and business to
organize; (5) aid to veterans and to "the ill, the aged and the unemployed,
and to the constant building up of agriculture"; (6) removal of trade barriers,
except insofar as tariffs were needed to protect the livelihood of American
farmers and workers.[62]

Jenkins thanked the former president for his six-point program and told
him the GOP members had come from "from this recess very much agitated,"
especially the younger ones. All had ideas and the steering committee had in
mind the "important task of working up some sort of brief platform or declaration of principles." He intended to pass Hoover's six-point program on to
the drafting committee for their use and told the former president he would
"let you know the reaction we get."[63]

When the Truman administration proposed universal military training
during peacetime, the former president was opposed. He was pleased by a
poll he conducted of congressman concerning the issue, which showed less
than 20 percent in both houses favoring enactment before the end of the
war.[64] When the atomic bomb was dropped on Japan, Hoover concluded that
it had destroyed whatever arguments there were for peacetime conscription.
But if it were to be enacted, Hoover wrote Senator Taft, it should defer college students, at least, since the nation's defense in the future would obviously "depend upon trained engineers, doctors and scientists and men who
can undertake public service."[65]

A harbinger of a role that the former president was soon to perform came
in a letter from Ferdinand Eberstadt, a veteran of several wartime mobilization agencies, who sought Hoover's advice on reorganization of the military
section of the executive branch of the government. The request originated
with Secretary of the Navy James Forrestal, and it solicited his views "concerning the essential elements of the military organization which will give
promise of most effectively meeting our military responsibilities."[66] This early
opportunity to be of service to the cause of reorganization of the executive
branch of the government was, however, missed by Hoover as he was on a
fishing trip in the West and was unable to answer the query until nearly a
month later, by which time Eberstadt had already submitted his report.[67]

In September, however, Hoover wrote O'Laughlin,

> You will remember that we had some conversation about my supporting Tru-
> man's re-organization plan. I am not especially enthused about the way they
> handled my help on the food question, inasmuch as they adopted practically
> every major recommendation and gave us no credit whatever. But if it is desir-
> able, I would be glad to go through with a letter to somebody in the Senate
> or the House. I think the matter is before the House Committee, and I think
> they have reported out something. If this is true, would you let me know what

Committee it is and what sort of report they made, and I will try to write something to the ranking Republican member.[68]

On October 1, he wired and wrote Congressman George Bender that the reorganization bill "giving authority to President Truman to reorganize the executive departments" provided "a sensible procedure and makes the proper exceptions and I favor it." He told Bender that the "overlap, waste, and conflict of policies between executive agencies have been a scandal" through six successive presidents and 35 years.[69] Truman thanked Hoover for his help ten days later.[70]

In November of 1945 Hoover mailed off another editorial to the *Los Angeles Times*, in which he took up another postwar issue. As a result of the war he found all nations striving for a higher degree of self-sufficiency, seeking to make themselves less dependent upon foreign trade. Inevitably this would produce higher tariffs everywhere to protect new industries, and America would also "experience the stimulus to self-sufficiency." As president, Hoover had, he said, advocated international cooperation to reduce tariffs, and this had been one motive for calling the World Economic Conference in London in 1933. Roosevelt had chosen, instead, a policy of bilateral reciprocal trade agreements. In comparing the Hoover years with the period of 1935–1938 under FDR, however, Hoover found that the percentage of imports on which tariffs had applied grew substantially during the Roosevelt years. Roosevelt's promises to reduce tariffs had not been kept, and the reciprocal trade policy had neither increased American foreign trade nor preserved peace.[71] He furnished the tariff figures to Congressman Thomas Jenkins, who promised to present them in a speech on the floor of the House.[72]

The operations of the United Nations Relief and Rehabilitation Agency continued to draw Hoover's criticism. In November 1945 he suggested the creation of a distinctly American organization to handle America's relief work in postwar Europe and found support for the idea in Congress.[73] Congressman Jenkins, chairman of the Food Committee, wrote Hoover in late November that there was "quite a strong sentiment against doing anything further for these countries than to give them the $550,000,000" that had already been approved for UNRRA.[74] When Hoover met with a UNRRA representative late in the month, he suggested strengthening the organization, especially through the recruitment of experienced American personnel.[75] Early in December he insisted that UNRRA should do something to aid Finland, and the agency did allocate supplies to help the Finns.[76] But Hoover still did not consider that UNRRA was as effective as the American Relief Administration (ARA) had been under his leadership after World War I. He wrote one correspondent, "U.N.R.R.A. scarcely parallels the A.R.A. We relieved 18 countries and coordinated the food supplies of 9 more . . . U.N.R.R.A. up to date has given relief to only 5 countries plus the displaced persons. The A.R.A. looked after those also after the last war."[77]

Now 71, Hoover seemed intent at last on reducing his activities. He told John Bricker, "Just 'making a speech' is out of my life hereafter. When I am bursting to say something, I look around for a forum."[78] He was disappointed by the lack of interest Republicans were showing in his proposed declaration of principles.[79] And so much of what was happening in Washington seemed still to have a through-the-looking-glass quality that defied understanding. When he learned of proposals that the United States should share the secrets of the atomic bomb with the Soviet Union, Hoover wrote, "Here we are building up a vast military establishment directed to Russia; there is no one else to harm us. And now we propose to give her military power over us. Why not give her half our fleet?"[80] He derived some satisfaction, however, from the knowledge that a number of books were being written that were not kind to Roosevelt, and Hoover was himself keeping three secretaries busy seven days a week at work on his own memoirs, which he expected to complete in the spring of 1946.[81] He was also busy refuting rumors spread by columnist Walter Winchell that he planned to remarry.

But late in January 1946 Hoover took time out to write a short piece for the Dutch Treat Club. He suggested, however, that author Clarence Kelland should put his own name on the piece, since, as Hoover put it, "I would never be forgiven for such frivolity." Such "frivolity" certainly deserves quoting:

> Now that we presumably have peace our diplomacy has a real job of converting its pre V-E day promises into the post V-J day realities. It is doing this job of converting the war output of idealism fairly competently. It is done chiefly with words. The ammunition of diplomacy is words and naturally they have to be bent around difficult corners if they are to make a conversion in such a fashion that nobody will detect them. Some people have wistful notions that diplomatic words, phrases and slogans kept the same meaning for at least a year or two. But that is only the aspiration of iconoclasts or foolish people who don't want ideas all the time slipping from their intellectual grasp. However, it is the sign of a good diplomat to have a genius for changing meanings on us right in the middle of the game. This changing the meaning of words is one of the triumphs of the true art.
>
> For instance, that word "appeasement." It is a term of vile reproach never to be used any more now that Hitler is buried. Moreover, we have to get over the hump of giving something to Joseph Stalin like a "sphere of influence" over 150,000,000 people in a dozen independent nations, all of which cynics might say was appeasement and that it was a violation of the Four Freedoms and the Atlantic Charter. But that is easy. We just call it (Yalta definition) "establishing a broad democratic basis."
>
> We did start the war with a Pied Piper's tune called the Four Freedoms and the Atlantic Charter. It was especially charming to idealists and left wingers. All that was to be applied "everywhere" and was to be the glory of man right after V-E day. But the diplomats lost the charter somewhere on the road to Teheran and at once insisted with eloquence that,

like the Ten Commandments and the Sermon on the Mount, it might take 2,000 years to get it over. When the dumb complained that this might be after World War X instead of World War II, diplomacy said, "We shall never recognize any government that did not conform." However, having put the Atlantic Charter and the Four Freedoms a long way off in this diplomatic way, then they decide to recognize various states provided they take two ministers into their Communist governments who "represent broad democratic interest" and who will be cooperative. They haven't yet mentioned that they will have to cooperate with 10 or 15 Communist ministers plus the secret police. However, that phrase fixes everything up beautifully except that these Communists have seized all American property "in the public interest." We will, no doubt, get over that hump by crediting it on Lend-Lease or something. Another example of preparing us for the worst with words was when our diplomats vested the Communists with the command of the underground in half a dozen nations. They did not like the sound the [word] Communist would make in the United States so they called them "partisans."

Also, when Soviet Russia annexed the economic and moral control of Manchuria, the same as she had done before the Japanese took it away from her forty years ago, the diplomats called it "reestablishing Chinese authority." When Dictator Vargas of Brazil proclaimed his Fascist government he was called "a democratic leader" by our diplomats who also said it was "the firm policy of the United States never to interfere in the domestic affairs of other nations." But when Dictator Peron appeared in Argentina, our Ambassador tried to upset him because he is a "fascist."

Perhaps some suggested definitions might help.

"Appeasement"—giving away something that belongs to somebody else.
"Cooperation"—giving away something that belongs to somebody else.
"Democracy"—now includes single-party government secret police to educate the voters.
"A Dictator"—depends on who he is.
"Open covenants openly arrived at"—when they are opened up later on.[82]

When President Truman appealed to the American people to conserve food so that it could be used to meet the famine overseas, Hoover supported the appeal with a statement asking that it "be supported by the whole American people." He called for special provision of food for undernourished children and mothers over the whole of Europe, including Germany, to combat the high infant mortality rate. "Peace and progress," he pointed out in words familiar from his campaigns in behalf of food relief to wartime Europe, "will not be restored if those who survive are to be infected by a generation of men and women stunted in body and distorted in mind." He was confident, Hoover said, that the need for increased food exports could be met entirely by "voluntary action to eliminate waste and unnecessary consumption and . . . without compulsory rationing, since the voluntary approach had worked during World War I."[83]

Hoover also supported Senator J. William Fulbright's effort to have the United States government finance intellectual exchanges between America and other nations. When asked by Fulbright for his views, Hoover wrote that he supported the proposal, and he went on to describe the work that the Belgian-American Educational Foundation had done in that field under his leadership, as well as his own efforts, as secretary of commerce and president, to establish such exchanges with ten countries, using war debts for financing.[84] Fulbright told Hoover he believed the former president's support would help and said he hoped that "this time we have more success in persuading our own government to promote this program." However, Hoover had to decline Fulbright's invitation to testify in behalf of his bill, since the former president was to be on a fishing trip to Florida on the date of the hearings.[85] Hoover was meanwhile launching his own major effort to promote the cause of international understanding by collecting documents in Europe for the Hoover War Library. In late January he lunched with General Dwight Eisenhower and pressed for liberalization of travel restrictions in Germany for Hoover War Library people seeking materials. According to Rickard's diary, Hoover was "very much impressed with the General, who [was] apparently not in sympathy with the White House and State Department in their handling of occupation of Germany, and carrying out [Henry A.] Wallace's plan for near extermination of Germany industry."[86]

Before leaving for Florida, Hoover delivered the Lincoln Day speech to the National Republican Club in New York City. In a nationally broadcast speech, the former president declared, "Today the great issue before the American people is free men against the tide of Statism which is sweeping three-quarters of the world—whether it be called Communism, Fascism, Socialism or the disguised American mixture of Fascism and Socialism called 'Managed Economy' now being transformed into a further ambiguity, the 'Welfare State.' This growth of statism has been nourished by the confusion of a great war. And it can grow still more by continued excessive taxation and by creeping inflation." The voters, he charged, were not being given a choice on fundamental issues, for both parties had "straddled" on those issues. The GOP and the American people needed "a fundamental and constructive philosophy of government" that would "reach far deeper than the froth of slogans or platform planks designed to appease every pressure group." Government must only be the "umpire and mediator" of economic life, not the dictator or operator of the economy. The government must be motivated by a philosophy based on "the concept that man can accomplish more by cooperation outside the government than by coercion from the government." He told his listeners, "There are fields where cooperation can be properly aided by government, but government swollen with power and laden with burdens becomes something above and apart from the governed. It becomes the enemy of the governed, increasing its prerogatives with fanatical zeal. To delineate the appropriate boundaries of the government which preserve such a philosophy and principles is the task of the statesmanship for which this country is waiting." Government must stimulate men's initiative and moral rectitude, while statism, on the contrary, strangled and undermined them.[87]

Hoover's fishing trip to the Florida Keys was destined to be a short one. Secretary of Agriculture Clinton Anderson phoned the former president in New York City on February 25, 1946, only to learn that he was in Florida fishing. Anderson left a message that he was eager to confer with Hoover about both the domestic and European food problems and to emphasize the urgency he offered to send "a special plane—land or amphibious—to wherever he might be to take him to Washington and to return him to Florida." According to a memorandum of the conversation, Anderson said, "Mr. Hoover had always been very helpful to him, had given him the best advice he had ever received last July, and that everything Mr. H. had told him at that time had worked out as HH said it would." Anderson said he did not want "to move in this problem without Mr. Hoover's knowledge and advice." Anderson assured Hoover that this was "not a politically cooked up arrangement, but they were solely interested in conservation." Anderson wanted Hoover to be the honorary chairman, "but in any event they needed his advice and . . . they did not want to choose the actual chairman who would do all the work without Mr. Hoover's approval."[88]

Hoover responded with a telegram the next day in which he advised against any committee organization outside of the government, such as Anderson seemed to be proposing, and arguing once again that the secretary of agriculture should have all control over food centralized under him. His advice on that score had been ignored repeatedly, but he offered it once more. In Hoover's view "only an official of cabinet rank and an existing organization can organize and direct the quick campaign that is needed now because food from the United States after the end of June will be of no avail in this famine and it is thus already very late to start." He suggested immediate steps to prevent hoarding and waste and unnecessary consumption and outlined measures to encourage substitution of foods as well as to control food exports and imports. The next step, Hoover advised, was to conduct a survey of the amounts and types of foods that were in surplus in the world, and "how much of each kind you can export from the United States without injury to public health." He could not, Hoover told Anderson, advise him on this latter phase of the problem since "it would require me to do exhaustive investigations at home and abroad and I assume you already have such information." He then suggested that a national organization, modeled after the World War I–era US Food Administration, be formed, with state and county food administrators to encourage conservation and the use of substitute foods.[89]

Anderson replied that Truman had asked him "to invite you formally" to a conference at the White House and that he would have the former president picked up by a navy plane and flown from Florida to Washington.[90] Hoover arrived looking "tanned and fit" and immediately called upon Americans to voluntarily consume less food, eliminate waste, and use substitutes in order to help relieve famine abroad. He then met with Truman, Anderson, and others. Hugh Gibson wrote to his wife, "It is a pity this step was not taken at the time we went down [to Washington] last year. The Chief told him everything that was going to happen just as it has happened since, and made [Truman] a memorandum of suggestions as to what steps should be taken. Needless to say, none of them have been taken and the situation has got rather out of hand . . . At any rate, it is good that something is being envisaged and we can hope that we shall come to grips with the subject after all this delay."[91] A few days later Gibson wrote further that Hoover had "picked up a bad cold flying north." It was, Gibson said, "too early to tell what will come of the conference in Washington, but I am not overoptimistic. None of them seem to have the vision that is needed to lay down a program and put it over to the people."[92]

The meeting resulted in the creation of the Famine Emergency Committee (FEC), with Herbert Hoover as honorary chairman. The committee, composed initially of twelve civic leaders, called for a 25 percent reduction in American consumption of wheat and wheat products and all possible savings of food, oils, and fats. The FEC intended to work through hotels, restaurants, and industry groups to formulate conservation measures. Truman called the meeting "the most important meeting, I think, we have held in the White House since I have been President." Hoover expressed confidence that the American people would respond to calls for voluntary conservation and described the United States as "the last reservation [sic] from which starvation can be halted." The FEC, he said, was calling for "a four-months sacrifice by the American people" in order to hold "together Western civilization against chaos." He insisted that Germany, Austria, and Japan would also have to be included in the relief program, not only for humanitarian reasons, but also for the safety of American occupation troops in those countries.[93]

Matters moved rapidly thereafter. Hoover was at first doubtful that much would result, since he had come to the conclusion that Truman was not very bright and seemed incapable of grasping the points the former president had tried to make. He told Rickard that he could not "believe this country ever was governed by such a mediocre type of man," and he despaired "of our ever accomplishing any constructive policy either international or domestic."[94]

But soon there were rumors in Washington that Hoover would be asked to travel to Europe to make a survey of the food situation, and on March 5, Gibson wrote his wife, "What a day! This morning I was called out of bed by a telephone call from the Chief in Washington. He said that the President had just sent the Secretary of Agriculture to see him to ask if he would undertake to do a flying trip all over Europe and prepare a report on the food situation. He accepted on the spot. Of course the trip should have been made when he first suggested it last May, but he did not take the trouble to rub it in."[95]

Writer Will Irwin furnished a humorous sidelight on Hoover's new involvement in famine relief, when he described the reaction of the director of the New York play *Lute Song* to the former president's appearance in the audience after his return from Europe. According to Irwin,

> on the first New York night of Lute Song I stood in the back of the house waiting for the curtain to go up on the first act. The director stood beside me. "You see that bulky man on the center aisle, eighth row?" I asked. "That's Herbert Hoover." "Do you know if there are any of those aeroplane safety straps in the house?" he asked. "Why?" I asked. "Because I want to send an usher to strap him to his seat before the second act opens," said the director. 'If I don't, he'll dive over the footlights and relieve that famine and there won't be any more show!'"[96]

By mid-March it was clear that the itinerary for Hoover's trip would have to be broadened to include more of the world than Europe, since, as Gibson pointed out, "the food problem is global and . . . it ought to be attacked on a world scale."[97] Hoover had told Secretary Anderson, "Aside from anything we can do in the United States in conserving food by human beings and animals, the greatest possibility of further covering the gap in supplies lies in mobilizing the Latin American states to join with us in conservation, reduction of imports, and expansion of their exports where they have such."[98] As he prepared to leave for Europe on the first stage of his inquiry, the former president received a warm telegram from labor leader John L. Lewis:

> On the eve of your departure to aid the suffering peoples of other lands I extend the greetings of an old friend with earnest wishes for your complete success and a safe return to your own country. You are undertaking a task which no other citizen has the wisdom or ability to perform, yet I am sure you will succeed and will be followed by the blessings of the millions whom you succor. As a duty to your fellow citizens and as a favor to your friends, please conserve your strength and safeguard your health on your arduous journey.[99]

Hoover was 71 years old and already suffering the effects of a cold he had caught during the flight north from Florida. Nevertheless, one Hoover friend estimated after his death that Truman had added ten years to the former president's life by putting him to work.[100]

Reviewing the new responsibility that the former president had taken on, *US News and World Report* wrote,

> Mr. Hoover, at 71, is in obviously robust health. His hair has turned from gray to white since he left the Presidency, but his step is brisk and his voice is vigorous. He still prefers the double-breasted blue suits that were characteristic of his White House days, but the famous high stiff collar that became a cartoonists symbol is often replaced by one that is low and soft.
>
> He has been busy. Speeches, usually critical of Administration policy— although he favored giving President Roosevelt dictatorial powers during

the war—have been numerous. A number of these have severely criticized
the war food program. Mr. Hoover still thinks the country should have
a national food administrator in charge of production, distribution and
prices . . . What the Administration will think of these ideas, however, is
the subject of some uncertainty.[101]

Newsweek observed that "under his calm, elderly, and gentle appearance,
the man seemed above all else a dramatic symbol of sympathy and hope." It
continued,

> The vast, impersonal forces of war and famine which had brought a con-
> tinent to chaos a generation ago had done their dreadful work again. And
> once again Herbert Hoover's organizational genius for feeding millions
> was in demand.
>
>   In the gray light of LaGuardia Field, on March 17, a chilly Sunday-
> morning group of spectators watched the former President climb into the
> big Air Transport Command C-54 and saw it vanish into the overcast.
> Thirty years after his rise to world eminence as the man who fed Europe,
> Hoover was going back on a similar mission.
>
>   If there was any irony in the situation, nothing in Hoover's benevolent
> aspect betrayed it. His smile was faint, but no fainter than it had been in
> the last two years of his Presidency and through the thirteen subsequent
> years since he left the White House.[102]

   The formation of the FEC, with Hoover as its "honorary" head was a
clear repudiation by the Truman administration of the efforts of UNRRA and
its head, Herbert Lehman. One student has noted that Lehman was already
disturbed over the lack of cooperation he was receiving from the American
government, and the formation of the FEC under Hoover "only confirmed
Lehman's resolution to resign." According to Milton Gustafson, "[Lehman]
felt that the problem could not be solved by a committee, especially one
headed by an old isolationist. When Truman asked Hoover to make a worldwide survey of food needs—including countries already expertly surveyed by
UNRRA—Lehman correctly assumed that the United States was moving
toward relief controlled strictly by the United States."[103] It is certainly true
that the international approach to famine relief symbolized by the UNRRA
efforts was being rejected by the United States, but it was more than an issue of
international versus national control of relief. Also at issue was the destination
of American food supplies. In his meeting with President Truman on May 28,
1945, Hoover had argued that those parts of Europe under Soviet domination
should be left to the USSR to feed, and he found Truman in agreement. Yet
European food relief under UNRRA was going largely to countries within the
Soviet zone of influence, and under the UNRRA agreement the Soviet Union
was not only free of any obligation to furnish food supplies, but could, as an
invaded country, even ask for UNRRA aid itself.[104]

Lehman tendered his resignation as head of UNRRA at a meeting of the UNRRA council in Atlantic City in mid-March, graciously terming Hoover's plea for voluntary food conservation "most praiseworthy and sure to lead to substantial results" but expressing doubts that it would be sufficient and the belief that government controls would have to be instituted. Lehman also called for feeding the Allies first and the defeated enemies last, a stance that was also at variance with Hoover's position. Meanwhile, the UNRRA officials showed their own concern for food relief and conservation by each breakfasting on three slices of toast, one corn muffin, one roll, cereal, fruit, bacon or ham and eggs, and coffee.[105] If all Americans showed that degree of cooperation with the food conservation effort, then Lehman's prediction of its insufficiency would doubtless be validated.

On March 16, Hoover appealed over nationwide radio for Americans to conserve food in order to avert famine for five hundred million people. He was joined by Congresswoman Clare Boothe Luce, who made the same plea.[106] The former president then flew to Europe for the first leg of his round-the-world food survey. He and his staff flew in a C-54 dubbed "The Faithful Cow," while a group of reporters, including newsreel cameramen, accompanied him in a C-47. The C-54 was a deluxe version operated by the Air Transport Command, with a private room in the forward part of the aircraft in which Hoover spent most of his time with a fair degree of privacy except when he played gin rummy with Hugh Gibson.[107]

In Paris Hoover again expressed opposition to food rationing, telling reporters that the American people would respond to a call for voluntary service to humanity. Hoover added, "This is the most prodigious call they have ever received in history, and I am sure they will answer it magnificently." "Here's how I see my job," he told reporters in Paris. "After the latter was I directed food supplies for a large part of Europe. Now I've been called back again like an old family doctor."[108] Lehman disagreed with Hoover over rationing, continuing to maintain the typical New Deal reliance on compulsion—in this case food rationing—but it was the former president whose views now prevailed in food relief matters. On March 26, the FEC rejected rationing, and two days later Truman expressed his opposition to it, as well.[109]

Meanwhile, Hoover and his entourage were traveling through Europe, obtaining data, making recommendations, and seeking to remove bottlenecks. Hoover was also acquiring materials for the Hoover War Library. In Italy the former president called upon Pope Pius XII to gain his cooperation in impressing Catholics, especially those in Latin America, with the necessity to conserve and export food. Hoover later credited the pope's assistance for the cooperation that the FEC received from Argentina and other South American countries. Frank Mason, who was part of Hoover's entourage, reported that the former president did no sightseeing and worked at a "dizzying pace," but he added that "The Chief thrives on it, and appears to be in perfect health."

At every stop they seemed to bring long overdue sunshine to the city they were visiting, with their hosts invariably reporting that it was the best weather they had experienced in weeks. In Switzerland Hoover and some of the others bought cheap watches. While in India, the former president remarked that "Mr. Gandhi and I have one thing in common. As a common mark of our humility, we each carry dollar watches." In India Hoover also had a suit made for him in 12 hours by a New Delhi tailor. Several of those in "The Faithful Cow" bought Egyptian puzzle rings and went nearly crazy trying to assemble them, causing Hoover to remark that "it would be an appropriate idea to buy a few of these rings for one's worst enemy—and watch them lose their minds and become harmless."[110]

As for the results in the countries visited, Hoover summarized them as follows:

Poland: We suggested to the Polish authorities that they should make an appeal to Russia for one-half of their food program; stating that the Russians had taken a great deal more than this quantity of cereals out of Poland and Germany that it would be justice if they contributed to this extent . . .

Finland: I suggested to the Finns that they make an application to the Russians for a further 100,000 tons of cereals, Russia already having furnished them 60,000 tons. I suggested that they represent that their people could not do hard labor on the present rations and that it would be impossible for them to continue to pay the hideous indemnity in commodities imposed upon them unless they could maintain the vigor of their workmen . . .

Sweden: I secured an agreement from the Swedes whereby they would cancel all of their contracted imports, reduce their rations, and get through on their present supply until the crisis was over. They further agreed to enhance their fish exports and place something over 100,000 tons of fish at the disposal of the authorities in Germany.

Norway: We impressed upon the Norwegians the necessity of continuous fishing, as they had stopped fishing for four days a week due to lack of opportunity to dispose of the fish and a shortage of salt. We later set up arrangements with American authorities in German to send agents to Norway and to ship them salt . . .

Great Britain: We insisted that as they had too much supply in their pipe line—being two months, or about 1,000,000 tons of cereals—they should release 500,000 tons to the general food pool. We suggested also that they should reduce the cereal consumption of Great Britain from 400 grams daily to at least 350, or perhaps 300, grams, as the ration contrasted badly with 200 to 250 grams daily across the Channel. They seemed to think this was too much of a hardship, but we pointed out that their calorie intake stood at 2,900 (against the normal of 2,200 calories for public health), compared with the masses of Europe on less than 1,800 calories and millions of people on less than 1,500. They subsequently released 200,000 tons from the pipe line and have put on a voluntary drive to reduce cereal consumption.

Belgium: We proposed to the Belgians that they must reduce their bread ration from 400 to 300 grams daily, so as to reduce their imports during the crisis, their subsidiary caloric intake being sufficient to stand this.

Holland: We suggested that they reduce their [bread] ration of 400 grams to 300 grams daily, in order to reduce their imports during the crisis, they having sufficient collateral food to do this.

Denmark: We suggested that they should increase their child feeding program in Germany and Austria with their surplus dairy and meat products. They promised to increase the program from the present 20,000 children up to 40,000 children.

Germany: We emphasized the necessity of the American authorities obtaining the maximum amount of fish from Sweden and Norway.

Austria: I emphasized to General Clark that he should insist that the Russians provide their quota of initial supplies to UNRRA, the British and Americans having undertaken to supply each one-third of the initial stock, each contributing 30,000 tons. So far as I have heard, he had only gotten 4,000 tons out of the Russians.

Yugoslavia: We found they had imported 120,000 tons of Army rations, of which they had sold 30,000 tons in the black market, and had furnished Tito's army with a large amount. We suggested that they at least use the balance in opening soup kitchens through the famine area, principally Dalmatia.

Egypt: I secured a contribution of 30,000 tons of wheat and millet, to be given to the Greeks and Italians, and an agreement that in another month, when prospects were secure, they would furnish an additional 30,000 tons of wheat, millet or rice, and that if the crop came in satisfactorily they would loan up to 200,000 tons, to be replaced later in the year. They do not produce very much of a surplus but their crop comes in June and could be used up to September [harvest] in crisis countries.

Iraq: We discovered that there were considerable surpluses in Iraq, amounting to 125,000 tons of coarse grains and 140,000 tons of dates, which could be exported at once. We found also that due to their early crops, they could ship a further 100,000 tons into India out of the new crop, to arrive in time to help over the Indian crisis . . .

India: We found that there was no food control in Punjab or the Sind; that while these two Provinces produce little beyond their necessities, yet their crop of wheat comes in early enough so that they could ship it into the rice famine areas during the latter part of July and August, this to be replaced by overseas imports at a later date. They were very reluctant to do anything of the kind.

Australia: I broadcast to Australia for an expedition of their supplies to India. They have approximately 1,000,000 tons of wheat remaining from the harvest of last January, which it had been intended would be spread over the year. I cabled to the Australian Food Minister, who responded courteously and informed me that he was reinforcing railway transportation through the interior with trucks, that he was loading Naval vessels, and he hoped to get his whole surplus into India in time . . .

Siam: We found a deplorable situation in that the Siamese had 1,500,000 tons surplus rice from the harvest of last November, but that due to British demands for this as an indemnity and with the inability of the Siamese Government to purchase it with their inflated currency or to transport it with their wrecked railroads or highways, nothing had been done . . .

China: I protested vigorously to T.V. Soong at the sale of UNRRA supplies in the Shanghai market . . . We found that of the UNRRA imports up to that time, 70,000 tons [out of 260,000] were en route to the famine areas but probably not over 20,000 tons had ever been delivered to the starving people.

Japan: The only suggestion we could make in regard to Japan and Korea was to set up a strong claim for the return of some part of the 1,500,000 tons of surplus food abstracted [sic] by the Russians from Manchuria . . .

General: The most important extracurricular activity of all has been the determination of the minimum food programs that will get the different nations over the crisis. When we started, the Combined Food Board had announced a 11,000,000 ton (or 43 per cent) gap in cereal supplies. By agreement in most cases, we cut the programs of import of various nations by 4,000,000 tons and still left them enough to get by on; and on the other hand, we developed between 3,000,000 and 4,000,000 tons additional supplies, so that the gap has been reduced to between 3–4,000,000 tons. And we have proposed measures to solve this.

I have also proposed that Europe widen child-feeding to 40,000,000 sub-normal children and the entire revamping of the world food organization, to begin in September.[111]

At the end of their European travels, Hoover spoke to an international emergency conference on European grain supplies in London and told them, "Hunger sits at the table thrice daily in hundreds of millions of homes . . . The world uses the words 'starvation' and 'famine' very loosely; some travelers glibly report there is now widespread death-dealing famine on the Continent of Europe. In modern civilization whole nations do not lie down and die. The casual observers do not realize that famine would have already struck great groups and classes were it not for past overseas supplies and that it is inevitable, unless we land for the next months every ton of overseas food that we can summon." He called the present crisis "the most critical food period in all history," with "20 millions of children . . . badly undernourished . . . steadily developing tuberculosis, rickets, anemia, and other diseases of sub-normal feeding. Unless they are better fed many will die and others . . . will furnish more malevolents."[112]

In April Truman seemed to question whether voluntary food rationing was really taking hold in the United States. He asked Hoover to return to interrupt his famine survey and return to the United States to make speeches that would stimulate support for food conservation, but the former president refused to do so unless ordered.[113] He talked to Truman by telephone from Cairo and convinced him that the trip should go on.[114] Instead of returning to the United States to give speeches, Hoover broadcast one from Cairo to the United States as part of a joint program with President Truman, new UNRRA head Fiorello LaGuardia, and Secretary of Agriculture Clinton Anderson. In his speech, Hoover described for Americans the plight of people in Europe and outlined a program of international action for dealing with the problem that included a voluntary reduction in American consumption of bread to 200 grams per day as part of a general reduction in consumption of wheat products by 40 percent and fats by 20 percent. He told Americans,

> The burden will be heavy on the American people, but we cannot do more than this. Europe and other countries must look to other sources for the balance of their food. This present world crisis is unique among all crises of history. For this crisis has a definite terminal date. That date is the arrival of the next harvest. It is therefore a short pull. If every source of supply were scraped to the bottom of the barrel we can pull the world through his most dangerous crisis, and the saving of these human lives is far more than an economic necessity to the recovery of the world. It is more even than the path to order and to stability and to peace. Such action marks the return of the lamp of compassion to the world. And that is part of the moral and spiritual reconstruction of the earth.[115]

From Japan Hoover issued a press release:

> Japan must have some food imports. Without them, all Japan will be on a ration little better than that which the Germans gave to the Buchenwald and Belsen concentration camps. It is an impossible concept that the American flag fly over such a situation. Aside from any Christian spirit, food imports are required if the American boys here are not be endangered by disorders and not involved in the sweep of epidemics that are inevitable from starvation. Moreover, unless there are food imports the people will not have the stamina to work upon reconstruction or in the fields for the next crop.[116]

After the stops in Asia, Hoover returned to the United States early in May, only to discover that threatened strikes were likely to disrupt the shipment of food from the United States overseas. The *New York Times* reported,

> If the transportation strikes now threatening in this country take place, many millions of persons living in the world's starvation areas will die, Herbert Hoover said here today as he returned from a world-circling trip investigating famine conditions for President Truman. Reading a prepared statement at a press conference . . . the former President said that "the potentiality of famine" was so imminent that if the coal strike continued "hundreds of thousands will die in the famine areas from delayed food shipments." "If the railroad strike takes place it will mean death to millions," he continued. If the shipping strike takes place it will be a holocaust . . . Mr. Hoover said that the world was "faced with the greatest potential famine in all human history," adding: "There is only

30 to 60 days supply of food in the famine area of 27 nations. They have five months to go until the next harvest."

The *Times* added, "The 72-year-old head of President Truman's Famine Emergency Committee looked more fit than might be expected of one who was just ending an arduous eight weeks survey trip of more than a score of European and Asiatic countries."[117]

Hoover submitted his report to President Truman on May 13. Hoover and his team told the president they were confident that with rigorous conservation and better cooperation between nations the remaining food deficit of approximately 3.6 million tons could be overcome. "The cooperation of Russia and the Latin American states," they suggested, "would greatly aid in meeting the problem."[118] The former president obviously considered Latin America important to the struggle against famine, having enlisted the assistance of the pope for that effort.[119] Two days later the president responded to the Hoover mission and report by writing the former president that he recognized "the collection of the basic facts had been an arduous and difficult task," and Hoover and his group had "provided a great service to your country and to humanity in making possible for each of us to know better the extent of world distress and to measure the magnitude of our responsibilities." He now asked Hoover to go to South America for a further survey, and Hoover consented. He told a news conference that the grain deficit could be surmounted if surplus grain producing nations would adopt "further vigorous conservation measures," but he refused to support rationing, telling the press that he wished to "be allowed to keep out of the domestic controversy" over rationing.[120] In his recommendations to Truman, however, the former president opposed rationing, arguing that voluntary food conservation was the answer.[121]

The following day Truman and Hoover met, and the former president suggested a telegram to Stalin that would encourage the Soviet Union to participate more in the relief effort. According to Hoover's aide-memoire of the conversation, "in the course of conversation, the President mentioned his difficulties with the Russians. I told him there was only one method of treating the present group of Russians and that was with a truculent spirit. They treated us that way and we should be truculent. Even he were to present a gold watch, it should be presented in a truculent mood. It would be more highly appreciated."[122] Rickard found Hoover looking well and alert after his round-the-world trip and particularly pleased with his success in having found food in unexpected places like Egypt and Iraq.[123]

When Fiorello LaGuardia, head of UNRRA wired Hoover to complain that some of the former president's remarks could be construed as criticism of that organization, Hoover responded, "I attach a table herewith showing the facts as to my statement that UNRRA covered only 20% of the world's food problems. The fat and oil situation runs about the same ratio. This statement was no reflection upon the great burden of UNRRA but the global picture we must overcome as a whole."[124]

On May 25, Hoover again decried the interference of the labor leaders with the food relief effort, telling the press, "The power over food or no food to half of the people in the United States and hundreds of millions in famine areas has now been taken over by half a dozen people who have never been elected to that power by the American people. While American cities have some reserves, most famine areas have none. Every delayed ship costs the lives of human beings."[125]

A few days later Hoover left once again at the president's bidding, this time on the tour of Latin American countries. *Time* magazine wrote,

> Back to Washington came Herbert Hoover after a 35,000 mile tour of twenty-five food-short countries. After reporting to the President he broadcast to the nation what he had seen: "The grimmest spectre of famine in all the history of the world . . . Hunger hangs over the homes of 800 million people . . . over one-third of the people of the earth." Even after whittling diets to a "bedrock" 1,500 daily calories, after stringently paring allocations of food to a subsistence minimum, Hoover conservatively figured that there still remained a "tragic gap" of 3,600,000 tons between world needs and world surpluses of exportable breadstuffs. This, said he, is "the whole amount necessary to save 40 million people." Could more food be taken from the beaten enemy? Said Hoover: "There are Americans who . . . believe in an 'eye for an eye,' a 'tooth for a tooth' . . . No one is the enemy of children . . . and to keep 500,000 American boys in garrison among starving women and children is unthinkable." . . . At the President's request Food Ambassador Hoover would continue his famine mission by a trip to South America to spur contributions there. But the hope of the world was still the vast U.S. granary. Would the U.S. keep its promise to win the race? Or was it too fat?[126]

Ray Lyman Wilbur wrote, "I am delighted that you have come into your own again."[127]

CHAPTER 10

On the Road at 71

Food Relief

Shortly after Hoover left for his fact-finding trip to Latin America, the *Columbus Evening Dispatch* of Ohio editorialized,

> Herbert Hoover has left for a thirty day tour of Latin America as a special food emissary of President Truman. His departure comes only a few days after he concluded an intensive round-the-world study of the food situation at the behest of the White House. Mr. Hoover's willingness to undertake these arduous assignments underscores both his deep patriotism and his high qualifications. The former president could not reasonably have been criticized had he politely refused. He is past 70, and the mere physical strain of an odyssey such as he recently completed would tax the strength of younger men, not to mention the effort required to obtain and appraise the desired data. Few men in public life have been so shamelessly abused and ruthlessly smeared for selfish ends, and Mr. Truman, whatever his merits in his own right, is the successor or political heir of the man who inspired the attacks. The fact that Mr. Hoover was requested to do the food survey job is the best testimony possible to his preeminence in this field. It emphasizes again both the lack of qualified men in the present administration and the petty vindictiveness of the Roosevelt administration in failing to avail itself of his services throughout the twelve years of real or fancied emergencies including the very real and tragic crisis of war.[1]

On June 19, Taft wrote Hoover asking for the "opportunity to explain fully [the] situation of OPA [Office of Price Administration] legislation to you before you make any statement with reference to it," but on the same day that Taft penned his letter Hoover's name entered the price control controversy.[2] Newspapers that day reported that Hoover had warned in telephone conversations with administration officials that "failure to maintain price ceilings on meats would wreck this government's endeavors to provide grain for the world's famine areas." They also reported that Hoover was returning from Latin America ahead of schedule in order "voice his views on congressional limitations on the administration's price control bill." The next day, Hoover denied that he had come back early to protect OPA or to preserve the controls on meats and also said he had never discussed the question over the phone with anybody in the Truman administration.[3] Later in the month Hoover traced the confusion to the fact that he had thought he was talking to William L. Batt, head of the US Rubber Board about rubber for Argentina, and not about meat restrictions.[4]

In late June, Hoover returned from the 25-day food survey of Latin America that elicited promises from the countries there of over two million tons of food to help fight the world famine. Argentina had been especially cooperative, and this led Hoover to intervene with the president concerning the low state of US relations with Latin America, especially Argentina under Juan Peron.[5] For the next few months Hoover and his close associates were involved in efforts to expedite US-Argentine economic relations and to procure the sale of American Liberty Ships to Argentina for transport of food to Europe.[6] The trip, however, took its toll on the former president. While in Caracas, Venezuela, he had slipped in the bathtub, causing a contusion in his back.[7] A few days after his return, Hoover wrote a friend, "Every molecule in my body yells at me that it is tired. I am just going away for a rest."[8]

Hoover was no doubt cheered, however, by a letter from John Callan O'Laughlin that indicated the Truman administration was giving serious consideration to reversing the decision of Secretary of Interior Ickes during the New Deal years and changing the name of Boulder Dam back to Hoover Dam. The White House appeared to agree that Hoover had been treated shabbily by Ickes. O'Laughlin also gathered that Truman intended to continue to consult Hoover "from time to time about national matters" and that the president was pleased with the fine service Hoover had rendered in the course of his famine survey.[9] A week later O'Laughlin wrote further that the president was "giving sympathetic consideration to rechanging the name of Boulder Dam to that of Hoover Dam." He told Hoover that "with the mood he is in and the gratitude he is expressing, I feel confident the decision will be favored."[10]

Ever since his February press release that supported Truman's plea for voluntary food conservative, Hoover had been active through press releases, speeches, and reports that sought to rally public support for the food relief effort. In what he hoped would be his last effort in behalf of food relief he spoke over the Canadian Broadcasting Company from Ottawa on June 28, in what he told Canadians was his "final report upon my food mission to 38 nations." He thanked the Canadians for their contribution, noting that four nations—Canada, the United States, Argentina, and Australia—had taken up 90 percent of the "overseas burden of relief to this, the greatest famine in all human history." He had "traveled some 50,000 miles visiting all of the important famine and food-deficit areas in the world," he said, "and all of the major food-surplus areas excepting South Africa and Australia," where he had "discussed crops, animals, calories, rations, stocks, ships, railroads, supplies and hunger with the Presidents, the Prime Ministers, the food officials of each of these nations." His function, Hoover said, had "been mostly advisory—or perhaps persuasive would be a better word," and he was "deeply indebted for the most extraordinary welcome and cooperation accorded to me and my associates."[11]

The danger of mass starvation he felt had now been averted everywhere but in China, "where transportation to the interior and inadequate organization has rendered relief only partially successful." The problems elsewhere were hardly over, however, as Hoover warned that the countries devastated by war "will not have fully recovered their ground crops nor have restored their flocks and herds during the next year." This meant that the "food situation of the world in the next year will not be easy, but next year in my view will not be one of such dreadful crisis and drastic regimens as the one which we are now in." World food agencies were being consolidated under an International Emergency Food Council [IEFC] of the United Nations. He was still especially concerned, however, with the food requirements of children, and he suggested that special efforts be made by the new agency to furnish a higher caloric intake to the young. "We cannot have recovery of civilization in nations with a legacy of stunted bodies or distorted and embittered minds," he told his listeners. This latter recommendation would lead eventually to the creation of the United Nations International Children's Fund.

After years of deafness on the part of Washington, Hoover at last found his recommendations concerning food questions were being adopted under the direction of Chester Davis, operational head of the FEC. The FEC now included local famine emergency committees and retail famine committees, housewife pledges, and even a youths' auxiliary famine emergency organization. The effort was intended to continue until at least the August harvest.[12] A complication arose in July when President Truman vetoed a bill extending the Office of Price Administration because it contained terms he would not accept, thus allowing the price control of OPA to expire on July 1, 1946. Hoover was disappointed because he had "secured substantial modifications" in Congress of the legislation in order to meet the president's objections. He told Chester Davis that he thought the President was able to exert "indirect control" under his "war powers" over grain, meat, and fats if OPA could not be extended. He was, he told Davis, going west for six weeks since "when the pressures of action let down I found I was very tired in most of my molecules."[13]

A week later Julius Klein wrote the former president that Secretary of Agriculture Clinton Anderson wanted him to travel to Washington upon his return from the West in order to consult "on the food situation and outlook."

Klein wrote, "I learn elsewhere that he has certainly been 'carrying the torch' for you in a big way in the face of the usual sharp criticism from all too familiar sources, both Republican and Democratic. He asked me to assure you that you are still 'ace high' with the president who 'is at your command for any- thing within reason.' Both he and Anderson seemed to feel deeply and genu- inely indebted to you—as they should be!"[14] Anderson himself wrote to tell Hoover how much he appreciated "the trips you have made and the wonderful advice you have given as well as the great influence you have been in the world food problems." He was, he said, "very hopeful that as the international food council [IEFC] progresses we may find some basis upon which your unusual experience and clear thinking can be utilized by us."[15]

Politics

Hoover's service in behalf of the Truman administration did not silence his opposition to the president's policies in other areas, particularly in foreign relations. On the last day of 1945, Hoover decried the agreements reached by Secretary of State James Byrnes with the Soviet Union as "the last installment of appeasement." In the former president's view the United States had in all its dealing with the Russians "appeased . . . at the expense of the liberty and freedom of more and more human beings."[16] Hoover had tried to stiffen Tru- man's attitude toward the Soviets, as in his meeting with the president after the European food survey, but apparently with little success. In the summer of 1946 he still regarded foreign relations as "half of our national problems" and as part of his effort to enhance Bricker's national stature he suggested that the Ohioan go to Europe after his election to the Senate since it "would place you in a position to speak authoritatively."[17]

Hoover was also concerned that the 1948 presidential race not find Repub- licans repeating what he regarded as the mistakes of 1936, 1940, and 1944. The "Republican New Dealers," as he described them, had won fewer total votes than local GOP candidates in 1940 and 1944, which meant to the for- mer president that "people went to the ballot box, voted for the local Repub- lican candidates, but believed that, as a choice of New Dealers, they preferred Roosevelt." In 1948 the GOP needed a "candidate who will stand up and fight the whole pack" of New Dealers and their communist and fellow-traveler allies. "I believe we could have won before on this line," he wrote a friend, "and I am even more sure of it now."[18]

Probably because of the FEC, Hoover took fewer partisan positions in 1946 after being called to serve by President Truman. But he remained on the offensive where other issues were concerned. In his birthday statement in August, Hoover lashed out at the Morgenthau Plan for the "pastoralization" of Germany, warning, "The dismemberment of the German state and the attempt to reduce the German people to a level of perpetual poverty will some day break into another world explosion."[19] According to John J. McCloy, both

he and Henry L. Stimson likewise opposed the Morgenthau Plan and welcomed Hoover's speeches in opposition to it. It was one of the rare times that
Hoover and Stimson agreed on anything.[20]

Contrary to the idealism that surrounded American intervention in
World War II, Hoover concluded that instead of freedom having expanded as
a result of the conflict, "it has shrunken to far fewer nations than a quarter of
century ago. And in addition there are at least 15,000,000 in concentration or
forced-labor camps who are slaves in every sense of the word. Several scores
of millions more are practical serfs." Hoover was concerned about the depletion of American reserves and industrial equipment as a result of the war, and
he outlined three major policies that the nation should follow:

> In the economic field we must now conserve our resources, improve
> our equipment and reduce our spending. We must end our role of Santa
> Claus. Now that world famine No. 2 is about over we should announce
> that our economic relations with other nations are a two-way street. And
> balanced traffic at that.
>
> In national defense we should hold the atomic bomb until there is real
> cooperation for lasting peace, which must include general disarmament in
> the world—Allies as well as enemy countries . . .
>
> We should devote ourselves to cooperation in the U.N. to maintain
> peace, and to do so appeasement must cease. To hold up the banner of the
> world we should at all times assert the principles of the Atlantic Charter
> for which we fought the war and to which all other nations pledged them-
> selves.[21]

Ironically, while Hoover was unsympathetic to the Soviet Union's defensive objectives in establishing control over its Eastern European perimeter
nations, he was quick to advocate a similar move by the United States in the
Pacific. Late in August 1946, he argued that America should retain the Pacific
islands that had been liberated from the Japanese by US forces "because
we must extend our perimeter of defense." The United States could not be
accused of imperialism in doing so, he argued, since it was not economic
interests that were sought but "simply looking after our own defense and the
defense of the world."[22] Secretary of the Navy James Forrestal expressed public support for Hoover's position.[23]

Shortly before the 1946 congressional elections, Hoover wrote General
Douglas MacArthur to remind him of a conversation between them in Tokyo
during the former president's famine survey travels. At that time he had suggested MacArthur could perform a role for the United States comparable to
that of "John the Baptist when he came out of the wilderness." He now told
the general that he should give three speeches after the congressional elections, "when politics will have gone into abeyance." He told MacArthur that
"the whole nation will listen to you as to no other man—and they would like

the opportunity to pay some tribute for your unparalleled service." There were, Hoover said, "three great fields of weakness in the country":

1. Morals, both in public and private life, have greatly degenerated during recent years. The heart-breaking scandals in public office exposed by Congressional investigations, the fearful increase in crime, divorce, blatant extravagance in living are part of it.
2. Our democracy is not working. We are in a muddle between left-wing and right-wing thinking. The left-wing regimentation of recent years has created a million bottlenecks in production and distribution and is at last breaking down in shortages and other supplies in the midst of plenty. The Administration still holds to the Roosevelt notion that it is possible to have totalitarian economics and at the same time preserve other freedoms . . .
3. Frustration in international relations is sweeping over the country. Obviously, America's Second Crusade for freedom and independence of nations wound up with less freedom, fewer independent nations, with Russia the real victor in the war and all the world menaced by her. The world is squarely faced with Asiatic versus Western civilization. Western civilization cannot stand the shock of either Communism dominating the world or of another world war. Strength by the United States in preparedness and sense and courage in diplomatic action can prevent both.

With his "fresh mind, a new approach and . . . oratorical endowment," MacArthur could "handle such old subjects with new light and inspiration."[24]

MacArthur, however, declined Hoover's suggestion as action inappropriate for an active duty military officer and pleaded the necessity for him to continue with his service in Japan. He had there, he said, "sure control . . . in spite of Russia and the Reds, but if I leave the situation might easily relapse into something quite different—possibly one inimical and hazardous to the United States." Moreover, he was certain that the merit of anything he might say "would be vitiated by the charge that it represented not so much a patriotic but a political effort," as "a disguised effort to enter the political race."[25]

The former president took no role in the 1946 congressional elections but predicted a GOP landslide. The prospect of a GOP victory led Mark Sullivan to write Hoover that he would like to be with the former president at the Waldorf Astoria to watch the election returns, because, Sullivan said, "I have always had in anticipation that return of conservative thought in America would be not merely vindication of you, but more than that a direct consequence of your constancy of personality and the course to which you bent your back when many were saying that capitalism and the Republican Party were dead."[26] When Republicans swept into control of both houses of Congress for the first time since the 1928 election, Hoover, too, regarded it as "much more than just another Congressional election." He explained, "The whole world, including the United States, has been for years driving to the left on the totalitarian road of 'planned economy'" America is by this election the first country to repudiate this road. And it defines that the Republican Party is the party of the right. We are again moving to the goal of free men. This decision of the United States will have a profound effect on nations which have been following along the road to the left."[27] European newspapers quickly predicted that the Republican victory and Hoover's statement meant the possibility that American economic policy might now be used to strengthen conservatives in Europe against leftists through strategic use of credits and other devices.[28]

Hoover soon followed up his first reaction to the GOP victory by adding that the election represented a demand by the country that "this creeping collectivism be swept into the sewer." Both political parties now needed "to expel those who are so minded that they can take their title from the Moscow heaven instead of Yorktown." And he laid down the legislative steps that he argued were necessary to reverse the collectivist trend in America. First, all the war powers and war agencies needed to be repealed and liquidated, thus ridding the nation of "half a million bureaucrats." Second, income taxes should be reduced by 20 percent, and twice that sum should be cut from expenditures. Third, the people must be relieved "of labor tyrannies." The right to strike, he insisted, was "no more unlimited a right than the right of free speech is unlimited—we must find a way of relieving our economy from the blight of [work] stoppages or we shall send ourselves again into the morass of depression that will end recovery from this war for years." Fourth, the United States must "dig out the Communist infiltration into our government and expose it to daylight." Fifth, the misdeeds of government officials must be exposed. In foreign affairs, the problem was communist imperialism, but Hoover found a positive sign in that the government had "about six months ago abandoned appeasement and has put up some resistance. It should be stiffened even more, because it is only toughness that they understand." The United States must also remain armed, "especially in the air," and keep the atomic bomb.[29]

Late in November, Chester Davis brought Hoover up to date on the fight against famine, writing that since his August letter the FEC and the local committees had been on a "stand-by" position. However, a review of the situation showed it to be still precarious. He told Hoover the situation showed a "world balance of supplies of wheat and cereals" that was still "most unfavorable"; the United States had adequate surpluses to meet the needs, but the "major famine emergency problem" was now in "transportation—internal movement, shortage of boxcars—" which had resulted in exports shipments falling "seriously behind commitments, primarily because of the maritime strikes of a few weeks ago . . . Our country must now export more than a million tons a month through June, 1947, if the 400,000,000 bushel goal is to be realized." This could be easily met if it weren't for the shortage of boxcars.

The situation was different from that at the time the FEC had been formed, when the primary problem had been procuring food. "The current problems," Davis wrote, "great as they are, do not seem to me to fall within the purview of the famine emergency committee" but rather fell under a cabinet committee Truman had appointed. Therefore, Davis suggested that the FEC continue in a "stand-by" status, and he asked Hoover for his views.[30] Hoover agreed that the FEC was "essentially a conservation committee and no conservation seemed necessary in view of the limitations on transport." There was, then, no reason to do anything but allow the FEC to "be moribund until something turns up."[31]

On the same date that he wrote to Davis, Hoover wrote President Truman:

> I should like to take this occasion to make a recommendation as to the world food situation which confronts us this harvest year. First, the United States should never again place the distribution of American food or relief into international control (except for the rehabilitation of children). The experience with UNRRA should be enough . . . The supplies to all schemes for international control of American food or relief as that can only end in foreign control of American farmers' prices and production. Second, whatever food we should decide to contribute to nations unable to find purchase resources should be sold with undertakings to pay the cost with interest. However insecure the credit may be, the requirement ultimately to pay is the only real check on wasteful demands and wasteful distribution. Third, it is time to end government charity (except as mentioned to children). It is my opinion also that the time has come to end even government credits for any purpose except to prevent starvation— and even here we should require some percentage of their exports at some future date to be set aside to repay us. Fourth, if the United Nations should set up some rehabilitation of European children, the United States should contribute; but as we would be the major contributor the direction of it should be American. If they do not create such an institution, we should make an appropriation to the American Red Cross to carry on such work.[32]

When Republicans prepared to take control of the House and Senate, the former president received many requests for his views on possible labor legislation.[33] On December 12 he discussed the subject with GOP congressional leaders, and on December 21 he wrote Senator Taft that he was glad the Ohioan had taken the chairmanship of the Senate Labor Committee. He told Taft of the many requests he had received from House Republicans, including Charles Halleck, for his views on labor legislation and recounted for Taft his experience with attempts to settle labor problems while secretary of commerce, including the Railway Mediation Act of 1926. The central idea in that legislation had been a mediation commission to intervene if a strike were imminent: "Upon failure of bargaining, mediation, conciliation and arbitration, an Emergency Commission of disinterested persons is appointed to investigate and declare a fair settlement with stay of strikes for 30 days for the Mediation Board to act, and an additional 30 days for the

Emergency Commission to act . . . This central idea appears in the Case
bill to be applied to all public utilities. I have long thought, and there is in
my opinion daily confirmation, that this is the right line in checking upon
strikes."[34] Hoover hoped, though, that the Democrats would take the leadership in proposing corrective labor legislation since it would be "easier to
accomplish and [the] Democrats will take responsibility." A few days later he
published an article, "The Right to Strike," in *This Week* magazine, in which
he pointed out that

> because everybody has more cash in his pocket and in the Bank, there is
> an illusion which always comes with the ending of war and its inevitable
> inflation. That illusion is that we have grown richer and more prosperous.
> The contrary is the case. The fact is, the American people have been ter-
> ribly impoverished. That impoverishment will develop later and recovery
> from it depends upon two things.
>
> First, on whether our people are willing, at least for a few years, to
> work more efficiently than ever before and thus restore their lost wealth.
>
> Second, recovery depends on what progress we can make in the ap-
> plication of labor-saving devices, new methods, new inventions and sci-
> entific discoveries, which increase the productivity of each individual and
> of the nation.

These requirements would be disrupted by continued labor conflict such as
had occurred in 1946. A "new idea has now grown up around the use of the
strike," Hoover wrote: "that this weapon can be employed for political and
ideological purposes and that it can be used so as to injure and endanger the
people at large that in their misery they or the government will be forced to
do the strikers' bidding. It is the people who suffer." A dozen labor leaders
now wielded "power over the life and living of the people greater than the
government. They have never been elected by the people. Years of battle
by the people finally eliminated such oppressions by business leaders."
Strikes now endangered "the life and living of hosts of people not party to
the dispute." New forms of collective bargaining and mediation were now
required before strikes were resorted to, and "the judicial machinery of the
country should be given power and penalties to end any strike which the
President, through the Attorney General, declares constitutes a danger to
large numbers of innocent people." Hoover also favored, he said, provision for compulsory arbitration. Americans "must master the difficult art
of working together. No country can move forward when its machinery
stands idle."[35]

In that same month he wrote Congressman Harold Knutson to suggest tax
revisions. Taxes, he wrote, were hamstringing small businesses, causing them
to sell "out to big business as being more profitable to take the capital gains
tax than to struggle on unable to save out of income tax or to plow in profits

as other major earnings are taken in taxes." Taxes were destroying initiative, since there was "very little incentive to produce activities," and Hoover called for changes in the income and corporation taxes.[36]

In his year-end review of Hoover's busy 1946, Edgar Rickard wrote,

> There is no doubt that the sniping at him by his enemies, and having no basic position, naturally was tending to depress him to the point of feeling that he was being deprived of a usefulness which his long experience and active, alert mind, deserved. His appointment by President Truman proved timely, and overnight he shook off his depression and entered into his job with the same keen enthusiasm and wise planning which made him successful. No one seems to question for a moment that his trip around the world saved the world from a terrible disaster.

Hoover had also, Rickard wrote, been "called to Washington and secretly gave his views to leading Republican legislators on labor legislation." Asked to put his views in the form of bills, he had substantially completed the task before leaving for Florida for a fishing trip shortly before Christmas.[37]

On the Road Again

In mid-January 1947, Secretary of War Robert Patterson asked Hoover to make another foreign trip, this time to Germany. The former president agreed to do so, but the mission would have to be for President Truman and he must first give his wife, sons, and grandchildren a vacation he had promised them. That agreed upon, Hoover also insisted that his survey not deal alone with food but also include a survey of general economic conditions and that he be allowed to make his findings public. He did not believe that Truman would agree to his terms, but on January 18, 1947, Truman asked him in writing to make the trip. The president wrote that the situation was improved over the previous year, but "a serious situation in food still exists in certain areas, particularly those in Europe occupied by our forces and for which we therefore have a direct responsibility."[38] Hoover responded that he wished to be of service but that he thought the scope of the mission should be broadened beyond a mere survey of food requirements. It would, he pointed out, "come as a great shock to our people that the American taxpayer for a second year must expend huge sums to provide money for the enemy peoples," and he was convinced that his mission should also study what could be done in Germany to increase her exports and thus enhance her ability to become "self-supporting." Without some indication of how and when American charity could be expected to end, "the Congress and the taxpayer are left without hope."[39] After a visit with Truman in Washington three days later, with his face sunburned from three weeks on a Florida houseboat, the two agreed on the "formula" that made Hoover's trip an economic mission devoted to food and its collateral problems.[40]

The 1947 trip was of shorter duration and covered only Germany and Austria, but Hoover was approaching his seventy-third birthday, and flying in an unpressurized DC-4 aircraft he suffered a hearing impairment that would lead to the loss of his hearing and force him to wear a hearing aid.[41] Upon his return, he confided to Edgar Rickard that as a consequence of unheated hotels and frigid conference rooms he had never been warm at any time during the three-week trip.[42] On March 18, Hoover submitted his report to the president, which contained his "conclusions upon the problem of reviving German industry and thus exports with which to relieve American and British taxpayers from their burden in preventing starvation in Germany." His report pointed out that American and British taxpayers were contributing nearly $600 million per year to fight famine in the American and British occupation zones and that the expense was "likely to be even greater after peace unless the policies now in action are changed." There was, Hoover argued, "only one path to recovery in Europe" and that was through production. The European economy was so "interlinked" with that of Germany that "the productivity of Europe cannot be restored without the restoration of Germany as a contributor to that productivity."[43]

The Allied "level of industry" policy, adopted in March 1946, was a product of the Morgenthau Plan type of vengeful thinking toward Germany. However justified, that policy was woefully ignorant of the realities of the European economy's interdependence and the importance of a healthy Germany for European prosperity. The program called for the reduction and removal of Germany's heavy industrial plants and the reduction of her industry to a level deemed capable of maintaining in Germany the average European standard of living. Already during his 1946 trip to Europe, Hoover and his associates had been exposed to concern expressed by other European leaders over the inability of Germany to import from them under the new policy, since the Germans could not produce the needed exports to trade for their goods. Hoover argued that the policy was destructive of European economic recovery, for it not only slashed fertilizer production, which affected Germany's ability to grow food, but it also reduced her production of the items she had previously exported to the point where she was now forced to import many of them. Germany needed heavy industry, since the light industries could never, in Hoover's view, "be expanded to a point where she will be able to pay for her imports."

From the beginning of his planning for peacetime with Gibson, Hoover had emphasized the need for a nonpunitive peace that could produce rapid economic recovery. Now he suggested a "new economic concept in peace with New Germany." It consisted of four items:

> 1. We should free German industry, subject to a control commission, which will see that she does no evil in industry, just as we see that she does not move into militarism through armies and navies. The difference between this concept and the "level of industry" concept is the

saving of several hundred millions of dollars a year to the American and British taxpayers. It is the difference between the regeneration and a further degeneration of Europe.

2. The removal and destruction of plants (except direct arms plants) should stop.

3. A further obstacle to building Germany as an essential unit of European economic recovery arises from the Russian Government's acquiring a large part of the key operating industries in their zone. Germany in peace must be free from ownership of industry by a foreign government. Such ownership can thwart every action of control or of up-building by joint action of other nations. German industry must be operated by Germans if any international control is to work, if she is to recover production and is to serve all nations equally.

4. There can be no separation or different regime of the Ruhr or Rhineland from the New Germany. That is the heart of her industrial economy.

Hoover also called for a "quick and sound" peace settlement in Germany, but if the Soviet Union (and perhaps France) would not cooperate, he advocated that "the Anglo-American zones should abandon the destruction of plants, the transfer of plants for reparations and the 'level of industry' concept, and start every plant, 'heavy' as well as 'light,' which can produce non-arms goods." This alone would relieve American and British taxpayers of the continued burden of feeding the Germans, since it would make it possible for them to pay for imports of food without relying on "American loans and charity." If the Soviet Union and France would not cooperate in the economic unification of the four zones, then a "self-sustaining economic community" should be built "out of the Anglo-American zones alone." Following Hoover's advice a new, higher "level of industry" was fixed for the Anglo-American zones in August, and the movement, already begun, for economic unity of the two zones was stepped up.[44]

Hoover's position agreed with that of the British, who could afford even less than the United States the continued cost of food relief in their zone of Germany, and it was also shared by many Americans in Germany, but it ran against the grain of those in the administration who carried over from the Roosevelt years the desire to impose a draconian peace on the Germans and reduce them to poverty levels of economic activity.[45] Late in January, however, Hoover met with Secretary of State George Marshall and Undersecretary of State for Economic Affairs William Clayton, and, according to the *New York Times*, the three "considered the necessity of integrating Mr. Hoover's mission to Germany, including his observations and the results of his study, with the department's over-all policy for bringing about an economically integrated Germany." Hoover was reported as being pessimistic about the possibilities of "bringing about a self-sustaining Germany."[46]

Yet Hoover's influence on the change of policy in the Truman administration has been largely ignored by historians. It is difficult to come to any other conclusion, however, than that Hoover's influence was probably the greatest of any other single individual. The former president not only advised President Truman on policies toward Germany but also put the matter in concrete economic terms that were difficult to ignore—the cost to the United States in terms of food relief for a prostrate Germany. And he could bring to the support of any changes a leading foreign policy voice among Republicans, an important consideration when Congress was now controlled by a GOP majority that looked to the elder statesman for leadership. General Lucius Clay, US commander in chief in Germany, later wrote, "Mr. Hoover did much to change thinking at home so that it would become possible for us to reform and stabilize German currency, to stop dismantling of German industry, and to permit free competitive enterprise to begin the rebuilding of Germany to provide, among other products, coal from the Ruhr needed throughout western Europe."[47] And when Hoover visited Germany in 1954, he was hailed by the German Chancellor Konrad Adenauer, who told him, "We . . . owe it to your political farsightedness, to your comprehensive knowledge of economic life, that we could again build up our country and our economy after the ravages of the Second World War . . . The limitations upon our economy were relaxed and, thanks to the magnanimous aid of the American people, we could begin the reconstruction of our native land."[48]

In February Hoover testified before the House Committee on Foreign Affairs in support of Truman's request for $350 million to be used for relief assistance, and he also met with Secretary of State George Marshall on the eve of Marshall's mission to Moscow. When the issue of possible economic assistance to Greece arose, Hoover told Senator Vandenberg that if the United States aided that country it should state forthrightly that the aid was designed to save the country from communism. In mid-March Hoover again spent three days in Washington testifying before congressional committees dealing with European economic and food problems.

Hoover continued to support the $350 million relief appropriation, even as he continued to press for adoption of his amendments in what was now a Republican-controlled Congress. In April Senator Vandenberg wrote the former president after he had testified for the Senate Foreign Relations Committee, "I shall submit your complete program of suggestions to the Committee. We shall collide with heavy opposition at certain points. On others the State Department (at my urgent request) has shown some disposition to approve your ideas." Vandenberg was certain that Hoover's amendments would make it "a better Bill."[49] When the appropriation passed, Major General William H. Draper Jr., economic adviser to the headquarters, European command, wrote Hoover, "There is no question in my mind that your report on food saved the day for our deficiency appropriation and I hope will prove equally effective with respect to the 1948 appropriation. Both Germany and all of those interested in the attainment of American objectives in Europe owe you a deep debt of gratitude."[50]

Hoover was also a voice of realism when consulted about Japan the follow-ing month. Responding to a request for his views, the former president wrote to Secretary of War Robert Patterson, "At the outset I wish to say that when I think of the white crosses over tens of thousands of American boys in the Pacific and the millions of butchered Chinese, I sympathize emotionally with Draconian measures of punishment. But when we look to the real interest of the United States and the future peace of the world, we must confine punish-ment to the war leaders and realize that we must live with this 80,000,000 peo-ple." Hoover's advice for Japan was similar to that he had given concerning Germany—namely, "that there must be a revolutionary change in the whole concept of 'levels of industry,' 'plant removals' for reparations and destruction of peace industry plants, if the Japanese people are to produce enough exports to pay for their food and other necessary imports, or become a stable and peaceable state." The policies in force, he suggested, had been made partly upon inadequate data at the time they were made, and he now suggested two changes in those policies: (1) allow as reparations only the machine tools and equipment from factories that could not be converted to peacetime produc-tion, assessing the value of other plants and compelling Japan to pay the value over a period of years as reparations while retaining the factories; (2) eliminate the concept of "levels of industry" entirely and replace it with "a few absolute prohibitions such as monopolies, arms manufacture, aircraft construction, speed (but not size) of ships, and install a general watch to see that industry is devoted to peace-time production."[51]

As with Germany, Hoover viewed the recovery of Japan as essential to the recovery of her neighbors and also as the only way to get Japan "off the back of the American taxpayer." He concluded his advice to Patterson by writ-ing, "Finally, may I say that what the world needs today above all things is recovered peace-purpose productivity. The United States does not possess the strength to bear the deficient productivity which now dominates industry all over the world. Chains on any productive area are chains on the whole world. We need a larger vision of the primary basis of world peace which is productivity. Otherwise there will be a disintegration of Western Civilization everywhere."

A few days later Hoover wrote to Secretary of State George C. Marshall, enclosing a copy of the letter to Patterson. He told Marshall that he could not "too strongly express my anxiety over the situation in both Germany and Japan. In my view they are the major fronts of Western Civilization. If the ideologic front is lost in Germany all Western Europe and even the Near East is lost. The Japanese is [sic] the real ideologic dam against the march of Com-munism in Asia." Germany and Japan should have "priority over shipments of food to any other country." As military occupier of those countries, the United States assumed a special responsibility for them, and food shortages would "only promote frustration at our efforts in democratization" as well as place a burden upon the American taxpayer. He closed by assuring Marshall that he perhaps understood "the burdens upon you more fully than any other person."[52] The secretary of state responded that additional wheat supplies were being sent to Germany and that additional aid to Japan was also being considered, "but there appears to be a little more time for decision." Marshall also told Hoover that he would keep him advised and "it may be that I will have to call on you for some assistance."[53]

Again, it is difficult to avoid the conclusion that Hoover had a decisive influence on the change of policy toward Japan, for largely the same reasons as in the case of Germany. That Hoover's advice concerning Japan tended to make more use of the perceived threat of expansion by the Soviet Union and its presumed surrogates in Asia, than in the case of Germany, almost certainly did not diminish its effectiveness, since those arguments meshed with the concerns of the Truman administration over the same issue.

Reorganization

Meanwhile, the outlines for the former president's next major contribution of public service had been developing. In September 1945, as noted earlier, Hoover offered his support for Truman's efforts to obtain from Congress authority for reorganization of the executive branch of the government.[54] That proposal, however, made little progress in the Democrat-controlled Congress, and the Republicans offered their own proposal upon taking control in January 1947, when Congressman Clarence J. Brown of Ohio, an old Hoover ally, introduced a bill and requested Hoover's views on the subject. Hoover responded,

> I do not know how many dozen commissions have been invited by Congress and by every President since Taft to make recommendations for consolidation and improvement of the government and executive branches. The reason all these failed is because they had no real power. If a commission were set up with the power to issue orders, it might be worthwhile, but without the power to correct the matter is just no use. Once during my administration I requested from the Congress authority to make these changes by executive order, provided there was no Congressional disapproval for a period of 30 days during which the order was to be tabled. Even this power was not granted. Where changes must be ratified by the Congress it has been impossible to reconcile the differences arising over new proposals of any kind—and that has been the sad state of affairs for 40 years. If you want to reorganize the government give the President the power to do it, or give a joint Congressional committee the power to do it, or some independent committee the power to do it, but you will never see any real changes if they are subject to ratification by Congress.[55]

Brown responded that he "had somewhat of the same thoughts on the subject . . . and [was] mindful of the difficulty involved in getting such authority from Congress." He suggested that a study be made as a first step, which should then be followed by granting authority to "some individual or group to carry out the findings and recommendations of the commission."[56]

Foreign Commitments

As Brown's bill began its slow path through congressional hearings, the problem of America's overseas economic commitments loomed larger and larger in Hoover's thinking. Nearly two years earlier, the former president had addressed the Executive's Club of Chicago in September 1945 on the question of postwar loans. At that time he had favored "such financial assistance under safeguards and defined fiscal policies," but if the United States acted "without wisdom and without regard to experience, far from curing the ills of the world, we will make them worse." Reviewing the history of American financial assistance to Europe during and after World War I, Hoover came to two conclusions: "First: When our government makes postwar loans in excess of a few tens of millions, they are only going to be partly repaid at best. Second: Loaning money is a poor road to international friendship. Despite all this, there is one over-riding necessity. We want to aid our allies to recovery, and we want within all of our capacities to help them." Hoover had proposed a 12-point program that included (1) declaring a worldwide moratorium on all intergovernmental war debts for five years and then joining with the Allies "in settling the disposition of all these debts," while insisting "that all weapons that we have sent on lend-lease should be destroyed"; (2) considering all further requests for assistance from the standpoint of "how much further burdens we can assume to aid others and still remain solvent"; (3) taking time to ascertain the actual needs of borrowing nations; (4) making loans only for specified productive purposes; (5) promoting the exchange of surplus commodities among those nations that possessed them; (6) reducing all financial assistance to statements in terms of commodities that might be purchased in the United States, thus assuring the employment of Americans in producing the commodities; (7) requiring that in exchange for assistance the recipient nations impose "no quotas against us, no discriminatory tariffs against us, no dumping of goods against us, no cartel operations against us" and promise "that no propaganda against the American system of life will be carried on." After listing the other points, Hoover concluded that in helping Europe the United States must keep its feet on the ground and "limit our help to what our taxpayers can afford. We should consider our own employment. We should organize our aid so as to minimize any ill will that might arise over these transactions."[57]

Hoover's recommendations to the Truman administration with regard to Germany and Japan in 1946–47 had in large part derived from his desire to liberate American taxpayers from the enormous load they were bearing for the relief of those countries. His worries were increased with the enunciation of the Truman Doctrine in early March of 1947 and its accompanying request for a $400 million appropriation to assist Greece and Turkey. Hoover suggested to Senator Vandenberg that the Truman administration be asked some hard questions in connection with the proposal, among them (1) Was there any chance the Soviets might react by declaring war against the United States? (2) If the Soviet Union did declare war, could Greece resist such an invasion with the help of the United States? (3) What evidence was there that if the Greek government became dominated by communists it would or could spread communism to other parts of the Mediterranean or the Middle East? (4) What evidence was there that the national security of the United States would be affected by communist governments in Greece and Turkey? (5) If Greece was threatened, why did the United States not ask for action from the United Nations? (6) Would the United States permit elections in Greece, and would the United States "retire from Greece" in the event an elected government there requested that we do so?[58]

Hoover now found himself increasingly queried as to America's ability to undertake the commitments that the Truman administration was asking of it. When a State Department official sought his advice in late March, Hoover responded with a long letter. He told Colonel C. Tyler Wood, "We both wish to see proper relief to those in need and we are both trying to protect the American taxpayer by proper safeguards. In my public statement at the hearings before the House Foreign Relations Committee, I made a series of suggestions which I believed would build constructively to these ends. Some of these suggestions were adopted in the Bill as reported out. Some of your suggested further amendments to meet my original proposals do not seem to me to go far enough to accomplish those purposes." Hoover insisted that the countries to be aided should be designated in the bill so as to avoid "blank-check legislation" and that the bill should be amended to indicate that "not more than $15,000,000 of this appropriation shall be used for countries other than Greece, Hungary, Italy, Poland, Austria and China."

Hoover also objected to allowing the recipient countries to "do their own purchasing in the United States," since it would lead to "competitive bidding." Instead, he suggested the bill be amended to ensure that all "procurement of American supplies shall be through the United States Government agencies unless otherwise designated by the President." The bill should also, he told Wood, begin to insist "upon some sort of repayment," in order to "bring to an end expectations of constant governmental charity from the United States." Moreover, if recipient countries produced a surplus from their harvests of 1947, they should be required to deliver the amount of that surplus, up to the amount of American aid received, "to representatives of the United States at seaports or acceptable frontier railway points for use in relief by the United States of other countries." Moreover, countries likely to be self-sufficient after the 1947 harvest should receive no aid after that time. The former president also advocated cutting off aid "to countries maintaining military establishments which, in the view of the President, are beyond the requirements to main public order within their countries."⁵⁹ Hoover sent copies of his correspondence and recommendations to Congressman Charles Eaton, with a note that he was "not desirous of making any public issues of such questions."⁶⁰ He also sent copies to Congressman John Vorys and asked him to share it with Congressmen Walter Judd and Christian Herter, since he did not have "a large enough secretarial staff to be documenting the whole government."⁶¹

Many of Hoover's friends and acquaintances were appalled by the Truman Doctrine. One wrote him in late April to ask him to go on the attack, since "you can drive a sane wind across this miasmal morass and there is no other voice to do it. The people seem to be hypnotized."⁶² But Hoover responded that he could not speak yet, for "the time is not ripe from my point of view."⁶³

Early in March 1947, Hoover wrote Senator Alexander Wiley that the Senate Judiciary Committee was considering various bills that would terminate the war powers given to the president. He was, Hoover wrote, concerned that the powers over food exports and imports be continued, since if they lapsed "all control of international food will go by the board," foreign countries "with money will be able to grab more than their share of our food."⁶⁴

On March 12, Hoover wrote President Truman that he was convinced $350 million was "more than can be properly spent in 1947, and especially so if other nations contribute." Since the United Nations was proposing another fund for the relief of children, Hoover suggested that the present bill be amended rather than another appropriation made later. He suggested as amendments to the $350 million appropriation bill the following:

A. That no relief shall be extended other than with the products of the United States and their transportation.
B. That such relief shall be limited to food, seed, fertilizers and medicine.
C. That no obligation or promise shall be made as to a definite period of relief beyond month to month.
D. That any relief given shall be distributed under the supervision of agents of the United State and to their satisfaction.
E. That no relief shall be extended to any countries where food, seed, fertilizers or medicine are being exported or removed during the calendar year in which relief is being extended.
F. That every country to which relief is extended shall obligate themselves to pay therefore at some future date.
G. That such payments shall take precedence over any reparations.
H. That they shall obligate themselves that should they have an exportable surplus from the 1947 or 1948 harvest, they will repay the United States by return of like amounts of good before December 1, 1947 or December 1, 1948 . . .
I. That an administrator of relief should be appointed under the Secretary of Agriculture. Notwithstanding any other provisions, the President is authorized to transfer from this fund an amount equal to 57

percent of any fund raised by the United Nations for the special feeding of children, such allotment not to exceed $50,000,000.[65]

When Congressman John Taber, chairman of the House Appropriations Committee, sought the former president's views concerning the $725 million appropriation requested by the War Department for the relief of Germany, Japan, and Korea in the next fiscal year, Hoover supported it, saying, "These enormous sums are inescapable for the next year unless millions of people under our flags are to die of starvation." But he again insisted that steps must be taken to "bring these burdens upon our taxpayers to an end." The difficulty still lay, he observed, in the "delay by Russia in making peace with Germany and Japan, together with the Allied policies of reparations and industrial demilitarization," which had "paralyzed the industrial productivity of these nations" so that they were still "unable to make substantial exports and are not contributing, as they otherwise would, to their own support."[66]

Once again Hoover hammered at his theme that if Russia and France would not cooperate with the United States and Great Britain in the economic unification of Germany, the Anglo-American zones should be unified economically "so as to restore their industrial production and exports," and they should insist that the French zone be incorporated into the bizonal area. Hoover also suggested a separate peace treaty with this bizonal area if "the next conference of Foreign Ministers does not succeed in more constructive policies." The whole "levels of industry" approach should be suspended in both Germany and Japan, and restrictions should be placed only on "a few specified industries, such as shipping and aviation." A peace treaty should be made with Japan "at once" by "as many nations as wish to adhere." The whole world was suffering, Hoover pointed out, because of the delay in the restoration of productivity in these two nations, because "the whole world is an interlocked economy, and paralysis in two great centers of productivity is a world disaster." He repeated his argument that Germany and Japan were vital to the defense of Western civilization and that if they were lost both "Europe and the Far East are lost." The Soviet Union was obviously obstructing recovery for as long as possible in order to bleed the United States while paying for relief. Concluding, Hoover called for "coordination of all aid which we are extending for relief and reconstruction abroad," because the "resources of the United States are not unlimited and we are carrying over 90 percent of these burdens."

Now that Hoover's advocacy of separate peace treaties was in the open, *Newsweek* magazine labeled it the "Hoover Doctrine" and wrote,

> The years had softened many of the harsh judgments that were made of Herbert Hoover during the early '30s. At 72 the nation's only living ex-president, and its leading authority on international relief, he was now

listened to with respect even by those who had once pilloried him. Where
Franklin D. Roosevelt had studiedly ignored the man he defeated in 1932,
Harry S. Truman had sought his counsel and used his experience.

In the State Department's gleaming new headquarters and on Capitol
Hill, what Hoover had to say last week about the interdependent problems of world prosperity and world peace met serious consideration and
no little approbation.[67]

The United States, Hoover had argued, "could not indefinitely support the
world's poorhouses" after paying out $14 billion to date, with an additional $5
billion earmarked for the current fiscal year. The only solution was to make a
separate peace, without the participation of Russia if necessary, and to concentrate on building economic self-sufficiency in order to liberate the American
taxpayer of the enormous burden of food relief. *Newsweek* wrote,

> At the State Department and in Congress, the reaction was the same.
> Those who discussed Hoover's statements, whether privately or for the
> record, approved them on the whole. However, the majority believed that
> his proposals were premature . . . But Rep. Charles A. Eaton, chairman of
> the House Foreign Affairs Committee, called Hoover's plan "a proposal
> for facing the realities." He said it should have "the most serious consid-
> eration without thought of politics." Taber approved it unconditionally.
> Rep. John M. Vorys, Ohio Republican, asserted that "the way for us to get
> along with Russia now is to arrange to get along without her."
>
> In cloakroom and corridor discussions, the sentiment was that appli-
> cation of the Hoover plan should not be "too quick on the trigger." But
> the emphasis was on the words "too quick." Representatives and senators
> were willing to "try once more." But if the new effort failed, like Hoover
> they wanted to "do something." It was up to the Russians.[68]

Time magazine summarized Hoover's proposals for separate peaces with Germany and Japan, and the abolition of the destruction of peacetime industries
in those countries, as the "Hoover Way."[69]

Hoover's suggestion of separate peace treaties apparently came as a surprise
to Secretary of State Marshall, since the former president had not consulted
with the State Department before suggesting it to Taber. But O'Laughlin
noted that Vandenberg had "advocated the proposal you . . . made in your
letter to Mr. Taber," and since Vandenberg and Marshall were close it would
seem to indicate that Marshall believed "it would be helpful for Vandenberg
to support your view."[70] Hoover told O'Laughlin that if "Marshall only knew
it he would find the Taber statement had universal editorial support. When
something commends itself to the *New York Times*, the *Chicago Tribune, Daily
News, Scripps Howard*, Philadelphia papers, etc., it must have touched American feeling." It might even give Marshall "a background in negotiating with
the Russians."[71] O'Laughlin responded that Marshall would doubtless have

welcomed the Taber letter if it had been written after the Balkan treaties had been ratified. He added, "Of course, he knew the country generally had approved your proposal, but, as I have said, he did not want anything whatever placed in the way of ratification. However, it is my judgment, and now that the treaties have been ratified, I am convinced it is now that of Marshall, that your letter was a valuable contribution, for it precipitated comment that showed the country does not intend to permit the Communists to continue to keep the entire world in a state of war."[72]

Meanwhile, the former president's relations with GOP congressmen and with the War Department remained close. Secretary of War Patterson wrote Hoover that "in your recent testimony and press statement . . . you have done everything that one man can do, and more than any other living man would be able to do, in giving aid to the War Department toward the successful discharge of this [food relief] responsibility."[73]

Hoover was muting his criticism of Truman's policy somewhat because Congress was in the process of renaming Boulder Dam after the former president, and Hoover wanted to be sure that Truman signed the name change into law. Secretary of Interior Harold Ickes had abruptly and spitefully changed the designation of that dam to Boulder during the early years of the New Deal, although many mapmakers had not made the change, but now the intended name seemed about to be restored. Rickard's diary for April 22, 1947, noted that Hoover "would like to have the Hoover Dam matter clear, as he wants to make some public remarks re administration." Hoover was convinced the nation was headed for an economic slump and that Truman had not helped the situation with his speeches.[74] The bill passed the Senate on April 23, and on May 2, 1947, Truman signed the name change. A wrong had at last been righted after over a dozen years. *Time* magazine observed, "Paying tribute to the man whose special talents he has used on several occasions, President Truman last week signed the joint congressional resolution restoring the name of Hoover to Boulder Dam. He used four pens, asked that they all be sent to the nation's only living ex-President." But Hoover could barely appreciate the moment as he was in the Waldorf suffering from a miserable cold he had caught while being rained on during fishing in New Jersey.[75]

Rickard noted in his diary for May 22 that Hoover was "playing [an] important role in the deliberations and actions of Republican Senators and Congressmen." The former president was leaving for Washington in a few days and had arranged to have ten congressmen breakfast with him. He had been offered the use of Blair House during his stay by the Truman administration but had declined it since it would "not provide [the] independence he desires," and he also worried that Blair House might be bugged.[76] Meanwhile, the Truman administration was making use of former Hoover relief associates in dealing with relief problems in Europe and was asking Hoover to recommend other administrators.[77]

Late in May, the former president was commended by Ernest T. Weir, chairman of National Steel and former finance chairman of the GOP, for his report on Germany. Weir himself had just returned from a tour of Germany and Austria with a committee of businessmen under the auspices of the War Department. He told Hoover that he thought the economic recovery of Germany would be a much "better and more effective method of permanently stopping the spread of Communism in Europe . . . than the one based on the so-called Truman Doctrine." Weir continued,

> I want to confirm my statement to you that I believe the Republican Party must come out with a definite foreign policy, because the present one of simply endorsing the Administration's program not only is ineffective so far as permanently helping the balance of the world is concerned, but certainly is destructive to us from a political point of view. In my opinion, you are the only man who can draw up this policy intelligently, and I hope you will do so. If you do take on this obligation, a number of us, who have some influence within the Party, will do everything in the world to have it endorsed.[78]

Weir also wrote to Taft that he was "thoroughly convinced that the rehabilitation of Germany, as recommended by Mr. Hoover and unanimously endorsed by this Committee, is the surest way to prevent the spread of Communism in Europe."[79] Taft agreed that "Germany is the key to the situation."[80]

Secretary of State Marshall's enunciation of the European Recovery Plan (ERP) or Marshall Plan at Harvard in early June led to new requests for Hoover's assessment of the "capacity of the United States to continue its aid to the world, and, at the same time, to effectively meet the continuing problems involved in achieving a sound domestic economy."[81] Hoover mailed off eight suggestions to Senator Styles Bridges in the middle of the month: (1) all US foreign economic relations should be under a single coordination; (2) excessive exports must be prevented in order to avoid inflation; (3) if necessary to prevent famine, America should increase its export surplus of food by voluntary conservation and alteration of some trade practices; (4) the government should monitor the quantity of goods and services that could safely be exported and limit purchases of commodities by curbing gifts and loans; (5) the government should prepare to stockpile for defense certain surplus commodities from abroad, thereby aiding those nations economically by the purchases; (6) countries receiving American aid should be required to cooperate with the United States in measures to reduce the relief burden, promote productivity, and bring about peace; (7) the United States should attach conditions to gifts and loans related to security and inspection of use; and (8) resources should be concentrated in areas where Western civilization could be preserved.[82] Bridges wrote Hoover a few days later that he "must be pleased by the widespread attention our exchange of letters received" and that his office had received "a fine response" to the exchange of letters.[83] Taft, too, wrote that Hoover's letter "certainly expresses my views, and I hope we can follow it up."[84]

Hoover was less than enthusiastic about the Marshall Plan, writing to O'Laughlin, his conduit to the State Department,

> Perhaps you can clear up a few mysteries for me. Why issue an invitation to Europe to gang up on the United States? Why ask Russia to join them in view of the Truman doctrine which was a flat declaration of a Western civilization bloc? Why this sudden switch? Do they realize that the first necessity of economic recovery is peace in Europe? Will they demand (if Russia joins) that she sign a peace with Austria and Germany such as we demand? Do they believe that they can separate Russia into economic cooperation without political cooperation? Do they think we will aid Italy and the satellite states without suspension of reparations? Do they think any Republican Congress will give aid to Russia in view of all that has happened? Or to the satellite states? They set in train some bad moments. And if they want Republican cooperation (and many Democrats) why don't they consult somebody?[85]

Clearly Hoover felt he should have been consulted. When Truman subsequently appointed a special nonpartisan committee of 19 domestic leaders to determine the capability of the United States to assist Europe economically, Hoover's name was conspicuously and surprisingly absent from the list, although it did contain GOP senators Vandenberg and Wallace White.[86]

Obviously stung by his omission from the committee, despite his well-known expertise, Hoover wrote O'Laughlin, "No one could be more relieved than I to read this morning's paper and find my name left off the list of the new fact-finding committee on our ability to pay Europe. Baruch tells me of his relief also. Had we been on the list it would have been difficult enough to refuse. My advices are that Marshall resents my epistles to Taber and Bridges as intrusions on his exclusive field—the making of foreign policies. Vandenberg is also upset and poisons Marshall." Marshall, Hoover decided, was out of his element in assuming that the "desperately selfish" politicians of Europe were motivated "from the same altruism which animates this more comfortable land of our own." Hoover felt, however, that his letter to Taber had accomplished two useful purposes: (1) it had "shown the country that there is another foreign policy than the isolationism of [Colonel Robert] McCormick and the appeasement of [Henry] Wallace," and (2) it had helped to get the relief appropriation passed. It had also shown Republicans "that there were more constructive ideas besides those of the Republican crumb-eaters of the State Department," by whom he clearly meant Vandenberg. He found over four hundred newspapers, ranging from the *Chicago Tribune* to the *New York Times* and *New York Herald Tribune*, and including the Scripps-Howard and Hearst papers, had supported the letter to Taber editorially, and the letter to Bridges, too, had enjoyed "astonishing" press support. Hoover predicted a gradual erosion of GOP support for Truman's foreign policies and an eventual awakening in the White House to the fact that "the publicity crumb-eaters cannot deliver the Republicans."[87] Clearly Hoover was willing to support bipartisanship in foreign policy only so long as he was a player in its formulation. Truman's failures to consult him before launching the Marshall Plan, and his omission of the former president from the advisory council, had cost the administration his support, while whose Republicans who did continue to support the president had now been labeled as "crumb-eaters" by the former president.

Late in June Hoover developed his own proposal for European reconstruction and mailed it off to Bernard Baruch. In it he expressed strong doubts about the ability of the United States to carry out the reconstruction of Europe by itself and dealt with the long-term effects he felt were likely to flow from the granting of economic aid directly from the United States to the recipient nations. The United States, he wrote, had only a limited ability to aid Europe and should be assisted by other countries like Argentina, Canada, and South Africa in the reconstruction effort. Direct loans between governments created "a political liability" that did not exist when such loans were made through government-supported agencies. The political liability lay in the fact that such direct loans became a political issue when time came for repayment, as they had after World War I. It was European opposition to repayment, then, Hoover argued, that had contributed to the rise of isolationism in the United States. Thus something like the World Bank should be the vehicle for financing and directing European reconstruction, and the United States could subscribe its contribution through purchase of debentures in the World Bank, with other capable nations doing likewise. This would remove the political character from the relationship between lenders and borrowers and would broaden the effort to include other nations besides the United States, while it would also provide as security to the lender the "portion of all assets of the World to which their ration of debenture holdings entitle them." It would give the whole reconstruction program "the character of an international cooperative action" and would "tend greatly to establish the international money exchanges and thus promote private transactions."[88]

But when Hoover went into greater detail in a further memorandum to Baruch on July 3, he gave American economic assistance a political character that was inconsistent with the internationalization of that assistance he had insisted upon his the earlier memorandum. As in his earlier letter to Taber, Hoover now sought political concessions from recipient nations, including their assistance in making an immediate peace settlement with Japan. France should get no aid unless it joined its zone of Germany with the American and British zones and should join the United States and Britain in making a separate peace with the western zone if the Soviet Union continued to obstruct a peace settlement with a unified Germany. Nations receiving aid from the United States should also cease extracting reparations from the defeated enemies and should abandon the "levels of industry" policy. The Soviet Union and its satellites should be barred from receiving aid, and efforts should be concentrated on Britain, France, Italy, the western zone of Germany, Austria, Greece, Turkey, Holland, Belgium, Finland, China, and Japan.[89]

The Western European nations should also be required to return to the prewar six day workweek until their economic crisis was ended, since the American sacrifice was unwarranted if the Europeans were unwilling to make those things they could produce for themselves. The United States should also insist that the Western European nations create "a customs and transportation union" that would increase productivity and be "a practical first step toward a United Nations of Europe." Only now did Hoover turn to alternatives to direct American loans to the needy countries. One alternative was for the United States "to stockpile . . . as part of national defense all the durable commodities of which we are or would be in short supply." Perhaps one-half billion dollars per year could be spent in relief-seeking countries through such purchases. The other alternative was the use of the World Bank as Hoover had advocated in his earlier note. The former president cautioned Baruch that his ideas were "not for publication or circulation," his purpose having been only to "give you personally my ideas as I will be away for two months or so."[90]

Hoover did, however, send to Senator Taft a copy of his memorandum to Baruch two weeks later. The two had earlier begun to consult on their response to the Marshall Plan, at which time Taft wrote Hoover,

> I read with great interest your letter to Senator Bridges, which is the best analysis of the subject anyone has offered. The chief characteristic of the Administration is the complete lack of analysis when they get down to figures. I felt that Arthur Vandenberg made a mistake in suggesting a special commission be appointed by the President. Such a commission has now been appointed, but [Averell] Harriman is its chairman, and the staff will presumably be selected by the Administration . . . Neither do I like the implication that if we are capable of exporting more goods we should, therefore, do so, regardless of the wisdom, either from our standpoint or that of the countries of Europe.

Taft said he was "prepared to support some additional lending," but it should be limited to food and to materials and supplies needed to get the European economy operating once again. He feared that the "European nations will agree on some global plan and global figures which Marshall may accept, and then we [Congress] will be in the wrong if we try to cut it down to a reasonable plan."[91]

In sending Taft a copy of the Baruch memorandum, Hoover told the Senator he was "really very much alarmed" that the Marshall Plan was "an invitation to gang up on the United States; it looks like committing the United States without authority of the Congress—until afterwards. Of course all of us want to do what we can, but we do not want to exhaust this country."[92] A broader implication of the Marshall Plan was that the secretary of state had succeeded in dividing the world, but Hoover was not certain the present division along the Iron Curtain and Manchuria would continue, "for nations will remain within their present allotted places only so long as they work the two now competitive Santa Clauses."[93] Taft responded to Hoover's memorandum and letter by writing that, without having yet studied it completely, he fully agreed with the former president's position on the whole question. Like Hoover, Taft was concerned that the Marshall Plan had been offered in such a way that it "invites the foreign nations to gang up and make unreasonable demands. Instead of making them come to us and imposing conditions on our assistance, we . . . seem to be begging them to let us help them as if it were to our financial or economic advantage to do so." The only advantage Taft could see for the United States was that the plan met this country's "desire to see peace and prosperity in the world."[94]

In September the former president was largely immobilized by a crippling attack of shingles. Rickard found him in a "pitiful condition," with his right arm paralyzed, an unusual development in shingles according to Hoover's doctor. The symptoms were, in fact, closer to those of polio than to the usual ones of shingles. However, the doctors consented to a Hoover speech at Madison Square Garden since they thought it would be good for his morale.[95]

In October Hoover resumed his critical analysis of the Marshall Plan as it was unfolding, mailing a memorandum via Taft to Congressman Christian Herter and also sending a letter directly to the Massachusetts congressman. In the memorandum Hoover again raised ten familiar points. The United States should assist needy nations to the fullest extent consistent with a healthy economy and adequate national defense, because the collapse of Western Europe would be detrimental to "our civilization" and to "the future progress of the United States and the Western Hemisphere." Nor would the "spiritual character of the American people" permit "hunger and cold" to exist as long as they had the ability to prevent it. While Europe and Asia were incapable of giving support to the United States in the event of a war with the Soviets, "their continued neutrality is of importance." But the United States should not pledge any long-term aid unless the recipient nations were willing to make "the necessary effort to restore their productivity," and the American people must recognize that the aid would not be repaid even if it was called a loan. The recipient nations should understand that such aid was a privation for Americans and that the American ability to give aid was limited. And aid should be unified and should be administered more consistently than in the past.[96]

All aid should be divided into two categories, Hoover wrote. The first category—including food, fertilizer, coal, and cotton—could be called "relief" goods, and any proceeds from the sale of these goods by recipient governments should be deposited to the account of the United States. The other category of goods, which the former president called "depletion" goods, were those commodities that represented a drain on American natural resources and that would have to be replaced by purchases from abroad at some point, as with oil and metals. These items should be paid for by the recipient governments in kind "to the full extent that exports of a given country to the United States permit." The balance should be secured by some form of collateral. Recipient countries should cooperate in obtaining oil from the Persian Gulf nations in order to supply their energy requirements. Finally, Hoover insisted again that Congress should "deny aid to any country which fails to cooperate with us in making immediate peace with Germany and Japan" and which did not abandon the policy of destroying the industrial capacity of those defeated nations. "The recovery of both the productivity of Europe and Asia will depend upon the restoration of industry in Germany and Japan," he wrote. "It is simply crazy for us to build up productivity in foreign countries out of American resources, and at the same time, to tear down productivity in these two areas."

The next month, Henry L. Stimson, now outside the government, tried to enlist Hoover for membership on a Citizens' Committee for the Marshall Plan whose members also included such lights as Dean Acheson, Herbert Lehman, Robert Patterson, Winthrop Aldrich, and John Winant.[97] The former president responded that he was "in favor of doing all that we can," but he again insisted on "certain essential safeguards on any such operation," and he had, he told Stimson, "the arrogance to believe that I have had more experience with these questions than any living person." If those safeguards were included, he would be glad to support it, but if not he wanted to be "free to state these safeguards in any support," and therefore he preferred not to join the committee until the details of the plan were spelled out in full.[98] Stimson was certain that Marshall's plan would "not permit indiscriminate giving or giving without proper safeguards," but he asked Hoover to let him know "what you regard as these essential safeguards."[99] There is no indication whether Hoover did so, but he did not join the committee.

While Hoover and his former secretary of state were at odds over the Marshall Plan, as they had been over so many issues dating back to the Hoover presidency, Hoover and Alf Landon were in accord. Landon wrote the former president in mid-November that he supported Hoover's position on the Marshall Plan and that he had scheduled a speech a few days hence for which he solicited Hoover's views on the European situation and Truman's policies. Landon also told him he had written Congressman Joseph Martin that "Congress should set up a board to administer whatever fund it provided, and you should be on it."[100] Hoover responded that he felt "great discontent with everything going on in connection with this program, but there seems to be no hope of much alteration at the present time due to the pressure now being exerted and the unwillingness of our people [in Congress] to fight it."[101] Landon was disappointed to learn from Hoover that congressional Republicans did not seem to putting up much of a fight. He considered Truman's message on aid to Europe "so general in its terms that it largely leaves the formulation of a program up to them." He told Hoover he planned to visit him within a few weeks to discuss the situation.[102]

For some, however, it appeared that Hoover was already exerting too much influence on the foreign policies of the Truman administration. As early as April 1946, the executive board of the United Electrical, Radio and

Machine Workers, a left-wing union with the Congress of Industrial Organizations attacked Truman because of the influence of Hoover, Vandenberg, and
other Republicans on his foreign policies.[103] More important, in September
1947, former vice president Henry A. Wallace, now editor of the liberal *New
Republic*, lashed out at the Truman administration in a speech that charged
that while there had been no resemblance between the foreign policy views
of Hoover and Roosevelt, within 46 days after FDR's death "Mr. Hoover
was welcomed to the White House." Now, two years later, Wallace charged,
"it is Hoover's thinking which guides our foreign policy." Specifically, Wallace pointed to Hoover's recommendations following his trip to Germany in
which the former president had advocated the rebuilding of German industry.
This policy, Wallace observed, had now become "the very core of our entire
program for European reconstruction."[104] It is curious that what was so obvious to Wallace has been obscure to so many historians.

CHAPTER 11

Rolling Back the New Deal

Politics

Wallace's speech to "progressives" was clearly a campaign effort looking to the 1948 presidential election. Despite his many other activities, Hoover was also thinking ahead to the election. In late October 1947 he expressed the belief that Taft could be elected president if he won the GOP nomination.[1] Hoover and Taft had worked closely together in the postwar years, not only on food relief and foreign policy matters, but also in labor legislation. Hoover had been much encouraged when the Taft-Hartley Labor Act was passed by Congress, writing the Ohioan that he had "restored representative government to mastery in its own house." The new law had restored some of the balance missing since the passage of the Wagner Labor Act during the Roosevelt years. The continuation of powerful labor organizations, possessing more power even than the federal government, would have meant, Hoover wrote Taft, "disaster to every hope of free men." He was also glad, he told the senator, "to see the adoption of my favorite gadget of a secret ballot of the workers as the final stage of collective bargaining before a strike that jeopardizes widespread public interest."[2]

Dewey and Taft were again the leading contenders for the 1948 GOP nomination, and both visited Hoover in October 1947, they having concluded, too, that the race was between them. According to Hoover's aide-memoire of their visits, the two contenders wanted the former president to get them together at the proper moment and obtain a pledge from each to support whichever appeared to have a definite lead in convention delegates. This would prevent a stalemate which might open the door for nomination of a dark-horse candidate. Privately, Hoover expressed a preference for Taft, but said he could accept Dewey over either Stassen or Eisenhower, two others who were being mentioned as possible nominees.[3] But by mid-November, Hoover doubted the ability of any Republican to beat Truman, whom he regarded as very adept at playing politics with national and international issues.[4] Hoover warned Republicans that if they were to enjoy any success against the president in 1948 they would have to learn to do the same.[5]

On the eve of his seventy-third birthday in August 1947, Hoover viewed the world with some optimism and expressed a hopeful outlook for "continued Western Civilization" in an interview. Although the Soviet Union was displaying its typical truculence, Hoover believed the Soviets were gradually being "isolated" and that their "instrument of ideological penetration" was weakening outside of Russia and her satellites. The arrested productivity of Germany and Japan were the great obstacles to world economic recovery, he repeated, and he again advanced his proposal for immediate peace with Japan, whether the Soviet Union joined it or not. He added,

> Another year after the war's end finds the earth without peace, little recovery in production, increasing danger of starvation abroad and alarms of another world war. One nation alone, by refusal of cooperation and destructive acts is responsible. If we are to reverse this tide of disaster, then free nations have but one of two possibilities, first, cooperation from Russia, which is improbable, second, making peace among the peoples outside Russia and her satellites, together with subjugation of her international poison squads, which is possible. If neither is done then an armed United States can live in reasonable comfort, use our food surplus to stave off starvation and want, even if it means isolation, which is most undesirable.[6]

In February the head of the Joint British-American Food and Agriculture Administration in Bizonia, as the merged British and American zones were referred to, wrote a Hoover intimate that the recommendations Hoover had made one-and-a-half years earlier were "now belatedly being partially put into force. The British and American zones are being merged economically, and administratively on the German and the British-American side so far as economic matters are concerned."[7] A few months later he wrote that Hoover might be interested "to know that the Child Feeding and School Lunch Program which his report on this situation started 2 years ago is still known by the Germans as the Hoover Child Feeding & School Lunch Program." General Lucius Clay, US commander in chief in Germany, later wrote, "The child feeding program did more to convince the German people of our desire to recreate their nation than any other action on our part."[8]

As for the Marshall Plan, Hoover insisted again it was more important to world economic recovery to make an immediate peace with Germany and Japan so that those two nations might be restored to productivity. With the $2.5 billion that the United States and Great Britain were being forced to spend on food relief there thus freed, most of the rehabilitation needs of Western Europe could be financed. If the foreign ministers' meeting in

November did not result in Soviet cooperation over Germany, then the United States, Britain, and France should organize a German government in their unified zones and make a separate peace with it. If other countries refused to cooperate with the United States in doing so, then America would "be driven into some degree of isolation." However, the former president clearly hoped the other nations would cooperate, since "isolationism which contemplates the further degeneration of Western Civilization is no asset to American progress."[9]

Landon wrote Hoover in November of the Marshall Plan that it seemed to him "as partners in the enterprise of reconstructing western civilization we have a right to ask that these countries put their house in order. I mean, the restoration of sound fiscal and economic policies so that people will be encouraged to go to work." He was giving a speech and asked for Hoover's views on "the European situation, and the Administration's policies."[10] Hoover replied that he had "great discontent with everything going on with this program, but there seems to be no hope of much alteration at the present time due to the pressures now being exerted and the unwillingness of our people to fight it." While he agreed on the need to prevent hunger and cold, the methods of restoring the people to productivity had not, Hoover thought, "been adequately taken care of."[11] Landon could not understand why the Republicans in Congress were not putting up a fight, since "the President's message was so general in its terms that it largely leaves the formulation of a program up to them." He was planning a visit with Hoover to discuss it.[12]

Reports of purges behind the Iron Curtain in November fanned Hoover's hopes that they indicated a growing opposition to the Soviet government, and he expressed confidence that the "restiveness" there "ultimately would blossom into revolution." He was certain "that the Communist ridden peoples will sooner or later throw off their chains." Europe's greatest problem, on both sides of the Iron Curtain, was the shortage of food and fuel, and free enterprise was "the only road to productivity." Noting that the United States, with its free economy, was providing most of the food and fuel to free Europe, he pointedly observed, "Had we in this hemisphere yielded to the economic utopias of either Eastern or Western Europe, I venture to say that hardly a ton of food or fuel would be moving overseas. Sooner or later the utopia-seeking nations will notice these facts and their peoples will resume the only road to freedom from hunger and cold."[13] In June he had delivered a speech at Princeton in which he pointed out the progress America had made under its "right-wing system of freedom." He told the students,

> The terrible reactionaries have filled the land with Legislatures, town councils, a free press, orchestras, bands, radios, juke boxes and other noises. It has a full complement of stadiums, ball players and college yells. Furthermore, they have sprinkled the country with churches, laboratories, built 10,000 schools and a thousand institutions of higher learning. And somehow these right-wing taxpayers are squeezing out the resources which maintain a million devoted

teachers, 100,000 able professors and the keep of 2,000,000 youngsters in colleges and universities. Possibly another ideology could do better in the next 200 years. But I suggest we had better continue to suffer the evils of right-wing freedom than to die of nostalgia.[14]

In December Senator Vandenberg asked the former president to testify on the Marshall Plan before the Senate Foreign Relations Committee, but Hoover demurred with the news that his doctor had ordered him not to travel so much.[15] He suggested, instead, that he prepare a short memorandum for the committee for release to the press, with the understanding that he might testify later.[16] Vandenberg agreed and suggested that Hoover's statement be released and read into the committee's record shortly after it had concluded hearing from the government's side in late January.[17] Hoover mailed off his memorandum to Vandenberg on January 18 and released it to the press. The memorandum listed three reasons the United States should help with European recovery: (1) because "the spiritual character of the American people" compelled them to "prevent hunger and cold to the full extent of their surplus, and even to the extent of personal self-denial"; (2) to bring about the defeat of communism in Western Europe and to stimulate economic and political unity among the nations there; and (3) because "the project builds for peace in the world." But there were very great dangers in the project. On the one hand was the possibility of failure, and on the other lay the danger that "the volume of exports and finance proposed may accelerate an already serious inflation; that it further delays our recuperation from the war; that it drains our natural resources and continues excessive taxation; all of which might bring depression and thus destroy the strength of the one remaining source of aid to a world in chaos." It was imperative, he admitted, to take some risks, but he was compelled "by conscience to say that the plan as presented should have certain constructive modifications and more safeguards."[18]

The effects of the decisions made by those directing the plan would pervade virtually every aspect of American economic and foreign policy, and the policies should be directed by a group representing all the areas of its impact, he told Vandenberg. China, Germany, Japan, Korea, and perhaps more countries, should be added to the original list of 16, since the "food supply and reconstruction of industry" in these 4 countries were "inseparable from the 16 countries." Again, Hoover insisted that recipient countries be required to abandon restraints upon enterprise and economy, balance their budgets, and curb inflation, since this would lead to the flow of American private capital into those countries and reduce the burden on the American taxpayer. He also again insisted that recipient countries cooperate with the United States in making a separate peace with Japan and in establishing a trizonal union in Germany, thus stimulating economic recovery in those countries and freeing money then being spent on relief to be used, instead, for reconstruction. Hoover opposed appropriating Marshall Plan money for 4-year periods, since no one could foresee the course the recipient economies would follow, and he worried that even the proposed commitment for the first 15 months would be too great a strain on American taxpayers when added to the cost of food relief. In a variety of ways, Hoover recommended alterations to the bill that would reduce the drain on American taxpayers, the economy, and natural resources. His memorandum attracted harsh editorial criticism from the *New York Times* and *New York Herald Tribune*.[19]

The former president had by now begun to regard the Truman administration's foreign policy more negatively, in part because he saw so few of his suggestions for the Marshall Plan being adopted.[20] He had become convinced that Marshall was a poor administrator and considered his continuation of the policy of dismantling German industry especially inexcusable.[21] The previously close relations between Hoover and Marshall had gradually deteriorated, apparently disrupted by the pressure upon Marshall by Democrats in Congress who, like Henry Wallace, complained of the impression abroad in the country that it was Republicans like Hoover and Undersecretary of State Robert Lovett who were having the greatest influence on Truman's foreign policies. According to columnist Drew Pearson, Marshall had, in fact, been called upon by 17 Democrat members of the House to explain his close ties with Hoover and other Republicans. The meeting had been distorted by Pearson, but it made relations between Hoover and Marshall more difficult.[22]

Meanwhile, Hoover had testified on behalf of the St. Lawrence Seaway Bill, and Senator Wiley told him in late December that he was looking forward to "speedy action" on it. He told the former president, "I have had occasion again and again to cite the splendid testimony which you made before my subcommittee of the Senate Foreign Relations Committee in support of the seaway." He was sure that Hoover's "long record of approval of this resolution will count as a very strong factor in the ultimate vote for the seaway."[23]

Rickard noted in early January 1948 that Hoover was "working hard on his analysis of the Marshall Plan, but does not want to make it public until as many other witnesses as possible have their say. It has been rewritten many times."[24] Early in March 1948, John Callan O'Laughlin sought to arrange a meeting between Hoover and Marshall to restore their previous amity. O'Laughlin told the former president that Marshall was particularly anxious for such a meeting "as there is a number of matters he would like to talk over with you."[25] Hoover responded positively and a meeting was arranged for March 22.[26] Whether the meeting with Marshall was responsible or not, Hoover appeared more conciliatory toward the Economic Recovery Plan (ERP) bill that was before the House of Representatives in another memorandum he wrote two days after that meeting.[27] Writing to Speaker of the House Joseph Martin, the former president observed that many of his recommendations had been incorporated into the bill, but others were still absent. He then pressed for adoption of the remainder of his recommendations but concluded by saying, "I realize that many approach this gigantic experiment with great apprehension and a realization of the sacrifices it will mean to our people. All legislation must be the result of compromise. However, if it should produce economic, political and self-defense unity in Western Europe, and thus a major dam against Russian aggression, it would stem the tide now running so strongly against civilization and peace. The plan, if well devised and under a capable Administrator, stands a good chance of success. I believe it is worth taking the chance."[28]

Thus either as a result of his conference with Marshall or from his satisfaction that some of the changes he had suggested were now in the bill, or both, Hoover began to modestly support the bill in Congress. He wrote to Bernard Baruch, "It is somewhat interesting to note that although the administration defamed all of my recommendations to Senator Vandenberg, a great many of them were essentially adopted and no doubt some of these others will be inserted. If these people would only send for us in advance, you and I could have shortened this whole legislation by at least two months."[29]

When John J. McCloy, president of the International Bank for Reconstruction and Development, asked for his views on the bank's policies in July 1948, Hoover responded that such views as he had were "more in the nature of impressions arising out of the changing times—and of less help than I could wish." He wrote,

1. It seems to me that events have abundantly proved the original concept of the Bank as a major world-war reconstruction agency, lending money on adequate security with assurance of repayment was an illusion. The physical, material, and political destruction of the war proved so great that there is . . . little security obtainable and little possibility of repayment such as this institution must have.

2. With a few exceptions major finance or reconstruction in these areas must be gifts, whatever other name they may be called by . . . the total sums are so huge, that they cannot be repaid . . .

3. So long as these illusionary sums hang around the world's neck, many of them purporting to be loans, they effectively block the possibilities of sound credit operations in those areas.

4. It may be argued that even in the presence of these huge obligations it is possible to make loans for special reproductive purposes and that by agreement from the increment of production such advances can be repaid . . . With currencies in the present state such assurances would be doubtful.

5. I therefore doubt that the World Bank can perform any but minor functions in the major E.R.P. [Marshall Plan] countries for some time to come. If it is to be operated as a real bank and not as a relief agency, I suggest that it must exclude any but minor operations in countries (a) with vast relief and war obligations until these are settled in some fashion by which real security can be given, and (b) until freedom and real stability of exchange is established.

6. The question before the [Advisory] Council seems to be that of what service the World Bank may perform in the meantime. If these limitations are correct, then the field of the Bank for the present must be mostly the old neutrals and countries like those in Latin America and the Near East, which are not bogged down with huge war obligations or artificial exchange and not in need of relief."

The Bank should also "confine itself mostly to loans to governments for improvement of transportation, communications and irrigation projects." The "support of American private investors in the Bank's securities" could not be justified in any other business.[30]

Late that month, Hoover wired Congressman Halleck his thoughts on prices, telling him,

One. The place where increased prices hit hardest is food and fuel. There has not been much recent increase in clothing or rent, nor likely to be much in the immediate future.

Two. There cannot be the slightest doubt that ERP and other relief shipments have increased prices not only of food and fuel, but of building materials . . .

Three. These impulses to rising prices are flatly an administration responsibility for were shipments confined to our actual surplus production by careful buying prices would not have been affected; commodity speculation and black market would have been avoided.

Four. No doubt wages and prices have been pressed up by inflationary effect of expanded credit and currency, both created by this administration . . .

Five. The facts bearing on these matters should be developed and if the above assumptions are correct, then the following simple action would display the administration's responsibility to the nation and at the same time roll back or halt further increased living costs, without transgression of fundamental Republican philosophy.

a. Give the President authority or require him to issue no permits either to government or private agencies for export of food and coal or building materials at prices higher than those at some previous date to be determined . . . The very threat of such action would reduce prices and action under it would hold them down.

b. Criticism would be that it might halt shipments to ERP countries. This would not only be temporary, but as to food they now have harvests in hand which will last different countries from five to eleven months, and there could be no starvation. Lower prices would be to their benefit if they expect to pay for our commodities and in any event would secure them in larger volume . . .

c. On the Fiscal side, the Federal Reserve Board should be vigorously examined. They have not used their powers over interest, open market operations, bank credits, and margins on speculative stocks and commodities. If they need more powers in these directions and to cover consumer credit, they should be given them. They will never use them.

d. In respect to iron and steel products and other building materials, there should be an immediate investigation of why they have not taken steps during the past 18 months to secure their production from Germany instead of export from the United States . . . It is foolhardy to take these commodities from our short supply and at the same time feed German workmen on charity from the American taxpayer . . .

e. All this will require vigorous unafraid investigation of relief by the House of Representatives committees other than Foreign Affairs . . . If the situation is as serious as the President represents, then the most serious investigation should be undertaken.[31]

Government Reorganization

Late in July 1947, the Republican Congress passed and Truman signed into law an act that established a committee to study and make recommendations concerning reorganization of the executive branch of the federal government. A new phase of Hoover's public service was launched when he accepted the chairmanship of the new Commission on Organization of the Executive Branch of the Government. The former president had suffered that serious attack of shingles during the late summer and early fall, however, and was able to do very little work. He described his bout with the disease as having "developed into a rather unusual form of paralysis of the muscles in my right arm and therefore hangs on for a long time—although the total medical profession in New York seems confident that they can get rid of it in time."[32] He was without any use of his right arm for several week. When Hugh Gibson suffered an attack of the disease in 1954, Hoover sent him some observations on his experience with the malady:

1. The doctors give you codein [sic], which disturbs your digestive track [sic];
2. They put colloden on you and take off your skin when they remove it;
3. They say martinis are bad for you;
4. Occasionally they are kind and give you a shot of morphine but sternly warn you not to get too much joy out of it;
5. At this point you can laugh for they carry away the needle;
6. And having admitted they know nothing and can do nothing about it, they send you a bill.[33]

On September 29, however, he issued a statement on the new commission, describing it as "the most formidable attempt yet made for independent review and advice on the business methods of the Executive Branch of the Federal Government." The commission, he noted, had been organized not only with the cooperation of both houses of Congress but also with that of the president and both political parties, and to keep it free of partisan politics the commission was not to make a report until after the 1948 election. The purpose of the commission was not to uncover wrongdoing, Hoover said—that was the responsibility of other agencies of the government,—but rather to look for ways to secure "efficiency and economy," thus reducing the cost of government for the taxpayer. In his statement, the former president reviewed the growth of the federal bureaucracy since before World War I, noting that federal civilian employees now outnumbered those of all state and local governments combined. The commission would also seek ways to relieve the president of the "intolerable labor and inadequate control imposed upon him by the multitude of independent establishments." It would especially concern itself with regulatory agencies that combined within them legislative, executive, and judicial powers and with defining "Federal as against state and local responsibilities." Relations between citizens and their government must be streamlined. The new chairman concluded, "There are a score of other areas which should be effectively explored. There is no hurry imposed upon this Commission, but the great responsibility involves the utmost thoroughness and the widest use of all the special abilities in the country."[34]

Through the fall and winter of 1947 Hoover busied himself with organizing the specialized "task forces" of the Commission on Organization of the Executive Branch of the Government and inaugurating the work of the commission. Hoover told reporters he had accepted service on the commission "with the direct understanding" that it would be his last service to the nation.[35] Privately, he told Senator Alexander Wiley he was convinced that "if we are to preserve our Government from death by the asphyxiation of centralization, we must restore responsibility and power in the states. And we are proposing to examine this question to the bottom."[36]

Reviewing Hoover's 1947, Edgar Rickard recorded in his diary that the former president had received many honors during the year, including the renaming of Hoover Dam and various magazine and newspaper tributes. But, Rickard added, he had "paid dearly for all this by impairment of health and this has been a very bad year from him. For weeks after his return from Europe in March he suffered from impaired hearing. In April a most serious attack of stomach ailment which laid him up for weeks and surely will require an operation. In August he contracted shingles in California, which left him with a paralyzed right arm which only now, six months later, is beginning to show improvement." But none of this, Rickard marveled, even the "constant pain in right arm and shoulder deterred him from constant work, particularly in organizing his committee. He has three women as secretaries and a research man, working constantly . . . While not generally vindictive, there is no doubt that he gets satisfaction from the many recent books deflating and debunking F.D.R."[37] In late February, the former president was still getting painful daily massages and was doubtful about attending the annual Bohemian Club encampment. He also had his staff researching his early involvement in the Cooperative for Assistance and Relief Everywhere (CARE) to establish his position as its originator.[38] Later, in 1953, he would submit a memorandum to Henry Cassitt for an article in the *Saturday Evening Post* that traced the concept to "Food Drafts" set up by the American Relief Administration after World War I and then resurrected after World War II by the "sale of actual packages of food which would be delivered in Europe." Capital had been obtained "from some 20-odd relief organizations" and "from the Army some millions of '10 to 1' tinned rations" had been secured at a small price, as well as the "services of some of the men who had participated in the World War I Relief Administration. The name 'C.A.R.E.' was decided upon as indicating the associations which co-operated."[39]

As the "task forces" proceeded with their investigations, Hoover monitored the political situation as the conventions drew near. It was a foregone conclusion that Truman would be nominated by the Democrats, although Hoover thought many Democrats might desert the president from a conviction that he could not win in November.[40] The GOP situation was still unclear. In March there was an effort to promote Vandenberg for the nomination, but Hoover was cool toward the senator from Michigan, and he believed the candidacy of General Douglas MacArthur would be foolhardy since "left-wingers" would smear him for his involvement in suppressing the bonus marchers in 1932.[41] Taft was clearly Hoover's choice, and Hoover counseled that the Ohioan should put great effort into the campaign in Nebraska since a big win in the primary there might assure his nomination. But above all, the former president was concerned that either Taft or Dewey should win the nomination and not some compromise candidate. He was insistent that Taft and Dewey must agree that one or the other would be the nominee.[42]

Late in March 1948 Cold War tensions were heightened as the result of a communist coup in Czechoslovakia. Hoover's reaction was more temperate even than Taft's. In a public letter to Paul Smith of the *San Francisco Chronicle* Hoover expressed his conviction that the Truman administration was "putting on a fear and war blitz in order to intimidate the Congress into appropriations, etc., and possibly to create a sense of emergency which would be helpful in the forthcoming [political] campaign." But Hoover was convinced that the Soviets did not want war, nor would they be ready to wage war for five to twenty years. The coup in Czechoslovakia he viewed as only a case of the Soviets "consolidating areas conceded to them by Roosevelt and Churchill." The real danger to the West was not from military invasion but from communist fifth columnists, and that was why he had supported the Marshall Plan. The United States ought to build up Western Europe as a buffer area against communism and pull its troops out as soon as possible; it should aid the Western Europeans in building their self-defense capability, "but we should enter no military alliances or military guarantees" lest the European countries "lie down and do nothing for themselves." In closing, Hoover recalled that he had expressed opposition over the years to American relations with the Soviet

Union, and especially to the American alliance with them during World War II. He told Smith, "I felt deeply at that time—and have ever since—that we were aligning ourselves with wicked processes and that the old biblical injunction that 'the wages of sin are death' was still working. We see the consequences today."[43]

Hoover's enhanced stature as a result of his prominence in the postwar years led potential Republican candidates not only to seek meetings with him but also to make sure that such meetings were publicized. In June 1947 Harold Stassen sought such a meeting and asked if Hoover objected to his answering in the affirmative if he were queried by reporters concerning any meeting with the former president. Hoover responded cheerfully that he had "no objection to anyone knowing that I keep good company."[44] In April of the following year, Stassen again sought a meeting with the former president.[45] When Taft won the Ohio primary early in May, giving him what appeared to his campaigners to be a commanding lead for the nomination, Congressman Clarence Brown, Taft's campaign manager, pressed for a meeting with Hoover and told him, "With your help victory seems certain."[46]

Hoover was convinced that Henry A. Wallace's third-party candidacy on the Progressive ticket would help Taft more than Dewey against Truman.[47] However, the former president adhered to a policy he had maintained consistently since leaving the White House in 1933 of refusing to publicly support any of the candidates for the GOP nomination, and so he refused to endorse Taft. In 1952 he would break with that policy, perhaps because of Taft's failure in 1948, but in 1948 he limited his role to broker in the convention. He had earlier suggested to both Taft and Dewey that the leader at convention time should be endorsed by the other in order to ensure that no stalemate developed that might open the door to nomination by a less-qualified dark horse as had happened with Willkie in 1940. Both agreed, and when Taft's bid faltered, Hoover told the Ohioan that "for the good of the Party he should retire and support his rival."[48] As a result, Dewey was nominated for the second time and Republicans looked forward confidently to victory in November.

In his fourth successive address to a GOP convention since he left the White House, Hoover dealt with the grave crisis he viewed as facing America and the world

> Liberty has been defeated in a score of nations. Those governments have revived slavery. They have revived mass guilt. They have revived government by hatred, by exile, by torture. Today the men in the Kremlin hold in their right hands the threat of military aggression against all civilization. With their left hands they work to weaken civilization by boring from within.
>
> These tyrants have created a situation new in all human experience. We saved them from Hitler, but they refuse to cooperate with us to establish good will or peace on earth. Thus today a powerful nation, dominated

by men without conscience, finds it useful to have neither peace nor war in the world.

Whether some of us, who foresaw that danger and warned of it, were right or wrong, and whatever the terrible errors of American statesmanship that helped bring it about, we are today faced with a world situation in which there is little time for regrets.

The only obstacle to the annihilation of freedom has been the United States of America. Only as long as America is free and strong will human liberty survive in the world.

The United States must assist in building strength and unity in Western Europe in order to "restore a balance of power in the world able to restore the hordes from the Eurasian steppes who would ruin Western Civilization." And the United States must shoulder "increased armament to assure that no hostile force will ever reach this hemisphere." But the American economy must not be exhausted by all these burdens "or the last hope of the world is lost." American aid to other countries must not be used for "non-essentials, for profligacy, or for inefficiency," and there must not be "a perpetual dependence of Europe and Asia upon the United States." Moreover, the reconstruction of Europe must include Germany.

At home America must restore freedom from the infection of "creeping totalitarianism" that had inserted "its tentacles into our labor unions, our universities, our intelligentsia, and our Government." The real problem was with "fuzzy-minded people who think we can have totalitarian economics in the hands of bureaucracy, and at the same time have personal liberty for the people and representative government in the nation." Such "totalitarian liberals" had "provided the ladders upon which the Communist pirates have boarded the Ship of State" in every country where the communists had taken control. Hoover concluded by telling the delegates, "My fellow Republicans, from the inevitable passing of years, this is indicated as probably the last time I will meet with you in Convention. That does not mean I shall spend my days with less concern and less watchfulness of the deep currents which will determine the future of American life. But this does warrant my speaking from my heart of this great concern." He asked the delegates to "face the truth that we are in a critical battle to safeguard our nation and civilization" and to choose leaders "who seek not only victory but the opportunity to service in this fight."[49] It was the first of several "farewells" that the former president would address to Republican conventions.

A newspaperman who was present wrote to O'Laughlin that he "would have been very proud to have been present at the performance of Mr. Hoover, and his reception by the tremendous crowd. Never in his 74 years has he had a higher moment. It was astounding. They drew the man to their hearts as they had forgotten to do through his long period of public service. They seemed to be trying to make up for their lapse of affection and understanding." And

Hoover's speech, he wrote, had been "the high spot of whole Convention."[50] Spargo wrote that he and his wife had "listened to the great ovation given you by the convention at Philadelphia with hearts filled with inexpressible joy and gratitude. We are glad to have lived to hear it. I am glad that your two sons were present to witness what was nothing short of an acknowledgement of the rightness and wisdom of the leadership they [the GOP] had not the vision or courage to follow while the opportunity existed."[51] Hoover told John Hamilton that after the speech he received a handwritten note from President Truman telling him that the speech was the greatest made "since Lincoln's Gettysburg Address."[52]

Of interest is the fact that Hoover's convention speech provided the inspiration for the formation of the Freedoms Foundation. In February 1949, Ken Wells wrote the former president that the foundation had been formed, sizable funds had been committed, and E. F. Hutton had provided the organization expenses. General Eisenhower, Senator Taft, and Harold Stassen had agreed to take a personal part in the awards program. Wells wrote, "Our inspiration came from your address last June 22 in Philadelphia. Mr. Hutton has earnestly sought a means to extend your thoughts again and again to all Americans that they might know the truth—and thus be free." The foundation had enough money to make several awards to people who "by their actions defend the spirit and philosophy of the constitution and Bill of Rights—and who build a zeal for personal responsibility and understanding and belief in liberty." These awards would be larger than the Nobel Prize, and they believed that the foundation could "take the initiative away from the Yankee Doodle communists in government and public life today."[53]

After writing a magazine tribute to the former president in 1947, author Eugene Lyons penned a complimentary biography, *Our Unknown Ex-President: A Portrait of Herbert Hoover*. While busy himself with writing his memoirs, Hoover was determined to see that Lyons's book was published and given adequate publicity and promotion to make it a success. Edgar Rickard's diary records a meeting of May 10 in Lyons's apartment to discuss methods to ensure a wide sale of the book. The meeting was attended by several Hoover intimates, including journalist George Sokolsky, as well as three representatives from the publisher, Doubleday. The publisher, Rickard wrote, had "not planned to spend much, and must be coerced into doing something."[54]

In May Hoover also ventured again to Washington where he urged Republicans in Congress to pass a pending bill that would admit a number of displaced persons to the United States. He wrote to ex–American Relief Administration (ARA) associate Hallam Tuck, then executive secretary of the International Refugees Association in Geneva, Switzerland, that the "old obstacle" still remained—"what will the others do?" Hoover had advocated that the United States take the lead by accepting at least two hundred thousand, with a promise to take more if other nations joined in.[55]

Herbert Brownell, Dewey's convention manager, expressed interest in conferring with Hoover soon after the convention, writing the former president that he recalled the "fine help that you extended to me during the 1944 campaign."[56] When Brownell visited him he conveyed to Hoover the same message from Dewey that the New Yorker had delivered in person in 1944—that he wanted no speeches from the former president in the campaign. Although he expected the 1948 campaign to be similar to that in 1944, Hoover did not "see how it is possible to lose the election."[57] He did not expect to participate in the campaign because of the burden of his work with reorganization commission and other activities, but when both Truman and Congressman Sam Rayburn took verbal potshots at him a few days later, Hoover wrote to Mark Sullivan that Truman seemed to be running "me for President again. If so, I may have to change my mind about not making any speeches in this campaign."[58] Following the Truman attack, several of Hoover's friends encouraged Dewey to defend the former president, but Dewey refused. Hoover told John Hamilton later, "I really believe that by 1948 the people of the country had reestablished me in their affections, but apparently the Governor held to the opinion that I was still political poison."[59]

In August the former president traveled once again to his West Branch birthplace to celebrate his seventy-fourth birthday. Columnist Anne O'Hare McCormick wrote of the experience,

> The former President's homecoming speech was the counterpart in personal terms of the address he delivered at the Republican convention a few weeks ago. In Philadelphia he was the elder statesman calling upon the party he once led to be equal to its opportunity and responsibility in a crucial hour of American history. In West Branch he was the country boy grown old and mellow and renowned. The burden of his speech was not that he is self-made but that he is America-made, the product of this society and this system. He has seen far more of this tortuous and tortured world than most political leaders, and the sum of his experience, distilled into this testament, is that there is nothing like America.[60]

Newsweek, after recalling the "seventeen emotion-crammed minutes" that he had been cheered at the GOP convention a week weeks earlier, described the birthday celebration for the former president in West Branch as "the climax in the restoration of Herbert Hoover to public esteem." It observed, "But to Hoover the celebration meant more than a personal vindication. It also meant vindication for his ideas—ideas which had been jeered at during the depression, but which had since regained respect."[61]

Hoover was troubled by the crisis with the Soviets over Berlin that followed closely after the coup in Czechoslovakia. The former president was concerned that the United States should avoid a confrontation with the Soviet Union and concentrate its energies on organizing for defense of the Western Hemisphere. Hoover told Rickard that the United States should have agreed well before this to the use of a Russian currency in Berlin and might thereby have avoided the blockade. The realities of the situation were that if the Soviets decided they wanted the United States out of Eastern Europe "they could close Austria overnight."[62]

O'Laughlin passed his concerns on to Secretary of State Marshall, who agreed with Hoover but insisted, according to O'Laughlin, "that to give in on Berlin would be the signal for further aggressive advances by the Soviets."[63] Hoover was convinced, however, that if war did break out the United States would be unable to prevent a Soviet occupation of France and Great Britain, and that their knowledge of that inclined those two countries toward neutrality in the event of any showdown between the United States and the USSR.[64] Marshall assured O'Laughlin that, on the contrary, the British and French were more insistent on standing fast over Berlin than was the United States and that their support could be relied upon if hostilities actually broke out.[65]

Hoover considered Truman's diplomatic recognition of the new state of Israel to be a purely political act to aid his reelection prospects, and he predicted, wrongly as it turned out, that the Arab nations would eliminate the Israeli state within ten days.[66] Among the few bits of advice that he gave Dewey in the campaign was to take up the battle against "the destruction and removal of non-military manufacturing plants from Germany." Although the Truman administration denied this was still happening, Hoover had evidence that the process was still going on, with the result that German exports had been stifled to the point where it was still requiring "us about $600,000,000 a year to keep Germans alive and in idleness and constant degeneration." It also meant that the United States was spending "one-third more" on the Marshall Plan than was necessary.[67] Late in September *Newsweek* magazine reported that Hoover and others were trying to dissuade Dewey from appointing John Foster Dulles as his secretary of state if he were elected. Hoover wrote a denial to the magazine and sent a copy to Dewey, who responded that he had not seen the article but would "have known it would be false in any event."[68]

Hoover's relations with the Dewey campaign were congenial, and he phoned the campaign directors periodically with suggestions, but he took no active role in the campaign, being preoccupied with the work of the reorganization commission. When queried by publisher Roy Howard on possible topics for Dewey's campaign speeches, Hoover responded,

1. Open with a sharp speech on the American system of freedom, the debauchery of its four protections, the courts, the Congress, local government . . .
2. Reorganization of the Federal Government, economy in Government, reduction of bureaucracy, restoration of local responsibility.
3. Revision of taxes so as to encourage incentives and protect the small business man. Debate on the mass of hidden taxes that fall on the "common man."
4. Agriculture.

5. Conservation of natural resources.
6. The dealings with Russia from Teheran to Potsdam; its consequences to freedom and peace. Include the surviving Morgenthau Plan for Germany which costs the taxpayers a billion a year for relief and demoralizes all Europe.
7. The Communist infiltration of our Government, in our universities and labor unions. Control of Communists by some system of public exposure, such as registration, etc.[69]

When asked by Rickard why women disliked Dewey, Hoover replied that it was because the New Yorker was "arrogant, ruthless and super-sensitive."[70]

Hoover told a Nebraska friend that he doubted "whether the Republican committee wants me to take any part in the campaign, and I know that I am too much overburdened with work to take on anything of the sort," but he added, "If there was a difference between success and failure . . . I would certainly feel it my duty to do so—but otherwise this job of reorganization of the federal government is just about all the load that I can carry, plus the other obligations which I already have."[71] He was irritated, however, that Truman had "taken cracks at me."[72]

On September 30 the 74-year-old former president registered to vote in New York for the first time, having until that time voted in California.[73] Partly because Hoover hoped for a Dewey victory, he resisted all pressures to push the commission's work through to completion before the election.[74] Still, the New Dealers had begun to realize that the report of the commission would be highly critical of the Roosevelt and Truman administrations, and Hoover knew they would try to prevent its publication, but they dared not attack the commission before the election. Hoover clearly hoped and envisioned that the election of Dewey to the presidency, together with a friendly, GOP-dominated Congress, would make it possible for the report to be used to roll back much of the New Deal. As *US News and World Report* put it, "if Mr. Truman, who has approved the plan, goes out in January, his successor will be Thomas E. Dewey, a man who has a reputation for driving toward efficiency in Government. He is expected to give his backing to a plan aimed at making the Federal Government more efficient. And Mr. Hoover, as a former President, may have more influence upon the country now than he ever did while he was in the White House."[75]

However, Hoover's hopes were dashed when Truman was reelected in one of the great upsets of American political history. In analyzing the election, the former president concluded that the Dewey campaign had ignored two crucial issues—the positive accomplishments of the GOP-dominated eightieth Congress and of the Republican Party. Speeches should have been delivered during the campaign, he wrote, defending the GOP record in the eightieth Congress for (1) liberating the worker through the Taft-Hartley Act; (2) transforming emergency agricultural price supports into a fixed policy of the government—an action approved by all farm leaders, but not sufficiently publicized during the campaign; and (3) lowering taxes. Speeches should have also defended the GOP. When Truman attacked the party as representing "big business and private interests," Dewey or others should have recited the list of regulatory legislation for which the GOP was responsible—legislation that in Hoover's view constituted "the most fundamental revolution in the economic history that the modern world has seen" by abandoning laissez faire and preventing monopoly in America. Republican speakers should have also blunted Democratic charges on conservation by pointing out that "every one of the great conservation services of the country today was created by the Republicans."[76]

Predictably, Hoover also argued that the GOP candidates should have attacked FDR for his failure to cooperate in halting the bank panic of 1933 and should have called attention to the recovery of the rest of the world from the depression within two years, while New Deal policies had forced the United States "to wallow in depression until 1940." The candidates might also, he wrote, have attacked FDR's foreign policies at Teheran and Yalta and Truman's at Potsdam, which in Hoover's view had "wrecked peace in the world" and enslaved hundreds of millions of people. Had such speeches been made, he believed, "it would have created pride and confidence in the Republican party" and would have brought more votes to the GOP ticket. He concluded, "One of the prime obligations of the presidential campaign is to put on an education of the people of the great public issues. It is the only time when the people listen and no one can convey this educational work except the Candidate for President. It was totally avoided and the Party was frustrated." Yet Hoover himself had not participated in the campaign. He would not make the same mistake in 1952.

After 16 years in an opposition role, Hoover now faced another 4 years of the same. The Truman victory was all the more disappointing to Hoover for the implications it would undoubtedly have for the recommendations of what was now being called the Hoover Commission.[77] Clearly it would be more difficult to get many of them adopted. But late in November Truman wrote Hoover that it seemed to him "satisfactory progress" was being made. He wanted soon to have a meeting with Hoover "on the whole subject," and he believed "we can really accomplish some good results as you and I are fully acquainted with what is necessary to make the government run more efficiently."[78] The commission's report was now absorbing all Hoover's time, and he wrote to Arch Shaw late in November that he had "just had to cut out everything for the present."[79] Clearly Truman's victory meant that the report would take a somewhat different tone than if Dewey had been elected president. As the recommendations of the various task forces of the commission were submitted and circulated for comments among the commission members, some were deliberately leaked in order to test public reaction before they were incorporated in the full report.[80] Still, Hoover doubted that the president would give the recommendations his unqualified support, and even if he did there would be opposition from within the bureaucracy to any change.[81]

    Rickard found Hoover "not elated" after the former president's chat with
Truman in early December. Hoover was still smoldering as a result of attacks
on his presidency by Truman during the campaign, after what Hoover considered the development of a cordial relationship between the two that ought
to have precluded such behavior. John Hamilton later recalled that Hoover
had made up his mind "he would never see Truman again as long as he lived,"
but when Truman called him to the White House Hoover could not refuse
from a sense of duty. But on his way to Washington, Hamilton said, Hoover
had "made up his mind he was going to have the first word," and when "he
entered the President's office, before the latter could say anything, he said to
him, 'Mr. President, I would be less than frank if I didn't tell you that your
Boston speech was both personally offensive to me and I believe uncalled
for.'" According to Hamilton's recollection of what Hoover told him, Truman
had instantly apologized, saying, "I feel the same way about it. It was one of
those damned speeches that someone had written for me, and when I got into
the part when I attacked you, I wasn't smart enough to know how to improvise
at the moment, and then I remembered the speech had been released to the
press and I had to go through with it."[82] Hoover told Rickard that three of
Truman's appointees on the commission were trying to prevent full publication of its report. They had, he said, gone along until the election, but then
began giving trouble, since "any real, vicious New Dealer does not want the
misrule of the last 15 years exposed, or the Wholesale reduction of Gov't
Employees with votes." In January, Hoover complained that he was having a
hard time getting full attendance at commission meetings, and he insisted on
full support for the final form of any task force report.[83] In February he was
pleased that Congress approved his plan to give the president authority to
initiate reforms but was disappointed that it had excluded the military from
the authority. When Truman phoned him on February 6, Hoover impressed
on the president the necessity to reverse the congressional exclusion of the
military services, since "a great deal of the reorganization of the defense establishment could be accomplished under such powers of budget, accounting,
procurement of supplies, etc., all of which apply to the military establishment
and . . . if such exception were made for that department, it would be not only
a complete block on these reforms but also on the transfer of certain civilian agencies out of that department and the transfer of some military agencies into it." Hoover found Truman "in complete agreement with me," and
he suggested that the president work with congressional leaders to get the
exemption withdrawn.[84]

    Three days later Hoover visited Truman to discuss again the "exemption
of the defense services from the full effect of the reorganization plan," and the
president told Hoover he would see if the Senate could remove the exemption.
Hoover also discussed with Truman the consolidation of all medical services,
of transportation, and of public works. He found Truman in full agreement
on all points, including the recommendation that there be boards of review

outside the White House.[85] Hoover hoped that Truman would be able to get the military included but found two of Truman's cabinet members—Forrestal and Acheson—blocking all efforts to do so.[86] Rickard noted that the former president looked well and "his mental capacity is extraordinary."[87]

In January, Hoover sent Truman a suggestion for transplanting five hundred thousand displaced Palestinian Arabs to the Tigris-Euphrates River Valley of Iraq. At present they were living in squalor and would require upwards of $15 million per year, Hoover estimated, "merely to provide subsistence with no real solution of the problem," and the United States would likely have to pay most of it. The ancient irrigation systems of the five hundred thousand to six hundred thousand acres of arable land in the Tigris-Euphrates area, however, could probably be restored to modern operation with under $50 million of expenditure and would (1) provide a permanent solution to the problem, (2) would ease Palestinian tensions, and (3) "would constitute a friendly gesture from the west to all Arab countries."[88] Truman responded a few days later that he had been "working on just such a plan" but "didn't know how far we can get with it."[89]

From early February until early March, a stream of reports went from the commission to Congress, recommending a total of 273 specific changes in the administrative structure of the executive branch of the government. The first report dealt with general management of the executive branch and recommended the creation of a clear line of responsibility and command, reduction of the 65 agencies reporting to the president by two-thirds, grouping of agencies and field services by function and purpose, the use of standard nomenclature, and the creation of a presidential staff secretary position and an office of personnel, as well as other reforms. As for personnel management, the commission recommended that the Civil Service Commission devote itself to setting and enforcing personnel standards rather than hiring and that hiring be turned over to the various departments and agencies, each of which should be given its own personnel officer. In one of its most important recommendations the Hoover Commission called for the creation of a new Office of General Services (later established as the General Services Administration), which would be directly responsible to the president and would supervise supply, records, maintenance, and building management operations throughout the government, except for the Post Office and Defense Departments. The commission also recommended changes in the handling of inventories, rents, record maintenance and management, traffic management, and purchases.

Other recommendations called for the Post Office Department to be placed on a business basis, that the postmaster general should cease to be a party official, that the postal service be decentralized into 15 regions under regional directors, that postmasters and top officials be named by the president without need for Senate confirmation, and other reforms. An area receiving the most sweeping recommendations for changes was the State Department. The commission recommended giving the secretary of state a clear line of command over the department and the Foreign Service. It also recommended that the department concentrate solely on making and coordinating foreign policy and that the department's personnel be merged with the Foreign Service into a single Foreign Affairs Service to serve at home and abroad. The commission wanted the State Department out of such functions as direction of occupied areas, granting visas, munitions export control, and other nondiplomatic functions. As for agriculture, the Hoover Commission recommended that overlapping responsibilities between the Agriculture and Interior Departments be ended by placing all major land agencies in the Department of Agriculture, and it also recommended that the department be organized into seven operating divisions, along with other reforms.

The commission suggested reorganization of the Defense Establishment to strengthen civilian control, with greater authority for the secretary of defense and the demotion of the secretaries of the army, navy, and air forces to undersecretaries of defense. It recommended that the chairman of the Joint Chiefs of Staff be named by the secretary of defense as his single link to his military advisors and that the secretary be given authority over the preparation of the defense budget, among other reforms. The Veterans Administration (VA) should turn over VA insurance to a separation corporation, and the administration's management should be streamlined to correct bureaucratic defects. The commission recommended performance budgets, under which funds were sought for specific functions, activities, and projects. It recommended groupings of kindred activities under the Departments of Labor and Commerce, including the transfer of some activities from other departments and agencies. Most transportation functions, for example, would be placed under the Department of Commerce. Included was a suggestion that the Commerce, Agriculture, Interior, and State departments establish an interdepartmental committee to end overlapping between their functions.

Turning to the Treasury Department, the commission recommended that it be reorganized along functional lines as the real government fiscal center, with the Reconstruction Finance Corporation, Federal Deposit Insurance Corporation, and Export-Import Bank transferred to its jurisdiction and nonfiscal functions like the Narcotics Bureau and Coast Guard transferred out. The Treasury Department should also serve as the central agency to examine lending agencies such as the Federal Farm Mortgage Corporation, the Home Owners Loan Corporation, and the Home Loan Bank Board.

The commission recommended the liquidation of thirty government enterprises, the consolidation of others, and the incorporation of still more. It urged higher salaries for the members of regulatory commissions and criticized their inadequate planning. It also suggested the conversion of the Interior Department into a public works agency that would have responsibility for the flood control and river and harbor development work that was then the responsibility of the Army Corps of Engineers. Authority for all public works should be concentrated in the Interior Department, except for grants-in-aid programs, and nonpublic works functions such as the Bureau of Land Management and the Fish and Wildlife Service should be removed. The Selective Service System should be moved to the Labor Department, along with the Bureau of Employees' Compensation, the Employees' Compensation Appeals Board, and other labor-oriented agencies and activities.

In another major recommendation, the Hoover Commission suggested the creation of a new cabinet department to supervise all welfare and educational programs. It also would take over such functions as those of the Federal Security Agency and the Bureau of Indian Affairs. It also proposed creation of a United Medical Administration that would oversee military and VA hospitals, the Public Health Service, and part of the Food and Drug Administration. Since the State Department should be limited to strictly diplomatic functions, the commission recommended the creation of an administrator of overseas affairs, who would be responsible for occupied and dependent territories, the European Cooperation Administration (ECA), and other such activities. It also recommended the establishment of a National Science Foundation to regulate interdepartmental research. In sum, the recommendations of the commission mirrored Hoover's opposition to waste and duplication in the federal bureaucracy, as well as his general philosophy against a bloated central government and his preference for state and local responsibility. The recommendations were largely concerned with methods by which costs might be reduced and activities curtailed and consolidated in the interest of efficiency and economy.[90]

Truman phoned Hoover early in February 1949 to express his appreciation and satisfaction with the commission's report. Thus began the cooperation between the two to ensure that legislation would be passed by Congress to implement the recommendations[91]. However, their cooperation was not as close as Hoover would have liked. A few days after the report was released, he met with Truman to discuss the recommendations that had been made, as well as some others that he felt strongly about but that the commission had been unable to agree upon.[92] Truman was not willing to commit himself to support all the recommendations, especially those which involved "the shifting of functions from one department to another," because it would be necessary, he told Hoover, to consider those carefully and to take into account the views of the responsible officials within the administration.[93] Hoover agreed with the president's desire to "keep a free hand," but he argued that some of the reforms could be carried through Congress if the two of them could agree to cooperate in supporting them. Under this category Hoover included "agreement upon the broad principles that the quasi-legislative and quasi-judicial functions are outside the executive arm; that there should be unification of public works and also of medical service and the grouping of certain lending agencies under the Secretary of the Treasury. All enable me to be of more service in holding this work in the nonpartisan field. Therefore, it has seemed to me that such personal understanding from time to time would forward our common purpose."[94] Although he continued to express his support for the commission's recommendations, Truman refused to enter into any such partnership with Hoover.[95] But whenever reorganization legislation that the president considered desirable became stalled in Congress, Truman was quick to call upon Hoover for assistance with Republican members.[96]

Newsweek was pessimistic about the "chances for an over-all reorganization of the government," because "the 81st Congress was as reluctant to give the necessary power to Mr. Truman as previous Congresses had been to let Hoover and Roosevelt have them." The problem was that every "government department had friends on Capitol Hill fighting to protect it from any shakeup in which it would lose power and prestige." Against the influence of the pressure groups was arrayed the prestige of Hoover and Truman, and "equally as important, perhaps, was the widespread support the plan was enlisting among taxpayers."[97]

It was never Hoover's style to rely on the natural course of events but rather to ensure that desirable actions were nudged along. Thus he early concluded that the commission's recommendations would require considerable publicity and lobbying if they were to overcome the resistance of bureaucrats and lobbyists for special interests.[98] Fortunately, he had offers of financial support for a campaign in behalf of the commission's report, and he aided in the formation of a Citizens' Committee for the Hoover Commission, headed by Dr. Robert L. Johnson, president of Temple University. Some two thousand telegrams were sent out to recruit members in March, and Hoover hoped to have the committee well enough organized by the end of that month that it would be able to enlist the support of congressmen who, until then, had felt unable to go against the organized opposition to specific reforms. While the former president maintained close relations with the committee, he did not participate publicly in its efforts to mobilize public opinion.[99] He continued, however, to do his own part in behalf of the recommendations by his speeches, radio talks, and testimony before congressional committees.

In March, Hoover spoke to the Radio Executives Club in New York and told them the government had become "a Gulliver's estate with threads spun around it until it had been rendered almost helpless." The Hoover Commission, he asserted, was "probably the last chance we have to free it from its bonds." The problem was that everybody in the government applauded reforms "in every branch except their own. By the time it is all over we expect an aggregate of 100 per cent of those affected to resist reforms." The commission, he told the executives, would have to rely on an aroused public opinion if the proposed reforms were to be accomplished, and he did not know what the result would be. The commission, he said, would have its final meeting in April and in the meantime he intended to go Florida and "do nothing but fish and rest."[100]

Hoover's principal problem continued to be with reforms of the military establishment, where the major obstacle continued to be Secretary of Defense

James Forrestal. In March, the former president complained to Rickard that Forrestal had been "disloyal" and that he had lost "all faith in him." Although Forrestal's title was secretary of defense, there was as yet no Department of Defense, Forrestal presiding over what was called the National Military Establishment (NME). Forrestal was about to be replaced by Louis Johnson, a man with whom Hoover had experienced only limited contact. The former president told Rickard he was disturbed "that there is so much organized opposition in Washington against his entire report, and so far he has not mustered any very large number of Senators or Congressmen who would be willing to go to bat for it." He was hoping, however, that his new Citizens' Committee would "bring unprecedented pressure to bear on Congress," since he did not expect Truman to be of much help.[101]

Johnson turned out to be more cooperative than Forrestal had been, and this made Hoover less pessimistic about the possibilities of reform in the military establishment in April than he had been in March. Truman had also exerted pressure on Senator Alben Barkley to straighten out the reorganization bill in that body, and Truman told Hoover that Barkley had promised to do so if Hoover could get Senate Republicans to go along.[102] Hoover promised to travel to Washington to do so, and a few days later he testified before a Senate committee on the military reforms, it being his intention, he told Rickard, "to take on one Department at a time and not rush too many plans before Congress and the President." Truman wrote that he appreciated "very much what you said before the Finance Committee of the Senate."[103] The former president had now also resorted to a hearing aid, his hearing having continued impaired since the trip to Europe.[104] In April Hoover gave five talks in one week over the radio to rally support for the reforms the commission had proposed.[105]

On May 7, Hoover issued a press statement concerning the tentative agreement of the Senate Armed Services Committee on the revised bill consolidating the armed services. It was, he said, "a nationally important step in the reorganization of the government, and through Senator Harry F. Byrd's able amendments it includes reforms in budgeting and accounting." All members of the committee, along with Secretaries Forrestal and Johnson and Ferdinand Eberstadt, chairman of the task force, deserved, Hoover said, "public appreciation for their fine teamwork."[106]

Meanwhile, the former president was disturbed by the activities of some of his fellow Republicans. In his Lincoln Day dinner speech in February, Dewey had again drawn a distinction between the GOP "old guard" and what Dewey chose to regard as his "reform" group in the party. Hoover worried that the New Yorker was following Theodore Roosevelt's divisive tactics, which had cost the Republican Party so dearly early in the century.[107] He was also shocked when Senator Robert Taft supported public housing legislation in Congress, concluding that the Ohioan was pursuing a path of naked political expediency in advocating what was to Hoover socialistic legislation.[108]

Hoover's views also continued to be sought in connection with matters unrelated to reorganization. Late in April 1949 Congressman Robert Doughton, chairman of the House Ways and Means Committee, solicited his views on pending legislation related to Social Security. Noting the enormous expenditures of the federal government caused by the Cold War and assistance to Europe, Hoover warned that the American economy was "up to the limit of endurance under this load. I believe we should go slow and hold further additions to this burden to the absolute minimum. When the cold war is over, we can afford many more domestic improvements." Hoover considered the actuarial basis of the Social Security system to be flawed and expected that within five to ten years "the general taxpayer will be forced to make up the annual deficit."[109]

The system, he said, should be placed on a "pay-as-you-go" basis, with an increase in benefits but no expansion of the coverage, and federal grants should be given to the states in order to provide funds for those "actually in need," because "the real and urgent problem is the need group," and the Social Security system could not solve their problems for "many years." Beyond that, the former president suggested a study to find a simpler system that would eliminate the dual administration of both federal and state programs. He thought a "careful inquiry might disclose an entirely different system which would avoid the huge costs of administration and the duplication, which would substitute some other forms of taxation, more simple and more direct for its support, and which would give more positive security to the aged than this complicated system." "I believe," he told one congressman, "some other system must be found if there is to be real protection in old age."[110]

Hoover sent Eisenhower a copy of his letter to Doughton, and Ike responded that he "most definitely" agreed with Hoover's views, but "unfortunately my own expressed conclusions lack not only the clarity but the authority that characterize yours." He thanked Hoover for "sending to the chairman of the Ways and Means Committee such a forceful exposition of common sense as applied to a very intricate and significant movement in our national life."[111]

Another of his concerns was with the expansion of federal welfare agencies, which he saw as having a deadening effect on individual and local responsibility. Such activities did have "a place in American life provided the cloak of welfare is not used as a disguise for Karl Marx," he wrote, but their effect was to dry up public support for private welfare agencies on the theory that the government should do it all. For Hoover, the "essence of our self government lies in self government outside of political government," with the "fabric of American life woven around our tens of thousands of voluntary associations." It was from these, not from bureaucracy, that "inspirations of progress spring," and it would mean an end of American civilization if they were replaced by government. Without their "spur to official progress," even governmental activities would deteriorate, for the "greatest and in fact the only impulse to social progress is the spark of altruism in the individual human being."[112]

In June the former president was also queried concerning his views on federal aid to education. He decried the effect of logrolling in sending federal assistance even to states that did not need help. He also opposed the growth of federal bureaucracy that must inevitably follow such a scatter-gun approach to education assistance and was alarmed at the extent to which the federal government was dictating state and local educational policies. The "grants-in-aid system" he regarded as "a prime instrument in centralizing the government of the people in Washington." Safeguards against federal dictation should be spelled out in greater detail in any future bills, and aid should be limited only to the approximately 12 states that genuinely needed it, with need defined in terms of educational standards rather than on economic calculations. If such an approach were followed he calculated that the proposed appropriation in Congress could be sliced by about half, unnecessary bureaucratic expansion could be halted, and the "camel's head" of federal bureaucratic control of education could be cut "out of approximately 80% of the nation's educational tents." In Hoover's view, "To place a Federal bureaucracy over the whole national system will be, in my mind, a disaster to educational progress—no matter what legal limits are put on it or what advantages are painted."[113]

In mid-June Hoover wrote Truman that he had received from the Budget Bureau drafts of reorganization plans that were to be sent to Congress under the Reorganization Act. Hoover called the president's attention to the fact that Congress had requested of the Hoover Commission that it put its recommendations into legislative drafts and that this had been done in many cases, with the bills then pending before congressional committees. There were, he told Truman, "two distinctive types of action": "First. Those reorganizations which can be accomplished under your authority in the 'Reorganization Act of 1949' by the submission of 'plans.' Second. Those that will require special legislation outside of these authorities." Hoover argued that the two should not be confused, and he separated for Truman those reforms that fit under the two categories. The first included authority to make certain transfers of agencies and responsibilities between departments; the second included reforms in the VA and the Post Office Department and reorganization of the personnel services. He told Truman "that in the present favorable atmosphere in Congress we might get substantial items through this session." He pointed out that the State Department Reorganization Act had already been passed, the Armed Services Reorganization Bill had passed the Senate, and the Procurement, Disposal of Property and General Service Administration bill had passed the House and had been approved by the Senate committee. He suggested that Truman push for the passage of four other bills already in the hands of Congress and that any others be held over until the next session.[114]

Ten days later Hoover testified before the House Armed Services Committee in behalf of the Senate version of the Defense Reorganization Bill. In his prepared statement, Hoover told the congressmen that the Senate bill was closer to the recommendations of the Hoover Commission. Hoover said,

> I believe it is generally agreed that the National Security Act of 1947 did not accomplish the high hopes of unity of command, civilian control of the financial and business operation of the military forces and the economy that was expected of it, and that the central weakness lies in the lack of clear authority and responsibility assigned to the Secretary of Defense.
>
> I may well comment that legislation on the lines of the Senate Bill has been recommended by President Truman, the late Secretary of Defense, James Forrestal; the present Secretary of Defense, Louis A. Johnson; former Secretary of War, Robert P. Patterson; Secretary of Air, W. Stuart Symington; Ferdinand Eberstadt, Chairman of our Task Force, and many others familiar with the problem. There is added indication of the need for this legislation as it was unanimously approved by the Senate Committee on Armed Services and passed the Senate without a consequential dissent.

Hoover then went on to defend the bill on efficiency and economic grounds.[115]

The very next day, the nearly 75-year-old former president testified before the Senate Committee on Expenditures in the Executive Departments in behalf of seven reorganization plans submitted to Congress by Truman that would take effect if not vetoed by Congress. These included such items as establishing a Department of Welfare to replace the Federal Security Agency, the transfer of certain bureaus to the Department of Labor, reforms in the Post Office Department, the National Security Council, National Security Resources Board, Civil Service, Maritime Commission, and the transfer of the Public Roads Administration to the Department of Commerce.[116]

A few days later Hoover wrote Truman that the Hoover Commission had "strongly recommended the gathering together of functions relating to transportation into a rounded division of [the Commerce] department and to place them under four bureaus: merchant marine, civil aviation, high-way transportation and railroad transportation." This would require the transfer of eight agencies in all or in part into the department but would produce "less overlaps and duplications and relieve your office from the burdens of five agencies or parts of agencies which now have 'independent' status and insufficient supervision." He told Truman he thought there was "great favor in the Congress for such a transportation division."[117] Truman responded that he was working with the Budget Bureau "on these plans and programs" and hoped "to have as many of them ready for the new Congress as we possibly can." Again, he expressed his appreciation for Hoover's help, but one gets the impression that matters were moving so rapidly that the president was having difficulty keeping up with them.[118]

Three days later Hoover called attention to the slump in metal prices and recommended that the government stockpile strategic metals to keep the prices up and eliminate unemployment. He wrote that the government could not lose money since national and world demand would make it possible in future to sell any stockpiles at more than was paid for them. Hoover admitted that his family owned "some minor interest in mines," but this involvement served to give him "practical knowledge of what is going on."[119] Truman responded that he had already made the stockpiling recommendation both to Congress and to the Munitions Board, and he feared that "some of our backward-looking 'economy-minded' Senators" would knock out the stockpiling appropriation, even though "common sense would dictate that now is the time to make these stockpiles of nonferrous metals."[120]

The opportunity to serve in the United States Senate, which Hoover had sought unsuccessfully after Hiram Johnson's death in 1945, was offered to him in 1949. The retirement of Senator Robert Wagner of New York created a vacancy, and New York Governor Thomas Dewey offered to appoint the former president to fill out the remainder of the session. This time Hoover declined the appointment, writing to Dewey on July 6, "I have given the matter prayerful consideration and I feel you must appoint some younger man. I will not be physically able to undertake the necessary strain of the nomination and election campaign four months hence or, if successful, to again repeat such a campaign in 1950. The Republican Party needs young blood on its fighting fronts." Hoover also saw little prospect for constructive service in the month that remained in the current session of Congress, and he believed his most useful service to the nation lay in "occasional special investigation or advice in fields where I have some experience, and with an entire independence of view." He could not "be so helpful to the country if I surrender such independence to re-enter" the active political field.[121] Dewey appointed John Foster Dulles, instead, and the fact that the seat had been offered first to Hoover was not made public so as not to detract from Dulles's appointment.[122]

In late July, Joseph Kennedy penned the former president a long note as Hoover approached his seventy-fifth birthday. Kennedy wrote,

> You have had the acclaim of the American people; you have had the criticism of the American people; and now in the twilight of your life, the American people have come to realize that Herbert Hoover is one of our few capable, understanding men in the public life of this generation. You will pardon me, I know, if I take some credit for being a factor in your return to government service four years ago. I realized then that the government was losing the services of the only clear-headed man that it was my pleasure to talk with. Your work for the last four years, which is the only period with which I am familiar, is one of the most astounding contributions to American life. I feel very sorry that Mrs. Hoover is not here to have the great satisfaction of seeing that the American

344   *H O O V E R*

people have finally realized that in her husband they have had one of the great
fighting forces for the kind of America we all want to live in.¹²³

On August 10, Hoover spoke at his seventy-fifth birthday celebration at
Stanford University, his alma mater and site of the Hoover Institution on
War, Revolution and Peace. Hoover began by observing of the library,

> It is now thirty-four years since this Library on War, Revolution and
> Peace was founded. Over these years friends of the Library have con-
> tributed over $3,450,000 towards its support. And of priceless value have
> been the millions of documents and materials furnished freely by hun-
> dreds of individuals and threescore governments.
>
> This institution is not a dead storage. It is a living thing which over
> the years will correct a vast amount of error in the history of these trou-
> bled times. It will also teach the stern lessons of how nations may avoid
> war and revolution.
>
> Not being a government institution, it has never received a dime from
> government sources, and its scholars therefore can be as free as the Sierra
> winds in its use and the expression of objective truth.

The former president then turned to the world and to the next generation. "If
America is to be run by the people," he said, "it is the people who must think."
He continued,

> And we do not need to put on sackcloth and ashes to think. Nor should
> our minds work like a sundial which records only sunshine. Our thinking
> must square against some lessons of history, some principles of govern-
> ment and morals, if we would preserve the rights and dignity of men to
> which this nation is dedicated.
>
> The real test of our thinking is not so much the next election as it is
> the next generation . . .
>
> We must wish to maintain a dynamic progressive people. No nation
> can remain static and survive. But dynamic progress is not made with dy-
> namite. And that dynamite today is the geometrical increase of spending
> by our governments—Federal, state and local.

Hoover described the growth of bureaucracy, dependency, and the cost
in taxes for Americans to pay for it. A major reason for the increase was the
rise of pressure groups, but "aggression of groups and agencies against the
people as a whole is not a process of free men." The implications should not
be debated just in legislative halls but "in every school" and "in every corner grocery." He concluded, "My word to you, my fellow-citizens, on this
seventy-fifth birthday is this: The Founding Fathers dedicated the structure of
our government 'to secure the blessings of liberty to ourselves and our posterity.' We of this generation inherited this precious blessing. Yet as spendthrifts

we are on our way to rob posterity of its inheritance. The American people have solved many great crises in national life. The qualities of self-restraint, of integrity, of conscience and courage still live in our people. It is not too late to summon these qualities."[124] The *New York Times* regarded Hoover's speech as a "test for liberals," admitting that the "more the Government becomes the distributing agency of the people's money, the more its economic power grows and the faster we move in the direction of bureaucracy and a state-directed economy."[125] Arthur Krock wrote that Hoover's "statistical method" had made an "obvious impression" in Washington. But despite the "powerful voices" now being recited for reduced federal spending, Krock wrote that they were "pushing a stone uphill and (up to now), like Sisyphus in the underworld, has seen it roll down again . . . That may happen again, regardless of Mr. Hoover's warning of the consequences as he sees them."[126]

Collier's magazine observed Hoover's seventy-fifth birthday by noting that the former president had "been deluged with criticism," and "for years his political opponents unjustly held him responsible for the depression of the thirties. His distinguished career of public service was forgotten in a storm of insult and criticism." *Collier's* continued,

> A lesser man of lesser faith might well have grown bitter. He might have retired to a life of prosperous idleness which Mr. Hoover could always have had and which he always scorned.
>
> Instead, Mr. Hoover patiently endured his role of scapegoat. Rather than become embittered, he seemed to grow in warmth and understanding. He began to display some of the wit that he had so carefully concealed during his years in the White House. And in the last few years Americans have begun to take a little stock and think something good about Herbert Hoover.

Now Hoover's "crowning achievement" had come with his service as chairman of the Hoover Commission—"an exhausting as well as exhaustive labor that has won him the gratitude and respect of the entire country." *Collier's* concluded, "We are happy that Mr. Hoover's deserved reward of public esteem has come to him in his lifetime. We salute him on his birthday as a wise statesman, a steadfast guardian of America's great traditions, and a cheerful believer in a future based on those traditions."[127]

A few days later Hoover was invited to become honorary chairman of the Freedoms Foundation, but he replied that he had "arrived at a time in life when I cannot take on any more responsibilities. To 'lend' one's name gives one such a responsibility and implies to the public that I am exercising a part in the management—which I simply cannot do."[128] In fact, on his way back to New York from California Hoover was stricken with a gall bladder attack on the train and had to spend five painful hours until a doctor could meet the train at Elko, Nevada, to give him shots of morphine, sulfa, and penicillin so that he could continue on the train. Doctors and ambulances were alerted along the rest of the route to Chicago in case the former president needed them. But after a few hours of sleep, Hoover recovered enough to resume a gin rummy game with his secretary, telling reporters "It'll take more than this to finish me."[129]

The draft of his memoirs had, meanwhile, been reaching immense proportions, only a small portion of which would ultimately appear in published form. Work was sporadic on them, however, as Hoover's time was largely taken up with trying to get the Hoover Commission's recommendations adopted and with answering queries for his position on various issues.

In September a familiar theme reemerged—a declaration of GOP principles. A midwestern acquaintance wrote Hoover that some "prominent men here in Kansas City" had been "having some quiet conferences with the object of trying to formulate some suggestions to be sent to the Republican National Committee and other Republican leaders in the East." They had in mind "a concise and succinct Declaration of Principles" that would begin with an endorsement of the Hoover Commission Report and then add other items that the GOP could lay before the millions of "young Republican men and women, under thirty years of age, who want to be Republicans but have no fixed views of what the Republican Party stands for."[130] Hoover suggested a "resounding declaration against 'me too' policies; against the Welfare State; demanding a reduction of Government expenses; no deficits and a reference to our report would help." He agreed that the GOP and the country needed "to hear from the grassroots."[131]

In October, Hoover heard from General Douglas MacArthur in Tokyo that the Japanese government wanted a foreword from Hoover for a Japanese-language edition of the reports of the Hoover Commission. The Japanese had used the American example to launch their own governmental reorganization effort.[132] Hoover did send a foreword to MacArthur for the Japanese and took the opportunity to write the general, "Many of us on this side of the Pacific are getting very impatient with the failure of our government to insist upon a peace with Japan even if it does not include the obstructionist governments. One reason is that we would like to see you home again. We need reinforcements if our own way of life is not to be lost in this wilderness of a 'welfare state.'"[133]

As 1949 neared an end the recommendations of the Hoover Commission seemed to have acquired considerable momentum in Congress, encouraging Hoover to believe that a significant proportion of the suggested reforms would actually be adopted. The former president was pleased with the reception the work of the Citizens' Committee was receiving and with the growing public interest in the commission's report.[134] Secretary of Defense James Forrestal had opposed many of the commission's recommendations for the military structure, but when Forrestal was replaced by Louis Johnson there was a more positive attitude in the Defense Department. Evidence of a more cooperative attitude could be seen in Johnson's offer to send a military aide to meet Hoover's train when he arrived from New York to testify before the House Armed Services Committee and in his offer to fly Hoover back to New York in a military aircraft any time he chose to leave.[135]

In his testimony before the House Armed Services Committee on October 21, 1949, Hoover emphasized the necessity for teamwork in defense. The Defense Unification Act, which was an outgrowth of the Hoover Commission's recommendations, had, he pointed out, been "insistently demanded by the country by experienced officials and twice fully canvassed by the Congress. It was the outgrowth of lack of unity in command and huge waste in the last war followed by a continuing disunity and waste in peace." The Hoover Commission had "recommended a form of organization that should solve these questions," he said. "I see nothing in these hearings that would change those recommendations." From the standpoint of both efficiency and economy, Hoover argued, the Defense Unification Act should stand.[136]

In late November, Hoover received encouragement from Senator Henry Cabot Lodge Jr., when Lodge praised the purpose and work of the Hoover Commission and asked Hoover and his associates to prepare "a definite program of legislative action necessary to carry out the Commission's recommendations essentially and faithfully. The danger exists that without such a program the Congressional effort may bog down in piece-meal disagreements over technicalities and interpretations." "We need," Lodge concluded, "a program of specific legislation to effectuate the new government structure which the Commission proposes."[137] Hoover responded, "We will do just that and will consult you about it."[138]

In mid-December Hoover went on the attack again against government waste and in behalf of the commission's reforms. In a speech before a national reorganization conference he called for a bipartisan crusade for economy in government. The former president admitted that progress had been made in reorganizing the government along the lines the Hoover Commission had recommended, but the "most urgent" reforms had not been enacted—reforms that he said would not only save billions for taxpayers but would also make the federal government more efficient. The alternative to enacting such money-saving reforms, Hoover warned, was finding two "Frankensteins" striding the United States—higher taxes or inflation. From Truman in Florida came a promise to the delegates at the conference that he intended to continue to push the commission's reforms through Congress.[139]

An encouraging message also came from the director of the budget in January, when he wrote Hoover, "This Budget reflects somewhat of what you have hoped to attain in the field of Federal budgeting. It is certainly a step, and I hope a fairly extensive step in the right direction."[140] Hoover agreed that the "new Budget in the adopting of the performance principle is the greatest step in the advance of this problem since 1920." He was sorry, he wrote the director, that "few people on this earth will ever fully understand its importance to good government."[141] Gradually Hoover could feel that he was again making a real contribution to the shape and practices of the federal government as he saw the reforms recommended by the Hoover Commission being adopted. But he was unhappy because when Truman presented the commission's recommendations to Congress he had "so altered their contexts as to ruin the ultimate results."[142]

Hoover was also cheered by Republican activities in digging out evidence of the influence of communists and "fellow-travelers" in the federal government that he had for so long criticized. He wrote Congressman Richard Nixon in January, "The conviction of Alger Hiss was due to your patience and persistence alone. At last the stream of treason that existed in our Government has been exposed in a fashion that all may believe."[143] He was similarly supportive of the investigations by Senator Joseph McCarthy, and he objected to efforts of those like Senator Millard Tydings to obstruct McCarthy's probes.[144]

Hoover was also convinced "that the continuous pressures upon the anti-communist National Government of China contributed to the breakdown of prestige and strength of Chiang Kai-shek and the encouragement of Mao Tse-tung." He told Senator William Knowland that he opposed recognition of the communist government of China and favored continued support for the Chiang Kai-shek government on Taiwan and the defense of that island and adjacent islands, to (1) create a "wall against communism in the Pacific"; (2) protect Japan and the Philippines; (3) prevent Chinese diplomatic establishments abroad from becoming "nests of Chinese conspiracies"; (4) prevent another communist member of the UN Security Council; (5) keep the Chinese communists from participating in peacemaking with Japan; (6) provide at least a "symbol of resistance" that would provide "a better basis for salvation of southeastern Asia"; and (7) to ensure "there would be at least a continued home of some time turning China in the paths of freedom again."[145] Knowland released Hoover's letter to the press and told him it had been "given an excellent play in all the newspapers of the Country and I think it has done a great deal to help focus attention on this important part of the world."[146] Hoover also suggested to Patrick Hurley, former ambassador to China, that he publish the story of his failure to achieve peace between the nationalists and communists in China, since it "might stem the undoubted determination of these left-wingers to recognize and support Mao Tse-tung and the communization of China."[147]

Hoover and Knowland were not, however, averse to providing food relief to deal with the famine conditions in China that followed the conclusion of the civil war there. The two conferred over the telephone late in March, with the result being a proposal from Knowland to Secretary of State Dean Acheson that surplus American food supplies be directed to the Chinese people, on condition that the people be notified of source of the relief via the Voice of America and other channels and that the food be supplied to all who needed it and not only to those who supported the communist government. Knowland suggested the creation of a relief commission similar to the Commission for

Relief in Belgium (CRB) under Hoover during World War I, with the distribution of food to be handled under the supervision of committees made up of both Chinese and American members. This should be done, Knowland told Acheson, "as a humanitarian move without in any way necessitating the recognition by this government of the regime in whose area the famine conditions prevail."[148] Acheson believed, however, that for the time being "the disadvantages of attempting to offer governmental relief outweigh the advantages." He did not, however, discourage private relief initiatives.[149]

A few weeks later, Hoover added that the whole "China discussion relates to a segment of the cold war against Communism upon which we are now spending over $20 billion a year." The war, he told Knowland, was being fought "on many fronts—the European front, the Mediterranean front, the Far Eastern front and the home front." The security of Taiwan "would admittedly strengthen the Asiatic front," and American military leaders had hitherto considered it "a necessary part of the defense of our boys now stationed on the Asiatic front." But, he said, if the military now changed its mind and said defense of the island was no longer of importance or if they considered war with the Soviet Union a likely outcome of US defense of the island, then Hoover "would bow to their judgment." But three questions still remained in either case, and the answer to the first was that the United States should not recognize communist China. As for the second, the question of what to do about the Chiang government of Taiwan, Hoover did not come out forthrightly now for the defense of the nationalist government there, but he did say that American policy "should be determined now so as to save further embarrassments in the future." The third question concerned the people of Taiwan. Hoover pointed out that their population was only slightly less than that of Greece and that the Atlantic Charter had promised self-determination. Although he did not come out forthrightly for their defense, his memorandum for Knowland implied more support for their independence from communist China than for the Chiang government.[150]

Knowland replied that he did not think a statement from Hoover along the lines of his memorandum was appropriate at the moment, since the seizure of consulates by the Chinese communists had created "a great deal of opposition to recognition from the President's own Party and it does not now look as though recognition is imminent." The question remained, however, whether the United States was to commit itself to the defense of Taiwan or to regard any communist aggression against that island as a logical extension of the civil war. Here the issue revolved, in Knowland's mind, around the importance of Taiwan for American security, and on that conflicting views had been given since 1945 and were still being given. Certainly the opinions of General MacArthur, supreme commander in the Far East, and Admiral Radford, commander in chief in the Pacific, should be solicited before any decision was made by the State Department.[151] For Hoover, the "crux of the situation" was the recognition of communist China and whether "the proposed sacrifice" of Taiwan was "part of that program."[152]

In May, Hoover wrote Knowland again that "recognition of the Moscow satellite government in China would be a further surrender in the cold war which General Bradley intimates we are losing" and would be "a further acceptance of the sweep of the Kremlin's aggressive militarism, agnosticism and Red imperialism." He added, "It is a system of immorality and without compassion that we cannot accept. It would plant another nest of Communist propagandists and agents in Washington and in every Chinese Consulate over the land. It would betray millions of Chinese still struggling against a slave state." "If the United Nations is ever to be useful to the human race," he told Knowland, "it must free itself of Communist domination—not add to it."[153] Later that month Hoover wrote again, "It looks like we will have to go into battle over Truman's promise not to oppose Mao Tse-tung's entry into the United Nations."[154]

In February 1950, Allan Nevins, author of a negative review in the *Saturday Review* of Hoover's *Challenge to Liberty* in 1934, importuned the former president to do an interview for the Columbia University oral history project. Not surprisingly, Nevins received a reply from an assistant secretary, who informed him that Hoover was away and that his commitments made it unlikely that he would have time to meet with Nevins.[155] It was a tragic loss to the Columbia Oral History Collection that might have been avoided had someone else but Nevins requested an interview.

Curiously enough, the former president was silent during the early months of 1949 when the idea of American commitment to the defense of Europe under the North Atlantic Treaty Organization (NATO) concept was evolving. Perhaps this silence was due to the overlap between that debate and the final months of the Hoover Commission's work and because Hoover was involved in the bipartisan effort to get the commission's recommendations adopted by Congress. Not even in Edgar Rickard's diary of his private conversations with Hoover is there any indication that the former president was monitoring the Senate debate over the treaty.

But a year later, when the business of the Hoover Commission had ceased to require so much of his time, Hoover began to devote attention to the NATO issue. After meeting with Senator Kenneth Wherry in May, Hoover sent him a memorandum dealing with Secretary of State Acheson's forthcoming visit to Europe to consult with leaders of NATO. There were, he wrote Wherry, "grave questions in this matter as to which the American people need information. In fact, we need a foreign policy." Hoover reiterated his concern that the United States was "economically overstrained" and still unable to give Americans the "services and relief of taxes that they should enjoy." The enormous strains on the economy and on taxpayers were due to the "Marshall Plan, the subsidizing of European armament and the demands of our own defense."[156]

Before appropriating more money the people needed to know what the administration's policies were and what the policies were of the European nations "for whom we are making huge sacrifices and efforts." Referring to newsmagazine assessments of Western Europe's puny military strength in comparison with that of the Soviet Union, Hoover wondered whether the time had not come "when we should find out beyond any question of a doubt whether the Nations of Western Europe and Southern Asia are willing to do far more themselves for their own defense." How many of them would stand with the United States against the Soviets if the cold war heated up? Hoover suggested that the will of the Marshall Plan recipient nations should be tested by insisting that they use approximately three billion dollars in counterpart funds for defense purposes and that they also be asked "to contribute something still more out of taxation." It was unfair to ask American taxpayers to shoulder greater burdens for people who were unwilling to do more for themselves.

With the United States already overextended economically—and overtaxed, according to Hoover's view—a new factor intruded to further drain the American economy when the communist government of North Korea invaded the Republic of Korea (South Korea) in June 1950. Hoover quickly supported American assistance to the South Koreans with a public statement: "When the United States draws the sword, there is only one course for our people. Like others, I have opposed many of our foreign policies, but now is not the time to argue origins, mistakes, responsibilities, or consequences. There is only one way out of such situations as this: that is to win. To win we must have unity of purpose and action."[157] He wrote Truman that he would "be glad to be of any service within my limitations at this time."[158] Truman responded with warm appreciation for Hoover's statement of support and added that if events required, "you may rest assured that I will want your help and advice."[159]

But as was so often the case, Hoover's public support masked serious private reservations. He was far from happy with the size of the American military commitment in Korea, and the limited assistance provided by other UN members was evidence to him that he had been correct in his doubts concerning the usefulness of the United Nations and of the will of the Western European nations to stand with the United States to resist communist aggression. When Senator Homer Ferguson solicited his views in mid-July concerning a UN resolution Ferguson had proposed to "brand any nation assisting the North Koreans directly or indirectly as an aggressor against the United Nations," Hoover told him their thinking ran "exactly on the same line. We must know who are with us and with what?"[160] As matters stood, he told Ferguson, the United States might perhaps have the support of Canada and Australia in a war with Russia. This was not much to show for the enormous expenditure of economic and military aid to Western Europe. After the Korean situation had been resolved, Hoover would "pull back our military actions to the Western Hemisphere. A war with Russia, with the support we now have in sight, could never end until we were economically exhausted—and we will be [economically exhausted] by a condition of huge armament for a few years even if we have no war with Russia."[161]

In a July 11 speech at the dedication of the William Allen White Memorial in Emporia, Kansas, Hoover called for every American to support the president in meeting the challenge in Korea. He recalled that he and White had been together at the Versailles Peace Conference after World War I, where they had "grieved over its political settlements" and dealt "with the bloody rise of Communism in the world." The two had then supported American entry into the League of Nations, and with the renewed outbreak of war in Europe in 1939 both had been "opposed to American's joining in the war," but after Pearl Harbor "both gave undeviating support to our Government." Hoover told his audience, "Today there is but one enemy of peace in the world," and that enemy was Marxist-Leninism. "War," Hoover argued was "justified only as an instrument for a specific consequence. That consequence for America was lasting peace." But the United States had strayed from that major objective in four ways. For one, its purposes had been "confused in both wars by crusades with glorious phrases about the personal freedom of man," ignoring that "we cannot change ideas in the minds of men and races with machine guns or battleships." The United States should "never again enter upon such a crusade" but should concentrate on its own defense. Second, the United States had mistakenly concentrated on winning battles rather than on winning a lasting peace. Third, in the peace settlements after the two world wars, the United States "departed from our true path and left many nations in such a plight as to become the prey of others. We yielded to the spirits of greedy imperialism in other nations and of vindictiveness and revenge," thereby sowing "the dragon's teeth of still another war." Fourth, the attempts to suppress aggression through international bodies had failed, because the League of Nations had "turned into an instrument to protect imperial spoils of war" and the United Nations had "turned into an instrument to protect Red imperialism." Hoover advocated reorganizing the United Nations "without the Communists in it," turning it into an instrument of defense against Communist aggression as it seemed to be doing in Korea.[162]

In his annual talk to the Bohemian Club encampment a few days later, Hoover dropped the characteristic levity and gave his listeners a serious review of the problems that faced the United States in the summer of 1950. For one, the United Nations was not functioning effectively as an instrument against communist aggression, and it would be even less effective if the Peoples' Republic of China (PRC) were admitted to the Security Council. The United States should make clear that it would use its veto, if necessary, to deny membership to the PRC. Korea had also demonstrated that Western Europe, with the exception of Great Britain, lacked the will for a war with the

Soviet Union and even the will to prepare for its own defense. Despite the fact that the manpower and industrial capacity of Western Europe were greater in 1950, the nations there had only one-fifth the army divisions they had put into the field for the two world wars, and a successful ground war could not be fought against the Russians with such numbers. The United States must rely on air and sea power to defend itself.[163]

The United Nations should demand that its members "refrain from economic, military or other aids to any" aggressor nations like North Korea. If the Soviet Union vetoed such a resolution, they should be kicked out of the UN. Another possibility was to introduce a resolution "denouncing Russia as an aggressor for having given military aid to [North] Korea," and even to impose "economic sanctions against Russia and her satellites for giving aid to an aggressor." If the United States proved unable to bring about increased solidarity and commitment among the noncommunist nations in resisting Soviet aggression, then it should "retreat into the Western Hemisphere to save our own civilization from exhaustion." Hoover did not consider that a desirable course of action, but the United States possessed the capacity to be self-sufficient if necessary.

As for the growing revelations of communists and their sympathizers in the government and other institutions, Hoover suggested laws against conspiracy and treason so that the government could "move directly against any publication or any persons attending any meeting of Communists where subversive activities were discussed." Intellectuals might believe in, or sympathize with, "abstract Communism, for that was part of academic freedom, but when such ideas moved from theory to subversive action they ought to be targets of the FBI." The former president had no patience for anyone who refused to take a loyalty oath to the government, but he was not in favor of a federal law to compel it. In conclusion he told the Bohemian Club group, "Today most of the American people have abandoned that supreme fantasy of all history which has been promoted since the Russian Revolution. That folly was the hallucination that this was one world. There are two worlds. One world is militaristic, imperialistic, aggressive, atheistic, and without compassion. The other world still holds to belief in God, free nations, human dignity and peace."

When Senator Taft asked for his views concerning any economic controls that might be needed because of the Korean War, Hoover responded that the United States was simultaneously involved in both a minor war and in a preparedness program for a major war. While the Korean War would cause "scarcely a ripple" in the American economy, the preparedness effort required some controls to curb inflation. These included prohibition of hoarding and the accumulation of excessive inventories, limitations on installment credit, increased excise taxes on nonessentials to discourage unnecessary buying, and cuts in government expenditures. No controls were needed on commodities and processing, and he did not advocate all-embracing price, wage, and rationing controls at the present time, only some controls over materials and manufacturing that were a military necessity. "Our greatest domestic danger at this time," he told Taft, "is shock hysteria in the public which leads the Congress to unnecessary surrenders of freedom."[164]

When Louis Johnson left the new Defense Department that had been created largely as a result of the Hoover Commission's recommendations, he wrote Hoover to "thank you for the friendship and support you have so consistently manifested, over a period of so many years. I shall always treasure the high privilege that has been accorded me, in having been permitted to put into effect the recommendations of the Hoover Commission with respect to the Department of Defense." It was the work of the commission, and Hoover's own efforts, he conceded, that were largely responsible for the reforms having been enacted.[165]

As the 1950 congressional elections approached, the 76-year-old former president contemplated what his role should be, writing one correspondence that he had "agreed to some work in this campaign as I believe it is the last chance for our country as we have known it."[166] When he was asked to give speeches, Hoover responded that he had been "awaiting the outcome of this three ring circus in foreign relations (plus a gall bladder attack) before settling anything in the nature of a public address." He had decided that any speech would be most effective if it were not in a "partisan frame" but was rather an analysis of where the Truman policies were leading the country. But a few days before Hoover was to deliver his major speech over CBS, Truman was scheduled to give one of his own, so that the former president decided he would have wait and see what Truman had to say before preparing his own speech.[167] He found Republican candidates "fighting well all over the country" but handicapped by voter preoccupation with the war in Korea.[168] Hoover's speech would in large part be an "I told you so" effort. As he wrote Felix Morley, "I was roundly denounced when I spoke out on the UN some months ago—but they had come to it. Likewise, I was the first fellow that demanded the protection of Formosa [Taiwan] and was denounced as a war monger—so I do not expect to find any favor from these quarters."[169]

In his speech on October 19, Hoover traced the course of America's relations with the Soviet Union from the time the nation "first entered this swamp of lost statesmanship when we recognized the Communist government in 1933," through the communist attempts to subvert the US government, the Soviet's wartime alliance against Germany, and her broken agreements and vetoes by the Soviet Union in the United Nations. The Russians had engineered the attack on South Korea, he charged, and "every day they engage in defamation of the American people." Soviet expansion could only be contained through "an effective organized phalanx of the non-Communist world," but Western Europe had shown no disposition to join in such an effort. They could muster only thirty active army divisions against the Soviet potential of 175 divisions, and the United States could only supply a minor part of the deficiency. Despite all the loans and gifts from the United States, the Western Europeans had created no significant defense capability by 1950. This meager result from American sacrifices was, Hoover said, "deeply disappointing to a growing body of Americans." Americans were beginning to question whether the Europeans, except for Great Britain, had "the will to fight, or even the will to preparedness." It was time for the United States to demand more than words from those nations; the United States should be willing to help Europe, but only Europeans did "most of it themselves—and do it fast." As for suggestions that ten American combat divisions should be sent to Europe, Hoover insisted that such an action could result only in "a slaughter of American boys unless many times that number were standing by their sides. We should say, and at once, that we shall provide no more money until a definitely unified and sufficient European army is in sight. And further that ten American divisions will not be landed until then."[170]

It was time, Hoover insisted, for the other nations of the world to help in shouldering the burden of their own defense, for the United States could not "long endure the present drain on our economy." He added, "But if we do not find real military action of powerful strength in Western Europe; if there is no definite and effective mobilization of the other members of the United Nations so as to take up the major burden of their own defenses, then we had better reconsider our whole relations to the problem. In that event, we had better quit talking and paying and consider holding the Atlantic Ocean with Britain (if they wish) as one frontier, and the Pacific Ocean with an armed Japan and other islands as the other frontier." Hoover had made it clear that he did not want to retreat from the communist front and would only contemplate doing so if the other nations of the world were unwilling to man that front with the United States. If not, then the United States should settle for "an uneasy peace within the economic burdens which the United States can bear." Hoover's speech was his opening effort in what would come to be referred to as "the Great Debate."

A few days before the election, Hoover invited Robert Johnson, head of the Citizens' Committee, to dinner at the Waldorf Astoria with 16 others, including Bernard Baruch and Dwight Eisenhower. He told Johnson,

> The reason for this little get together is to consider what might be done in respect to one phase of reducing inflation dangers. There is need to secure public support for reduction and post-ponement of nonmilitary expenditures which have increased in the Federal, State and local levels by about $22 billion since 1939. Part of this increase is of course necessary. Some of the gentlemen invited have suggested that a non-partisan, rapid, brief mobilization of existing public groups might be effected without difficulty or expense if leadership could be provided. It is solely to get your thinking on the matter for some sort of complete, effective organization that I am asking you to sit with us.[171]

Disappointingly, however, nothing resulted from the conference, and Hoover
suggested that the Citizens' Committee add the call for postponement of
spending to its campaign for enactment of the Hoover Commission reforms.[172]

By this time the issue of communist subversion in the federal government and elsewhere had become a major controversy, largely as a result of
the investigations and charges of people like Senator Joseph McCarthy. Late
in 1950 the controversy brought Hoover another invitation to service from
President Truman, who wrote that he had decided to appoint a bipartisan
commission from all segments of American life to investigate the extent of
the alleged communist penetration into the government. He proposed to
appoint Hoover as chairman of the committee, and Truman told him that if
he would serve, it "could not only restore the confidence of the people in the
organization of the government, but could help the foreign policy situation
very much."[173]

Hoover told the president that despite his age he did not "wish to ever
refuse service to the country," but he doubted that there were "any consequential card-carrying Communists in the government or, if there are, they
should be known to the FBI." The real source of lack of confidence in the
government, he suggested, came from the conviction that there were people
there (not Communists) who had "disastrously advised on policies in relation
to Communist Russia" and that they were still in the government. To investigate the past and present behavior of such people would require a widespread
and extensive inquiry, and Congress would probably duplicate its efforts by
conducting its own, anyway. Hoover concluded,

> Therefore, it seems to me that any inquiry as to "Communists in the govern-
> ment" by an informal commission would not be likely to satisfy the public or
> to restore confidence. I dislike indeed to respond in terms of declination to any
> request of yours, as I would like greatly to be helpful to you in these troublous
> [sic] times. In that direction, may I suggest that a statement might be issued by
> you that you would be glad if the Congress would either create such a com-
> mission, or would itself make an inquiry on the broadest basis such as I have
> outlined, both as to the past and present. That very statement by you would
> greatly restore confidence in the administration's foreign policy makers.[174]

CHAPTER 12

The Great Debate

Opening Fire

On September 26, 1950, the North Atlantic Council announced agreement on the establishment of a unified force for the defense of Europe. On December 18, General Dwight D. Eisenhower was designated as supreme commander of the NATO armed forces. On the same day that Eisenhower's selection was announced, influential liberal columnist Walter Lippmann lashed out at Truman's foreign policies. Americans, he wrote, had been "shaken" by the "demonstration of misinformation, miscalculation, and misjudgment at the highest levels of decision and command" involved in the decision to allow "virtually all of the American Army and all of its reserves" to be "sucked into a peninsula of Asia in the presence and in defiance of overwhelmingly superior forces." It was time, Lippmann wrote, for a new doctrine to guide American policy, one in which the "central principles" would be "that North America is an island, a continental island to be sure, but still in relation to the Old World an island. The people of North America can never meet on even terms the armed forces of the Eurasian Continent." Lippmann added, "The true American doctrine—both in defense and offense—is to recognize limitations of and to exploit the advantages of our island character—our inferiority in manpower, our superiority in technology and in production, the oceans of sea and air around us which offer the means of a flexible defense and a highly mobile offense."

The American people, he said, wanted "to increase the military power of the United States and to get out of entanglements like Korea. There is little doubt, I think, that the main tide is running in the direction of an armed isolation." Lippmann concluded, "Our allies abroad will be well-advised, therefore, for their own security as well as for our own, to work with and not against an American withdrawal from the overextended commitments of the Truman doctrine." In his column the next day Lippmann added, "The new doctrine will have to found the defense of the United States and of the Atlantic community upon seapower and airpower—and along with them upon a diplomacy which is conceived and is planned by men who know the limitations and also the advantages of sea and air power."[1]

It was one of the few times that Hoover and the noted columnist had been in agreement, although Hoover's own emphasis was on air power. As early as 1947 the former president had begun to formulate a position on American defense policy founded in air power. For some time he had carried on a correspondence with Bonner Fellers, a retired general and former MacArthur aide who in 1947 became director of public relations for the Veterans of Foreign Wars (VFW). Early in September Fellers wrote Hoover that he had convinced the VFW to take up advocacy of peace through air power at its convention that year. If the convention approved, "the principal VFW objective for next year in the Congress and with the American people will be the creation of an American air force in being second to none." Fellers asked Hoover to pass along to Senator Taft an article he had written on "Our National Security," and Hoover did so.[2] Taft responded that he agreed entirely with Fellers's position, since "common sense demands that we maintain a complete superiority in the air."[3] This emphasis on air power for American defense would soon become a basic principle in the Hoover-Taft approach to American military policy.

Even as Lippmann was writing his columns, Hoover was busy preparing a speech he had scheduled for December 20. He regarded the speech as one of the most important he had given. He wrote to Raymond Moley and others, "In an 'emergency' on June 29, 1941, I made an appraisal of the forces moving in the world. I advised arming to the teeth and a policy of watching and waiting before we committed ourselves. I pointed out the obvious disaster if we jumped in. I was proved right after infinite losses to our country." Hoover predicted that this new speech was "likely to be no more welcome than the one ten years ago."[4] To Taft he wrote, "The task I am setting in my speech . . . is to align us against commitment of American forces in Europe—or anywhere else until we can see clearly what support we will have this time." Aware that he was likely to be criticized for his position, Hoover added, "I hope I may have some defense if that becomes necessary." He did not, he told Taft, "expect our Eastern seaboard press to be any more enthusiastic" about this speech than they had been about the one in June 1941.[5]

Senator William Jenner wrote Hoover a few days before the speech that he had learned from Wherry of the former president's planned speech, and he told Hoover, "Never have the American people stood in such dire need of wise and courageous American leadership; therefore, I want you to know how heartened I am that you are again going to raise your voice in a grim warning of where we are headed and of what we must now undertake to do if we are to save these United States". He assured the former president of his "whole-hearted support."[6]

Hoover's speech was delivered as American forces reeled back in Korea before the onslaught of Chinese Communist "volunteers." The former president had advised General MacArthur weeks before not to pursue the North Korean armies north to the Yalu River but to "stop and dig in on the short line across Korea—and then use his Air Force on any armies north of that area." He had advised this because of the "oncoming winter, the impossibility of an adequate campaign in those mountains and temperature," as well as "to await the summation of action in the United Nations and in Europe, and the inadequacy of the forces which had been provided for in Korea."[7]

Hoover's speech began with a survey of the global military situation. By contrast with the eight hundred million people and over three hundred combat army divisions of the communist world, only the British Commonwealth and the United States had shown any disposition to defend the free world. Between them there were about three hundred million people, and only about sixty combat divisions, but powerful air and naval forces. From this Hoover concluded that it was impossible to defeat the Soviet Union and its satellites in a land war. Moreover, the United States was "already economically strained by government expenditures." Hoover argued for the defense of the "Western Hemisphere Gibraltar of Western Civilization" and, through the use of air and sea power, for defense of the Atlantic and Pacific oceans, with Great Britain as the frontier of American defense in the Atlantic and Japan, Taiwan, and the Philippines as the American frontier in the Pacific.[8]

Such a strategy meant that the United States must concentrate on the development of air and sea forces rather than a large army. In this way the United States could, after the initial large expenditures on planes and ships, cut its military expenditures, balance its budget, and free itself "from the dangers of inflation and economic degeneration." Economically strong, the United States could continue to feed the hungry of the world and to assist other countries in arming themselves against communism. But before the United States furnished any further military aid to Europe, those nations must demonstrate their determination to defend themselves by organizing and equipping combat divisions in numbers adequate to "erect a sure dam against the Red flood." That must be done before the United States landed "another man or another dollar on their shores." To act otherwise would be to encourage another Korea, which "would be a calamity to Europe as well as to us." America's policy toward Europe should be one "of watchful waiting." This was not isolationism, Hoover argued, but just the opposite. And eventually, he hoped, "the millions of non-Communist peoples of the world" would awaken to their dangers, and "the evils of Communism and the disintegration of their racial controls will bring their own disintegration."

Hoover's office reported a "tremendous, favorable response" after the speech, with the telephone ringing continually and a flood of telegrams that began even before he had returned to the office from delivering it. Not one response had been unfavorable.[9] The gauntlet was now down and the "Great Debate," as the media referred to it, had warmed up, for Hoover's position was in stark contrast to that of the Truman administration's commitment to the defense of Western Europe, a commitment symbolized by Eisenhower's imminent departure for Europe to take command of Western defense forces there. A check through the *Congressional Record* for a comparison of comment in Congress concerning the December 20, 1950, speech with that for the June 1941 speech found that there had been little comment over the earlier speech in contrast "with the amount of comment which the speech of December 20, 1950 is receiving in the Record."[10]

Typically press coverage of the debate distorted Hoover's position into advocacy of withdrawal to the Western Hemisphere, when in fact the former president had only offered that as an alternative should the Western European nations not shoulder more of the burden of their own defense. The *Wilmington Star* of North Carolina wrote of the debate, "Meanwhile, nothing has been in the news in a long time so capable of provoking discussion. American newspapers, largely guided by their party affiliations—as was Mr. Hoover—were prompt to seize upon his New York speech and give it commendation or condemnation." It found "commendation" by the *Seattle Times*, the *San Francisco Chronicle*, the *Indianapolis Star*, and the *Atlanta Constitution*, with condemnation by the *New York Times*, the *Washington Evening Star*, the *Pittsburgh Post-Gazette*, and others.[11] Hoover's own clipping service indicated that newspapers with over 31 million in circulation supported him fully (with another 3.7 million giving partial support), while those with under 11.5 million (mainly in New York and Washington, DC) were opposed.[12]

The internationalist *New York Herald Tribune* was charitable enough to admit that Hoover's position was not "isolationist," since it embraced not only the Western Hemisphere but also Britain, Japan, Taiwan, and the Philippines, but it coined a new term to describe the Hoover doctrine—"retreatism." Retreatism, it admitted, had gained "increased stature" because of Hoover's advocacy of it, and it represented "a body of opinion that must be reckoned with in the formation of American policy," because it appealed "to the angry frustration which events in Korea have aroused and because it offers what purports to be a cheaper way to defend America than by assisting allies."[13] Raymond Moley, in *Newsweek*, wrote that it "would be wholly irrational and bitterly unfair to call this isolationism. It will be called that, however, by some people who believe that there should be no limits on American commitments of blood and money, anywhere, any time or in any form." He added, "This program so earnestly presented by Herbert Hoover should be American policy. And to hasten the day when it can be American policy, the Republican Party should adopt it as its own."[14] From the other side of the aisle in the Senate came a warm note from Senator Harry Byrd: "Your address was a powerful one and made a most profound impression upon the country. I have received a large number of letters commending it."[15]

Senator Homer Ferguson wrote the former president that he had "done a marvelous job in arousing the American people to the dangers of our present course of action." He told Hoover, "Support for your views runs strong in every mail we received. And the great debate you touched off will clarify the principles that have long been clouded in the propaganda of those who deal irresponsibly with the American national interest." The American people, he added, were "not falling" for the attempt to label Hoover an isolationist with their smear tactics.[16] Another Senator, Thye of Minnesota, wrote a friend that Hoover's position was "significant, particularly as it gave warning to the countries of Western Europe that they must do something themselves." Congressman Lawrence H. Smith, of Wisconsin, a member of the House Foreign Affairs Committee, wrote Hoover that his speech had "rung the bell. People everywhere are talking about it. Republicans in Congress should make it the rallying point for a new approach in foreign policy."[17][18]

For the liberal magazine *The Nation*, however, Hoover's speech indicated that he had been "captured" by world communism, for if his advice were followed it would mean the "Russians would be free, for all we cared, to grab what they could get, including what they want most in the world—the industrial power of the Ruhr, Belgium, and France with which to combine the vast man-power of Russia and China." Although Hoover had declared his opposition to "appeasement," *The Nation* averred, "inevitably his doctrine smells to Europeans not merely of isolationism but of appeasement." *The Nation* concluded,

> It appears, then, that one wing of the Republicans, claiming to be the fiercest opponents of communism, have dealt what may prove a deadly blow to democratic prestige the world over. They have afforded Moscow a wonderful opportunity to sow the seeds of doubt and dissension among our allies; they have encouraged the "neutralist" elements in Europe; they have weakened the position of the American, British, and French negotiators, who may shortly sit down with the Russians in a new effort to reach an understanding on Germany and other outstanding issues. It will not be easy to repair the damage that has been done; it may not be possible to do so at all unless the Republican Party redefines its policy in plain terms and convinces the world that it is not seeking an escape from reality to a hemispheric ivory tower.

The other major liberal journal, the *New Republic*, opened its pages to Harold Ickes, hardly a foreign policy expert, who wrote that Hoover was "about the last man to be taken seriously by the American people on international relations." The former secretary of the interior argued that Hoover "would be held in higher esteem and respect if he should desist from his untimely and badly-conceived advice, the only effect of which is to confound and confuse, not only the people of the United States, but the nations to which we have given the right to look to us for succor in our common peril." It was especially ironic, Ickes wrote, that Hoover was attacking Truman's policies after it was the president who had made Hoover—this "Presidential DP [displaced person]"—chairman of the commission on reorganization of the federal government, thus giving him the "chance to rehabilitate himself in the public opinion that he had forfeited by his unfortunate administration of American domestic and foreign affairs during his Presidential term."[19]

Such criticism, Raymond Moley pointed out in *Newsweek*, ought not to blind critics to the fact that Hoover "was speaking the minds of millions of Americans." "Nor," Moley said, "should the shock occasioned in Europe by Hoover disturb us, because it will take some plain speaking to awaken the nations over there to their deadly peril." Moley explained that Hoover wanted to make sure that "before we wander vaguely in pursuit of various 'points,' including Point Four, we take note of what should be called Point One. And that is to make sure beyond all doubt that we are strong within the area described and that we waste none of our power in peripheral defenses which in sound military judgment we cannot defend. To weaken ourselves through indiscriminate adventures is to make of ourselves a poor protector when genuine needs arise."[20]

President Truman quickly reiterated the position of his administration that Western Europe's defense was vital to the security of the United States.[21] Hoover would no doubt have agreed with both the *Herald Tribune* and Truman if only the Europeans, themselves, were as committed to their defense as American internationalists were. This was the point that both of his critics neglected to mention. When Senator H. Alexander Smith championed the Hoover doctrine in the Senate, the former president wrote him, "I know how difficult it is to defend this creature—but you did a great job and I am grateful." He suspected that "Congress is going to get a jolt of public opinion such as it has not seen for a long time."[22]

Hoover was correct, as members of both houses of Congress were inundated with mail and wires in support of the Hoover doctrine. Richard Nixon wrote the former president on December 22 that he had "already received over 100 wires this morning indicating enthusiastic approval of your speech last night." He told Hoover he was "sure your comments will have an excellent effect in developing a more realistic approach to the critical problems we face today."[23] Former New Deal brain truster Raymond Moley also supported Hoover's doctrine in his newspaper column and in *Newsweek* magazine and wrote to Hoover, "I don't think a speech was ever at so necessary a moment in so clearly reflecting the feeling of the country." Moley opined that it would be "of immense help in creating a real Republican policy in the new Congress."[24] Felix Morley wrote that Hoover's anticipation of a "strongly hostile" reaction had been unjustified. "Of course," he wrote, "there has been the conventional sniping from professional New Deal apologists, but so far as we have an independent press it seems to me that the reaction has been quite strongly favorable." He added, "If the Europeans have any real desire to unite for self-preservation your speech will stimulate it. If they have no such desire, you have at least pointed to the course that we shall eventually have to follow."[25] Landon wrote Hoover that it had "been a long time since a talk by anyone has rung the bell as your last one has done." The Kansan decried the misinterpretation of the speech by administration spokesmen but found general understanding and agreement on "the kernel of your talk and that is that we can't save people who are unwilling to save themselves."[26] Felix Morley found support for Hoover's position building and said that the "New Deal columnists who have had everything their way for so long are running around in circles down here [Washington]."[27]

John Foster Dulles, Republican member of Truman's State Department, delivered a speech nine days after Hoover's that was widely billed as the administration's "reply" to Hoover, although Dulles wrote Hoover that it was an invention of the press since he intended the speech to be, instead, "a year-end discussion of the critical international situation." Dulles admitted that his point of view would be somewhat different from Hoover's but added that he agreed with much of what the former president had said and hoped that Hoover would agree with much of what he had to say. "I think it is very healthy to have a great nation debate upon the grave issues of our time," he wrote. Enclosing a copy of the letter to Hoover with one he wrote to Taft, Dulles told the senator, "The State Department publicity people pulled this one on me. Actually, as you will see, my speech tonight pretty much represents the strategic concept which you and I discussed."[28]

Dulles's speech erected a "straw man" in describing advocates of making the United States a Gibraltar of self-defenses and then demolished them. On the contrary, Dulles said, in the event of a Soviet invasion, "there is only one effective defense for us and for others. That is the capacity to counterattack. That is the ultimate deterrent." Dulles urged an increase in America's air power, a bigger navy, increased stockpiles of weapons, and a greater ground force to discourage aggression, and he insisted that they be started immediately, regardless of sacrifice.[29] The speech seems scarcely to have caused a ripple among the public, despite the ballyhoo of newspapers like the *New York Times*. The *Times* found the response to the speech to be "insignificant" and "disappointing," which it admitted was "in sharp contrast to the heavy public response resulting from the Hoover speech." Democratic senator Herbert Lehman, a supporter of Truman's foreign policy, admitted that his office had received "only two pieces of mail on Dulles, whereas the Hoover mail was still arriving."[30] The *Houston Post* found Dulles's arguments filled with "defects in his reasoning, some contradictions and inconsistencies which leaves one far from convinced or assured."[31] In fact, Hoover was no advocate of an American Gibraltar, nor would he have disagreed with much Dulles said except for his advocacy of a larger ground army.

Senator Taft joined the fray with a speech in the Senate on January 5, 1951, that took up many of the same points Hoover had posed two weeks earlier and propounded similar policies. He, too, called for reliance on air and sea power for defense not only of the Western Hemisphere but also of the Atlantic and Pacific—everywhere that it was possible to exclude communism by other than the use of land armies. He added, "Of course, Mr. Hoover's recent speech was completely misrepresented by the Administration press in this regard. He did not advocate retirement to the American continent. He only urged that emphasis be place on our defense of the Atlantic and Pacific oceans, as it should be particularly if all our allies should abandon us." Taft, though, broadened the scope of the American defense perimeter to include Indonesia, Australia, and New Zealand, even while he joined Hoover in opposing the commitment of American ground troops for the defense of Europe until those nations showed a greater disposition to defend themselves. And like Hoover, Taft expressed concern over the implications for the American economy of the massive expenditures on defense under Truman. Echoing the former president, Taft argued that the United States "must not so extend" itself "as to threaten economic collapse or inflation, for a productive and free America is the last bastion of liberty."[32] The senator regarded his speech as fundamentally "in accord with Mr. Hoover's theory, although I . . . tried to make it somewhat less uncompromising."

Hoover's speech attracted the predictable distortions and smears, despite widespread support from newspapers and the public, and so did Taft's. Taft wrote a friend that "the international press in the East and the New Deal columnists are determined to involve us in the project of a large American army in Europe, and they are doing everything possible to smear statements like that of President Hoover or my own."[33] When Senator Knowland queried him concerning the editorial and other responses to his speech, Hoover forwarded to him a breakdown from his clipping service that showed newspapers with 68 percent of the circulation supported his position, those with 8 percent showed partial support, and only those with 24 percent were opposed. The only areas showing significant opposition to his program were in the Southern and South Atlantic states. But influential newspapers in New York City opposed it.[34]

A typical distortion was that offered by the moderator of the "American Forum of the Air," in mid-January, when he summarized Hoover's position as follows: "He wants the United States to pull out of Europe and Asia; to preserve this Western Hemisphere Gibraltar. He would cut off all aid to Western Europe until it showed spirit and strength in defending itself against Red Russia. Administration leaders have called this isolationism, a wave of defeat and frustration, an act of appeasement." Fortunately, Senator Everett Dirksen was present in this instance to point out that the description had omitted Hoover's call for defense of the Atlantic and Pacific oceans, with the American frontiers in distant Great Britain, Japan, Formosa, and the Philippines. Moreover,

Hoover was willing to aid Western Europe if it showed willingness to aid in its own defense. His opposite number, Senator Paul Douglas, supported the stationing of American troops in Europe but agreed with Hoover that the Western European nations should do more to defend themselves.[35]

When the *New York Herald Tribune* tried to make an issue between Stassen and Hoover over the former's speech in mid-January, Stassen, too, wrote the newspaper that it was in error: "I believe that President Hoover's position has been partly misinterpreted by both the administration and by the Republican Senators who claim to adopt it. His basic premise is that if the western European nations are not determined to defend themselves and do not themselves rearm, we cannot attempt to defend them on the ground. This is certainly sound." Stassen also agreed with Hoover that first priority in American defense should be given to "the building of an extremely powerful American Air Force."[36]

Air Power

Encouraged by the response to his December 20 speech, Hoover set to work gathering ideas for a follow-up speech that would reply to his critics. He wrote to General A. C. Wedemeyer late in December, "There will be more of this debate—probably more observations from me in the latter part of January."[37] During that month, Hoover began to circulate drafts of a proposed speech among his advisers.[38] The former president received further stimulus to go back on the attack from a *New York Herald Tribune* story on January 28 that reported the Democratic National Committee was circulating among Democratic congressmen a paper that described Hoover and Taft as "false prophets of doom," who were now advocating the same "wrong" policies they had supported before World War II. Just as the two "isolationists" had supposedly misjudged the situation from 1939 to 1941, so now they were off the mark again, and two men so completely "wrong" a decade earlier were certainly not to be judged competent in the present circumstances.[39] The Democratic policy paper was for Hoover a perfect example of the tendency of that party to confront opposition with smears rather than to debate issues on their merits.

Senator Karl Mundt wrote Hoover in mid-January to encourage him to again discuss the international situation. He told the former president, "The basic concept which you developed in your last speech has met with wide acceptance, but slowly and surely those who have perverted it and distorted it have been making headway by the very volume and vigor of their attacks, rather than by the logic of their analysis and answers. It might be that the time is propitious now to reiterate and expand upon your earlier suggestion."[40]

Hoover's speech of February 9, 1951, was directed at the smears and distortions. Instead of shrinking from comparisons with his position before World War II, Hoover furnished quotations from his speech of June 29, 1941, in which he had questioned the wisdom of America allying itself with Russian communism against Germany and added, "Need I remind you that the grip of Communism in this decade has spread slavery from 200,000,000 to 800,000,000? And we have no peace." American foreign policy should be based on certain "stark realities," the first of which was the impossibility of defeating the Soviet Union's massive army in a land war, given the small number of combat divisions then available among NATO nations. Another was the desirability and possibility of defending the Western Hemisphere and making it self-sufficient. He was not advocating "isolationism," Hoover pointed out, "but if other nations should fail, we may be isolated by force of circumstances and against our will." A third reality was the finite economic capacity of the United States, which was being strained by the burdens imposed by the Truman administration and which could lead to economic chaos for the nation and make it easy prey for Stalin. A fourth factor was the inability of the United Nations to be "a substantial protection from Communist aggression." Before obligating itself in Europe, the United States must take into consideration the commitments it had already made in Korea, Japan, and elsewhere. The NATO treaty provided only that its membership would aid one another in the event of attack. There had been no attack. The Truman administration had earlier denied any intention of stationing American ground troops in Europe, but it was now apparent that he intended to do exactly that, even though there had been no attack. With the great disparity between Soviet strength and that of the NATO countries it was apparent that many more American divisions would have to be sent.[41]

His critics disposed of, Hoover now returned in the remainder of the speech to his own doctrine. The American air threat to the Soviet Union, he insisted, was "far more powerful than pouring American divisions into the reach of this Asiatic horde." And while a ground war would necessarily have to be a defensive one, through the use of air power the United States could go on the offensive. Moreover, air power would be less of a strain on the economy. Hoover calculated that for the same amount of money required to maintain even ten American divisions in Europe for a year, the United States could "purchase and man 390 B-36 long range bombers compared to 60 of them at present," and the annual cost of maintaining the bombers would be only one-third that for the ten army divisions. But Hoover's speech revealed that he had somewhat altered his doctrine since the December 20 speech. Like Taft, the former president was now more explicit in advocating the use of American air and sea power in an offensive role to aid Western Europe if it were attacked by the Soviets. Hoover also reiterated that both Japan and West Germany should be given their independence under representative governments. He said, "During 100 years these nations were the great dams against these Russian-controlled hordes. In the last war we may have been engaged in a great crusade for freedom of mankind, but we certainly destroyed these two dams." Only in the event that the Western European countries continued to ignore their own defense should the United States as a "prudent nation, have in mind a second line of air and naval defense based upon the foreign shores of the Pacific and Atlantic Oceans both North and South, and I may add the Mediterranean and Indian Ocean." What he proposed was neither retreat nor withdrawal. "The essence of the program I have proposed is to effectively restrain our enemies from attack upon our allies or ourselves. It is the best chance of peace—even if it is an uneasy peace."

Advocates of air power were delighted with Hoover's speeches, but that of February more than that of December 20. Bonner Fellers wrote in *Human Events* that the logic of Hoover's and Taft's speech was "compelling," the "essence" of it being "a pragmatic, resourceful attempt to deter war, win it if war comes, and in any event avoid the slaughter of millions of our youth on the Eurasian mainland." A powerful American air force was the solution to the dilemma posed by the nation's inability to numerically "right the world's balance of war." Fellers wrote, "To succeed in a program of containment we must be able to strike quickly, not just on the European fronts but anywhere about and within Russia's far-flung borders. Only air power has the range, speed and flexibility to perform such a mission . . . More than anything else, Russia fears air power. It is the one weapon against which Russia's terrific ground forces, enormous distances, and winters are impotent."[42]

The use of American air power as an offensive weapon against the Soviet Union had not been set forth clearly in Hoover's December speech, although it was in his February address. The shift in the two speeches from an emphasis on defense to the offensive use of air power against the Soviet Union in the event of war stemmed in large part from the influence of Major Alexander P. de Seversky, a noted exponent of air power since before World War II. In a press release of January 16, Seversky sharply criticized Hoover's December position for being "a purely defensive strategy based on the Navy and Air Force. But we know that defense has never won a war and never will. It would leave the initiative to the enemy in the wishful hope that the Soviets, if left alone, will disintegrate with time. It would also contemplate abandonment of our Western Allies—an unnecessary step if our strategy is right."[43] Hoover subsequently wrote to Seversky concerning his criticism, and the two men began a correspondence in which the aviator acquainted the former president with the offensive capabilities of air power.

Queries from Congress

Meanwhile, Hoover's counsel was being sought from Washington concerning other matters. When Senator Hugh Butler asked his advice on committee appointments in that body, Hoover recommended Taft for foreign relations, since his "major job on labor is now mostly finished, Dirksen on the "expenditures committee," and Nixon on the judicial committee that was likely to be conducting "more left-wing investigations." When his views concerning possible wage and price controls during the Korean conflict based on his World War I experience were sought by Senators Ferguson and Capehart, the former president responded with the familiar advice he had offered ineffectually during World War II. The "essential principles" he told them again were as follows:

1. A single responsible administrator over a group of related activities— sometimes with an advisory board . . .

2. Large responsibilities were placed upon the representatives of the producers, manufacturers and distributors . . . The purpose was to secure the maximum cooperation from the men who had the 'know-how.' Their sons were also in the war . . .

3. The general method of price control was by agreement with producers' 'war committees' of raw materials, food, etc. as near as possible to the point of production. From that point on, prices were held by allowing the normal manufacture or trade markups . . .

4. While restricting the production of many nonessentials, we paid no attention to the frills of life . . . We dealt only with essentials and staples.

5. We secured a large part of our enforcement in prices, production and distribution through the 'war committees'; that is, the manufacturers' committees watched the producers, the wholesalers watched the manufacturers, the retailers watched them both, and the price method being simple, the consumers watched them all.

"In World War II," Hoover wrote, "the controls were set up on the European-bureaucratic force basis of World War I and everybody knows its failures."[44]

When Hoover was invited by Democratic Senator Tom Connally to testify before a joint hearing of the Senate Foreign Relations and Armed Services Committees on the issue of sending American ground forces to Europe, the former president suggested that "before I can be of help to the Committees some further action by them is necessary." He urged them to gather "much more information and experienced independent opinion," particularly concerning the "political, military, preparedness intentions and actions of the European members of the North Atlantic Pact." The restrictions against "active and reserve military officers expressing views not approved by the Defense Department should be forthwith removed and such men should "be assured against any reprisals." Former diplomats and other civilians with experience in Europe should also be called to testify. Once these steps had been taken, Hoover said he would be willing to testify.[45]

Meanwhile, General Dwight Eisenhower had testified before the House and Senate, and Senator Knowland condensed the general's testimony for Hoover. According to Knowland, Eisenhower told the congressmen and senators he believed "the morale of western Europe can be raised sufficiently to establish forces in being for the defense of that area of the World," but he did not believe it was possible "to set a mathematical formula for the number of American troops to be sent to Europe vis a vis the number to be furnished by the other signatories" of the NATO agreement. The "bulk" of the forces, however, would be supplied by the Europeans, and Knowland was somewhat assured by the likelihood that "we would not be placing the percentage we have in Korea," although he would like a clearer definition of what percentage the "bulk" was likely to constitute, since it could "anything from 51% up to 90%."[46]

Hoover did, however, testify before the Senate Foreign Relations Committee on February 27 in behalf of the Wherry Resolution. Introduced by Senator Kenneth Wherry of Nebraska, that resolution would have expressed it as the "sense of the Senate that no ground forces of the United States should be assigned to duty in Europe for the purposes of the North Atlantic Treaty, pending the adoption of a policy with respect thereto by Congress."[47] In his testimony, Hoover rebutted all arguments advanced for stationing US ground forces in Europe and raised his familiar arguments against such an action. He concluded that "there is only one real salvation for Europe at the present moment. That is, to build up the air and naval power of the United States and Britain so as to overwhelm Russia in case of attack."[48] Wherry wrote Hoover that if his resolution was not adopted, it meant "that the President will have the sole authority to use a pool of 3,500,000 men where he chooses and where he pleases."[49] Hoover, however, was pessimistic that the Wherry Resolution or its counterpart in the House would pass, telling Congressman Frederick Coudert Jr. that the "next two weeks will probably determine that Congress has lost all its powers in these matters."[50]

Fellers found Hoover's testimony "marvelous" and told him it would "do a world of good," while Seversky wrote the former president, "From a professional military point of view, your second speech was much closer to the strategic concept we airmen entertain, and your statement before Congress, from our point of view, was nearly perfect.[51]" Hoover was himself convinced that the Senate hearings had awakened the public mind to the possibility that Truman's policies might draw the United Sates into a Korea-type war in Europe, and he was certain that "the American people, outside selected circles, are ninety percent with us." Taft agreed that Hoover's testimony had helped arouse public support for the Wherry Resolution. He had heard nothing but the highest praise for the testimony and he told Hoover, "I believe the smear tactics have failed, and whether we win or lose we will have the majority of the people with us."[52]

In mid-February *Human Events*, the conservative journal, carried a story that suggested a plot by the Truman administration to divert Hoover from his leadership in the Great Debate. It read,

> When the former President visited Mr. Truman last week, few suspected that
> the interview (initiated by Truman) concealed an attempt to divert Mr. Hoover

from his present foreign-policy crusade. Officially, the meeting was concerned with famine relief for India; Mr. Truman wanted Hoover's advice on the matter. Quite probably that was the only intent of the President. However, we learn from reliable sources that White House advisors were seeking to get Mr. Hoover out of the country, to interrupt his active participation in the Great Debate over foreign policy. And they persuaded Mr. Truman to ask the former President to go to India to investigate food conditions. Whether Mr. Hoover saw the trap or not, he declined the suggestion saying that all relevant data for reaching a decision on Indian relief reposed in the Department of Agriculture. This episode is significant because it shows that the Administration remains troubled by the influence of Hoover's speeches on the people. Even after the Eisenhower report, the Hoover utterances carry weight—in large part because no one can accuse the former President of political ambitions.[53]

Early in March Hoover wrote radio commentator Fulton Lewis Jr. that he believed the hearings had "reoriented the public mind in an unexpected quarter." He explained,

> Marshall's statement that they propose to send four divisions (without a limit on more divisions) to Europe has awakened the American people at last to the fact that an army of American boys is to be sent to Europe despite all promises to the contrary. Hitherto, all our prophecies that this is the end result of the Eisenhower and other commitments the public did not take very seriously. Now the reaction is simple. They don't want to take the step through the door of a ground war like Korea again. We get licked for the present, but I believe the American people outside selected circles are 90% with us.[54]

While the Senate debated the Wherry Resolution, Hoover addressed a dinner meeting of House and Senate Republicans in Washington on March 13, the purpose of which, Representative Clarence Brown told him, was to "clarify the [international] problems and help them consolidate their position for the coming battle." The meeting was off the record but nevertheless made its way into the newspapers. At the meeting, Hoover lashed out at the "infantry generals" of the Pentagon who could not grasp the strategic potential of air power, and he argued that the deterrent posed by long-range American air power was more likely to prevent the outbreak of World War III than the stationing of ground troops in Europe. It was time for civilian control to be reestablished over the armed forces through the reassertion of congressional responsibilities of American foreign and military policies. Clearly the Western Europeans were not worried about the possibility of a Soviet invasion, else they would have done more to arm themselves—and some Europeans had, in fact, begun to suspect that the United States was seeking a war with the Soviets in which Western Europe would be the battleground.[55] A month after Hoover's talk, the mystery of the press coverage was uncovered when the manager of the Willard Hotel, where the dinner had been held, discovered that a zealous reporter had drilled a hole through the partition behind Hoover and a stenographer had listened and taken notes.

By late March the former president concluded that the Great Debate had probably been lost, "but we can at least hope that posterity will realize that we did our best in their protection."[56] Early the next month the Senate did vote by a narrow margin of 49 to 43 to permit four US divisions to be sent to Europe as part of the NATO force, with the stipulation that Truman must seek approval from Congress before increasing these forces. The Wherry Resolution was then tabled. Senator Taft, who from the beginning had been more compromising than Hoover on the issue, voted both for the four divisions and to table the Wherry Resolution, confident that the point had been made and that Congress had established control over any increase in the American commitment.[57]

Revisionism

Coincidental with Hoover's inauguration of the Great Debate, revisionist historians had launched a timely attack on the foreign policies of the Roosevelt administration of a decade earlier. At the American Historical Association meeting in December 1950, Professor Charles C. Tansill of Georgetown University and Dr. Harry Elmer Barnes, formerly of Smith College, presented a panel in which FDR's policies came under fire for "allowing an unalerted Pearl Harbor to be attacked even though [Roosevelt] knew the attack was coming; of paving the way for Communism's present death grip on China by turning Japan into an enemy of the United States, and then, in World War II, destroying Japan as a bulwark against Russia." Tansill reasoned, "If Japan could be maneuvered into firing the first shot, America could enter a crusade on two fronts. Thanks to the breaking of the Japanese code, Roosevelt and his coterie of advisers had advance knowledge of Japan's intention to strike." Barnes attacked the dominance of the history profession by "court historians"—those who had worked for the federal government during and after the war—who were committed to defending Roosevelt against the truth, as raised by revisionist historians. Barnes argued, "The attitude of the public during war time has been maintained by means of propaganda. The United States is likely to undertake the third crusade before it is fully aware of the real causes and disastrous results of the second." But the revisionist historians, he charged, were being hamstrung by unsympathetic publishers and smear artists, so that the "very existence of historical science is being threatened" and could only be saved by publishing the facts "before the chains are fastened on us and the lock is closed." He concluded, "A robust revisionism is our only hope of deliverance, if there be one, at this late date."[58]

Distinguished historian Charles Beard, himself author of a damning work on FDR's pre–Pearl Harbor policies (*President Roosevelt and the Coming of the War*, 1941 [1948]) had earlier noted that "anybody who deviates a hair's breadth from the Roosevelt line is in trouble, not only from the professional smear Bund but also from 'scholars.' I have been through the mill myself."[59] As Joan Hoff has pointed out, Hoover was actively encouraging the revisionists by seeking financial support for them and by providing them with material from his own extensive files. Beard began to consult with Hoover for source material as early as 1945 and received help from both Hoover and his former undersecretary of state William Castle.[60] Such revisionist works not only served to vindicate Hoover's position in 1939–1941 but also aided his fight against the new interventionism of the 1950s.

Hoover also welcomed books that seemed to expose the culpability of the Roosevelt administration in the attack on Pearl Harbor. When Admiral Robert Theobald's book, *The Final Secret of Pearl Harbor: the Washington Contribution to the Japanese Attack*, appeared in 1954, Hoover wrote to Admiral Pratt that Theobald was "right that Roosevelt created the war, but he is wrong that they held out the fleet in Pearl Harbor as bait. The facts are that they expected the attack to take place on the Philippines or thereabouts, which accounts for their gross neglect as to Hawaii."[61]

MacArthur

In the spring of 1951 the Great Debate was overshadowed by the dramatic dismissal of General Douglas MacArthur from his command of UN forces in Korea by President Truman. Convinced from intelligence reports that the Chinese effort in Korea was ebbing for lack of supplies and modern weapons, MacArthur had suggested a battlefield cease-fire to the Chinese commander, thereby undercutting Truman's diplomatic efforts in behalf of an armistice. Worse, from the administration's standpoint, MacArthur coupled his offer of a cease-fire with threats of possible military action against China itself if a cease-fire were not forthcoming. Direct military attacks on Chinese Manchuria had already been advocated by all four major veterans' organizations in December 1950, including the Veterans of Foreign Wars, the American Legion, the Disabled American Veterans, and AmVets.[62] MacArthur's action, however, was in clear opposition to Truman's policies and in defiance of the president's "gag" order to the general. When MacArthur went further by implicitly criticizing Truman for his failure to make use of Nationalist Chinese troops from Taiwan, in replying to a letter from Congressman Joseph Martin, the president relieved the general of his command.

Hoover's suite in the Waldorf Tower quickly became the headquarters for orchestrating the general's return to the United States. Bonner Fellers, who had served as secretary to MacArthur during the war and through the first months of the occupation of Japan, now acted as liaison between Hoover and the general. When MacArthur expressed his intention to return to the United States by ship, Hoover insisted that he fly back, instead, to reach the United States as soon as possible. Clearly, if the general returned by ship the furor over his dismissal would have ebbed by the time he reached the United States. According to Fellers, MacArthur told him to inform "the chief" that if Hoover would advise him what he should do he would follow his advice, and when he was back in the United States he would "take [Hoover's] advice and that of no one else." Fellers later recalled that when he passed the message to the former president, Hoover "started giving [advice] right then over the phone—quite a bit—so much that I again called [MacArthur] back that night."[63]

Hoover suggested the content for MacArthur's speeches, recommended that he deny for the present reports that he had accepted a $100,000-a-year position with Remington Rand Corporation, since it would lower his "stature at this critical moment," and arranged for a great homecoming for the general in San Francisco, enlisting the assistance of William Randolph Hearst.[64] Hoover also apparently helped engineer the invitation to the general to speak before Congress.[65] Fellers told MacArthur that Hoover had also advised him to ignore the "yells of 'creating disunity.' There are things far worse for a nation than disunity over policies. The worst is wrong policies that kill the flower of a people."[66] Hoover described for MacArthur the division over American foreign policies, as exemplified by the Great Debate. But while others allied with Hoover in the fight against Truman's foreign policies eagerly sought MacArthur's active and effective support of the Hoover position, the former president counseled the general not to align himself with either side but to "speak above them."[67]

MacArthur later told newsman Richard Berlin that he had expected to slip off unnoticed to a hotel upon his arrival in San Francisco and then to fly east unrecognized. He felt discouraged, even disgraced. But the tumultuous welcome Hoover had helped arrange in San Francisco buoyed his spirits.[68] MacArthur subsequently followed much of Hoover's advice, and Bonner Fellers, in reminiscing later, concluded that the general's speech before Congress reflected much of Hoover's influence. He estimated "that possibly half of the points in the speech had been more or less suggested by Mr. Hoover."[69]

Hoover stayed silent on foreign policy while the debate over the Wherry Resolution and the furor over MacArthur's return to the United States revealed the discontent with Truman's policies. Late in May he confided that he had reduced his public speaking because there was little to add to what he had already said. "You have had about two billion words on the subject during the last month," he told Arch Shaw, "and an astonishing amount of lies from men in high places. I intend to keep still until after this burst of words and lies have gone by."[70] In July, though, he returned to the offensive with a memorandum to Senators Homer Ferguson and Kenneth Wherry and to journalist George Sokolsy that listed the essentials of a bipartisan foreign policy. Bipartisanship, he wrote, could only be obtained through "cooperation of the Administration with the Republicans in the United States Senate and House of Representatives," who were the only "representatives of the Party who can make effective commitments in respect to bi-partisan policies. It no doubt increased the efficiency of the State Department to hire Republicans," he observed in an obvious reference to John Foster Dulles, but "the American people should not be deceived into thinking it constitutes bi-partisan action," because such Republicans were not "acting under the authority of the Republican members of the Congress." Bipartisanship also meant that the administration should not seek to "avoid the spirit of the Constitution" by making executive agreements and other commitments that did not require the approval of the Senate, and there could not be bipartisanship without consultation with congressional Republicans in the early stage of any agreements made.[71] Ferguson delivered a speech to the Senate on July 30 based on Hoover's memorandum, while Wherry responded that he agreed "with it completely and have taken this position many times publicly."[72]

In August the former president traveled to his native Iowa and addressed twenty thousand people in 96-degree heat at the state fair. At 77 years of age now, Hoover called for a reawakening of interest in the "Old Virtues"—integrity, truth, honor, patriotism, economy in government, self-reliance, thrift, and self-sacrifice, as well as decency in public life. He attacked the "cancerous growth of intellectual dishonesty in public life which is mostly beyond the law." He saw greater danger in America's "complaisance with evil," "public toleration of scandalous behavior," and "cynical acceptance of dishonor" than he did in foreign threats to the United States. Noting the revelations of corruption in the Truman administration, Hoover wondered how the Founding Fathers of the Republic would have reacted to "the 'sacred honor' of the five per centers, mink coats, deep freezers and free hotel bills? Or favoritism in government loans and contracts? Or failure to prosecute evil-doers, cancerous rackets and gambling rings with their train of bribed officials all through the land." The issue in American life, he insisted, was "decency in public life against indecency." He also attacked secrecy in foreign policy, charging that the Teheran and Yalta agreements, "which sold the freedom of half a billion down the river," could never have been approved if they had been "submitted to the American people for debate and to the Congress for decision." "And there is where we lost the peace and wandered into this land of hot and cold wars."[73] Former defense secretary Louis Johnson wrote Hoover that it "was a magnificent address . . . and sorely needed!"[74]

Reorganization

During 1949 and 1950 a substantial number of the recommendations of the Hoover Commission had been implemented, by administrative decree, executive order, or congressional legislation. During 1951, however, little was accomplished in putting the remainder of the recommendations into force. The *New York Times* found that "little more than lip service" had been paid to the recommendations in 1951 by comparison to 1949–1950, and it argued,

"This is not good enough when the efficient working of democratic government is at stake, not to mention total savings estimated at $5.4 billion annually." Noting that there would be twenty separate measures for reform before Congress when it convened, the *Times* continued, "In our view it would be the best kind of politics for the so-called 'leadership' in Congress to take an active part in furthering some of these essential reforms in governmental reorganization. We don't think it is true that the people are uninterested. We think that next November they will be very interested in knowing just how much of the Hoover proposals have been adopted, how much rejected—and why."[75] When Hoover went on the attack once again in December concerning the scandals in the Truman administration, he argued that those scandals "would not have occurred if the Hoover Commission's recommendations on political appointments had been accepted more than two years ago."[76]

Foreign Policy

The Great Debate, despite Senate consent to the stationing of four divisions of American troops in Europe, was far from over. Felix Morley aided Hoover in writing another speech on the issue and strongly encouraged the former president to give it.[77] The speech went through numerous revisions, with the early drafts proposing a mutual withdrawal of US and Soviet troops from a zone in Europe that would begin with Germany and then be broadened. The US troops, having been sent to Europe by President Truman, were now envisioned by Hoover as potential bargaining chips to bring about concessions from the Soviet Union. The plan would have included the unification and neutralization of Germany after the joint US-Soviet withdrawal, followed by a general withdrawal by both the Soviet Union and the United States from European countries.[78] In the final draft of the speech that was delivered on January 27, 1952, however, these elements were missing, probably because in an election year Hoover did not wish to propose anything that might embarrass his choice for the GOP presidential nomination, Robert Taft.[79]

Less than two weeks before Hoover's speech, General Hoyt R. Vandenberg, US Air Force chief of staff, told the Economic Club of New York City that the United States needed a 143-group air force. The decision of the secretary of defense and the Joint Chiefs of Staff to press for an air force that large, he told them, had been reached as the result of "a long hard look at the realities of the world struggle against communism." An air force of that size would give the United Sates, he said, "a force so powerful that even a would-be aggressor would shrink from the cost of challenging it; or, if its power to deter should not be enough, a force capable of engaging instantly and effectively in a world of survival." In words that echoed those of Herbert Hoover in previous speeches, Vandenberg told his audience, "It seems to me self-evident, on the basis of the Korean experience, that neither this nation nor its allies can afford to adopt a strategy calling for an endless line of garrisons along the entire perimeter of Communist power." The Soviet Union, he argued, was "primarily vulnerable to air power—both land-based and carrier-based."[80]

Hoover's speech of January 27 found the nations of Western Europe had made no appreciable progress in arming themselves in the year since the Great Debate. The only improvement in the defense of Europe stemmed from the presence of the American divisions there, and the European attitude concerning the possibility of a Soviet invasion was still "profoundly different from the attitude of Washington." Only in this country was there the kind of "war psychosis" that led to air raid drills. Europeans recognized that had the USSR wanted to overrun Western Europe they could have done so at any time in the previous five years, and their failure to do so was proof to the Europeans that the Soviets harbored no such desire. Whether the Europeans were correct or not in this assumption, it did "contribute to Western Europe's lack of hysteria and their calculation of low risk and, therefore, their lack of hurry to arm." The complacence of the Europeans required that United States reevaluate its own policies. A "prairie fire of revolution" had been ignited against the West in Asia and the Middle East, while in Korea Americans continued to die. Americans, already groaning under the weight of a war economy, would soon begin to feel the full impact of the gigantic increases in government spending and taxes that were spawning the irresistible forces of inflation. Hoover again advocated reliance upon air and sea power to defend the free world, which "could better halt the spread of Communist imperialism." Hoover told his listeners that he firmly believed "a third world war is neither necessary nor inevitable."[81]

The speech received plaudits from numerous retired generals and admirals, including two former chiefs of naval operations, cabinet officials, and diplomats. He gathered their comments together and released them to the press the following month.[82] Lieutenant General Leslie Groves, overseer of the atomic bomb project during World War II, issued his own statement, which read,

> I hope that Mr. Hoover's words will not be ignored as they were a year ago just because they make unpleasant reading. As he points out, the great danger of our position is overextension in international commitments, both economic and military. It will take courage to revise our present policies, to admit our mistakes, and even to accept minor and, we hope, temporary defeats. As Mr. Hoover suggests, our military policy should be based on air and sea where our great technical capabilities can be put to best advantage, rather than on the ground where the number of bayonets is of prime importance.[83]

Taft told Hoover that he had read the speech with "great pleasure and approval." Though he doubted that "anyone who is actually responsible for foreign policy in early '53 could at that time take as drastic action as you proposed," if nominated and elected he would "move in the same general direction." He believed the speech would "have a substantial effect on future American policy."[84]

Publicity and apparent support for Hoover's position also came from a highly unlikely source. In what Harrison Salisbury, correspondent in Moscow, described as a "most unusual" action, *Pravda*, the organ of the Central Committee of the Communist Party in the USSR, published the January 27 speech in full, together with a two-column, front-page editorial that described Hoover's critique of American foreign policy as based on realistic facts. And, Salisbury wrote, the *Pravda* analysis was reprinted by "three other important Soviet newspapers—the military organs *Red Star* and *Red Fleet* and the Moscow party organ *Moscow Pravda*." This constituted, Salisbury observed, "a major event in Soviet discussion." Salisbury found Western diplomats in Moscow pondering the significance of it all. He speculated that the Soviets had concluded Hoover's views represented such a sizable body of American opinion that Truman's policies might be changed in a direction that Moscow believed would "reduce the danger of a third World War." Salisbury concluded, "While a good many conclusions might be drawn from these facts, one that seems to be indisputable to the Russians is that Mr. Hoover's program is less likely to lead to a third world war than that of Mr. Truman."[85]

The reception by the Truman administration was, however, less hospitable, especially in the Pentagon. Bonner Fellers wrote Hoover that his speech had "caused near consternation in the Army Division of the Pentagon. General [J. Lawton] Collins, who was quite upset, canceled his appointments for the day, called in some dozen top brass to plan how best to meet your views, especially those relating to the Europeans providing their own ground defenses." According to Fellers, Collins had told the other officers, "We can't take this," and the army had "decided to launch a press, radio and magazine educational campaign to discredit your speech" by calling in "key reporters and commentators and then leak such secret briefing information as is necessary to establish a basis to undermine your views."[86]

That same month the former president received a request from the GOP National Committee for his views on a statement that had been prepared for use by convention delegates in formulating the foreign policy plank of the Republican platform at the convention. The statement called for repudiation by the United States of the Teheran, Yalta, and Potsdam agreements because they had been "unilaterally violated by the Soviet government and hence are now no longer binding on the United States," because they had not been "submitted to the Senate in treaty form for approval and hence the action of the executive was unconstitutional, and because "they violated the principles of the Atlantic Charter" and had resulted in the "enslavement of Albania, Bulgaria, Czechoslovakia, Hungary, Poland, Rumania, and Yugoslavia." Such a statement would serve notice to the Soviet Union that the United States did not recognize their domination of these peoples, would give those nations encouragement in maintaining their "moral resistance" to communism, and would also regenerate American diplomacy. It would also rally "the foreign language groups in the United States" behind the GOP as the party committed to the "liberation" of their motherlands.[87] Except for the omission of Latvia, Estonia, and Lithuania from the list of enslaved peoples, this was classic Hoover, and he responded that the proposal "seems good to me."[88]

Politics

Typically, Hoover began in 1951 to monitor the campaigns for the GOP, convinced, as he wrote one correspondent on the last day of 1951, that "only the election of a Republican President will save this country. But first we must nominate somebody who has no taint of 'me-too-ism.'"[89] To ensure this, Hoover interested himself again in the nomination of Senator Robert A. Taft. The only obstacle seemed to be the popularity of General Dwight D. Eisenhower, but in April 1952 the former president tried to convince himself that Ike's popularity had peaked and that Taft would now come on.[90] Felix Morley considered Taft's nomination and election so essential that he suggested the former president break with his practice since 1933 of not supporting any candidate for the nomination and come out openly for Taft's nomination. General Robert Wood even suggested Hoover might consider going to the convention as a New York delegate and lead the movement for Taft in the voting. Morley wrote Hoover of Wood's suggestion, "Of course any such action would bring you down to the arena of politics and would, therefore, temporarily diminish your influence in the vital role of elder statesman. On the other hand, it would also emphasize the vital importance of the coming nomination and would give enormous stimulus to the Republican unity which is shaping up in spite of a relative handful of dissidents." Morley thought Wood's suggestion worthy of consideration.[91]

Hoover, however, continued to maintain a public appearance of impartiality through the preconvention months, even though he was active privately in the Taft campaign to an extent unprecedented for the former president in any previous preconvention campaign. John D. M. Hamilton, Taft's eastern manager in 1952, recalled that Hoover had made connections for him in the East—including one with Governor Charles Edison (Democrat) of New Jersey—which were extremely valuable, and when the campaign ran short of money, helped the Taft forces obtain contributions, including $5,000 from Joseph P. Kennedy (Democrat) for the New Hampshire primary campaign.[92]

It soon developed that the nomination would hinge upon the decision reached by the convention over the question of the seating of rival Taft and Eisenhower delegates from several Southern states. Great publicity was given to the charge that the Taft campaigners had "stolen" a number of delegates in those states. Hoover tried to arrange a compromise over the disputed delegates with Senator Henry Cabot Lodge, of the Eisenhower forces, but failed.[93] The former president was incensed over the tactics of the Eisenhower organization before and during the convention in Chicago, charging that the pressure applied upon the delegates was reminiscent of the 1940 Willkie "blitz" and seemed to have been arranged by the same operators.[94]

The contrast between Taft and Eisenhower seemed to offer a clear choice for those who favored an American military and foreign policy based on air and sea power instead of a large standing army and commitments in Europe and elsewhere. As the first commander of NATO troops in Europe, Ike seemed to represent all that Hoover and the supporters of his doctrine opposed, while Taft's position had been consistently close to Hoover's own. This perception of the issues brought such air power advocates as Bonner Fellers, A. C. Wedemeyer, and Seversky into the Taft campaign. Early in July Seversky send Hoover a personal message that he intended to distribute to GOP delegates in support of Taft's nomination, and he solicited Hoover's comments on it.[95] Seversky's memorandum made the familiar points and drew contrasts between Taft and Eisenhower, with the latter described as "a military man in the tradition of old-style surface warfare," whose obsolete ideas could lead American youth to be "committed to useless slaughter in Europe and Asia without the slightest chance of preserving our way of life." His memorandum called for the election of a civilian as president, one who recognized that any future war could be won only through "global command of the air—a command as clear cut and decisive as was Britain's global command of the seas in an earlier period." Hoover considered the appeal "a clear cut statement and a good one."[96]

The GOP's elder statesman made his second "farewell appearance" before a Republican convention on July 8, 1952. In a month he would be 78 years old. His address dealt with what were by now familiar refrains—the usurpation of power by the federal government, the loss of freedom in America, the poisoning of the American economy with fascism, socialism, and Keynesianism, the burgeoning of the federal bureaucracy—before he turned to foreign policy. Here, too, the refrain was familiar—the betrayal of freedom for hundreds of millions of people by Roosevelt-Truman surrenders at Teheran, Yalta, and Potsdam. Despite the $35 billion dollars of aid poured into Western Europe by the United States, the nations there still showed no serious disposition to defend themselves against the massive military strength of the Soviet Union. He looked at the economic burden placed upon the American people by Truman's overseas commitments and concluded, "If free men are to survive in America we must reduce spending and taxes." Truman was following "the road to militarism in the United States. That is at its base a threat to all freedoms." The only alternative to bankruptcy and militarism was to rely on air and sea power for America's defense. "I do not propose that we retreat in our shell like a turtle," Hoover insisted. "I do propose the deadly reprisal strategy of a rattlesnake." He closed with his farewell and added that he would continue the fight "for those principles which made the United States the greatest gift of God to free men."[97]

Hoover tried once more to engineer a compromise over the disputed delegates, this time by interceding with GOP national chairman Guy Gabrielson, and when that failed Hoover abandoned all pretense of impartiality in the convention.[98] Upset with the tactics of the Eisenhower campaigners, he publicly endorsed a candidate for the GOP nomination for the first time since he had left the presidency. In a press statement on July 9, Hoover said,

> I have not for many years taken public part in convention choice of candidates, but on this occasion when the issues are so vital to our country, my conscience demands that I speak out. I favor Senator Taft, whom I have known since he was associated with me in World War I. Senator Taft has long proved his forthrightness, integrity and absolute devotion to the public interest, and he has had long experience in government. His leadership in the Senate has provided the Republic Party with a fighting opposition to the currents of collectivism in the country. This convention meets not only to nominate a candidate, but to save America. I have been deeply distressed at the acrimonious discussion in the convention. I can only hope that it shall cease for the sake of our party and the country.[99]

But Hoover's endorsement was an act of desperation, for it was already clear that the uncommitted delegates in such key states as Michigan, California, Pennsylvania, and Minnesota would not support Taft in the struggle over the contested delegates and probably would support Ike for the nomination. Bowing to the inevitable, Hoover began to cast about for a new candidate who might be able to stop the Eisenhower bandwagon and settled on MacArthur, who agreed to accept the nomination if it were offered to him.[100]

Eisenhower's momentum was unstoppable, however, and he was nominated on the first ballot. Disappointed, Hoover nevertheless told reporters, "Being a Republican, I shall vote the Republican ticket."[101] The terseness of his statement, without any reference to supporting the ticket, revealed his disappointment with the result and his disgust with the tactics of the Eisenhower camp. The former president wrote to Taft, "I am sorry, beyond expression. We did our best."[102] The senator responded that he could not "adequately express my gratitude for the support you gave me throughout the nomination campaign, for your public statement, and for your letter of regret." He was "deeply disappointed," not only because he was fearful of what "we may get in the way of government" if Eisenhower were elected, but also because of the sacrifices that had been made by his supporters in the losing cause. "As far as I am concerned," he concluded, "I am probably better off individually."[103]

Hoover told GOP chairman Guy Gabrielson that he had handled the convention "with great urbanity and fairness in a most difficult situation," and added, "We are now in uncharted waters."[104] In his reply, Gabrielson alluded to Dewey's support for Eisenhower and wrote that "it looks as though we are going to be called upon to rescue [the GOP] again from the Governor of New York." A bright spot for Hoover at the convention was the emergence of Senator Everett Dirksen. Hoover wrote him, "This is just to say that you are the one who emerged from the convention as the leader of our kind of

Republicans. Some day we may be able to stop the left-wing domestic and misdirected foreign policies."[105] Taft agreed that the conservative wing of the party must now work to free the GOP of New Deal influences in order that it might win the election and "thereafter conduct a government based on sound Republican principles. We can still carry on that fight both before and after the election."[106]

A month before the convention, *Time* magazine published a notable one-page profile of the former president, writing, "The unremarked phenomenon of Herbert Hoover is that he has been so long out of a regular job and has kept himself so busy." He was now working on his memoirs, writing in pencil, "doing a good deal of crossing out and writing over, sitting at a large desk from which, by stretching, he can look down 31 stories on the disordered world." The former president was attacked by his enemies as "a hopeless reactionary" and regarded by his friends "as a last hope of sensible liberalism." "His voice," *Time* wrote, "is low and husky, and as he talks, he abstractedly fingers a couple of worn coins. As on an old coin, the familiar face has grown a little indistinct. Heavy frame spectacles sometimes slip down to the end of the short nose; around the turned-down mouth, the once plump bull-terrier cheeks now sag mastiff-like." It added,

> In the past 16 years, the ex-president has delivered more than 50 carefully considered, formal lectures to his fellow countrymen. But he has not limited himself to exhortation. He has thrown himself into many worthy projects: into programs of relief for the hungry; into studies of such topics as revolution, war & peace, and the chaos in the executive department of the U.S. Government (from this last, he produced the monumental Hoover Commission Report); into organizations like the Boys' Clubs and the Salvation Army in which he takes his participation very seriously. A friend remembers him traveling west by train one day, getting a wire from the Salvation Army which urged him to buy a doughnut in the Army's doughnut campaign. Hoover promptly wired back: "I will buy a doughnut."

"Age," *Time* reported, "does not trouble him." And

> he grudgingly wears a hearing aid, bolts his food, and smokes recklessly . . . The man who upheld Prohibition as his stern executive duty now drinks two Martinis before dinner. He relaxes in the evening by preoccupiedly playing gin rummy or canasta with some of his group of loyal friends . . . To his Waldorf suite comes a steady stream of callers, including Republican Congressmen and foreign officials. He spends part of every day with these visitors, assiduously pumping them. He is one of the best-informed private citizens in the U.S.
>
> The suite is his haven and his watchtower. From the wall of the imposing living room, a portrait of Lou Henry Hoover gazes down on her husband's pipes, his blue and white porcelain and his solemn books. Three women secretaries wait on him. He seldom dictates answers to his

mountainous correspondence, merely pencils a line across a letter which
gives the clue as to what he wants the answer to be.

Time concluded its essay by observing, "Hoover spent a few bitter and silent
years after the country discarded him. Few people cared whether he had anything to say or not. Now a large number of people think he is right, so that
even those who disagree with him listen to him with uneasy attention. He
is an embarrassing old man who cannot be squelched. At 77, the Chief says
invincibly: 'They're not going to shut me up.'"[107]

The Campaign

Taft shared Hoover's lack of warmth for the GOP candidate and revealed no
inclination to give Eisenhower active support. Alarmed by the coolness of the
conservatives toward his campaign, Eisenhower soon tried to build bridges to
both Hoover and Taft. He wired Hoover on July 29 that he was sorry to have
missed him at the convention and said he hoped they could meet at the former president's "personal convenience" to talk about about the Hoover Commission's recommendations and Hoover's views "on many other questions
facing us today." He reported "gratifying evidence of developing team work
and cooperation among major elements of the Republican Party" but added
that "to bring this to full success we of course need your help."[108] Hoover
responded with little enthusiasm that he had "a number of long established
commitments on the [West] coast" but that a meeting could be arranged when
he returned east "after August."[109]

Taft, too, had put off any meeting with Eisenhower until September and
had formulated conditions that Eisenhower would have to agree to before he
would support the nominee in the general election. In late August it appeared
that the two rivals might not get together, but Eisenhower soon felt the
effects in his campaigning of the lack of a unified party behind him, so in
mid-September the two met at Eisenhower's headquarters on Morningside
Heights in New York City. As a result of their conference, Taft felt that he
had obtained enough concessions from the nominee in budget, taxation, and
labor matters to permit him to support the general.[110] It was a conference that
unified the party, and conservatives like Hoover could now support the GOP
nominee.

It was by now customary for newspapers and magazines to pay tribute to
the elder statesman at each birthday. *Collier's* marked his seventy-eighth by
writing,

> We hope that Herbert Hoover's seventy-eight birthday, on August 10th,
> will be a happy one. And if the former President finds satisfaction in a
> long life of continuing accomplishment, we believe that it will be. In the
> past year Congress has put into practice still more of Mr. Hoover's wise

recommendations for government reorganization. The Hoover memoirs were read by millions when they first appeared in *Collier's*. Two volumes which have appeared in book form spent several weeks on the best-seller list, and the third volume, to be published September 3rd, should enjoy a similar success.

We wish that we had space to publish all the many letters, expressing the respect and esteem of his countrymen, which we received when the memoirs were appearing in this magazine. But we can assure Mr. Hoover that they reflected an abiding gratitude for his many years of public service. And this assurance, together with the recollection of the spontaneous ovation he received at the Republican National Convention, should help convince Mr. Hoover that after 20 years away from public office he is, to reverse the slogan of one of his political opposites, the unforgotten man.[111]

In mid-August, Hoover wrote his old friend Clarence Kelland that after two weeks "in circulation" he had found "one thing stands out." He explained,

> The candidate who has the courage to come out flat and say our experiment in Western continental Europe has been a failure; that we must recall our 400,000 army and 50,000 American women and children from the jeopardy they are in (either they are in terrible jeopardy or all this stuff is a fake); that we love the British and the U.N., and he could continue that the Western Europeans seem satisfied they are in no danger—such a candidate would carry this country—labor, the farmers, the middle class, the youngsters and mothers.
>
> And I cannot be reconciled to any policy to continue on a road which will inevitably lead to a ground war with the Communists, with our certain defeat and the destruction of all human freedom for centuries.[112]

He told General Wedemeyer that he did not see any "slugging" on foreign policy, with Dulles's proposals "sheer bulk." If Eisenhower would follow the advice contained in his letter to Kelland, the general would "sweep the country." If not, he feared the GOP would go "down the Whig slide." He could not, he said, make a speech for Eisenhower that did not include the point that he disagreed "with the foreign policies of either Eisenhower or Stevenson—and I shall continue to oppose them," but "I do want to see a change in Washington and can support that." But, he told Wedemeyer, "such a speech would be no good to Ike."[113] He was perfectly content, Hoover said, to be ignored in the campaign, since he wanted "to be free to oppose important policies which are not in the best interests of our people."[114]

Hoover now waited for a call from Eisenhower. Meanwhile, he leaped to the defense of the vice presidential nominee, fellow Californian Richard M. Nixon, when Nixon came under attack over the "slush fund" issue. After Nixon made his famous televised "Checkers" speech, the former president issued a press release: "From intimate acquaintance with Senator Nixon since before he entered public life, I can say that if everyone in the city of Washington possessed the high level of courage, probity and patriotism of Senator Nixon this would be a far better nation. There can be but one end of this campaign of smear. The Republican Party will be firmer in the heart and confidence of the American people."[115]

Finally Hoover received the long-awaited wire from the nominee. According to Bonner Fellers, Hoover learned that the farther west Eisenhower campaigned, the more people asked him if he were supported by Hoover, and when he reached California he was told he could not carry the state without Hoover's endorsement.[116] Whether this was true or not, Eisenhower did wire Hoover on October 7 that he had tried to reach him by telephone before leaving New York for his western campaign but the former president had been out of town. He had then expected to meet Hoover in California, but the former president was not there, either. He now hoped to meet with the elusive Hoover in New York when he returned there on October 16.[117] The former president quickly responded that if Eisenhower wanted his participation in the campaign, October 16 would be too late to make effective arrangements. He told Ike, "If you request it, I will prepare and deliver a major address in your support . . . However, I want you to feel perfectly free to make such a decision. If you believe it better that I stay out of a public part of the campaign, it will in no way dim my prayers for your success."[118]

Approval was evidently conveyed to Hoover in some way, for he went on the air over CBS radio and television on October 18 with his lone campaign speech. It was the speech that Hoover had for so many years hoped Republican candidates would make, and it was doubtless one of the best and most heartfelt of his public career. He first told his listeners that he had come out of what he "had hoped was final retirement from political activities" and had done so "at General Eisenhower's request" because he believed "General Eisenhower and the Republican ticket should be elected." Hoover addressed his talk especially to the 40 percent of voters—approximately forty million in number—who had "come of age since there was last a Republican Administration in Washington," since those forty million knew "little of the Republican Party's background of principles, or its forward-looking constructive accomplishments" after twenty years of "misrepresentations" by the Democrats. He called attention to seven major such misrepresentations. Reviewing the GOP's record of legislation designed to curb the excesses of big business, beginning with the Sherman Antitrust Act and the Interstate Commerce Act, he rebutted the misrepresentation of the party as the instrument of big business privilege. Tracing the origins of the Great Depression to World War I, and voicing his familiar assertion that recovery had begun in 1932 only to be retarded by fear of the New Deal and the consequences of New Deal legislation, Hoover rebutted the misrepresentation that the GOP had caused the depression and that FDR had rescued the American people.[119]

The former president then reviewed GOP legislation and other actions establishing the Departments of Labor and Commerce, ending the 12-hour workday and establishing the Railway Mediation Board, the Bureau of Housing, Civil Service Commission, and other initiatives, to put to rest the charge that the GOP was "reactionary" and opposed to change and reform. He pointed out that the Republican Party had originated "practically the whole idea and all of the agencies of Federal conservation of natural resources" to refute the claim that the GOP was anticonservation. Comparing the record of publicized corruption in twenty years of Democratic rule with that of the GOP before 1933, he ridiculed the claim that the Republican Party was corrupt. Describing the GOP's internationalist efforts to preserve peace through the Washington treaties, the Kellogg-Briand pact, the World Economic Conference, and other such initiatives, Hoover undermined the assertion that the Republican Party was incapable of preserving peace and was isolationist. And comparing the 80,000 membership roll of the US Communist Party in 1943, with the 13,000 membership in 1932, he refuted the charge that the "Republican depression" had fueled the growth of communism in the United States. Hoover concluded by warning his young listeners that these misrepresentations were not "ancient stuff" but rather still indicated "the character of the party seeking by such means to retain their hold on Washington."

Judging from Hoover's correspondence, the speech was well received. One writer said it had "an almost unbelievable impact, especially on the younger generation."[120] Eisenhower warmly acknowledged the speech, and Hoover told him it had obviously met with favor, for there had been 35,000 requests for copies.[121] On October 22, Hoover wrote Clarence Kelland of the irony in the fact that the GOP National Committee, "after refusing to pay for the electronics of that speech (for which we had to pass the hat) has now ordered 35,000 copies."[122] By November 17, Hoover reported to Eisenhower that the number requested had grown to over 130,000.[123] Shortly before delivering the speech, Hoover wrote John Wheeler of the North American Newspaper Alliance that he was "again and finally going out of politics as soon as I finish a speech for Ike."[124]

Privately, Hoover's indictment of twenty years of Democratic rule was more severe than anything he was saying in the campaign. That indictment, though, was summed up in a memorandum he sent to Senator William Knowland on October 25, with a notation: "Perhaps some of it may be of use to you." In it, Hoover pointed to the encroachment of the federal government's power at the expense of state and local governments, with the result that the federal bureaucracy had grown in twenty years from 580,000 to 2,500,000 with the addition of "almost a thousand of government agencies. In fascist fashion, they dictate and give orders and favors to our citizens. In "many states there are more Federal officials than State, Municipal and County government employees, including the police." The Democrats had also taken the United States into "two great wars" that had resulted in the Yalta agreement that "planted the Communist hob-nail boots in China." "Out of all this came the 'police action' in Korea where we have already lost 122,000 dead, wounded and missing American boys." Roosevelt and Truman had also added more than $230 billion to the national debt—an "increase from $150 for every man, woman and child to $1500 for every one of you and a chain around the neck of every new baby." Federal taxes had "increased from an average of about $16 for each man, woman and child to about $430 for every one of them. Inflation had reduced the value of the dollar to only 48 cents from $1.00, so that as a result of taxes and inflation it would now require an income of $8,000 per year to buy as much as $3,000 per year would when FDR took office." Hoover added other charges—"creeping socialism" by the New Deal and Fair Deal, the penetration of communists and their sympathizers into government and labor unions, corruption, and "intellectual dishonesty"—as manifested by the "growing use of half-truths, poison smears and slogans, creation of fear, horror techniques and perversion of simple, well understood expressions," including the perversion of the term "liberalism."[125]

On November 6, 1952, the former president stationed himself in front of the television set in his Waldorf Tower suite to watch the election returns, confident that after twenty years a Republican would be returned to the White House. Stopping off en route to the Eisenhower suite in the Commodore, Clare Boothe Luce found Hoover "as close to happy" as she had ever seen him. A few hours later, when the results were known, Eisenhower joined his supporters briefly to thank them for their assistance, then returned to his suite where he collapsed on the bed exhausted from the long campaign. Mrs. Luce, who had served as something of a "pipeline" for Hoover's suggestions to the nominee during the campaign, now told the president-elect that before he went to sleep there was one more thing he must do. He must telephone the elderly man in the Waldorf who had been waiting twenty years for this moment. Mrs. Luce dialed the phone and caught Hoover just as he was readying himself for bed. At her suggestion, Eisenhower told Hoover that he would try to bring as much integrity to the presidency as Hoover had and that he would count heavily on the former president for his advice.[126] Hoover had waited a long time to hear those words from a Republican president.

CHAPTER 13

███████████████████████████

The Republican Years

Hoover and Eisenhower

Hoover did find some cause for concern in the 1952 vote. Having criticized past GOP presidential candidates for running behind the vote totals of the party's local candidates, he now faulted Eisenhower for running ahead of them. He blamed it on the fact that Ike had run a campaign "centered upon an individual and little interest in the Party as such." From this he concluded that the battle in behalf of conservative ideals was far from over.[1] Clearly the president's commitment to Republicanism was suspect in the Hoover-Taft wing of the party, but Hoover's own commitment to the party had been equally questioned by party leaders in the 1920s. In fact, the parallels between Hoover and Eisenhower were many and striking. Like Ike, Hoover had been considered too "liberal" by many party regulars when he entered the White House. Both had earned their reputations in wartime—Hoover as administrator of relief and head of the US Food Administration during World War I, and Eisenhower as leader of the Allied military forces in Europe in World War II. Both had built their reputations largely as administrators, for even Eisenhower's military laurels rested primarily on his ability to deal with the complex problems of directing a multinational army and controlling subordinates who frequently clashed with him over strategy while championing their own national interests. And both Hoover and Eisenhower became more committed and orthodox in their Republicanism after they had departed from the White House.

When Henry Hazlitt proposed in *Newsweek* that outgoing presidents should have the option of resigning immediately after the election in favor of the president-elect, Hoover criticized the proposal as impractical. "A new President," he wrote Hazlitt, "has been too busy with his campaign to select a Cabinet and his major officials. Without such officials to enter office with him, he would be helpless." He could not select such officials before the election, since that "would create many political liabilities." Still, Hoover believed the interregnum could be shortened to one month.[2]

Hoover was cheered by numerous letters after Election Day that hailed Eisenhower's victory as the culmination of his own twenty years of labor in behalf of the party. Congressman Joseph Martin wrote, "No one has contributed more to the upbuilding of the Republican Party than you have, and I know the election Tuesday was a great vindication to you. Truth and justice at last prevail."[3] In fact, the word *vindication* was used repeatedly to describe Hoover's relation to the election. Another correspondent wrote that the election represented "the splendid vindication by millions of American voters of those political principles which you consistently espoused and defend against attack, and worse, indifference." Similarly, he continued to receive plaudits for his campaign speech in Eisenhower's behalf. But the former president was convinced that the cabinet would be filled with "pre-Convention Ike men. The solace is that it cannot be as bad as the last."[4]

But only silence emanated from the camp of the president-elect. Except for the phone call from the Commodore to the Waldorf Astoria on election night, there was neither acknowledgment from Eisenhower of Hoover's contribution to the election nor any recognition of the former president's stature in the party. Not until December 23 was he invited to lunch with the president-elect along with his secretary of state-designate, John Foster Dulles, and Dr. Arthur S. Flemming, president of Ohio Wesleyan University. Flemming had served on the Hoover Commission and was now part of a three-man committee named by the general to evaluate a study of the organization of the executive branch of the government that was being conducted by Temple University.[5] Apparently encouraged by the talks, Hoover reactivated the Citizens Committee for the Hoover Report in early January 1953, and in that same month he attended the first inauguration of a Republican as president of the United States since he himself had taken the oath in March 1929.[6]

Active at 78

In January Hoover's close friend Felix Morley penned a long portrait of him for *Pathfinder* magazine. Morley wrote that at 78 Hoover now yielded "somewhat to the persuasion of those who warn that there are limits to his physical endurance," but he retained "a lot of the vigor that . . . has taken him to almost every country on the globe. If his limbs are a little stiff his mind is certainly as quick and limber as ever." Describing his work, Morley wrote,

> Mr. Hoover has an enormous correspondence from all over the world, which is punctiliously acknowledged. Then there are his educational and charitable interests, such as Stanford University, the Carnegie Institute, the Huntington Library and the Boys' Clubs of America, for all of which

Mr. Hoover serves as an active trustee.

Then "the Chief," as his helpers call him, advises on the continuing work springing from the report of the Hoover Commission on reorganization of the Federal bureaucracy. He serves, as always without compensation, in an advisory capacity for the World Bank and other international agencies. He has more requests for appointments than could be fitted into a 70-hour week. And he no sooner finished the last volume of his Memoirs than he started another book which is requiring the more painstaking research because its revelations of some as yet unwritten history may well prove startling.

Morley concluded, "A number have tried to smear him—this modest man who grows vehement only when the essential virtue of this country is attacked. But the smears have not stuck. The little minds cannot for long successfully assail the great. Only temporarily does the prophet lack honor in his own country."[7]

At the age of 78, Hoover remained remarkably active. Consulted by Congress and the Eisenhower administration concerning possible reforms in the Defense Department and the Social Security Agency, he received an appreciative letter from the president for his support of the plan for reorganization of the Social Security Agency.[8] Still distressed over the organization of the civil service system, Hoover sought reforms there and tried to enlist the support of *Readers' Digest* in the effort. His special concern was "that somewhere between 1500 and 2000 policymaking and policy-advising officials are now frozen into the Civil Service," which meant that Eisenhower could not really get "possession of the Government unless he can appoint or re-appoint these people." An administration whose policies had been mandated by the people and that had been entrusted with the responsibility to implement those policies ought to have "policy-making officials of their choice."[9]

The former president was also laying the foundation for a crusade that he would wage for several years against public power—government ownership and operation of electric utilities—that had been so much a part of Roosevelt's New Deal. In mid-March he wrote Joseph M. Dodge, the new director of the budget, for figures on federal power enterprises. He told Dodge that the Hoover Commission under Truman had been unable to compare the efficiency of public power versus private utilities because of "the shortcomings of the Federal enterprises' accounting methods," which had not furnished the information required by law of private enterprises, thus making it impossible for the commission's accountants to draw up comparisons. He wrote Dodge, "With the background of the Commission's information and my own engineering experience, I have thought I could be of service to further develop this subject and some alternatives. These expenditures now enter in a large way into the budget. I believe it would be of service to your work if the whole investment and operation of these enterprises could be determined." He hoped that the information he asked for from Dodge would make possible the comparisons that should be made. He added that he planned "to open this whole Pandora's Box in an address on April 11th. I start off by absolving the present administration of any part of it." The address would kick off Hoover's final assault on the New Deal.[10]

Although the promised material did not reach him in time for the speech, Hoover was able to assemble enough information from other sources to deliver the speech at the Case Institute of Technology on April 11. He reminded Dodge to send it to him, however, since he intended to continue on the attack and the additional information "could more fully indicate possible saving and revenues which might be of use in your many labors."[11] In the April 11 speech Hoover called for the US Government to "get out of the business of generating and distributing power as soon as possible" and gave three "first steps" by which that could be done, reducing the annual investment by the government in power enterprises by $600 million per year and also rescuing free enterprise "from this variety of creeping socialism." The three steps included (1) making no further appropriations for steam-generating plants or hydroelectric power generation, since, if such projects were economically feasible, "private enterprises will build them and pay taxes on them"; (2) ceasing appropriations for multipurpose dam projects unless the power generated by them was to be leased to private enterprises or states or municipalities or regional authorities for distribution; (3) establishing a temporary commission to reorganize the entire federal venture into the power business.[12]

Hoover presented figures that showed the public sector of power production had grown from less than 1 percent of the national total in 1933, to 20 to 25 percent by the middle of 1953. He recommended that the temporary commission he had suggested should (1) revise accounting methods of public power projects to divide fairly the cost between the various functions of multipurpose dams so that the real burden to taxpayers caused by the subsidized cheap power rates would be made apparent; (2) investigate the actual cost and prospective return for each major project contemplated; (3) formulate methods and standard terms for leasing out generating plants, transmission lines, and electric power to provide for interest payments, amortization, and arrears on the federal investment; (4) work out procedures for local or state agencies to share in the cost of future capital outlays for generating facilities when they were part of multipurpose dam projects.[13]

Hoover received "the usual left-wing attack by their battalions, regiments and corps" for his speech, with Eisenhower's secretary of the interior, Douglas McKay, among those expressing "unqualified disagreement."[14] From the perennial Socialist Party candidate for president Norman Thomas, a Hoover ally in his attempts before and during World War II to get food relief to Europe, came a challenge to debate the relative merits of public versus private ownership.[15] Hoover replied,

While I do not expect you to agree with my address, it is certain from your letter that you have not read the full text, which I am sending you. You suggest a debate, but your mistaken conception of my views, your extension of my speech to include the sale of all public owned electric plants, dams, post offices, forest and public lands to corporations would seem to be setting up wholly false premises for such a debate. In any event, I am associated with no person or organization who holds such views or objectives as you imply. Therefore, I could designate no one to undertake such a debate.[16]

Foreign Relations

In mid-March, Hoover raised the possibility of again proposing a mutual US-Soviet withdrawal from European nations. In a draft letter describing his proposal, he wrote that he had presented the idea "to our officials for tentative consideration" a year earlier, and now he wondered if there was "anything practical in the idea." He then outlined his plan:

> The idea I am suggesting for consideration is that we . . . should now propose a unified, disarmed and neutral Germany and Austria, withdrawal of all foreign military forces—Russian and Allies—leaving them with a constabulary for internal defense. It might be proposed that guardianship of any such arrangement be assigned to the United Nations, with the right of constant inspection of activities on the borders as well as control of neutrality within Germany. We might propose that Germany's neutrality be guaranteed by all powers . . . I do not suggest that in considering this idea that it be complicated by any proposals of world disarmament except Germany and Austria. If other Western Europe States should wish to arm, it will give them time to build up their defenses. I do not suggest that we, or Britain, abandon our great deterrent on Russian military aggression—our air and naval forces. If accepted, it would enable us to reduce our dangers of war on the European flank for some years, strengthen our deterrents, reinforce our own defenses and somewhat reduce our excessive military expenditures by decreasing our ground troops . . . If the Russians should favor such a proposal it might be followed with a later proposal as to Korea, and to Indo-China, but I would not think that the German-Austrian proposal should be complicated by including them at the start.

Even if the Russians rejected such a proposal, Hoover thought "it might be good propaganda as to our constructive efforts to find peace," especially "in the Middle Eastern, South Asian, and Latin American countries, but even among the people of the Soviet Union." His proposal, he said, was intended to go to several intimates for their "confidential reactions."[17]

General Albert Wedemeyer, now vice president of AVCO Manufacturing, quickly pointed out defects in Hoover's plan. It was based, he noted, on "two very weak and uncertain premises: 1) That the Soviet Union would abide by such an agreement, and 2) That the Germans themselves would accept such a status of impotency when surrounded by bristling guns of distrustful and unfriendly countries." Wedemeyer suggested, instead, allowing West Germany to create an army of sixty divisions and requiring the other NATO members to furnish eighty, which, together with supporting units from the United States, should be an adequate dam against Russian aggression.[18] Obviously disappointed by the reactions to his plan, Hoover wrote that because the lower house of the German parliament had ratified membership in NATO, he had suspended any further work on his proposal.[19]

The former president questioned, though, the movement to rearm Germany as a member of NATO. He wrote Admiral William V. Pratt,

> The Germans have always been the major enemy of Russia. They are the only race on the Continent with the virility and military ability to again threaten Russia. It may be possible that [Stalin's successor], uncertain of his position, will want to divert Russia into a foreign adventure. Suppose he said we will not have an armed Germany, that he will neutralize and refederate that state, that we [USSR] have no designs on the rest of Europe and then occupied Western Germany, which they could do in three weeks. Where would we be? We would have 550,000 American hostages in Soviet hands which could be distributed in Russian centers. They must thus defy us to drop atomic bombs. But beyond that I do not believe there is a government on the Continent that would join us in a war on Russia. Especially as all our Army on the Continent would have disappeared.

From such reasoning, Hoover decided the United States "should go a little slow until we can better appraise this new [Soviet] regime."[20] In May he concluded that the British disagreed with America's military policies and were advocating his "line." He told Admiral Pratt, "Whether they will break away and try to make peace with the Kremlin is in the balance."[21]

Hoover and other air power advocates were shocked, however, when the first Eisenhower budget slashed the air force objective of 143 groups down to 110 or 120. Fellers wrote Hoover, "The Republican policy to establish American Air Supremacy advocated by you and Senator Taft has been abandoned."[22] Hoover did not feel disposed openly to criticize a Republican administration, however, over this or any other issue. As he wrote Ferdinand Eberstadt on another issue late in May 1953, "I am still regarded by many of the public as a Republican leader," and if he opposed the administration this would "at once be heralded as a split in the Party." The reality was that Eisenhower's was "the only Republican Administration we can have or hope to reelect in our time." He did not rule out the possibility, however, that some other issue might eventually compel his "conscience to speak up."[23]

In April Arthur Krock reported in the *New York Times* that the Eisenhower administration was moving "methodically and at a more rapid pace" to carry out its campaign promises, including that of "taking the Government out of competition with private business to the utmost practical degree." Krock wrote that both the executive branch and Congress had "made long steps toward that goal and have listened with interest to advice from former President Hoover that it make an even longer one."[24] Encouraged, the former president wrote that he was confident the administration was "making progress in cleaning up the mess" in Washington. He knew from his years investigating that "mess" as head of the Hoover Commission what a task it would be. He wrote one correspondent, "It will be a slow job, but I am in hopes such progress will have been made by 1954 that we can carry the Congressional elections."[25]

Reorganization

Meanwhile, Senator Homer Ferguson and Congressman Clarence Brown were proposing legislation that would create a new Commission on Organization of the Executive Branch of the Government. The new bill differed from that which had established the first Hoover Commission in several important respects. For one, the Ferguson-Brown bill was forthright in calling for the elimination of "non-essential services, functions, and activities which are competitive with private enterprise." For another, it did not require that the new commission consist of an equal number of Democrats and Republicans. And finally, the new bill would also provide the commission with the power to subpoena witnesses and to recommend legislation or constitutional amendments.[26] Queried by Brown as to possible appointees for the new commission, Hoover wrote, "The House Committees have declared themselves for private enterprise. Unless that Commission is set up under men who believe in it, certainly I want no part of it." After suggesting several possible members, including Lewis Strauss, Hoover added that it "would be a good thing if the President appointed Dr. Arthur Flemming from his official staff. As you know, he was a member of our Commission."[27]

Hoover's own crusade against government ownership continued to be concentrated on federal power projects. On June 8 he dined at the White House, and the following day he prepared a memorandum for the president on "Projects for Navigation, Flood Control, Irrigation and Electric Power." In it, Hoover pointed out that the price tag for all projects authorized by Congress or proposed by government agencies or local communities would be approximately $50 billion. Many of these would have to be delayed or postponed due to the state of the economy. Hoover again suggested a "Commission for Review" to examine all such projects and decide which should be continued or begun. By "a nation-wide review of our Federal electric power now in operation," the commission could also determine "which could be more profitably administered by private enterprise or by the municipalities or the States or by a combination of States covering river basins." Private enterprise and state participation should also be brought into the financing of such projects. Hoover insisted, "Our purpose must be to restore the vitality and responsibility of local government in the administration of these projects. By doing so we can give release of the States from Federal dictation and remove taints of Socialism." In a cover letter to Lewis Strauss, by whom the memorandum was to be transmitted to Eisenhower, Hoover added that "by the character of his appointments on the new Commission for Reorganization of the Government now passed by Congress," the president could accomplish the creation of the "Commission of Review" that he had recommended in the memorandum.[28] A few days later Hoover sent Senator Herman Welker of Idaho a copy of his April speech, adding that he had sent it because "it would appear that the President has now adopted this policy."[29]

When newspaper publisher Richard Lloyd Jones wrote Hoover of his concern that the Eisenhower administration was very "casual in its attitude toward its campaign promises to the people," Hoover responded that the word "disturbed, scarcely expresses my views." He added, "My difficulty is that unless we can re-elect this administration, the Republican Party is ended—and with it the end of free men as you and I would have them. I have felt there is some hope that forces in Europe will take the solution into their own hands. Opposition to the Roosevelt-Truman regime at least relieved frustration."[30]

On July 10, 1953, President Eisenhower signed into law the Ferguson-Brown bill creating the new Commission on Organization of the Executive Branch of the Government, and three days later he wrote Hoover to ask if the former president would serve on it.[31] With Hoover's consent, the president named him as one of four presidential appointees to the commission, along with Attorney General Herbert Brownell, Dr. Arthur S. Flemming, director of defense mobilization and a member of the first Hoover Commission, and Democrat James A. Farley, postmaster general under Roosevelt. Vice President Nixon, acting for the Senate, appointed two Republicans and two Democrats, as did Speaker of the House Joseph Martin. Both Senator Ferguson and Congressman Brown, sponsors of the legislation, were selected. In appointing three Republicans and one Democrat, Eisenhower created a Republican majority of seven to five on the commission, which was permitted under the law. The GOP majority, however, diminished the aura of nonpartisanship that had surrounded the work of the first commission, and it laid the basis for later criticism of the commission's recommendations.[32] Of his new responsibilities, Hoover told the press, "Unending public chores seem to have become my privilege in life."[33]

Early in 1953, Hoover's longtime, close friend, Ohio senator Robert A. Taft, was afflicted with cancer. Now majority floor leader of the GOP-controlled Senate, Taft fought a courageous battle against the disease. Despite his own advanced age, the former president managed frequent visits to Taft's bedside. In July, Hoover flew to California for his annual visit to the Bohemian Club encampment. By this time Taft's malignancy was well advanced, and on the last day of July he died. In a statement to the press, Hoover recalled that the two had been devoted friends "for over thirty-five years since he joined in public service during the first World War." He described Taft as "more nearly an irreplaceable man in American life than we have seen in three generations."[34]

The next day, Hoover delivered his annual off-the-record talk at the Bohemian Club, beginning with an appraisal of the international situation. Stalin's death, he now concluded, would lead to a period of relative tranquility in Soviet relations with the rest of the world until a new leader was able to consolidate his hold on the government. He still believed that the primary focus of Soviet expansionist aims was in Asia, not in Western Europe, but he found the Western European nations no better prepared now to defend themselves than they had been three years earlier. Again he called for a reappraisal of American policies toward Europe. Of the new Hoover Commission, as it was already being called, he noted that this one had "far wider powers" than the first one, including the authority to "make recommendations for surgery on everything except the Congress and the Judiciary." That he viewed the new commission as an opportunity to wage renewed warfare on the remnants of the New Deal and Fair Deal is clear, for he told his listeners,

> The Commission can at least serve to expose certain overall growths in the Federal Government during the past 20 years which cry for remedies. The first is to lessen this invasion of State and local governments by a Federal bureaucracy from Washington. The survival of free men rests on local governments.
>
> The second is to make a contribution toward lessening Federal expenditures, toward balancing the budget and toward reducing taxes. This continued inflation, unless quickly stopped, will undermine all freedom in the United States.
>
> The third is creeping Socialism. The Federal Government has to-day more than 500 activities in economic competition with the private citizens. The new authority specifically requires us to propose surgical operations on these spots. Among them is the so-called public power. My objections are not directed against building dams for water conservation or for generation of electric power. I do object to the use of power distribution to socialize the electric industry.

The commission, he said, "could do a better job if we had dictatorial powers, and the right to have about one man hung every month without trial." Its main purpose was "to help clean up the mess which General Eisenhower inherited. But it will take time." Hoover ended his talk with a eulogy of Senator Taft.[35]

Now that he was back in the business of reorganizing the federal government, Hoover considered it best "to keep still on any partisan matter for the present," since he was trying to put the new commission "on a non-partisan basis—or at least bipartisan."[36] He told GOP national chairman Leonard Hall that he would not be able to make speeches "for some months to come. I have to be careful if I am going to do the job now in front of me."[37] No doubt Hoover was aware of concern already being expressed that the commission planned an all-out assault on the New Deal. As one Brooklyn College professor put it in a letter to the *New York Times*, the new Hoover Commission, "if permitted, will serve as the front for the Republican party to turn the clock back to the Nineteen-twenties and the political philosophy of Herbert Hoover."[38] Certainly the potential for that happening with a committee dominated by Republicans and headed by Hoover, working together with a Republican White House and Congress, seemed enormous. The surprise reelection of Truman in 1948 had blunted such a wide-scale assault on the New Deal by the first commission; the concern now was with the possibility that Republicans might lose control of Congress in 1954 before the new commission finished its work.

Hoover was elected chairman by the new commission at its first meeting late in September 1953, and he outlined the task before the new Hoover Commission in a press release. He pointed out that the first commission had made a total of 273 recommendations for reforms in the government, of which about 122 remained as "unfinished business." Those earlier recommendations had primarily dealt with reform of the executive agencies of the government, and one result of its work had been that the heads of agencies had been granted greater authority to affect their own reorganization "toward greater efficiency and the elimination of waste." But many of the problems in those areas remained, since they could not be solved by individual agencies and Hoover had suggested that the new commission "specialize in such fields," including such multiagency problems as "the methods and problems in accounting, budgeting, and procurement of supplies and personnel." The president was also still overburdened by "an appalling number of agencies" that reported only to him and that lacked adequate supervision or overlapped with other agencies. Some activities—like housing, medical services, and lending—were participated in by a number of different agencies. And Hoover pointed out that the new commission was specifically charged with inquiring into areas where the government was competing with private enterprise. It would proceed as the earlier commission had, "by setting up task forces composed of men and women who have had experience in these fields and who are independent of any special interest."

The former president had already drawn up lists of prospective task force members and had won at least grudging approval of them from the commission, as well as the authority to name other members without consultation with the commission. A study of the second Hoover Commission notes, "As a result the membership of all the task forces eventually was named by the former President even though the 1947 Commission had voted as a body on such appointments."[39] In selecting the areas of inquiry for the task forces and naming their members, Hoover had clearly put his own stamp on the commission's inquiry and likely recommendations to a far greater degree than with the first commission. More so than the first one, this commission deserved description as the Hoover Commission.

From the very first meeting there was uneasiness on the part of some of the members of the commission, especially with the scope of the inquiry by the task force on water and power resources, which some of them felt to be an echo of Hoover's April speech in which he had made clear his antipathy to federal involvement in the generation and distribution of electric power. The *New York Times* wrote, "While commission members declined to be quoted, some privately expressed the fear that the issue could be prejudged."[40] Another issue that would later draw some criticism was Hoover's refusal to provide for the selection of a vice chairman, even though the legislation establishing the commission clearly mandated that one should be chosen. It has been suggested that Hoover's failure to put the question to the commission stemmed from "his desire to retain unrestricted control over the Commission since he may have found the presence of Vice-chairman Dean Acheson a personal hindrance in 1949."[41] While this may well have been one factor, another was doubtless the fact that both Senator Ferguson and Congressman Brown, the cosponsors of the legislation establishing the commission, desired the post. Brown was especially opposed to Ferguson becoming vice chairman, since the senator was a comparative latecomer to the movement for a commission, while Brown had originated it.[42] Thus Hoover may have left the vice chairmanship vacant to avoid alienating either of these friends.

The commission's inquiry into public power was the lightning rod that drew most criticism of the commission's work. Only weeks after the first meeting of the commission, the *New York Times* observed that the water and power resources task force, headed by retired admiral Ben Moreel, now chairman of Jones and Laughlin Steel, would, if it followed Hoover's personal inclination, probably reflect the advice of the former president's April speech. However, the newspaper argued that the issue of public power was more complicated than that. While there were some areas in which private enterprise might be more efficient, there were others in which public ownership seemed essential. The *Times* hoped that the task force would approach the issue with an open mind and would "contribute new ideas in this field."[43] A few days later, two public power interest groups—the American Public Power Association and the Cooperative League—charged that the Moreel task force was stacked in its membership with opponents of public power. The American Public Power Association found not a single one of the 25 members of the task force who was a public power advocate, and it feared the task force would simply recommend specific methods for implementing the views Hoover had outlined in his April speech.[44]

In late November, smarting under criticism for having promoted a man to an important position in his administration who later turned out to be a spy, Truman lashed out at his critics. Dewey wrote Hoover, "On the other hand, for twenty years the Democrats lied about you and your administration. As late as 1952, Adlai Stevenson was running against you for President. It mystifies me why it should be proper for Democrats to lie and lie and lie about a Republican former President and improper for the Republicans to tell the truth from the record about a former Democrat President. The distinction completely eludes me." And Dewey said so in a speech on December 16, 1953.[45] Hoover responded that he thought "somebody ought to point out that the Democratic Party gained power and held it for 20 years by lying about the Hoover Administration." He did not know if "the Republican Party can hold power for 19 years or more by telling the truth about the Roosevelt and Truman administrations."[46]

At the end of the year Hoover wrote Hugh Gibson that he had been "working at my job in Washington 3 to 4 days a week since mid-September."[47] It was a remarkable work schedule for a man who was less than a year away from his eightieth birthday. Herbert Brownell later recalled of his service on the Hoover Commission, "Joe Kennedy and I sat together and we really admired Mr. Hoover. He worked like a Trojan. That's my recollection of him during that time—how hard continuously he worked. He just begrudged every minute we took out for a sandwich and coffee in the middle of our all day meetings, you know, because he wasn't getting anything done. We used to joke with him a little about it, and he would laugh about it but he'd go right on with business during the lunch."[48] Hoover reported that the initial "coldness . . . even some hostility" in his relations with the Eisenhower administration had gradually "evaporated," but "I am not in any inner circle of influence." With the exception of a few people in the administration, he described himself as "in an outer darkness." He found hopeful signs, however, that his "three year campaign on obsolete methods of war" had "now had a mite of acceptance as witness the budget which will be presented next month."[49] He reiterated this latter point to another friend and added that there was also a growing awareness in Washington that "Europe does not intend to help itself so long as we keep up the money stream. If these tendencies continue, we may see daylight." As for the reorganization committee, Hoover wrote that he had "taken on a most trying job merely in the hope that I can contribute something to keep the ADA [the liberal Americans for Democratic Action] from running the United States."[50]

The next month he wrote Hugh Gibson that his job was giving him no "joy" but that "the State Department has decided to go back to my recommendations of four years ago and begin there, which is something." He was about to leave for a fishing trip in Florida to "recuperate from some rough sessions with the politicians in my new commission. My relations with the New Dealers four years ago were more pleasant." He did find pleasure, however, in the fact that "the administration, without admitting it, has adopted my proposals in the Great Debate—of course without any acknowledgment as to where they got it. Anyway it is all to the good. And somehow the republic lives."[51] Indeed, by the time he wrote to Gibson in mid-January 1954, the "New Look" defense policy of the Eisenhower administration was clear, and it was compatible with the former president's views in its emphasis on air power, nuclear weapons, and flexible response.

While avoiding partisan speeches during his work on the Hoover Commission, the former president continued to preach on issues that were dear to him. In January 1954 he told the International Ben Franklin Society that the federal government had shown "some lack of adherence" to Franklin's notions of thrift. He noted that for Franklin government borrowing and debts "were the road of sorrow and in general the destroyers of liberty."[52] Two months later he predicted that if the recommendations of the new Hoover Commission were followed they would save between $5 billion and $7 billion per year. He told the National Press Club that he did not expect all the recommendations to be adopted, however, since about two hundred pressure groups "occupy themselves pressuring the Government for more spending or in opposing any reductions."[53]

Foreign Relations Again

Hoover could not free himself of foreign policy issues even while pursuing his work on the commission. Late in 1953, a small group of opponents of the admission of the People's Republic of China into the United Nations launched a drive to secure the signatures of several hundred prominent Americans on a petition opposing such a move. Hoover agreed to sign the petition in September.[54] When word of the petition leaked out, the organizers were so deluged with requests by others to sign that they changed the movement to the Committee for One Million. Charles Edison, Congressman Walter Judd, and former diplomat Joseph C. Grew sought Hoover as a sponsor in order attract financial support and further signatures.[55] Hoover did so, issuing a statement in January at their request, which said, "One of the greatest dangers the cause of freedom faces today is uncertainty in the minds of both governments and peoples abroad as to the position of the United States in relation to Communist China. The nations in the far East are in constant danger of their aggression. In the meantime, they work and conspire to break down the morals of these free peoples of Asia; endeavor to create disunity and spread lies about the stand of the United States." The Committee for One Million was clarifying the position of the United States, he said, by its activities.[56] An old foreign policy ally in Kansas was not, however, a supporter of the petition being circulated by what he termed "Hoover's committee." Alf Landon did not favor admission of the PRC into the UN, but he did wish to preserve flexibility in American foreign policy in the event it might some day be possible to "woo this government away from the Kremlin."[57] Thus the two septuagenarian GOP statesmen were at odds over the issue, and Landon spoke out in Kansas against the petition campaign.

In January 1954 the proposed Bricker amendment was an issue in American politics. That amendment, introduced by Hoover's friend Senator John Bricker of Ohio, was intended to place restrictions on the treaty-making power of the White House and was, in part, a reaction to the perceived abuses in that regard during the Roosevelt and Truman years. Eisenhower showed a disposition to compromise over the issue, and Hoover favored it but did not take a strong public position on the issue, although he almost certainly would have done so had a Democrat occupied the White House. In February he wrote Admiral Pratt he was "convinced that some amendment will be passed sooner or later. It may be reduced to Presidential Agreements as distinguished from Treaties."[58] In fact, however, the Bricker amendment failed passage.

Meanwhile, the former president was still smarting under the attacks Truman had made on him during the 1952 campaign. When James Farley invited him to attend a dinner honoring Truman's seventieth birthday, Hoover declining, telling the former postmaster general that his "presence there would cause a mass of gossip and ventilation of old issues, more especially in this case, in view of Mr. Truman's personal attacks upon me." Obviously hoping that Farley would pass his feelings on to Truman, Hoover wrote,

> I have never made a personal attack upon him, and I gave much of my energies for nearly four years to aiding his Administration. We have differed on public policies, but that is the legitimate and necessary process of American life. I have had a higher opinion both of Mr. Truman personally and of many of his policies than many of my political colleagues. I have no desire to avoid meeting him. Indeed, I am confident the time will yet come when he and I can join to forward matters of public interest.[59]

In April 1954 Senator Alexander Wiley solicited Hoover's views on possible revisions in the United Nations Charter, since the charter provided that revisions might be proposed at the 1955 meeting of the United Nations. Hoover responded that the United Nations should be retained, even though it had not "fulfilled expectations." Pointing to similarities between the League of Nations and the United Nations, Hoover observed that they had both suffered from a dissolution of the spirit of wartime unity and neither was prepared for "the destructive effect upon peace or upon the organizations by totalitarian governments," which were, "by nature militaristic and aggressive and, therefore," were "poor material upon which to build international laws and morals." Both the League of Nations and the United Nations had been rendered "impotent to prevent aggression by a major power" due to the dominance and disparate views of those powers, and neither organization had been able to make any progress toward disarmament for the same reasons. The failures of both organizations had also led to a resurgence of balance of power concepts, the formation of alliances, and the division of the world into armed camps.[60]

Hoover saw, however, little likelihood that the situation could be changed by alterations in the charter so long as the Cold War continued. Any such changes, he said, would have to "await a great change in the whole Communist attitude." In the meantime, the United Nations should continue to "build toward more unity in the field of pacific action to settle disputes especially among secondary nations; in the promotion of scientific research; exchange of knowledge; public health; philanthropy; and such contributions to general prosperity as are possible." He noted suggestions that Secretary of State Dulles had made for revisions, implying approval of them, and added one new suggestion: "That all treaties suggested by [the United Nations] subsidiary economic, social or other organizations for submission to nations should be subject to revision and approval by the Security Council before their submission to individual nations."

During May and June of 1954 the French reeled before attacks by the communist Viet Minh in Indochina and British Prime Minister Winston Churchill visited the United States. A visitor late in June drew Hoover out at length on the subject of world affairs in an eight-hour conversation. He found Hoover convinced that Eisenhower would not send ground forces to aid the French in Indochina and of the opinion that such an intervention would have been "much worse than Korea" and "the end of the Republican Party" if Eisenhower did embark upon it. Such an American intervention in Southeast Asia would be "just what Russia would like to have us do." He opposed the creation of a Southeast Asian military alliance but was concerned over Japan's necessity to trade with her Asian neighbors, and so he favored, instead, an "Asian economic alliance" that would include Burma and India. He recognized the tenseness of the current world situation but did not "share the view that if we start drawing in our horns and minding our own business that Russia will advance every foot we retreat until we will eventually find North America standing alone in a communist world." This "unreasoning fear" Hoover called "silly." It ignored, he pointed out, the forces of nationalism, "the fact that no people anywhere like to live under the Russian yoke," and "the fact that the farther Russia spreads out the weaker the control."[61]

Later that same month Hoover told the Hall of Fame Dinner in Chicago his ideas on how the United States might get along with other free nations. First, Americans must recognize "that there are wide differences in social inheritances, economic and political objectives in each of the free nations" and that "military alliances or peacetime collective action can endure only as long as there are common objectives and purposes among the participants." But those "interests, objectives, and policies . . . constantly shift with this rapidly changing scene," as could be seen in the shift of American policies and attitudes toward the Soviet Union, Germany, and Japan. Americans must also recognize "that the atomic bomb and the steady growth of Communist military strength have contributed to shift the policies of some of the free nations." The United Nations was paralyzed by the communist members and by the lack of unity among the free nations, with the result that many free nations had been "forced into a multitude of military alliances," while others had sought refuge in neutrality, and "some of our military allies are faltering in the march." American must realize that collective security through the United Nations was nonexistent and that the world was back to the old concepts of balances of power and "ancient forms of diplomacy." Moreover, in dealing with "these gigantic problems of today we must have patience, tolerance, and understanding of these differences of interests and objectives of the free nations" and should not expect miracles of those who "must pilot our foreign policies." But Americans should not abandon hope in the United Nations, nor should they give up "the ideal that someday, somehow, unity for peace can be built in the world." Americans should recognize the importance of nationalism in the world and not denigrate it at home, for love of country was a source of strength that could keep the country free. Finally, Hoover concluded that "our people must realize that our own right arm plus some deterrents unhealthy to the aggressor are our major reliance for our defense."[62]

In early August, President Eisenhower invited the most famous fisherman in America to join him on a fishing trip to Colorado, and Hoover, who rarely turned down a fishing opportunity, agreed.[63] Eisenhower then wrote to the former president describing the fishing possibilities in the Denver area. He told Hoover that he need not "be especially terrified at the prospect of living on my cooking for a couple of days." He explained,

> My culinary reputation is pretty good—but my repertoire is limited. It is only after about four days that my guests begin to look a little pained when they come to the dinner table. It is a grand place to loaf and we will have absolutely no one with us except my great friend who owns the place, and possibly my brother Milton.
>
> The little stream has many pools that can be fished easily from the bank. Even if you should be compelled to cross the stream occasionally, you will find it remarkably easy to wade.
>
> I cannot tell you how delighted I am at the prospect of the two of us having a period together in such a quiet retreat.[64]

Hoover scribbled his reply on the letter, "I will be at the airport in Washington on August 30 to undertake a charming prospect."

Before the fishing trip, the former president journeyed to his birthplace in West Branch, Iowa, where he gave a speech. Of all Hoover's birthday celebrations, the eightieth was certainly the most spectacular. *Time* described the preparations in the small town of a population of 769:

> The Lions International club pushed a campaign to get the town's modest homes gleaming with new paint, and front yards trimmed to the quick. Work was rushed on the new elementary school so that the famous guest could dedicate it. The night before the big day, the Women's Society of Christian Service of the Methodist Church stored gallons of pickled beets and great bowls of applesauce in the demonstration refrigerators of Rummels' appliance store on Main Street. At midmorning the ladies began carrying the food to a special luncheon tent along with 60 fried chickens, cords of fresh sweet corn, and the

100-egg birthday cake baked by Mrs. Harold Heick.[65]

The *New York Times* reported that church and service groups from West Branch and surrounding small towns would man sandwich stands to serve the fifty thousand guests attending, while church women would serve an "old-fashioned Iowa dinner" that included fried chicken, Iowa corn on the cob, tomatoes, apple sauce, cake, and ice cream to two hundred invited guests.[66]

In his speech to the assembled throng, Hoover argued that the division of powers between the federal and state governments, as well as between the three branches of the federal government, had "become seriously confused, corroded and weakened during the twenty years before this Administration," as the federal government under Roosevelt and Truman had reached out to absorb "many of the vital functions of state and local government." The result had been a burgeoning of the federal bureaucracy, and innate in bureaucracy were "three implacable spirits," which he described as "self-perpetuation, expansion of their empires, and demand for more power. Bureaucracy rushes headlong into the visions of the millennium and sends the bills to the Treasury." In foreign relations there had been "a special encroachment of the Executive upon the legislative branch. This has been through a new type of commitment of the United States to other nations"—joint statements with foreign officials that committed America "without the specific consent of the elected representatives of the people." Hoover reviewed such commitments, which had "resulted in a shrinking of human freedom over the whole world" and to the "jeopardies of the 'Cold War.'" A by-product had been the shrinking of American freedoms through "crushing taxes, huge defense costs, inflation and compulsory military service." Such misuse of power must be forever made impossible. The present world situation had confirmed, in Hoover's view, his predictions as an opponent of intervention in World War II. But far from being pessimistic about the nation's future, Hoover told his audience, "There are voices in our country who daily sound alarms that our civilization is on the way out. Concentrated on the difficulties of our times, they see an early and dour end for us. But civilization does not decline and fall while the people still possess dynamic creative faculties, devotion to religious faith and to liberty. The American people still possess those qualities. We are not at the bedside of a nation in death agony."[67]

Hoover's West Branch speech, though, only touched the tip of the iceberg of his feelings about the course of America's foreign relations during the Roosevelt and Truman years. In September he wrote a long memorandum "simply to file away for the record" that is much more revealing of his views. He began by noting, "The state of mind of all thinking Americans is one of complete frustration over our foreign policies." Despite the obvious aim of "the Kremlin to spread Communism over the earth by infiltration, conspiracy or military conquest," the United States had from 1933 to 1946 undertaken "military alliance and political collaboration and appeasement with the Kremlin," and then "from 1942 to 1950 we undertook at the same time to support the Chinese Nationalists and collaboration and appeasement with the Chinese Communists." He added, "The result has been a long line of tombstones over 21 free peoples and 900,000,000 human beings engraved with the words, "Recognition of Communist Russia, 1933," "The Atlantic Charter, 1940," "The Tacit Alliance with Russia, 1941," "The Moscow Conference, 1942," "Casablanca, 1943," "Teheran, 1943," "Yalta, 1945," "Potsdam, 1945," "Hiroshima and Nagasaki, 1945," "United Nations, 1945," "The Marshall Mission to China, 1946," "Death of China, 1950," "The Aggression Against Korea, 1952," "Indo-China, 1954," "The Defeat of the European Defense Community, 1954." Recognition of the Soviet Union had brought communist conspirators into the United States who, along with fellow travelers, attained important positions in the federal government where "(a) they influenced American national policies to further Communist calamities upon civilization; and (b) they stole our national secrets of policy and of military invention, including both the A- and H-Bombs."[68]

By the alliance with Stalin and Churchill during the war not only was communism spread over the world but the unconditional surrender policy "destroyed the German 1000-year dam against the swarming of Asiatic hordes over Western Europe and the Japanese 75-year dam against the spread of Russian conquest of Asia." The United Nations had only resulted in "the spread of further Communist infiltration; the frustration of every effort to secure peace, and a world forum for the defamation of the United States." The policy of containment, launched in 1946, had led to the stationing of three hundred thousand American servicemen in Europe, air bases on the periphery of the Soviet Union, "gigantic giveaway programs of money, commodities, and arms under the Marshall Plan and other agencies, to a total expenditure of $70 billion, or enough to have rebuilt every subnormal home, school, and church in the United States." When the communists began in 1950 a "policy of military aggression by their satellite countries," the United Nations had responded in Korea, but the "nations who voted for this action in the United Nations, have about 1,500,000,000 inhabitants and armed forces of about 2,000,000 men. Yet those who voted contributed only 5% of the United Nations Armies. We, with 10% of the number of inhabitants, furnished 95% of the military forces and lost 150,000 casualties." The Allies, notably Great Britain, had intervened to prevent victory in Korea and MacArthur had been removed. Allied compromise in Korea was regarded among Asians as a defeat for the United States and the United Nations, and that defeat had been followed by another in Indochina for the West. By supporting Britain and France in retaining their overseas empires, the United States had been given "the stigma of colonial exploitation which we little deserve in view of our long history of sympathy with peoples trying to be free"

The conclusions that Hoover drew from all this were as follows: "We must at last recognize one positive fundamental in international life. The economic and expansion aims, ideals, objectives, traditions, fears, hates and national interests in all nations are different." The United States must also recognize the power of the spirit of nationalism in other nations. Military alliances could only endure so long as "the aims, ideals and interests and safety of nations run parallel." The policies of Italy, France, and the nations of South Asia were also profoundly influenced by the presence of powerful communist parties in those countries. NATO was still utterly incapable of putting up any significant defense against a communist attack. More and more nations were embracing a new international phenomenon—neutralism—together with an emphasis on "peaceful coexistence." These forces meant that "the whole North Atlantic Treaty Organization has gone with the wind" and not even Britain or Japan could be counted upon as an ally any longer in the event of a war with the Soviet Union. Hoover wrote, "That there is failure and disaster which besets our present policies should be now evident. We have tried cooperation with the Kremlin. We have tried since the war to find peace by (a) diplomatic organization; (b) military alliances for 'containment'; (c) resistance of Communist satellite aggression; (b) economic support to nations. All of these policies have gone by the board. There is no wonder that thinking Americans are in a state of total frustration over our national policies."

What should the United States do to cope with the new situation in the world? First, Hoover concluded, the government should be frank with the American people about "where we find ourselves," admitting that "a new line of foreign policies must be worked out." The United States should not oppose movements toward neutralism, since to oppose them would be futile in any case. Nor should the United States oppose "any agreements between nations and Russia looking to 'peaceful coexistence.' If they think they can get protection from aggression by those means we ought [not] to object to their trying it." The United States might keep "a feeble flame of resistance alive by arms and subsidies to such governments as pledge themselves there will no 'neutralization' agreements to 'peaceful coexistence.'" That might include such nations as Germany, Belgium, Holland, Greece, Spain, and Turkey, but "we should furnish nothing more even to these countries except upon request. Then we could make our demands as to what they intend to do, and how?" Economic aid should be ruled out as "an antidote to Communist penetration," because "no amount of American activities could so rebuild European lower classes' standard of living as would counteract Communist infiltration and much of our aid is blatantly diverted to the rich, not the poor." West Germany should be given complete independence and be allowed to rearm, so that they could "rebuild the only safety of Western Europe—the German dam. Whether Russia would sit by and see Germany re-arm itself is problematical but it is worth trying." Japan could "only survive by raw materials from China and that market for manufactured goods," so the United States "should encourage her to set up all such trade relations" with China in order that American subsidies to offset her deficit in trade could be eliminated.

Most of America's rehabilitation measures should be concentrated in Latin America—"and there only upon their request and upon our stipulation that their governments set up their own organization for this purpose to which we could contribute on a 50-50 basis. These steps are essential to maintain wise use and to maintain their own national pride." Meanwhile, the United States should "build our air, atomic and missile weapons intensively and at once to such dimensions as will deter any Communist attack upon us. We should build our radar and other electronic defenses to the utmost degree." Ground armies, "except for internal defense," he now considered obsolete, as well as battleships. Money currently being spent on foreign military and economic aid should be diverted instead to America's own economic rehabilitation. The United States "should cease to support colonial exploitation even by our friends" and "reaffirm the American doctrine of freedom of peoples." And finally, Hoover concluded, "above all, we should realize that only in our own strong arm and the Western Hemisphere is our safety and sanctuary. We should not destroy them by chasing mirages."

In October, two months after his eightieth birthday, Hoover hosted an "after-glow" party at his Waldorf suite for his guests at various Bohemian Club encampments over the years. In a talk to the group, he touched on many topics including the work of the reorganization committee. He gave them one example of the "nightmare" they were confronting:

> The Federal Government is engaged in 1500 socialistic business enterprises in competition with the citizens; it has $25 billion invested in them; 12 agencies give contrary advice on the weather; and 41 agencies give assorted medical service. That does not include the Federal Hospitals of which there are 38 in the New York area alone—each with empty beds. The Government possesses obsolete commodities costing $30 billion and that does not include 22 years' supply of toilet paper. After listening to lists of some of these commodities, I suggested to the Pentagon that I had no doubt the General who fought the first battle with gun powder kept his crossbows in storage for 40 years.

Of the controversy that was still being generated by Senator Joseph McCarthy's charges of communists in the government, Hoover told his guests "I may mention that Moscow has not stopped recruiting agents among our fuzzy-minded intellectuals just because Senator McCarthy is to be stopped by Senator [Ralph] Flanders. McCarthy is the seventh King-pin to be bowled over by the left-wingers in ten years. But we still have two King-pins standing up. They head other Congressional Committees at work on this job." The former president argued that such committee investigations of communists were vital.[69]

Turning to foreign relations, the former president detected a rise in the spirit of nationalism everywhere but in the United States. The atomic and hydrogen bombs, he suggested, had "transformed all our alliances, all allegiances and all international relations," for no matter how much other nations might wish to support the United States, they would no longer dare to go to war with the Soviet Union lest they be obliterated by Soviet nuclear weapons. The funneling of American money into the pockets of other nations had won no dependable friends for the United States, he concluded, but "they still want our money." As for the United Nations, he found no one convinced "that this organization could or would protect us from a major military aggression," but it ought to be retained if only because "they have electronic devices by which we can give and receive the best oratory of denunciation in five languages all at once." There was also always the possibility that the United Nations might one day become "a rallying point for unity in the free nations," and if it did nothing else it made contributions in public health. On the positive side, he found "less war tensions in the world than a year or two years ago," and there had recently been advances and technology of revolutionary import, with no sign that the pace was slackening. And the resultant increases in productivity, he noted, had "produced a higher standard of living than we had before the second World War."

In October Hoover accepted an invitation from Chancellor Konrad Adenauer to visit West Germany, and late in the month Adenauer called on him in New York to finalize the details of the trip that was scheduled for late November.[70] Before he left for Germany, the off-year elections of 1954 swept the GOP out of control of Congress, which boded ill for the prospects of the Hoover Commission recommendations when they reached Congress. A few days before he left for Germany Hoover wrote Clarence Kelland that he hoped conservative Democrats would join with conservative Republicans in the Congress "in opposition to further socialism," but he did not expect much help from "middle-of-the-road Republicans." He predicted that the Hoover Commission report would "throw many jolts against all this, but beyond registering, it will not likely be decisive." He still hoped that the GOP would eventually awaken to the fact that the United States was not a socialist country. Hoover expressed his satisfaction with Dulles, Secretary of Defense Charles Wilson, Secretary of the Treasury George Humphrey, Secretary of Agriculture Ezra Taft Benson, and presidential assistant Sherman Adams. "The trouble," he wrote, "comes from other quarters from outside the White House and the Cabinet." He was leaving for Germany, he told Kelland, "to help Adenauer, for he is the only bulwark against the sweep of Socialism over Europe."[71]

Adenauer greeted Hoover at the airport upon his arrival in Germany, and hailed the former president "as one of the great men of the world who has placed himself in the service of humanity."[72] At a dinner hosted by Adenauer, Hoover was described as a great American who had helped pave the way for West Germany's recovery from the ravages of war.[73] In a speech in the West German capital of Bonn, Hoover expressed his faith in a healthy German nationalism. He reiterated his belief that Germany had "before now been the bastion of Western civilization which deterred its destruction by Asiatic hordes. My prayer is that Germany may be given the unity and full freedom which will restore her to that mission in the world." The fundamental reason for the presence of US armed forces in Europe, he said, was not the defense of the United States, which could be done more cheaply, but to preserve Western civilization in Europe and the freedom of the peoples there. He again expressed hope that other European nations would take up more of the burden of their own defense, warning that the patience of the American people was not inexhaustible. Tensions with the Soviet Union seemed to be abating, but Hoover warned that "from our many years' experience with the Communists we should learn more about what peaceful coexistence means. What we must await are works rather than words."[74] West German president Theodor Heuss told Hoover, "Your name is blessed by millions of nameless people."[75] When he left Germany a few days later the former president recalled that when he had visited the country eight years earlier it had appeared that it would be "many, many years" before the Germans would be on their feet again, and he described their accomplishments since then as "brilliant." "Today," he told Adenauer, "under your wise statesmanship, West Germany is about to attain her independence and to become a partner in the defense of freedom from the common danger."[76]

After he had reported to President Eisenhower on the trip, the president responded by writing that he had noted "with great satisfaction" that Hoover's trip "had been as successful as I knew it would be and a real tribute to the humanitarian spirit of America which you personify. Let me thank you for your readiness to undertake this mission. At this decisive moment in the history of American-German relations, it would be hard for me to think of any man more eminently qualified to convey to the German people the feelings of friendship with which the American people welcome the return of Germany to the family of Western nations." Hoover confided to a friend, however, that he had not enjoyed the trip, because "I had to deliver four speeches, attend four banquets, eat four luncheons and meet hundreds of people. I am glad to get back home and to work. However, Chancellor Adenauer was kind enough to say that I helped him to win the election."[77] Although Hoover was now in his eighties, this was not the last overseas mission the president would ask him to undertake.

The Hoover Commission

Hoover now immersed himself once again in the work of the second Hoover Commission, and in mid-February 1955 the commission's first report was submitted to Congress. It recommended a government employment program to attract and retain more top talent, including the creation of a "senior civil service group" of nonpartisan, well-paid professional administrators who possessed special skills and experience; higher pay for top administrators; improved training programs; and greater use of merit pay increases.

The report also called for revisions to be made in the conflict-of-interest rules and in reduction-in-force procedures; the extension of civil service to cover more government employees, including US marshals and customs officials; and the payment of "prevailing wages," especially to employees in lower wage brackets. The report estimated that nearly $50 million per year could be saved from reductions in employee turnover if these reforms were adopted.[78]

A week later the second report was released, dealing with paperwork and the reduction of red tape. Estimating that $255 million could be saved if its recommendations were put into effect, the report called for a presidential executive order that would create a paperwork management program under the supervision of the General Services Administration, with an official in each government agency responsible for eliminating nonessential reports and copies of letters and for simplifying forms.[79]

The third report, issued a week after the second, recommended the closing of uneconomical federal hospitals and an end to excessive building of new ones. It called for an end to free medical care for merchant seamen and restrictions on care for veterans with non-service-connected disabilities, as well as contributory medical and hospital insurance for civilian employees of the government and dependents of servicemen stationed in the United States. It recommended the creation of an advisory council to coordinate federal medical services and suggested that most of the hospitals and clinics of the Public Health Service be closed and that armed forces hospital services be regionalized. It also called for the creation of a national library of medicine, the creation of a central authority for medical care in the event of a nuclear attack, and reorganization of the Food and Drug Administration.[80]

While the reports of the task forces flowed into the commission, were debated and modified, and the result recommendations were passed on to Congress or the White House, Hoover wrote a friend that he had "never worked harder nor longer hours than on the present job." He had "little hope that our views will be adopted, but at least the American people will know what their government is doing." He was not "as frightened over wars and rumors of wars as much as Washington and the Press" were, he added, but wrote, "To keep up such tensions is good setting for military legislation and spending. With 8,000,000 persons, directly or indirectly being employed in the Military field and the present inflation of every business activity, we would have a bigger bump than that of 1931 if peace came all of a sudden. And with an unbalanced budget inflation is still working."[81]

On April 28, a Hoover Commission staff luncheon discussed the attacks that Democrat Wright Patman was making on the Hoover Commission recommendations in Congress. According to Neil MacNeil, Hoover listened in silence and then said, "Gentleman, there is a tradition that every dog must have at least one flea. It's only proper that we should have one."[82] The next day, Hoover met with Eisenhower in the White House at the president's request. The former president took the opportunity to press upon Ike his recommendations about Mutual Security. In an aide-memoire of their conversation, Hoover wrote,

> I told him of our Task Force work and their support to continuing a large part of the program. Also I told him that we were interested in the method of organization and certain policies to be followed.
>
> I suggested he could cure much of the opposition and improve the organization if he would at once by executive order transfer certain parts of the program to other agencies than the State Department. I suggested that he at once transfer: Military Assistance support to NATO; Korea Relief, Off-Shore Procurement and probably "Direct Defense Support" to the Department of Defense where they really belonged; and set up his new International Co-operation Administration as a coordinating agency by appointing the Director a member of the many coordinating Councils and Boards.

Other functions of the old Foreign Operations Administration (FOA), he suggested, should be transferred to the Departments of Commerce, Agriculture, the Export-Import Bank, and so on. According to Hoover's aide-memoire, Eisenhower "liked the idea and returned at once to the Cabinet Meeting where he proposed these ideas. He subsequently instructed the Budget Director to draw up the necessary executive orders. The Director consulted with me and we set the matter en train."[83]

The fourth report of the commission was the most controversial to date and barely passed the commission by a narrow 7-5 vote with three Democrats and two Republicans dissenting. The report called for sweeping changes in federal lending activities, including major shifts to private enterprise, and cited potential savings of $200 million per year. Included were proposals that the Production Credit Corporation, Agricultural Marketing Act Revolving Fund, Federal Farm Mortgage Corporation, and loans for college house construction all be liquidated; that crop loans to farmers under price supports be substituted for the present purchase agreements; that the Rural Electrification Administration (REA) be put on a self-supporting basis and merged into private enterprise; that Federal Housing Administration (FHA) programs be reorganized to obtain financing from private sources subject to federal regulation; that the president be allowed to raise the down-payment requirements for FHA-insured loans; and that the Export-Import Bank end short-term commercial loans and become the only federal source of long-term exports and loans to foreign governments. It also called for the Small Business Administration and other lending agencies to raise their interest charges to cover their operating costs and pay interest to the Treasury equal to the cost of money to the government and for the Federal National Mortgage Association, Federal Intermediate Credit Banks, and Banks for Cooperatives to be merged with private enterprise through "mutualization." The commission also asked Congress to review the International Monetary Fund to determine whether it was still needed by the United States. It was the strongest assault on the legacy of the New Deal yet.[84]

The fifth report, on the transportation functions of the federal government, was less controversial. It recommended the appointment of a transportation director in the Defense Department to strengthen central direction of transportation functions and urged pay raises for government traffic management personnel, an end to government shipping of private automobiles abroad for servicemen, the transfer of mail from military to civilian aircraft, greater use by the military of commercial cargo and passenger ships and tankers, and more group movements of military personnel to replace individual movements; it scored the unnecessary and uneconomical use of government ships in competition with commercial shippers and pointed out that such practices were at odds with the aim of Congress to build a strong, privately operated American merchant marine.[85]

Even Hoover joined with five other members of the commission in abstaining from the vote on some of the proposals in the report on federal legal services and procedures but agreed to their submission to Congress for consideration. The report urged the establishment of a US administrative court for tax, labor, and trade regulations, as well as the creation of a career legal service. The objective was to separate the administrative and judicial functions that had been combined in some federal agencies and thus give greater protection against abuses of power and arbitrary bureaucratic actions.[86] The report on federal surplus property followed a few days later and urged that a catalog of all federal property be compiled. It criticized the federal government for sloppy inventory keeping and lack of coordination between government agencies, which had combined to produce a huge accumulation of government supplies, especially by the armed forces.[87]

In the midst of the commission's work, Hoover agreed to testify in person before the Senate committee considering changes that might be made in the United Nations Charter. He told the committee he did not believe "that under present circumstances the Charter can be very effectively amended because of the Communist veto in the Security Council," but he suggested that amendments be proposed anyway "and ventilated to the world at large." He then repeated the recommendations he had made in his memorandum a year earlier, which were in turn the suggestions he had made in 1945. When asked if he thought the Soviet Union should be expelled from membership, Hoover responded that "we have to go on and worry with the Russians and with the hope that things may be better sometimes."[88] The *New York Times* noted that anti-UN members of Congress had expected support from the former president in their efforts to reduce the power of the United Nations or to take the United States out of it, but his testimony had given them no "comfort."[89]

A few days later the Hoover Commission report on federal buying of food and clothing went to Congress, claiming potential savings of $340 million per year if new central agencies were created in the Defense Department to buy and distribute and control supplies for the armed forces. It urged the abolition of competitive bidding and expected savings if the General Services Administration (GSA) began to handle all government purchases except those under farm price-support programs. It urged "cross-servicing" arrangements between the GSA and the armed forces.[90]

The next round of recommendations in mid-May were controversial, when the commission urged the federal government to eliminate over one thousand enterprises that were competing with private business, including the Postal Savings system, and advocated an increase in parcel post rates, an end to chemical research by the Tennessee Valley Authority (TVA), and an increase in the price of TVA-produced fertilizer to cover all costs, including the loss of taxes that could otherwise have been obtained from private producers.[91]

Embroiled in controversy over some of the commission's recommendations, Hoover now took to the stump to strengthen support for them. Early in May he told the Chamber of Commerce of the United States that the federal budget could be balanced "overnight" if the recommendations were implemented. Some of the problems the commission discovered in the government arose, he said, from the "fabulous growth of the Federal Executive branches by about fourteen times the size of twenty-five years ago." Others were "due to obsolete legislation which obstruct progress," while still others were from "the tenacity of Government agencies to the idea that their empires are sacrosanct." Some were due to "the pressure groups that profit from the present set up of these agencies and resent all change," and some were "due to the primary emotion of all bureaucracies that their sleep be not disturbed." Later in the month he told the National Industrial Conference Board that if all the recommendations were adopted they would save taxpayers $6 billion per year and produce a return of $7 billion to the Treasury as a result of the liquidation of government agencies and functions that competed with private business.[92]

Obviously eager to have the commission's work behind him, Hoover wrote a friend in late May that for "five months I haven't been able to let go of this bear's tail for an hour. But on June 15 I expect to have him finished and then see my friends again."[93]

The commission's recommendations on federal storage urged more modern operations and a wider use of private warehouses with claimed savings of $235 million per year. It found considerable duplication of storage space by the armed forces and proposed that the GSA be authorized to force coordination in the storage of civilian records. The commissions also recommended expansion of civilian and military research and development, especially in weapons development, asked for more federal assistance to medical research, and cited inadequate public and state support for medical schools. It proposed a standing committee of scientists in the Department of Defense to spur weapons development.

There was little agreement within the commission on its recommendations dealing with foreign aid, with Hoover being the only member who supported the entire report. A majority of the members argued that the recommendations should have included one for reduction in foreign aid. The report did point out that certain nations no longer needed extensive aid and argued that technical aid to the original NATO countries should end, that aid for large manufacturing or industrial projects in Asia should not be undertaken except perhaps in Japan, that the United States should not duplicate the programs of the UN, and that all overseas nonmilitary personnel of US agencies should be put under the chief of the US diplomatic mission in whatever country they were stationed.

The next report was one dear to Hoover's heart. It called for the rates charged for power by federal power projects to be raised to cover the costs that private utilities must pay, including taxes; it urged that the Federal Power Commission should set the rates; and it suggested that charges be levied against users of inland waterways constructed by federal funds, that a water resources board be established to advise on all water and hydroelectric power projects, and that the federal government undertake no development projects when state and local governments or private interests could do them. It also recommended that so far as possible all new federal power facilities should be self-financing. The commission next attacked the waste in federal real estate management, noting that some agencies were buying property while others had idle land and buildings. It urged that the Bureau of the Budget and the GSA be given greater control over federal real estate management.

Since the Hoover Commission was due to expire on June 30, the reports were being issued at a more rapid pace in May and June. One of the most important recommendations was the one advocating changes in preparation of the federal budget and the form of congressional appropriations, which the commission estimated could save $4 billion per year through the adoption of private business methods. It recommended new powers and staff for the Bureau of the Budget to control spending and perform management duties, proposed an accounting office under an assistant budget director to plan for accounting and budgeting in executive agencies, and also suggested that the bureau place its own experts in major agencies, with each agency to have a controller chosen with the help of the assistant budget director. It urged that Congress limit its practice of obligating funds years ahead of disbursal and suggested that the budget and appropriations be shifted from an "obligational" basis to "accrued expenditures," which would end large balances of unspent appropriations.

The commission held its final meeting on June 24 and paid tribute to Hoover, who hailed the contribution made by the commission members.[94] Two days later the *New York Times* wrote, "For former President Herbert

Hoover the last public service is done."⁹⁵ With the expiration of the Hoover Commission on June 30, it reported, "Mr. Hoover, its chairman for eight years, at 81, and with forty-one years of almost constant and almost wholly unpaid public service behind him, will retire to private life."⁹⁶ There was some irony in the fact that the same newspaper had similarly retired the former president after the first Hoover Commission had expired. The reporter who interviewed Hoover found "traits the public rarely sees. He was warm and friendly, a hint of humor lurking in his speech. With a well-caked black briar pipe clutched in his left hand, he rose to shake hands. The high starched collar had been replaced by a shirt with almost no starch at all." Hoover told that the press that the commission's recommendations on the civil service were the "nearest my heart's desire." Of the philosophy that guided the commission's work, he said, "The purpose was to save the taxpayers money. But more important than savings was the realization that whole social and economic foundation is based on private enterprise."

Two more reports were issued after the final meeting of the commission. The first recommended the creation of a fourth branch of the Defense Department—a civilian-run Defense Supply and Service Administration—which it estimated could save $2 billion per year. The commission also proposed modifying the conflict-of-interest laws so that appointees to government position would not be required to liquidate "lifetime business" interests, but requiring them instead to take an oath that they would not participate in decisions affecting their financial interests.

The last, and one of the most controversial reports, was the one on water resources and power, although it was less sweeping than the suggestions of the task force. The commission recommended higher rates for electricity produced by federal agencies like the TVA; a ban on new generating projects by the federal government if state, municipal, or private funds were available; permission for private companies to buy a "fair share" of federal power for resale; requirements that agencies like the TVA finance themselves by issuing public securities; that government cease its preferential treatment in power sales to nonprofit agencies like cities and cooperatives; that government cease building transmission lines where nonfederal agencies could provide the service; and that Congress adopt a clear statement on national water supply. It also advocated that a "user charge" be placed on inland waterways; that a water resources commission be created to advise the president; and that the rates for federal electricity be made high enough to provide payments in lieu of taxes to state and local governments such as private utilities would pay. The commission report, however, did not follow the task force recommendation that called for the sale of federal power facilities to private enterprise.

In a memorandum to Congressman Charles Halleck, Hoover pointed out that the commission's recommendations "generally follow the policies of the Eisenhower Administration insofar as they have been declared." As examples, he listed the following:

1. The Commission, like the President, urged the imperative necessity to develop our water resources.
2. Both the President and the Commission urged the construction of more multiple-purpose dams for navigation, irrigation, flood control, and hydro-electric power.
3. The President is reported to have remarked at one time that there was "creeping socialism" in the public power area. The Commission stated that it was clear that in this field the Government was conducting activities competitive with private enterprise.
4. The President urged that States and municipalities participate in the cost of multiple-purpose dams. The Commission endorsed this policy.
5. The President urged the "partnership" participation of private enterprise in those projects where hydro-electric power was involved. The Commission strongly endorsed this policy.
6. The Administration also urged that private enterprise develop hydro-electric power dams and made such a policy clear in the case of the Hell's Canyon Dam in Idaho and several others. The Commission strongly endorsed this policy.
7. The President called attention to the dangers to the inhabitants of created Federal power monopolies in regions. The Commission reports emphasize the same idea.
8. The Commission endorsed the Administration policy that existing power projects should not be sold.
9. The Secretary of the Interior and the President have opposed any further Federal construction of steam plants. The Commission states the same policy.
10. The Secretary of the Interior states there should be no construction of new transmission lines where private utilities can do the job equally well. The Commission endorsed this policy.
11. The President suggested that TVA should issue its own securities to the public for further financing instead of calling upon the Treasury. The Commission endorsed this and urged that this method be applied to the other great power groups now being operated by the Government.
12. The President has erected a coordination at the Washington level . . . The Commission strongly supported better coordination at this level and goes a step further by proposing that the present committees be transformed into a single permanent Water Resources Board composed jointly of civilians and cabinet members.
13. The President has urged better coordination at the River Basin level. The Commission urges such organization.[97]

At a news conference on June 30, Hoover brushed aside criticism of the water resources and power report and made public the more drastic recommendations of the task force. He noted that the commission estimated that a total of $8.5 million per year might be saved if all the recommendations of the commission were adopted, and the Treasury could receive $15 billion through the recovery of investments, liquidation of liabilities, and property sales. When asked if he thought there was a need for yet a third commission, Hoover replied that if so, "somebody else" would have to organize it.[98] The expiration of the Hoover Commission signaled yet another "retirement" for the former president. The liberal *New Republic*, always a Hoover critic, remarked that it "was not a completely happy ending. Criticism had reached a new peak of bitterness with the publication of the Commission's report on Water Resources and Power. The Administration and Congress have been very slow to act on the Hoover group's recommendations, and it is unlikely that many of them will be put into effect despite Mr. Hoover's claim that the resulting savings would balance the budget and permit a $2 billion tax cut." It was a sharp contrast, the magazine observed, with the first Hoover Commission, but the first had been nonpartisan while the new commission had been "weighted with conservatives" and its recommendations "gave off the musty scent of long-stored goods." It concluded,

> It has been almost 23 years since Herbert Hoover lost the Presidency. For most of this time he has lived in a political netherworld, his name synonymous with Depression, his high collar the symbol of the unenlightened conservative. But now the time is back in joint for Mr. Hoover. It is prosperity again, as it was when he was elected to the Presidency in 1928. His Party is again in power, and it has granted him the opportunity of making a final testament to the country of his years in public life. Ninety-five percent of the press has hailed his efforts; he was applauded as he left the conference room last week. The dark memories of the New Deal are past. In his own eyes, Hoover has been finally redeemed. And now he can retire.[99]

The *New York Times* reported that Hoover had gone back to the Waldorf from Washington, packed his fishing gear, and left for a fishing trip to California.[100]

A press release from the commission recommended that 33 independent agencies then reporting to the president be placed under the supervision of "some official within the President's office." It noted that the commission had made 145 "administrative" recommendations that could be carried out by the various departments and agencies and 167 that required congressional legislation. The commission identified fifty administrative actions that had already been taken and forty bills that had been drafted to cover many of the legislative recommendations. But the *New York Times* found that "the Administration and Congress have been so slow to act upon this year's Hoover reports that one can fairly wonder how many of them will be put into effect at all." It found this in marked contrast with the enthusiasm that had been shown for the recommendations of the first Hoover Commission.[101]

Hoover was prepared for opposition and criticism, writing fellow commission member, Clarence Brown, "I expect a lot of venom from the left."[102] Brown was encountering criticism of the commission's recommendations in the House and he wrote Hoover, "I am sure you appreciate it is not easy for me to, almost singlehanded, combat those, both in and out of Government, who for their own selfish reasons would like to belittle and besmirch the efforts of the Hoover Commission."[103]

Hoover was not very sanguine that the recommendations requiring legislation would be adopted, but he was encouraged that those capable of being put through by administrative action were "being rapidly adopted by the Republican administration." He feared, though, that "we may have to await a Republican Congress to have rapid motion in the legislative matters." But, no matter what the rate of adoption, he thought the reports would "have educative value."[104] Hoover also thought the predictions in the press of his retirement were a bit premature, writing one friend, "If the history of the first Commission on Organization is any guide, I will, in the next few years, be before 20 Congressional Committees explaining what we meant and 20 audiences trying to convince pressure groups the error of their ways." He was, the former president said, "neither going to get 'retirement,' nor do I want it."[105]

Democratic Senator John McClellan, chairman of the Senate Committee on Government Operations, later recalled that "at the expiration of both the Commissions [Hoover] headed, he returned to the Treasury of the United States a 'surplus.' That is, he got the job done without spending all the appropriation that the Congress gave him—a rarity, I regret to say, in Washington today." This indicated to McClellan that Hoover lived "up to the principles of good government for which he so squarely stands."[106]

CHAPTER 14

The Ageless One

Reorganization

The issue was all so very plain for the former president. As he told the *US News and World Report* in August, "In the Commission's work, the large majority favored the philosophical foundation under which we would operate. It's very simple—that the whole social-economic system of this country is based on private enterprise, properly regulated to prevent unfair competition and to prevent monopolies; that the Government should provide those services which people cannot do for themselves." It was to this test, he said, that the commission had submitted all the agencies it had examined. "That part of our work was not so much a matter of savings as strengthening our vital structure of individual, State and local government rights." But in addition to "trying to strengthen the philosophical foundations of our country," the commission had also tried to reduce expenses without injuring the security of the nation or disturbing "the justifiable social services of the country."

When asked if there had been enthusiasm demonstrated in Congress for the recommendations of the commission, Hoover responded that he "couldn't say one way or the other," but he added, "With the philosophical foundation I told you about a minute ago, I imagine that all the 'left-wingers' in the Congress are opposed to everything we suggested." The federal government was "immensely too big," he observed, because it had "undertaken functions which ought to be left to the States and the people." Although approximately 70 percent of the recommendations of the first Hoover Commission had been adopted, it had taken six years. Asked how much the first commission had saved the taxpayers, Hoover pointed to the General Services Administration (GSA), created as a result of the first commission, which already showed specific savings of $150 million per year and might have saved more had it not been for the enormous budget increases related to the Korean War. Asked how much success he expected in getting the recommendations of the second commission through Congress, Hoover replied that he expected even more, "because we have a more emphatic public opinion between us now." He admitted, however, that "there is a very considerable element who are on the 'left-wing' side who do not believe in these recommendations."[1]

The "left-wing" was not long in being heard from. In September the *Democratic Digest* printed an attack on the second Hoover Commission in the name of the Democratic national committee. The article implied that the commission had been politically partisan, that Hoover had stacked the task forces with adherents to his own philosophy, and that even President Eisenhower did not approve of the commission's recommendations. It was typical of the type of smearing that the former president had endured for twenty years, without any effort by the *Digest* to deal with the recommendations of the commission on their merits, and Hoover responded with a statement on August 16 denouncing the "infamous smear" and pointing out that the commission had "never divided upon political grounds," that every "recommendation was by a majority and was voted for by some if not all of the five Democratic members." As for the president's attitude, Hoover pointed out that Eisenhower had already "directed the Departments to set up machinery for the implementing of the Commission's administrative recommendations."[2]

During 1955 and 1956 the former president delivered a number of speeches on the work of the second Hoover Commission and even consented to a first appearance on *Meet the Press* in order to acquaint the public with the work of the committee. After the broadcast, the moderator, Lawrence Spivak, wrote Hoover that when he did finally decide to retire, "there is a place for you in television." He thought the former president had done "a wonderful job" during the broadcast and concluded, "The only criticism I have to make—and it really isn't a criticism—is that you did not smile more frequently, because when you did your face lighted up in an extraordinary way and brought out qualities of humor and kindliness which are not often enough associated with your greatness." Hoover, had he wrote, "looked and sounded vigorous and fifteen years younger than your chronological age."[3] A letter writer to the *St. Louis Post*-Dispatch described Spivak's "kidgloves" treatment of Hoover on the television show "like an art lover looking at the Mona Lisa in the Louvre . . . was Lawrence Spivak of Meet the Press questioning Herbert Hoover."[4] Through such appearances and the renewed work of the Citizens Committee for the Hoover Report, Hoover sought to build public support for the commission's recommendations to ensure that they would be implemented.[5] Rolling back the New Deal was not an easy task.

The former president also continued to speak out on political and international issues. Of the forthcoming Geneva summit conference, he told the press he foresaw the possibility of "an endurable peace for years to come" but cautioned that it was by no means a "lasting peace."[6] When Eisenhower challenged the Soviet Union to exchange full military information with the

United States, Hoover described it as a "master stroke" by which the Soviets were confronted with the problem of demonstrating the sincerity of their professed desire for world peace. Eisenhower's challenge, Hoover told the press, had "really put the Russians in a spot this time."[7]

Life in the Eighties

For his eighty-first birthday, August 10, 1955, Hoover traveled to Newberg, Oregon, where he had spent much of his childhood. There he delivered a nostalgic speech on the "American Way of Life," which included reminiscences of his boyhood among the Oregon forests and lakes. Such reminiscences, he mused, would probably be considered "an expression of longing to go backward in American life," and while he denied it, he did lament that "during the last score of years our American way of life has been deluged with criticism." It was important, though, to "occasionally mention something good about ourselves," including the unequaled level of American productivity and standard of living and the constantly improving health and life expectancy. He listed other positive features of America and concluded that "freedom of mind, of spirit, and of initiative still lives in America . . . Here alone, even with all its defects, is human dignity not a dream but an accomplishment."[8] Despite the optimism of his speech, however, Hoover was more pessimistic in writing: "I don't like for the American people, each with their own problems, to be as discouraged over the future as I am."[9]

With Truman's departure from the White House in January 1953, the ex-president "club" was doubled after Hoover had been the only member for nearly a score of years. Although Hoover had declined an invitation to attend a seventieth birthday dinner for the Democratic former president in 1954, Truman paid a courtesy call on Hoover in New York City in mid-October 1955, and later in the month the GOP elder statesman joined the sponsors of the Harry S. Truman Library, Committee of the Southwest, in seeking to raise $200,000 in that part of the country as part of the $2 million needed to build the library in Independence, Missouri.[10]

In October Ruth Inglis penned a portrait of the former president for *American Mercury* in which she wrote of Hoover's relief activities at the time of World War I and observed that "one of the cruel disappointments of his life was the denial to him of the opportunity to serve his government in a similar way during World War II." She continued, "It is almost a miracle—indeed a measure of the man—that Hoover did not become bitter during the long years from 1933 to 1947, when his unheeded warnings were proved all too true while he stood by helplessly. Despite the accuracy of his predictions in both domestic and foreign affairs, Hoover does not sing the 'I Told You So' blues. His is a creative and constructive nature as well as a practical one." After describing the two Hoover Commissions, Inglis wrote, "In the best and historic meaning of the words, Herbert Hoover has always been a great patriot and a great liberal.

Those who have thought otherwise might well examine their own thinking to see to what extent they have been influenced by a diabolical propaganda machine long ago exposed. Hoover's life is an open book. His record is clear and unblemished. From the earliest days of his career down to the present, in word and deed, his life has been devoted to the furtherance of the freedom and welfare of mankind."[11]

On November 6, 1955, NBC television aired a production of "A Conversation with Herbert Hoover," during which the former president pointed out,

> I've never accepted compensation either for relief or for federal service, except in this sense—that I have at times taken federal salaries and expended them on matters that are outside my own needs and use. I was led to that by an over-all question of conviction of my own . . . [I]t happened that I had prospered in my profession, at a time when the income tax was only one percent. I was able to save a competence, and I felt that I owed to my country a debt that was unpayable and I had no right to ask her to pay me, so that that was the practice right up until this year.[12]

In November Hoover was again pressed into service by President Eisenhower, when he was asked to represent the United States at the Armistice Day ceremony at Arlington National Cemetery, where he laid a wreath on the Tomb of the Unknown Solder. It was a day, Hoover remarked, for consecrating the nation once again to peace. "And we dedicate ourselves," he added, "to maintain respect of nations for our preparedness and our might to defend ourselves against aggression."[13] In December the octogenarian looked ahead to 1956: "As I have launched about 300 reforms needed in Washington, I shall have to spend my next months with Congressional committees and government agencies bent on devices to avoid them. However, it is a blessing to keep busy. To be sure of that, I am at odd times writing some more volumes to be published after I have passed on. That delay is in order that I won't need meditate on the reviews which this great center of intelligence [New York] will produce."

He had decided to spend the holidays in Florida fishing, he added, "because out in a skiff on the blue water and with no radio, television, telephone or tabloids with their scoops of murders, and with only a bonefish for an objective, one can recover some stability from the jars and shocks of the time."[14]

Hoover was also distressed by the increasing prevalence of internal subversion throughout the world. He wrote Admiral Pratt that the "whole containment policy is being broken down under the impact of Communist internal conspiracies. Unless the West is prepared to hold the Persian Gulf, the Arab States, and North Africa away from the Communists—by force, it necessary—we had better get into our own shell and establish the outposts to warn us of attack."[15]

The trip to the keys for fishing was part of Hoover's annual routine that included part of the summer spent in the West fishing in Oregon, visits to San Francisco and Stanford University, and time at the Bohemian Club encampment among the redwoods. Part of the winter was spent pursuing bonefish and other varieties of game fish off the Florida coast. The rest of the time Hoover divided between the New York apartment and activities in Washington, adding an occasional trip for speechmaking. He also continued his work on behalf of the Hoover Commission's recommendations, and he remained abreast and vocal concerning world and domestic affairs.

Politics

Before he left for Florida, Hoover made a second appearance on *Meet the Press*, thereby creating a situation that he later referred to as the "Double Cross." During the telecast, the former president referred to the burdens of the presidency and innocently proposed "an Administrative Vice President" to relieve some of those burdens, but the suggestion set off a hornet's nest since he seemed to be proposing a change of constitutional importance. When he was called to testify on his proposal before the Senate Subcommittee on Government Organization, Hoover found his position undercut by the White House. Understandably, Eisenhower feared that the public would interpret such a proposal as evidence that the president did not feel capable of handling all the duties of his office after his heart attack of September 1955 with the 1956 presidential campaign already under way.[16] Hoover felt betrayed by Eisenhower, but Truman also opposed his proposal.[17]

In other respects, too, Hoover had begun to feel estranged from the Republican in the White House. When one correspondent suggested of the Eisenhower administration that "one would almost think the New Deal was still doing business," Hoover agreed that it was "the Neo-New Deal."[18] And despite his campaign against public power the Senate had approved a bill for Niagara power that meant for him only more "creeping socialism."[19] Meanwhile, Hoover was withdrawing more and more into writing. One secretary wrote that he had been as "busy as ten bird dogs" with the work on his books, while another confided, "At the moment the chief is busy on four different books! We can't write another two—yes I know that HH can!"[20]

His estrangement from the Republicans in Washington drained the former president of any enthusiasm for a repeat performance of his quadrennial "farewell" to the GOP convention in 1956. Instead, he had planned a fishing trip over the week of the convention. But when queried by GOP national committeeman Leonard Hall about an appearance, Hoover responded, "I had made other plans than attending this year's convention. I said last time that was my last appearance. If the President wishes me to do it, I will see what I can do to rearrange matters."[21] A request did come from Eisenhower that read, "You exemplify in more ways than I am sure you realize the dignity and spirit of the Republican Party, and I know that every delegate to the Convention would be keenly disappointed, as would I, if you were not there to lend your counsel and advice."[22] Hoover had, he wrote a friend, planned to leave "for the woods of Wyoming until both my birthday and the convention were over." But he would honor the request from the president to speak.[23] To Eisenhower, Hoover replied, "I am also much more than even grateful for a President who has, amid stupendous difficulties, kept the world at peace and lifted American public life again to the levels of integrity. As you wished I will make a short speech at the Convention. It will not be an earthquake."[24]

Before the convention, Hoover relaxed in the Bohemian Grove woods and delivered his yearly off-the-record speech. In a long speech filled with humor, the former president surveyed domestic issues from taxes to academic freedom. Discussing the efforts of the Hoover Commission to eliminate some government operations, he told his fellow revelers, "The most permanent thing in our system is a temporary government agency." He added, "If you will look into the road blocks in trying to escape from this manifestation of Karl Marx, you will find a combination of bureaucracy, its pressure groups, Americans for Democratic Action, the so-called liberals, and the local Chambers of Commerce. The Chambers shiver that some job in their locality may be lost." Besides his traditional survey of domestic and international conditions, the former president told his fellow revelers why so many presidents took up fishing: "There are some 18,000,000 potential voters who bought fishing licenses last year. The way to interest them is to join them, and get photographed in the act. Moreover, as all men are equal before fishes, this is the sport to demonstrate fealty to the Common Man." There were also "certain secret political complexions of fishing," he told them. "The Ancient Greeks and Romans sought auguries of the future by examining the entrails of sheep. In these days the augury of forth-coming political events is done with a dead fish, and several still cameras and TV close-ups." As for presidents fishing, he said, "The simple reason is that the American people concede privacy on only two occasions. Fishing and prayer—and presidents cannot pray all the time, even if the activities of the public need it. Moreover, if the President wants to leave the White House, no citizen questions the purity of his motives if is just going fishing. Any other destination requires a press conference and a press release."[25]

On the eve of his eighty-second birthday, Hoover told the press he detected an ebbing of world tensions, but he refused to estimate the prospects for peace. He did, however, credit President Eisenhower and Secretary Dulles with having contributed an "enormous amount" toward a reduction in world tensions. The former president was described by reporters as "ruddy and in good health" and somewhat apologetic for having slowed down to only a twelve-to-fourteen hour workday. He was opposed to retirement, which meant centering one's life on ills and pills and associating only with others having the same preoccupation. He told reporters, "Any oldster who keeps at even part-time work has something worth talking about. He has a zest for the morning paper and his three meals a day. The point of all this is not to retire from work or you will shrivel up into a nuisance to all mankind." The *New York Times* added,

> On his annual summer visit to the West Coast, Mr. Hoover has fished four or five days in the Mackenzie River of Oregon, his favorite trout stream. He has attended the annual encampment of the Bohemian Club . . . He has sat in at board meetings of many organizations of which he is chairman or a member. He has helped launch a financial drive for a Stanford medical center as honorary chairman of the campaign. He keeps a staff of eight secretaries and research assistants on the move here and in New York. Although Mr. Hoover's speechmaking now is limited, he receives fifty or sixty letters a day asking him to give talks. Once in a while, one invitation draws an affirmative answer. After that address, his secretaries are swamped with mail.[26]

The 1956 Republican national convention marked the centennial of the party. In his speech before the convention on August 21, Hoover noted that in each of his past six convention appearances he had stressed "our responsibility to maintain the safeguards of free men," and he opined that this remained "America's most vital issue." Freedom was "threatened and even overwhelmed by the revival of old ideas and the spread of a host of new ideas dangerous to free men." The Eisenhower administration had reduced international tensions, however, and had "stemmed the malign forces which have beset us from within and without," while increasing prosperity and maintaining "two vital forces in the minds of free men"—integrity and religious faith. It was the responsibility of the centennial convention of the Republican Party to "generate a spirit which will rekindle in every American a love not only for his country but a devotion to its true ideals." He told the delegates he only had faith in the future of the nation because of "the genius of our people, their devotion to personal liberty, and their sustaining religious beliefs."[27]

In the Democratic convention that year, the son of Hoover's old friend Joseph P. Kennedy was nearly nominated for the vice-presidential spot on the ticket. John F. Kennedy had served in the House of Representatives before moving on to the Senate in 1952. As chairman of the Senate subcommittee responsible for reviewing the legislative recommendations of the Hoover Commission, he had been in close touch with Hoover. Another Kennedy son, Robert, had worked with the second Hoover Commission until he resigned in February 1954. Hoover's own son, Herbert Jr., was an undersecretary of state in the Eisenhower administration. In September 1956, Hoover wrote Joseph Kennedy, "You and I need another joint session. I don't know that we can do anything about things. At least we can take satisfaction in two sons in public life who are carrying on the battle."[28] Kennedy replied that they both could "take immense satisfaction in the jobs being done by Herbert Jr. and Jack, but I was thrilled to read while abroad of the way you 'stole the show' while on stage at the Republican convention."[29]

The Republican elder statesman had one other consolation in 1956. Although there was much that he found objectionable in Eisenhower's policies, the president did not regard him as a pariah to be shunned at campaign time. In 1956 the Eisenhower campaign again sought his assistance in making a speech on nationwide television. The director of public relations for the GOP National Committee gushed to him in mid-October, "We are delighted at your consent to make this important telecast, and I am sure it will be one of the most important in the entire campaign. I know how well your speech at the convention was received throughout the country, and I am sure your talk will be instrumental in swinging many millions of votes for President Eisenhower."[30] The chairman of Citizens for Eisenhower in Philadelphia asked Hoover to help in that city. Pennsylvania, he said, was likely to be crucial for Eisenhower's reelection, and Philadelphia would affect the state's vote. The city had gone for Stevenson in 1952, and Eisenhower's camp wanted "an informal press, radio, or television interview with you when you arrive in Philadelphia on Tuesday, October 23, to receive the Systems and Procedures Association award."[31] Hoover's new popularity with the party doubtless amazed him, but he had to decline the Philadelphia arrangements since he did not plan to accept the award in person.[32]

Nevertheless, Hoover did give a brief speech in behalf of the Eisenhower-Nixon ticket on October 29. The speech was only five minutes in length and was delivered in a New York studio of CBS. The objectives of the American people, he said, were the "advancement of peace in the world and preparedness for defense in the meantime," as well as an ever-rising standard of living and maximum employment, economy in government, reduced taxes, a balanced budget, a stable dollar, care of those unable to care for themselves, "public improvements which the people or the States cannot accomplish for themselves," governmental integrity, and the preservation of freedom against encroachment by government. "In these vital aspects of American life," Hoover asserted, "the Eisenhower Administration has already succeeded or is driving toward these objectives." The Democratic candidate, he suggested, would "have an uphill battle against these accomplishments." He concluded that the voters of America would "be happier if you vote for President Eisenhower, Vice President Nixon and a Congress friendly to them. Anyway, may God bless you all."[33]

Foreign Affairs

In 1956 the veteran of numerous relief activities also became involved in what was to be his last international relief activity. The refugee problems that resulted from the Hungarians' revolt against their Russian masters in 1956 were made to order for Hoover's talents and energies and for the pool of aging, but experienced, relief workers who remained active from the days when he had directed them in earlier such efforts. In late October 1956 Dr. Tibor Eckardt called a meeting of prominent Hungarian Americans at which the group decided to form a group named First Aid for Hungary that was incorporated on November 5, 1956, with Hoover as honorary chairman. Working through a field office in Vienna, the organization was soon shipping medical supplies to 5 hospitals inside Hungary and had established 17 first-aid stations on the Austro-Hungarian border, 4 field kitchens in Austria, and 3 mobile field pharmacies in the border area. They also supplied materials to Hungarian refugees immigrating to the United States.[34] Hoover also advised the White House on how the governmental aspect of the refugee problem might be handled. First Aid for Hungary was, in the words of one Hoover associate, "intended to mean just that"—a first-aid, temporary type of program. The main task was left to the larger organizations and to governments.[35] By February 1959 Hoover concluded that the organization had fulfilled its "first-aid" function and that future and larger relief efforts would have to be dealt with by government agencies. First Aid for Hungary ended its operations that month.[36]

In response to Hoover's letter of congratulation on the 1956 election, Vice President Richard Nixon wrote the former president a long reply in January in which he expressed his "deep appreciation for the counsel, friendship and support you have so generously given to me during the ten years I have been in public life." He continued,

> I recall also the memorable occasion when I was your guest at Cave Man [at Bohemian Grove] just after I had won the nomination for the Senate, but before the election that November. I remember, too, the messages you never failed to send me after each victory, and the strong support you gave me at the time of the so-called "fund" controversy during the 1952 campaign.
>
> I particularly valued the advice you have given me on those occasions when we have met in either New York or Washington. Incidentally, as you no doubt have noted, my report on the Hungarian refugee situation reflected several of the suggestions you had made. I am presently urging within the Administration an approach to aiding people inside Hungary along the same lines you used so successfully in the Russian relief program of 1922.

He hoped, Nixon told the elder statesman, "that in the future I can continue to have the benefit of your experience and judgment as they are applied to some of the problems which we face in government."[37]

Early in January 1957 Hoover was asked to testify before the House Foreign Affairs Committee on Eisenhower's request for standby authority to use American armed forces in the Middle East and for $400 million to be used for economic assistance in the region.[38] Hoover was then in Florida recovering from cold and bronchitis. Advised against a trip to Washington by his doctor, he sent instead a telegram containing his support for Eisenhower's proposals.[39] The former president had been concerned about the Middle East situation for some time, especially over evidence that the Soviet Union was increasing its influence in that vital part of the world through "international conspiracies." Clearly this was a major departure from the strategy he had advocated during the Great Debate.[40]

Hoover wired the chairman of the House Foreign Affairs Committee that he could condense his views on the president's proposals into one sentence: "On the understanding that these proposals extend only to Russian Communist military aggression and to economic aid I am in full agreement with the President."[41] When Senator Alexander Wiley requested his views on the same topic, Hoover wrote that he certainly supported Eisenhower's proposal "that the United States should use its military forces to aid Middle East states to repel any military aggression" and also his proposal for "continued economic aid to the region." It was, he said, "essential to the peace of the world that the Soviet government should be under no misapprehension as to our position with respect to any military aggression which they might contemplate in the Middle East."[42] Yet neither Eisenhower's proposal nor Hoover's support took into account the major danger in the region, which was internal subversion rather than overt military aggression.

Through 1957 Hoover remained active in monitoring the progress of the recommendations of the second Hoover Commission through Congress, particularly those relating to budgeting and reorganization of the Defense Department. In this he worked closely with Senator John Kennedy and with Congressman Clarence Brown.[43] In April he wrote Senator Kennedy his appreciation for his efforts in behalf of the Commission's recommendations, and Kennedy responded, "I want to thank you very kindly for your gracious letter . . . in which you commented on my activities in behalf of S434 which would implement what I know you would consider one of the most important recommendations of the second Hoover Commission." He told Hoover that he "greatly appreciated" Hoover's approbation.[44] In July Hoover visited Independence, Missouri, to join Chief Justice Earl Warren, Eleanor Roosevelt, Senator William Knowland, House Speaker Sam Rayburn, Congressman Charles Halleck, and others for the dedication of the Truman Presidential Library. In a short speech, Hoover opined that it was "of extreme importance that we do not concentrate the history of the United States in Washington, D.C. I am happy to witness an event wherein the history of the American people is being brought closer and closer to them."[45]

After typically celebrating his birthdays in West Branch, where he was born; in Newberg, Oregon, where he grew up; or at Stanford University, Hoover spent his eighty-third birthday in a different locale—aboard an American President Lines liner that was named after him, *The President Hoover*. Feted by 125 guests, including Anne Rogers, star of the road company of *My Fair Lady*, who led them in singing "Happy Birthday" to the former president,

Hoover recalled that the same shipping line had earlier named a ship after him just before World War II. "Unfortunately," he said, "that ship was a casualty in the last war." It had been a struggle, he noted, to keep his name on ships and heavenly bodies. He explained,

> One astronomical observatory in Europe named a star in my honor. Another, to get me nearer to home, named a planet for me. They each placed a Greek suffix to my name, which seemed to qualify me to associate with the stars and planets named after the Greek gods on Olympus.
>
> Suddenly some committee in some association of astronomers decided living persons could not have such distinctions. Despite the Greek suffix, I was taken off of Olympus. But my astronomer friends, like my American President Line friends, were sturdy men, and now I am back both in the stars and on the sea.[46]

The Historian

In September 1957, Hoover wrote columnist David Lawrence that he had been "greatly impressed by your penetrating analysis of the Wisconsin Senatorial election in this morning's papers." He then turned to a theme dear to his heart since the Landon campaign in 1936:

> You might give thought to the idea that conservatives of both parties are putting on sit-down strikes against their Presidential (and possibly some other) candidates . . . The sit-down strikes by conservatives can of course be of three varieties—voters go to the polls and vote their local tickets and do not vote for their Presidential candidate, or they can vote for the opposition Presidential candidate, or they can stay at home.
>
> You might think over the following corroboration of the conservative sit-down. In both Dewey elections it can be demonstrated that many Republican conservatives did not like his attitudes, as shown by the fact that he ran behind the local Republican vote by somewhere from 1,000,000 to 1,500,000 votes . . .
>
> It would seem that this sit-down strike by conservatives may be only a minority but may be effective in defeat of the candidate of their party.
>
> The assumption by candidates that they must cater to the "liberal" vote and that the conservatives must go along is a fallacy.[47]

Now in his eighties, the elder statesman's speeches had grown shorter and less frequent, his travel to all but his accustomed haunts more circumscribed. He continued with his busy writing schedule and sounded occasional "blasts" from his apartment in the Waldorf Tower, writing an old friend late in 1957,

> I have gone into this comfortable monastery not to illuminate the margins of old manuscripts like the monks of old, but to write manuscripts myself and occasionally peep out and say something to the American people. I get hundreds

of supporting editorials on these occasional peeps, but of course nothing happens. They, however, comfort me that I am still sane. The first book will be out
in April or May on *The Ordeal of Woodrow Wilson*. It will illustrate some lessons
on the old war and prove that Woodrow Wilson would be a "reactionary" in
present estimation. It is friendly to Wilson and I hope you will like it.[48]

Even during his fishing trips to Florida, Hoover was putting in many hours
at his writing. A secretary at that time recalled later that her "favorite remi-
niscence is the period between 3:30 and 4:00 [p.m.], when Mr. Hoover would
assemble us all in the dining room. He'd settle back with a huge mug of coffee
and a pipe which constantly went out, and he'd tell stories of his wonderful
experiences. In addition to ourselves, the audience might include former vice
president Nixon, heads of corporations, Senators, and the top executives in
the country. It was a wonderful time."[49]

The Ordeal of Woodrow Wilson was published in 1958 and is a unique historical document—a study of one president of the United States written by
another president of the opposing political party who worked with him during a crucial point in American history. While much of the book actually
deals with Hoover's own activities during the armistice period, the portrait of
Wilson it presents is a sensitive and sympathetic one. Hoover first argues that
Wilson's "liberalism" was, like his own, at variance with the modern definition of the term. He writes of Wilson, "As a Jeffersonian Democrat, he was a
'liberal' of the nineteenth century cast. His training in history and economics
rejected every scintilla of socialism, which today connotes a liberal." Instead,
Wilson's philosophy had been based on a regulated free enterprise system,
with federal intervention "justified only when the task was greater than the
states or individuals could perform for themselves." He then recounted the
story of "the President's plans, his obstacles, his methods, his successes and
the causes of the tragedy which came to him in his efforts to bring lasting
peace to the world."[50] One reviewer of the book wrote, "Hoover's book is
essentially a documentation, a blueprint of the Wilsonian ordeal. He shows
in detail how Wilson captured the imagination of a warshocked world with
the promise of a just peace and a League of Nations to tidy up the international madhouse. He then shows how Old World hatreds and greeds,
together with homegrown suspicions, turned Wilson's dream into a patch-
work of drab compromises."[51]

For the most part, Wilson scholars reacted positively to the book. Arthur
Link, the leading Wilson biographer, hailed the book for its "really large contribution to our knowledge of the events of World War I and the peace conference, because it presents the first detailed account of Mr. Hoover's own
enormous labors during this period," after his memoirs had only told "a small
part of the story." "Indeed," Link concluded, the "great merit of this volume lies in the fact that it is more a personal memoir than a biographical
study," and he concluded that it was "Mr. Hoover's finest book."[52] Harrison

Salisbury wrote in the *New York Times* that Hoover's reason for writing the book "becomes clear almost from the opening page. It lies in Mr. Hoover's admiration for Wilson's ideals. The two men may have represented warring political parties, but Mr. Hoover makes no secret of the fact that Wilson was his guiding light."[53] Another *Times* reviewer added, "Any reader, not a professional student of Wilson's last years, will find this book a revelation."[54]

Peeps

Senator Estes Kefauver queried Hoover in January of 1958 concerning his views on what should be done in the event of the inability of a president to perform the duties of his office, an issue that seemed particularly relevant and timely because of Eisenhower's two serious illnesses during his first term. Kefauver wanted the former president to testify before his subcommittee on constitutional amendments relating to the question of where he would "place the responsibility for determining the President's inability to perform the powers and duties of his office."[55] Hoover wrote from the Key Largo Anglers' Club in Florida that in the interests of the separation of powers, and because of the mandate given to the president's political party by his election, "a President's inability to serve or his possible restoration to office should be determined by the leading officials in the Executive Branch, as they are of the party having the responsibilities determined by the election." He told Kefauver "a simple amendment to the Constitution (or possibly statutory law) could provide for such a commission made up from the Executive Branch to make the determination required."[56]

The following month the 83-year-old former president left his "monastery" to deliver two "peeps" to the American people. He spoke at Washington's Birthday ceremonies at Valley Forge, Pennsylvania, and delivered virtually the same speech he had made there in 1931. Again he argued for the individual against "the deadening restraints of Government," but with government ready to "equally assure his fair chance, his equality of opportunity from the encroachment of special privileges and greed or domination by any group or class."[57]

A few days later he spoke to the New York Chamber of Commerce on the economic recession that had gripped America. He called the recession a "minor slump in business and employment" and recalled for his audience that "once upon a time my political opponents honored me as possessing the fabulous intellectual and economic power by which I created a worldwide economic depression all by myself. At least I might claim from these tributes that I must know something about depressions." Hoover's advice was to put a freeze on wage and price increases, eliminate waste, and reduce nonessential government spending until the budget was balanced. He found hopeful signs that Eisenhower was at least following the latter policy, but Hoover advocated pushing beyond a balanced budget "to the point where we can have a tax reduction. That would be the greatest possible stimulant to recovery." But taxes could be reduced only if there were corresponding cuts in government expenditures or a balanced budget. And the way to do so was to look at the recommendations of the second Hoover Commission.[58]

Those recommendations were, in fact, making progress. Democratic Senator Hubert Humphrey, chairman of the Senate reorganization committee, reported early in February 1958 that 270 recommendations of the second commission had been put into effect either wholly or in part. He calculated that this represented about 53 percent of the total, but other recommendations were still under study because of "revolutionary change" that they proposed.[59] Hoover was doing everything he could to assist passage of a bill through Congress that would implement some of the commission's recommendations in the Defense Department. Although Clarence Brown worked hard in Congress to get the bill passed, not all Hoover Commission members approved of it. Ferdinand Eberstadt, in fact, resigned from the lobbying group because he felt that the bill was alien to the commission's mission to promote efficiency or economy and was so "vague in its requests for grants of authority that no one can tell whether they should or should not be granted." His impression was that the bill was primarily "a political response to the public clamor that arose at the time Sputnik went up" and would do nothing to eliminate the deficiencies in the Department of Defense, which were "far more deficiencies of policies and decisions."[60]

Hoover responded that he, too, was unhappy with the failure of the recommendations of the two Hoover Commissions to make more of a "dent on their operations," but he argued that "any shake-up might be useful as the organization could not be worse than it is."[61] On June 11 the president wrote Hoover that he appreciated the former president's "telegram in respect to defense reorganization." "As you indicate," Ike wrote, "in the interest of unity, efficiency and the greatest military strength at the least cost, the need is urgent to vest clear-cut authority in the Secretary of Defense." Differences of opinion had developed between Congress and Eisenhower on certain provisions of the bill, he told Hoover, but the former president's telegram to Congress had "powerfully" supported "the basic approach which I have been striving to advance, and I am most grateful to you for it."[62]

As the former president neared his eighty-fourth birthday, Eisenhower dispatched him yet again on a foreign mission, this time to represent the United States during its "official days" at the Brussels World Fair in June.[63] Although recovering from the removal of his gall bladder, Hoover agreed to make the trip.[64] Another leading American, Vice President Richard Nixon, went abroad during May and learned vividly the discontent that existed in Latin America toward the United States. After his return he visited Hoover at the Waldorf Tower for an hour and emerged to report that the former president had given him "some constructive suggestions with regard to United States policy toward Latin America."[65]

Hoover's own trip was less eventful. Spirited to Brussels aboard the presidential airplane *Columbine*, he was met at the airport by Prince Albert and Belgian and American officials. He stayed in the simple quarters of the Foundation Universitaire, an institution for exchange students which he had helped found, met with old Belgian and American comrades from his relief days, was received in audience by King Baudouin, and visited the Dowager Queen Elizabeth at her palace. On America's Independence Day he gave a speech at the fair. Hoover told his audience that "in this climate of friendly competition, criticism of other nations would be entirely out of place," but it was appropriate "that the representatives of a particular nation should interpret here the ideals, the aspirations, and the way of life of his own people." He reminded the Europeans that since Americans were descended from every nation in Europe they therefore had "some responsibility for these invisible forces radiating from my country." There were, he noted, two "major methods of government among free peoples"—the American form, "where the executive is separated from the legislative powers, and the election of the individual executive and legislative officials is for fixed terms," and the parliamentary form that "combined the legislative and administrative powers, and their officials are periodically subject to election—all at the same time."[66]

Since World War I, Hoover noted, there had been a proliferation of "fractional political parties" in Europe, which hampered the ability of governments to govern effectively. "The American method is not perfect," he admitted, "but for 182 years it has sustained stability in our country through every crisis and in the main, brought an orderly progress in the midst of new inventions and ideas." The American system, he concluded, might have "uses for other free men." Hoover touched on the economic progress of America and the "spiritual and moral impulses and ideals which motivate the lives of peoples." After dealing with technological advances, he turned to "the false legends, misrepresentations, and vicious propaganda" that were being disseminated concerning the United States and that often depicted it "as living under the control of wicked men who exploit our economic life through gigantic trusts and huge corporations." The former president picked such misrepresentations apart. Far from being imperialistic, as some charged, the United States had "willingly borne back-breaking taxes" without any hope of returns in order "to aid in protecting the freedom of mankind and to relieve people from poverty." They had fought and died in three great wars "that more freedom would come to mankind and that the world might have a lasting peace," while after none of these victories had the United States asked "for an acre of territory, except a few military bases to protect the free nations." Nor had the United States ever sought "reparations or economic privileges" but on the contrary had "made gigantic gifts and loans to aid nations in defense and reconstruction, including Communist Russia." He told his audience, "I would not have believed in the face of this worldwide record that peoples with a free press could be imposed upon by such propaganda," but such "misrepresentations and propaganda are inciting physical attacks upon American citizens, upon our officials, and abuse of our country." If they continued, he warned, they could lead to a resurgence of isolationist feeling in the United States.

Premier Gaston Eyskens proclaimed the following day "Hoover Day" in Belgium. Hoover spoke on the Belgian relief work he had headed and on the Belgian American Educational Foundation that had resulted from it. The foundation had granted nearly two thousand fellowships to Americans and Belgians. Premier Eyskens was one of four Belgian premiers who had benefited from such a fellowship, and he paid tribute to Hoover's career of public service and spoke of the esteem and love all Belgians felt for him. That day the former president left for his return to the United States.[67] On July 7 he reported to Eisenhower that he had "completed your mission to Belgium," and "judging by both the Belgian, the continent and the American press, your idea proved of value. Certainly the Belgian people are grateful to you for this and many other reasons. I am indebted to you for the honor of representing you and for your making the path smooth with the *Columbine*."[68]

The *New York Times* called the dispatch of Hoover to Belgian "an unusually felicitous idea" and described his speech as "a very good one, indeed." The former president, it wrote, had spoken "with a vigorous forthrightness" on "the elements of strength in our form of government and political society," and his "reply to the constant criticism of the United States was thoughtful and well taken." The editorial concluded, "Once more Mr. Hoover has been an honor to his country."[69]

The next month the *New York Times* wrote, "Herbert Hoover, who marks his eighty-fourth birthday today, engaged in good-natured polemic against the Russians, offered cautious advice on foreign affairs, extolled the virtues of fishing, and gave an account of an ex-President's private life in an interview last week." It reported that the former president had invited the press and television newsmen into his "comfortable monastery" in the Waldorf Tower and had given them "an hour's display of the Hoover wit." If the Soviets wanted peace, he told them, they must "stop conspiring to upset free governments and stop the hate talk about the United States and other free countries." He did not expect that the Russians would do so but said, "We are all hopeful there is going to be a change of mind and heart and if they make an attempt at it we will grasp it with both hands." The newspaper reported of Hoover's private life that he had kept himself busy at writing during 1958 with the help of four secretaries and a research assistant. He had received 1,620 invitations to speak and accepted 30. "I'm my own 'ghost,'" he told reporters, "and I revise and revise to make my speeches. I revised those thirty speeches 154 times." He had also written 55,952 letters, "not counting acknowledgments," had taken "part in the dedication of the Truman Library, a school and nine of the forty-one new Boys Clubs of America clubhouses, was active in fundraising for twelve causes, received ten honors, and published another book." He had also found time for trout fishing on the Mackenzie River and had pursued bonefish in two trips to the Florida Keys. It would have added up to a formidable year for a man half Hoover's age. His birthday, the *Times* reported, would be spent in Greenwich, Connecticut, with his son Allan and his family, where "he throws dignity and Quaker sobriety to the wind and has a romping good time."[70]

Reorganization Again

Undoubtedly Hoover's most memorable birthday gift was the passage of the bill by Congress that provided for reorganization of the Department of Defense along the lines recommended by the second Hoover Commission.[71] Hoover wrote Congressman Brown that he had received news of the passage from Brown "while out fishing." He told the Ohio congressman, "There has never been in my long experience such an example of legislative ability and persistence as you demonstrated in this legislation. You have my unbounded admiration. And I hope the Department will carry it forward, for it can be of immense national service."[72] With the passage of this act, the Citizens' Committee for the Hoover Commission Report disbanded. Hoover claimed that the adoption of the commission's recommendations had now reached the point where they were saving taxpayers "upwards of $3,000,000,000 a year." The Citizens' Committee estimated that 64 percent of the commission's recommendations had so far been adopted, with both the Defense Department reorganization bill and the modernization of the federal budget system having been signed into law in 1958. Charles Francis, chairman of the Citizens' Committee called these "two of the most significant and far-reaching recommendations ever made in the name of the bipartisan Hoover Commission."[73]

Newsweek took this occasion to review the work of the second Hoover Commission and its results in October 1958. The Citizens' Committee, it noted, had "struggled against great odds," with the public more apathetic where the second commission's recommendations had been concerned, government bureaucrats unsympathetic, and even the White House sometimes uncooperative. The magazine added, "Even so, the Citizens Committee, by mobilizing public opinion and bombarding Washington with thousands of letters, was extraordinarily successful. In all, some 60 per cent of the Hoover Commission's 314 recommendations were adopted by Congress or implemented by the President, at an estimated savings to the taxpayers of between $3 billion and $4 billion. One of the committee's most notable successes was the new law putting budget expenditures on an annual basis, thus saving many millions in holdover appropriations." *Newsweek* then listed the major proposals that had been implemented, including the inauguration of a government-wide program to reduce paperwork and cut storage costs, liquidation of the assets of the Reconstruction Finance Corporation, streamlining of the Pentagon's research and development programs, higher salaries for career technicians and other federal employees with professional and scientific skills, establishment of a Federal Career Executive Board to offer greater career incentives for management personnel, elimination of duplicate hospital services in the same area of the country by more than one military service, greater utilization of private business for the government's "housekeeping" chores, the curtailment of about six hundred federal activities that were in competition with private business, and increased use of commercial vessels and airlines for routine shipments and travel by the Department of Defense, as well others. But _Newsweek_ also found many other proposals still pending, including some that were dearest to Hoover's philosophy.[74]

The _New York Times_ also lauded the work of the Hoover Commissions in a November 2 editorial, noting that the reports of two commissions "represented a milestone in the history of American Government, for they included far-reaching proposals that took form in the Reorganization Act of 1949, the Military Unification Act of the same year, creation of the General Services Agency and the Department of Health, Education and Welfare, improvements within the State, Labor and Post Office Departments and the Bureau of Internal Revenue, and the passage of the Defense Reorganization and modern budgeting acts this year." But the _Times_ added,

> No discussion of the work of the Hoover Commission can be complete, however, without pointing to the fundamental reforms that have been proposed and not yet acted upon because they are politically unpalatable, or because there are powerful special-interest lobbies working against them or for other equally bad reasons. Outstanding is the need for reorganization of the Veterans' Administration and veterans' service, and also the unification of the vast array of Federal medical services. Of equally great importance is the necessity for reorganization of our natural resource agencies, with special attention to elimination of competition among them and to coordination of river development policies. Even without the help of the Citizens Committee, strong leadership at the top of the government could do much to clear up the major unfinished business in the field of organization reforms.[75]

The Man in the White House

Hoover, though, had never entertained great hope that his "conservative" philosophy would be strongly supported by the Republican in the White House. He had only modest expectations when Eisenhower was first inaugurated in 1953, and six years of the Eisenhower presidency did not lessen his concern for the future of the GOP. Eisenhower and other Republican candidates seemed still to assume that they must court "liberal" voters, since "conservative" voters had nowhere else to go and would support GOP candidates in any case. For Hoover that assumption was a "fallacy," and he saw his views borne out by the 1958 midterm elections, in which GOP defeats demonstrated that "Republican radicalism can get nowhere."[76] After the election Hoover wrote that the Republican Party still did not "seem to comprehend that the only way they can live as a vital party is on the conservative side." The position of the self-styled "liberal" or "modern" Republicans had already been "fully preempted by the opposition." Republicans must embrace four major issues: (1) the problem of communism; (2) the necessity for "preservation of the American way of life and freedom, itself, from socialism"; (3) the necessity to reduce expenditures and balance the budget to head off inflation; and (4) the need to free the people from the domination of "wicked" labor unions. The GOP, he maintained, could "save the foundation of American life by these corrections."[77]

Meanwhile, as a result of the passage of PL85-745 of 1958, Hoover, as an ex-president, would begin to receive a pension of $25,000 per year, with the first check, minus withholding, due him on September 30.[78] Hoover returned the W-4 that was mailed to him by the Secretary of Treasury and wrote, "I gather I am now a government employee. All of which will complicate both my life and my annual income tax return!"[79]

Hoover was now more critical of Eisenhower's domestic policies, he having mellowed toward the president's foreign policies. He supported the president in his military intervention in Lebanon, calling it "the only course possible if the freedom of nations is to be protected from militarist conspiracies."[80] Appearing on the conservative *Manion Forum*, the former president opined that the greatest problem before the United States was "to find some road to lessen the repeated tensions created by the Communists over the world," such as their provocations over Berlin. Behind the tensions between the two great superpowers lurked "the dangers of a war more dreadful than mankind has ever known." The free world had spent forty years seeking "a workable relationship or some basis of peace with the Communists," learning from bitter experience that the Reds harbored entirely different concepts of international relations than did the rest of the world—based, he concluded, on no "code of morals such as that to which we must adhere." The USSR had violated a long list of treaties, and before the United States could consider any future agreements with them, such as reduction or limitation of military capabilities, there must be set up "independent machinery to enforce such agreements on both sides." He noted with approval that "President Eisenhower has stood firm on this principle."[81]

Nothing that the European nations had done since the Great Debate had erased Hoover's disillusionment with them. He wrote Richard Berlin of the Hearst newspapers in September 1958, "Between you and me it amounts to the fact that no nation in Europe either can nor intends to join with the United States in a nuclear war with Russia—and the American people have never been plainly told this bare fact. However, these European alliances improve the propaganda front." The European nations were simply too close to the Russian borders to put up any defense, and their only hope was "a victory by the United States." Hoover's familiar conclusion was that "the only real balance of power available to us is the Western Hemisphere if we keep Communist governments out."[82]

Others were not as charitable toward the occupant of the White House as Hoover was, Richard Lloyd Jones writing Hoover after the 1958 electoral defeats that Eisenhower had "set out to destroy the Republican party and he has succeeded. We desperately need a Herbert Hoover of thirty years ago."[83] When Senator Barry Goldwater asked him for a copy of the draft of Republican principles that he had submitted to the resolutions committee of the 1958 convention, Hoover sent one and wrote the Arizonan,

> I felt that a short statement in commonly understood terms without emotional phrases would be carried in people's minds and pockets as the dictum of a Party to which they would like to belong.
>
> I did not win out. Except for a line or two, it was wholly rejected by the Resolutions Committee.
>
> That "platforms" are outdated was evident as the newspapers seldom noticed the 1956 version.
>
> I do not wish this published or circulated under my name . . . I have moved entirely out of the political world.[84]

In April it was announced that the Hoover Birthplace Foundation was erecting a library at West Branch to house the former president's papers, which would be transferred there from the Hoover Institution at Stanford. It was expected that the library would be open by November, and it was expected that Hoover would be there for the opening.[85]

Life at the Waldorf

Hoover appeared on the nationally televised *Meet the Press* on the day before his eighty-fifth birthday in 1959. The leader of the Soviet Union was soon to visit the United States, kindling hopes that better relations between the two superpowers would result. Hoover was less sanguine, warning that the "tactics of the communists may change, but their determination to dominate the world continues." He did foresee the possibility of tensions temporarily lessening, however, thus tiding the world over to "a period in which there may be hopes for greater steps to peace." Hoover was confident that the president would not "compromise with or appease the evil forces in this world."[86]

When newsman Chet Huntley asked him which of his services to the nation had made him proudest, Hoover pointed to his relief activities. His work on government reorganization had been "a very happy job, but it had some good consequences, and some were indifferent." He now estimated that 70 percent of the recommendations of the first commission had been adopted, but only claimed 30–40 percent for the second, which was far less than the estimate of the Citizens' Committee. He repeated his warning that the United States had involved itself in too many foreign crises and that the nation badly needed to "clean up our own household" because of the dangers from inflation, unbalanced budgets, and the "huge growth of crime." Asked if there was any hope of the GOP ever again becoming the majority party in the United States, Hoover responded, "Being a longtime Republican, I'm always in hope." The broadcast ended on a health note:

> Mr. [Bob] Considine: I've got a good question, Mr. President: On the eve of your 85th birthday, how do you feel?
>
> Mr. Hoover: I feel physically perfect.
>
> Mr. Considine: Good.
>
> Mr. Hoover: About 68 I should think.
>
> Mr. Considine: Good.

In his birthday statement to the press the next day, Hoover told them he had "six jobs as yet uncompleted." He was keeping an eye on the dangers to the country, hoping to be of service if needed; he was writing three volumes on the history of his relief activities under the title *An American Epic*; he was still working with the Boys' Clubs of America; there were his continuing efforts to build up what was now called the Hoover Institution on War, Revolution and Peace; he was responsible as a trustee or chairman of a dozen institutions; and he attended baseball games. He had not, he told the press, retired.[87] Two days before his birthday he had thrown out the first ball at the "Old Timers" game at Yankee Stadium with millions of baseball fans watching on television. The *New York Times* found Hoover's "eye is still good and his arm strong. Few would have suggested that he would be celebrating his eighty-fifth birthday today. But it is typical of the man that he seems to get stronger as he gets older."[88]

Meanwhile, Hoover continued to leave his "monastery" to deliver his occasional "peeps." As indicated by his mention of it in the *Meet the Press* interview, the former president had become increasingly concerned over the growth of crime in the United States. In June, *This Week* magazine published his short article, "We Must Know More about Crime," in which Hoover argued that the information on crime was deficient, particularly that which gave data on the relative efficiency of the various procedures and methods of justice in stemming crime. Hoover recommended a special census by the Census Bureau that would include the names of all criminals arrested during the previous two years, together with details of the crime and the disposition of the case. This would provide needed information on the ratio of arrests to crimes, the length of time before arrest, and the length of time spent in prison for each category of crime. Such data might indicate where the judicial system had been "lax or effective." "The story from this Census," he suggested, "might bring realization to the American people that freedom in the United

States is in more jeopardy from crime than from all the Communist conspiracies within our borders."[89]

Hoover clearly believed, however, that at this point in his life he could make his greatest contribution through the completion of the books he was writing rather than by public activities, particularly when the latter now exerted a greater strain upon him. A normal day found him working for 10 to 11 hours, but if he awakened during the night he was likely to write again until he was sleepy. He rose at 7 a.m., and after breakfasting at 9:00 he began his writing, assisted by his secretaries and research assistants. After lunch at 1 p.m., he napped at 2 p.m., but by 3:00 he was back at his desk writing until 5:30, whereupon he read the afternoon newspapers and watched the 6 p.m. newscast. At 7:15 guests arrived for dinner, and Hoover indulged in the one dry martini he allowed himself daily. Evenings were filled with conversation or canasta playing. By 10:00 he was preparing for bed. Author Jim Bishop, profiling the former president for *American Weekly* magazine, wrote, "He is alone, yet not lonesome. He is accustomed to doing his own thinking and his own work. At the age of 85, no one helps this man—this rock—with his shoes or his tie. He believes in God and he subscribes to the credo that God will help those who help themselves. Don't forget, he plans to complete four more books."[90]

But Hoover did remain somewhat active publicly. In December 1959 he became a member of the board of trustees of the conservative Americans for Constitutional Action, but on the condition that it would not require any work of him. This group, whose board included former New Jersey governor Charles Edison, Robert E. Wood, Edgar M. Eisenhower, and Felix Morley, dedicated itself to the election of candidates for public office who subscribed to conservative, constitutional principles.[91] And Hoover could not resist an occasional opportunity to give his views on the state of the world and to wage his personal war against the ideas of Karl Marx. In February 1960 he told the Eastern Area of United Presbyterian Men that America was "plagued with the infection of Karl Marx in both the thinking of our people and the affairs of our government." That infection had been "frozen in" by the time Eisenhower took office, having been spread through the nation "by deluded and misled men and by disguised organizations, fronts and cults" who, like "hermit crabs" had crawled "into such terms as 'liberal,' 'progressive,' 'public electric power,' 'managed economy,' 'welfare state,' and a half dozen others." But experience had demonstrated conclusively that government-managed commerce and industry led to dictatorship. Another crisis was the moral slump in America and the failure of the judicial system to imprison criminals. "I know of nothing in the Scriptures," Hoover told the Presbyterian men, "which advocates the release of mad dogs on the streets. In fact, I interpret Christ's words on 'casting into outer darkness' to include an effective sentence in prison."[92]

When Republicans asked their former president for yet another "farewell" at their 1960 convention, Hoover tried to avoid it. When the subject was first raised early in March, he wrote to Congressman Clarence Brown, "I will be on the edge of my eighty-sixth year with many commitments that I have to complete. I have already said four farewells to these bodies, which would seem to be enough. Also my advice on these occasions has had but little effect. Therefore, with your great art in political sciences, can you not bury this request?"[93] To another correspondent he wrote that he had "concluded some time ago not to enter upon this campaign. That is the job of the vigorous younger generation."[94] In April he also declined the president's request that he represent Eisenhower at the dedication of two memorials of the American Battle Monuments Commission in Belgium, writing the White House, "In order to conserve my strength for already existing obligations and administrative burdens, I am not able to take on additional commitments."[95]

Republicans refused, however, to heed Hoover's pleas. He was told that if he would just make a personal appearance at the convention there would be a ceremonial presentation to him of a gold convention badge, which would be televised to the nation and could be watched on large screens by the delegates.[96] This and other such proposals finally prompted a letter from the former president to GOP national chairman Thruston Morton:

> It seems certain that you and many of our leaders are going all around Robin Hood's barn to get me into the Chicago convention! All together these ideas include such things as taped television recordings to be put on screens in the convention hall, live TV with statements from distant cities, and a message to be read at the convention. I, of course, will do anything that I can physically manage to help the party. From all this discussion, I have decided that if you think it important for me to take part in the convention, the direct thing for me to do is to go to Chicago and make a short address. I can do this if it is staged in the earlier part of some evening session and on live nationwide TV. This plan would enable me to fly from San Francisco (where I will be) to Chicago during the day, retire at some hour like 10:00, and return to San Francisco the next morning. This plan would avoid all the above complex arrangements.[97]

The convention scheduled his speech for 8 p.m., and Hoover set to work drafting a speech. This one was destined to be his last personal "farewell" appearance before a GOP convention.[98] But he had also scheduled two speeches in California and a television appearance for September. As he wrote Patrick Hurley, there would be "no summer vacation for me," for between speeches he was "chained to my desk."[99]

Six weeks before the convention, John D. M. Hamilton called on Hoover and found "his mind was as bright and clear as ever," although there was evidence of some physical deterioration since they had last met. In a two-hour talk they ranged over a variety of topics. Hoover was convinced there would be no war with the Soviet Union soon, since he considered the United States superior in every category of war-making potential except ground troops. He was still uncomfortable, however, with the stationing of American ground troops in Europe. He felt flattered that all the potential Democratic candidates for their party's nomination had been to see him except Adlai Stevenson and Hubert Humphrey, and he attributed this courtesy to his friendship with Truman. As for the Republican ticket, the assumption was that Vice President Richard Nixon would head it, and their discussion was about potential running mates. Hoover expressed a preference for Senator Barry Goldwater but recognized that the GOP was unlikely to nominate two candidates from the western states. Of the eastern possibilities, he preferred Henry Cabot Lodge over Nelson Rockefeller because of the former's qualifications and experience in the United Nations and because of his concern that Rockefeller was too liberal.[100]

Meanwhile, Hoover had appeared on the nationally televised talk show *Person to Person* in May and expressed his lack of interest in a proposed senate seat for former presidents. "Twenty years ago I would have been enthusiastic about that," he told reporters, "but at my time of life, I don't look on the prospect of sitting on a hard cushion for several hours a day and listening to speeches as being attractive."[101] In mid-June he spoke at the laying of the cornerstone of the $12 million United Engineering Center in New York City, where he told the audience the "unextinguishable spark in the minds of men to be free" might yet save progress and civilization despite the inroads of communism. Communism controlled six hundred million people, he estimated, but progress in the past century had flowed from "free and productive minds in the civilized parts of the world—that is, the nations possessed of independence and personal freedom."[102]

On July 25, the former president flew from California to Chicago for his speech to the convention. That night he told the delegates, "I had not expected to speak at this Convention. In each of your last three Conventions I bade you an affectionate good-bye. Apparently my good-byes did not take. And I have been bombarded with requests to do it again for the fourth time. Unless some miracle comes to me from the Good Lord this is finally it." Although he briefly alluded to foreign dangers and to domestic political, economic, and social issues, Hoover concentrated primarily on what he described as "a frightening moral slump" in the United States, part of the reason for which lay in the Marxist infection, which was a destroyer of all morals. Religious institutions and other agencies dedicated to character building in youth needed help, and the nation in general needed "a rebirth of that great spiritual force which has been impaired by cynicism and weakened by foreign infections." He called that force nationalism—a belief in America. "The re-echo of the word America," Hoover maintained, "might resurrect conscience away from crime and back to manhood." It might also restrain the selfish demands of special interest groups and stimulate "anew the initiative and enterprise of tens of thousands of our youth who from fear of the future seek refuge in the bureaucracies of industry and government, and it might bring about insistence "upon a revision of our weakened courts." Hoover called upon Republicans to "stop this moral retreat, to lead the attack and recapture the meaning of the word—America."[103] A few days later he confided, "I am just too old to be traveling about. The trek to the Convention proved it."[104]

Hoover had earlier expressed a preference for Lodge as vice presidential candidate and his choice was well known, so he was no doubt cheered when Lodge was chosen as Nixon's running mate. The *New York Times* had reported that fact before the choice was made, and after the nomination it reported, "Mr. Nixon's choice was bolstered . . . sources said, by the fact that President Eisenhower and former President Hoover also wanted Lodge."[105]

Freed of his duty to the convention, Hoover returned to California, where he spoke to the press and the Union League Club of San Francisco a week later. After discussing his own activities, the former president turned to the issue of civil rights and opined "that the states and local governments must and in the end will, obey the law of the land as declared by the Supreme Court." Hoover did not believe, however, that "the Federal Government should ever use force against the states, except in rebellion." He criticized the federal government for failing to adopt the remainder of the recommendations of the Hoover Commission, but found consolation in "the likelihood that both parties in this campaign will attack the other for this failure." He called for "an entire reorganization our tax laws," because they were "destroying initiative." The problem of food surpluses could be solved by the federal government leasing "for 20 years all the marginal land for an annual rental and leave the farmer to live on his farm, but to use it for food supply to his family and to release it to pasturage and reforestation." As for the surpluses that already existed, he would "say to every nation of low standard of food supply—send your ships here and you can get it for nothing." He continued in opposition to federal aid to education and to disarmament without adequate controls, and supported continued nuclear testing, both above and below ground. He continued to oppose admission of the People's Republic of China into the UN and suggested that if "the Communists and African groups become a majority, its usefulness to the United States is likely to be less than nothing." He was against summit conferences, arguing that the president's voice was more powerful from the White House. And he was obviously not opposed to US military action against Cuba. "Too many people," he told his audience, "rise in horror that any action on our part would be an act of aggression," but "when a man comes at you with a dagger pointed at your heart, it is not aggression to kick his pins out from under him."[106]

As for himself, Hoover told the Union Leaguers that he saw "about 1000 people individually a month. They mostly want something. I answer an average of 1000 letters a month. I have made 14 different sized speeches this year, 1960; I have a responsibility in the management of a dozen Scientific, Educational and Charitable enterprises. I am working on 4 books under the title, *An American Epic*."

Back in his comfortable "monastery," Hoover submitted to yet another birthday interview. Of the possibility that Americans might vote against the Democratic nominee, John F. Kennedy, because he was a Catholic, Hoover opined, "I think it's a dreadful idea. I abhor bigotry in every form." He refused to answer other political questions, though, since he had received "many touching tributes" from both Democrats and Republicans on his birthday and did not want to be "offensive to my many friends on the other side." He would, however, vote for the GOP candidates. The thousands of letters he had received for his "moral slump" speech at the Republican convention convinced him that "some force is stirring our people beyond the satisfactions of increasing standards of living." As for Soviet premier Khruschev's assertion that the grandchildren of this generation would live under communism, Hoover answered, "Well, that ain't so." He supported the Twenty-second Amendment to the Constitution, which limited the presidency to two terms for one person, because "eight years in the White House is enough exhaustion for any mortal." As for his own work, he was still putting in ten hours a day, sometimes seven days a week, on his books. The second volume of *An American Epic* was to be published the following month, the third was in page proof, and a fourth was "in the oven"—in the process of being written.[107]

Politics Again

Both presidential candidates in 1960 were well known to Hoover. The former president, together with his son, Herbert Jr., had been instrumental in encouraging Richard Nixon to enter politics for the first time in 1946, and they had maintained close contact ever since. On the Democratic side, John F. Kennedy was the son of Hoover's longtime friend Joseph P. Kennedy, and the former president had worked closely with the nominee when Senator Kennedy chaired the subcommittee reviewing the legislative recommendations of the second Hoover Commission. Hoover appears to have grown somewhat disenchanted with Nixon during the campaign due to the nominee's failure to call on him during his travels.[108] Hoover did not take an active part in the campaign but did offer Nixon advice. After the first televised Nixon-Kennedy debate, Hoover suggested that reporters be eliminated from any further debates as their questions showed that they were "prejudiced and laying deliberate traps for Nixon." He also suggested that the GOP nominee stop agreeing with Kennedy's "goals" during the debate, since, he said, "Kennedy's goals are not those of the people from whom Nixon must get his votes," and the goals were "evil—they are stupendous spending (with inflation); they are socialism disguised as a 'welfare state.'" In Hoover's view, Kennedy was clearly determined to set up "a new and greater New Deal." The GOP elder statesman also suggested that Nixon do a better job of making up for his subsequent television appearances, since, in the words of one broadcaster whom he quoted, "Nixon looks like a made-over stiff."[109]

After the four debates that had been scheduled between the two candidates, Kennedy challenged Nixon to yet a fifth confrontation. On October 20, Nixon met with a number of friends and advisers at the Waldorf to discuss the challenge. Among those present were Hoover and Thomas E. Dewey. Hoover's advice was to decline the challenge by claiming that Nixon's time was all "booked up."[110] This was Nixon's position the following day, but he modified it slightly a day later, consenting to another debate if the time could found in his schedule. The time was, of course, not found, and a fifth debate was never held.[111] Hoover also suggested to GOP national committee chairman Thruston Morton that Nixon attack the Democratic spending proposals and point to the inflation and higher taxes that must result. He suggested that Nixon draw a contrast by promising "reduced expenses of government" that would include demands that Europe take over 80 percent of the foreign aid program, the liquidation of "government activities in competition with private enterprise," and the implementation of "Hoover Commission recommendations."[112] Hoover, however, found the campaign confusing and disappointing since "the great vital issues to our future" were not being mentioned.[113] On Election Day, eight years of GOP occupancy of the White House came to an end, as Kennedy narrowly defeated Hoover's fellow-Californian.

CHAPTER 15

The Grand Old Man of the Grand Old Party

The New President

Soon after the election, the former president departed for the Florida Keys on another fishing trip. By coincidence, both of the 1960 presidential candidates were also relaxing in Florida in January—the president-elect in Palm Beach and Nixon in Key Biscayne. On January 11 Hoover traveled to Palm Beach for a reception in his honor on the eve of the dedication of Hoover Dike, an 85-mile-long structure that contained the waters of Lake Okeechobee. Construction on the dike had started during his administration and was being renamed for him the following day.[1]

At the reception, both Joseph Kennedy and the president-elect called on Hoover. Joseph Kennedy may have suggested to the former president at this time the desirability of a meeting between his son and Nixon to demonstrate postelection unity to the public, although Hoover later told Nixon that the elder Kennedy had phoned him with the suggestion.[2] Joseph Kennedy apparently told Hoover that if he would arrange for Nixon to receive his son, he would make sure that the president-elect called on the vice president. According to Hoover's account, Nixon was at first reluctant but finally consented to meet with Kennedy. When news broke that the two had met, Hoover traced the source of the "leak" and learned that it had come from the Nixon "camp."[3]

In mid-January Nixon wrote Hoover another appreciative letter, thanking the former president for his "aid in the battles in which it was my lot to be involved." "But above all," he told Hoover, "I want you to know how much I have appreciated those occasions when you have so generously given of your time and energy to advise me on issues on which I had to make decisions. Our breakfasts and other meetings in your apartment in the Waldorf

447

are among the most cherished memories of my fourteen years of government service."[4] Hoover told Nixon, "You will discover that elder statesmen are little regarded by the opposition party until they get over 80 years of age—and thus harmless."[5]

Shortly after the election, Hoover wrote a former Hoover Commission task force member that he had "a curious feeling that you and I may be surprised by favorable consequences of the election in important directions."[6] Clearly Hoover was referring to the possibility of further action on the remaining Hoover Commission recommendations by a president who had worked with him on those recommendations as a senator. A month later he wrote that he was especially hopeful that 1961 would see "further implementation of the Commission recommendations." The former president found bases for hope, too, in the fact that during 1960 more had been accomplished in getting recommendations adopted than in any other year since the Commission had made its reports to Congress, and the results were especially gratifying in the defense area. Moreover, Kennedy, he wrote, was "fully familiar with the recommendations and during the past campaign cited their further implementation as a means he would use to increase efficiency and reduce governmental expenditures."[7] Hoover was now serving as honorary chairman of the Committee of Hoover Commission Task Force Members, which had replaced the Citizens' Committee as the lobby for adoption of the commission's recommendations.

For this and other reasons, Hoover was drawn to the new president despite the perceived ideological gap between them. Despite his eighty-six years, the former president flew to Washington for Kennedy's inauguration, only to find the Washington airports closed due to bad weather.[8] Kennedy obviously felt close to the GOP elder statesman, too, seeking his advice at the reception in Palm Beach. Hoover told Kennedy that he had none but not to worry since "everybody has advice for a new President."[9] In March 1961 President Kennedy sought Hoover as honorary chairman of the national advisory council for his new Peace Corps, but the former president declined, arguing that he was too busy to be of much help.[10] The following month, George McGovern invited him to become honorary chairman of the advisory committee for Kennedy's Food-for-Peace program, but again Hoover declined for the same reason, although he offered to give advice if it were needed.[11] Hoover took advantage of the opportunity to suggest to McGovern a survey to locate the truly hungry peoples of the world, and he also insisted that those nations that possessed the resources to buy food should be eliminated from consideration by the agency. However, "antagonism of some nations to the United States" ought not to disqualify them from receiving relief if they truly needed it, and Hoover said he would "not eliminate even Red China if they would accept control of distribution by American staff." Guarantees were needed in any case, he told McGovern, to ensure that food reached the intended recipients, and this could best be done by the creation of "joint commissions comprising their own nationals and Americans."[12]

Meanwhile, on April 17, 1961, the Bay of Pigs invasion by anti-Castro exiles took place. Denied promised air support by the Kennedy administration, the invaders were crushed in less than 72 hours by Castro's forces. Hoover was critical of Kennedy's handling of the affair, telling journalist Richard Berlin that despite his Quaker loathing for war, he would have ordered "the necessary forces into the Bay of Pigs, and I would decimate that Cuban army while they're there, because it's going to have to be done some time and you should do it now and not kill the lives of innocent civilians. I'd end the thing forthwith."[13] Embarrassed by the fiasco, Kennedy, in the words of the *New York Times*, "sought the counsel of two elders of the Republican party . . . in his quest for national solidarity in what he has called a period of peril." On April 28 the president called on both Hoover and Douglas MacArthur in their respective apartments in the Waldorf Tower, spending twenty minutes with Hoover and over an hour with the general.[14] According to Hoover's aide-memoire of their conversation, he "assured the President of his support in any action he must take to defend the United States." This nation was entitled to defend itself against such menaces as Cuba presented under the Monroe Doctrine, he told Kennedy, and that doctrine had never been repealed. Hoover regarded the presence of a communist regime 90 miles from the United States "an intolerable menace to the safety of our country" and "a center of conspiracy to overthrow all free governments in this hemisphere by violence." It was also "daily perpetrating every form of brutality and violation of primary human rights" within Cuba. He suggested two options to Kennedy: (1) an air strike to destroy Castro's military equipment, followed by an invasion by Latin American troops "to restore order and a free election"; or (2) "leave him alone in his accumulating miseries." Hoover preferred the second method for the time being, but he promised to support Kennedy in whichever course he chose.[15]

A week later former vice president Nixon also called on Hoover and MacArthur while on his way to the Midwest for a series of speeches in "loyal opposition" to the Kennedy administration. After 45 minutes with the former president, during which they discussed foreign policy and other subject matter of his forthcoming speeches, Nixon emerged from his suite to say that he was "always amazed" at the way the 86-year-old Hoover stayed "on top of world affairs."[16]

Slowing Down?

Hoover, confided, however, that his doctors had advised him if he wanted to complete all his projects he must "not go out nights," "must not eat anything except this list (which excludes all good food except cranshaw melons)," "must not climb steps or hills," "must not take automobile rides of more than two or three miles," and "must not ride in vibrating planes—i.e., go only where the jets go."[17] The diet must have especially been painful for Hoover, whose cook recalled that he was a rapid and voracious eater who was fond of steaks and roast beef for dinner, stews and chops or fish for lunch, and eggs every day for breakfast along with grapefruit and melons, as well as Canadian or Irish bacon. Hoover also enjoyed salads with his meals, and pumpkin or apple pie for dessert, sometimes substituting baked apples or ice cream or pastry.[18] He also liked to eat cheese and crackers and always had a stone that he struck matches on to light his pipe.[19] And every day before his health failed, he had two martinis.[20] Hoover rarely dined alone, perhaps once per month, and was addicted to canasta playing with his guests, often with his neighbor at the Waldorf, William Nichols. Nichols also recalled sharing in Hoover's "wonderfully warm routine of Christmas tree trimming, Christmas eve dinners, Christmas morning package opening."[21] He had his baseball visits down to the annual Old Timers game and the World Series, since he didn't want to risk catching a cold "for anything less than a major game."[22]

He no longer, he said, felt "any great bitterness about Franklin Roosevelt" and had, he told an interviewer, "forgiven all my enemies except one—Charles Michelson, the paid smearer. He was the most unfair person that ever ran loose." Hoover indicated a Chinese jar, 600 years old, with a figure half man and half wolf, and referred to the figure as the "Michelson of his day." He had, he told a reporter, "certainly liked" the change in the public's attitude toward him. "Public life and representative government," he said, "is a tempest and leaves many scars. But finally the public gets a better understanding and likes you more." As for the "recipe for a long life," he told the reporter, "Never retire. Keep working. If you retire you've got nothing to think about but your ills and pills, and pretty soon you're spending all your time with other people who have nothing to think about but their ills and pills. It becomes a self-multiplying thing. You have to have some occupation. You have to keep looking forward with some hope about the future."[23] From a 90-year-old friend came the warning to the nearly 87-year-old Hoover that "one loses a lot of strength between 87 and 90."[24] Hoover replied, "It is good to hear from you despite your gloom over what is coming to me these next three years. However, I can finish my job in three years more so that fact is cheerful."[25] As it turned out, the former president had only slightly more than three years to live.

In late June Hoover traveled to Philadelphia for a nationally broadcast speech in Independence Square, where he told his young listeners that "the validity of our beliefs in freedom is at stake on a global battleground." He warned them, "You will inherit the costly burden of our defense against the implacable foe who lurks in the Kremlin. While we hope for the cooperation of other nations in the defense of mankind, in the end the safety of America must rest upon our own well-armed right arm, whatever sacrifice this entails. I am confident of your courage. What I am saying to you is not a recital of trite banalities, for these rights and responsibilities are the base of our American way of life, and, in fact, of our civilization." Hoover recalled that he had "lived and worked in countries of free men, of tyrannies, of Socialists, and of Communists," had "seen liberty die and tyranny rise," had "seen slavery again on the march." Each homecoming to the United States "was for me a reaffirmation of the glory of America."[26] The following month he paused on his way to the Bohemian Club encampment to speak in favor of support for privately financed institutions of higher education as part of a $100 million fund drive for his alma mater, Stanford University.[27] A friend wrote early in August to Hoover, "You certainly do get around. One day I get a note from you from Key Largo [Florida], and the next from Waldorf Towers, and then from the Mark Hopkins Hotel [San Francisco]. Your courage in undertaking long trips is most notable."[28]

The former president also monitored the progress of the second Hoover Commission's recommendations in Washington. In June he wrote to Kennedy calling his attention to the fact that a Senate bill embodying recommendations for further reforms of budgeting and accounting, which Kennedy had sponsored as a Senator, had passed the Senate and was now in a House committee. Hoover wondered if any of the Kennedy's assistants "could help get the bill before the House."[29] Kennedy responded that he would "endeavor to do everything possible to ensure House consideration of the measure," and he told Hoover, "Within the Executive branch we are continuing to make budget improvements along the lines recommended by your Commission, including particularly the extension of cost-based budget practices. We expect to achieve most of the benefits which we had in mind a few years ago under the legislation which was then enacted."[30]

In July, just weeks before his eighty-seventh birthday, Hoover traveled to California to attend the annual Bohemian Club encampment and attend a few directors' meetings. The *New York Times* reported, however, that the former president had been "saying yes to so many invitations . . . that he already has agreed to what a colleague calls 'a fantastic schedule,' that began with a speech to business and financial leaders in San Francisco." Looking, the *Times* said, "unusually fit," Hoover made a plea for support of non-tax-supported institutions of higher education like Stanford University. He also called upon all Americans to support President Kennedy in putting up a solid front "to the enemy who lurks in the Kremlin." After his vacation in the Bohemian Club encampment, Hoover also planned to dedicate a new Boys' Club in south San Francisco.[31]

Two days before his eighty-seventh birthday the former president submitted to another interview by the press. One reporter found "the once brown hair is thin and gray. The step is slow and deliberate. The voice is thin and lacks some of its old decisiveness. But the spirit is still vibrant." Hoover again underscored the increase in crime, blaming it on "the restrictions upon our courts and the practices which have developed within them." He suggested the American Bar Association "look into the methods of the British courts where is no such appalling record as that in the United States." He deni-grated charges that Americans were "soft." "Too much attention is paid to what goes on in the cities," he told reporters. "Out in the countryside, in the small towns, on the farms, Americans are just as patriotic as they ever were, ready to meet any emergency, any challenge."[32]

In late October, Eisenhower stopped off at Hoover's apartment for break-fast and later wrote him, "As always I enjoyed the opportunity to exchange views—on a wide variety of subjects—with you."[33] President Kennedy also extended the former president the courtesy of a "year-end briefing" by John McCone in January 1962 and solicited his opinion concerning the propos-als made in his January 24 speech to Congress. Hoover responded to that speech by writing that he was "in agreement with both the gravity of our situ-ation in foreign trade and with your major proposals for legislation." Hoover reminded the President that, when president, he had sought authority over tariffs somewhat similar to that which Kennedy was asking from Congress as part of his Trade Expansion Program.[34]

In July 1962, Hoover responded to a story in the June 18 issue of *US News and World Report*, which averred that Hoover was the only president whose wealth had approached that of JFK. He wrote to David Lawrence,

> This statement is not true. There have been several Presidents of comfortable fortunes. Among them—Franklin D. Roosevelt. The amount of his fortune is clear from the probate of his will. When in the White House, my assets were not one-half those of Franklin Roosevelt . . . Perhaps I may add that my modest competence was made not from inheritance, but from hard work in my twenty years of engineering practice. Since I retired from my profession and entered public service to direct the Belgian Relief Commission over forty-three years ago, I have never accepted any payment—not even personal expenses—from any private organization (except some royalties on articles and books). More-over, I have devoted my payments from the Government to charity or public service, retaining nothing for the use of myself or family. I know it may seem absurd to some, but I have had the belief that as my country had given me schooling, a profession and great opportunities, I deserved no pay from her but rather service from me without payment.[35]

Hoover opposed admission of the People's Republic of China into the United Nations for the balance of his life, furnishing a message for a Com-mittee for One Million rally in September that said, "Over the years I have opposed the admission of Red China to the United Nations and my views are the same today."[36] Some of the same people who opposed PRC admission to the United Nations were also against UN military action against the attempt of Katanga to split away from the Congo and establish an independent African state. Hoover refused to join in a general protest against the UN action but did issue a press statement in December that deplored American assistance to the United Nations in the suppression of the Katangan movement, saying, "It is a sad day for the American people when American resources are applied to the killing of people who are seeking for independence and self-government free from Communist domination."[37]

Early in 1962 Hoover enjoyed what would be his last visit to Key Largo in pursuit of the beloved bonefish. He confided to a friend that he had been instructed by his doctor "to remain in this land of escape until New York reforms its weather habits," and he would not return to New York until some time in April.[38] Hoover's secretary described his life in Florida on this last trip: "We live aboard the boat, we fish—after bonefish and big ones—we go sightseeing for we have a car with us, we cruise about—and life is not strenuous or dressy."[39] In mid-February she reported, "At the moment the Chief is bonefish champ of the KLAC [Key Largo Anglers' Club] and is on board with a 9 3/4-pound bonefish and also on the board for a tarpon!"[40]

In that same year the former president agreed to join former presidents Truman and Eisenhower as honorary chairmen of the Atlantic Council, a group formed by former secretary of state Christian Herter to promote unity in the Atlantic community.[41] He also sent a message of support to a rally of the Young Americans for Freedom, a conservative young people's group inspired by conservative intellectual William F. Buckley Jr.[42] Afterward he wrote Senator Barry Goldwater that he had heard the rally was a "great triumph for you and the Young Americans for Freedom," but more important, it had "established a great movement of conservative thought in our country. And we have needed that leadership for a long time."[43] He told Goldwater that there was "not much that I can do in this campaign, but let me know through [Herbert Jr.] of any service I can do and it will be done."[44]

In March, Hoover joined former president Truman in supporting President Kennedy's resumption of nuclear testing, telling reporters, "We can do no other if we are to survive."[45] When astronaut Scott Carpenter was welcomed to New York City after his voyage into space, Hoover ignored his doctor's advice and joined Truman at a luncheon in Carpenter's honor. He told reporters that Carpenter "has given us a lift and he has given us prestige all over the world."[46] A month later Hoover made his final visit to California, where he told the press that he sympathized with the president in the current economic downturn: "He came in just before a big bust in the stock market and with a Congress opposed to him. He's going down the same weary path, and my sympathies are with him." Hoover was obviously referring to his own experiences after the stock market crash in 1929. He also expressed his bewilderment with the pace of technological change in the 1960s, remarking of the Telstar satellite broadcasts, "The electronics men have just got beyond my comprehension. I belong to a generation that just doesn't grasp all that."[47]

On his eighty-eighth birthday, Hoover returned to his birthplace of West Branch, Iowa, for the dedication of the new Herbert Hoover Presidential Library located but a stone's throw from the restored two-room cottage in which he had been born. Repaying his Republican friend for Hoover's appearance at the dedication of his own presidential library several years earlier, Truman was on hand for the ceremonies at West Branch and led the crowd in singing "Happy Birthday" to Hoover. An estimated 45,000 people showed up to pay tribute to Iowa's most distinguished son. Reporters found the GOP elder statesman speaking with a firm voice, though "thin of hair and slightly stooped." In his speech, he called on Americans to acknowledge that the United Nations had "failed to give us even a remote hope of lasting peace" but had, instead, "added to the dangers of wars which now surround us." The failure was due to the communist nations who, "for forty years, have repeatedly asserted that no peace can come in the world until they have overcome the free nations." The result was that they had "destroyed the usefulness of the United Nations to preserve peace." Hoover now suggested,

> The time is here. If the free nations are to survive, they must have a new and stronger world-wide organization to meet this menace. For purposes of this discussion I may call it the Council of Free Nations. It should include only those nations who are willing to stand up and fight for their freedom and their independence.
>
> The foundations for this organization have already been laid by the forty nations who have taken pledges in the five regional pacts and they have obligated themselves to assist each other with military forces against aggression. And there are other free nations who should join.

He did not suggest that his proposed council should replace the United Nations, but "when the United Nations is prevented from taking action, or if it fails to act to preserve peace, then the Council I have suggested of free nations should step in." He suggested an analogy with the Concert of Europe, which had maintained peace in Europe after the Napoleonic wars.[48]

A few days after his speech, Senator J. William Fulbright, Arkansas Democrat, endorsed Hoover's proposed Council of Free Nations on the *Issues and Answers* radio and television program.[49] President Kennedy said the proposal deserved study but told reporters that the real challenge was to breathe new life into existing organizations, like NATO, rather than create new ones.[50]

In that same month, Hoover wrote to a friend and public opinion surveyor on a subject long dear to him:

> I am wondering if you could make a direct attack, with statistical proof, that Republican leaders have—ever since Landon—held to the belief that the Regular Republicans would vote for them in any event, and that they had need to fish in liberal waters for support. The result of which has been that Regular Republicans (conservatives) have, directly or indirectly, engaged in sit-down strikes. I believe that you could show that the sit-down was a large element in the defeat of Landon, Dewey, Willkie, and Nixon . . . I believe you and I agree that both psychologically and in practice that there is room in the American scene for only two political parties—one really conservative and one really liberal—and

until Republican leaders frankly use the word "conservative" and adopt such policies, they have little chance of winning elections.[51]

Hoover clearly expected that such an article would aid Barry Goldwater, the conservative candidate for the GOP nomination.

Slowing Down

Despite his advancing age, the former president had only slightly curtailed his travel and activities in 1962. The winter fishing trip, extending into the early months of 1962, the annual trek to California, and the birthday visit to Iowa constituted a good deal of travel for one who turned 88 in that year. By now the former president was physically unable to go fishing but would see the party off when their boat left the pier and then greet them upon their return to find out if they'd had any luck. It would, however, be his last year of travel. Shortly after his birthday, Hoover entered the hospital in New York City for what was described as an annual checkup. Predictions that he would be released within a few days were revised when tests disclosed a growth on the interior of his large intestine. Surgery was performed and doctors reported, "The pathological study revealed an ulcerated polyp of the transverse colon. A portion of the polyp had undergone malignant change. There was no evidence of any spread beyond the polyp. A segment of the colon which included the polyp was removed and no recurrence is anticipated."[52] The prognosis was too optimistic, but Hoover would live for two more years.

After his release from the hospital in mid-September 1962, Hoover returned to his "comfortable monastery" high in the Waldorf Tower, where he was for a time allowed no phone calls, no visitors, and no work. Early in October he wrote a friend, "I expect that next week I will be able to put on pants."[53] That month he watched developments in the Cuban missile crisis and was consulted, along with Truman and Eisenhower, by President Kennedy before the US government replied to Khruschev's proposal for ending the crisis.[54]

In December, Hoover addressed a poignant letter to another aging former president, Harry Truman, in which he told him,

> Yours has been a friendship which has reached deeper into my life than you know. I gave up a successful profession in 1914 to enter public service. I served through the first World War and after, for a total of about 18 years. When the attack on Pearl Harbor came, I at once supported the President and offered to serve in any useful capacity. Because of my varied experiences during the first World War, I thought my services might again be useful, however there was no response. My activities in the second World War were limited to frequent requests from Congressional committees. When you came to the White House, within a month you opened the door to me to the only profession I knew, public service, and you undid some disgraceful action that had been taken in the prior years. For all of this and your friendship I am deeply grateful.[55]

Shortly after Pearl Harbor Hoover had begun to research and write fragments of what he planned to be an exposure of what he regarded as the fallacies of the foreign policies of the Roosevelt administration. The project began to be referred to as the "magnum opus" by those around him and was gradually broadened to include the record of appeasement of the Soviet Union under FDR and his successors. By the 1960s, with his other books completed, the one consuming ambition of the aging states- man was to complete the work before he died. Felix Morley recalled that Hoover "had so much in his mind, so much in his experience, that he was anxious to get down on paper while he was still alive—things which he knew; which he knew other people did not know about, which were the very stuff of history." "Well into his eighties," Morley noted, "his desk was always littered."[56]

Neil MacNeil recalled that Hoover wrote in longhand on legal pads and had a dish on his desk with sharpened pencils that were kept sharp by his secretary. MacNeil added that Hoover

> literally worked day and night, even in his late 80s . . . He was an old man in a hurry. He felt that he didn't have enough time to get done half the things he wanted to do before he passed on. He was pressing for them . . . He worked day and night and it never used to bother him. He had people in for 9:00 breakfast. He'd work all morning . . . In the morning, the secretaries would come in and find a lot of work. What happened was the old boy would get up at night, put in two or three hours at his desk, and leave all this work for them to do in the morning, enough to start them all off and keep them going again, and then he'd go back to bed until he got up for breakfast.[57]

Hoover's health, however, began to interfere with his plans. He wrote an old friend late in January 1963,

> I have taken a licking with a setback thrown in. However, I am doing better now. But I am not allowed any more journeys away from New York. I do see people, play a limited amount of canasta, and above all am trying to finish five more books before my time runs out. The book on fishing will be out in May. The fourth and fifth volume of *An American Epic* is in the last stages of comple- tion. But the big job of three volumes on "Who, When & How we got into the Cold War" has already had 20 years of work and requires two more. I hope to leave them as a sort of "will and testament" before I finally vanish.

Intimates, including radio commentator Hans V. Kaltenborn, had read them, he reported, and they were "enthusiastic that they are great and needed books." Hoover obviously chafed at the continued confinement in the apart- ment, but his doctors had admonished him that he could "provide any climate in your present abode, so why go out into the cold and meet a dozen kind of bugs which wish to kill you!"[58] While there would obviously be no fishing trip to Key Largo, Hoover still wistfully hoped that he might once more be able to take part in the Bohemian Club encampment in the summer.

In February, Hoover responded to a query about food relief for Communist China by writing,

> It is true that I directed, on behalf of the American people, the relief of the hideous famine in Communist Russia from 1920 to 1923. But whether I would do it today for Communist China is a somewhat moot question. I am 88 years-plus, and have recently been through major surgery from which I have not yet fully recovered. As to the matter of relief itself to China from the United States, I would recommend it if they would accept the conditions of the Riga Agreement (see Volume III of my An American Epic); all of which they very likely would not accept. Therefore, that is likely to be also 'moot.'[59]

Early in 1963, Hoover was saddened by litigation in the courts over the operation of the Belgian American Education Foundation, when some of the heads of the foundation were taken to court because they had allegedly done things that were not in the best interests of the foundation. Hoover wrote W. Hallam Tuck, then on the foundation's board of directors, that he had never in his life "been so saddened by disloyalty and dishonesty of men whom I had trusted. By the organizations I have created I have given them a living over most of these years. The one redeeming thing in this experience is your loyal fight for me. I owe you an unpayable debt."[60]

In June 1963, the former president was again stricken with gastrointestinal bleeding and received transfusions. His sons Allan and Herbert Jr. were in constant attendance in his apartment.[61] The *New York Times* reported, "Once a remarkably robust man, Mr. Hoover has appeared thin and drawn, almost frail, the last nine months."[62] Yet a few days later the doctors termed the former president's recovery from the latest bout "almost miraculous."[63] On his eighty-ninth birthday, however, the elder statesman was for the first time unable to meet with reporters for his annual session. He was in poor health and unable to walk, but the *New York Times* reported, "His condition, however, is improving steadily and he is impatient to complete another book, one he considers his magnum opus, a history of the last 30 years." It added that Hoover's books were "an important source of revenue for the Boys' Clubs of America, to which he gives the royalties." And even though he could not meet with the press, Hoover issued a brief statement in which he said, "I may be permitted to remark that I have lived a long time and have seen great changes in this world of ours, and that the longer I live and the more I see, the more confidence I have in the American system of constant goodwill and service to other nations, and of free enterprise and personal liberty. We have a great way of life—let's keep it that way."[64]

It must have cheered the former president, however, to hear from the Democratic chairman of the House Committee on Government Operations, the committee that had "the chief responsibility on the House side for consideration of matters relating to the Hoover Commissions and their work," that "even after many years, the Commissions on Organization of the Executive

Branch of the Government, which you headed, continue to hold and attract much interest." He told Hoover, "Their findings and recommendations are still used as points of reference or departure in the consideration of proposals affecting Government organization."[65]

The following month he wrote a friend that he was "making slow progress, but my major job, the case history of the Second World War and its betrayal of freedom is now completed except my staff overhaul to check every sentence for its accuracy. The staff can now complete it in about another year."[66] He was, he wrote Mrs. Joseph Kennedy, confined to a wheelchair like her husband, but "I am in a better way than he for I have begun to walk with the help of two good nurses."[67] When a youthful visitor told him she was happy with her life as it was, Hoover's expression, she recalled, "was one of total horror, and he said, 'How can you say a thing like that, because I want more. I want to write a better book. I want to have more friends—I just want more—and I think you should never sit back and say, 'I want the status quo.'"[68] According to Felix Morley, the former president felt he had outlived his time, but since he had been given the additional years through no virtue on his part, he felt compelled to make good use of them.[69] Still Hoover enjoyed an occasional football and baseball game, especially the annual Old Timers baseball game, although in his final year or two he was watching them on the television from his wheelchair.[70]

By early November 1, 1963, he could tell Clarence Kelland he had experienced "a little luck": "Blood transfusions seem to have restored my red blood cell percentage. Hence, I am doing everything except walk and function as an intellectual. The *Readers Digest* have accepted the Magnum Opus and it will probably start in about six months. They seem much excited by it, and I am full of forebodings as to mud volcanoes which will arise from the left who are still adept in that field."[71] A few weeks later, the aged elder statesman, who felt he had outlived his time, grieved for a young president struck down by an assassin's bullet before his time. Hoover told the press, "I am shocked and grieved to learn of President Kennedy's assassination. He loved America and has given his life for his country. I join our bereaved nation in heartfelt sympathy for Mrs. Kennedy and their two children."[72]

Journalist Richard Berlin later recalled that he was in a hunting lodge in Canada when he got a phone call from the White House. Lyndon Johnson told him he needed all the help he could get and had arranged for Eisenhower and Truman to visit him, but he also wanted to talk to Hoover. Johnson told Berlin that if Hoover couldn't visit him, he would travel to New York, instead.[73] The following week, Johnson went to New York for Herbert Lehman's funeral and afterward visited Hoover with Chief Justice Earl Warren and Robert Wagner.[74] Johnson recalled for the press that Hoover had conveyed to Johnson through Hoover's son his willingness to help the new president in any way he could, although acknowledging that there was little he could contribute at his age. Hoover also expressed his appreciation for Johnson's support of the Hoover Commission recommendations during his years in the Senate. The former president was also visited by Jackie and Robert Kennedy soon after JFK's assassination, while Hoover was still in his sickbed.[75]

At about the same time, Hoover wrote his sister, "I have had some bad luck this year: too much time in bed, six good nurses, five good doctors, 12 pills daily! We have been making some good progress against them, and I am promised I will defeat them before I pass the 100 mark, so that is my health report. And I am doing everything to help."[76]

On Christmas Day, President Johnson phoned the former president and told a press conference a few days that Hoover had given him "some very constructive suggestions on the operations of the Federal Government that grew out of his retirement. We are studying those suggestions. We are applying them where they are appropriate. The Hoover Commission reports have been very carefully evaluated since I became President."[77]

Albert Wedemeyer visited the former president early in February 1964 and wrote,

> He was sitting up in a chair in his bedroom. He has a tiny Siamese kitten which craws all over him, and when I entered took a dim view of my intrusion, so much that the little rascal jumped from the Chief's lap and then up into mine and when I tried to fondle it the little devil bit me. This amused the Chief a great deal. Actually, he was glad to have it jump out of his lap into mine because he was adjusting his earphones and the little rascal kept pulling it out of his ear and biting the cable to the battery.

Wedemeyer found Hoover had "lost considerable ground" but had "a wonderful sense of humor as always." They chatted for about an hour and discussed the 1964 presidential campaign, with the former president expressing doubts that Barry Goldwater could defeat Johnson, if the Arizonan were the GOP nominee, unless the Bobby Baker scandal cost the president votes in the North and his Civil Rights stand hurt him in the South.[78] Former vice president Richard Nixon also called on Hoover, according to a memorandum in the Hoover papers, and asked for the elder statesman's support in gaining the 1964 nomination. But, according to the memorandum, Hoover replied "that at 90 years—with six nurses and five doctors, I was under instructions not to get into any more controversies." He had, according to the memorandum, given "the same reply to his principal opponents."[79]

Later in February Hoover was again stricken with internal bleeding, combined with a respiratory ailment. In a few days, however, the crisis passed and the *New York Times* reported that he had been able to sit up in bed to eat his breakfast. It added, "As a nurse approached with his scrambled eggs he said to her, jokingly, 'Faster, faster.'"[80] The following month, Congressman Charles S. Gubser, who represented Hoover's old district of Palo Alto, California, paid tribute to the former president in the House of Representatives and was joined by many other congressmen who added their remarks.[81] Hoover wrote

Gubser, "Never have I received a greater get-well incentive than yours and your comrades' in Congress. I do not feel I deserve such a tribute, but if anything will get me feeling completely well again, you and your colleagues have made a major push in that direction."[82] Incredibly, Hoover had begun to contemplate writing yet another book. In mid-April 1964, he wrote Bonner Fellers, "I am doing another book. It covers recent history I didn't touch on [in] my previous volumes. You and I played a role in the arrangements for General MacArthur when he returned from Tokyo. Do you have a diary or other notes you made at that time which I could have copies to amplify my own material? I will return them to you promptly."[83]

Some of Hoover's intimates hoped that he would support Senator Goldwater for the Republican nomination, and at some point in the California primary campaign the former president did dictate a letter to Senator William Knowland to be used in support of the Arizonan if it were considered useful.[84] In the letter, Hoover said that a "great need of the Republican Party and indeed a need of the two-party system is for a fighting campaign. Senator Goldwater can make such a campaign." The statement was never mailed to Knowland, however, on the advice of one of Hoover's intimates, journalist Neil MacNeil. Goldwater did visit Hoover in May, however, and according to Jeremiah Milbank Jr., who accompanied the senator, Goldwater and Hoover had a high regard for one another.[85]

In May 1964, Hoover accepted another honorary degree—his last. By his reckoning it marked the ninetieth such award, one for each year of his life, making him probably the all-time champion in that regard. Included in the total were over twenty from foreign institutions.[86]

In July 1964 the elder statesman was not able to make another "farewell" appearance before his party's convention. Instead he prepared a message to be read to the delegates by Senator Everett Dirksen of Illinois.[87] Hoover's message was a familiar declaration of those principles he had long encouraged Republicans to adhere to. The United States, he concluded, could only "survive by bending together the forces of free men—men of religious faith, of loyalty to our American traditions, of integrity in public office, who deeply love our country." And he told the audience, "We hold the long record of the Republican Party gives the best assurance that these principles will prevail in the United States, and with the help of God they will."[88] Dirksen told the audience that "the grand old man of the Grand Old Party is listening to this program. What better way to exhilarate his spirit than to give him an ovation to lengthen his span of years. Let him hear you."[89]

In the midst of the convention, Goldwater phoned Hoover to inform him he had tapped Congressman William Miller of New York to be his vice-presidential nominee and asked Hoover for any comments or objections he might have, adding, "We miss you."[90] Goldwater had also tried to visit Hoover a few days earlier in New York but found him resting. The former president wired Goldwater that he regretted not having been available at the time of his visit and also his disappointment that he could not "take part actively" in the campaign, but he promised to issue a statement in Goldwater's behalf whenever the nominee asked him to do so.[91] The Arizonan paid another courtesy call on Hoover in early August.[92] Bonner Fellers recalled that he had seen Hoover for the last time when he called on him while in New York to attend a Goldwater rally in Madison Square Garden shortly before Hoover's final attack. Fellers found the former president in his bathrobe, still determined to write another book. He recalled that Hoover "was strong for Goldwater. He didn't think that he was going to be elected, and I was so dumb that I thought he might be."[93]

The "grand old man of the Grand Old Party" received numerous tributes as he approached his ninetieth birthday. Dr. Howard Rusk wrote in the *New York Times* of the inspiration Hoover had supplied for the creation of UNICEF and the support he had given to that organization.[94] Again, Hoover was unable to hold his annual meeting with the press but instead issued a birthday statement. He expressed optimism that American freedoms would continue to grow, including those that were not granted specifically by law—the freedom to choose one's method of livelihood, to buy or not to buy, and to venture into new pursuits and to protect one's success. He concluded, "In short we have freedom of choice. And the product of our freedom is the stimulation of our energies, initiative, ingenuity and creative faculties." He again deplored the rise in crime and juvenile delinquency and the continued denial in some parts of the country "of an equal chance to our Negro population."[95] New York and the governors of fifteen other states proclaimed August 10 Herbert Hoover Day, and birthday parties were held for the former president at numerous Boys' Clubs.[96]

A week later Congressman Craig Hosmer suggested the former president as a candidate for the 1965 Nobel Peace Prize, noting that under the terms of Dr. Alfred Nobel's will members of Congress were eligible to recommend living persons for the award.[97] This initiative led to numerous letters written in the final months of Hoover's life by congressmen, senators, academics, and others supporting him for the award.[98] Tragically, Hoover's death a few months later ended his candidacy for an award that would so fittingly have crowned his many humanitarian efforts.

For as long as he was able, Herbert Hoover labored at his magnum opus. Ben Moreel later recalled that "his consuming ambition in those days and in his last years was to finish this one book on Communism." He told Moreel it "was the one thing he wanted to do before he died." Hoover told his friends, according to Joseph F. Binns, "'You know, I don't have too much time to finish what I'm doing,' but he would continue to work and his work became almost the center of his life." In the final months of his life, Hoover consented to fewer and fewer appointments in order to devote his time to the book.[99]

Neil MacNeil recalled that the former president had used every resource in order to put together the story of what had happened to American foreign policy as a result of the diplomatic recognition of the Soviet Union by Roosevelt in 1933, using the research staff of the Hoover Institution and combing through thousands of documents from all over the world. MacNeil added that Hoover's son Herbert Jr., as undersecretary of state under Eisenhower, had been able to gather materials for his father from the State Department archives and that Hoover had also drawn upon his acquaintanceship with world statesmen and the diaries and correspondence of prominent Americans. According to MacNeil, Hoover had completed two and one half of the projected three volumes, working virtually down to the day that he died. A number of people were entrusted with reading and commenting on the work, and the staff at the Hoover Institution was given the task of checking the accuracy of what he had written. He wanted the book published regardless of the consequences for him and the costs, because he considered it, said MacNeil, "a public duty." However, some close friends of the former president, as well as members of his family, opposed publication on the grounds that it might diminish Hoover's image and reopen old sores and attacks upon him that had for years been laid to rest.[100]

On October 3, Barry Goldwater wrote Hoover to thank him for his support so far in the campaign, telling him, "This campaign will chart the course of conservatism in America for years to come, and I am counting on your continued efforts to help make it a success."[101] But Hoover was not to participate in the campaign, nor was he to live long enough to witness the defeat of the first Republican candidate since his own race in 1932 who embodied the principles he believed in. At 3:55 p.m. on Saturday, October 17, 1964, the cancer in his system unleashed its final assault and the aged statesman was soon in critical condition. On October 20, at 11:35 a.m., Herbert Hoover died.[102]

The body of the former president lay in state first at St. Bartholomew's Episcopal Church in New York City, where an estimated 17,500 mourners paid their last respects to him on the first day. On October 22 the political campaign ceased for a day as the presidential and vice-presidential candidates of both parties flew to New York to attend the funeral services. Also on hand were Bernard Baruch, James Farley, Mrs. Joseph Kennedy, Mr. and Mrs. Richard Nixon, Robert Kennedy, John Connally, Mayor Robert Wagner, and other leaders of American life. The large and elaborate St. Bartholomew's was a stark contrast to the small, plain Friends' meeting house in West Branch where Hoover had worshipped as a child.[103] But the simplicity of the service was closer to that of his youth.

The casket was then transported by train to the nation's capital and covered the four blocks from Union Station to the Capitol on a caisson drawn by seven horses. To the sound of a dirge, the procession slowly made its way through a crowd 4 and 5 deep, while cannons executed a 21-gun salute and 48 jet fighters streaked overhead in groups of 3. In the Capitol the former president lay in state on the same catafalque on which Presidents Lincoln and Kennedy had rested.[104] The end of Hoover's long journey ended where it had begun over 90 years before, when his casket was flown to Cedar Rapids, Iowa, whence it was taken to West Branch for a simple burial service on October 25. Five thousand mourners met the plane in Cedar Rapids, and 75,000 were on hand for the burial service.

Since the transfer of Lou Henry Hoover's remains from her burial site at Stanford University to West Branch, the two have rested atop a grassy knoll overlooking the area where the young Bert lived and played. Visiting the knoll, sheltered by a half-circle of pines, and the two plain, flat marble slabs covering their graves, a visitor on a summer's morning can glimpse rabbits and squirrels frolicking in the spacious and well-manicured park. A short distance away, a stream of visitors can be seen sightseeing amid the buildings of Hoover's youth—the cabin in which he was born, the blacksmith shop in which his father labored, the meeting house in which the family worshipped—and entering the Hoover Museum to acquaint or reacquaint themselves with the accomplishments of a remarkable man. And in the rear of the one-story limestone museum, scholars labor at the desks of the Hoover Presidential Library, sifting through the materials of a busy life.

The magnum opus on which Hoover labored for over twenty years of his life, and which he considered so important that he drove himself to try to complete it in the final months of his life, has never been published. This "last will and testament" to the American people is still under lock and key.[105] But Herbert Hoover, son of a small-town Iowa blacksmith, was himself an American "magnum opus" and an "American epic." The *New York Times* editorialized, "In the death of Herbert Hoover the United States has lost a man who has long deserved to rank as its Eldest Statesman."[106] James Reston wrote that Hoover "had the last laugh. He convinced most of his critics in the end and outlived the rest of them. And few politicians manage to do that."[107]

Conclusion

Although Hoover clearly relished the sobriquet of *elder statesman*, it is equally clear that the term only rarely applied to him during the three decades after he left the presidency. He was too active and far too contentious during most of that time to fit the usual image of elder statesman. At some points, in fact, the former president resembled a pit bull more than an elder statesman.

Historian Craig Lloyd once described Herbert Hoover as an "aggressive introvert" in his book by that title (Columbus, OH, 1973). A case could equally be made that the former president was a reluctant extrovert. He fairly burst with things to say, advice to give, and services to render, and yet he was always reluctant to do so without prodding, a plea for assistance, a request for counsel. And it was usually the case that the prodding, pleas, or requests must be made public, lest it be inferred that he was forcing himself on somebody's attention. This was especially true during the Democratic years that took up two of the three decades he lived after leaving the White House.

Such a response was natural considering that Hoover was subjected to smearing and neglect by the Democrats from his presidency onward and that he even suffered from many members of his own party. The result was that the advice and service of a remarkably able man were certainly underutilized during much of his postpresidency, largely because of the image created for him by the spin doctors of the 1930s and 1940s. This association with the Hoover manufactured by Charles Michelson and his successors meant that his ideas and services were often rejected without regard to merit simply because acceptance of them might tend to the former president's credit.

There seems little doubt that the breadth and depth of Hoover's knowledge of the world—especially of domestic and international economic matters—was intimidating for lesser minds, and such minds were in the ascendancy during the 1930s and 1940s in both political parties. Hoover had every reason to be contemptuous of the abilities of Roosevelt, his cabinet members, Truman, and the assorted Republican candidates who ran against them. Few of them could see beyond the politically expedient, and few could grasp—as Hoover did with consummate skill—all the pieces in the intricate chessboard that made up the American and the world economies.

In defiance of the caricature of Hoover that has been drawn by many historians it is tempting to wonder if the reelection of Hoover in 1932 might not have produced recovery from the depression during his second term from a combination of the improvement that began all over the world in the summer of 1932, including the United States, and the results of the World Economic Conference in 1933 if it had had been handled more skillfully than it was by his successor. Well aware of the interdependency of the world economy, Hoover would have worked for economic cooperation in solving the depression, rejecting the isolationist approach of Franklin Delano Roosevelt. Such a course may well have also resolved many of the tensions that contributed to the outbreak of World War II.

Nothing brought out the pit bull instinct in Hoover more than the "infections" of Karl Marx that he saw threatening the world and even pervading American politics. For the former president there was little to choose between the statism of fascism and that of communism. Both were inimical to the liberty of the individual. Growth in the power of the central government could only come at the expense of the freedoms of the people. The loss of economic freedoms must inevitably lead to the attrition of all other freedoms before long.

Hoover worried that the early seizure of power over the economy by the New Deal would, after their inevitable failures, lead to demands for even more power. "Planned economy" and "welfare state" were for the former president only appealing slogans that masked the loss of individual freedom in America, even as they had done in other countries. Accordingly, Hoover battled against such ideas within the Republican Party, determined to maintain the GOP as the party of traditional liberalism or "conservatism," and he tried to forge the party into a formidable challenger against a Democratic Party that seemed infected with statist objectives. In international affairs he tried to alert Americans to the dangers posed by American foreign policies that could only contribute to the expansion of communism and the "enslavement" of millions, and he dedicated himself to maintaining America's economic and military strength in the face of such foreign challenges.

One can trace this leitmotif through most of Hoover's words and actions after he left the presidency. His struggles with Landon, Willkie, Dewey, and even Eisenhower over GOP principles and programs were only partly from personal ambitions. More than that, they stemmed from his conviction that only he could lead the party back to its basic principles and away from the New Dealism that tainted his rivals, as did his efforts to commit the Republican Party to those principles through declarations and convention platforms.

His opposition to American recognition of the Soviet Union and the People's Republic of China was based on his concern that it would lead to the cancerous growth of communism in the United States through the creation of new nests for subversion. He was a staunch opponent of American entry into World War II because of his conviction that the defeat of Germany and Japan could only result in the enslavement of more peoples by the Soviet Union and the emergence of that nation as an even greater threat to peace and the security of the United States. He also feared that American entry into the war would lead to the loss of political and economic freedoms at home under the Roosevelt administration.

The seeming contradiction in his reluctance to aid Western Europe to the extent advocated by the Truman administration is resolved by noting Hoover's concern that the Soviet Union would benefit greatly if the United States were drained economically by undertaking more commitments abroad than it could bear and his fear that American manhood might similarly be "bled" on remote battlefields defending a free world that showed little disposition to aid America in its sacrifices. At the same time, he supported postwar arrangements with Germany and Japan that would permit them to recover rapidly so that they might resume as much as possible their prewar role as "dams" against Russian expansion in Europe and Asia.

Hoover's emphasis on food relief during and after World War II was not so intimately tied to this leitmotif, being in large part purely humanitarian, but his opposition to the internationalization of such relief and his insistence in the postwar period that the recipients know the origins of the food indicate his desire that the food should simultaneously serve a political purpose in the struggle for allegiance among the world's peoples.

The two Hoover Commissions are graphic examples of the former president's desire to purge as much as possible the legacy of New Deal statism from the federal government, with reductions in the size of the bureaucracy and the transfer of many of its functions back to the state and local governments, and to individuals, whence they had been usurped by the New Deal.

And through it all, the former president sought to wage that same battle against the infection of Marxism through his books, from *The Challenge to Liberty* down to the unpublished "magnum opus" that was so important to him and through the support he gave and found for other authors and journals that shared his point of view.

In his battles, "the Chief" commanded a battalion of loyal followers who committed themselves and a portion of their assets to support his point of view. Indeed, his support seemed to grow more intense as one ascended the intellectual ladder and it included leading journalists, authors, ex-diplomats, and some of the most successful business and financial leaders. Such support enabled Hoover to exert a much greater influence than if he had been dependent on his own voice and resources alone. But more important than any other single factor was Hoover's dedication and a capacity for hard and constant work that made him a marvel for those familiar with his regimen.

After the death of Senator Robert A. Taft, Hoover described his Ohio friend as "more near to an indispensable man than any in America," but the term more accurately describes Hoover himself. At times it seemed as if Hoover and his dedicated followers were alone in their struggle to preserve the Republican Party as an American alternative to the alien statism that was pervading America. Hoover lived to see the nomination, at last, of a Republican presidential candidate in 1964 who could carry the torch that age and infirmity required he pass on. He anticipated, but did not live to see, Barry Goldwater's defeat in 1964. But the victories of Ronald Reagan and the conservative Republican sweep of Congress in 1994 could probably not have occurred had not Hoover kept the torch of traditional American liberalism alive from 1933 to 1964. It is in this enduring sense that Hoover deserves most of all the title of "elder statesman."

Afterword

by George H. Nash

The publication of the late Gary Dean Best's impressive volume brings to completion one of the most ambitious historical undertakings of recent decades. The Herbert Hoover Biography Project was conceived nearly forty years ago during the centennial celebration of his life in 1974. At that time the trustees of the Hoover Presidential Library Association recognized that no adequate biography of America's thirty-first president existed. There were, to be sure, a number of popular and journalistic accounts—some of them astute and entertainingly written—but none that could be considered broadly authoritative, deserving the lasting attention of serious scholars.

In 1975 the Library Association acted to fill this gap by commissioning a definitive, scholarly biography of Mr. Hoover. It is worth pausing to reflect upon these terms of reference. *Definitive*: thorough, dispassionate, and comprehensive, yielding a standard reference work of enduring (rather than ephemeral) value. *Scholarly*: judicious, uncensored, and accurate, based on exhaustive archival research and striving for impartiality. The aim was neither to praise Hoover nor to pillory him but first and foremost to understand him: an enigmatic figure who has long stood in the shadows of our national narrative.

The implications of this conceptualization of the project were profound. For such an endeavor, no arbitrary timetable could be fixed, nor any preset number of words and pages. The venture was to become what the Librarian of Congress Daniel Boorstin once defined as a "great enterprise": "one for which a reliable timetable is impossible. By definition it is what has never before been accomplished." "Only rarely," said Boorstin, "is some great project of intellectual circumnavigation accomplished in a predicted time."[1]

At the outset, few if any of those associated with the Hoover Biography Project foresaw its ultimate dimensions. Indeed, if Hoover himself is looking down today on this now finished, six-volume study of his life, he may well be chuckling. It has taken a team of biographers nearly as long to write about him as he himself spent on the public stage.

Hoover might be amused, but not surprised, by the amount of intellectual circumnavigation required to take his measure. If *The Life of Herbert Hoover* series has proven to be unusually hefty and wide-ranging, it is largely because its subject was no ordinary man.

Consider, for a moment, the sheer breadth and magnitude of his career. Born in 1874 in a little Iowa farming community, Hoover was orphaned before he was 10. By the time he was 21, he had worked his way through Stanford University and had entered his chosen profession of mining engineering. At the age of 24, he was superintendent of a gold mine in the desolate outback of Western Australia. By the age of 27, he had managed a gigantic coal-mining enterprise with nine thousand employees in northern China and had survived a harrowing brush with death in the Boxer Rebellion. By 1914, at the age of 40, Hoover was a sophisticated and extraordinarily successful mining engineer who had traveled around the world 5 times and had business interests on every continent except Antarctica.

During World War I, Hoover, residing in London, rose to prominence as the founder and director of the Commission for Relief in Belgium, an institution that provided desperately needed food supplies to more than nine million Belgian and French citizens trapped between the German army of occupation and the British naval blockade. His emergency relief mission in 1914 quickly evolved into a gigantic humanitarian enterprise without precedent in world history. By 1917 he was an international hero, the embodiment of a new force in global politics: American benevolence.

When America declared war on Germany in 1917, Hoover returned home and became head of the US Food Administration, a specially created wartime agency of the federal government. As US Food Administrator and as a member of President Woodrow Wilson's War Cabinet, he endeavored to stimulate domestic food conservation and food production, to control surging inflation of food prices, and to create surpluses of foodstuffs for export to America's allies, who faced privation and even starvation if the necessary supplies were not delivered to them through the German submarine blockade. In the titanic struggle of 1917–18, food joined ships and soldiers as a critical component of victory over the enemy. "Food Will Win the War" was Hoover's slogan. As the architect and implementer of America's food policies, he was one of the nation's most important war leaders.

At the conflict's victorious close in 1918, President Wilson dispatched Hoover to Europe to organize food distribution to a continent careening toward disaster. There, for ten grueling months, he directed American-led efforts to combat famine and disease, establish stable postwar economies, and in the process check the advance of Bolshevik revolution from the East. It was a Herculean undertaking of immense complexity, entailing the purchase and shipping of food from all over the earth and then the distribution of it in more than twenty strife-torn nations.

A little later, between 1921 and 1923, Hoover's American Relief Administration administered a massive, emergency relief operation in the interior of Soviet Russia, where a catastrophic famine—Europe's worst since the Middle Ages—had broken out. He did so at the request of Russia's anxious but suspicious Communist leaders, who wanted his help but feared his militant anti-communism. Millions died before Hoover's food shipments and aid workers could reach all the starving, but millions more survived thanks to Hoover's provision. At its peak of operations, his organization fed upwards of 10 million Russian citizens a day.

All in all, between 1914 and 1923 the American-born engineer-turned-humanitarian directed, financed, or assisted a multitude of international relief endeavors without parallel in the history of mankind. Nearly 34 million metric tons of food were delivered to the lands and peoples imperiled by World War I and its aftermath. The monetary value of this sustenance exceeded $5,234,000,000—a figure that, in today's currency, would top fifty billion dollars. For most of this incredible undertaking, Herbert Hoover had high administrative responsibility.

No one can say precisely how many people owed their lives to his exertions. But reasonable inferences about the number of beneficiaries can be drawn. By one possibly conservative estimate, prepared by this author some years ago, between 1914 and 1923 more than 83,000,000 men, women, and children in more than 20 countries received food allotments for which Hoover and his associates were at least partially responsible. This figure does not include the belligerent populations (120,000,000) of America's principal wartime allies (Great Britain, France, and Italy) who received critically needed foodstuffs from the United States in 1917–18—a form of "foreign aid" that cannot be considered humanitarian assistance in the ordinary sense of the term.

Eighty-three million people—it is a staggering figure. But whether this estimate is high or low, Hoover's standing in the annals of organized humanitarianism is incontestable. As someone remarked a number of years ago, Herbert Hoover was responsible for saving more lives than any other person in history.

In 1919, the "food regulator for the world" (as General John J. Pershing called him) returned from Europe an international luminary. He was hailed as the "Napoleon of Mercy." He became known at the "Great Humanitarian." Just 45 years old, he was at the threshold of political stardom in his native land.

During the Roaring Twenties Hoover ascended still higher on the ladder of public esteem. As secretary of commerce under Presidents Warren Harding and Calvin Coolidge, he quickly became one of the three or four most influential men in the US government—and in all American public life. He seemed ubiquitous: it was said of him that he was secretary of commerce and undersecretary of every other department. He took time in 1922 to write a book titled *American Individualism*, in which he expounded his understanding of the American sociopolitical system and its undergirding principles.

(A dozen years later he would publish another book of political philosophy: *The Challenge to Liberty*.) In 1927, with President Coolidge's blessing, Hoover orchestrated a relief operation for more than six hundred thousand displaced victims of the great Mississippi River flood in the lower South—the worst natural disaster in American history. His success added even more luster to his humanitarian reputation. The very next year, the "master of emergencies" (as admirers called him) was overwhelmingly elected president of the United States—without ever having held an elective public office.

Then came the bitter ordeal of the White House years and the most severe economic trauma this nation has ever experienced. During his tormented presidency, Hoover strained without stint to return his country to prosperity while safeguarding its political moorings. His labors—even now widely misunderstood—seemed unavailing, and in the election of 1932 his fellow citizens' verdict was harsh.

Before his term as chief executive, Hoover's career trajectory had curved unbrokenly upward. Now it headed pitifully down. "Democracy is not a polite employer," he later wrote of his defeat at the polls. This was putting it gently. In 1933 he left office a virtual pariah, maligned and hated like no other American in his lifetime.

And then, astonishingly, like a phoenix, he slowly rose from the ashes of his political immolation. Now came the final phase of Hoover's career: his remarkable ex-presidency, chronicled so ably and meticulously by Professor Best. During Hoover's thirty-one-and-a-half years as a former president (the longest such span, as of this writing, in American history), "the Chief," as his intimates called him, resolutely refused to fade away. A crusader for the principles of what he now called "historic liberalism," he fought fervently against the New Deal of Franklin Roosevelt, which he saw as a dangerous, collectivistic assault upon America's free society and constitutional order. Having observed abroad the unpalatable character of life under statism, he could not bring himself to acquiesce in silence at home.

Sinclair Lewis once observed that the secret of success is to "make the seat of your pants adhere to the seat of your chair for long enough." This was one of Hoover's secrets also. Endowed with generally excellent health, amazing drive, and tremendous stamina, he also possessed two other attributes that profoundly shaped his later years: a determination to vindicate himself and his political ideals and a philosophy of life that exalted good works and practical achievement. All this is carefully documented in Professor Best's volume.

Late in his life, Hoover told one of his grandchildren, "When you stop wanting to know, then you start to die." Even as the infirmities of age crept up upon him, he seemed driven by an urge to know and especially to teach: about his experiences in office, about the meaning of America, and about the threats posed by what he called "pernicious" ideologies to the land he loved.

And so, until very nearly the end, Hoover lived strenuously. Even in his mideighties he worked as many as 12 hours a day. Between the ages of 85 and

90, he published 7 books. Throughout his public career he wrote incessantly. A bibliography of his published writings and addresses contains over 1,200 entries.

When Hoover died in 1964, he had lived ninety phenomenally productive years, including a full fifty in the public eye. It was a record that in sheer scope and duration may be without parallel in American history.

This is the story that *The Life of Herbert Hoover* has attempted to tell, in six lengthy volumes.[2] Although the four contributors to the series—Kendrick A. Clements, Glen Jeansonne, Gary Dean Best, and the author of this Afterword—do not invariably agree in our interpretations, I am confident that we share a core conviction: Herbert Hoover is one of the few Americans who has truly deserved a multivolume biography.

Although Professor Best's book formally completes the Hoover Biography Project, in one sense the story of our thirty-first president's life continues to be written. Each year, in the burgeoning archives of the Herbert Hoover Presidential Library in Iowa and the Hoover Institution in California, researchers of all ages examine aspects of his career. History is "a conversation without end," someone has said. Hoover is not immune from this unceasing process of rediscovery and reappraisal.

Thus in recent years we have witnessed the publication of such illuminating studies as Hal Elliott Wert's *Hoover the Fishing President*; Timothy Walch's scholarly anthology *Uncommon Americans: The Lives and Legacies of Herbert and Lou Henry Hoover*; and Bertrand M. Patenaude's *The Big Show in Bololand: The American Relief Expedition to Soviet Russia in the Famine of 1921*.[3] Since 2000 Hoover's wife (whose papers were only opened for research in the mid-1980s) has herself been the subject of discerning biographies by Anne Beiser Allen, Dale C. Mayer, and Nancy Beck Young.[4] Relevant articles and monographs too numerous to mention continue to appear.

Undoubtedly the most unusual recent contribution to Hoover scholarship has come from none other than Hoover himself, nearly half a century after his passing. In the book before you, Professor Best alludes to an unpublished "magnum opus" on which the Chief was working intensively during his final years: a highly critical study of President Franklin Roosevelt's foreign policies and their baneful impact upon the world. It grew, in Best's words, into an account of the "appeasement of the Soviet Union under FDR and his successors." By the early 1960s, Best observes, Hoover's "one consuming ambition" was to complete this gargantuan document before he died. He confided to a friend that he wanted to publish it without regard to cost or controversy as "a public duty."[5]

After Hoover's death in 1964, his heirs—concerned, it seems, that release of such a thunderbolt might reopen old political wounds—decided not to proceed to publication. Instead, they placed his manuscript in storage, where, for nearly half a century, it remained. At the time Professor Best completed work on his own volume several years ago, the mysterious tome was still unpublished and unavailable for research.

In 2009 the Herbert Hoover Foundation authorized the editing of the Magnum Opus for publication. In 2011 the Hoover Institution Press duly published the final version, under the title *Freedom Betrayed: Herbert Hoover's Secret History of the Second World War and Its Aftermath.*[6] His numerous earlier drafts and relevant research files—filling two hundred archival boxes—were simultaneously made public for the first time.

Freedom Betrayed was the culmination of an extraordinary literary project launched by Hoover during World War II. Originally conceived as volume 5 of a projected multivolume set of his memoirs, the "War Book" (as he first called it) initially focused on his battle against President Roosevelt's foreign policies before Pearl Harbor. As time went on, Hoover widened his scope to include Roosevelt's foreign policies during the war, as well as the war's darker consequences: the vast and terrible expansion of the Soviet empire and the eruption of the Cold War against the Communists. As a historian of these events, Hoover became interested not only in the diplomatic blunders of the Roosevelt administration vis-à-vis Joseph Stalin but also in the influence on Roosevelt of advisers who proved to be Communists or their willing accomplices. To Hoover the "calamity" of the Cold War was the direct result of misjudgments by American leaders between 1933 and 1953—failures that enormously strengthened our postwar enemy, the Soviet Union. To prove this thesis became the intent of what Hoover and his staff informally called the Magnum Opus.

In its final form, *Freedom Betrayed* was part memoir and part diplomatic history. For two decades Hoover wrote and repeatedly revised it, producing what may be the most ambitious and systematic work of World War II revisionism ever attempted. He considered it to be his most important book and his "will and testament" to the American people. He wanted it to be an irrefutable indictment of the "lost statesmanship" of his presidential successor. To Hoover, FDR's prewar and wartime diplomacy had made the world safe for Stalinist Russia, triggering a dangerous, *third* world war—the Cold War—against a "Communist giant which our own leaders helped build."

In a way, the Magnum Opus was the former president's summa. Nearly one thousand pages long, it is a comprehensive synthesis of the convictions and arguments relating to World War II that Professor Best gleaned so carefully from Hoover's correspondence and speeches. As such, it enriches and complements Professor Best's narrative, and vice versa. The serendipitous appearance in print of *Freedom Betrayed,* so close to the publication of the final volume of the Hoover Biography Project, underscores the truth that historical research never ends—not, at least, so long as treasures like the Magnum Opus remain to be mined and exploited.

Freedom Betrayed also exemplifies a trait that Professor Best takes note of in his book: Hoover was never content to leave the judgment of his legacy to others. Not only was he one of the eminent public figures of the twentieth century; along the way he also became his own archivist and his own biographer. Historians can be grateful that this indefatigable mining engineer, humanitarian, and statesman had the historical consciousness, foresight, and resources to document and explain his life journey.

Why did he choose the kind of life that he led? This, perhaps, is the final question, and in an autobiographical statement composed around the time of World War I, he came as close as he ever did to providing an answer. "There is little importance to men's lives," he wrote, "except the accomplishments they leave to posterity." It is "in the origination or administration of tangible institutions or constructive works" that men's contributions can best be measured. "When all is said and done," he asserted, "accomplishment is all that counts."[7]

Hoover lived a life of phenomenal accomplishment. True to his creed, he founded or guided an imposing array of institutions that improved the lives of countless people: the Commission for Relief in Belgium, American Relief Administration, Belgian American Educational Foundation, American Child Health Association, Finnish Relief Fund, and many more. Between 1933 and 1964 three institutions in particular became the beneficiaries of his labors: the Hoover Institution on War, Resolution and Peace ("probably my major contribution to American life");[8] the Boys Clubs of America movement; and, toward the end, the Herbert Hoover Presidential Library. Upon each he left a perdurable imprint; each in a way conferred upon him the secular immortality that I think he craved.

Some of his accomplishments were, and always will be, controversial. His political philosophy and vision of America will probably never gain universal appeal. But in the end we must forever grant him this: Herbert Hoover secured his place in history the old-fashioned way. He *earned* it.

Notes

Chapter 1

1. Ably described in his *Interregnum of Despair* (Urbana: University of Illinois Press, 1970).
2. Lou Henry Hoover to Allan Hoover, February [11?], 1933, Allan Hoover Papers, Herbert Hoover Presidential Library (hereafter cited as HHPL).
3. Lou Henry Hoover to Allan Hoover, February [8?], 1933, ibid.
4. Lou Henry Hoover to Aunt Lillian Weed, January [4?], 1933, ibid.
5. Lou Henry Hoover to Allan Hoover, February [2?], 1933, ibid.
6. Lou Henry Hoover to children, November [18?], 1932, ibid.
7. Lou Henry Hoover to Allan Hoover, February [11?], 1933, ibid.
8. Gary Dean Best, *Pride, Prejudice and Politics* (Westport: Praeger, 1991), p. 21. Cites W. Ross Livingston to Joseph A. Broderick, March 4, 1933, Raymond Moley Papers, Hoover Institution (hereafter cited as HI).
9. Best, *Pride, Prejudice, Politics*, p. 23. Cites Rexford Tugwell Diary, February 19, 1933, Franklin D. Roosevelt Presidential Library (hereafter cited as FDRPL).
10. Rexford Tugwell Diary, February 19, 1933, FDRPL. The details of Hoover's efforts to enlist FDR's cooperation and the correspondence that passed between them can be found in Timothy Walch and Dwight M. Miller, eds., *Herbert Hoover and Franklin D. Roosevelt: A Documentary History* (Westport: Greenwood Press, 1998), pp. 129–47.
11. Rexford G. Tugwell, "The Protagonists: Roosevelt and Hoover," *Antioch Review* 13 (December 1953): 419.
12. Edgar Rickard Diary, March 5, 1933, HHPL.
13. "Press Statement Urging Support of President Roosevelt's Bank Holiday Proclamation," Herbert Hoover Special Collections: Articles, Addresses and Public Statements, 1915–1964, HHPL.
14. *New York Times*, March 8, 1933.
15. Ibid., March 9, 1933.
16. Ibid., March 10, 1933.
17. Herbert Hoover to David Reed, March 10, 1933, Herbert Hoover Papers, HHPL.
18. Edgar Rickard Diary, March 15, 1933, HHPL.
19. *New York Times*, March 17, 1933.
20. Ibid., March 21, 1933.
21. Ibid., March 22, 1933.
22. Saul Pett to Herbert Hoover, June 13, 1961, Herbert Hoover Papers, Post-Presidential Subject File, Associated Press, HHPL.
23. *Washington Post*, March 3, 1933.
24. *Chicago Tribune*, March 2, 1933.
25. *Baltimore Sun*, March 4, 1933.
26. *New York Herald Tribune*, March 3, 1933.

27. Lou Henry Hoover to Dolly Gann, November 1, 1941, and to Lena Yost, March 13, 1942, Lou Henry Hoover Papers, HHPL.
28. Lou Henry Hoover to Helen Boone, March 26, 1937, ibid.
29. Lou Henry Hoover to Allan Hoover, May [25?], 1933, Allan Hoover Papers, HHPL.
30. Hoover to Henry Allen, January 18, 1947, Herbert Hoover Papers, HHPL.
31. Clarence Kelland to Neil MacNeil, January 27, 1957, Neil MacNeil Papers, HHPL.
32. Lou Henry Hoover to Allan Hoover, undated [1941?], Allan Hoover Papers, HHPL.
33. Edgar Rickard Diary, July 14, 1938, HHPL.
34. Mark Sullivan to Henry Robinson, November 21, 1932, Mark Sullivan Papers, HI.
35. Jeremiah Milbank Jr. interview, p. 10, Oral History Collection, HHPL.
36. Sullivan to Robinson, November 21, 1932, Mark Sullivan Papers, HI.
37. Jeremiah Milbank Jr. interview, p. 12, Oral History Collection, HHPL.
38. Edgar Rickard Diary, March 15, 1933, HHPL.
39. Ibid., August 16 and August 28, 1933.
40. *New York Times*, February 26, 1933.
41. Ibid., March 5, 1933.
42. Hoover to John Callan O'Laughlin, March 31, 1933, John Callan O'Laughlin Papers, Library of Congress (hereafter cited as LC [copies available at HHPL]).
43. Edgar Rickard Diary, April 6, 1933, HHPL.
44. Ibid., April 14, 1933.
45. Ralph Heppe to Lawrence Richey, April 19, 1933, and Paul Sexson to Heppe, April 22, 1933, Herbert Hoover Papers, Post-Presidential Subject File, Associated Press, HHPL.
46. Hoover to George H. Lorimer, June 1, 1933, Herbert Hoover Papers, HHPL.
47. Hoover to Lewis Strauss, May 16, 1933, Strauss Papers, HHPL.
48. Hoover to Mark Sullivan, April 10, 1933, Mark Sullivan Papers, HI; Hoover to Paul Wooton, September 9, 1933, Herbert Hoover Papers, HHPL.
49. Hoover to Strauss, July 31, 1933, Strauss Papers, HHPL.
50. Hoover to Walter Hope, August 9, 1933, Herbert Hoover Papers, HHPL.
51. Hoover to Strauss, August 23, 1933, Strauss Papers, HHPL.
52. Hoover to Simeon Fess, May 9, 1933, Herbert Hoover Papers, HHPL.
53. O'Laughlin to Hoover, June 17, 1933, John Callan O'Laughlin Papers, LC.
54. Ibid., June 20, 1933.
55. Hoover to Everett Sanders, July 5, 1933, Herbert Hoover Papers, HHPL.
56. Bertrand Snell to Hoover, July 11, 1933, ibid.
57. Hoover to Strauss, July 5, 1933, Strauss Papers, HHPL.
58. O'Laughlin to Hoover, April 7, 1933, and Hoover to O'Laughlin, April 10, 1933, John Callan O'Laughlin Papers, LC.
59. O'Laughlin to Hoover, July 14 and July 21, 1933.
60. Lou Henry Hoover to Marie Sullivan, May 10, 1933, Lou Henry Hoover Papers, HHPL.
61. Lou Henry Hoover to Allan Hoover, August [6?], 1933, Allan Hoover Papers, HHPL.
62. Ibid., October [3?], 1933.
63. Draft statement enclosed with Hoover to O'Laughlin, October 12, 1933, John Callan O'Laughlin Papers, LC.
64. Hoover to Strauss, October 11, 1933, Strauss Papers, HHPL.
65. O'Laughlin to Hoover, October 9, 1933, John Callan O'Laughlin Papers, LC.
66. Sullivan to Hoover, October 21, 1933, Mark Sullivan Papers, HI.
67. Hoover to O'Laughlin, October 12, 1933, John Callan O'Laughlin Papers, LC.
68. Draft statement enclosed with Hoover to O'Laughlin, October 12, 1933, ibid.
69. Hoover to Strauss, October 4, 1933, Strauss Papers, HHPL.
70. *New York Times*, September 29 and 30, 1933.
71. "Report of Progress to the Economic Club of Chicago by the Committee on Recent Economic Changes," October 26, 1933, enclosed with Arch Shaw to Hoover, November 13, 1933, Herbert Hoover Papers, HHPL.
72. Arch Shaw to Hoover, November 13, 1933, ibid.
73. *Chicago Tribune*, November 20, 1933.

74. Hoover to Will Irwin, December 1, 1933, Herbert Hoover Papers, HHPL.
75. Hoover to Whiting Williams, December 20, 1933, ibid.
76. Fess to Hoover, November 28, 1933, ibid.
77. O'Laughlin to Hoover, January 24, 1934, John Callan O'Laughlin Papers, LC.
78. Walter F. Brown to Hoover, November 29, 1933, Herbert Hoover Papers, HHPL.
79. Remarks by Hon. Bertram Snell, *Congressional Record*, Vol. 78, Part 2 (February 1, 1934), p. 1798.
80. Hoover to Snell, telegram, February 2, 1934, Herbert Hoover Papers, HHPL.
81. Lou Henry Hoover to Agnes Morley Cleaveland, May 18, 1945, Lou Henry Hoover Papers, HHPL.
82. Lou Henry Hoover to Allan Hoover, undated [1934?], Allan Hoover Papers, HHPL.
83. "Collectivism Comes to America: Roosevelt's First Term, 1933–1936" (unpublished manuscript, April 1950), p. 209. Filed under *The Memoirs of Herbert Hoover, Vol. 3*, "The Aftermath," Herbert Hoover Papers, Special Collections: Books, HHPL.
84. Hoover to Edward Eyre Hunt, September 14, 1933, Herbert Hoover Papers, HHPL.
85. Hoover to John Wheeler, April 25, 1934, ibid.
86. For example, Gertrude Lane to Hoover, January 26, 1934, ibid.
87. Hoover to Howard Heinz, March 7, 1934, ibid.
88. Arthur Ballantine to Hoover, March 27, 1934, and Hoover to Ballantine, April 5, 1934, ibid.
89. Hoover to Ashmun Brown, March 13, 1934, ibid.
90. Minutes of the Republican National Committee meeting, June 5, 1934; report of the continuation of the Republican National Committee meeting, June 6, 1934, Republican National Headquarters.
91. *New York Times*, June 7, 1943; *New York Herald Tribune*, June 7, 1934.
92. Report of the continuation of the Republican National Committee meeting, June 6, 1934, Republican National Headquarters.
93. R. B. Creager to Hoover, telegram, June 6, 1934, Herbert Hoover Papers, HHPL.
94. *New York Herald Tribune*, June 7, 1934.
95. Quoted in *New York Times*, April 3, 1934.
96. *New York Times*, April 3, 1934.
97. Ibid., April 1, 1934.
98. Hoover to Theodore Joslin, April 10, 1934, Herbert Hoover Papers, HHPL.
99. Hoover to Lane, July 9, 1934, ibid.
100. Hoover to White, July 31, 1934, William Allen White Papers, LC.
101. Hoover to Strauss, May 17, 1934, Strauss Papers, HHPL.
102. Edgar Rickard Diary, July 14, 1934, and Hoover to Hugh Gibson, August 23, 1934, Herbert Hoover Papers, HHPL.
103. Herbert Hoover, *The Challenge to Liberty* (New York: Charles Scribner's Sons, 1934), pp. 203–4.
104. White to Book-of-the-Month Club, telegram, August 15, 1934, William Allen White Papers, LC.
105. Hoover to White, August 23, 1934, ibid.
106. *New York Herald Tribune*, September 5, 1934.
107. *The Nation*, October 17, 1934.
108. Gary Dean Best, *Nickel and Dime Decade* (Westport: Praeger, 1993), p. 6. Cites Best, *Pride, Prejudice, Politics*.
109. Best, *Nickel and Dime*, pp. 6–7.
110. *Saturday Review*, October 6, 1934.
111. *Manchester Guardian*, September 28, 1934.
112. Will Durant to Hoover, October 8, 1934, Herbert Hoover Papers, HHPL.
113. Glenn Frank to Hoover, October 23, 1934, ibid.
114. *Washington Post*, September 28, 1934.
115. Quoted in *New York Times*, August 12, 1934.
116. "Collectivism Comes to America," p. 211.
117. Edgar Rickard Diary, February 26, 1935, HHPL.
118. "America's Conservative Revolution," *Antioch Review* 15 (June 1955): 204.

119. A description of the Bohemian Grove encampment can be found in the Edgar Rickard Diary, July 19 through August 2, 1947, HHPL.
120. Lou Henry Hoover to Charlotte Kellogg, October 27, 1933, Lou Henry Hoover Papers, HHPL.
121. Lou Henry Hoover to Allan Hoover, May 14, 1934, Allan Hoover Papers, HHPL.
122. Hoover to Gibson, August 23, 1934, Herbert Hoover Papers, HHPL.
123. *New York Times Magazine*, May 27, 1934.
124. Ibid.
125. Ibid.
126. *Washington Post*, July 29, 1934.
127. Clapper to wife, July 22, 1934, Raymond Clapper Papers, LC.
128. *New York Times*, July 19, 1934.
129. Ibid., August 14, 1934.
130. Strauss to Hoover, May 4, 1934, Strauss Papers, HHPL.
131. Hoover to O'Laughlin, May 11, 1934, John Callan O'Laughlin Papers, LC.
132. Edgar Rickard Diary, June 21, 1934, HHPL.
133. Best, *Pride, Prejudice, Politics*, p. 71. Cites *New York Herald Tribune*, September 4 and September 28, 1934; *New York Times*, September 25, 1934; and *Wall Street Journal*, September 5, 1934.
134. Hoover to Will Irwin, August 23, 1934, Will Irwin Papers, HI.
135. Best, *Pride, Prejudice, Politics*, p. 72. Cites *Chicago Tribune*, August 27, 1934.
136. Best, *Pride, Prejudice, Politics*, p. 75. Cites *New York Herald Tribune*, October 18, 1934.
137. Hoover to O'Laughlin, August 31, 1934, John Callan O'Laughlin Papers, LC.
138. Henry Fletcher to Hoover, August 31, 1934, Herbert Hoover Papers, HHPL.
139. Hoover to Henry Allen, October 17, 1934, ibid.
140. Lester Dickinson to Hoover, November 1, 1934, ibid.
141. Shaw to Hoover, October 4, 1934, ibid.
142. See, for example, Henry Allen to Hoover, November 6, 1933, George Akerson to Hoover, November 21, 1933, and Arch Shaw to Hoover, June 6, 1934, Herbert Hoover Papers, HHPL; Mark Sullivan to Hoover, April 30, 1934, Mark Sullivan Papers, HI.
143. James Farley to Franklin D. Roosevelt, August 1, 1935, transmitting an account by student Grey of Hoover's comments on January 19, 1935, Franklin D. Roosevelt Papers, FDRPL.
144. Edgar Rickard Diary, February 11, 1935, HHPL.
145. "Address of Herbert Hoover before the National Republican Club of New York on Lincoln's Birthday," February 12, 1935, Herbert Hoover Papers. Special Collections: Articles, Addresses and Public Statements, 1915–1964, HHPL.
146. Hoover to White, January 12, 1935, William Allen White Papers, LC.
147. Hoover to Strauss, January 12, 1935, Strauss Papers, HHPL.
148. "Statement on Going Off the Gold Standard," Tucson, Arizona, February 20, 1935, Herbert Hoover Special Collections: Articles, Addresses and Public Statements, 1915–1964, HHPL.
149. *New York Times*, February 21, 1935.
150. *New York Herald Tribune*, February 22, 1935.
151. *New York Times*, February 22, 1935.
152. Hoover to Arthur Hyde, February 25, 1935, Herbert Hoover Papers, HHPL.

Chapter 2

1. *New York Times*, February 22, 1935.
2. Reprinted in Herbert Hoover, *Addresses Upon the American Road, 1933–1938* (New York: Charles Scribner's Sons, 1938), pp. 40–44.
3. Hoover to Walter Hope, January 14, 1935, Herbert Hoover Papers, HHPL.
4. Hoover to William Allen White, February 25, 1935, William Allen White Papers, LC.
5. White to Hoover, March 4, 1935, ibid.

6. *New York Times*, March 24, 1935.
7. Ibid., March 25, 1935.
8. Hoover to Orville Bullington, April 24, 1935, Herbert Hoover Papers, HHPL.
9. Hoover to Bullington, February 28, 1935, ibid.
10. Edgar Rickard Diary, April 7, 1935, HHPL.
11. Hoover to Gertrude Lane, April 23, 1935, Herbert Hoover Papers, HHPL.
12. Edgar Rickard Diary, June 9 through June 12, 1935, HHPL.
13. Hoover to Christopher Morley, February 4, 1935, Herbert Hoover Papers, HHPL.
14. Hoover to Ashmun Brown, May 15, 1934, ibid.
15. Harry W. Morris, "Republicans in a Minority Role, 1933–1938" (Ph.D. dissertation, University of Iowa, 1960), pp. 110–13.
16. Hoover to White, May 10, 1935, William Allen White Papers, LC.
17. Hoover to Harrison Spangler, May 10, 1935, Arthur Hyde to Hoover, May 10, 1935, and Spangler to Hoover, May 13, 1935, Herbert Hoover Papers, HHPL; White to Frank Knox, June 26, 1935, William Allen White Papers, LC.
18. Morris, "Republicans," pp. 114–15.
19. Hoover to Walter Head, May 15, 1935, Herbert Hoover Papers, HHPL.
20. Edgar Rickard Diary, June 9 through June 12, 1935, HHPL.
21. White to Walter Newton, June 26, 1935, William Allen White Papers, LC.
22. Hoover to Channing Pollock, June 22, 1935, Herbert Hoover Papers, HHPL.
23. *Salt Lake Tribune*, June 23, 1935.
24. Hoover to Edmund E. Lincoln, June 27, 1935, Herbert Hoover Papers, HHPL.
25. Hoover to Spangler, July 24, 1935, ibid.
26. Memo by D. M. Reynolds, May 1, 1935, ibid.; memo of a telephone conversation with Hoover, May 6, 1935, Mark Sullivan Papers, HI.
27. See, for example, Lincoln to Hoover, June 24, 1935, forwarded to Brown, June 26, 1935, and Hoover to Brown, September 10, 1935, Walter Brown Papers, Ohio Historical Society.
28. Reprinted in Hoover, *Addresses, 1933–1938*, pp. 63–74.
29. *Time*, October 14, 1935.
30. *Collier's*, October 12, 1935.
31. Hoover to Brown, telegram, September 30, 1935, Herbert Hoover Papers, HHPL.
32. Reprinted in Hoover, *Addresses, 1933–1938*, pp. 75–86.
33. Edgar Rickard Diary, November 16, 1935, HHPL.
34. Hoover to Brown, November 27, 1935, Herbert Hoover Papers, HHPL.
35. Charles Hilles to Henry Fletcher, November 18, 1935, copy in Herbert Hoover Papers, HHPL.
36. Hoover to Ballard Dunn, September 21, 1935, ibid.
37. Hoover to Gen. George Van Horn Moseley, October 21, 1935, ibid.
38. *Newsweek*, November 23, 1935.
39. *Literary Digest*, November 23, 1935.
40. Edgar Rickard Diary, October 12, 1935, HHPL.
41. *Chicago Tribune*, November 9, 1935.
42. Hoover to John Spargo, September 22, 1935, Spargo Papers, University of Vermont.
43. *New York Times*, November 30, 1935.
44. O'Laughlin to Hoover, November 30, 1935, John Callan O'Laughlin Papers, LC.
45. Hoover to Charles F. Scott, December 7, 1935, Herbert Hoover Papers, HHPL.
46. Reprinted in Hoover, *Addresses, 1933–1938*, pp. 87–100.
47. Ibid., pp. 101–13.
48. Hoover to O'Laughlin, January 24, 1936, John Callan O'Laughlin Papers, LC.
49. Hoover to James P. Goodrich, January 25, 1936, Herbert Hoover Papers, HHPL.
50. Robert G. Simmons to Hoover, February 10, 1936, ibid.
51. See, for example, Hoover to Hyde, January 27, 1936, and Harry Chandler to Hoover, January 28, 1936, ibid.
52. Alan Fox to Hoover, February 4, 1936, ibid.
53. *New York Times*, January 5, 1936.

54. Ibid., January 11, 1936.
55. Ibid., January 17, 1936.
56. Reprinted in Hoover, *Addresses, 1933–1938*, pp. 114–25.
57. Edgar Rickard Diary, February 26, 1936, HHPL.
58. Reynolds to Hoover, February 5, 1936, Herbert Hoover Papers, HHPL.
59. Reprinted in Hoover, *Addresses, 1933–1938*, pp. 126–41.
60. Edgar Rickard Diary, March 11, 1936, HHPL.
61. Donald R. McCoy, *Landon of Kansas* (Lincoln: University of Nebraska Press, 1966), pp. 244–46.
62. Edgar Rickard Diary, March 27, 1936, HHPL.
63. *New Republic*, March 11, 1936.
64. Reprinted in Hoover, *Addresses, 1933–1938*, pp. 142–58.
65. Rickard to Spargo, April 3, 1936, Spargo Papers, University of Vermont.
66. Edgar Rickard Diary, April 14, 1936, HHPL.
67. Lawrence Richey to George Getz, April 9, 1936, Herbert Hoover Papers, HHPL.
68. Edgar Rickard Diary, May 6, 1936, HHPL; O'Laughlin to Hoover, May 11, 1936, John Callan O'Laughlin Papers, LC.
69. Reprinted in Hoover, *Addresses, 1933–1938*, pp. 159–72.
70. Dunn to Hoover, April 27, 1936.
71. Morris, "Republicans," p. 163; George Henry Lobdell Jr., "A Biography of Frank Knox" (Ph.D. dissertation, University of Illinois, 1954), pp. 263–64, 266, 274.
72. "Statement to the Press," Chicago, May 18, 1936, Herbert Hoover Special Collections: Articles, Addresses and Public Statements, 1915–1964, HHPL.
73. Edgar Rickard Diary, June 9 through June 11, 1936, HHPL.
74. Reprinted in Hoover, *Addresses, 1933–1938*, pp. 173–83.
75. Edgar Rickard Diary, June 9 through June 11, 1936, HHPL.
76. Chester Rowell to Myrtle, June 11, 1936, Chester Harvey Rowell Papers, Sanoian Special Collections Library, California State University, Fresno.
77. Edgar Rickard Diary, June 9 through June 11, 1936, HHPL.
78. Rickard to Mills, June 13, 1936, copy in Spargo Papers, University of Vermont.
79. "Collectivism Comes to America: Roosevelt's First Term, 1933–1936" (unpublished manuscript, April 1950), p. 260. Filed under *The Memoirs of Herbert Hoover, Vol. 3*, "The Aftermath," Herbert Hoover Papers, Special Collections: Books, HHPL.
80. Ibid., pp. 270–71.
81. William Starr Myers Papers, Princeton University.
82. Edgar Rickard Diary, June 12, 1936, HHPL.
83. See, for example, A. C. Mattei to Hoover, June 14, 1936, Herbert Hoover Papers, HHPL.
84. Hoover to Walter F. Brown, June 23, 1936, Herbert Hoover Papers, HHPL.
85. *New York Times*, July 5, 1936.
86. Willard Kiplinger to Ben Allen, July 10, 1936, Benjamin Shannon Allen Papers, HI.
87. Allen to Kiplinger, July 23, 1936, ibid.
88. Charles P. Taft to Robert A. Taft, July 28, 1936, Robert A. Taft Papers, LC.
89. Robert A. Taft to Charles P. Taft, July 30, 1936, ibid.
90. Alfred Landon to Hoover, August 7, 1936, Alf M. Landon Papers, Kansas Historical Society.
91. Hoover to Newton, August 15, 1936, Herbert Hoover Papers, HHPL.
92. Hoover to Bullington, July 9, 1936, ibid.
93. Transcript of telephone conversation between Landon and Hoover, September 2, 1936, ibid.
94. Hoover to Landon, September 2, 1936, ibid.
95. "Taxation," address before the American Metal Mining Congress, Denver, Colorado, September 30, 1936, Herbert Hoover Special Collections: Articles, Addresses and Public Statements, 1915–1964, HHPL.
96. Newton to Hoover, September 26, 1936, Herbert Hoover Papers, HHPL.
97. Edgar Rickard Diary, September 28, 1936, HHPL.
98. Ibid., October 5, 1936.

99. William Honnold to Hoover, June 24, 1936, and Hoover to Honnold, June 26, 1936, Herbert Hoover Papers, HHPL.
100. Reprinted in Hoover, *Addresses, 1933–1938*, pp. 201–15.
101. Ibid., pp. 216–27.
102. "Collectivism Comes to America," p. 281.
103. Raymond Moley, *27 Masters of Politics* (New York: Funk and Wagnalls, 1949), pp. 26–27.
104. Harold L. Ickes, *The Secret Diary of Harold L. Ickes* (New York: Simon and Schuster, 1953), vol. 1, p. 639.
105. Bascom N. Timmons, *Garner of Texas* (New York: Harper Brothers, 1948), p. 208.
106. Hoover to Ogden Mills, November 4, 1936, Herbert Hoover Papers, HHPL.
107. Edgar Rickard Diary, November 30, 1936, HHPL.
108. White to Jay Darling, December 15, 1936, William Allen White Papers, LC.
109. Lewis Strauss to Hoover, November 6, 1936, Herbert Hoover Papers, HHPL.
110. Hoover to Hyde, January 1, 1937, ibid.
111. Hoover to White, January 9, 1937, William Allen White Papers, LC.
112. Edgar Rickard Diary, December 31, 1936, HHPL.
113. Landon to Richard Lloyd Jones, January 1, 1937, Alf M. Landon Papers, Kansas Historical Society.
114. Shaw to Hoover, undated [January 31, 1937?], Herbert Hoover Papers, HHPL.
115. John D. M. Hamilton interview, pp. 28–30, Oral History Collection, HHPL.
116. Karl A. Lamb, "The Opposition Party as Secret Agent: Republicans and the Court Fight, 1937," *Papers of the Michigan Academy of Science, Arts, and Letters* 46 (1961): 540–41.
117. Reprinted in Hoover, *Addresses, 1933–1938*, pp. 229–36.
118. Edgar Rickard Diary, February 24, 1937, HHPL.
119. Hoover to O'Laughlin, February 26, 1937, John Callan O'Laughlin Papers, LC.
120. Landon to Amos Pinchot, March 11, 1937, Alf M. Landon Papers, Kansas Historical Society.
121. John D. M. Hamilton interview, pp. 21–28, Oral History Collection, HHPL.
122. Edgar Rickard Diary, April 18 and April 19, 1937, HHPL.
123. Hoover to Hamilton, April 23, 1937, Herbert Hoover Papers, HHPL.
124. Hoover to White, May 11, 1937, ibid.
125. Alison Reppy to Spargo, May 24, 1937, Spargo Papers, University of Vermont (copy in Herbert Hoover Papers, HHPL).
126. *New York Times*, May 14, 1937.
127. Ibid.
128. Ibid., May 21, 1937.
129. Landon to William Hard, May 10, 1937, Alf M. Landon Papers, Kansas Historical Society.
130. Edgar Rickard Diary, May 19, 1937, HHPL.
131. Hard to Hoover, telegram, June 11, 1937, Herbert Hoover Papers, HHPL.
132. Hoover to Hard, June 21, 1937, ibid.
133. Edgar Rickard Diary, May 27, 1937, HHPL.
134. Rickard to Spargo, August 27, 1937, Spargo Papers, University of Vermont.
135. Reprinted in Hoover, *Addresses, 1933–1938*, pp. 243–63.
136. Hoover to Robert D. Blue, August 21, 1937, Herbert Hoover Papers, HHPL.
137. Hoover to Reynolds, July 8, 1937, ibid.
138. Hoover to Dunn, July 9, 1937, ibid.
139. Landon to Mossman, August 10, 1937.
140. Bertrand Snell to Hoover, August 9, 1937, Herbert Hoover Papers, HHPL.
141. Hoover to Spangler, August 21, 1937, ibid.
142. Hoover to Jacob Allen, August 21, 1937, ibid.
143. Spangler to Hoover, August 25, 1937, ibid.
144. Hoover to Spangler, August 28, 1937, ibid.
145. Hoover to Arthur Ballantine, August 28, 1937, ibid.
146. Hoover to Chester Rowell, September 8, 1937, ibid.
147. Edgar Rickard Diary, September 13, 1937, HHPL.

148. Landon to Hard, September 13, 1937, Alf M. Landon Papers, Kansas Historical Society.
149. Knox to Hoover, September 13, 1937, Herbert Hoover Papers, HHPL.
150. *Washington Post*, September 19, 1937.
151. Ibid., September 23, 1937

Chapter 3

1. *New York Times*, September 23, 1937.
2. Ibid., September 24, 1937.
3. Edgar Rickard Diary, September 20, 1937, HHPL.
4. Ibid., September 25 and September 28, 1937.
5. *Cleveland News*, September 30, 1937.
6. *Baltimore Sun*, September 28, 1937.
7. *New York Times*, October 15, 1937.
8. Richard Lloyd Jones to Alf Landon, September 25, 1937, Alf M. Landon Papers, Kansas Historical Society.
9. Landon to Jones, September 27, 1937, ibid.
10. Frank Altschul to Landon, November 3, 1937, ibid.
11. Hoover to Theodore Roosevelt Jr., August 25, 1937.
12. Hoover to John Hamilton, October 5, 1937, Herbert Hoover Papers, HHPL.
13. Landon to Sen. John Townsend Jr., October 6, 1937, Alf M. Landon Papers, Kansas Historical Society.
14. See, for example, Landon to Knox, October 14, 1937, and Landon to Vandenberg, October 14, 1937, ibid.
15. Hoover to Frank Lowden, October 8, 1937, Herbert Hoover Papers, HHPL.
16. *New York Times*, October 13, 1937.
17. Ibid., October 21, 1937.
18. Ibid., October 24, 1937.
19. *Palo Alto Times*, October 20, 1937; Hoover to Harrison Spangler, October 23, 1937, Herbert Hoover Papers, HHPL.
20. Reprinted in Herbert Hoover, *Addresses Upon the American Road, 1933–1938* (New York: Charles Scribner's Sons, 1938), pp. 264–75.
21. *New York Times*, October 27, 1937.
22. *Time*, November 8, 1937.
23. Ben S. Allen to Hoover, October 28, 1937, Herbert Hoover Papers, HHPL.
24. *New York Times*, October 24, 1937.
25. John Hamilton to Landon, November 2, 1937, Alf M. Landon Papers, Kansas Historical Society.
26. "An Abstract of the Stenographic Report of a Meeting of the Republican National Committee Held at Chicago, November 5, 1937," Republican National Headquarters.
27. *New York Times*, November 7, 1937.
28. Donald R. McCoy, *Landon of Kansas* (Lincoln: University of Nebraska Press, 1966), p. 373.
29. *New York Times*, November 6, 1937.
30. Hoover to Frank Knox, November 6, 1937, Herbert Hoover Papers, HHPL.
31. Knox to Hoover, November 9, 1937, ibid.
32. See, for example, Spargo to Allison Reppy, November 8 and November 27, 1937, Spargo Papers, University of Vermont (copies in Herbert Hoover Papers, HHPL).
33. See, for example, Hoover to Spangler, November 11, 1937, Herbert Hoover Papers, HHPL; Landon to Henry Fletcher, November 16, 1937, Alf M. Landon Papers, Kansas Historical Society.
34. See, for example, Hoover to Spangler, December 2 and December 9, 1937, Herbert Hoover Papers, HHPL; Fletcher to Landon, November 23, 1937, and January 31, 1938, and Landon to Fletcher, February 1, 1938, Alf M. Landon Papers, Kansas Historical Society.
35. *New York Times*, October 17, 1937.

36. Reprinted in Hoover, *Addresses, 1933–1938*, pp. 276–80.
37. Ibid., pp. 281–86.
38. Hoover to Spargo, December 10, 1937, Spargo Papers, University of Vermont.
39. Memo enclosed with Hoover to Lewis Strauss, March 4, 1937, Strauss Papers, HHPL.
40. Gary Dean Best, *Pride, Prejudice and Politics* (Westport: Praeger, 1991), pp. 157–74.
41. Ibid., pp. 175–88.
42. Edgar Rickard Diary, October 11, 1937, HHPL.
43. Ibid., October 18, 1937.
44. Ibid., November 22, 1937.
45. Hoover to John Bricker, November 1, 1937, Herbert Hoover Papers, HHPL.
46. Hoover to James Howell, November 2, 1937, ibid.
47. Hoover to Ashmun Brown, December 29, 1937, ibid.
48. William Allen White to Hoover, January 31, 1938, William Allen White Papers, LC.
49. Reprinted in Hoover, *Addresses, 1933–1938*, pp. 287–99.
50. *San Francisco Chronicle*, December 19, 1937.
51. Hoover to Gertrude Lane, December 15, 1937, Herbert Hoover Papers, HHPL.
52. Hoover to H. Alexander Smith, January 25, 1938, ibid.
53. Hoover to John Hartigan, September 19, 1935, ibid.
54. Edgar Rickard Diary, November 12, 1936, HHPL.
55. Ibid., December 7, 1936.
56. Hoover to Smith, January 25, 1938, Herbert Hoover Papers, HHPL.
57. John Callan O'Laughlin to Hoover, December 13, 1937, John Callan O'Laughlin Papers, LC.
58. Hoover to Smith, January 25, 1938, Herbert Hoover Papers, HHPL.
59. Bertrand Snell to Hoover, January 27, 1938, ibid.
60. *New York Times*, December 15, 1937.
61. Hoover to Smith, January 3, 1938, Herbert Hoover Papers, HHPL.
62. Hoover to O'Laughlin, February 8, 1938, John Callan O'Laughlin Papers, LC.
63. Lou Henry Hoover to Mr. and Mrs. Hugh Gibson, undated [March, 1938?], Lou Henry Hoover Papers, HHPL.
64. Perrin Galpin, "Through Europe with Mr. Hoover," Herbert Hoover Papers, Post-Presidential Subject File, Trips: 1938 European Trip, HHPL.
65. *Newsweek*, February 28, 1938.
66. Galpin, "Through Europe."
67. Edgar Rickard, "High Lights of Various Incidents and Opinions of H.H. on His Return From Europe, Gained By Me from Various Personal Talks With Him and Listening In On His Talks With Other Individuals," Herbert Hoover Papers, Post-Presidential Subject File, Trips: 1938 European Trip, HHPL.
68. Galpin, "Through Europe."
69. Rickard, "High Lights."
70. Press release, March 8, 1938, Herbert Hoover Special Collections: Articles, Addresses and Public Statements, 1915–1964, HHPL.
71. Galpin, "Through Europe."
72. "Interview with the London Press," March 18, 1938, Herbert Hoover Special Collections: Articles, Addresses and Public Statements, 1915–1964, HHPL.
73. Strauss to Hoover, telegram, March 16, 1938, Strauss Papers, HHPL.
74. Edgar Rickard Diary, March 18 and March 19, 1938, HHPL.
75. Reprinted in Hoover, *Addresses, 1933–1938*, pp. 309–24.
76. Arch Shaw to Hoover, April 22, 1938, Herbert Hoover Papers, HHPL.
77. Raymond Clapper to White, April 4 and April 11, 1938, William Allen White Papers, LC.
78. White to Hoover, April 4, 1938, ibid.
79. Hoover to Will Irwin, April 6, 1938, Herbert Hoover Papers, HHPL.
80. Hoover to Ellery Sedgewick, April 25, 1937, Herbert Hoover Papers, Post-Presidential Subject File, *Atlantic Monthly*, HHPL.

81. Best, *Pride, Prejudice, Politics*, p. 151. Cites Clapper Diary, Raymond Clapper Papers, LC; *New York Herald Tribune*, June 17, 1937; *Wall Street Journal*, June 18, 1937.
82. Hoover to Dorothy Arnold, July 29, 1937, Herbert Hoover Special Collections: Articles, Addresses and Public Statements, 1915–1964, HHPL.
83. Hoover to Snell, April 10, 1938, Herbert Hoover Papers, HHPL.
84. Best, *Pride, Prejudice, Politics*, p. 194. Cites *Barron's*, March 21, 1938, and Clapper to Landon, March 30, 1938, Raymond Clapper Papers, LC.
85. Hoover to J. William Ditter, telegram, April 1, 1938, Herbert Hoover Papers, Post-Presidential Subject File, Reorganization Bill, HHPL.
86. "Press Interview in Chicago," April 4, 1938, Herbert Hoover Special Collections: Articles, Addresses and Public Statements, 1915–1964, HHPL.
87. "Press Interview in San Francisco," April 7, 1938, ibid.
88. Hoover to Snell, April 10, 1938, Herbert Hoover Papers, HHPL.
89. Hoover to William Castle, April 9, 1938, ibid.
90. Reprinted in Hoover, *Addresses, 1933–1938*, pp. 325–34.
91. Reppy to Hoover, April 5, 1938, Herbert Hoover Papers, HHPL.
92. White to Hoover, April 4, 1938, William Allen White Papers, LC.
93. Shaw to Hoover, June 9, 1938, Herbert Hoover Papers, HHPL.
94. Reprinted in Hoover, *Addresses, 933–1938*, pp. 335–42.
95. Ibid., pp. 343–54.
96. A. C. Mattei to Hoover, May 9, 1938, Herbert Hoover Papers, HHPL.
97. Best, *Pride, Prejudice, Politics*, pp. 195–96. Cites *Barron's*, May 9, 1938; *New York Herald Tribune*, May 12, 1938; *Barron's*, April 4, 1938.
98. Best, *Pride, Prejudice, Politics*, p. 197. Cites *Magazine of Wall Street*, May 7, 1938, p. 78.
99. Best, *Pride, Prejudice, Politics*, p. 197. Cites *United States News*, April 25, 1938.
100. Glenn Frank to Hoover, telegram, June 20, 1938, Herbert Hoover Papers, HHPL.
101. Hoover to Frank, June 26, 1938, ibid.
102. Smith to Hoover, July 5, 1938, ibid.
103. See, for example, William Gross to Hoover, August 5, 1938, ibid.
104. A copy of the declaration can be found in Herbert Hoover Papers, Post-Presidential Subject File, Campaign 1938–39: Republican Program Committee, HHPL.
105. Smith to Hoover, August 15, 1938, and Shaw to Hoover, August 26, 1938, Herbert Hoover Papers, HHPL.
106. Chester Rowell to Hoover, August 14, 1938, ibid.
107. Hoover to Gross, August 11, 1938, ibid.
108. Hoover to Shaw, August 15, 1938, ibid.
109. Hoover to Mark Sullivan, July 16, 1938, Mark Sullivan Papers, HI.
110. Hoover to Spargo, August 11, 1938, and Spargo to Hoover, August 31, 1938, Spargo Papers, University of Vermont.
111. Will Irwin, "Herbert Hoover Tells 'What America Must Do Next,'" *Liberty Magazine*, July 16, 1938.
112. Edgar Rickard Diary, July 31 and August 1, 1938, HHPL.
113. "Address at Reception to Republicans," August 6, 1938, Herbert Hoover Special Collections: Articles, Addresses and Public Statements, 1915–1964, HHPL.
114. Reprinted in Herbert Hoover, *Further Addresses Upon the American Road, 1938–1940* (New York: Charles Scribner's Sons, 1940), pp. 3–20.
115. Hoover to Stuart Lake, October 12, 1938, Lake Papers, Huntington Library.
116. Reprinted in Hoover, *Further Addresses*, pp. 21–38.
117. *New York Times*, October 18, 1938.
118. Ibid., October 28, 1938.
119. Reprinted in Hoover, *Further Addresses*, pp. 39–57.
120. See John Canning to Hoover, October 21, 1938, Herbert Hoover Papers, Post-Presidential Subject File, California Picketing Act, HHPL.
121. Hoover to Sanborn Young, September 3, 1938, ibid.
122. Ray Lyman Wilbur to Hoover, October 31, 1938, ibid.

123. Hoover to Paul Smith, telegram, November 4, 1938, ibid.
124. Best, *Pride, Prejudice, Politics*, p. 202. Cites *Newsweek*, October 17, 1938; *New York Herald Tribune*, November 5, 1938; *New York Times*, November 1, 1938.
125. See, for example, Landon to Don Berry, November 16, 1938, Alf M. Landon Papers, Kansas Historical Society.
126. See, for example, Will Irwin to Hoover, November 12, 1938, Herbert Hoover Papers, HHPL.

Chapter 4

1. Gary Dean Best, *Pride, Prejudice and Politics* (Westport: Praeger, 1991), pp. 203–4. Cites *New York Times*, November 13, 1938; *United States News*, November 14, 1938; Joseph Alsop to his mother, November 15, 1938, Alsop Papers, LC.
2. Hoover to Miles Jones, November 15, 1938, Herbert Hoover Papers, HHPL.
3. "Press Statement on Congressional Election Returns," November 9, 1938, Herbert Hoover Special Collections: Articles, Addresses and Public Statements, 1915–1964, HHPL.
4. "Preliminary Analysis of Gubernatorial Election Returns," enclosed with O. Glenn Saxon to Hoover, December 1, 1938, Herbert Hoover Papers, HHPL.
5. Edgar Rickard Diary, November 24, 1938, HHPL.
6. Hoover to William Honnold, November 12, 1938, Herbert Hoover Papers, HHPL.
7. H. L. Mencken to William Allen White, November 23, 1938, William Allen White Papers, LC.
8. Will Irwin to Hoover, November 12, 1938, Herbert Hoover Papers, HHPL.
9. R. B. Creager to Hoover, November 12, 1938, ibid.
10. Hoover to Irwin, November 16, 1938, ibid.
11. Dr. Julius Klein to Hoover, November 14, 1938, Julius Klein Papers, HI.
12. John Spargo to Edgar Rickard, November 14, 1938, Spargo Papers, University of Vermont.
13. See, for example, William Castle to Hoover, October 18, 1938, and Hoover to Castle, October 19, 1938, Herbert Hoover Papers, HHPL.
14. *New York Times*, January 27, 1938.
15. Reprinted in Herbert Hoover, *Addresses Upon the American Road, 1933–1938* (New York: Charles Scribner's Sons, 1938), pp. 300–308.
16. Hamilton Fish Jr. to Hoover, telegram, January 17, 1938, Herbert Hoover Papers, HHPL.
17. Reprinted in Herbert Hoover, *Further Addresses Upon the American Road, 1938–1940* (New York: Charles Scribner's Sons, 1940), pp. 85–92.
18. Hoover to Walter Lichtenstein, October 3, 1938, Herbert Hoover Papers, HHPL.
19. "Broadcast Protest at Jewish Persecution over Station KSFO, San Francisco," November 14, 1938, Herbert Hoover Special Collections: Articles, Addresses and Public Statements, 1915–1964, HHPL.
20. Edgar Rickard Diary, November 25, 1938, HHPL.
21. "Statement on Entrance of Refugee European Children into America; Telegram to Lewis Strauss," January 13, 1939, Herbert Hoover Special Collections: Articles, Addresses and Public Statements, 1915–1964, HHPL.
22. *New York Times*, April 23, 1939.
23. Reprinted in Hoover, *Further Addresses*, pp. 93–103.
24. Harry Chandler to Hoover, February 7, 1939, Herbert Hoover Papers, HHPL.
25. Frederick Libby to Hoover, telegram, February 13, 1938, ibid.
26. Fish to Hoover, February 4, 1939, ibid.
27. Hoover to Boake Carter, February 4, 1939, ibid.
28. See Hoover to Castle, December 12, 1938, ibid.
29. W. G. Andrews to Hoover, January 23, 1939, ibid.
30. Address of Senator Styles Bridges over the National Broadcasting Company network, February 20, 1939. Press release filed in Herbert Hoover Papers, HHPL.
31. Quoted in Bainbridge Colby to Hoover, February 23, 1938, ibid.
32. Hoover to John Callan O'Laughlin, March 25, 1939, John Callan O'Laughlin Papers, LC.

33. Ibid., April 14, 1939.
34. Hoover to William Starr Myers, December 28, 1938, Herbert Hoover Papers, HHPL.
35. Reprinted in Hoover, *Further Addresses*, pp. 58–68.
36. Hoover to Frank Taggart, February 22, 1939, copy in Mark Sullivan Papers, HI.
37. Edgar Rickard Diary, February 22, 1939, HHPL.
38. Alf Landon to John Henry, August 28, 1939, Alf M. Landon Papers, Kansas Historical Society.
39. Hoover to Thomas Dewey, March 10, 1939, Herbert Hoover Papers, HHPL; Donald R. McCoy, *Landon of Kansas* (Lincoln: University of Nebraska Press, 1966), pp. 417–18.
40. For Simpson's activities, see Judith Stein, "The Impact of the New Deal on New York Politics: Kenneth Simpson and the Republican Party," *New York Historical Society Quarterly* 56 (January 1972): 39–53; McCoy, *Landon*, p. 401ff.
41. Dewey to White, July 1, 1939, and White to Dewey, July 5, 1939, William Allen White Papers, LC.
42. Henry to Landon, February 25, 1939, Alf M. Landon Papers, Kansas Historical Society.
43. Jacob Allen to Ben Allen, January 22, 1939, Herbert Hoover Papers, HHPL.
44. John Mott to Hoover, February 23, 1939, ibid.
45. Hoover to Arthur Hyde, telegram, March 11, 1939, ibid.
46. Ben Allen to James Selvage, April 11, 1939, ibid.
47. See, for example, Landon to Henry, February 28, 1939, and Henry to Landon, March 18, 1939, Alf M. Landon Papers, Kansas Historical Society.
48. Arthur Free to "Charley," March 20, 1939, copy enclosed with Free to Hoover, March 23, 1939, Herbert Hoover Papers, HHPL.
49. Hoover to Arch Shaw, March 24, 1939, ibid.
50. Edgar Rickard Diary, December 15, 1938; Paul Mallon to Selvage, April 7, 1939, ibid.
51. Hoover to William Gross, April 21, 1939, ibid.
52. Hoover to Wilbur Matson, April 11, 1939, ibid.
53. Harrison Spangler to Hoover, April 17, 1939, ibid.
54. Hoover to James Goodrich, April 25, 1939, ibid.
55. Will Loomis to Justus Craemer, May 22, 1939, copy enclosed with Craemer to Hoover, June 3, 1939, ibid.
56. Edgar Rickard Diary, May 31, 1939, HHPL.
57. Frank Fetzer to Ben Allen, June 12, 1939, June 21, 1939, and June 27, 1939, Ben Allen Papers, HI.
58. Hoover to Thomas Campbell, June 24, 1939, and Campbell to Hoover, June 30, 1939, Herbert Hoover Papers, HHPL.
59. Hoover to C. C. Moore, August 28, 1939, ibid.
60. Edgar Rickard Diary, June 7, 1939, HHPL.
61. Reprinted in Hoover, *Further Addresses*, pp. 197–207.
62. Ibid., pp. 208–14.
63. Edgar Rickard Diary, June 5, 1939, HHPL.
64. Hoover to Mark Sullivan, June 21, 1938, Mark Sullivan Papers, HI.
65. Reprinted in Hoover, *Further Addresses* pp. 104–15.
66. Hoover to Castle, April 10, 1939, Herbert Hoover Papers, HHPL.
67. Hoover to Orville Bullington, April 11, 1939, ibid.
68. Hoover to O'Laughlin, June 20, 1939, John Callan O'Laughlin Papers, LC.
69. Reprinted in Hoover, *Further Addresses*, pp. 116–28.
70. Ibid., pp. 129–38.
71. Ralph Brewster to Hoover, telegram, July 5, 1939, Herbert Hoover Papers, HHPL.
72. "Let's Keep Women and Children Out of the Trenches," *Christian Herald*, August, 1939, Herbert Hoover Special Collections: Articles, Addresses and Public Statements, 1915–1964, HHPL.
73. Will Durant to Hoover, July 6, 1939, Herbert Hoover Papers, HHPL.
74. O'Laughlin to Hoover, July 8, 1939, John Callan O'Laughlin Papers, LC.

75. See, for example, Hoover to Sen. Arthur Capper, July 14, 1939, Herbert Hoover Papers, HHPL.
76. Hoover to O'Laughlin, July 18, 1939, John Callan O'Laughlin Papers, LC.
77. Paul Shoup to Hoover, July 24, 1939, and Hoover to Shoup, July 31, 1939, Herbert Hoover Papers, HHPL.
78. Hoover to O'Laughlin, August 28, 1939, John Callan O'Laughlin Papers, LC.
79. *Montana Standard*, Butte, Montana, August 27, 1939.
80. Hoover to Walter Head, August 30, 1939, Herbert Hoover Papers, HHPL.
81. "Broadcast on Outbreak of European War," San Francisco, September 1, 1939, Herbert Hoover Special Collections: Articles, Addresses and Public Statements, 1915–1964, HHPL.
82. Hoover to O'Laughlin, September 4, 1939, John Callan O'Laughlin Papers, LC.
83. Hoover to Castle, September 14, 1939, Herbert Hoover Papers, HHPL.
84. "Bart" to "Dave," August 24, 1939, Robert A. Taft Papers, LC.
85. Nathan MacChesney to Frank Knox, August 11, 1939, Nathan MacChesney Papers, HHPL.
86. Hoover to Walter Newton, September 3, 1939, Herbert Hoover Papers, HHPL.
87. Robert Simmons to Hoover, August 18, 1939, ibid.
88. Selvage to Hoover, August 22, 1939, and Hoover to Selvage, August 27, 1939, ibid.
89. Hoover to Simmons, August 28, 1939, ibid.
90. Edgar Rickard Diary, September 13, 1939ff., HHPL.
91. Ibid., September 21, 1939.
92. Gross to Hoover, September 9, 1939, Herbert Hoover Papers, HHPL.
93. Henry to Landon, September 8, 1939, Alf M. Landon Papers, Kansas Historical Society.
94. Jacob Allen to Ben Allen, September 11, 1939, and Jacob Allen to Hoover, September 20, 1939, Herbert Hoover Papers, HHPL.
95. Hoover to Jacob Allen, September 16, 1939, ibid.
96. See A. C. Mattei to Hoover, May 9, 1938, and articles of incorporation for Constitutional Publications, Inc. therein, ibid.
97. See Hoover to W. K. Kellogg, January 7, 1942, ibid.
98. See Hoover to James Howell, September 7, 1939, Howell to Hoover, September 12, 1939, and Hoover to Howell, September 14, 1939, ibid.
99. Rickard to Lou Henry Hoover, September 29, 1939, Lou Henry Hoover Papers, HHPL.
100. George Henry Lobdell Jr., "A Biography of Frank Knox" (Ph.D. dissertation, University of Illinois, 1954), pp. 301–303; Steven M. Mark, "An American Interventionist: Frank Knox and United States Foreign Relations" (Ph.D. dissertation, University of Maryland, 1977), pp. 215–17.
101. Hoover to Charles Tobey, September 27, 1939, Herbert Hoover Papers, HHPL.
102. Edgar Rickard Diary, September 14, 1939, HHPL.
103. Ibid., September 19, 1939.
104. White to Knox, September 23, 1939, William Allen White Papers, LC.
105. See Herbert Hoover, *An American Epic, Vol. 4: The Guns Cease Killing and the Saving of Life from Famine Begins, 1939–1963* (Chicago: Henry Regnery, 1964), pp. 1–97.
106. See, for example, Edgar Rickard Diary, September 20, 1939, HHPL.
107. Hoover to Christian Herter, September 14, 1939, Herbert Hoover Papers, HHPL.
108. Reprinted in Hoover, *Further Addresses*, pp. 139–57.
109. See "The Allies Can't Lose: Interview with Roy Howard, Editor, New York World-Telegram," October 3, 1939, Herbert Hoover Special Collections: Articles, Addresses and Public Statements, 1915–1964, HHPL.
110. Hoover to Leland Cutler, October 5, 1939, Herbert Hoover Papers, HHPL.
111. Edgar Rickard Diary, October 7, 1939, and October 10, 1939, HHPL.
112. See, for example, Gross to Hoover, October 5, 1939, Herbert Hoover Papers, HHPL.
113. Hoover to Styles Bridges, October 11, 1939, ibid.

114. "Memorandum on Neutrality Bill Sent to Several Senators, Congressmen and Others," October 11, 1939, Herbert Hoover Special Collections: Articles, Addresses and Public Statements, 1915–1964, HHPL.
115. "News Reel Re: Embargo Repeal," October 11, 1939, ibid.
116. White to Hoover, October 11, 1939, William Allen White Papers, LC.
117. Hoover to Arthur Vandenberg, October 12, 1939, and Vandenberg to Hoover, October 13, 1939, Herbert Hoover Papers, HHPL.
118. Hoover to Vandenberg, October 17, 1939, Herbert Hoover Papers, HHPL.
119. Hoover to Castle, October 20, 1939, ibid.
120. "Neutrality Bill Broadcast," October 20, 1939, Herbert Hoover Special Collections: Articles, Addresses and Public Statements, 1915–1964, HHPL.
121. Edgar Rickard Diary, October 19, 1939, HHPL.
122. See, for example, Gross to Hoover, October 20, 1939, and Hoover to Gross, October 21, 1939, Herbert Hoover Papers, HHPL.
123. Edgar Rickard Diary, October 26, 1939, HHPL.
124. Hoover to Shaw, October 28, 1939, Herbert Hoover Papers, HHPL.
125. Knox to White, October 27, 1939, William Allen White Papers, LC.
126. Landon to White, October 30, 1939, ibid.
127. Castle to Hoover, November 8, 1939, and Hoover to Castle, November 10, 1939, William R. Castle Papers, HHPL.
128. Vandenberg to Hoover, November 6, 1939, Herbert Hoover Papers, HHPL.
129. Hoover to Vandenberg, November 7, 1939, ibid.
130. Hoover to O'Laughlin, November 6, 1939, John Callan O'Laughlin Papers, LC.
131. Edgar Rickard Diary, October 6, 1939, HHPL.
132. Alan Fox to Hoover, October 31, 1939, Herbert Hoover Papers, HHPL.
133. Fox to Larry Richey, November 3, 1939, ibid.
134. Daniel Willard to Hoover, November 3, 1939, and Hoover to Willard, November 19, 1939, ibid.
135. L. O. Hartman to Hoover, November 20, 1939, and Hoover to Hartman, November 26, 1939, Herbert Hoover Papers, Post-Presidential Subject File, Peace Proposal by Howard P. Davis, HHPL.
136. Howard Davis to Hoover, November 23, 1939, ibid.
137. Hoover to Kenneth Simpson, December 3, 1939, Herbert Hoover Papers, HHPL.
138. Hoover to Rickard, December 5, 1939, ibid.
139. "Interview—*Editor and Publisher*," December 23, 1939, Herbert Hoover Special Collections: Articles, Addresses and Public Statements, 1915–1964, HHPL.
140. *New York Times*, October 21, 1939.
141. Ibid., December 15, 1939.
142. Ibid.
143. *Newsweek*, December 15, 1939.
144. *Time*, December 18, 1939.
145. Edgar Rickard Diary, December 16, 1939, HHPL.
146. Ibid., December 31, 1939.
147. Ibid., January 3, 1940.
148. Hendrik Van Loon to Hoover, National Committee on Food for the Small Democracies Records (hereafter NCFSD Records), HI.
149. Hoover to Rickard, telegram, December 6, 1939, ibid.
150. *Time*, December 18, 1939.
151. "Interview—*Editor and Publisher*," December 23, 1939, Herbert Hoover Special Collections: Articles, Addresses and Public Statements, 1915–1964, HHPL.
152. Edgar Rickard Diary, December 15, 1939, HHPL.
153. Hoover to Risto Ryti, telegram, December 18, 1939, NCFSD Records, HI.
154. Hoover to Ryti, telegram, December 23, 1939, ibid.
155. Stephen Wise to Hoover, telegram, November 29, 1939, Herbert Hoover Papers, Post-Presidential Subject File, American Jewish Congress, HHPL.

156. Hoover to Wise, December 4, 1939, ibid.
157. Wise to Hoover, telegram, December 13, 1939, ibid.
158. Hyde to Hoover, December 15, 1939, Herbert Hoover Papers, HHPL.
159. See, for example, MacChesney to Monte Appel, December 15, 1939, and Appel to MacChesney, December 16, 1939, Nathan MacChesney Papers, HHPL.
160. Hoover to A. H. Kirchhofer, January 1, 1940, Herbert Hoover Papers, HHPL.
161. Hoover to Sewell Avery, November 4, 1939, ibid.
162. Jacob Allen to Hoover, telegrams, December 15 and 16, 1939, ibid.
163. Jacob Allen to Hoover, December 18, 1939, ibid.

Chapter 5

1. Robert Taft to Hoover, January 25, 1940, Herbert Hoover Papers, HHPL.
2. William P. Langer and S. Everett Gleason, *The Challenge to Isolation: The World Crisis of 1937–1940 and American Foreign Policy* (New York: Harper & Brothers, 1952), pp. 337–38.
3. Hoover to William Harbison, May 8, 1940, Herbert Hoover Papers, Post-Presidential Subject File, Food for the Small Democracies (Belgium, Holland, Poland, Denmark and Norway), HHPL.
4. Edgar Rickard Diary, January 3, 1940, HHPL.
5. Norman Davis to Hoover, January 17, 1940, NCFSD Records, HI.
6. "Press Statement on Ending of Finnish Russian War and Its Peace Terms," March 13, 1940, Herbert Hoover Special Collections; Articles, Addresses and Public Statements, 1915–1964, HHPL.
7. Hoover to Rickard, April 2, 1940, NCFSD Records, HI.
8. Hoover to committee members and state chairmen, April 13, 1940, ibid.
9. Lou Henry Hoover to Joel and Helen Boone, March 10, 1940, Lou Henry Hoover Papers, HHPL.
10. Lewis Strauss to Glenn Frank, January 19, 1940, Glenn Frank Papers, Pickler Memorial Library, Truman State University.
11. Arch Shaw to Hoover, January 29, 1940, Herbert Hoover Papers, HHPL.
12. Frank to Hoover, February 28, 1940, ibid.
13. Alan Fox to Hoover, February 1, 1940, ibid.
14. Hoover to Edward Lyman, February 24, 1940, and attachment, ibid.
15. Results from Lewis Strauss poll and Queens postcard poll, enclosed with Fox to Hoover, February 14, 1940, ibid.
16. William Gross to Hoover, February 16, 1940, ibid.
17. Reprinted in Herbert Hoover, *Further Addresses Upon the American Road, 1938–1940* (New York: Charles Scribner's Sons, 1940), pp. 69–81.
18. John G. Mott to Hoover, February 5, 1940, Herbert Hoover Papers, HHPL.
19. Hoover to Mott, February 8, 1940, ibid.
20. Harold Jones to David Ingalls, February 15, 1940, Robert A. Taft Papers, LC.
21. Undated memorandum, David Ingalls to John Henry, ibid.
22. *Washington Evening Star*, February 29, 1940; Edgar Rickard Diary, February 29, 1940, HHPL.
23. Edgar Rickard Diary, March 21, 1940, HHPL.
24. Hoover to Rickard, April 2, 1940, NCFSD Records, HI.
25. Edgar Rickard Diary, March 10, 1940, HHPL.
26. See, for example, Thomas Campbell to Hoover, April 5, 1940, Herbert Hoover Papers, HHPL.
27. Edgar Rickard Diary, April 9, 1940, HHPL.
28. William Starr Myers to Hoover, April 9, 1940, Herbert Hoover Papers, HHPL.
29. Edgar Rickard Diary, April 15, 1940, HHPL.
30. Ibid., April 17, 1940.
31. Hoover to Arthur Hyde, April 15, 1940, Herbert Hoover Papers, HHPL.
32. James Selvage to Gross, April 19, 1940, ibid.

33. Rickard to John Spargo, April 22, 1940, Spargo Papers, University of Vermont.
34. Orville Bullington to Larry Richey, May 30, 1940, Herbert Hoover Papers, HHPL.
35. Hoover to Walter Newton, May 11, 1940, ibid.
36. Memorandum, April 28, 1940, John Callan O'Laughlin Papers, LC.
37. Reprinted in Hoover, *Further Addresses*, pp. 158–71.
38. Arthur Vandenberg to Hoover, April 23, 1940, Herbert Hoover Papers, HHPL.
39. Hoover to Vandenberg, April 24, 1940, ibid.
40. See Herbert Hoover Papers, Post-Presidential Subject File, Food for the Small Democracies (Belgium, Holland, Poland, Denmark and Norway), HHPL.
41. W. K. Kellogg to Hoover, July 25, 1940, and Hoover to Kellogg, telegram, July 29, 1940, Herbert Hoover Papers, HHPL.
42. "Press Statement on Production for National Defense," May 17, 1940, Herbert Hoover Special Collections: Articles, Addresses and Public Statements, 1915–1964, HHPL.
43. Hoover to Joseph Martin, May 17, 1940, Herbert Hoover Papers, HHPL.
44. "National Defense," radio address, May 27, 1940, Herbert Hoover Special Collections: Articles, Addresses and Public Statements, 1915–1964, HHPL.
45. *New York Times*, May 29, 1940.
46. "Press Statement on Advisory Defense Commission," May 29, 1940, Herbert Hoover Special Collections: Articles, Addresses and Public Statements, 1915–1964, HHPL.
47. William Starr Myers Diary, May 29, 1940, William Starr Myers Papers, Princeton University.
48. Hoover to Arthur Free, May 29, 1940, Herbert Hoover Papers, HHPL.
49. *New York Times*, May 21, 1940.
50. Frank Knox to William Allen White, William Allen White Papers, LC.
51. Hoover to John Bricker, June 7, 1940, Herbert Hoover Papers, HHPL.
52. "The Nine Horsemen and America," published in *Liberty* magazine, June 5, 1940, Herbert Hoover Special Collections: Articles, Addresses and Public Statements, 1915–1964, HHPL.
53. Karl Mundt to Hoover, June 8, 1940, Herbert Hoover Papers, HHPL.
54. *San Francisco Chronicle*, June 26, 1940.
55. See, for example, Edgar Rickard Diary, April and May 1940, HHPL.
56. Ross Laird to Richey, May 24, 1940, Herbert Hoover Papers, HHPL.
57. Hoover to Newton, May 11, 1940, ibid.
58. Edgar Rickard Diary, May 26, 1940, HHPL.
59. Ibid., May 29 and May 31, 1940.
60. Ibid., May 29, May 31, and June 3, 1940.
61. Mark Sullivan to Hoover, May 2, 1940, and Hoover to Sullivan, May 3, 1940, Herbert Hoover Papers, HHPL.
62. Arthur B. Dunne to Taft, May 24, 1940, and Taft to Dunne, May 31, 1940, Robert A. Taft Papers, LC.
63. "Political Outlook for 1940," Opinion Research Corporation, May 21, 1940.
64. Edgar Rickard Diary, June 3, June 6, June 7, and June 10, 1940, HHPL.
65. Miles W. Jones to Hoover, June 8 and June 14, 1940, Herbert Hoover Papers, HHPL.
66. Hoover to Robert Simmons, June 7, 1940, ibid.
67. Alf Landon to Arthur Capper, June 5, 1940, Arthur Capper Papers, Kansas Historical Society.
68. Simmons to Hoover, June 7, 1940, Herbert Hoover Papers, HHPL.
69. *New York Times*, June 18, 1940.
70. Ibid., June 19, 1940.
71. Richey to Charles Tobey, telegram, May 20, 1940; Tobey to Hoover, May 23, 1940; Hoover to Tobey, May 24, 1940, Herbert Hoover Papers, HHPL.
72. *New York Times*, June 21, 1940.
73. "Press Statement on Cabinet Change," June 20, 1940, Herbert Hoover Special Collections: Articles, Addresses and Public Statements, 1915–1964, HHPL.
74. Press release, June 21, 1940, Hoover Papers, Post-Presidential Subject File, Campaign 1940, Polls, Fox, Allen, HHPL.

75. Hoover to Simmons, June 7, 1940, Herbert Hoover Papers, HHPL.
76. Christian Herter to Richey, June 11, 1940, and Edgar Queeny to Hoover, June 13, 1940, ibid.
77. Hoover to R. B. Creager, June 11, 1940, ibid.
78. See *New York Times*, June 13, June 16, and June 18, 1940.
79. Ibid., June 19, 1940.
80. Ibid., June 20, 1940.
81. Ibid., June 23, 1940.
82. Ibid., June 25, 1940.
83. Edgar Rickard Diary, June 13, 1940, HHPL.
84. *New York Times*, June 14, 1940.
85. *Editor and Publisher*, June 29, 1940.
86. Samuel F. Pryor interview by the author, July 9, 1980.
87. Reprinted in Herbert Hoover, *Addresses Upon the American Road, 1940–1941* (New York: Charles Scribner's Sons, 1941), pp. 205–23.
88. *New York Times*, June 26, 1940.
89. Ibid.
90. Ibid.
91. *Editor and Publisher*, June 29, 1940.
92. James Selvage interview, p. 25, Oral History Collection, HHPL.
93. Edgar Rickard Diary, June 28, 1940, HHPL.
94. Pryor, interview.
95. *New York Times*, June 26, 1940.
96. Ibid., June 27, 1940.
97. "Interview with the Press," June 26, 1940, Herbert Hoover Special Collections: Articles, Addresses and Public Statements, 1915–1964, HHPL.
98. Edgar Rickard Diary, June 27, 1940, HHPL.
99. *New York Times*, June 28, 1940.
100. Edgar Rickard Diary, June 28, 1940, HHPL.
101. John D. M. Hamilton interview, pp. 34–35, Oral History Collection, HHPL.
102. Donald R. McCoy, *Landon of Kansas* (Lincoln: University of Nebraska Press, 1966), p. 373.
103. Walter F. Brown to Hoover, July 1, 1940, Herbert Hoover Papers, HHPL.
104. John G. Mott to Hoover, July 11, 1940, ibid.
105. *New York Times*, July 1, 1940.
106. Hoover to Thomas Dewey, July 17, 1940, Herbert Hoover Papers, HHPL.
107. Hoover to Brown, July 26. 1940.
108. Edgar Rickard Diary, September 12, 1940, HHPL.
109. Memorandum of August 15, 1940, John Callan O'Laughlin Papers, LC.
110. Hoover to O'Laughlin, August 15, 1940, ibid.
111. Hoover to James Wright, August 19, 1940, Herbert Hoover Papers, HHPL; Edgar Rickard Diary, August 24, 1940, HHPL.
112. Hoover to Newton, August 26, 1940, Herbert Hoover Papers, HHPL; Edgar Rickard Diary, September 11, 1940, HHPL.
113. Hoover to Samuel Crowther, August 27, 1940, Herbert Hoover Papers, HHPL.
114. Hoover to O'Laughlin, August 5, 1940, John Callan O'Laughlin Papers, LC.
115. "Statement to the Press on Naval and Air Bases," September 4, 1940, Herbert Hoover Special Collections: Articles, Addresses and Public Statements, 1915–1964, HHPL.
116. Reprinted in Hoover, *Addresses, 1933–1938*, pp. 14–26.
117. *New York Times*, September 19, 1940.
118. Edgar Rickard Diary, September 20, 1940, HHPL.
119. Ibid., September 28, 1940.
120. O'Laughlin to Hoover, September 27, 1940, John Callan O'Laughlin Papers, LC.
121. Edgar Rickard Diary, September 29, 1940, HHPL.
122. Ibid., September 28, 1940.
123. Hoover to Gross, October 7, 1940, Herbert Hoover Papers, HHPL.

124. Hoover to O'Laughlin, October 11, 1940, John Callan O'Laughlin Papers, LC.
125. Reprinted in Hoover, *Addresses, 1933–1938*, pp. 224–39.
126. Mark Sullivan to Hoover, October 26, 1940, Herbert Hoover Papers, HHPL.
127. "Remarks on War-Trend of the Roosevelt Administration," as quoted by the *San Francisco News*, October 22, 1940, Herbert Hoover Special Collections: Articles, Addresses and Public Statements, 1915–1964, HHPL.
128. "Reply to President Roosevelt's Accusations on Armament and Defense," October 31, 1940, ibid.
129. Reprinted in Hoover, *Addresses, 1933–1938*, pp. 34–51.
130. Ibid., pp. 240–56.
131. Hoover to Sullivan, November 3, 1940, Herbert Hoover Papers, HHPL.
132. Hoover to Hugh Gibson, October 4, 1940, NCFSD Records, HI.
133. Edgar Rickard Diary, August 20, 1940, HHPL.
134. White to Hoover, October 24, 1940, William Allen White Papers, LC.
135. *Commonweal*, November 29, 1940.
136. Hoover to Kenneth Wherry, November 4, 1940, Herbert Hoover Papers, HHPL; Edgar Rickard Diary, November 6, 1940, HHPL.
137. Hoover to Mrs. Harold Brunson, November 7, 1940, filed with Robert Simmons correspondence, Herbert Hoover Papers, HHPL.
138. Hoover to Gross, November 7, 1940, ibid.
139. Hoover to Sullivan, November 9, 1940, Herbert Hoover Papers, Post-Presidential Subject File, Campaign 1940, Candidates, Willkie, HHPL.
140. "Press Statement on Election of Mr. Roosevelt and Mr. Wallace," November 7, 1940, Herbert Hoover Special Collections: Articles, Addresses and Public Statements, 1915–1964, HHPL.
141. "Press Remarks against Centralization in the National Government," as quoted by the *San Francisco Chronicle*, November 11, 1940, ibid.
142. Edgar Rickard Diary, November 14, 1940, HHPL.

Chapter 6

1. Edgar Rickard Diary, November 16, 1940, HHPL.
2. Ibid., November 21, 1940.
3. Hoover to John G. Mott, November 27, 1940, Herbert Hoover Papers, HHPL.
4. Edgar Rickard Diary, December 4, 1940, HHPL.
5. Hoover to Bison, November 29, 1940, NCFSD Records, HI.
6. See correspondence for November and December 1940 in ibid.
7. Hoover to John Callan O'Laughlin, telegram, December 3, 1940, and O'Laughlin to Hoover, December 5, 1940, John Callan O'Laughlin Papers, LC.
8. Hoover to William Castle, December 20, 1940, NCFSD Records, HI.
9. Memorandum of a meeting with Joseph Kennedy, November 22, 1940, Herbert Hoover Papers, HHPL.
10. Hoover to R. Douglas Stuart, December 6, 1940, Herbert Hoover Papers, Post-Presidential Subject File, America First Committee, HHPL.
11. Hoover to Robert Taft, January 6, 1940, Herbert Hoover Papers, HHPL.
12. Reprinted in Herbert Hoover, *Addresses Upon the American Road, 1940–1941* (New York: Charles Scribner's Sons, 1941), pp. 55–62.
13. William Allen White to Ray Lyman Wilbur, January 17, 1940, William Allen White Papers, LC.
14. Reprinted in Hoover, *Addresses, 1940–1941*, pp. 63–65.
15. Ibid.
16. Hoover to Taft, January 6, 1941, Herbert Hoover Papers, HHPL.
17. Hoover to Walter Newton, January 25, 1941, ibid.
18. Hoover to Robert E. Wood, January 14, 1941, ibid.

19. Donald R. McCoy, *Landon of Kansas* (Lincoln: University of Nebraska Press, 1966), pp. 456–57.
20. Raymond Clapper to Alf Landon, January 16, 1941, and Landon to Clapper, January 20, 1941, Alf M. Landon Papers, Kansas Historical Society.
21. John Spargo to Hoover, January 16, 1941, Herbert Hoover Papers, HHPL.
22. Hoover to Arthur Vandenberg, January 24, 1941, Herbert Hoover Archives, HI.
23. Vandenberg to Hoover, January 27, 1941, ibid.
24. Hoover to O'Laughlin, January 26, 1941, John Callan O'Laughlin Papers, LC.
25. William Gross to Hoover, telegram, November 8, 1940, Herbert Hoover Papers, HHPL.
26. "Press Remarks against Centralization in the National Government," as quoted by the *San Francisco Chronicle*, November 11, 1940, Herbert Hoover Special Collections: Articles, Addresses and Public Statements, 1915–1964, HHPL.
27. Ben Allen to Hoover, November 13, 1940, Herbert Hoover Papers, HHPL.
28. Kenneth Wherry to Hoover, November 19, 1940, ibid.
29. Herbert Clark to Hoover, November 26, 1940, and Hoover to Clark, November 28, 1940, ibid.
30. See, for example, Arthur Capper to Landon, January 23, 1941, and February 1, 1941, Alf M. Landon Papers, Kansas Historical Society.
31. Landon to Capper, January 4, 1941, ibid.
32. Taft to Landon, telegram, February 5, 1941, ibid.
33. O'Laughlin to Hoover, February 24, 1941, John Callan O'Laughlin Papers, LC.
34. Edgar Rickard Diary, January 31, 1941, HHPL.
35. Hoover to O'Laughlin, February 18, 1941, John Callan O'Laughlin Papers, LC.
36. Taft to Hoover, February 25, 1941, Herbert Hoover Papers, HHPL.
37. Hoover to Castle, March 1, 1941, ibid.
38. Castle to Hoover, April 19, 1941, William R. Castle Papers, HHPL.
39. *An Act to Further Promote the Defense of the United States*, Public Law 77-11, U.S. Statutes at Large 55 (1941) 31–33.
40. Memorandum to Hoover from William H. Tuck, January 24, 1941, William Hallam Tuck Papers, HHPL.
41. Hoover to Hendrik Van Loon, February 21, 1941, NCFSD Records, HI.
42. Hoover to O'Laughlin, February 23, 1941, John Callan O'Laughlin Papers, LC.
43. O'Laughlin to Hoover, February 24, 1941, ibid.
44. Jay Darling to Mark Sullivan, April 2, 1941, and Sullivan to Hoover, April 9, 1941, Herbert Hoover Papers, HHPL.
45. Reprinted in Hoover, *Addresses, 1940–1941*, pp. 147–55.
46. Memorandum of a meeting with Cordell Hull, February 28, 1941, Herbert Hoover Papers, HHPL.
47. Edgar Rickard Diary, February 28, 1941, HHPL.
48. Ibid., March 7, 1941.
49. "Press Release—Rejoinder to British Embassy Note," March 10, 1941, Herbert Hoover Special Collections: Articles, Addresses and Public Statements, Appendix, HHPL.
50. Edgar Rickard Diary, March 25, 1941, HHPL.
51. Memorandum of a meeting with Sir Gerald Campbell, March 26, 1941, Herbert Hoover Papers, HHPL.
52. Hoover to Hull, March 27, 1941, ibid.
53. Edgar Rickard Diary, March 28, March 31, April 10, and April 25, 1941, HHPL.
54. *The Nation*, May 3, 1941.
55. Hoover to O'Laughlin, March 9, 1941, John Callan O'Laughlin Papers, LC.
56. Landon to Franklyn Waltman, March 21, 1941, Alf M. Landon Papers, Kansas Historical Society.
57. Hoover to Castle, March 20, 1941, William R. Castle Papers, HHPL.
58. Reprinted in Hoover, *Addresses, 1940–1941*, pp. 66–76.
59. Hoover to Samuel Crowther, April 1, 1941, Herbert Hoover Papers, HHPL.
60. Hoover to Ben Allen, April 2, 1941, ibid.

61. Hoover to Arthur Hyde, April 5, 1941, ibid.
62. Hoover to O'Laughlin and enclosed copy of a letter to an undisclosed recipient, April 7, 1941, John Callan O'Laughlin Papers, LC.
63. "A Survey—the American Scene Today," undated memorandum by Hoover, copy enclosed with Robert Richardson to O'Laughlin, May 26, 1941, John Callan O'Laughlin Papers, LC.
64. Hoover to Charles Tobey, May 9, 1941, Herbert Hoover Papers, HHPL.
65. Reprinted in Hoover, *Addresses, 1940–1941*, pp. 77–86.
66. Charles Dawes to Hoover, telegram, May 12, 1941, Herbert Hoover Papers, HHPL.
67. Alexander Wiley to Hoover, May 13, 1941, ibid.
68. Raymond Moley to Hoover, May 17, 1941, ibid.
69. Robert Wood to Hoover, May 26, 1941, Herbert Hoover Papers, Post-Presidential Subject File, America First Committee, HHPL.
70. *New York Times*, June 23, 1941.
71. Address by Robert Taft broadcast over CBS, June 25, 1941, release copy in Herbert Hoover Papers, HHPL.
72. Reprinted in Hoover, *Addresses, 1940–1941*, pp. 87–102.
73. Memorandum of a conversation with Truman Smith, June 1, 1941, Herbert Hoover Papers, HHPL.
74. *New York Times*, July 1, 1941.
75. Address by Alf Landon broadcast over CBS, July 20, 1941, release copy in Herbert Hoover Papers, HHPL.
76. Hoover to O'Laughlin, June 26, 1941, John Callan O'Laughlin Papers, LC.
77. Hoover to Hyde, June 6, 1941, Herbert Hoover Papers, HHPL.
78. Hoover to Joseph Scott, August 27, 1941, ibid.
79. Hoover to Ben Allen, June 4, 1941, ibid.
80. Hoover to Hull, June 3, 1941, ibid.
81. Hull to Hoover, June 28, 1941, ibid.
82. Paul D. Boone to Landon, May 28, 1941, Alf M. Landon Papers, Kansas Historical Society.
83. Frank Knox to Landon, "received June 11, 1941," ibid.
84. Landon to Knox, June 16, 1941, ibid.
85. Hoover to Landon, June 27, 1941, Herbert Hoover Papers, HHPL.
86. Robert Hutchins to Hoover, telegram, June 29, 1941, ibid.
87. Landon to Hoover, July 7, 1941, and Hoover to Landon, telegram, July 12, 1941, ibid.
88. Landon to Hoover, July 25, 1941, ibid.
89. Joseph Kennedy to Hoover, telegram, July 29, 1941, and Landon to Hoover, telegram, July 29, 1941, ibid.
90. Landon to Hoover, August 4, 1941, ibid.
91. *New York Times*, August 6, 1941.
92. Arch Shaw to Hoover, telegram, June 30, 1941, Herbert Hoover Papers, HHPL.
93. Hoover to Fulton Lewis Jr., July 1, 1941, ibid.
94. Taft to Hoover, July 3, 1941, ibid.
95. Edgar Rickard Diary, June 30, 1941, HHPL.
96. Hoover to Boake Carter, July 14, 1941, Herbert Hoover Papers, HHPL.
97. Hoover to Roy Woodruff, July 13, 1941, ibid.
98. Hoover to Taft, July 14, 1941, and Hoover to J. William Ditter, July 14, 1941, ibid.
99. Taft to Hoover, July 16, 1941, ibid.
100. Woodruff to Hoover, July 18, 1941, ibid.
101. Robert Wood to Hoover, August 21, 1921, ibid.
102. Wendell Willkie to White, August 29, 1941, and White to Willkie, September 4, 1941, William Allen White Papers, LC.
103. Edgar Rickard Diary, July 27, 1941, HHPL.
104. Harrison Spangler to Hoover, September 11, 1941, Herbert Hoover Papers, HHPL.
105. Hoover to Spangler, September 17, 1941, ibid.
106. Broadcast of July 20, 1941, Alf M. Landon Papers, Kansas Historical Society.

107. Hoover to Castle, July 23, 1941, Herbert Hoover Papers, HHPL.
108. Hoover to Castle, September 4, 1941, ibid.
109. Reprinted in Hoover, *Addresses, 1940–1941*, pp. 103–14.
110. Chester Bowles to Hoover, September 17, 1941, Herbert Hoover Papers, HHPL.
111. Edgar Rickard Diary, October 21, 1941, HHPL.
112. Hoover to John G. Mott, September 12, 1941, Herbert Hoover Papers, HHPL.
113. Hoover to Joseph Scott, September 14, 1941, ibid.
114. Hoover to Charles Teague, September 22, 1941, General Accessions: Teague, Charles, HHPL.
115. "Statement about the results of a questionnaire on national defense question answered by Stanford University faculty members," October 1, 1941, Herbert Hoover Special Collections: Articles, Addresses and Public Statements, Appendix, HHPL.
116. Karl Mundt to Hoover, October 20, 1941, Herbert Hoover Papers, HHPL.
117. Hoover to Mundt, October 21, 1941, ibid.
118. Hoover to Vandenberg, October 29, 1941, Herbert Hoover Archives, HI.
119. Vandenberg to Hoover, October 31, 1941, ibid.
120. Hoover to Wesley Stout, telegram, September 17, 1941, Herbert Hoover Papers, Post-Presidential Subject File, *Saturday Evening Post*.
121. "The First American Crusade," published in the *Saturday Evening Post*, November 1, 8, and 15, 1941, Herbert Hoover Special Collections: Articles, Addresses and Public Statements, 1915–1964, HHPL.
122. Mundt to Hoover, October 30, 1941, Herbert Hoover Papers, HHPL.
123. Julius Klein to Ernest Klein, November 3, 1941, Julius Klein Papers, HI.
124. Hoover to Wallace White, November 5, 1941, Herbert Hoover Papers, HHPL.
125. "Shall We Send Armies to Europe? And A Way to National Unity," address before the Union League Club, Chicago, November 19, 1941, Herbert Hoover Special Collections: Articles, Addresses and Public Statements, 1915–1964, HHPL.
126. Hoover to O'Laughlin, February 8, 1938, John Callan O'Laughlin Papers, LC.
127. Hoover to O'Laughlin, July 31, 1939, ibid.
128. Hoover to O'Laughlin, August 5, 1940, ibid.
129. Castle to Hoover, undated but July 1941, Herbert Hoover Papers, HHPL.
130. Hoover to O'Laughlin, August 30, 1941, John Callan O'Laughlin Papers, LC.
131. Hoover to Taft, August 3, 1941, Herbert Hoover Papers, HHPL.
132. Hoover to Castle, September 4, 1941, ibid.
133. Hoover to O'Laughlin, September 6, 1941, John Callan O'Laughlin Papers, LC.
134. Hoover to O'Laughlin, November 16, 1941, ibid.
135. Bowles to Hoover, November 29, 1941, Herbert Hoover Papers, HHPL.
136. Hoover to Bowles, November 29, 1941, ibid.
137. "The Desvernine Incident," entry for November 23, 1941, filed in Herbert Hoover Papers, Post-Presidential Subject File, Pearl Harbor, Hoover Diary of Events, HHPL. See also, in the same file, Hoover's memorandum of February 10, 1942.
138. Ibid., November 29, 1941.
139. Ibid., November 30 and December 1, 1941. According to Baruch's memoirs, it was Raymond Moley who phoned him to arrange the meeting with Desvernine. See Bernard Baruch, *Baruch: The Public Years* (New York: Holt Rinehart Winston, 1960), pp. 288–91.
140. Entry for December 2, 3, 4, and 5, 1941, Post-Presidential Subject File, Pearl Harbor, Hoover Diary of Events, HHPL.
141. Robert Sherrill, "Backdoor to War," *Inquiry*, May 14, 1979, pp. 25–27.

Chapter 7

1. John D. M. Hamilton interview, p. 25, Oral History Collection, HHPL.
2. Hoover to Robert Taft, December 8, 1941, Herbert Hoover Papers, HHPL.
3. Hoover to William Castle, December 8, 1941, William R. Castle Papers, HHPL.

4. Hoover to Taft, December 8, 1941, Herbert Hoover Papers, HHPL.
5. "Statement to the Press—Japanese Attack on Pearl Harbor," December 8, 1941, Herbert Hoover Special Collections: Articles, Addresses and Public Statements, 1915–1964, HHPL.
6. Hoover to Boake Carter, December 11, 1941, Herbert Hoover Papers, HHPL.
7. Taft to Hoover, January 3, 1942, ibid.
8. Memorandum, April 26, 1945, filed in Herbert Hoover Papers, Post-Presidential Subject File, Food, World Wars I & II, Food Prices, Conservation and Consumption, HHPL.
9. Alf Landon to Hoover, January 9, 1941, Alf M. Landon Papers, Kansas Historical Society.
10. Hoover to John Callan O'Laughlin, January 19, 1941, John Callan O'Laughlin Papers, LC.
11. A. E. Bowman to Hoover, February 18, 1942, filed in Herbert Hoover Papers, Post-Presidential Subject File, Food, World Wars I & II, Correspondence, HHPL.
12. Hoover to Bowman, March 7, 1942, ibid.
13. Landon to Raymond Springer, January 13, 1942, Alf M. Landon Papers, Kansas Historical Society.
14. Hoover to Herbert Clark, December 19, 1941, and Hoover to Ruth Simms, December 18, 1941, Herbert Hoover Papers, HHPL.
15. Taft to Hoover, January 3, 1942, ibid.
16. Hoover to Wallace Meyer, November 21, 1941, Herbert Hoover Papers, Post-Presidential Subject File, Charles Scribner's Sons, HHPL.
17. Whitney Darrow to Hoover, December 23, 1941, ibid.
18. Hoover to Darrow, December 29, 1941, ibid.
19. Hoover to Raymond Moley, January 17, 1942, Herbert Hoover Papers, HHPL.
20. Hoover to Clarence Kelland, January 19, 1942, ibid.
21. Lou Henry Hoover to Florence Stewart, June 24, 1942, Lou Henry Hoover Papers, HHPL.
22. Raymond Moley to Hoover, January 15, 1942, Herbert Hoover Papers, HHPL.
23. William Barrett to Hoover, January 12, 1942, ibid.
24. Taft to Hoover, January 3, 1942, ibid.
25. Hoover to O'Laughlin, January 19, 1942, John Callan O'Laughlin Papers, LC.
26. Hoover to William Mitchell, January 27, 1942, Herbert Hoover Papers, HHPL.
27. Hoover to Edward Borchard, January 30, 1942, ibid.
28. Hoover to W. K. Kellogg, January 17, 1942, ibid.
29. Chester Bowles to Hoover, September 17, 1941, ibid.
30. Bowles to Hoover, November 28, 1941, ibid.
31. Hoover to Kellogg, January 7, 1942, ibid.; Edgar Rickard Diary, December 30, 1941, HHPL.
32. Hoover to Allen Dulles, January 21, 1942, Herbert Hoover Papers, Post-Presidential Subject File, Council on Foreign Relations, HHPL.
33. Dulles to Hoover, February 2, 1942, ibid.
34. Hoover to Richard Lloyd Jones, February 18, 1942, Herbert Hoover Papers, HHPL.
35. Hoover to Jones, February 26, 1942, ibid.
36. Hoover to O'Laughlin, February 24, 1942, John Callan O'Laughlin Papers, LC.
37. O'Laughlin to Hoover, February 25, 1942, ibid.
38. For example, Hoover to Landon, February 16, 1942, Alf M. Landon Papers, Kansas Historical Society.
39. Clipping with Hoover to Landon, February 16, 1942, ibid.
40. Collady to Landon, February 25, 1942, ibid.
41. Taft to Hoover, February 24, 1942, Herbert Hoover Papers, HHPL; Landon to Taft, March 3, 1942, Alf M. Landon Papers, Kansas Historical Society.
42. Landon to Hoover, March 7, 1942, Alf M. Landon Papers, Kansas Historical Society.
43. Hoover to Mrs. Ogden Reid, March 10, 1942, Herbert Hoover Papers, HHPL.
44. Raymond Clapper to Landon, June 15, 1942, Alf M. Landon Papers, Kansas Historical Society.
45. Landon to Clapper, July 7, 1942, ibid.
46. Hoover to O'Laughlin, March 30, 1942, John Callan O'Laughlin Papers, LC.
47. Hoover to Hugh Gibson, telegram, April 11, 1942, Hugh Gibson Papers, HI.
48. Gibson to Perrin Galpin, April 16, 1942, NCFSD Records, HI.

49. Hoover to Ray Lyman Wilbur, March 28, 1942, Herbert Hoover Papers, HHPL.
50. "Report of Committee on Resolutions," filed with Taft correspondence, ibid.
51. Hoover to O'Laughlin, April 22, 1942, John Callan O'Laughlin Papers, LC.
52. "Report of Committee on Resolutions," filed with Taft correspondence, Herbert Hoover Papers, HHPL.
53. Reprinted in Herbert Hoover, *Addresses Upon the American Road, 1941–1945* (New York: Van Nostrand, 1945), pp. 160–71.
54. Arthur Capper to Hoover, May 22, 1942, Herbert Hoover Papers, HHPL.
55. Albert Wedemeyer interview, pp. 5–6, Oral History Collection, HHPL.
56. Taft to Hoover, May 15, 1942, Herbert Hoover Papers, HHPL.
57. Hoover to Landon, May 29, 1942, Alf M. Landon Papers, Kansas Historical Society.
58. O'Laughlin to Hoover, May 21, 1942, John Callan O'Laughlin Papers, LC.
59. Capper to Hoover, May 22, 1942, Herbert Hoover Papers, HHPL.
60. Landon to Hoover, June 2, 1942, and Hoover to Landon, June 5, 1942, Alf M. Landon Papers, Kansas Historical Society.
61. Edgar Rickard Diary, April 26, 1942, HHPL.
62. Ibid., May 2, 1942.
63. Hoover to O'Laughlin, June 5, 1942, John Callan O'Laughlin Papers, LC.
64. "An Interesting Parallel," Herbert Hoover Papers, Post-Presidential Subject File, Welles, Sumner, HHPL.
65. Hoover to Robert Wood, June 10, 1942, Herbert Hoover Papers, HHPL.
66. Wood to Hoover, June 15, 1942, ibid.
67. Edgar Rickard Diary, June 23, 1942, HHPL.
68. Ibid., June 24, 1942.
69. Lou Henry Hoover to Florence Stewart, June 24, 1942, Lou Henry Hoover Papers, HHPL.
70. Hoover to O'Laughlin, May 19 and June 9, 1942, John Callan O'Laughlin Papers, LC.
71. Hoover to O'Laughlin, June 9, 1942, ibid.
72. Hoover to Landon, June 2, 1942, Herbert Hoover Papers, HHPL.
73. Edgar Rickard Diary, July 9, 1942, HHPL.
74. Hoover to Taft, July 9, 1942, Herbert Hoover Papers, HHPL.
75. Hoover to Stanley Washburn, July 13, 1942, ibid.
76. *Time*, July 6, 1942.
77. Herbert Hoover and Hugh Gibson, *The Problems of Lasting Peace* (New York: Doubleday, Doran and Co., 1942).
78. See, for example, William Allen White to Capper, June 16, 1942, Arthur Capper Papers, Kansas Historical Society, and White to James Wadsworth, June 16, 1942, William Allen White Papers, LC.
79. White to Landon, July 10, 1942, William Allen White Papers, LC.
80. Capper to White, June 26, 1942, Arthur Capper Papers, Kansas Historical Society; Taft to Hoover, July 14, 1942, Herbert Hoover Papers, HHPL.
81. Hoover to Taft, July 19, 1942, Herbert Hoover Papers, HHPL.
82. Leon Stoltz to Chauncey McCormick, May 26, 1942, Herbert Hoover Papers, HHPL.
83. Harold Burton to Hoover, August 14, 1942, Herbert Hoover Papers, HHPL; Burton to Hugh Gibson, August 14, 1942, Hugh Gibson Papers, HI.
84. Burton to Hoover, August 31, 1942, Herbert Hoover Papers, HHPL.
85. *New York Times*, June 21, 1942.
86. Hoover to Gibson, July 18, 1942, Hugh Gibson Papers, HI.
87. Hoover to Julius Klein, July 31, 1942, Julius Klein Papers, HI.
88. White to Hoover, August 4, 1942, Herbert Hoover Papers, HHPL.
89. Hoover to O'Laughlin, March 10, 1942, John Callan O'Laughlin Papers, LC.
90. Hoover to O'Laughlin, March 30, 1942, ibid.
91. Edgar Rickard Diary, April 26, 1942, HHPL.
92. Hoover to O'Laughlin, April 10, 1942, John Callan O'Laughlin Papers, LC.
93. Hoover to Philip Bancroft, September 4, 1942, Herbert Hoover Papers, HHPL.
94. Hoover to O'Laughlin, August 3, 1942, John Callan O'Laughlin Papers, LC.

95. Hoover to Arch Shaw, September 12, 1942, Herbert Hoover Papers, HHPL.
96. Hoover to Arthur Sulzberger, September 12, 1942, ibid.
97. Hoover to Taft, August 3, 1942, ibid.
98. Hoover to Taft, August 22, 1942, ibid.
99. Taft to Hoover, September 1, 1942, ibid.
100. Hoover to Shaw, August 19, 1942, ibid.
101. Hoover to Gibson, August 20, 1942, Hugh Gibson Papers, HI.
102. Hoover to O'Laughlin, August 24, 1942, John Callan O'Laughlin Papers, LC.
103. Landon to Hoover, October 13, 1942, Alf M. Landon Papers, Kansas Historical Society.
104. Hoover to O'Laughlin, October 26, 1942, John Callan O'Laughlin Papers, LC.
105. "Statement to the Press," November 4, 1942, Herbert Hoover Special Collections: Articles, Addresses and Public Statements, 1915–1964, HHPL.
106. Hoover to Joseph Martin, November 6, 1942, Herbert Hoover Papers, HHPL.
107. Hoover to Robert Simmons, November 9, 1942, ibid.
108. Hoover to Castle, December 1, 1942, ibid.
109. Edgar Rickard Diary, November 23, November 24, and November 25, 1942, HHPL; Hoover to Herbert Lehman, November 24, 1942, Herbert Hoover Papers, HHPL.
110. Edgar Rickard Diary, December 3, 1942, HHPL; Hoover to Lehman, November 25, 1942, Herbert Hoover Papers, HHPL.
111. Memorandum, December 3, 1942, filed with Lehman correspondence, Herbert Hoover Papers, HHPL.
112. *New York Times*, December 3, 1942.
113. Norman Thomas to Hoover, November 27, 1943, Herbert Hoover Papers, HHPL.
114. Hoover to Wilbur, December 13, 1942, Ray Lyman Wilbur Papers, HI.
115. Edgar Rickard Diary, November 5, November 7, and November 18, 1942, HHPL.
116. White to Hoover, November 30, 1942, Herbert Hoover Papers, HHPL; Landon to White, November 30, 1942, William Allen White Papers, LC.
117. William Hutchinson to Landon, November 30, 1942, Alf M. Landon Papers, Kansas Historical Society; Hoover to White, December 2, 1942, Herbert Hoover Papers, HHPL.
118. Hoover to McCormick, November 10, 1942, Herbert Hoover Papers, HHPL.
119. See, for example, Ellsworth Barnard, *Wendell Willkie: Fighter for Freedom* (Marquette: Northern Michigan University Press, 1966), pp. 382–84; Edgar Rickard Diary, December 11, 1942, HHPL.
120. Walter Brown to Taft, December 9, 1942, Brown Papers, Ohio Historical Society.
121. Hoover to White, December 9, 1942, Herbert Hoover Papers, HHPL.
122. Hoover to Wilbur, December 13, 1942, Ray Lyman Wilbur Papers, HI.
123. Taft to Brown, December 17, 1942, Brown Papers, Ohio Historical Society.
124. Barnard, *Wendell Willkie*, p. 384.
125. *New York Times*, December 17, 1942.
126. Wendell Willkie to Hoover, telegram, December 17, 1942, Herbert Hoover Papers, HHPL.
127. Hoover to Willkie, December 20, 1942, ibid.
128. Hoover to Landon, December 21, 1942, Alf M. Landon Papers, Kansas Historical Society.
129. White to Landon, December 28, 1942, William Allen White Papers, LC.
130. Hoover to Walter Lippmann, December 23, 1942, Herbert Hoover Papers, HHPL.
131. O'Laughlin to Hoover, December 19, 1942, John Callan O'Laughlin Papers, LC.
132. Hoover to White, January 5, 1943, Herbert Hoover Papers, HHPL.
133. White to Hoover, January 5, 1943, ibid.
134. Landon to Hoover, January 7, 1943, ibid.
135. Harrison Spangler to White, January 7, 1943, William Allen White Papers, LC.
136. Edgar Rickard Diary, January 6, 1943, HHPL.
137. Reprinted in Hoover, *Addresses, 1941–1945*, pp. 179–95.
138. Taft to Hoover, January 12, 1943, Robert A. Taft Papers, LC.
139. Hoover to Castle, January 17, 1943, Herbert Hoover Papers, HHPL.
140. *New York Times*, January 15, 1943.
141. Hoover to Shaw, January 15, 1943, Herbert Hoover Papers, HHPL.

142. Hoover to O'Laughlin, January 18, 1943, John Callan O'Laughlin Papers, LC.
143. "Food Supplies for this War," address before the National Industrial Conference Board, January 21, 1943, Herbert Hoover Special Collections: Articles, Addresses and Public Statements, 1915–1964, HHPL.
144. Edgar Rickard Diary, January 21, 1943, HHPL.
145. Hoover to Kent Cooper, January 6, 1943, Herbert Hoover Papers, HHPL.
146. Memorandum, January 8, 1943, filed with Halifax correspondence, ibid.
147. Edgar Rickard Diary, January 9, 1943, HHPL.
148. Hoover to O'Laughlin, January 10, 1943, John Callan O'Laughlin Papers, LC.
149. Taft to Hoover, January 12, 1943, Herbert Hoover Papers, HHPL.
150. Landon to Hoover, January 12, 1943, with enclosed memorandum, and Hoover to Landon, January 19, 1943, ibid.
151. Hoover to Martin, January 12, 1943, ibid.
152. Hugh Butler to Hoover, January 14, January 23, and January 30, 1943, ibid.; Edgar Rickard Diary, January 30, 1943, HHPL.
153. Castle to Hoover, February 10, 1943, Herbert Hoover Papers, HHPL.
154. Hoover to Martin, January 18, 1943, ibid.
155. William A. Baker to Hoover, November 18, 1942, ibid.
156. Hoover to Castle, January 17, 1943, ibid.
157. Hoover to Martin, January 19, 1943, ibid.
158. Memorandum, "Civilian Organization in War," filed with Martin correspondence, ibid.
159. Martin to Hoover, January 20, 1943, ibid.
160. See, for example, Hoover to George Aiken, January 31, 1943, ibid.
161. Hoover to Hugh Butler, January 31, 1943, and Butler to Hoover, February 3, 1943, ibid.; Edgar Rickard Diary, February 3, 1943, HHPL.
162. White to Hoover, February 5, 1943, Herbert Hoover Papers, HHPL.
163. *New York Times*, February 8, 1943.
164. Ibid., February 9, 1943.
165. Ibid.
166. Wickard to Hoover, telegram, February 6, 1943, and Hoover to Wickard, two telegrams, February 6, 1943, Herbert Hoover Papers, HHPL.
167. Taft to Hoover, February 7, 1943, and Hoover to Norman Thomas, February 15, 1943, ibid.
168. Frederick Libby to Hoover, February 15, 1943, and Thomas to Hoover, February 16, 1943, ibid.
169. Edgar Rickard Diary, February 9, 1943, HHPL.
170. *New York Times*, February 14, 1943.
171. Hoover to O'Laughlin, February 21, 1943, John Callan O'Laughlin Papers, LC.
172. O'Laughlin to Hoover, March 2, 1943, ibid.
173. Spangler to Landon, February 20, 1943, Alf M. Landon Papers, Kansas Historical Society.
174. Spangler to Landon, February 26, 1943, ibid.
175. White to Charles McNary, March 18, 1943, and White to Harold Stassen, March 18, 1943, William Allen White Papers, LC.
176. Harold Burton to Hoover, March 19, 1943, Herbert Hoover Papers, HHPL.
177. Ibid., copy of the resolution enclosed.
178. Hoover to Burton, March 23, 1943, ibid.
179. Arthur Vandenberg, ed., *The Private Papers of Senator Vandenberg* (Boston: Houghton Mifflin, 1952), pp. 41–43, 47.
180. Hoover to White, March 23, 1943, and White to Hoover, March 29, 1943, Herbert Hoover Papers, HHPL.
181. *New York Times*, March 16, 1943.
182. Ibid., March 23, 1943.
183. Ibid., April 4, 1943.
184. Castle to Hoover, March 22, 1943, Bernice Miller to Castle, telegram, March 24, 1943, and Castle to Hoover, March 25, 1943, Herbert Hoover Papers, HHPL.
185. Hoover to William Barrett, March 17, 1943, ibid.

186. Castle to Hoover, April 19, 1943, ibid.
187. Hoover to White, March 31, 1943, ibid.
188. White to [addressees not given], April 2, 1943, copy filed with White correspondence, ibid.
189. Landon to Hoover, March 26, 1943, Alf M. Landon Papers, Kansas Historical Society.
190. Hoover to Landon, March 29, 1943, ibid.
191. Landon to Hoover, April 3, 1943, ibid.
192. Wendell Willkie, *One World* (New York: Simon and Schuster, 1943), pp. 85–87.
193. Ibid., pp. 177–78.
194. Landon to John O'Donnell, May 8, 1943, and John Henry to Landon, May 8, 1943, Alf M. Landon Papers, Kansas Historical Society.
195. Hoover to Castle, April 24, 1943, Herbert Hoover Papers, HHPL.
196. Lehman to Hoover, March 4, 1943, ibid.
197. Hoover to Lehman, March 17, 1943, ibid.
198. White to Landon, May 11, 1943, William Allen White Papers, LC.
199. Hoover to Landon, telegram, May 15, 1943, Alf M. Landon Papers, Kansas Historical Society.
200. White to Roger Straus, May 15, 1943, William Allen White Papers, LC.
201. Landon to James Wright, March 29, 1943, Alf M. Landon Papers, Kansas Historical Society.
202. Spangler to Landon, May 29, 1943, ibid.
203. White to Spangler, April 6, 1941, William Allen White Papers, LC.
204. See Landon to Hoover, June 8, 1943, and Landon to O'Donnell, May 8, 1943, Alf M. Landon Papers, Kansas Historical Society.
205. Edgar Rickard Diary, May 27 and June 17, 1943, HHPL; Hoover to Earl Warren, June 9, 1943, Herbert Hoover Papers, HHPL.
206. Vandenberg, *Private Papers*, p. 54.
207. *New York Times*, June 11, 1943.
208. Chester Davis to Hoover, June 12, 1943, Herbert Hoover Papers, HHPL.
209. Hoover to Davis, June 19, 1943, ibid.
210. Hoover to Sam D. Goza, July 15, 1943, ibid.
211. Hoover to Kelland, July 21, 1943, ibid.
212. Hamilton to Hoover, August 2, 1943, ibid.
213. Albert Hawkes to Hoover, August 12, 1943, ibid.
214. H. Alexander Smith to Warren Austin, August 5, 1943, Warren Austin Papers, University of Vermont.
215. Ibid., draft of August 4, 1943, enclosed.
216. Austin to Fred Howland, August 7, 1943, ibid.
217. Austin to Vandenberg, August 19, 1943, ibid.
218. Edgar Rickard Diary, August 24, 1943, HHPL.
219. Hoover to John Bricker, August 30, 1943, Herbert Hoover Papers, HHPL.

Chapter 8

1. John Callan O'Laughlin to Hoover, June 5, 1942, John Callan O'Laughlin Papers, LC.
2. Hoover to Arthur Vandenberg, August 31, 1943, and Hoover to Warren Austin, same date, Herbert Hoover Papers, HHPL.
3. Reprinted in Herbert Hoover, *Addresses Upon the American Road, 1941–1945* (New York: Van Nostrand, 1945), pp. 71–94.
4. Hoover to Arch Shaw, telegram, September 8, 1943, Herbert Hoover Papers, HHPL.
5. Hoover to Charles Hebbard, April 6, 1943, ibid.
6. Chauncey McCormick to Hoover, September 8, 1943, ibid.
7. *New York Times*, September 3, 1943.
8. Printed in *Tennessee Republican Age* (February/March 1944), pp. 16–18.
9. Robert A. Divine, *Second Chance: The Triumph of Internationalism in America During World War II* (New York: Atheneum, 1971), p. 132.

10. Hoover to William Allen White, September 16, 1943, Herbert Hoover Papers, HHPL.
11. Austin to Boyd Edwards, September 14, 1943, Warren Austin Papers, University of Vermont.
12. White to Hoover, September 20, 1943, Herbert Hoover Papers, HHPL.
13. Ibid.
14. Robert Taft to Hoover, September 23, 1943, ibid.
15. Austin to Hoover, September 21, 1943, ibid.
16. Hoover to Austin, September 22, 1943, ibid.
17. Hoover to Taft, September 25, 1943, ibid.
18. Landon to William Hutchinson, June 8, 1943, Alf M. Landon Papers, Kansas Historical Society.
19. Henry Allen to Hoover, August 10, 1943, Herbert Hoover Papers, HHPL.
20. O'Laughlin to Hoover, December 19, 1942, John Callan O'Laughlin Papers, LC.
21. O'Laughlin to Hoover, September 17, 1943, ibid.
22. Hoover to Henry Haskell, November 6, 1943, Herbert Hoover Papers, HHPL.
23. H. V. Kaltenborn to Hoover, May 31, 1943, ibid.
24. Hoover to Landon, September 20, 1943, ibid.
25. Hoover to White, May 27, 1943, ibid.
26. John Foster Dulles to Hoover, October 5, 1943, ibid.
27. Hoover to O'Laughlin, June 15, 1942, ibid.
28. "Memorandum: Why a Negotiated Peace Is the Best Way Out of a Bad Situation in Which Only Stalin Could Win," enclosed with Frederick Libby to Hoover, April 29, 1943, ibid.
29. Hoover to O'Laughlin, May 9, 1943, John Callan O'Laughlin Papers, LC.
30. Landon to Frank Carlson, May 20, 1943, Alf M. Landon Papers, Kansas Historical Society.
31. Walter Lippmann, *U.S. Foreign Policy: Shield of the Republic* (Boston: Little, Brown and Co., 1950), chapter 10.
32. Hoover to Landon, November 2, 1943, Alf M. Landon Papers, Kansas Historical Society.
33. O'Laughlin to Hoover, November 8, 1943, John Callan O'Laughlin Papers, LC.
34. Taft to Hoover, November 9, 1943, Herbert Hoover Papers, HHPL.
35. Landon to Hoover, November 18, 1943, ibid.
36. Hoover to Roy Howard, November 2, 1943, ibid.
37. Haskell to Hoover, November 8, 1943, ibid.
38. Edward Anthony to Hoover, November 12, 1943, ibid.
39. Anthony to Hoover, November 19, 1943, ibid.
40. *New York Times*, November 11, 1943.
41. O'Laughlin to Hoover, December 3, 1943, John Callan O'Laughlin Papers, LC.
42. Hoover to O'Laughlin, December 9, 1943, ibid.; "Statement to the Press," December 8, 1943, Herbert Hoover Special Collections: Articles, Addresses and Public Statements, 1915–1964, HHPL.
43. Hoover to O'Laughlin December 13, 1943, and enclosed memorandum, John Callan O'Laughlin Papers, LC.
44. "Remarks over Columbia Broadcasting System to the Emergency Conference to Save the Jews of Europe," July 25, 1943, Herbert Hoover Special Collections: Articles, Addresses and Public Statements, 1915–1964, HHPL.
45. O'Laughlin to Hoover, December 7, 1943, John Callan O'Laughlin Papers, LC.
46. Hoover to O'Laughlin, December 9, 1943, ibid.
47. Hoover to Joseph Martin, March 31, 1943, Herbert Hoover Papers, HHPL.
48. Hoover to Fred Albin, April 5, 1943, ibid.
49. Hoover to Taft, April 7, 1943, ibid.
50. Bernard Baruch to Hoover, June 14, 1943, ibid.
51. Hoover to Arthur Krock, June 17, 1943, Krock interview, p. 9, Oral History Collection, HHPL.
52. "A Check-Up of the Food Front," June 8, 1943, Herbert Hoover Special Collections: Articles, Addresses and Public Statements, 1915–1964, HHPL.
53. *New York Times*, June 9, 1943.

54. Hoover to Arthur Hyde, June 18, 1943, Herbert Hoover Papers, HHPL.
55. Hoover to Arthur Krock, September 20, 1943, quoted in Krock interview, pp. 10–11, Oral History Collection, HHPL.
56. *New York Times,* September 16, 1943.
57. Roosevelt memorandum to Gen. Watson, March 9, 1943, and Patterson to Roosevelt, February 20, 1943, Roosevelt Papers, PPF 820, Franklin D. Roosevelt Presidential Library.
58. Thomas Jenkins to Hoover, September 27, 1943, Herbert Hoover Papers, HHPL.
59. Hoover to Jenkins, September 29, 1943, ibid.
60. Jenkins to Hoover, October 4 and November 18, 1943, ibid.
61. Guy Gillette to Taft, April 23, 1943, Robert A. Taft Papers, LC.
62. Hoover to Ray Lyman Wilbur, April 29, 1943, NCFSD Records, HI.
63. Wilbur to Food for Freedom, Inc., May 4, 1943, ibid.
64. Hoover to Herbert Lehman, June 23, 1943, Herbert Hoover Papers, HHPL.
65. Gillette to Taft, October 6, 1943, Robert A. Taft Papers, LC.
66. E. Stanley Jones to Hoover, October 15, 1943, NCFSD Records, HI.
67. Nevin Sayre to Elbert Thomas, November 2, 1943, copy in Robert A. Taft Papers, LC.
68. Norman Thomas to Elbert Thomas, November 2, 1943, copy in ibid.
69. Herbert Hoover, *An American Epic, Vol. 4: The Guns Cease Killing and the Saving of Life from Famine Begins, 1939–1963* (Chicago: Henry Regnery, 1964), p. 97.
70. Hoover to John Taber, May 15, 1944, Herbert Hoover Papers, HHPL.
71. Roy Dunn to Hoover, September 6, 1943, filed with Willkie correspondence, Herbert Hoover Papers, HHPL.
72. Hoover to Dunn, September 9, 1943, ibid.
73. Hoover to John Bricker, October 1, 1943, ibid.
74. White to Roger Straus, May 22, 1943, William Allen White Papers, LC.
75. Landon to Hoover, May 17, 1943, Alf M. Landon Papers, Kansas Historical Society.
76. Landon to Hoover, June 5, 1943, ibid.
77. Hoover to Thomas Dewey, October 15, 1943, Herbert Hoover Papers, HHPL.
78. Dewey to Hoover, October 16, 1943, ibid.
79. Unsent letter from Hoover to Dewey, January 26, 1944, and notation that Hoover telephoned instead, ibid.
80. Hoover to Henry Allen, November 12, 1943, ibid.
81. Landon to Herbert Feis, January 7, 1944, Alf M. Landon Papers, Kansas Historical Society.
82. Edgar Rickard Diary, January 7, 1944, HHPL.
83. Roosevelt to Hoover, telegram, January 7, 1944, Roosevelt Papers, PPF 820, Franklin D. Roosevelt Presidential Library.
84. *New York Times,* January 11, 1944.
85. Katherin Milbank to Neil MacNeil, April 6, 1957, MacNeil Papers, HHPL.
86. Clarence Kelland to MacNeil, January 27, 1957, ibid.
87. Edgar Rickard Diary, January 8, 1944ff.
88. Hoover to David Lawrence, November 1, 1943, Herbert Hoover Papers, HHPL.
89. Castle to Landon, January 31, 1944, Alf M. Landon Papers, Kansas Historical Society.
90. Hoover to O'Laughlin, February 7, 1944, John Callan O'Laughlin Papers, LC.
91. *New York Times,* February 3, 1944.
92. Hoover to Hugh Gibson, February 16, 1944, Herbert Hoover Papers, HHPL.
93. Hoover to Homer Mann, March 17, 1944, ibid.
94. Memorandum dated March 29, 1944, filed with Dewey correspondence, ibid.
95. Hoover to Landon, March 16, 1944, ibid.
96. Hoover to Bricker, March 11 and April 12, 1944, ibid.
97. Landon to Frank Carlson, April 7, 1944, Alf M. Landon Papers, Kansas Historical Society.
98. Hoover to Richard Lloyd Jones, April 13, 1944, Herbert Hoover Papers, HHPL.
99. Hoover to Dewey, April 10, 1944, ibid.
100. A copy of Bricker's speech is filed with Bricker correspondence, ibid.
101. Hoover to Dewey, May 1, 1944, ibid.
102. Robert Wood to Vandenberg, May 2, 1944, Robert E. Wood Papers, HHPL.

103. Wood to Vandenberg, May 3, 1944, ibid.
104. William Gross to Hoover, May 12, 1944, Herbert Hoover Papers, HHPL.
105. Hoover to Gross, May 15, 1944, ibid.
106. "Statement to the Press," May 25, 1944, Herbert Hoover Special Collections: Articles, Addresses and Public Statements, 1915–1964, HHPL.
107. Edgar Rickard Diary, May 26, 1944, HHPL.
108. Ibid., June 9 and June 11, 1944.
109. Ibid., June 13 and June 23, 1944.
110. "Freedom in America and the World," address before the Republican National Convention, June 27, 1944, Herbert Hoover Special Collections: Articles, Addresses and Public Statements, 1915–1964, HHPL.
111. *New York Times*, June 28, 1944.
112. Bascom Timmons interview, p. 22, Oral History Collection, HHPL.
113. According to Bricker, Hoover did not actually tell him to take the second spot but did indicate that Dewey was sure to be nominated and, by implication, suggested that the best Bricker could hope for was the second spot on the ticket. John Bricker interview, May 21, 1980.
114. *New York Times*, June 30, 1944.
115. Hoover to Michael Shannon, July 5, 1944, Herbert Hoover Papers, HHPL.
116. Hoover to Dewey and Bricker and enclosed memorandum, July 7, 1944, ibid.
117. Robert Harriss to Hoover, May 17, 1944, ibid.
118. Dewey to Hoover, July 18, 1944, ibid.
119. Hoover to John Hamilton, July 12, 1944, ibid.
120. Herbert Brownell to Hoover, August 17, 1944, ibid.
121. Herbert Brownell interview, pp. 3–4, Oral History Collection, HHPL.
122. Bonner Fellers interview, p. 14, Oral History Collection, HHPL.
123. John Hamilton interview, p. 26, Oral History Collection, HHPL.
124. Edgar Rickard Diary, September 13, 1944, HHPL.
125. Hoover to Mrs. Albert Simms, September 7, 1944, Herbert Hoover Papers, HHPL.
126. Edgar Rickard Diary, September 22, 1944, HHPL.
127. See, for example, ibid., September 26, 1944.
128. Hoover to Robert Simmons, September 21, 1944, Herbert Hoover Papers, HHPL.
129. Edgar Rickard Diary, September 29 and November 6, 1944, HHPL.
130. Hoover to William Barrett, August 4, 1944, Herbert Hoover Papers, HHPL.
131. Hoover to Gibson, July 14, 1944, Hugh Gibson Papers, HI.
132. Gibson to Hoover, July 25, 1944, ibid.
133. "Statement on the Death of Wendell Willkie," October 8, 1944, Herbert Hoover Special Collections: Articles, Addresses and Public Statements, 1915–1964, HHPL.
134. Frank Mason interview, p. 44, Oral History Collection, HHPL.
135. Edgar Rickard Diary, November 8, 1944, HHPL.
136. Hoover to Castle, November 17, 1944, Herbert Hoover Papers, HHPL.
137. Hoover to Mann, November 20, 1944, ibid.
138. Hoover to Edgar Queeny, November 29, 1944, ibid.
139. Albert Wedemeyer interview, pp. 5–6, Oral History Collection, HHPL.
140. Hoover to O'Laughlin, December 18, 1944, John Callan O'Laughlin Papers, LC.
141. Hoover to Wilbur, January 28, 1945, Herbert Hoover Papers, HHPL.
142. "Statement on the Yalta Agreement," February 12, 1945, Herbert Hoover Special Collections: Articles, Addresses and Public Statements, 1915–1964, HHPL.
143. Hoover to Wilbur, February 15, 1945, Ray Lyman Wilbur Papers, HI.
144. Castle to Hoover, February 16, 1945, Herbert Hoover Papers, HHPL.
145. Hoover to Landon, February 18, 1945, copy filed with Castle correspondence, ibid.
146. Hoover to Castle, February 18, 1945, ibid.
147. Castle to Hoover, February 26, 1945, ibid.
148. "Statement to the Press on the Death of Franklin Delano Roosevelt," April 12, 1945, Herbert Hoover Special Collections: Articles, Addresses and Public Statements, 1915–1964, HHPL.
149. Joseph Green interview, p. 31, Oral History Collection, HHPL.

Chapter 9

1. Edward Stettinius to Hoover, telegram, April 21, 1945, Herbert Hoover Papers, HHPL.
2. Hoover to Lewis Strauss, April 23, 1945, and Hoover to Stettinius, telegram, April 23, 1945, ibid.
3. Felix Morley, *For the Record* (South Bend, IN: Regnery Gateway, 1979), p. 416.
4. Hoover to Arthur Hyde, April 23, 1945, Herbert Hoover Papers, HHPL.
5. Hyde to Hoover, April 27, 1945, ibid.
6. Hoover to May Leavitt, April 24, 1945, May Hoover Leavitt Papers, HI.
7. Edgar Rickard Diary, April 16, 1945, HHPL.
8. Charles Tobey to Hoover, April 19, 1945, Herbert Hoover Papers, HHPL.
9. See John Coulter to Hoover, April 20, 1944; Bernice Miller to Frank Hanighen, May 30, 1944, Hoover to Hanighen, February 28, 1945, and Miller to Hanighen, April 7, 1945, ibid.
10. Edgar Rickard Diary, April 17, 1945, HHPL.
11. Reprinted in Herbert Hoover, *Addresses Upon the American Road, 1941–1945* (New York: Van Nostrand, 1945), pp. 111–23.
12. Hoover to Arthur Krock, April 2, 1945, Krock interview, p. 13, Oral History Collection, HHPL.
13. Reprinted in Hoover, *Addresses, 1941–1945*, pp. 124–36.
14. Raymond Moley to Hoover, April 16, 1945, Raymond Moley Papers, HI.
15. Frederick Libby to Edwin Borchard and Robert Taft, March 29, 1945, and enclosed statement, Robert A. Taft Papers, LC.
16. Hoover to Homer Capehart, April 26, 1945, Herbert Hoover Papers, HHPL.
17. Undated memorandum filed with Henry Stimson correspondence, ibid.
18. Memorandum of a conversation with Ralph Brewster, April 28, 1945, filed with Brewster correspondence, ibid.
19. *New York Times*, May 9, 1945.
20. Ibid., May 17, 1945.
21. Hoover to Taft with enclosures, April 11, 1945, Herbert Hoover Papers, HHPL.
22. Memorandum dated April 26, 1945, filed in Herbert Hoover Papers, Post-Presidential Subject File, Food, World Wars I & II, Food Prices, Conservation and Consumption, HHPL.
23. Edgar Rickard Diary, May 13, 1945, HHPL.
24. Ibid., May 14, 1945.
25. Memorandum dated May 15, 1945, filed with Joseph Kennedy correspondence, Herbert Hoover Papers, HHPL.
26. Memorandum dated May 15, 1945, filed with Stimson correspondence, ibid.
27. Taft to Hoover, May 23, 1945, ibid.
28. Hoover to Taft, May 25, 1945, ibid.
29. Hoover to Richard Davies, May 18, 1945, Herbert Hoover Papers, Post-Presidential Subject File, Food, Foreign Policy Association.
30. "Memorandum on Meeting with Gentlemen Sent to See HH by Secretary Stimson," May 23, 1945, Herbert Hoover Special Collections; Articles, Addresses and Public Statements, 1915–1964, HHPL.
31. Harry Truman to Hoover, May 24, 1945, Herbert Hoover Papers, HHPL.
32. Edgar Rickard Diary, May 26, 1945, HHPL.
33. Ibid., May 27, 1945.
34. *New York Times*, May 27, 1945.
35. Memorandum dated May 28, 1945, filed with Truman correspondence, Herbert Hoover Papers, HHPL.
36. Edgar Rickard Diary, May 30, 1945, HHPL.
37. *New York Times*, May 28, 1945.
38. "Personal Memorandum on Meeting with Secretary of War Stimson," May 30, 1945, Herbert Hoover Special Collections: Articles, Addresses and Public Statements, 1915–1964, HHPL.

39. "Letter and Memoranda to President Truman Following Conference with Him on May 28th," May 30, 1945, ibid.
40. Truman to Hoover, June 1, 1945, Herbert Hoover Papers, HHPL.
41. *New York Times*, June 7, 1945.
42. Castle to Hoover, June 2, 1945, Herbert Hoover Papers, HHPL.
43. Hoover to Wallace White, July 12, 1945, ibid.
44. Hoover to John Callan O'Laughlin, June 8, 1945, John Callan O'Laughlin Papers, LC.
45. Joseph Green interview, p. 41, Oral History Collection, HHPL.
46. O'Laughlin to Hoover, June 9, 1945, John Callan O'Laughlin Papers, LC.
47. Hoover to William Knowland, June 12, 1945, Herbert Hoover Papers, HHPL.
48. Thomas Jenkins to Hoover, June 11, 1945, ibid.
49. Hoover to Jenkins, June 20, 1945, ibid.
50. Raymond Buell, et al., to Hoover, July 8, 1945, and Christopher Emmet Jr. to Hoover, telegram, July 18, 1945, ibid.
51. Reprinted in Hoover, *Addresses, 1941–1945*, pp. 137–43.
52. Henry Allen to Hoover, August July 27, 1945, Herbert Hoover Papers, HHPL.
53. Hoover to Allen, August 1, 1945, ibid.
54. "The Challenge to Free Men," address before the Iowa Association of Southern California, August 11, 1945, Herbert Hoover Special Collections: Articles, Addresses and Public Statements, 1915–1964, HHPL.
55. Edgar Rickard Diary, January 13, 1945, HHPL.
56. O'Laughlin to Hoover, August 9 and August 11, 1945, John Callan O'Laughlin Papers, LC.
57. Edgar Rickard Diary, August 9 and August 10, 1945; see, for example, James Selvage to Hoover, August 9, 1945, Arnold Stifel to Hoover, August 9, 1945, Edgar Queeny to Earl Warren, copy of a telegram, August 9, 1945, and John Bricker to Warren, copy of a telegram, August 13, 1945, Herbert Hoover Papers, HHPL.
58. Hoover to Stifel, August 17, 1945, and Hoover to Selvage, August 17, 1945, ibid.
59. "Memorandum: The Outstanding Effects of Potsdam," August 8, 1945, Herbert Hoover Special Collections: Articles, Addresses and Public Statements, 1915–1964, HHPL.
60. "Address on Postwar Foreign Loans" before the Executives' Club of Chicago, September 17, 1945, ibid.
61. "The Republican Party and the Democratic Process," *Los Angeles Times* editorial sent to Norman Chandler, October 14, 1945, ibid.
62. Hoover to Jenkins, September 11, 1945, Herbert Hoover Papers, HHPL.
63. Jenkins to Hoover, September 13, 1945, ibid.
64. Hoover to Jeremiah Milbank, April 24, 1945, ibid.
65. Hoover to Taft, September 1, 1945, ibid.
66. Ferdinand Eberstadt to Hoover, August 20, 1945, ibid.
67. Hoover to Eberstadt, September 19, 1945, ibid.
68. Hoover to O'Laughlin, September 25, 1945, John Callan O'Laughlin Papers, LC.
69. Hoover to George Bender, October 1, 1945, Herbert Hoover Papers, HHPL.
70. Truman to Hoover, October 11, 1945, ibid.
71. "Old Man Tariff," *Los Angeles Times* editorial sent to Norman Chandler, November 6, 1945, Herbert Hoover Special Collections: Articles, Addresses and Public Statements, 1915–1964, HHPL.
72. Jenkins to Hoover, November 6, 1945, Herbert Hoover Papers, HHPL.
73. Hoover to Jenkins, November 8, 1945, ibid.
74. Jenkins to Hoover, November 24, 1945, ibid.
75. R. G. A. Jackson to Hoover, November 27, 1945, Herbert Hoover Papers, Post-Presidential Subject File, United Nations, UNRRA, Correspondence, HHPL.
76. Jackson to Hoover, December 8, 1945, ibid.
77. Hoover to Will Shafroth, December 29, 1945, Herbert Hoover Papers, HHPL.
78. Hoover to Bricker, October 12, 1945, ibid.
79. Edgar Rickard Diary, November 14, 1945, HHPL.
80. Hoover to Emmet, November 13, 1945, Herbert Hoover Papers, HHPL.

81. Edgar Rickard Diary, review of the year 1945, HHPL.
82. "Article for Dutch Treat Yearbook Sent to C. B. Kelland," January 30, 1946, Herbert Hoover Special Collections: Articles, Addresses and Public Statements, 1915–1964, HHPL.
83. "Statement to the Press Concerning World Food Crisis," February 9, 1946, ibid.
84. Hoover to J. William Fulbright, February 8, 1946, Herbert Hoover Papers, HHPL.
85. Fulbright to Hoover, February 11, 1946, ibid.
86. Edgar Rickard Diary, January 29, 1946, HHPL.
87. "The Obligation of the Republican Party," address before the National Republican Club, February 12, 1946, Herbert Hoover Special Collections: Articles, Addresses and Public Statements, 1915–1964, HHPL.
88. Memorandum of a telephone conversation, February 25, 1946, FEC file, Herbert Hoover Papers, HI. [*sic*]
89. Hoover to Clinton Anderson, February 26, 1946, ibid.
90. Anderson to Hoover, telegram, February 26, 1946, ibid.
91. Hugh Gibson to Mrs. Gibson, February 28, 1946, Hugh Gibson Papers, HI.
92. Gibson to Mrs. Gibson, March 3, 1946, ibid.
93. *New York Times*, March 2, 1946.
94. Edgar Rickard Diary, March 13, 1946, HHPL.
95. Gibson to Mrs. Gibson, March 5, 1946, Hugh Gibson Papers, HI.
96. Will Irwin to Hoover, March 11, 1946, FEC file, Herbert Hoover Papers, HI.
97. Gibson to Mrs. Gibson, March 13, 1946, Hugh Gibson Papers, HI.
98. Hoover to Anderson, March 15, 1946, FEC file, Herbert Hoover Papers, HI.
99. John L. Lewis to Hoover, ibid.
100. Morton Blumenthal interview, p. 32, Oral History Collection, HHPL.
101. *U.S. News and World Report*, March 15, 1946.
102. *Newsweek*, March 25, 1946.
103. Milton O. Gustafson, "Congress and Foreign Aid: the First Phase, UNRRA, 1943–1947" (Ph.D. dissertation, University of Nebraska, 1966), pp. 240–41.
104. *New York Times*, March 15, 1946.
105. Ibid., March 16, 1946.
106. Ibid., March 17, 1946.
107. Frank Mason to Julius Klein, March 22, 1946, Mason Papers, HHPL.
108. *Newsweek*, April 1, 1946.
109. *New York Times*, March 27 and March 29, 1946.
110. Mason to Klein, May 4, 1946, Frank Mason Papers, HHPL.
111. "Extracurricular Activities, draft #2," memorandum dated May 8, 1946, Mason Papers, Famine Relief Survey, General, HHPL.
112. *Time*, April 22, 1946.
113. Edgar Rickard Diary, April 16, 1946, HHPL.
114. Gibson to Mrs. Gibson, April 20, 1946, Hugh Gibson Papers, HI.
115. *New York Times*, April 20, 1946.
116. "Japanese Food Supply," May 6, 1946, Herbert Hoover Special Collections: Articles, Addresses and Public Statements, 1915–1964, HHPL.
117. *New York Times*, May 11, 1946.
118. Hoover, et al., to Truman, May 13, 1946, Herbert Hoover Papers, HHPL.
119. *New York Times*, May 11, 1946.
120. Ibid., May 13, 1946.
121. Ibid., May 14, 1946.
122. Memorandum dated May 16, 1946, filed with Truman correspondence, Herbert Hoover Papers, HHPL.
123. Edgar Rickard Diary, May 18, 1946, HHPL.
124. Hoover to Fiorello LaGuardia, May 19, 1946, FEC file, Herbert Hoover Papers, HI.
125. "Statement to the Press," May 25, 1946, Herbert Hoover Special Collections: Articles, Addresses and Public Statements, 1915–1964, HHPL.

126. *Time*, May 27, 1946.
127. Ray Lyman Wilbur to Hoover, May 21, 1946, FEC file, Herbert Hoover Papers, HI.

Chapter 10

1. *Columbus Evening Dispatch*, May 27, 1945.
2. Robert Taft to Hoover, June 15, 1946, Herbert Hoover Papers, HHPL; *New York Herald Tribune*, June 19 and June 20, 1946.
3. *New York Post*, June 29, 1946.
4. *New York Herald Tribune*, June 20, 1946.
5. Edgar Rickard Diary, June 21, 1946, HHPL.
6. See, for example, Julius Klein memorandum to Hoover, July 2, 1946, Hoover to William Leahy, July 3, 1946, and Leahy to Hoover, July 5, 1946, in FEC file, Herbert Hoover Papers, HI.
7. Edgar Rickard Diary, June 21, 1946, HHPL.
8. Hoover to Edward Anthony, June 25, 1946, FEC file, Herbert Hoover Papers, HI.
9. John Callan O'Laughlin to Hoover, July 5, 1946, John Callan O'Laughlin Papers, LC.
10. Ibid., July 13, 1946.
11. Reprinted in Herbert Hoover, *Addresses Upon the American Road, 1945–1948* (New York: Van Nostrand, 1948), pp. 259–66.
12. Chester Davis to Hoover, July 12, 1946, FEC file, Herbert Hoover Papers, HI.
13. Hoover to Davis, July 16, 1946, ibid.
14. Klein to Hoover, July 24, 1946, ibid.
15. Clinton Anderson to Hoover, July 25, 1946, ibid.
16. Hoover to O'Laughlin, December 31, 1945, John Callan O'Laughlin Papers, LC.
17. Hoover to John Bricker, August 17, 1946, Herbert Hoover Papers, HHPL.
18. Hoover to Wilbur Matson, October 10, 1946, ibid.
19. *New York Times*, August 13, 1946.
20. John McCloy interview, p. 8, Oral History Collection, HHPL.
21. *New York Times*, August 27, 1946.
22. Ibid., August 31, 1946.
23. Ibid., September 24, 1946.
24. Hoover to Douglas MacArthur, October 17, 1946, Herbert Hoover Papers, HHPL.
25. MacArthur to Hoover, October 31, 1946, ibid.
26. Mark Sullivan to Hoover, October 31, 1946, Mark Sullivan Papers, HI.
27. *New York Times*, November 6, 1946.
28. Ibid., November 7, 1946.
29. "Address at the National Industrial Conference Board," November 17, 1946, Herbert Hoover Special Collections: Articles, Addresses and Public Statements, 1915–1964, HHPL.
30. Davis to Hoover, November 26, 1946, FEC file, Herbert Hoover Papers, HI.
31. Hoover to Davis, December 3, 1946, ibid.
32. Hoover to Harry S. Truman, December 3, 1946, Herbert Hoover Papers, HHPL.
33. Edgar Rickard Diary, December 11, 1946, HHPL.
34. Hoover to Taft, December 21, 1946, Herbert Hoover Papers, HHPL.
35. "The Right to Strike," *This Week*, December 29, 1946, Herbert Hoover Special Collections: Articles, Addresses and Public Statements, 1915–1964, HHPL.
36. Hoover to Harold Knutson, December 21, 1946, Herbert Hoover Papers, HHPL.
37. Edgar Rickard Diary, review of 1946, HHPL.
38. Truman to Hoover, January 18, 1947, Herbert Hoover Papers, HHPL.
39. Hoover to Truman, January 19, 1947, ibid.
40. Memorandum dated January 22, 1947, filed with Truman correspondence, ibid.
41. Frank Mason interview, p. 17, Oral History Collection, HHPL.
42. Edgar Rickard Diary, February 23, 1947, HHPL.
43. Reprinted in Hoover, *Addresses, 1945–1948*, pp. 83–97.

44. Lucius Clay, *Decision in Germany* (Garden City, NY: Doubleday, 1950), p. 156.
45. Alan Kramer, *The West German Economy, 1945–1955* (New York: Berg, 1991), pp. 60–66.
46. *New York Times*, January 31, 1947.
47. Quoted in Louis P. Lochner, *Herbert Hoover and Germany* (New York: Macmillan, 1960), p. 197.
48. Quoted in ibid., p. 217.
49. Arthur Vandenberg to Hoover, April 22, 1947, Herbert Hoover Papers, HHPL.
50. William Draper to Hoover, April 25, 1947, ibid.
51. Hoover to Robert Patterson, May 7, 1947, ibid.
52. Hoover to George C. Marshall, May 12, 1947, ibid.
53. Marshall to Hoover, May 15, 1947, ibid.
54. Hoover to O'Laughlin, September 25, 1945, John Callan O'Laughlin Papers, LC.
55. Hoover to Clarence Brown, February 1, 1947, Herbert Hoover Papers, HHPL.
56. Brown to Hoover, February 4, 1947, ibid.
57. Reprinted in Hoover, *Addresses, 1945–1948*, pp. 3–13.
58. Hoover to Vandenberg, March 18, 1947, Herbert Hoover Papers, HHPL.
59. Hoover to C. Tyler Wood, March 29, 1947, ibid.
60. Hoover to Charles Eaton, March 29, 1947, ibid.
61. Hoover to John Vorys, March 29, 1947, ibid.
62. Garrett to Hoover, April 21, 1947, ibid.
63. Hoover to Garrett, April 23, 1947, ibid.
64. Hoover to Alexander Wiley, March 6, 1947, ibid.
65. Hoover to Truman, March 12, 1947, ibid.
66. Hoover to John Taber, May 26, 1947, ibid.
67. *Newsweek*, June 9, 1947.
68. Ibid.
69. *Time*, June 2, 1947.
70. O'Laughlin to Hoover, June 3, 1947, John Callan O'Laughlin Papers, LC.
71. Hoover to O'Laughlin, June 5, 1947, ibid.
72. O'Laughlin to Hoover, June 7, 1947, ibid.
73. Patterson to Hoover, June 13, 1947, Herbert Hoover Papers, HHPL.
74. Edgar Rickard Diary, April 22, 1947, HHPL.
75. *Time*, May 12, 1947.
76. Edgar Rickard Diary, May 22, 1947, HHPL.
77. Ibid., June 2, 1947.
78. Ernest Weir to Hoover, May 26, 1947, Herbert Hoover Papers, HHPL.
79. Weir to Taft, May 19, 1947, Robert A. Taft Papers, LC.
80. Taft to Weir, June 16, 1947, ibid.
81. Styles Bridges to Hoover, undated [May 1947?], Herbert Hoover Papers, HHPL.
82. Hoover to Bridges, June 13, 1947, ibid.
83. Bridges to Hoover, June 20, 1947, ibid.
84. Taft to "Julius," June 16, 1947, Robert A. Taft Papers, LC.
85. Hoover to O'Laughlin, June 16, 1947, John Callan O'Laughlin Papers, LC.
86. *New York Times*, June 23, 1947.
87. Hoover to O'Laughlin, June 23, 1947, John Callan O'Laughlin Papers, LC.
88. Hoover to Bernard Baruch, with memorandum, June 29, 1947, Herbert Hoover Papers, HHPL.
89. Hoover to Baruch, July 3, 1947, ibid.
90. Hoover to Baruch, July 4, 1947, ibid.
91. Taft to Hoover, July 11, 1947, ibid.
92. Hoover to Taft, July 16, 1947, ibid.
93. Hoover to O'Laughlin, July 23, 1947, John Callan O'Laughlin Papers, LC.
94. Taft to Hoover, August 13, 1947, Herbert Hoover Papers, HHPL.
95. Edgar Rickard Diary, September 20, 1947, HHPL.
96. Hoover to Christian Herter, October 30, 1947, Herbert Hoover Papers, HHPL.

97. Henry Stimson to Hoover, telegram, November 4, 1947, Herbert Hoover Papers, HHPL.
98. Hoover to Stimson, November 7, 1947, ibid.
99. Stimson to Hoover, November 12, 1947, ibid.
100. Alf Landon to Hoover, November 11, 1947, ibid.
101. Hoover to Landon, November 20, 1947, ibid.
102. Landon to Hoover, November 24, 1947, ibid.
103. *New York Times*, April 8, 1946.
104. Ibid., September 12, 1947.

Chapter 11

1. Edgar Rickard Diary, October 23, 1947, HHPL.
2. Hoover to Robert Taft, June 24, 1947, Herbert Hoover Papers, HHPL.
3. Edgar Rickard Diary, October 30, 1947, HHPL.
4. Ibid., November 13, 1947.
5. Ibid., December 18, 1947.
6. *New York Times*, August 10, 1947.
7. Stanley Andrews to Frank Mason, February 5, 1948, FEC file, Herbert Hoover Papers, HI.
8. Lucius Clay, *Decision in Germany* (Garden City, NY: Doubleday, 1950), p. 268.
9. *New York Times*, August 10, 1947.
10. Alf Landon to Hoover, November 11, 1947, Herbert Hoover Papers, HHPL.
11. Hoover to Landon, November 20, 1947, ibid.
12. Landon to Hoover, November 24, 1947, ibid.
13. *New York Times*, November 21, 1947.
14. "Bicentennial Anniversary of Princeton University," June 16, 1947, Herbert Hoover Special Collections: Articles, Addresses and Public Statements, 1915–1964, HHPL.
15. Arthur Vandenberg to Hoover, December 20, 1947, Herbert Hoover Papers, HHPL.
16. Hoover to Vandenberg, December 24, 1947, ibid.
17. Vandenberg to Hoover, December 30, 1947, and Hoover to Vandenberg, January 2, 1948, ibid.
18. Reprinted in Herbert Hoover, *Addresses Upon the American Road, 1945–1948* (New York: Van Nostrand, 1948), pp. 120–30.
19. Edgar Rickard Diary, January 23, 1948, HHPL.
20. Ibid., February 9, 1948.
21. Ibid., February 29, 1948.
22. John Callan O'Laughlin to Hoover, March 2, 1948, John Callan O'Laughlin Papers, LC.
23. Alexander Wiley to Hoover, December 23, 1947, Herbert Hoover Papers, HHPL.
24. Edgar Rickard Diary, January 9, 1948, HHPL.
25. O'Laughlin to Hoover, March 2, 1948, John Callan O'Laughlin Papers, LC.
26. Hoover to O'Laughlin, telegram, March 4, 1948, and O'Laughlin to Hoover, telegram, March 4, 1948, Herbert Hoover Papers, HHPL.
27. Reprinted in Hoover, *Addresses, 1945–1948*, pp. 131–37.
28. Hoover to Joseph Martin, March 24, 1948, Herbert Hoover Papers, HHPL.
29. Hoover to Bernard Baruch, March 24, 1948, ibid.
30. Hoover to John McCloy, July 5, 1948, ibid.
31. Hoover to Charles Halleck, July 28, 1948, ibid.
32. Hoover to Ray Lyman Wilbur, October 2, 1947, Ray Lyman Wilbur Papers, HI.
33. Hoover to Hugh Gibson, August 6, 1954, Herbert Hoover Papers, HHPL.
34. "Statement Concerning the Commission on Organization of the Executive Branch of the Government," September 29, 1947, Herbert Hoover Special Collections: Articles, Addresses and Public Statements, 1915–1964, HHPL.
35. *New York Times*, September 30, 1947.
36. Hoover to Wiley, December 27, 1947, Herbert Hoover Papers, HHPL.
37. Edgar Rickard Diary, review of 1947, HHPL.

38. Ibid., February 28, 1948.
39. "Memorandum on the Origin of C.A.R.E. for Mr. Henry La Cassitt's Article for the *Saturday Evening Post*," October 31, 1953, Herbert Hoover Special Collections: Articles, Addresses and Public Statements, 1915–1964, HHPL.
40. Edgar Rickard Diary, March 8, 1948, HHPL.
41. Ibid., March 9, 1948.
42. Ibid., March 19, 1948.
43. "Letter to Mr. Paul Smith of the *San Francisco Chronicle*," March 30, 1948, Herbert Hoover Special Collections: Articles, Addresses and Public Statements, 1915–1964, HHPL.
44. Harold Stassen to Hoover, May 28, 1947, and June 11, 1947, and Hoover to Stassen, June 13, 1947, Herbert Hoover Papers, HHPL.
45. Stassen to Hoover, April 14, 1948, ibid.
46. Clarence Brown to Hoover, telegram, May 6, 1948, filed with Taft correspondence, ibid.
47. Edgar Rickard Diary, February 19, 1948, HHPL.
48. "Remarks at the Bohemian Grove Encampment," August 1, 1953, Herbert Hoover Special Collections: Articles, Addresses and Public Statements, 1915–1964, HHPL. In his talk Hoover described the 1944 convention, but Taft was not a candidate in 1944, so it is clear that the meetings must have been held in 1948.
49. Reprinted in Hoover, *Addresses, 1945–1948*, pp. 67–73.
50. Frank D. Schroth to O'Laughlin, June 25, 1948, John Callan O'Laughlin Papers, LC.
51. John Spargo to Hoover, June 26, 1948, Herbert Hoover Papers, HHPL.
52. John Hamilton interview, part 2, p. 14, Oral History Collection, HHPL.
53. Kenneth Wells to Hoover, February 2, 1949, filed in Herbert Hoover Papers, Post-Presidential Subject File, Freedoms Foundation at Valley Forge, HHPL.
54. Edgar Rickard Diary, May 10, 1948, HHPL.
55. Hoover to William Hallam Tuck, May 13, 1948, Herbert Hoover Papers, HHPL.
56. Herbert Brownell to Hoover, July 24, 1948, ibid.
57. Hoover to Hugh Gibson, August 12, 1948, ibid.
58. Hoover to Mark Sullivan, September 6, 1948, ibid.
59. John Hamilton interview, part 2, p. 15, Oral History Collection, HHPL.
60. *New York Times*, August 11, 1948.
61. *Newsweek*, August 23, 1948.
62. Edgar Rickard Diary, October 23, 1948, HHPL.
63. O'Laughlin to Hoover, September 17, 1948, John Callan O'Laughlin Papers, LC.
64. Hoover to O'Laughlin, September 20, 1948, ibid.
65. O'Laughlin to Hoover, September 22, 1948, ibid.
66. Edgar Rickard Diary, May 15, 1948, HHPL.
67. Hoover to Thomas Dewey, July 2, 1948, Herbert Hoover Papers, HHPL.
68. Hoover to Dewey, September 20, 1948, and Dewey to Hoover, October 4, 1948, ibid.
69. Hoover to Roy Howard, August 26, 1948, ibid.
70. Edgar Rickard Diary, November 1, 1948, HHPL.
71. Hoover to Robert Simmons, September 2, 1948, Herbert Hoover Papers, HHPL.
72. Hoover to Mark Sullivan, September 6, 1948, Mark Sullivan Papers, HI.
73. Edgar Rickard Diary, September 30, 1948, HHPL.
74. Ibid., September 9, 1948.
75. *U.S. News and World Report*, September 24, 1948.
76. "Memorandum on the Election," November 17, 1948, Herbert Hoover Special Collections: Articles, Addresses and Public Statements, 1915–1964, HHPL.
77. Edgar Rickard Diary, November 2, 1948, HHPL.
78. Harry Truman to Hoover, November 26, 1948, Herbert Hoover Papers, HHPL.
79. Hoover to Arch Shaw, November 28, 1948, ibid.
80. See, for example, Stimson to Hoover, November 22, 1948, and Hoover to Stimson, November 30, 1948, ibid.; "Compensation of Top Government Officials," statement before the subcommittee of the Committee on Post Office and Civil Service, United States Senate,

Eightieth Congress, Second Session, December 13 and 14, 1948, Herbert Hoover Special Collections: Articles, Addresses and Public Statements, 1915–1964, HHPL.

81. Edgar Rickard Diary, December 4, 1948, HHPL.
82. John Hamilton interview, part 2, p. 25, Oral History Collection, HHPL.
83. Edgar Rickard Diary, January 28, 1949, HHPL.
84. Memorandum of a telephone conversation, February 6, 1949, filed with Truman correspondence, Herbert Hoover Papers, HHPL.
85. Memorandum of a telephone conversation, February 9, 1949, ibid.
86. Edgar Rickard Diary, February 18, 1949, HHPL.
87. Ibid., February 12, 1949.
88. Hoover to Truman, January 21, 1941, Herbert Hoover Papers, HHPL.
89. Truman to Hoover, January 25, 1949, ibid.
90. The detailed reports of the Hoover Commission were published in a series of pamphlets by the U.S. Government Printing Office. A condensed summary, intended for a general audience, was published as *The Hoover Commission Report on Organization of the Executive Branch of Government* (New York: McGraw-Hill, 1949).
91. Memorandum of a telephone conversation, February 6, 1949, filed with Truman correspondence, Herbert Hoover Papers, HHPL.
92. Memorandum of a telephone conversation, February 9, 1949, ibid.
93. Truman to Hoover, February 11, 1949, ibid.
94. Hoover to Truman, February 14, 1949, ibid.
95. Truman to Hoover, February 16, 1949, ibid.
96. Memorandum dated April 7, 1949, ibid.
97. *Newsweek*, February 21, 1949.
98. Edgar Rickard Diary, January 28, 1949, HHPL.
99. Ibid., April 9, 1949.
100. *New York Times*, March 11, 1949.
101. Edgar Rickard Diary, March 9, 1949, HHPL.
102. Memorandum dated April 7, 1949, filed with Truman correspondence, Herbert Hoover Papers, HHPL.
103. Truman to Hoover, April 12, 1946, ibid.
104. Edgar Rickard Diary, April 9, 1949, HHPL.
105. Ibid., April 22, 1949.
106. "Press Statement," May 7, 1949, Herbert Hoover Special Collections: Articles, Addresses and Public Statements, 1915–1964, HHPL.
107. Edgar Rickard Diary, February 10, 1949, HHPL.
108. Ibid., April 22, 1949.
109. Hoover to Robert Doughton, April 25, 1949, Herbert Hoover Special Collections: Articles, Addresses and Public Statements, 1915–1964, HHPL.
110. Hoover to Robert Kean, May 7, 1949, Herbert Hoover Papers, HHPL.
111. Dwight Eisenhower to Hoover, May 17, 1949, ibid.
112. Statement enclosed with Bernice Miller to William Nichols, May 19, 1949, ibid. The statement was later published by *This Week*, October 9, 1949.
113. Hoover to Samuel McConnell Jr., June 22, 1949, Herbert Hoover Papers, HHPL.
114. Hoover to Truman, June 19, 1949, ibid.
115. "Statement before the Armed Services Committee, House of Representatives," June 29, 1949, Herbert Hoover Special Collections: Articles, Addresses and Public Statements, 1915–1964, HHPL.
116. "Statement before the Senate Subcommittee on Post Office and Civil Service," June 30, 1949, ibid.
117. Hoover to Truman, July 4, 1949, Herbert Hoover Papers, HHPL.
118. Truman to Hoover, July 6, 1949, ibid.
119. Hoover to Truman, July 9, 1949, ibid.
120. Truman to Hoover, July 12, 1949, ibid.
121. Hoover to Dewey, July 6, 1949, ibid.

122. Dewey to Hoover, July 18, 1949, and Hoover to Dewey, July 26, 1949, ibid.
123. Joseph Kennedy to Hoover, July 26, 1949, ibid.
124. "Think of the Next Generation," August 10, 1949, Herbert Hoover Special Collections: Articles, Addresses and Public Statements, 1915–1964, HHPL.
125. *New York Times*, August 11, 1949.
126. Ibid., August 14, 1949.
127. *Collier's*, August 13, 1949.
128. Guy Rush to Hoover, August 18, 1949, and Hoover to Rush, August 22, 1949, Herbert Hoover Papers, HHPL.
129. *Time*, August 22, 1949.
130. Homer Mann to Hoover, September 25, 1949, Herbert Hoover Papers, HHPL.
131. Hoover to Mann, September 25, 1949, ibid.
132. Douglas MacArthur to Hoover, October 8, 1949, ibid.
133. Hoover to MacArthur, October 19, 1949, ibid.
134. Edgar Rickard Diary, December 14, 1949, HHPL.
135. Louis Johnson to Hoover, October 19, 1949, Herbert Hoover Papers, HHPL.
136. "Statement before the Armed Services Committee, House of Representatives," October 21, 1949, Herbert Hoover Special Collections: Articles, Addresses and Public Statements, 1915–1964, HHPL.
137. Henry Cabot Lodge Jr. to Hoover, November 22, 1949, Herbert Hoover Papers, HHPL.
138. Hoover to Lodge, November 25, 1949, ibid.
139. *New York Times*, December 13, 1949.
140. Frank Pace Jr. to Hoover, January 6, 1950, Herbert Hoover Papers, HHPL.
141. Hoover to Pace, January 9, 1950, ibid.
142. Edgar Rickard Diary, March 16, 1950, HHPL.
143. Hoover to Richard Nixon, January 22, 1950, Herbert Hoover Papers, HHPL.
144. Edgar Rickard Diary, March 8, 1950, HHPL.
145. Hoover to William Knowland, December 31, 1949, Herbert Hoover Papers, HHPL.
146. Knowland to Hoover, January 3, 1950, ibid.
147. Hoover to Patrick Hurley, February 2, 1950, ibid.
148. Knowland to Hoover, March 29, 1950 with enclosed copy of letter to Acheson, ibid.
149. Acheson to Knowland, April 6, 1950, filed with Knowland correspondence, ibid.
150. Hoover to Knowland, January 20, 1950, ibid.
151. Knowland to Hoover, January 23, 1950, ibid.
152. Hoover to Knowland, January 24, 1950, ibid.
153. Hoover to Knowland, May 6, 1950, ibid.
154. Hoover to Knowland, May 30, 1950, ibid.
155. Allan Nevins to Hoover, February 3, 1950, and Barbara Feldon to Nevins, February 15, 1950, ibid.
156. Hoover to Kenneth Wherry, May 6, 1950, and enclosed memorandum, ibid.
157. "Statement on the Korean Situation," recorded June 28, 1950, for broadcast on NBC *Voice of Events*, July 1, 1950, Herbert Hoover Special Collections: Articles, Addresses and Public Statements, 1915–1964, HHPL.
158. Hoover to Truman, July 1, 1950, Herbert Hoover Papers, HHPL.
159. Truman to Hoover, July 3, 1950, ibid.
160. Homer Ferguson to Hoover, July 17, 1950, ibid.
161. Hoover to Ferguson, July 20, 1950, ibid.
162. "World Peace and the United Nations," July 11, 1950, Herbert Hoover Special Collections: Articles, Addresses and Public Statements, 1915–1964, HHPL.
163. "Bohemian Club Speech (off-the-record)" July 30, 1950, ibid.
164. Hoover to Taft, August 13, 1950, Herbert Hoover Papers, HHPL.
165. Louis Johnson to Hoover, September 18, 1950, ibid.
166. Hoover to Hughston M. McBain, September 8, 1950, ibid.
167. Hoover to Guy Gabrielson, September 28, 1950, ibid.
168. Hoover to Edgar Rickard, October 13, 1950, ibid.

169. Hoover to Felix Morley, October 15, 1950, Felix Morley Papers, HHPL.
170. "Where We Are Now," October 19, 1950, Herbert Hoover Special Collections: Articles, Addresses and Public Statements, 1915–1964, HHPL.
171. Hoover to Robert Johnson, October 28, 1950, Herbert Hoover Papers, HHPL.
172. Hoover to Robert Johnson, November 18, 1950, ibid.
173. Truman to Hoover, November 25, 1950, ibid.
174. Hoover to Truman, November 26, 1950, ibid.

Chapter 12

1. Clipping filed in Herbert Hoover Papers, Post-Presidential Subject File, Foreign Policy, Opposition.
2. Bonner Fellers to Hoover, September 3, 1947, Herbert Hoover Papers, HHPL.
3. Hoover to Fellers, September 5, 1947, and Robert Taft to Hoover, October 11, 1947, ibid.
4. Hoover to Raymond Moley, December, 1950, Raymond Moley Papers, HI.
5. Hoover to Taft, December 18, 1950, Robert A. Taft Papers, LC.
6. William Jenner to Hoover, December 14, 1950, Herbert Hoover Papers, HHPL.
7. Hoover to Fellers, December 3, 1950, ibid.
8. "Our National Policies in this Crisis," December 20, 1950, Herbert Hoover Special Collections: Articles, Addresses and Public Statements, 1915–1964, HHPL.
9. *San Francisco Examiner*, December 21, 1950.
10. Arthur Kemp to Hoover, undated [December 1950 or January 1951?], Herbert Hoover Papers, HHPL.
11. *Wilmington Star*, December 23, 1950.
12. Hoover to William Knowland, January 11, 1951, Herbert Hoover Papers, HHPL.
13. *New York Herald Tribune*, December 22, 1950.
14. *Newsweek*, January 1, 1951.
15. Harry Byrd to Hoover, December 28, 1950, Herbert Hoover Papers, HHPL.
16. Homer Ferguson to Hoover, January 16, 1951, ibid.
17. Lawrence Smith to Hoover, December 23, 1950, ibid.
18. "Hoover's Folly," *The Nation*, December 30, 1950.
19. "Every Man a President," *New Republic*, January 8, 1951.
20. *Newsweek*, January 1, 1951.
21. Quoted in *New York Herald Tribune*, December 22, 1950.
22. Hoover to H. Alexander Smith, December 27, 1950, Herbert Hoover Papers, HHPL.
23. Richard Nixon to Hoover, December 22, 1950, ibid.
24. Moley to Hoover, December 21, 1950, ibid.
25. Felix Morley to Hoover, December 27, 1950, Felix Morley Papers, HHPL.
26. Alf Landon to Hoover, December 26, 1950, Herbert Hoover Papers, HHPL.
27. Morley to Hoover, January 5, 1951, Felix Morley Papers, HHPL.
28. John Foster Dulles to Taft, December 29, 1950, with copy of Dulles to Hoover, December 18, 1950, Robert A. Taft Papers, LC.
29. *New York Times*, January 3, 1951.
30. Ibid.
31. *Houston Post*, January 1, 1951.
32. "The Safety of the Nation," Robert A. Taft Papers, LC.
33. Taft to Ethan Shepley, January 8, 1951, ibid.
34. Knowland to Hoover, January 9, 1951, and Hoover to Knowland, January 11, 1951, Herbert Hoover Papers, HHPL.
35. "The American Forum of the Air," January 14, 1951, Herbert Hoover Papers, Post-Presidential Subject File, American Forum of the Air, HHPL.
36. Harold Stassen to Hoover, January 16, 1951, and enclosed copy of Stassen to *New York Herald Tribune*, same date, Herbert Hoover Papers, HHPL.
37. Hoover to Albert C. Wedemeyer, December 31, 1950, ibid.

38. See, for example, Hoover to Morley, January 24, 1951, and Morley to Hoover, January 26, 1951, ibid.
39. *New York Herald Tribune*, January 28, 1951.
40. Karl Mundt to Hoover, January 19, 1951, Herbert Hoover Papers, HHPL.
41. "We Should Revise Our Foreign Policies," February 9, 1951, Herbert Hoover Special Collections: Articles, Addresses and Public Statements, 1915–1964, HHPL.
42. Bonner Fellers, "The Real Deterrent," *Human Events*, January 24, 1951.
43. Press statement, January 16, 1951, filed with Alexander de Seversky correspondence, Herbert Hoover Papers, HHPL.
44. Hoover to Homer Capehart, February 5, 1951, ibid.
45. Hoover to Thomas Connally, February 17, 1951, ibid.
46. Knowland to Hoover, February 2, 1951, ibid.
47. Kenneth Wherry to Hoover, February 6, 1951, ibid.
48. "Defense of Europe," statement before the Senate Committees on Foreign Relations and Armed Services, February 27, 1951, Herbert Hoover Special Collections: Articles, Addresses and Public Statements, 1915–1964, HHPL.
49. Wherry to Hoover, February 6, 1951, Herbert Hoover Papers, HHPL.
50. Hoover to Frederick Coudert Jr., February 5, 1951, ibid.
51. Fellers to Hoover, February 27, 1951, and de Seversky to Hoover, March 19, 1951, ibid.
52. Taft to Hoover, March 5, 1951, Robert A. Taft Papers, LC.
53. *Human Events*, February 15, 1951.
54. Hoover to Fulton Lewis Jr., March 4, 1951, Herbert Hoover Papers, HHPL.
55. *New York Times*, March 14, 1951.
56. Hoover to Jenner, March 22, 1951, ibid.
57. James T. Patterson, *Mr. Republican: A Biography of Robert A. Taft* (Boston: Houghton Mifflin, 1972), pp. 480–81.
58. *Human Events*, January 17, 1951.
59. Charles Beard to Moley, September 15, 1948, Raymond Moley Papers, HI.
60. Joan Hoff Wilson, "Herbert Hoover Reassessed," Mark Hatfield, ed., *Herbert Hoover Reassessed*, Senate Document 96–63 (Washington, DC: USGPO, 1981), p. 112.
61. Hoover to Beard, December 17, 1945, and Hoover to Castle, December 16, 1945, Herbert Hoover Papers, HHPL.
62. Fellers to Hoover, December 7, 1950, ibid.
63. Bonner Fellers interview, pp. 17–18, Oral History Collection, HHPL.
64. Memorandum, April 13, 1951, filed with Douglas MacArthur correspondence, Herbert Hoover Papers, HHPL.
65. Richard Berlin interview, p. 6, Oral History Collection, HHPL.
66. Memorandum, April 14, 1951, filed with Douglas MacArthur correspondence, Herbert Hoover Papers, HHPL.
67. Memorandum, April 15, 1951, ibid.
68. Richard Berlin interview, p. 5, Oral History Collection, HHPL.
69. Bonner Fellers interview, p. 19, ibid.
70. Hoover to Arch Shaw, May 26, 1951, Herbert Hoover Papers, HHPL.
71. "Confidential Memorandum on the Essentials of Bi-Partisan Foreign Policy Sent to Senator Ferguson, Senator Wherry, and George Sokolsky," July 7, 1951, Herbert Hoover Special Collections: Articles, Addresses and Public Statements, 1915–1964, HHPL.
72. Ferguson to Hoover, July 31, 1951, and Wherry to Hoover, July 9, 1951, Herbert Hoover Papers, HHPL.
73. *New York Times*, August 31, 1951.
74. Louis Johnson to Hoover, August 31, 1951, Herbert Hoover Papers, HHPL.
75. *New York Times*, August 6, 1951.
76. Ibid., December 30, 1951.
77. Morley to Hoover, October 9, 1951, and Hoover to Morley, October 13, 1951, Felix Morley Papers, HHPL.
78. Morley to Hoover, October 15, 1951, ibid.

79. Morley to the author, July 18, 1980.
80. *New York Times*, January 16, 1952.
81. "The Year Since the Great Debate," January 27, 1952, Herbert Hoover Special Collections: Articles, Addresses and Public Statements, 1915–1964, HHPL.
82. *New York Times*, February 8, 1952.
83. Copy of Leslie Grove's statement enclosed with Bernice Miller to Bonner Fellers, January 29, 1952, Herbert Hoover Papers, HHPL.
84. Taft to Hoover, February 5, 1952, Robert A. Taft Papers, LC.
85. *New York Times*, February 5, 1952.
86. Fellers to Hoover, January 30, 1952, Herbert Hoover Papers, HHPL.
87. Arthur Bliss Lane to Hoover, January 23, 1952, Herbert Hoover Papers, Post-Presidential Subject File, Campaign 1952, Correspondence, HHPL.
88. Hoover to Lane, January 26, 1952, ibid.
89. Hoover to Hulett C. Merritt, December 31, 1951, Herbert Hoover Papers, HHPL.
90. Hoover to Wilbur Matson, April 24, 1952, ibid.
91. Morley to Hoover, October 12, 1951, Felix Morley Papers, HHPL.
92. John D. M. Hamilton interview, part 1, p. 49, Oral History Collection, HHPL.
93. Hoover to Henry Cabot Lodge Jr., telegram, June 26, 1952, and Hoover to Lodge, telegram, June 29, 1952, Herbert Hoover Papers, HHPL.
94. John D. M. Hamilton interview, part 1, p. 52, Oral History Collection, HHPL.
95. De Seversky to Hoover, July 1, 1952, Herbert Hoover Papers, HHPL.
96. De Seversky, "An Airman's Plea to All Republican Delegates," filed with de Seversky correspondence, ibid.
97. "Address at the Republican National Convention," July 8, 1952, Herbert Hoover Special Collections: Articles, Addresses and Public Statements, 1915–1964, HHPL.
98. See Hoover to Guy Gabrielson, July 3, 1952, Herbert Hoover Papers, Post-Presidential Subject File, Republican National Committee, Correspondence, HHPL.
99. "Statement to the Press Endorsing Senator Robert Taft as Republican Candidate for President," July 9, 1952, Herbert Hoover Special Collections: Articles, Addresses and Public Statements, 1915–1964, HHPL.
100. Albert C. Wedemeyer interview, pp. 26–27, Oral History Collection, HHPL.
101. "Statement to the Press after Mr. Eisenhower's Nomination as Republican Candidate for President," July 11, 1952, Herbert Hoover Special Collections: Articles, Addresses and Public Statements, 1915–1964, HHPL.
102. Hoover to Taft, July 11, 1952, Robert A. Taft Papers, LC.
103. Taft to Hoover, July 17, 1952, ibid.
104. Hoover to Gabrielson, July 23, 1952, Herbert Hoover Papers, HHPL.
105. Hoover to Everett Dirksen, July 23, 1952, ibid.
106. Taft to Robert Wood, August 8, 1952, Robert E. Wood Papers, HHPL.
107. *Time*, June 23, 1952.
108. Dwight Eisenhower to Hoover, telegram, July 29, 1952, Herbert Hoover Papers, HHPL.
109. Hoover to Eisenhower, telegram, July 31, 1952, ibid.
110. Patterson, *Mr. Republican*, pp. 576–78.
111. *Collier's*, August 16, 1952.
112. Hoover to Clarence Kelland, August 17, 1952, Herbert Hoover Papers, HHPL.
113. Hoover to Wedemeyer, August 29, 1952, ibid.
114. Hoover to Wedemeyer, October 7, 1952, ibid.
115. Press release, September 25, 1952, filed with Nixon correspondence, ibid.
116. Bonner Fellers interview, p. 25, Oral History Collection, HHPL.
117. Eisenhower to Hoover, telegram, October 7, 1952, Herbert Hoover Papers, HHPL.
118. Hoover to Eisenhower, telegram, October 8, 1952, ibid.
119. "The Constructive Character of the Republican Party," October 18, 1952, Herbert Hoover Special Collections: Articles, Addresses and Public Statements, 1915–1964, HHPL.
120. Joseph N. Pew to Hoover, November 6, 1952, Herbert Hoover Papers, HHPL.
121. Hoover to Eisenhower, October 21, 1952, ibid.

122. Hoover to Kelland, October 22, 1952, ibid.
123. Hoover to Eisenhower, November 17, 1952, ibid.
124. Hoover to John Wheeler, October 17, 1952, ibid.
125. Hoover to Knowland, October 25, 1952, ibid.
126. Clare Boothe Luce, interview by the author, August 12, 1980.

Chapter 13

1. Hoover to Joseph N. Pew Jr., November 10, 1952, Herbert Hoover Papers, HHPL.
2. *Newsweek*, December 1, 1952; Hoover to Henry Hazlitt, November 29, 1952, Herbert Hoover Papers, HHPL.
3. Joseph Martin to Hoover, November 7, 1952, Herbert Hoover Papers, HHPL.
4. Hoover to Clarence Kelland, November 18, 1952, ibid.
5. *New York Times*, December 24, 1952.
6. Ibid., January 7, 1953.
7. Felix Morley, "A Visit with an Elder Statesman," *Pathfinder*, February 18, 1953, p. 29 ff.
8. Dwight Eisenhower to Hoover, March 16, 1953, Herbert Hoover Papers, HHPL.
9. Hoover to Joseph Dodge, March 24, 1953, ibid.
10. Hoover to Dodge, March 18, 1953, and March 24, 1953, ibid.
11. Hoover to Dodge, April 10, 1953, ibid.
12. "Federal Socialization of Electric Power," address at the diamond jubilee of the Case Institute of Technology, April 11, 1953, Herbert Hoover Special Collections: Articles, Addresses and Public Statements, 1915–1964, HHPL.
13. *New York Times*, April 12, 1953.
14. Hoover to Sam McKelvie, April 20, 1953, Herbert Hoover Papers, HHPL.
15. Norman Thomas to Hoover, April 13, 1953, ibid.
16. Hoover to Thomas, April 14, 1953, ibid.
17. Draft letter, March 19, 1953, filed with Albert Wedemeyer correspondence, ibid.
18. Wedemeyer to Hoover, March 21, 1953, ibid.
19. Hoover to Wedemeyer, March 23, 1953, ibid.
20. Hoover to W. V. Pratt, March 9, 1953, ibid.
21. Hoover to Pratt, May 21, 1953, ibid.
22. Bonner Fellers to Hoover, May 10, 1953, Herbert Hoover Papers, HHPL.
23. Hoover to Ferdinand Eberstadt, May 28, 1953, ibid.
24. *New York Times*, April 19, 1953.
25. Hoover to McKelvie, April 20, 1953, Herbert Hoover Papers, HHPL.
26. Robert J. Huckshorn, "Congressional Reaction to the Second Hoover Commission," (Ph.D. dissertation, University of Iowa, 1957), p. 19.
27. Hoover to Clarence Brown, June 5, 1953, Brown Papers, Ohio Historical Society.
28. Hoover to Lewis Strauss, June 9, 1953, with enclosed memorandum, Herbert Hoover Papers, HHPL.
29. Hoover to Herman Welker, June 18, 1953, ibid.
30. Richard Lloyd Jones to Hoover, June 22, 1953, and Hoover to Jones, June 24, 1953, ibid.
31. Eisenhower to Hoover, July 13, 1953, ibid.
32. Huckshorn, "Congressional Reaction," pp. 21–22.
33. *Time*, August 17, 1953.
34. "Telegram to Mrs. Robert A. Taft on the Death of Her Husband," July 31, 1953, Herbert Hoover Special Collections: Articles, Addresses and Public Statements, 1915–1964, HHPL.
35. "Remarks at the Bohemian Grove Encampment," August 1, 1953, Herbert Hoover Special Collections: Articles, Addresses and Public Statements, 1915–1964, HHPL.
36. Hoover to Raymond Moley, August 6, 1953, Raymond Moley Papers, HI.
37. Hoover to Leonard Hall, telegram, August 27, 1953, Herbert Hoover Papers, Post-Presidential Subject File, Republican National Committee, Correspondence, HHPL.
38. *New York Times*, July 28, 1953.

39. Huckshorn, "Congressional Reaction," p. 25.
40. *New York Times*, September 30, 1953.
41. Huckshorn, "Congressional Reaction," p. 52.
42. Brown to Hoover, August 27, 1953, Brown Papers, Ohio Historical Society.
43. *New York Times*, November 13, 1953.
44. Ibid., November 16, 1953.
45. Thomas Dewey to Hoover, November 27, 1953, Herbert Hoover Papers, HHPL.
46. Hoover to Dewey, November 30, 1953, ibid.
47. Hoover to Hugh Gibson, December 19, 1953, Hugh Gibson Papers, HI.
48. Herbert Brownell interview, pp. 9–10, Oral History Collection, HHPL.
49. Hoover to Gibson, December 19, 1953, Hugh Gibson Papers, HI.
50. Hoover to Wilbur Matson, December 27, 1953, Herbert Hoover Papers, HHPL.
51. Hoover to Gibson, January 24, 1954, Hugh Gibson Papers, HI.
52. "Benjamin Franklin," address to the International Franklin Society, Inc., January 23, 1954, Herbert Hoover Special Collections: Articles, Addresses and Public Statements, 1915–1964, HHPL.
53. "Outlook for Further Reorganization," address to the National Press Club, March 10, 1954, ibid.
54. Hoover to Walter Judd, September 17, 1953, Herbert Hoover Papers, Post-Presidential Subject File, Committee for One Million, HHPL.
55. Joseph Grew, Charles Edison, and Walter Judd to Hoover, October 12, 1953, ibid.
56. Enclosed with Hoover to Edison, January 15, 1954, ibid.
57. Alf Landon to Morley, November 24, 1953, Raymond Morley Papers, HHPL.
58. Hoover to Pratt, February 12, 1954, Herbert Hoover Papers, HHPL.
59. Hoover to James Farley, March 27, 1954, ibid.
60. Hoover to Alexander Wiley, April 20, 1954, with enclosed memorandum, ibid.
61. "Memo of a Conversation with the Honorable Herbert Hoover" [by Kenneth Batchelder?], June 25, 1954, Herbert Hoover Papers, Post-Presidential Subject File, Foreign Policy, Printed Materials and Clippings, HHPL.
62. "Some National Problems," address at the Merchandise Mart, Chicago, June 24, 1954, Herbert Hoover Special Collections: Articles, Addresses and Public Statements, 1915–1964, HHPL.
63. Eisenhower to Hoover, telegram, August 2, 1954, and Hoover to Eisenhower, telegram, August 4, 1954, Herbert Hoover Papers, HHPL.
64. Eisenhower to Hoover, August 6, 1954, ibid.
65. *Time*, August 23, 1954.
66. *New York Times*, August 8, 1954.
67. "The Protection of Freedom," August 10, 1954, Herbert Hoover Special Collections: Articles, Addresses and Public Statements, 1915–1964, HHPL.
68. "Our Present Foreign Situation," memorandum of September 4, 1954, Herbert Hoover Papers, Post-Presidential Subject File, Foreign Policy, Unpublished Memo by Hoover, HHPL.
69. "Address at the 'After-Glow' Party Given by Mr. Hoover at the Waldorf-Astoria Hotel for His Guests at Various Bohemian Encampments," October 15, 1964, Herbert Hoover Special Collections: Articles, Addresses and Public Statements, 1915–1964, HHPL.
70. *New York Times*, October 13 and October 31, 1954.
71. Hoover to Kelland, November 19, 1954, Herbert Hoover Papers, HHPL.
72. *New York Times*, November 23, 1954.
73. Ibid., November 24, 1954.
74. Ibid., November 25, 1954.
75. *U.S. News and World Report*, December 3, 1954.
76. *New York Times*, November 27, 1954.
77. Anecdote by Neil MacNeil, December 1, 1954, MacNeil Papers, HHPL.
78. *New York Times*, February 14, 1955.
79. Ibid., February 21, 1955.

80. Ibid., February 28, 1955.
81. Hoover to Kelland, March 7, 1955, Herbert Hoover Papers, HHPL.
82. Anecdote by Neil MacNeil, April 28, 1955, MacNeil Papers, HHPL.
83. Memo of visit with President Eisenhower, April 29, 1955, filed with Eisenhower correspondence, Herbert Hoover Papers, HHPL.
84. *New York Times*, March 15, 1955.
85. Ibid., April 4, 1955.
86. Ibid., April 11, 1955.
87. Ibid., April 18, 1955.
88. "An Appraisal of the Changes in the Charter of the United Nations," statement before the Senate Foreign Relations Committee, April 21, 1955, Herbert Hoover Special Collections: Articles, Addresses and Public Statements, 1915–1964, HHPL.
89. *New York Times*, April 22, 1955.
90. Ibid., April 25, 1955.
91. Ibid., May 16, 1955.
92. Ibid., May 5, 1955.
93. Hoover to Edward Anthony, May 29, 1955, Herbert Hoover Papers, HHPL.
94. *New York Times*, June 25, 1955.
95. Ibid., June 26, 1955.
96. Ibid., June 30, 1955.
97. Hoover to Charles Halleck, June 29, 1955, Herbert Hoover Papers, HHPL.
98. *New York Times*, July 1, 1955.
99. *New Republic*, July 11, 1955.
100. *New York Times*, July 11, 1955.
101. Press release, June 30, 1955, Second Hoover Commission Records, General/Subject Files, Press Releases, HHPL.
102. Hoover to Brown, July 6, 1955, Brown Papers, Ohio Historical Society.
103. Brown to Hoover, July 8, 1955, ibid.
104. Hoover to Dewey, July 14, 1955, Herbert Hoover Papers, HHPL.
105. Hoover to Joseph Dodge, July 15, 1955, ibid.
106. John McClellan to Neil MacNeil, January 31, 1957, filed with anecdotes collected by MacNeil, MacNeil Papers, HHPL.

Chapter 14

1. "Government Is Too Big," *U.S. News and World Report*, August 5, 1955.
2. "Press Release Concerning the *Democratic Digest*'s Article in the September 1955 Issue, 'The Second Hoover Commission Abandons Reform for Revolution,'" August 16, 1955, Herbert Hoover Special Collections, Articles, Addresses and Public Statements, 1915–1964, HHPL.
3. Lawrence Spivak to Hoover, November 7, 1955, Herbert Hoover Papers, HHPL.
4. Quoted in Spivak to Hoover, January 13, 1956, ibid.
5. See William Hallam Tuck Papers, Citizens Committee for the Hoover Report, HHPL.
6. *New York Times*, July 9, 1955.
7. Ibid., July 26, 1955.
8. Reprinted in Herbert Hoover, *Addresses Upon the American Road, 1955–1960* (Caldwell, ID: Caxton Printers, 1961), pp. 79–85.
9. Hoover to Richard Lloyd Jones, January 11, 1956, Herbert Hoover Papers, HHPL.
10. Hoover to James Farley, March 27, 1954, ibid.; *New York Times*, October 14 and November 1, 1955.
11. "Herbert Hoover: Statesman Extraordinary," *American Mercury*, October, 1955.
12. Remarks on the NBC production of "A Conversation with Herbert Hoover," November 6, 1955.
13. *New York Times*, November 12, 1955.

14. Hoover to Wilbur Matson, December 20, 1955, Herbert Hoover Papers, HHPL.
15. Hoover to William Pratt, November 18, 1955, ibid.
16. Memorandum filed in Herbert Hoover Papers, Post-Presidential Subject File, United States Commission on Organization of the Executive Branch of the Government, Administrative Vice President Proposal, Documents on "Double Cross," HHPL.
17. *New York Times,* January 16, 1956.
18. George H. Quinion to Hoover, March 10, 1956, and Hoover to Quinion, March 13, 1956, Herbert Hoover Papers, HHPL.
19. Hoover to William Knowland, telegram, May 16, 1956, and Knowland to Hoover, May 17, 1956, ibid.
20. Bernice Miller to Loretta Camp, undated, and Camp to Miller, June 1, 1956, ibid.
21. Hoover to Leonard Hall, June 15, 1956, ibid.
22. Dwight Eisenhower to Hoover, July 2, 1956, ibid.
23. Hoover to Matson, July 17, 1956, ibid.
24. Hoover to Eisenhower, August 14, 1956, ibid.
25. "Speech at the Bohemian Grove," July 28, 1956, Herbert Hoover Special Collections, Articles, Addresses and Public Statements, 1915–1964, HHPL.
26. *New York Times,* August 10, 1956.
27. Reprinted in Hoover, *Addresses, 1955–1960,* pp. 93–98.
28. Hoover to Joseph Kennedy, September 19, 1956, Herbert Hoover Papers, HHPL.
29. Kennedy to Hoover, October 31, 1956, ibid.
30. L. Richard Guylay to Hoover, October 15, 1956, Herbert Hoover Papers, Post-Presidential Subject File, Republican National Committee, Correspondence, HHPL.
31. William Rawls to Hoover, telegram, October 21, 1956, Herbert Hoover Papers, Post-Presidential Subject File, Campaign 1956, Correspondence, HHPL.
32. Hoover to Rawls, telegram, October 21, 1956, ibid.
33. Reprinted in Hoover, *Addresses, 1955–1960,* pp. 101–3.
34. Report dated December 7, 1956, First Aid for Hungary Records, HI.
35. Perrin Galpin to Tuck, December 12, 1956, ibid.
36. Hoover to Tibor Eckardt, February 12, 1957, and memorandum from Galpin to Hoover, February 14, 1957, ibid.
37. Richard Nixon to Hoover, January 14, 1957, Herbert Hoover Papers, HHPL.
38. Thomas Gordon to Hoover, telegram, January 3, 1957, ibid.
39. Hoover to Gordon, telegram, January 6, 1957, ibid.
40. Hoover to Pratt, November 18, 1955, ibid.
41. Hoover to Gordon, telegram, January 6, 1957, ibid.
42. Hoover to Alexander Wiley, January 24, 1957, ibid.
43. Clarence Brown to Hoover, September 4, 1957, ibid.
44. John F. Kennedy to Hoover, April 23, 1957, ibid.
45. "Remarks Made at the Dedication of the Harry S. Truman Library," July 6, 1957, Herbert Hoover Special Collections, Articles, Addresses and Public Statements, 1915–1964, HHPL.
46. "Statement Made on the Occasion of His 83rd Birthday on the SS President Hoover," August 10, 1957, ibid.
47. Hoover to David Lawrence, September 3, 1957, Herbert Hoover Papers, HHPL.
48. Hoover to Matson, December 23, 1957, ibid.
49. Bernice Miller to Hugo Meier, February 1, 1958, ibid.
50. Herbert Hoover, *The Ordeal of Woodrow Wilson* (New York: McGraw-Hill, 1958), p. vii.
51. Quoted in *Book Review Digest 1958* (New York: H. W. Wilson, 1959), p. 537.
52. *New York Times Magazine,* April 27, 1958.
53. *New York Times,* April 17, 1958.
54. Ibid., April 28, 1958.
55. Estes Kefauver to Hoover, January 10, 1958, Herbert Hoover Papers, HHPL.
56. Hoover to Kefauver, January 20, 1958, ibid.
57. *New York Times,* May 6, 1958.

58. "Some Observations on Business Slumps and Recessions," February 27, 1958, Herbert Hoover Special Collections, Articles, Addresses and Public Statements, 1915–1964, HHPL.
59. *New York Times*, February 10, 1958.
60. Ferdinand Eberstadt to Hoover, May 6, 1958, Herbert Hoover Papers, HHPL.
61. Hoover to Eberstadt, May 14, 1958, ibid.
62. Eisenhower to Hoover, June 11, 1958, ibid.
63. Memorandum of a telephone conversation, April 11, 1958, filed with Eisenhower correspondence, ibid.
64. *New York Times*, May 6, 1958.
65. Ibid., May 21, 1958.
66. "Address Delivered at the Brussels Exposition," July 4, 1958, Herbert Hoover Special Collections, Articles, Addresses and Public Statements, 1915–1964, HHPL.
67. *New York Times*, July 6, 1958.
68. Hoover to Eisenhower, July 7, 1958, Herbert Hoover Papers, HHPL.
69. *New York Times*, July 7, 1958.
70. Ibid., August 10, 1958.
71. Brown to Hoover, August 15, 1958, Herbert Hoover Papers, HHPL.
72. Hoover to Brown, August 21, 1958, ibid.
73. *New York Times*, October 30, 1958.
74. *Newsweek*, October 23, 1958.
75. *New York Times*, November 2, 1958.
76. Hoover to Lawrence, September 3, 1957, and Hoover to Clarence Kelland, November 10, 1958, Herbert Hoover Papers, HHPL.
77. Hoover to Matson, December 19, 1958, ibid.
78. Robert Anderson to Hoover, telegram, September 12, 1958, ibid.
79. Hoover to Anderson, telegram, September 15, 1958, ibid.
80. "Press Release Concerning President Eisenhower's Use of United States Armed Forces in the Lebanese Crisis," July 15, 1958, Herbert Hoover Special Collections, Articles, Addresses and Public Statements, 1915–1964, HHPL.
81. "This Crisis in the Principles and Morals in International Relations," Manion Forum, April 5, 1959, ibid.
82. Hoover to Richard Berlin, September 6, 1959, Herbert Hoover Papers, HHPL.
83. Jones to Hoover, January 9, 1959, ibid.
84. Hoover to Barry Goldwater, April 30, 1959, ibid.
85. *New York Times*, April 5, 1959.
86. Reprinted in Hoover, *Addresses, 1955–1960*, pp. 66–75.
87. Ibid., p. 389.
88. *New York Times*, August 10, 1959.
89. Reprinted in Hoover, *Addresses, 1955–1960*, pp. 141–48.
90. *American Weekly*, August 9, 1959.
91. Ben Moreell to Bernice Miller, December 1, 1959, and Hoover to Moreell, December 11, 1959, Herbert Hoover Papers, Post-Presidential Subject File, Americans for Constitutional Action, Correspondence, HHPL.
92. "Some Observations on Current American Life," February 13, 1960, Herbert Hoover Special Collections, Articles, Addresses and Public Statements, 1915–1964, HHPL.
93. Hoover to Brown, March 7, 1960, Herbert Hoover Papers, HHPL.
94. Hoover to Frances Hazlitt, March 27, 1960, ibid.
95. Hoover to Wilton Persons, April 7, 1960, filed with Eisenhower correspondence, ibid.
96. Thruston Morton to Hoover, June 17, 1960, Herbert Hoover Papers, Post-Presidential Subject File, Campaign 1960, HHPL.
97. Hoover to Morton, June 22, 1960, ibid.
98. Morton to Hoover, June 23, 1960, and Hoover to William Nichols, June 29, 1960, ibid.
99. Hoover to Patrick Hurley, July 8, 1960, Herbert Hoover Papers, HHPL.
100. John D. M. Hamilton interview, pp. 19–24, Oral History Collection, HHPL.

101. "Transcript of Television Interview on 'Person to Person' with Charles Collingwood," May 13, 1960, Herbert Hoover Special Collections, Articles, Addresses and Public Statements, 1915–1964, HHPL.
102. "Remarks at the Laying of the Cornerstone of the United Engineering Center," June 16, 1960, ibid.
103. Reprinted in Hoover, *Addresses, 1955–1960*, pp. 156–161.
104. Hoover to Roy Roberts, July 30, 1960, Herbert Hoover Papers, HHPL.
105. *New York Times*, July 25 and July 27, 1960.
106. "Remarks before the Press and Union League Club," August 2, 1960, Herbert Hoover Special Collections, Articles, Addresses and Public Statements, 1915–1964, HHPL.
107. *New York Times*, August 10, 1960.
108. Neil MacNeil interview, pp. 85–86, and Walter Trohan interview (with Ray Henle), pp. 26–27, Oral History Collection, HHPL.
109. "The Great Debate," undated memorandum, filed with Nixon correspondence, Herbert Hoover Papers, HHPL.
110. Neil MacNeil interview, pp. 85–86, Oral History Collection, HHPL.
111. *New York Times*, October 22, 1960.
112. Hoover to Morton, September 15, 1960, with enclosures, Herbert Hoover Papers, HHPL.
113. Hoover to William Lamb, October 12, 1960, ibid.

Chapter 15

1. *New York Times*, January 9 and January 13, 1961.
2. For Nixon's account, see Richard Nixon, *Six Crises* (Garden City: Doubleday, 1962), pp. 403–410. Hoover also told his close friend Neil MacNeil that Kennedy's overture was by phone; see Neil MacNeil interview, pp. 80–81, Oral History Collection, HHPL.
3. Undated memorandum, filed with Nixon correspondence, Herbert Hoover Papers, HHPL.
4. Nixon to Hoover, January 15, 1961, ibid.
5. Hoover to Nixon, January 27, 1961, ibid.
6. Hoover to Ben Moreell, November 19, 1960, ibid.
7. Hoover to Charles Hook, December 20, 1960, ibid.
8. Hoover to John F. Kennedy, telegram, January 19, 1961, ibid.
9. *New York Times*, January 12, 1961.
10. Kennedy to Hoover, telegram, March 2, 1961, and Hoover to Kennedy, March 3, 1961, Herbert Hoover Papers, HHPL.
11. Bernice Miller to T. J. Reardon Jr., April 25, 1961, Herbert Hoover Papers, Post-Presidential Subject File, Food for Peace, HHPL.
12. Hoover to George McGovern, April 25, 1961, ibid.
13. Richard Berlin interview, p. 18, Oral History Collection, HHPL.
14. *New York Times*, April 29, 1961.
15. Memorandum dated April 28, 1961, filed with Kennedy correspondence, Herbert Hoover Papers, HHPL.
16. *New York Times*, May 5, 1961.
17. Hoover to David Packard, June 16, 1961, Herbert Hoover Papers, HHPL.
18. Daniel Rodriguez interview, pp. 14–19, Oral History Collection, HHPL.
19. Lowell Thomas interview, p. 13, ibid.
20. Bascom Timmons interview, p. 23, ibid.
21. William Nichols interview, pp. 25–26, ibid.
22. Quoted for approval in Saul Pett to Hoover, Jun 13, 1961, Herbert Hoover Papers, Post-Presidential Subject File, Associated Press, HHPL.
23. Ibid.
24. William Lamb to Hoover, June 9, 1961, Herbert Hoover Papers, HHPL.
25. Hoover to Lamb, June 13, 1961, ibid.

26. "The Inheritance of the Next Generation," address given at Independence Hall, June 27, 1961, Herbert Hoover Special Collections: Articles, Addresses and Public Statements, 1915–1964, HHPL.
27. *New York Times*, July 23, 1961.
28. Lamb to Hoover, August 3, 1961, Herbert Hoover Papers, HHPL.
29. Hoover to Kennedy, June 16, 1961, ibid.
30. Kennedy to Hoover, August 9, 1961, ibid.
31. *New York Times*, July 23, 1961.
32. Ibid., August 19, 1961.
33. Dwight Eisenhower to Hoover, October 23, 1961, Herbert Hoover Papers, HHPL.
34. Hoover to Kennedy, February 3, 1962, ibid.
35. Hoover to Lawrence, July 17, 1962, ibid.
36. Hoover to Marvin Libman, September 14, 1961, Herbert Hoover Papers, Post-Presidential Subject File, Committee for One Million, HHPL.
37. "Statement Supporting the Recommendations of Senator Thomas J. Dodd in Respect to Katanga," December 21, 1961, Herbert Hoover Special Collections: Articles, Addresses and Public Statements, 1915–1964, HHPL.
38. Hoover to Packard, March 6, 1962, Herbert Hoover Papers, HHPL.
39. Miller to Packard, January 2, 1962, ibid.
40. Miller to Hugo Meier, February 19, 1962, ibid.
41. *New York Times*, January 30, 1962.
42. "Statement Read at Rally of the Young Americans for Freedom," Madison Square Garden, March 7, 1962, Herbert Hoover Special Collections: Articles, Addresses and Public Statements, 1915–1964, HHPL.
43. Hoover to Barry Goldwater, March 11, 1962, Herbert Hoover Papers, HHPL.
44. Hoover to Goldwater, July 22, 1964, ibid.
45. *New York Times*, March 4, 1962.
46. Ibid., June 6, 1962.
47. Ibid., July 24, 1962.
48. "A Proposal for Greater Safety for America: The Assurance That We Are Not in the Decline and Fall of the American Way of Life," August 10, 1962, Herbert Hoover Special Collections: Articles, Addresses and Public Statements, 1915–1964, HHPL.
49. *New York Times*, August 20, 1962.
50. Ibid., August 23, 1962.
51. Hoover to Rogers Dunn, August 25, 1962, Herbert Hoover Papers, HHPL.
52. The *New York Times* extensively covered Hoover's illness from August 21 to September 5, 1962.
53. Hoover to David Packard, October 8, 1962, Herbert Hoover Papers, HHPL.
54. *New York Times*, October 29, 1963.
55. Hoover to Harry Truman, December 29, 1962, Herbert Hoover Papers, HHPL.
56. Felix Morley interview, p. 23, Oral History Collection, HHPL.
57. Neil MacNeil interview, pp. 58–59, 107, ibid.
58. Hoover to Clarence Kelland, January 31, 1963, Herbert Hoover Papers, HHPL.
59. Hoover to Donald Brownlow, February 4, 1963, ibid.
60. Hoover to William Hallam Tuck, April 23, 1963, quoted in Hilda Bunge Tuck interview, p. 10, Oral History Collection, HHPL.
61. *New York Times*, June 20, 1963.
62. Ibid., June 15, 1963.
63. Ibid., June 21, 1963.
64. "Statement by Mr. Hoover on His Eighty-Ninth Birthday," August 10, 1963, Herbert Hoover Special Collections: Articles, Addresses and Public Statements, 1915–1964, HHPL.
65. William L. Dawson to Hoover, June 13, 1963, Herbert Hoover Papers, HHPL.
66. Hoover to George Mardikian, September 26, 1963, ibid.
67. Hoover to Mrs. Joseph Kennedy, September 26, 1963, ibid.
68. Mr. and Mrs. William Nichols interview, pp. 10–11, Oral History Collection, HHPL.

69. Felix Morley interview, p. 24, ibid.
70. Neil MacNeil interview, p. 72, ibid.
71. Hoover to Kelland, November 6, 1963, Herbert Hoover Papers, HHPL.
72. "Statement on the Death of President John F. Kennedy," November 22, 1963, Herbert Hoover Special Collections: Articles, Addresses and Public Statements, 1915–1964, HHPL.
73. Richard Berlin interview, p. 2, Oral History Collection, HHPL.
74. *New York Times*, December 9, 1963.
75. Neil MacNeil interview, p. 63, Oral History Collection, HHPL.
76. Hoover to Hulda McLean, December 10, 1963, Herbert Hoover Papers, HHPL.
77. *New York Times*, December 28, 1963.
78. Albert Wedemeyer to Kelland, February 5, 1963, Wedemeyer Papers, HI.
79. Undated memorandum, filed with Nixon correspondence, Herbert Hoover Papers, HHPL.
80. *New York Times*, February 28, 1964.
81. *Congressional Record*, Vol. 110, Part 5 (March 25, 1964), pp. 5942–5949.
82. Hoover to Charles Gubser, April 5, 1964, Herbert Hoover Papers, HHPL.
83. Hoover to Bonner Fellers, April 18, 1964, ibid.
84. Draft letter to Knowland, filed with Goldwater correspondence, ibid.
85. See Ray Henle comments in Jeremiah Milbank Jr. interview, pp. 8–9, Oral History Collection, HHPL.
86. Dwight Miller (Hoover Library archivist) to author, November 19, 1998.
87. Hoover to Everett Dirksen, June 23, 1964, Herbert Hoover Papers, HHPL.
88. "Statement to Be Read at the Opening Night of the Republican Convention," July 13, 1964, Herbert Hoover Special Collections: Articles, Addresses and Public Statements, 1915–1964, HHPL.
89. *New York Times*, July 14, 1964.
90. Memorandum dated July 16, 1964, filed with Goldwater correspondence, Herbert Hoover Papers, HHPL.
91. Hoover to Goldwater, telegram, July 16, 1964, and letter, July 22, 1964, ibid.
92. *New York Times*, August 9, 1964.
93. Bonner Fellers interview, pp. 30–31, Oral History Collection, HHPL.
94. *New York Times*, August 9, 1964.
95. Ibid., August 10, 1964.
96. Ibid., August 11, 1964.
97. Ibid., August 17, 1964.
98. See Herbert Hoover Papers, Post-Presidential Subject File, Nobel Peace Prize, HHPL.
99. Joseph Binns interview, p. 20, Oral History Collection, HHPL.
100. Neil MacNeil interview, pp. 44–53, ibid.
101. Goldwater to Hoover, October 3, 1964, Herbert Hoover Papers, HHPL.
102. *New York Times*, October 19, 1964.
103. Ibid., October 24, 1964.
104. Ibid., October 26, 1964.
105. Allan Hoover to the author, May 5, 1980.
106. *New York Times*, October 21, 1964.
107. Ibid.

Afterword

1. Daniel J. Boorstin, "When Risks Are Worth Taking," *Christian Science Monitor*, August 6, 1981, p. 23.
2. For readers unfamiliar with the preceding five volumes in the Hoover biography series, they are as follows: George H. Nash, *The Life of Herbert Hoover: The Engineer, 1874–1914* (New York: W. W. Norton and Co., 1983); George H. Nash, *The Life of Herbert Hoover: The Humanitarian, 1914–1917* (New York: W. W. Norton and Co., 1988); George H. Nash, *The Life of Herbert Hoover: Master of Emergencies, 1917–1918* (New York, W. W. Norton and Co.,

1996); Kendrick A. Clements, *The Life of Herbert Hoover: Imperfect Visionary, 1918–1928* (New York: Palgrave Macmillan, 2010); and Glen Jeansonne, *The Life of Herbert Hoover: Fighting Quaker, 1928–1933* (New York: Palgrave Macmillan, 2012).

3. Hal Elliott Wert, *Hoover the Fishing President: Portrait of the Private Man and His Life Outdoors* (Mechanicsburg, PA: Stackpole Books, 2005); Timothy Walch, ed., *Uncommon Americans: The Lives and Legacies of Herbert and Lou Henry Hoover* (Westport, CT: Praeger, 2003); Bertrand M. Patenaude, *The Big Show in Bololand: The American Relief Expedition to Soviet Russia in the Famine of 1921* (Stanford, CA: Stanford University Press, 2002).

4. Anne Beiser Allen, *An Independent Woman: The Life of Lou Henry Hoover* (Westport, CT: Greenwood Press, 2000); *Dale C. Mayer, Lou Henry Hoover: A Prototype for First Ladies* (New York: Nova History Productions, 2004); Nancy Beck Young, *Lou Henry Hoover: Activist First Lady* (Lawrence, KS: University Press of Kansas, 2004).

5. See, in this volume, pp. 456 and 462.

6. George H. Nash, ed., *Freedom Betrayed: Herbert Hoover's Secret History of the Second World War and Its Aftermath* (Stanford, CA: Hoover Institution Press, 2011).

7. Herbert Hoover, "Information for Biographers" (n.d.; ca. World War I), Pre-Commerce Papers, Herbert Hoover Papers, HHPL, West Branch, Iowa.

8. [Hoover], "General Comment and Summary" (typescript, n.d., [May 1959?]), Hoover Institution Records, Series F-03, Hoover Institution Archives, Stanford University.

Bibliography

The only scholarly biography that deals comprehensively with Hoover's post-presidential years is my own *Herbert Hoover: The Postpresidential Years, 1933–64* (2 vols., Stanford, CA, 1983). Other, less extensive treatments can be found in David Burner, *Herbert Hoover: A Public Life* (New York, 1979), Joan Hoff Wilson, *Herbert Hoover: Forgotten Progressive* (Boston, 1975), and Richard Norton Smith, *An Uncommon Man: The Triumph of Herbert Hoover* (New York, 1984).

At the instance of Senator Mark O. Hatfield, approximately 30 essays were written to commemorate the fiftieth anniversary of Hoover's inauguration as president. These appeared first in Congressional Record and were then published in *Herbert Hoover Reassessed*, U.S. Senate Document No. 96–63 (Washington, DC, 1981). Several of these essays deal with the postpresidential years and offer useful insights. Two other anthologies also contain useful articles: Lee Nash, editor, *Understanding Herbert Hoover* (Stanford, CA, 1987), and Thomas T. Thalken, editor, *The Problems of Lasting Peace Revisited* (West Branch, IA, 1986).

As yet, only a few published articles deal with Hoover's postpresidential years, while general works on the period and biographies of other figures influential during these areas are of only marginal use for a study of Hoover. Research for this work, therefore, has relied primarily on manuscript sources, oral histories, and interviews.

Manuscript Collections
Herbert Hoover Presidential Library

Papers

George Akerson Papers
Arthur Ballantine Papers
William R. Castle Papers
Herbert Hoover Papers
Lou Henry Hoover Papers
Clarence B. Kelland Papers
Nathan MacChesney Papers
Neil MacNeil Papers
Frank Mason Papers
Felix Morley Papers
Edgar Rickard Diary

Harrison Spangler Papers
Lewis Strauss Papers
Charles Teague Papers
William Hallam Tuck Papers
Hugh Wilson Papers
Robert E. Wood Papers

Hoover Institution on War, Revolution and Peace

Benjamin Shannon Allen Papers
Citizens Committee for Reorganization of the Executive Branch of the Government Records
First Aid for Hungary Records
Perrin C. Galpin Papers
Hugh Gibson Papers
Herbert Hoover Papers
Edward Eyre Hunt Papers
Will Irwin Papers
Julius Klein Papers
May Hoover Leavitt Letters
Hulda Hoover McLean Papers
Raymond Moley Papers
National Committee on Food for the Small Democracies Records
Mark Sullivan Papers
United States Famine Emergency Committee Records
Albert C. Wedemeyer Papers
Ray Lyman Wilbur Papers

Franklin D. Roosevelt Presidential Library

Franklin D. Roosevelt Papers
Rexford Tugwell Diary

Huntington Library

Stuart Lake Papers

Kansas Historical Society, Topeka, Kansas

Arthur Capper Papers
Alf M. Landon Papers
Charles Scott Papers

Library of Congress

William Borah Papers
Raymond Clapper Papers
Henry P. Fletcher Papers
Frank Knox Papers
Charles McNary Papers
Ogden Mills Papers
John Callan O'Laughlin Papers

Everett Sanders Papers
Robert A. Taft Papers
William Allen White Papers
Walter Brown Papers
John Vorys Papers

Mudd Manuscript Library, Princeton University

William Starr Myers Papers

Ohio Historical Center

John Bricker Papers
Clarence Brown Papers
Walter Brown Papers
John Vorys Papers

Pickler Memorial Library, Truman State University

Glenn Frank Papers

Republic National Headquarters, Washington, DC

Republican National Committee Minutes

Sanoian Special Collections Library, California State University, Fresno

Chester Harvey Rowell Papers

University of Vermont

Warren Austin Papers
John Spargo Papers

In addition to manuscript collections, the following unpublished sources were used.

Oral Histories

Herbert Hoover Presidential Library Oral History Collection

Richard E. Berlin
Joseph F. Binns
Herbert Brownell
Thomas E. Dewey
Bonner Fellers
Joseph C. Green
John D. M. Hamilton

Neil MacNeil
Frank E. Mason
Jeremiah Milbank Jr.
Ben Moreel
William I. Nichols
James P. Selvage
Walter Trohan
Albert C. Wedemeyer

Columbia University Oral History Collection

Harvey H. Bundy
H. Alexander Smith
James W. Wadsworth

Interviews

John Bricker
Alf M. Landon
Clare Boothe Luce
Samuel Pryor

Correspondence

Allan Hoover
Felix Morley
Dwight Miller

Published sources that proved useful are cited in the notes.

Index

Printed and bound in the United States of America